Programming Languages:
Paradigm and Practice

McGraw-Hill Computer Science Series

Programming Languages:

Paradigm and Practice

SECOND EDITION

Doris Appleby
Marymount College

Julius J. VandeKopple
Marymount College

THE McGRAW-HILL COMPANIES, INC.

New York   St. Louis   San Francisco   Auckland   Bogotá   Caracas
Lisbon   London   Madrid   Mexico City   Milan   Montreal   New Delhi
San Juan   Singapore   Sydney   Tokyo   Toronto

McGraw-Hill

A Division of The **McGraw·Hill** *Companies*

PROGRAMMING LANGUAGES:
Paradigm and Practice

1 2 3 4 5 6 7 8 9 0 DOC DOC 9 0 9 8 7 6

ISBN 0-07-005315-4

This book was set in Palatino by Cecelia G. Morales.
The editor was Eric M. Munson.
The production supervisor was Richard A. Ausburn.
The design manager was Charles A. Carson.
Project supervision was done by Cecelia G. Morales.
R. R. Donnelley & Sons Company was printer and binder.

Appleby, Doris.
    Programming languages : paradigm and practice / Doris Appleby,
Julius VandeKopple. -- 2nd ed.
        p.   cm.
    Includes bibliographical references and index.
    ISBN 0-07-005315-4
    1. Programming languages (Electronic computers)   I. VandeKopple,
Julius.   II. Title.
QA76.9.A67   1997
005.13--dc20
                                                96-36525

http://www.mhcollege.com

For our students—may their future in computing be bright

CONTENTS

Preface   xii

PART I   **Preliminary Concepts**

0   Introduction   2
     0.0   In this Chapter   3
     0.1   Problem Solving   3
            Devices from Mathematics / Conceptual and Implementation Levels
     0.2   Language Paradigms   6
            Imperative Paradigms / Declarative Paradigms
     0.3   Practical Considerations   11
            From Low Through High to Very High Level / Programming in the Large / Special Problems
     0.4   Language Criteria   14
            Well-Defined Descriptions / Provability / Reliability / Fast Translation / Efficient Object Code / Orthogonality / Generality / Consistency and Common Notations / Uniformity / Subsets / Extensibility / Portability
     0.5   Summary   25
     0.6   Notes on References   25

1   Variables and Data Types   28
     1.0   In this Chapter   29
     1.1   Primitive Data Types   30
            Integer / Real / Character / Boolean / Pointer
     1.2   Variables   36
            Identifiers / Reserved Words and Keywords / Binding / Blocks and Scope / Activation Records
     1.3   Structured Data Types   47
            User-Defined Types / Aggregate Types / Type Issues
     1.4   Summary   61
     1.5   Notes on References   61

2   Abstraction   62
2.0 In this chapter   64
2.1 Data Abstraction   64
Data and the Store / Abstract Data Types / Generic Types
2.2 Control Abstraction   74
Branching / Iteration / Recursion / Exceptions
2.3 Procedural Abstraction   83
Procedures / Modules and ADTs / Classes of ADTs / Objects /
Concurrent Execution
2.4 Summary   94
2.5 Notes on References   95

PART II   Imperative Languages

3   Block Structure   98
3.0 In this Chapter   100
3.1 ALGOL 60   100
Historical Vignette: Design by Committee / Concepts from ALGOL
60 / Trouble Spots in ALGOL 60 / Language Specification
3.2 ALGOL 68   111
3.3 Pascal   113
Historical Vignette: Pascal and Modula-2: Niklaus Wirth / Philoso-
phy and Structure
3.4 Ada   117
Historical Vignette: Ada / Program Organization / Types / The
Generic Facility / Exceptions / The Ada Programming Support
Environment (APSE)
3.5 C   132
Historical Vignette: The Dynamic Duo, Dennis Ritchie and Kenneth
Thompson / Data Types in C / C Operators / C and UNIX /
The C Standard / Advantages and Disadvantages
3.6 Summary   145
3.7 Notes on References   146

4   Languages for Object-Oriented Programming (OOP)   148
4.0 In this Chapter   150
4.1 Programming with Objects   150
Messages, Methods, and Encapsulation / Early Notions of Objects
in Simula / Objects in Ada 83 and Ada 95
4.2 Classes and Polymorphism   162
Generic Procedures and Packages in Ada / Classes in Object Pascal /
Classes in C++ / Implementation of Inherited Classes

4.3 Smalltalk 175
Historical Vignette: Smalltalk: Alan Kay

4.4 Inheritance and Object-Orientation 177
Types and Subtypes in Inheritance Hierarchies / Multiple Inheritance / Language Exemplars / Dynamic Binding

4.5 Java 196
Java Language Constructs / The Java Application Programming Interfaces (APIs) / Compiling and Running a Java Program / HotJava and Applets / Program Types / Differences Between Java, C, and C++

4.6 Summary 206

4.7 Notes on References 206

5 Language Constructs for Parallel Processing 208

5.0 In this Chapter 209

5.1 The Paradigm 210

5.2 Multiple Processes 212

5.3 Synchronization of Cooperating Processes 213
Semaphores / Monitors / Rendezvous / Message Passing

5.4 Some Synchronization Solutions 221
Semaphores in ALGOL 68, C, and Pascal S / Monitor and Process Types in Concurrent Pascal / The Rendezvous in Ada and Concurrent C / Message Passing in Occam

5.5 Tuples and Objects 235
The Tuple-Space of Linda / Objects as Units of Parallelism

5.6 Managing Partial Failure 240

5.7 Summary 241

5.8 Notes on References 242

PART III Formal Languages and Automata

6 Formal Languages 244

6.0 In this Chapter 245

6.1 Formal Languages 246
Formal Languages Defined / The Chomsky Hierarchy of Formal Languages / Historical Vignette: Language Classifications: Noam Chomsky / Historical Vignette: Alan Turing: What Machines Can't Do

6.2 Regular Grammars   260
    Regular Expressions / Finite Automata (FAs, NFAs, and DFAs) /
    Applications
6.3 Context-Free Grammars (CFGs)   267
    Push-Down Automata (PDAs) / Parse Trees / Ambiguous
    Grammars / Applications / Normal Forms
6.4 Grammars for Natural Languages   279
6.5 Summary   281
6.6 Notes on References   282

PART IV Declarative Languages

7 **Logic Programming**   284
    7.0 In this Chapter   285
    7.1 Formal Logical Systems   286
        Historical Vignette: Aristotle / Proofs / Searching
    7.2 PROLOG   301
        Historical Vignette: PROLOG: Colmerauer and Roussel / Convers-
        ing in PROLOG: Facts, Rules, and Queries / PROLOG Implemen-
        tations / Applications / Strengths and Weaknesses
    7.3 Summary   321
    7.4 Notes on References   322

8 **Functional (Applicative) Programming**   324
    8.0 In this Chapter   327
    8.1 Features of Functional Languages   327
        Composition of Functions / Functions as First-Class Objects /
        No Side Effects / Clean Semantics
    8.2 LISP   330
        Historical Vignette: LISP: John McCarthy / The LISP Language
        (SCHEME Dialect) / Other Nonfunctional Features / Dialects /
        Common LISP
    8.3 Implementing Functional Languages   354
        Lazy Versus Strict Evaluation / Scope and Bindings / Garbage
        Collection
    8.4 Supporting Parallelism with Functions   362
    8.5 Other Functional Languages   364
        APL / ML / Others
    8.6 Summary   373
    8.7 Notes on References   374

9   Languages for Databases   376

9.0   In this Chapter   378
9.1   Hierarchical and Network Models   378
9.2   The Relational Model   380
      *Manipulating Relational Databases / SQL / Logic-Based Systems
      Using PROLOG*
9.3   Semantic Data Models   390
9.4   Object-Oriented Database Model   392
9.5   Summary   393
9.6   Notes on References   394

Appendix A   395
      Logical Calculi (for Chapter 7)

Appendix B   405
      The lambda Calculus (for Chapter 8)

Appendix C   411
      Software Sources

References   415

Index   429

Labs

2.1   Abstract Data Types: Ada/Pascal   71
2.2   Parameter-Passing Methods: Pascal   90
3.1   Blocks: Ada/Pascal   132
3.2   Combining Low and High Level Features: C   142
3.3   Fun with C Tricks: C   143
3.4   IDE Tools: Pascal/C   144
3.5   APSE Tools: Ada   145
4.1: Objects, Encapsulation, and Methods:
      Object Pascal/Ada/C++   161
4.2   Polymorphism: Object Pascal/Ada/C++   174
4.3   Classes and Inheritance: Object Pascal/C++   195
4.4   Objects and Object-Oriented Programming: Java   205
4.5   HTML to Be Used on the World Wide Web with Java   205
4.6   An Applet: Java   205
5.1   Simulation of Parallel Processing: Ada   232
5.2   Producers-Consumers: Pascal S/Occam 2/C-Linda   239
6.1   Regular Expressions: grep   265
6.2   EBNF: Paper and Pencil   277
7.1   Language Introduction: PROLOG   298
7.2   Cannibals and Missionaries: PROLOG   318

8.1   Getting Acquainted with LISP: SCHEME   347
8.2   A Palindrome Function: SCHEME   347
8.3   Programming Using Loops: SCHEME   347
8.4   Tracing and Debugging: SCHEME   348
8.5   Programming in SCOOPS: SCHEME   352
9.1   SQL: dBASE IV   389

PREFACE

LANGUAGE PARADIGMS

During the last 10 years, languages for programming computers have been organized into a hierarchy of paradigms, the major ones being those shown in Figure P.1 below.

A paradigm can be thought of as a collection of abstract features that categorize a group of languages which are accepted and used by a group of practitioners. A student who understands what distinguishes each paradigm and has some programming experience with at least one language in each paradigm can be considered basically educated in the subject matter of programming languages. We will discuss the notion of paradigm in Chapter 0, and provide descriptions exemplified by existing languages in the chapters that follow.

ORGANIZATION OF THIS TEXT

This book is organized on four principles:

- A good way to bring order into the sometimes confusing collection of high level languages is to study them paradigm by paradigm.

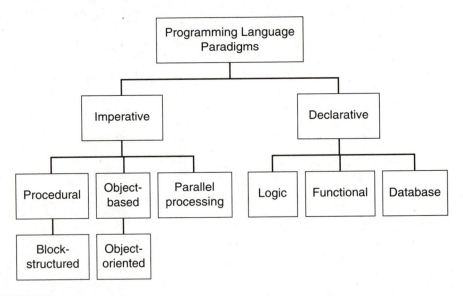

FIGURE P.1
A hierarchy of programming language paradigms

- Most people don't understand a language unless they actually use it.
- In order to use a language, you need an elementary language manual, which also acts as a tutorial.
- Everything a student needs to achieve the first three principles should be easily and inexpensively available.

To do this, we provide:

- A textbook
- Laboratory assignments using exemplary code
- Low-cost language MiniManuals, providing tutorials in the various languages used

The intended audience is students who can program well in at least one high level language. Knowledge of assembly language is not assumed, although it would be helpful in understanding some topics.

The text is divided into four parts, as illustrated in Figure P.2.

In the text, we start off with some basic concepts that can be found in almost any language. Rather than consider data as bit-strings, and a program as a sequence of instructions to manipulate those bits, we look at data, program control, and procedures at a higher or more abstract level. That done, we study the paradigms, one by one, with particular focus on an example language from each category. If the language is a particularly good example of a paradigm, it is called an *exemplar*. To provide hands-on practice with each paradigm, we have organized the student's work around weekly programming labs using the exemplars.

The text gives equal weight to the two top-level paradigms, imperative and declarative. It also emphasizes the theoretical foundations of different language types. Most programming languages have not developed simply as collections of useful computational features. Many have tried faithfully to implement mathematical theories, which provide the vocabulary and structure for solving problems and about which much has been proved. We have either incorporated these notions into the text itself or included them in brief appendices on underlying mathematical theory. Each programming language is presented as an example of one of the paradigms and, if applicable, as a model of a mathematical theory.

Any language, written or spoken, has syntax (form) and semantics (meaning). Linguistic theory has also influenced programming languages, so we have included Chapter 6 on the use of linguistics to write formal language definitions. This book blends theoretical foundations and history with practical programming experience in 12 example languages. A student could not expect to become competent in 12 different languages in the course of a single semester, but can at least see what they all look like.

From one to six formal programming assignments have been provided for most chapters. These labs, which can be implemented in either a closed or open lab setting, present substantial applications written in the example language under discussion. In addition, our colleagues have written five MiniManuals, each providing a tutorial on an individual exemplar language. These are available under separate cover. A complete teaching package includes the text, the laboratory assignments, whichever MiniManuals an instructor chooses, and the Instructor's Manual.

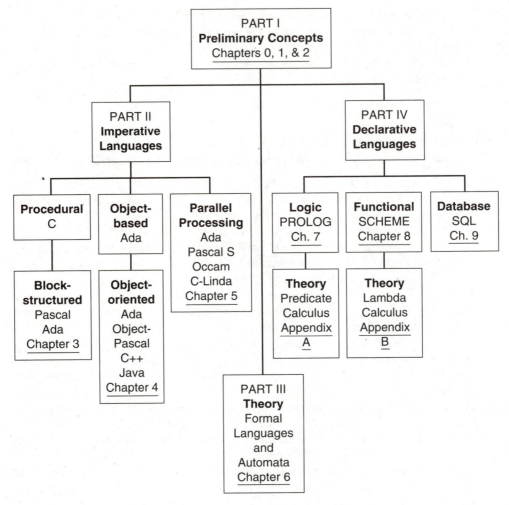

FIGURE P.2
Organization of the text

Part I: Preliminary Concepts

When the 1985[1] Pascal standard included two levels of the language, Pascal Level 0 and Pascal Level 1, the Australians on the standards committee complained that the usage of Level 0 was a "barbarism in the English language" [quoted in Cooper, 1983]. Agreed. Nonetheless, we have included an introductory Chapter 0, which

---

[1]The 1983 Standard [ANSI/IEEE-770X3.97, 1983] described only Level 0 Pascal, which did not include conformant arrays, which are in Level 1. The 1985 standard includes both Level 0 and Level 1.

explains the historical notion of scientific paradigms, discusses the abstract features of each of the paradigms above, lists concrete performance characteristics that every language must possess, and provides an introduction to language syntax. This chapter prefaces the technical work of the course.

Chapters 1 and 2 describe constructs implemented in all languages, with examples written in a Pascal/Ada-like pseudocode. In Chapter 1 we consider variables and data types and in Chapter 2 the concepts of abstraction for data, control constructs, and modules.

Part II: Imperative Languages

Part II deals with the imperative paradigm, which includes languages with facilities for assigning values to memory locations. Chapter 3 discusses procedural block-structured languages, with which most students have had some programming experience. Object-oriented languages are the subject of Chapter 4, with Ada, Object Pascal, C++, and Java as examples. Chapter 5 is devoted to the paradigm that includes languages for distributed programming, those that implement parallel processing. Here we will look, in addition to Ada, at shared memory models (Pascal S), message passing (Occam), and C-Linda, which implements concurrent processing using a memory organization called tuple space.

Part III: Formal Languages and Automata

Part III is a single chapter that looks at formal languages. Its organization follows Chomsky's hierarchy of language types, focusing on practical uses for programming languages. Special attention is given to type 2, the so-called context-free languages, which form the theoretical basis for the definitions of many existing languages. The study of formal languages and theoretical machines on which they can be implemented (theoretically) can constitute much of the material for a course in theoretical computer science. Some curricula do not include such a course or some students do not opt to take it as an elective. Thus we include this brief chapter for those who will not study formal languages in greater depth.

Part IV: Declarative Languages

Declarative languages are those based on relations or functions, in which the programmer does not consider the assignment of values to storage locations, but thinks in terms of functional values or the relationship of entities to each other when solving a problem. In Chapter 7, we look at PROLOG as an example of a language for logic programming. The SCHEME dialect of LISP is presented as a functional language in Chapter 8, and SQL is the example of a language for manipulating databases discussed in Chapter 9. Some of the theoretical material has been placed in appendices to facilitate the reading of these chapters.

HANDS-ON LABORATORY ASSIGNMENTS

Although a blueprint for lifetime learning may be the main goal of education, computing students also need to develop language skills. We have included laboratory assignments for both this skill-building needed for the world of work and the reinforcement that dealing with concrete languages provides for conceptual learning. A student who successfully completes a weekly lab will have gained some modest skill in several of the languages in this text.

Students approaching a language for the first time can use one of two methods:

- Start at the beginning learning basic constructs, while writing increasingly complex programs
- Look at model programs and modify or extend them as best they can.

We have generally used the second option in the 25 labs of this text, which allows some of the flavor of the individual languages to be seen. Students are then asked to modify the programs or add to them. A student could be assigned about half of these labs in one semester depending on the focus of the course. They can be done either as closed or open labs depending on an individual school's teaching environment. We have used both types of lab, and have found a combination where students do some work in a supervised lab and some on their own to be ideal. Each lab can be completed in approximately an hour and a half.

Laboratory assignments employ 12 different languages: Ada, C, C++, Java, SCHEME (LISP), Object Pascal, Pascal, PROLOG, SQL, and three languages for parallel processing: Occam, Pascal S, and C-Linda. Compilers and/or interpreters for all of these are available free or at minimal expense for the DOS operating system. Addresses where they are available can be found in Appendix C. Lab assignments can be found in the *Instructor's Manual.*

COURSE ORGANIZATION

In our experience, the Programming Languages course benefits students most if they actively program in several of the languages studied. But when they have lab in addition to classroom assignments, it is usually the latter that gets slighted. There are 241 exercises in the text, but none that requires computer solution. Thus, we would expect students to come to class prepared with answers to only some of the exercises, while successfully completing all the labs assigned.

These materials are intended for a one-semester or quarter course in Programming Languages, including a weekly closed, open, or mixed lab. The 25 lab assignments are far too many for a one-quarter or semester course, and an instructor may choose which to use depending on the focus of the course. Labs address particular language constructs, and some can be executed in a choice of language. The instructor may choose in which languages to provide programming experiences.

Table P.1 provides a listing of the Lab and Exercise resources and estimates of the time required to cover the various materials provided. A lecture is considered to be 75 minutes, and a lab may be from 0 to 2 hours. If students do not have a

TABLE P.1
Materials in this text

Chapter	Topic	#Lectures	#Labs	#Exercises
0	Introduction	1	0	17
1	Data Types	3	0	27
2	Abstraction	3	2	22
3	Block Structure	3	5	29
4	OOP	4	6	27
5	Parallel Processing	4	2	10
6	Formal Languages	3	2	35
7	Logic Programming	4	2	29
8	Functional Languages	5	5	14
9	Languages for DBMS	2	1	16
Appendix A	Logical Calculi	0	0	8
Appendix B	The lambda Calculus	0	0	7
Totals		32	25	241

scheduled lab, some time in class should be used to familiarize them with a lab assignment before they are asked to complete it on their own.

A typical undergraduate semester is composed of 15 weeks, or 13 if we exclude class periods used for testing and review. A class meeting 3 hours a week for lecture, plus once a week for a 1- to 2-hour lab, should be able to finish all 9 chapters of the text and complete 13 of the 25 labs. Selection of which labs to assign will depend on the focus of the course and which languages are available on campus. Some of the labs are available in a choice of language, and an instructor may want to have students do the same problem in two or more languages. For example, the second lab on parallel processing in Chapter 5 can be done in Pascal S, C-Linda, and Occam. Students would benefit from seeing all three languages. Ordinarily, students would be assigned a lab in only one of the languages in which we have implemented it, i.e., Ada, C, or Pascal for block-structured languages and Ada, C++, or Java for object-oriented languages.

Most semesters do not have thirty-two 75-minute lecture periods, but twenty-six, so choices must be made. Everyone should do Chapters 0–3, but after that, what to omit depends on what other courses are offered at a school. If students will have a full course on parallel processing, Chapter 5 can be skipped. If there is a course in theoretical computer science or in databases, Chapter 6 or Chapter 9 can be left out.

In a quarter system, one might omit Chapters 5, 6, and 9. These students could be expected to complete nine or ten labs.

HISTORICAL VIGNETTES

Readers can learn a little of what real people do from the historical vignettes on prominent language innovators. These are stories about real people who made lasting contributions to the development of programming languages. The earliest is Aristotle, who originated formal logic, and the most recent is the team that designed the Ada language for the United States Department of Defense.

TEACHING MATERIALS

Teaching materials in addition to the text include:

1. 241 pencil and paper exercises at the end of major sections of the text
2. Appendix C, containing sources for free or inexpensive software
3. An *Instructor's Manual* containing:
   - Solutions to the exercises in the text
   - 25 laboratory assignments. Instructors can provide their students with copies of the labs they want them to complete.
   - A diskette containing suggested solutions to the labs
   - Source code needed by students for completing the labs can be downloaded from http://www.mhcollege.com. Be sure to read the README file for a description of the contents of the directory.
4. Five low-cost language MiniManuals providing language tutorials sufficient for completing the labs

The programs are intended for distribution to students. Suggested solutions are for the instructor's use. These programs are substantial, and have been thoroughly tested to run on DOS, Windows, or UNIX workstations. They are well-written example programs to be modified or completed by the students.

The MiniManuals are language tutorials sufficient for completing the labs or for individual language workshops lasting a few days. Motivation for preparing the manuals was to present, briefly, the key features of each language, and to keep the cost of materials down for the course. The Programming Languages course is usually not successful if students do not have access to a manual for each language used, and full manuals tend to be either expensive or unavailable unless purchased with a compiler.

MiniManuals are available for:

Imperative Languages:
1. Ada
   by George Benjamin,
   Muhlenberg College

   Block-structured, object-oriented, and distributed paradigms

2. C and C++
   by Maryam Hastings,
   Marymount College, and
   William Hastings,
   Fordham University

   Block-structured and object-oriented paradigms

3. C++
   by William Hastings,
   Fordham University

   Object-oriented paradigm

Declarative:
4. SCHEME
   by Richard Hull,
   Lenore-Rhyne College

   Functional paradigm

5. PROLOG   Relational (logic) paradigm
   by Tom Hankins and Thom Luce,
   University of West Virginia
   College of Graduate Studies

NEW IN THIS EDITION

The first edition of this book was written by the first author, who is delighted to have worked in collaboration with the second author on this version. In response to suggestions by our reviewers, the first chapters on basic concepts and block structure were rewritten to include more concepts and fewer language examples, as students found switching from one language syntax to another confusing. Chapter 1 was split into the new chapters, 1 and 2, and rewritten in a Pascal/Ada-like pseudocode to clarify basic notions of typing, variables, data, control, and procedural abstraction, as well as implementation issues.

Chapter 4 (object-oriented languages) was expanded to include more material on these languages. Since some of the features of object-orientation have been added to the new Ada 95, we have included a discussion of these new features. The C/C++ MiniManual includes some material on objects, presenting them as an extension of C. In addition, we have added a new MiniManual just on C++, which looks at the whole programming enterprise from an object-oriented point of view. Students who already know C will be more interested in the new C++ manual, while those with no knowledge of C can see some C++ in the C/C++ MiniManual. The Pascal/Object Pascal MiniManual has been discontinued, because Pascal is considered by many to be a dying language and will soon be replaced by C++ as a first language for high school students.

We have added a discussion of the new Java language from Sun Microsystems and three new Java labs to Chapter 4. Java is available free from Sun by anonymous ftp over the Internet (see Appendix C).

Chapter 5 (distributed and parallel processing) includes more language examples and three new labs, implementing solutions to the producer-consumer problem in Pascal S, C-Linda, and Occam, as well as the Ada lab included in the first edition. The new labs were made practical for this PC-based course since inexpensive compilers and hardware have recently become available. Individual boards called transputors can be installed and interconnected in PCs and accessed through the Occam language. Linda is a programming paradigm that can be emulated in either C or Ada. Pascal S is a subset of standard Pascal.

Chapters 6 and 8 were completely rewritten for the sake of clarity and simplicity. The material on the predicate calculus (Chapter 7) was moved to an appendix, to be studied by students who have little knowledge of formal logic. We also moved the theoretical discussion of the lambda calculus (Chapter 8) to an appendix. Theoretical material for other chapters, which was separated from the main text in sections called "Theoretical Excursions" in the first edition, was simplified and included in the body of the text.

Material on languages that were treated only briefly in the first edition was deleted. Thus you will find only passing discussion of APL, BASIC, COBOL, SNOBOL, SETL, Modula-2, or special "little languages" here. We did, however, add some discussion of the typed functional language ML to Chapter 8.

Code was rewritten in both the text and the MiniManuals to conform to new versions of the several languages used.

ACKNOWLEDGMENTS

The Historical Vignettes were written by our former student, Laurie Sexton, who also served as research assistant, reader, and critic.

The MiniManual authors read materials related to the languages they were working with and offered many suggestions and corrections. They also wrote, tested, and debugged lab assignments using the languages addressed in their manuals.

Carol Torsone of the College of Saint John Fisher provided labs for Chapter 5 on parallel processing, in addition to that implemented in Ada by George Benjamin. Karen Appleby of IBM's Watson Labs wrote the three new Java labs.

The first edition benefited from careful readings by several reviewers who were anonymous to the first author at the time. We appreciate all their careful thought and comments. They are:

Jane Hill, Dickinson College; Jim Beug, California Polytechnic, San Luis Obispo; Jon Manney, North Carolina State University; Richard Salter, Oberlin College; Rob Lyndon, Ohio University; Walter Pharr, College of Charleston; Stan Seltzer, Ithaca College; Tom Meyers, Colgate University; Dale Hanchey, Oklahoma Baptist University; and David Jackel, LeMoyne College.

A second group of reviewers made many suggestions for changes to the second edition. They are:

Benjamin Zorn, University of Colorado at Boulder; Rajive Bagrodia, UCLA; Shermane Austin, City College of New York; Harold Grossman, Clemson University; Brian Molloy, Clemson University; Salih Yurttas, Texas A&M University; Ephraim Glinert, Rensselaer Polytechnic Institute; T. Ray Nanney, Furman University; Manuel E. Bermudez, University of Florida; Patty Brayton, Oklahoma City University; K.N. King, Georgia State University; and Donald Bagert, Texas Tech University.

And finally, we must acknowledge our editor, Eric Munson from McGraw-Hill. We needed his TLC to persevere through to the end from conception to final proofing. Without Holly Stark, Eric's able assistant, the book would never have seen the light of day.

Doris Appleby
Julius VandeKopple

PART I

Preliminary Concepts

In the first three chapters, we will look at basic concepts and notation that will be used throughout the book. We begin in Chapter 0 with the language paradigms that form the structure for our study of programming languages. Basic language terms included here also form a context for discussing features of individual languages in later chapters. Also, we will introduce notation that is commonly used in describing language syntax, the structure of valid language constructs.

Chapter 1 includes issues of data types, both those primitive to a language and structured types, defined by the user or formed with entries of other types. In looking at program variables, we consider their attributes and the time that these attributes are bound to the variable. These are important to a clear understanding of how a language works.

We look at concepts of abstraction in Chapter 2. In data abstraction, the data values and operations on those values are considered together. The sequencing of computer actions forms the basis for control abstraction. The section on procedural abstraction includes a discussion of parameter-passing methods, as well as an overview of program modularization and abstract data types.

CHAPTER 0
INTRODUCTION

0.0 In this Chapter	**3**	
0.1 Problem Solving	**3**	
Devices from Mathematics	4	
Algebra	4	
Logic	4	
Set Theory	5	
Function Theory	5	
Conceptual and Implementation Levels	5	
0.2 Language Paradigms	**6**	
Imperative Paradigms	8	
The Block-Structured Paradigm	8	
The Object-Based Paradigm	8	
The Distributed Programming		
Paradigm	9	
Declarative Paradigms	9	
The Logic Programming Paradigm	10	
The Functional Paradigm	10	
The Database Language Paradigm	10	
Exercises 0.2	10	
0.3 Practical Considerations	**11**	
From Low Through High to Very		
High Level	11	
Programming in the Large	12	
Special Problems	13	

Data Processing	13
Graphics	13
Real-Time Embeddings	14
Exercises 0.3	14
0.4 Language Criteria	**14**
Well-Defined Descriptions	14
BNF and EBNF	14
Semantics	17
Provability	18
Reliability	19
Fast Translation	20
Efficient Object Code	21
Orthogonality	21
Generality	22
Consistency and Common	
Notations	22
Uniformity	22
Subsets	23
Extensibility	23
Portability	23
Exercises 0.4	24
0.5 Summary	**25**
0.6 Notes on References	**25**

Introduction

Computer programs are used to solve problems, and there have been thousands of years of work in mathematics to this end. Programming languages are specified by rules for forming correct statements, organizing them into modules, submitting them to a compiler, which translates the code into a language understandable by a particular machine, and finally running the program, i.e., submitting input to the computer, which transforms it into output according to the instructions in the program. This chapter serves as an introduction to what is to come.

0.0
IN THIS CHAPTER

- Traditional mathematical methods for solving problems and how they have influenced the development of programming languages
- The hierarchy of language paradigms (types of languages): putting disparate languages into order
- Some practical considerations in the world of computer users
- Criteria for deciding whether a language is "good" or "bad"
- A brief introduction to the Backus-Naur and Extended Backus-Naur forms for describing language syntax

0.1
PROBLEM SOLVING

When we use a computer, we are attempting to solve a problem. It may be a business problem involving profit and loss, a scientific problem employing models of physical behavior, a statistical investigation assessing the chance of some event occurring, a linguistic exercise in interpreting natural language, or just plain word processing. People solved problems long before computers became commonplace, resulting in a wealth of experience to benefit from today.

Charles Hoare claims that "the primary purpose of a programming language is to help the programmer in the practice of his art" [Hoare, 1973]. This practice consists of program design, coding, documentation, and debugging. Classic problem-solving aids benefit programmers in many ways, including the design of programs.

Devices from Mathematics

Any problem that can be expressed symbolically or numerically is included in the realm of mathematics. Thus it is in this discipline that most computer languages are based. Mathematicians have worked on different ways to represent facts in economical and unambiguous ways. We can represent the addition of one and two by 1 + 2, PLUS(1,2), or ADD 0001 0010. These are three different syntaxes for the same idea. The syntax of a programming language is much closer to a formal language in the mathematical sense, than to the natural languages we use in everyday parlance. It is important to keep the distinction between natural languages, with their semantic ambiguities, and precise formal languages in mind. The study of programming languages themselves is much more straightforward when approached from a formal perspective than from custom. We will consider formal languages and their relationship to computing devices in Chapter 6.

Each mathematical or program statement has *syntax* (form) and *semantics* (meaning). The semantics for each of the representations of "one plus two" should adhere to the standard notions of the addition of two natural numbers. In any programming language, each statement must be both syntactically and semantically unambiguous. Furthermore, a compiler or interpreter must be able to decide whether a program is syntactically correct. If so, the run-time system must then execute the program in accordance with its semantics. Our understanding of these notions owes much to mathematicians and logicians.

Algebra

Mathematical problem solving has progressed through arithmetic, geometry, algebra, analysis, and their various extensions and subtopics. This large body of methodology has been automated, with user access made through high-level imperative programming languages, which will be defined in the next section. As much as possible, language notation, or syntax, conforms to accepted mathematical usage.

In addition to the problem-solving methods mentioned above, systems have been developed with their own mathematical languages and rules. Three of the most widely used are logic, set theory, and function theory.

Logic

Logic is the science of reasoning. If we follow its syntax and rules, we can deduce new facts from old ones. We will also know that the new facts are just as correct as the old ones were. For example, if "All birds can fly" and "Tweety is a bird" are true, we can deduce "Tweety can fly" applying rules from the predicate calculus.

To reason logically, we must first decide what constitutes a sentence or state-ment and what does not. This is specified by the syntax of the language being used in a particular system of logic. Among correctly written statements, some are true and some are not.

Around the turn of the century, mathematicians thought that all of mathemat-ics could be expressed in formal logic. Although this turned out to be untrue, just as it is untrue that all problems can be solved by computer, the methods developed have proved valuable in mathematics, linguistics, and computer science. We will look more closely at this in Chapter 7.

Set Theory

The theory of sets is another formalism. Hopes that it would capture all of mathematics were dashed in the early thirties when inconsistencies were discov-ered. Practitioners in many fields work comfortably with sets and find them advan-tageous for solving problems. Thus many programming languages incorporate sets directly into the available structures. One language, SETL2, which we will mention only briefly, is based entirely on sets.

Function Theory

After the failures of both formal logic and set theory to incorporate all of math-ematics, Alonzo Church attempted the task through functions. A function, as the word implies, specifies some sort of action or transformation of information. Ad-dition is a function which transforms two numbers into a third according to par-ticular rules. A computer program can be thought of as a function as well, transforming its input into its output. Languages based on functions have been especially useful in the field of artificial intelligence (AI). Although Church's origi-nal program to express all of mathematics through functions failed, the most popu-lar AI language, LISP (an acronym for list processing), owes both its syntax and part of its semantics to his Lambda-Calculus, which will be discussed briefly in Appen-dix B. We will look at LISP in Chapter 8.

The most general of all programming languages can be described using func-tions and can be used as input to the most general of all computers, the Turing Machine. We will discuss these theoretical matters briefly in Chapter 6.

Conceptual and Implementation Levels

Any programming language can be considered equivalent to any other, in that each changes values of the store.[1] They can, however, be quite different at both the con-ceptual and the implementation level. A language is organized around a particu-lar conceptual model. A LISP programmer does not bother with the store, but thinks in terms of functions, atoms, and lists. When programming in logic we consider

---

[1]The store of a computer is usually thought of as an array of cells in which values are kept. Each cell has a unique name that can be recognized through a legal identifier of a programming language. The store may be implemented variously in the hardware of different physical computers.

relations and clauses. When working in Pascal, we think "top down" in terms of procedures accomplishing particular tasks.

Once a language has been developed conceptually, it must be implemented so that its basic structures can be represented at the bit level. This is the job of the compiler designer, who also works at various conceptual levels. In this text, we will mention implementations, but will work largely at the conceptual level.

0.2
LANGUAGE PARADIGMS

The notion of scientific paradigms can be found in Thomas Kuhn's *The Structure of Scientific Revolutions*. He defines them as "universally recognized scientific achievements that for a time provide model problems and solutions to a community of practitioners" [Kuhn, 1962]. Peter Wegner extends the notion to programming language paradigms, which "may be defined intensionally by their properties or extensionally by one or more instances" [Wegner, 1988]. These terms, *intension* and *extension*, are borrowed from set theory. A set may be defined intensionally by describing the members of the set. For example, "S is the set of all black and white dogs" defines the set S intensionally. Any black and white dog is intended to be in S. D = {Spot, Snoopy, Tyge} is defined extensionally. D is built from the empty set $\varnothing$ by extending it three times, D = $\varnothing \cup$ {Spot} $\cup$ {Snoopy} $\cup$ {Tyge}.

The block-structured paradigm can be described intensionally as the set of all programming languages that support nested block structures, including procedures, or it can be described extensionally by listing particular languages with this feature, e.g., BlockStructuredLanguages = {ALGOL, Pascal, Ada, Modula, C}. In defining a paradigm, no attempt is made to insure that the list of language exemplars is exhaustive. Kuhn uses the term *exemplar* for an example that helps to define a paradigm. A single language incorporating all the features of a paradigm is thus an exemplary realization of the paradigm. We may investigate a particular paradigm by exploring the features of one or more representative languages. You will not be far wrong if you relate a language paradigm to a very good example language for a collection of related ideas.

A paradigm, and also its exemplars, is most useful when it is simple and clearly differentiates one language from another. Exemplars may be manufactured to serve as a model, as are some experimental languages, or may be already existing languages. We may say that Ada is "block-structured" and also "object-based." Thus Ada belongs to both the block-structured and object-based paradigms. Whether or not Ada can serve as an exemplar depends on your view of Ada.

In this text, we will explore the paradigms selected by Wegner and his colleagues as representing the languages predominantly in use today by significant groups of programmers and researchers.

Kuhn's essay has been widely praised and is considered to have raised the level of discussion about the nature of science. He claims that notable scientific achievements often precede the recognition of an abstract paradigm. Such achievements serve to define the legitimate problems and research methods in an area of scientific inquiry for succeeding generations of practitioners. When a significant new paradigm is made known, it attracts a group of adherents away from competing methodologies. It also must be open-ended enough to leave all sorts of problems to be solved. Examples of classic competing scientific paradigms are Aristotelian versus Newtonian dynamics, or Ptolemaic versus Copernican astronomy. A more recent example is the wave versus quantum theory of electrical current. Each serves a useful purpose in particular applications. Kuhn holds that "despite occasional ambiguities, the paradigms of a mature science can be determined with relative ease" [Kuhn, 1962].

Wegner believes that computer science is becoming, if not already is, mature and that the paradigms for programming languages fall into two classifications, imperative and declarative. *Imperative languages* specify how a computation is performed by sequences of changes to the computer's store, while *declarative languages* specify what is to be computed.

Kuhn holds that paradigms help specify appropriate puzzles to be solved, and that a scientist is motivated "to succeed in solving a puzzle that no one before has solved or solved so well" [Kuhn, 1962]. Wegner refers to problems in need of solution, rather than puzzles, and to paradigms as descriptions of "patterns of thought for problem solving" [Wegner, 1988]. These patterns are so elusive that, in practice, paradigms are abstracted from models of computation, example languages, and language features. The abstractions, and not the individual languages, are of major importance when considering programming languages as a group. We will deal with notions of abstraction in Chapter 2.

Kuhn traces new paradigms from the breakdown of an older one in an application. He comments that "retooling is an extravagance to be reserved for the occasion that demands it" [Kuhn, 1962]. A breakdown was recognized by the Department of Defense (DOD), which was floundering in a sea of software written in hundreds of sometimes unmaintainable and often fragile different languages. The development of the Ada language, now required for all Defense contracts, involved the simultaneous development of both paradigm and example.

Perhaps the most startling part of Kuhn's work describes scientific revolutions within their social context. When contrasting paradigms exist, the choice of which will hold sway is not always based on merit or proximity to "truth." One community or another decides which problems are more important to solve, and then supports the most promising paradigm for attacking them. This decision is sometimes made acrimoniously, with hostile camps supporting different models. Many criticisms were leveled at *The Structure of Scientific Revolutions* when it first appeared. There was confusion over the paradigm notion itself. In a postscript to the second edition [Kuhn, 1970], Kuhn attempts to separate the notion into two parts: the constellation of beliefs, values, and techniques shared by a community of practitioners, and the concrete models or examples themselves. He identifies four components of a discipline organized around a particular paradigm. The first he calls symbolic generalizations. These are the written rules or laws of the paradigm. Second are the beliefs of the community of practitioners, the particular ways of proceeding that appear to be most fruitful. Third are the values of a group about what is most important. Simplicity, such as is found in Pascal or pure LISP, might be valued more than widespread applicability, one of the goals of PL/I. The fourth and final component is the exemplars themselves, including the problems to be solved with their solutions.

Programming language paradigms and languages are not immune from champions and detractors. Certain languages become *linguae francae* for commercial, scientific, or other reasons. We will recognize all of Kuhn's four components as we look more closely at the paradigms and their particular language exemplars.

Imperative Paradigms

Imperative paradigms are those which facilitate computation by means of state changes. By a state, we mean the condition of a computer's random access memory (RAM),[2] or store. It is sometimes helpful to think of computer memory as a sequence of "snapshots," each one capturing the values in all the memory cells at a particular time. Each individual snapshot records a state.

When a program is entered, associated data exists in a certain condition, say an unsorted list off-line. It is the programmer's job to specify a sequence of changes to the store that will produce the desired final state, perhaps a sorted list. The store involves much more than data and a stored program, of course. It includes symbol tables, a run-time stack(s), an operating system and its associated queues and stacks, etc. The complete program, data, and even the CPU itself can be viewed as part of the initial state. The first task might be to input the unsorted list and the final one to output the sorted list. We will discuss the formal connections between languages and state transitions in Chapter 6.

The Block-Structured Paradigm

FORTRAN, the first language with program blocks, partitions the state into blocks representing subroutines and common data. FORTRAN blocks can be thought of as a flat file, where each block follows its predecessors. Because of this flat structure, FORTRAN is no longer considered to be a block-structured language, but is an example of a procedure-oriented language, where programs are executed through successive calls to separate procedures. FORTRAN's libraries of tested, useful procedures are one of its practical features.

The term *block structure* now refers to nested scopes. That is, blocks may be nested within other blocks, and may contain their own variables. The state represents a stack with a reference to the block currently active on top. In block-structured languages, the procedure is the principal building block of programs. Language examples are Ada, ALGOL 60, Pascal, ALGOL 68, and C.

The Object-Based Paradigm

The object-based paradigm describes languages that support interacting objects. An object is a group of procedures that share a state [Wegner, 1988]. Since data is

---

[2]The user can read or write to RAM in contrast to ROM, which is read-only memory.

also part of a state, data and all the procedures or functions that apply to it can be captured in a single object. Examples are Ada, where objects are called packages; Modula, where they are called modules; and Smalltalk, where objects are called (rightfully) objects. In C++, a collection of objects is grouped into a class.

The term *object-oriented* was originally used to distinguish those object-based languages that supported classes of objects and the inheritance of attributes of a parent object by its children. Ada 83 was considered to be object-based, but not object-oriented. Some features of the object-oriented paradigm have been added to Ada 95, but it is not considered to be fully object-oriented by some practitioners.

The Distributed Programming Paradigm

Concurrent programming has been divided into two broad categories, loosely or tightly coupled systems. The term *distributed* usually refers to languages for loosely coupled systems that support a group of programmers working on a particular program simultaneously and communicating through message passing over a communications channel, such as a point-to-point link or a local area network (LAN). In a loosely coupled distributed system, a language need not support simultaneous memory sharing, thus skirting some problems.

A tightly coupled system allows more than one running process to access the same memory location. A language associated with the system must synchronize the sharing of memory so that only one process writes to a shared variable at a time, and so that a process can wait until certain conditions are fulfilled before continuing to execute. Shared memory has the advantage of speed, because messages need not be passed.

Concurrent programming is associated with more than one CPU operating simultaneously in parallel, with or without data sharing. Multiple CPUs are not essential for this paradigm, however. What is essential is that work on a particular problem can be shared. Ada is perhaps the best-known language supporting concurrency. In Ada, two or more procedures execute independently. The sharing of results occurs through a process called a *rendezvous*.

Recently, work has been done on languages that blur the distinction between the loosely and tightly coupled paradigms. Languages such as Concurrent PROLOG, Linda, and Occam have some features of both. In Chapter 5 we will consider both the distributed and shared-variable paradigms.

Declarative Paradigms

A declarative language is one in which a program specifies a relation or function [Wegner, 1988]. When programming in the declarative style, we make no assignments to program variables. The interpreter or compiler for the particular language manages memory for us. These languages are "higher level" than imperative languages, in that the programmer operates more remotely from the CPU itself.

The three declarative paradigms are taken from mathematics: logic, the theory of functions, and the relational calculus.

The Logic Programming Paradigm

Logic programming is based on a subset of the predicate calculus, including statements written in forms known as Horn clauses. The predicate calculus provides axioms and rules so one can deduce new facts from other known facts. A Horn clause allows only one new fact to be deduced in any single statement. A system of Horn clauses allows a particularly mechanical method of proof called *resolution.*

A logic-based program consists of a series of axioms or facts, rules of inference, and a theorem or query to be proved. The output is true if the facts support the query and false otherwise. PROLOG is the exemplar for logic programming languages.

The Functional Paradigm

Purely functional languages operate only through functions. A function returns a single value, given a list of parameters. No global assignments, called side effects, are permitted. A program is a function call with parameters possibly calling other functions to produce actual parameter values. Such a function call might be:

```
DoPayroll(BalanceBooks(ComputeSalaries(EmployeeRecords), OldBooks))
```

returning the value NewBooks. During the running of DoPayroll, no changes would be made to either EmployeeRecords or OldBooks.

Functions themselves are first-class values which can be passed to other functions and returned as functional values. Thus functional programming provides the ability for a program (function) to modify itself, i.e., learn.

In practice, there are few purely functional languages, since basic side effects such as input and output are desirable. LISP is the best-known functional language. Pure LISP exists and has a devoted following, but production versions include many nonfunctional features.

The Database Language Paradigm

The properties that distinguish languages designed to deal with databases are persistence and the management of change. Database entities do not disappear after a program terminates, but live on indefinitely as originally structured. Since the database, once organized, is permanent, these languages must also support change. The data may change and so too may the relationships between data entities or objects.

A database management system includes a *data definition language* (DDL) for describing a new collection of facts, or data, and a *data manipulation language* (DML) for interacting with existing databases.

Database languages can be embedded in other programming languages for greater flexibility. An effort is also being made to make them easy to use, so nonprogrammers can manage the normal data of the world of business and affairs.

EXERCISES 0.2
1. Consider a language you know well and discuss it in terms of the four paradigm components mentioned by Kuhn.
    a. Symbolic generalization: What are the written rules of the language?
    b. Beliefs of the practitioners: What particular features of the language are believed to be "better" than in other languages?
    c. Values: What thinking or programming style did the originators believe best?
    d. Exemplars: What sort of problems can be solved most easily in the language?

2. If you know more than one language, repeat Exercise 1, comparing this second language with the first.
3. FORTRAN, standing for FORmula TRANslation, was the first language that tried to let programmers express their problems in familiar mathematical notation. Name some examples that are perfectly good algebraic formulas, but do not work well as programming expressions. What is the problem? You might consider both the limitations of computers as finite computational devices and the limitations of particular equipment, such as keyboards and visual displays. How about the symbols themselves?
4. ALGOL was the first ALGOrithmic Language. What devices must be implemented to deal successfully with algorithms?
5. If shortness of source code is valued, we might rank languages in terms of how many lines are needed to write code for a particular problem. APL, C, BASIC, Pascal, and COBOL are listed here in order from shortest to longest average program length. Discuss the features that promote brief code in languages with which you are familiar.
6. The most familiar recursive procedure is the factorial function,

```
FACT(0) = 1
FACT(n) = n * FACT(n-1), (n > 0)
```

Recursion is often implemented as a run-time stack, with a node pushed on the stack each time the function is called and popped off when no longer needed. Suppose a reference to the block of code for FACT is F. (Here "reference" refers to the memory address where the code is stored.) Draw the stack for FACT(3). What information other than F must be in each node of the stack to make the recursion work?

0.3
PRACTICAL CONSIDERATIONS

Computer programs are written to exploit the limits of computers and their problem-solving abilities. Sometimes their purpose is to solve efficiently some particularly tedious problem in the real world of science, industry, and business. Thus languages are designed to incorporate particular features desired by the potential users. Languages designed with particular users in mind include COBOL for the business community and Ada for the DOD.

From Low Through High to Very High Level

A language is considered low level if one can directly manipulate a machine's random access memory (RAM) using statements in the language. Those at the lowest level are machine dependent and assign values of 0 or 1 to individual bits. A simplistic assembly language program to initialize a five-element array to 0 is:

```
MOV #0,R2
MOV R2,428
MOV R2,430
MOV R2,432
MOV R2,434
MOV R2,436
```
(0.3.1)

After execution of the fragment, words 428–436 of RAM will contain the value 0. Equivalent code in Pascal is:

```
var                                                              (0.3.2)
   IntArray : array[1..5] of integer;
   I : 1..5;

begin
   for I := 1 to 5 do
      IntArray[I] := 0;
...
```

The Pascal code is easier to understand, but we have lost control over just which memory locations will house the array. The Pascal compiler does this, presumably, in an efficient manner.

In APL we can do the job with:

```
V <- 5 0                                                         (0.3.3)
```

Here the instruction is certainly quick and easy, but we have lost yet another element of control over the machine itself. When an APL program is executing, space must be found for the five-element vector V "on the fly."

```
V <- V,V
```

is also a perfectly good APL statement, which produces two copies of V catenated together, i.e., V is 0 0 0 0 0 0 0 0 0 0.

Languages such as APL, LISP, PROLOG, SETL2, and SNOBOL are called "very high level languages" because they allow the direct manipulation of complex data structures. In APL the basic structures are arrays and matrices; in PROLOG, relations; in SETL, sets and maps; and in SNOBOL, patterns, or sets of strings. The goal of these languages is to make programming easier. Program specification and "coding up" are to be done in one straightforward step.

The price paid for efficient writing of programs may be execution efficiency. Very high level programs often have large memory requirements and execute slowly. They are, however, very useful for prototyping, the trying out of preliminary versions of new systems. The languages are often easy to learn, so suitable for beginning students and for designers of programming languages and other computer applications. Compiler writers and machine builders are working to translate programs written in these languages directly into more efficient intermediate languages so that the expensive part of application development, the man-years of programmer time, can be minimized.

Programming in the Large

One of the things a computer does well is remember large numbers of facts. It can also process these facts much faster than any human. Just think of the possibilities when a group of human beings work with a group of computers on a particularly hard problem, such as predicting the weather. This is perfectly reasonable to tackle, since meteorologists know what sorts of data are needed and good equipment exists to measure this data. Managing a world economy, where daily local fluctuations in currency and bond rates affect markets world-wide is another problem of large proportions. Attempts at coordinating both human and machine efforts will be discussed in Chapters 4 and 5.

Special Problems

As computers have become more available, due to both increased capabilities and lowered prices, they are being used to accomplish more tasks. When a particular use becomes pervasive in an industry, it sometimes pays to develop both machines and languages specialized to the task at hand.

Data Processing

One of the first areas where computers were obviously useful was in handling massive amounts of data. Herman Hollerith's tabulating machine was first used in compiling the 1890 U.S. census. For the past fifty years, every sizable corporation has had a data processing (DP) department. Dickens's Bob Cratchit was the classic data processor with his account books and quill pen. As these tasks became mechanized, fourth-generation languages (4GLs) were developed to meet these special needs.

Why fourth generation? Although different authors divide languages up differently, a reasonable grouping is to call machine languages first generation, assembly languages second, and procedural languages third generation.[3] These last include FORTRAN, COBOL, ALGOL, Pascal, and C. Gary Hansen [Hansen, 1988] describes 4GLs as languages with the following five properties:

1. Database structures and programming
2. A centralized data dictionary containing information about system components
3. Visual programming, such as using a mouse with icons
4. A graded-skill user interface allowing novices as well as database experts to use the programs
5. An interactive, integrated, multifunction programming environment

Although a discussion of fully functional fourth-generation languages such as NOMAD and Application Factory is beyond the scope of this book, we include IBM's database language SQL in Chapter 9.

Graphics

Graphics is, of course, concerned with graphs, charts, and other visual representations of data. Here we need languages that can manipulate individual dots

---

[3]In this categorization of languages by generation, it is interesting that LISP fits nowhere. PROLOG is generally considered to be a language of the fifth generation, and Ada can be thought to be an extension of third-generation languages. Functional languages seem to be off in an unnamed generation by themselves.

(pixels) on a monitor or printing device. More difficult is incorporating a graphics language into an existing programming language. This is often the job of an Integrated Development Environment (IDE), which may include editors, debuggers, etc., as well. An IDE is not part of a language per se, but is sometimes packaged with a compiler.

Real-Time Embeddings

Computers can accomplish tasks other than the production of printed output from given numerical input. They may also signal apparatuses to do one thing or another, given certain conditions. In such a case, a computer and its languages may be embedded in another larger machine. Examples are medical monitors, which automatically regulate intravenous dosages depending on data taken from the patient, automatic pilots in airplanes, and the entire Strategic Defense Initiative (SDI). One of the primary purposes of the DOD-sponsored language, Ada, is to facilitate these real-time embeddings. We will see examples of language features supporting such activity throughout the text.

EXERCISES 0.3
1. Suppose we wish to print out the arrays defined in listings (0.3.1)–(0.3.3). Which would you expect to be printed the fastest? slowest? Why?
2. The BASIC language permits undeclared arrays of up to ten elements. Why do you think the designers forced users to declare larger arrays but not small ones?

0.4
LANGUAGE CRITERIA

There are, or have been, literally hundreds of programming languages. Many are no longer used, while the notions of others have been incorporated in other languages. Throughout this text, we will discuss the following criteria for considering a language meritorious. There are many other lists. These were first suggested by Barbara Liskov in a course at MIT and are reported in [Horowitz, 1984]. The criteria are interrelated, e.g., a language with a well-defined description may well be reliable and efficient, in part because of its description. We will merely define the terms here.

Well-Defined Descriptions

FORTRAN or PL/I programmers often worked as a group. If one didn't know or had forgotten how to write code to perform a particular task, the easiest thing to do was walk down the hall and ask a friend. The manuals were huge, poorly organized volumes that instructed by example more often than by any other means.

BNF and EBNF

The designers of ALGOL 60 rectified this by providing a tidy, eighteen-page language description. Language syntax is described in the formal Backus-Naur Form

(BNF), followed by programming examples. BNF is an example of a metalanguage, a language used to describe another language, in this case a programming language. BNF has symbols, called metasymbols, and rules of its own, which are used to define the syntax of the particular programming language in question.

By *syntax*, we mean a collection of statements formed by following a set of rules that differentiate valid from invalid programs. Syntax by itself gives no meaning to a language; it merely defines the collection of phrases and sentences that are valid combinations of the characters of the language. We will look at language definitions more carefully in Chapter 6. However, in order to understand the language descriptions that follow, you will need to understand a bit of BNF now.

BNF employs the metasymbols ::=, |, <, >, ., and boldface as follows:

Metasymbol	Meaning	(0.4.1)[4]
::=	is defined to be	
|	alternatively, or	
<something>	<something> is to be replaced by its definition	
something	A word written in boldface is called a terminal or *token* indicating an indivisible language element allowing no further replacements	

In the brief discussion of BNF that follows, we will use the Pascal-like pseudocode, used when describing language features in Chapters 1–3, as an example. We will start with the BNF definition for a pseudocode program shown in listing (0.4.2).

```
<program> ::= <program-heading>';'<program-block>                (0.4.2)
<program-heading> ::= program <identifier>
<program-block> ::= <block> program
<block> ::= <constant-definition-part>
              <type-definition-part>
                 <variable-declaration-part>
                    <procedure-and-function-declaration-part>
                       <statement-part>
<statement-part> ::= <compound-statement>
<compound-statement> ::= begin <statement-sequence> end
```

Pseudocode identifiers are described in BNF as:

```
<identifier> ::= <letter>|<identifier><letter>|<identifier><digit>     (0.4.3)
```

The BNF definition can be read as, "An identifier is defined to be a letter, or an identifier followed by a letter, or an identifier followed by a digit." Notice that the definition is recursive since <identifier> occurs on both the left and the right sides of the metasymbol, ::=. Letters and digits are defined to be:

```
<letter> ::= a|b|c|d|e|f|g|h|i|j|k|l|m|n|o|p|q|r|s|t|u|v|w|x|y|z     (0.4.4)[5]
<digit>  ::= 0|1|2|3|4|5|6|7|8|9
```

---

[4]In some versions of BNF, ::= is replaced by = or –>, and <something> by *something*. Tokens may be written in single quotes, to indicate their indivisibility, e.g., 'a' instead of **a**.

[5]Our pseudocode is not *case sensitive*, so the listing of lowercase letters implies the inclusion of uppercase letters as well.

Examples of identifiers are: q, Q, Soup, V17a, a34kTMNs, and MARILYN. To show that V17a conforms to the definition, we make the following substitutions:

```
<identifier>                                           (0.4.5)
<identifier><letter>
<identifier>a
<identifier><digit>a
<identifier>7a
<identifier><digit>7a
<identifier>17a
<letter>17a
V17a
```

Since BNF definitions are not always obvious, *syntax diagrams* or *railroad charts* have become popular, especially in elementary language manuals. The chart for an identifier is shown in Figure 0.4.1.

If one follows the arrows, the same restrictions as in the BNF definition are encountered. Our pseudocode is not case sensitive, so uppercase as well as lowercase letters may be used in the definition.

Individual characters are tokens, and our pseudocode has other tokens as well. Some of these are special symbols, such as +, -, =, ;, and ::=. Others are called word-symbols, which include *reserved words,* which may not be redefined within a program. Note that these reserved words always appear boldface. The BNF for these is:

```
<word-symbol> ::= program | const | type | procedure | function | var |   (0.4.6)
                  begin | end | div | mod | and | not | or | in | array |
                  file | record | set | case | of | for | to | downto | do |
                  if | then | else | repeat | until | while | with | nil
```

Identifiers are also tokens, as are numbers and strings.

BNF was extended in various ways, usually called EBNF (Extended Backus-Naur Form). Additional symbols defined for the International Standards Organization (ISO) 1980 Revised Standard for Pascal [ISO-DP7185, 1980] are as follows:

Symbol	Meaning	(0.4.7)
[something]	0 or 1 occurrence of something, i.e., optional	
{something}	0 or more occurrences of something	
(this | that)	grouping; either of this or that	

In EBNF the definition of an identifier can be shortened to:

```
<identifier> ::= <letter>{<letter>|<digit>}                (0.4.8)
```

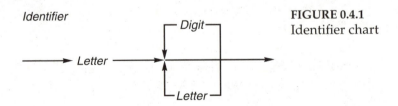

Identifier

FIGURE 0.4.1
Identifier chart

Notice the economy and clarity of style, with the recursion of the BNF definition eliminated.

We will now continue the definition of a program, started above in listing (0.4.2). The EBNF definition for <statement-sequence> is:

```
<statement-sequence> ::= statement{statement}
```
(0.4.9)

Instances of [something] and of (this | that) occur in the definition for a statement as follows:

```
<statement> ::= (<simple-statement> | <structured-statement>)                (0.4.10)
<simple-statement> ::= <empty-statement> | <assignment-statement> |
                       <procedure-statement>
<structured-statement> ::= <compound-statement> | <conditional-statement> |
                           <repetitive-statement | <with-statement>
<conditional-statement> ::= <if-statement> | <case-statement>
<if-statement> ::= if <boolean-expression> then statement [<else-part>] end if;
<else-part> ::= else statement
```

As an example of how this all works, we need first the applicable EBNF definitions for simple expressions. Then we will show that the simple expression A + B * 2 is syntactically correct.

```
1.  <simple-expression> ::= [sign] <term> {<adding-operator><term>}          (0.4.11)
2.  <term> ::= <factor> {<multiplying-operator><term>}
3.  <factor> ::= <identifier> | <unsigned-constant> | <function-designator> |
                 <set-constructor> | <expression> | not <factor>
4.  <unsigned-constant> ::= <unsigned-number> | <character-string> | <constant-identifier>
5.  <unsigned-number> ::= <digit-sequence> | <unsigned-real>
6.  <digit-sequence> ::= digit{digit}
7.  <adding-operator> ::= + | - | or
8.  <multiplying-operator> ::= * | / | div | mod | and
```

A *syntax tree*, showing the derivation of A + B * 2, is shown in Figure 0.4.2. Other EBNF definitions for pseudocode language constructs will be introduced in Chapter 1. Just how it is used should become clear as the various examples are encountered.

Semantics

A language must also be defined *semantically* by describing just what a particular construct means. For example, the expression (X < 3) means in pseudocode that X must have a value; that value is comparable to the integer 3, and the expression is true if value < 3, and false otherwise. Natural language is notoriously ambiguous, so efforts are being made to describe formally language semantics as well as syntax.

Two formal mathematical methods are being used to describe the semantics of languages. The first is axiomatic and the second denotational. Axiomatic semantics are based on the predicate calculus, which we will discuss in Chapter 7 when we study the declarative, logic-based language PROLOG. Axiomatic semantics

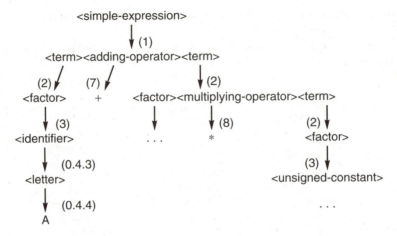

FIGURE 0.4.2

A syntax tree—parenthesized numbers to the right of each derivation indicate the rule used

make statements about programs that are either true or false at various stages in a program's execution. These statements are usually in the form of pre- and post-conditions, which are made before and after a statement such as a loop or procedure executes. If each condition can be proven true, regardless of the data input, the program will be guaranteed to be correct.

Denotational semantics is based on the theory of functions. We will study programming languages based on functions in Chapter 8. Each program and each procedure is associated with a (recursive) function. If program P is associated with function f_P and if $X_1, X_2, \ldots, X_n$ are inputs to P, then $f_P(X_1, \ldots, X_n)$ should produce a value corresponding to the desired output of P, given $X_1, X_2, \ldots, X_n$ as inputs.

A third semantic method is to describe a theoretical machine for a language and how it operates. A compiler writer's job would then be to implement this machine for a particular piece of hardware. The designer will have already guaranteed that the language operates correctly on the theoretical machine. We will see an example of such a machine in Chapter 7.

Formal semantic methods are important for several reasons. They provide, first, an unambiguous language definition; second, standards so that a language will not vary from implementation to implementation; and third, a basis for correctness proofs of both compilers and programs.

Provability

Proving with mathematical certainty that a program is correct is a slow-going process. C.A.R. Hoare believes, however, that "the practical advantages of program proving will eventually outweigh the difficulties, in view of the increasing costs of programming error" [Hoare, 1969]. Proving a program correct involves three steps:

first, proving that the program accomplishes the intention of the programmer; second, proving that the compiler correctly translates the syntax and semantics of the language used into machine code; and third, proving that the machine itself operates correctly.

One goal for any programming language is to prove that a compiler for the language accurately interprets it. This is often hard to do if the language definition includes natural language descriptions of what is meant by a particular bit of syntax. If syntax can be described in a formal language, and semantics described axiomatically, a compiler can be formally proved to fulfill both the syntactical and semantic definition of a language.

The syntax of Pascal was defined in BNF, and its semantics defined axiomatically by its designer, Nicholas Wirth, working with C.A.R. Hoare. PL/I was designed using the Vienna Definition Language (VDL), and ALGOL 68 was defined in a two-level vW-grammar—named for its originator, A. van Wijngaarden—which was too arcane for most users. These last two metalanguages form bases for proving compilers. If a language is defined in VDL, it includes a description of what happens when each statement of the language is executed theoretically on a theoretical computer. If a compiler faithfully implements the theoretical computer, program execution can be proved correct. The vW-grammar does not describe a theoretical computer, but does allow that part of semantics dealing with declarations to be defined in the grammar. Thus no grammatically correct programs can be generated that redeclare variables or define them in an inconsistent manner.

Reliability

Software is considered reliable if it behaves as advertised and produces results the user expects. When an error occurs, it should be easily detected and corrected. A programming language fosters the writing of reliable programs in often subtle ways. The goto statement is perhaps the most notorious language feature thought to result in unreliable programs [Dijkstra, 1968b]. The underlying problem here is that programs with many back-and-forth goto's are hard for anyone but the originator to read, and thus hard to modify or debug.

Unusual syntax features may also foster errors. The C language uses = as an assignment operator. x = 5 assigns the value 5 to the storage location designated for x. For comparisons, == is used. x == 5 compares the value of x to 5 and is either true or false, depending on whether x equals 5 or not. Since C allows assignments almost anywhere in a statement, the inadvertent substitution of = for the unfamiliar == may produce no error, only unintelligible results. Both Modula-2 and C identifiers are case sensitive. Thus Count and count represent distinct variables, which are easily confused by both a programmer and a subsequent reader.

A reliable language should be able to handle run-time errors. Arithmetic overflow occurs when an integer is computed that is larger than can be supported by the particular hardware involved. A variety of errors can occur during data input, from reading past the end of a file to an unallowed value entered interactively. These kinds of errors are called *exceptions*, and language provisions for dealing with them are called *exception handlers*. Aborting a program is not always acceptable, particularly for real-time applications.

For programming languages, reliability will usually refer to mechanisms that promote the writing, maintaining, and debugging of correct programs, and the subsequent handling of exceptions when a program runs.

Fast Translation

The programming languages we will consider in this text are usually machine independent. That is, a program written in the language can be translated and then run on a variety of different machines. A program we write is in *source code*. This must be translated into a language a particular machine can recognize, and eventually into *machine code* that can actually run. The machine on which a program will run is called the *host* and its language(s), *host language(s).* We put the alternate (s) after language here, because a machine may have more than one host language. Any machine must have an associated low level machine language written in binary code. It may also have a higher level machine-specific assembly language. Often it is practical to first translate source code into *target code*, which is intermediate between source and machine code. Target code may or may not be one of the host languages.

Translation of source code involves three steps: lexical analysis, syntactic analysis, and semantic analysis. Lexical analysis, or *scanning*, identifies which tokens represent values, identifiers, operators, etc. Syntactic analysis, called *parsing*, recognizes valid statements while rejecting invalid statements of the source language. Semantic analysis determines the "meaning" of a statement. Some translators can perform two or more of these three processes in a single pass over the source code.

Translators are either *interpreters* or *generative translators*, which generate target code. An interpreter is itself a program that translates a language expression or statement, computes, and then prints or otherwise uses its result. Interpreters are usually easier to write than generative translators, but execute more slowly. One advantage of an interpreter is that execution as well as syntax errors are detected as each statement is encountered, thus eliminating any doubt about just where any trouble lies. The LISP and PROLOG languages have both interpreters and compilers, the first being used for learning and experimentation, where line-by-line results are desirable. A compiler is usually more advantageous for large programs.

The most common parts of a generative translator are the *compiler, linker,* and *loader*. The compiler translates source code into machine-oriented target code, called *object code*. The linker links together independently compiled target code into a single *load module*, resolving differences among tokens. Its output may be in the same target code as its input but is free of references from module to module. Resulting code is thus *relocatable*, since it contains any information it needs and is independent of other program segments. The loader makes the final translation into machine code and loads the program into various memory locations. The output from the loader is an *executable module* in machine code. During each phase, entries are made into various tables, which keep track of the types of variables, storage addresses, etc.

It is important in some instances, e.g., an interactive application, that source code translate quickly. On the other hand, if a program will be compiled only once, and run often, compilation speed may not be a primary concern. Successful attempts have been made at one-pass compilers, which scan the source code only once, while some translators make many passes (e.g., some of IBM's first PL/I compilers, which made more than thirty passes to compile a complete program). Some factors affecting the number of passes needed by a particular compiler are [Tremblay, 1985]:

1. How much memory is available? Can both the source and object code being generated fit in memory simultaneously?
2. How fast is the compiler itself and how much memory does it require?
3. How large is the object program and how fast must it run? Must the object code be optimized?
4. What sort of debugging features are required for the source code?
5. What sorts of error detection and recovery is required for executable code?
6. How many people will be involved in writing the compiler? Would it be advantageous to let each write an independent pass accomplishing a single phase of the compilation process?

Efficient Object Code

After source code is compiled into object code, no further reference is made to the source language. Thus it is at compile time that matters of efficiency in both memory use and execution time must be considered. There is usually a trade-off between work that the programmer must do and work that the compiler can do. For example a language that has all type and variable declarations preceding other code can assign all memory locations at one time, speeding up compilation. The programmer will have to make these declarations, of course, before a program can be compiled.

Some compilers, called *optimizing compilers*, execute one or two more steps after semantic analysis to increase the efficiency of the compiled code. The first optimizations, such as eliminating common subexpressions, are machine independent, while final improvements depend on the particular machine on which the program will run. Very high level languages, where programs manipulate complex structures such as records, lists, relations, or sets, depend on optimizing compilers for efficiency. Programming languages run the gamut from ones like C, where the programmer can work very close to the CPU itself, to database manipulation languages (DMLs), where underlying physical structures are largely hidden. In the lower level languages, efficient object code often reflects the programmer's skill, while in very high level languages it depends on the skill of compiler writers.

Orthogonality

The word *orthogonal* comes from the Greek and refers to straight lines meeting at right angles. Random variables are considered to be orthogonal if they are independent. It is in this sense of independence that language features can be considered orthogonal. Here we mean that components are independent of each other and that they behave in the same way in any circumstance.

One example is in the concepts of types and functions. A type describes the structure of data items. A function is a procedure that is passed a finite number of parameter values and returns a single value to the calling procedure. In an orthogonal language, types are independent of functions, and no restrictions apply to the types of parameters that can be passed or to the type of value that can be returned. Thus we would be able to pass a function to a function, and receive a function back. LISP incorporates this particular feature, but certain inherent difficulties must be understood and dealt with.

ALGOL 68 was intended as an entirely orthogonal language. It has very few built-in constructs, and the programmer is able to build what is wanted by combining features. It never became popular in the United States, in part because it was too orthogonal. Programmers wanted special structures that behaved in predictable ways.

Nonorthogonality can be annoying and lead to errors. To the novice Pascal programmer, there seems to be no good reason why a function cannot return a record or that a file must be passed as a **var** parameter.

Generality

Generality is related to orthogonality. It refers to the existence of only necessary language features, with others composed in a free and uniform manner without limitation and with predictable effects. As an example of a lack of generality, consider the free union type in Pascal. A free union is a record that may have a field that varies in type depending on its use. We will consider free unions in Chapter 1. In such a record, the variant field variable might function as a pointer and not be directly accessible, for printing or other uses. At another time during the same run, it might be typed as an integer, with its value available for printing, arithmetic operations, etc. This feature is not general, because the storage location related to the variant field variables is not treated in a uniform manner and the effects are not predictable.

Consistency and Common Notations

As we have mentioned before, problems for computer solution are often conceived in the languages of mathematics. Thus the notation of programming languages should be consistent with the commonly used notations of this field. We use "−" to indicate subtraction and negative numbers. Thus 5 − 3 and −5 should be allowed in languages supporting integer arithmetic.

$1 \in \{1, 2, 3\}$ is the common notation for set membership, and is thus preferable to Pascal's 1 **in** [1, 2, 3]. However, not all character sets support $\in$, {, and }, so substitutions are sometimes made.

Uniformity

Related to consistency is uniformity.[6] By this we mean that similar notions should look and behave in the same way. One uniformity issue has to do with the necessity for begins and ends. Should every "end" be preceded by a matching "begin"?

---

[6]The same notions which we are calling uniformity here, following Liskov's definition, are called regularity by other authors.

Similarly, should every statement end with a semicolon (;)? In a completely uniform language, the answer would be yes to both questions.

Subsets

A subset of a language is an implementation of only part of it, without special features. The original specifications for the DOD language Ada allowed no subsets. Motivating this was the desire of the DOD to have its contractors produce software exploiting a full-featured Ada. After all, unnecessary features were not included. One of the disadvantages of this approach was that students could not begin learning the language until fully validated compilers were available; thus a corps of programmers did not exist until several years after the language had been completed.

Some languages are large, with many special components. These can run only on large machines and are unavailable to smaller companies and schools unless subsetted. Another advantage of subsets is incremental development of a language. By this we mean early release of a small core language, with other features being released as they are developed.

Extensibility

The converse of subsets is extensibility. A language may have a standard core, which is unvarying on every implementation, but various extensions. The advantages of subsets are enhanced when a language can be extended in useful ways. Beginning in 1968, the developers of COBOL (COmmon Business Oriented Language) adopted this approach by defining a "nucleus" that all compilers must meet. Eleven standardized modules were added, which may or may not be included in any given COBOL compiler. Ada 95 has adopted a similar modular approach.

Designers of Pascal used yet another approach, defining a small portable standard language, with some desirable features, such as graphics and string handling capabilities, missing. Implementers of Pascal added various enhancements, which made their compilers attractive to programmers, but the resulting programs less portable. For example, Standard Pascal has no string type, but almost all Pascal compilers provide one built into the language itself or in a special module to be included with most source files.

Portability

A language is portable if its programs can be compiled and run on different machines without the source code having to be rewritten. To achieve portability, national and international standards organizations have been established to produce language descriptions to which implementations must adhere. The most active of these are the American National Standards Institute (ANSI), British Standards Institution (BSI), International Standards Organization (ISO), and the Institute of Electrical and Electronics Engineers (IEEE). These groups have various official committees, which prepare and revise standards for different languages.

Standards can be developed after gaining some experience with a particular language, as with Pascal, or before a language is designed, as with Ada. Early standardization may perpetuate unrecognized poor design features, while delay fosters incompatible dialects. LISP is perhaps the language with the greatest unstandardized longevity. LISP was designed and implemented in the early sixties, but is only now being standardized to Common LISP. The standardized part will be only a small core, however, with different implementers free to make any extensions they wish.

EXERCISES 0.4

1. Complete the right side of the syntax tree of Figure 0.4.2.
2. Draw a syntax tree to demonstrate that the following are syntactically correct pseudocode expressions. Write the number of the rule used to the right of each substitution as in Figure 0.4.2.

   a. (3 + X) * Y   b. **not** (A **or** B)   c. 2 **or** A

3. Exercise 2c represents a syntactically correct expression that is semantically incorrect. If a compiler were written to implement our pseudocode, when might this error be trapped: during lexical, syntactic, or semantic analysis, or at run time?
4. Well-defined descriptions must be written for both the syntax and semantics of a language. Find the definition of a "for" statement in two different formalisms. Two possibilities are syntax diagrams in Pascal and EBNF for ALGOL 60 or Ada. Which do you find easiest to read?
5. Using the descriptions you found for exercise 4, look at the semantic definitions. Are they formal or natural language definitions? To find these semantic definitions, you may have to locate the official standard or report. Syntax charts often appear in textbooks, but the semantic definitions may be missing, with meaning explained in the body of the text or by example.
6. Use the EBNF statements in listing (0.4.10) to show that statement a below is syntactically correct, while statement b is not. Why is b ambiguous?

   ```
   a. if (N = 1) then print ('N WINS!'); else
          if (N = 2) then print ('N PLACES!'); end if;
      end if;
   b. if (M < 4) then if (M < 2) then print ('M WINS!')
          else print (M SHOWS OR PLACES!); end if;
   ```

7. When producing object code, optimization involves rearranging and changing operations to make the program run faster. One of these techniques is called *folding*, the process of computing at compile time arithmetic operations that are known [Gries, 1971]. Suppose our source code includes the following sequence of statements:

   ```
   H := 1 + 1; I := 3; B := 6.2 + I
   ```

   These can be optimized to

   ```
   H := 2; I := 3; B := 9.2
   ```

   Optimize the following sequences of statements:

   ```
   a. X := 10; Y := X / 2; Z := SQR(X) - (X + Y);
   b. X := 10; Y := X + Z; Z := SQR(X) - (X + Y);
   c. case I of
          1: Print (I * 2);
          2: Print (I * 3);
          3: Print (I * 4);
          else Print (I)
      end case;
   ```

8. If you are familiar with some assembly language, convert the code sequences of exercise 3 into both optimized and unoptimized assembly code.
9. Find as many as you can of nonorthogonal or nongeneral features of a language you are familiar with. For each, why do you think the restriction was made?

0.5
SUMMARY

We first looked at traditional methods for solving problems, which include algebra, logic, and function theory. We then discussed Peter Wegner's organization of programming languages into imperative and declarative paradigms. Imperative languages work by changing the values of computer memory, called the store, while the declarative style involves writing commands to perform some action, e.g., sort a list. Mechanisms hidden within the language itself then carry out the instructions. Algebra is the basis for most imperative languages, while the other two devices from mathematics form the basis for declarative languages.

The imperative paradigm is further divided into block-structured, object-oriented, and distributed languages. The first two group program ideas into program units called blocks or objects. Each may have data local to the unit. The object groups operations on data with the data itself.

The declarative paradigm includes, in addition to logic and function-based languages, a paradigm for database operations. These are often based on the theory of relations.

Not all languages fit neatly into one paradigm or another, with many having features of more than one. There are also languages designed to tackle special computing problems, such as graphic displays and those that run in real time, controlling other sorts of machines.

Languages must be reliable, understandable, efficient in terms of run time and space consumption, and must meet the needs of a community, be they scientists, business people, or nontechnical users. Each of these groups is used to a particular vocabulary and way of looking at things; thus a variety of languages exists and will most likely continue to do so.

0.6
NOTES ON REFERENCES

A well-written and fairly easy-to-read text on axiomatic semantics is [Gries, 1981]. The book has many easy examples, which allows for understanding, but that is also its drawback. Nowhere is a program of even average length or complexity analyzed using the pre- and post-condition methodology. [Tennent, 1976] and [Gordon, 1979] provide good introductions to denotational semantics. Both axiomatic and denotational semantics are considered in [Mandrioli, 1986].

The student interested in translators is referred to [Calingaert, 1988]. The coverage is on a "first book" level, with material restricted to the translation of procedural languages. Another interesting text is [Kamin, 1990], which considers LISP, APL, SCHEME, SASL, CLU, Smalltalk, and PROLOG through interpreters written in Pascal.

Brief overviews on programming languages, language design, control structures, data types, Pascal and Ada, database management and exception handling, experiences in designing new languages, and axiomatic language definitions are contained in an *IEEE Tutorial* volume [Wasserman, 1980]. The collection also includes original articles by leading language implementers.

CHAPTER 1
VARIABLES AND DATA TYPES

1.0 In this Chapter	**29**	
1.1 Primitive Data Types	**30**	
Integer	30	
Real	31	
Character	32	
Boolean	32	
Pointer	33	
Exercises 1.1	36	
1.2 Variables	**36**	
Identifiers	37	
Reserved Words and Keywords	37	
Binding	38	
Name Binding	38	
Address Binding and Lifetime	38	
Value Binding	39	
Type Binding	39	
Blocks and Scope	39	
Static Scoping	41	
Blocks	41	
Dynamic Scoping	42	

Activation Records	43
Exercises 1.2	45
1.3 Structured Data Types	**47**
User-Defined Types	47
Subrange Types	47
Enumeration Types	48
Aggregate Types	48
Arrays	49
Strings	51
Records	52
Union Types	53
Sets	55
Lists	56
Type Issues	57
Type Checking	57
Strong and Weak Typing	58
Exercises 1.3	60
1.4 Summary	**61**
1.5 Notes on References	**61**

CHAPTER 1

Variables and Data Types

Imperative languages provide an abstraction for machine code. Variables act as abstractions for memory cells, with names replacing references to machine addresses. The entry in a cell is associated with some type. Computer languages generally provide some primitive data types, such as character and integer. In many cases the data may take some structure, such as an array or record, so such capabilities are also generally supported.

A variable must be bound to the properties associated with it. Aside from its name and associated address, it should be bound to some type and a value. The time of this binding, whether during compilation or execution, becomes important in understanding a language. When we add functions and procedures, we must consider also the scope and lifetime of these variables.

1.0
IN THIS CHAPTER

When considering variables and type issues, it is helpful to look at both the basic concepts and some principles for their implementation. In this chapter we will consider:

- Primitive data types and their representation
- Binding of attributes to variables
- Blocks, scope, and implementation via activation records
- Structured types and their allocation
- Type checking and type compatibility issues

1.1
PRIMITIVE DATA TYPES

Languages provide the programmer with certain basic data types, specifying both the set of data items and a set of operations on them. The number of types vary, from pure LISP with one essential type, the symbolic expression or S-expression, to a rich language like Ada, with six basic types: enumeration, integer, real, array, record, and access, as well as types derived from these. The enumeration types we will present include character and boolean types.

Many languages include such primitive types as integer, real, character, boolean, and pointer. While the specifications of these types may vary between languages and machines, there are a number of common aspects. Note, however, that these all differ from aggregate types, such as arrays and records, which are composed of other types and will be discussed in section 1.3.

Integer

One of the most common primitive date types is *integer*. For many languages, the integer size may be determined by the word size of the target machine.[1] While several representations are possible, if a machine supports 2s-complement arithmetic with a 16-bit word, using one bit for the sign, the largest 15-bit value would be +32,767. Hence this would likely become the value of `maxint` on this machine for a language like Pascal. Clearly this can be a problem if we desire that programs be portable between target machines with different word sizes that support a common language.

Some languages like C and Ada also provide short integer and long integer types. These are generally implementation dependent on what hardware support is available and may use a byte or word for short integers, while long integers might be composed of double words or four words. Again, if portability is important, one must be aware of differences on target machines.

It is also becoming common for a language to support unsigned integers, in which positive values only are used. In this case, room is not needed for a sign bit so we can reach a maximum value of 65,535 on a 16-bit machine. The language C even includes unsigned short and long integers.

Some machines (such as the IBM 370) are able to store integers in decimal, rather than binary, format. In this *binary coded decimal* (BCD) representation, digits 0 to 9 are stored in four bits each, so that 0011 0101 would represent 35. Arithmetic operations need to be supported, and there may be a limit on the number of digits permitted. While a language may support a type such as BCD integers, it might not be supported by the hardware of the target machine. In this case, a compiler might either provide it in software or not support the type.

---

[1] This refers to the machine on which the resulting object code is to be executed.

These are not the only models, of course. The set language SETL2[2] permits an integer to be practically "infinite" in size, limited only by the memory available. Such a language can be particularly useful for mathematical problems involving large numbers.

Real

It is important to note that the computer representation of *real* numbers differs significantly from the concept in a mathematics course, in which most real numbers do not have an exact decimal representation. In computer languages, we must remember that the actual value may be represented only by an approximation. For example, **pi** and **sqrt**(2) have nonrepeating and nonterminating decimal representations in math, but must be approximated by some digital value for computer use.

The *fixed point* number representation specifies both a fixed number of digits and the position of the decimal (or binary) point. They are much like integers then, except for the radix (decimal or binary) point. They are available in languages like COBOL and PL/I. A sample declaration in PL/I is:

```
DECLARE TAX FIXED DECIMAL (8,2);
```

Here the variable TAX can represent a decimal number in the range from –999999.99 to 999999.99. Useful in working with monetary values, a machine may actually support such fixed point types as binary coded decimals (BCD), or they may be simulated by floating point numbers. While BCD is not supported on many machines, a fixed binary type would be. Note, however, that the specification for the exact number of binary digits to be used may not fit the byte or word structure of the machine.

A *floating point* number is based on the idea of scientific notation, in which we represent both the mantissa (fractional part) and the exponent of a number. The notation 3.2843E–4 is commonly used in printouts to represent $3.2843*10^{-4}$.

In order to use the built-in floating point commands and hardware, however, they are generally stored in binary, with some bits for the exponent and some for the fraction, as shown in Figure 1.1.1.

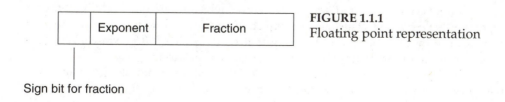

FIGURE 1.1.1
Floating point representation

Sign bit for fraction

---

[2]SETL (SET Language) and its successor SETL2 are very high level programming languages, developed at New York University, which are based on the mathematical notion of set theory. Their design features have made them useful in software prototyping.

It is interesting to note that successive numbers are not equally spaced as they are in the fixed point notation. For example, consider the following decreasing sequence of numbers with 2-digit fractional parts: 1.2E–3, 1.1E–3, 1.0E–3, 9.9E–4, 9.8E–4, etc. The step size between the first three is .0001, but it is .00001 between the last three.

Double-precision reals provide more bits for each of the exponent and mantissa. Standards for floating point binary arithmetic have been established by IEEE [IEEE-754, 1985]. While most languages provide no control over the precision of these reals (other than single or double precision), some languages like PL/I and Ada make provision for doing so.

Character

Characters are represented in the computer by numeric codes. ASCII (American Standard Code for Information Interchange) is the most common and is often supported by hardware.[3] For 7-bit ASCII, the codes from 0 to 127 represent both printable characters (*alphanumeric* characters) as well as a number of control characters, useful for printer and screen control. 8-bit codes provide extended character sets in the range 128 to 255. The Java language supports a 16-bit code called Unicode[4] in order to support more non-English characters. The numeric ordering of the codes provides a natural ordering of the characters themselves, hence relational operators may be used to compare them. While the source program and input data are generally characters, the strings representing numeric data may be converted to an integer or real representation as they are read.

In some languages, the char type may be used to represent objects other than single characters. In C, char can save space in place of short integers. Strings of characters are generally a more useful data type and are discussed later in this chapter.

Boolean

The *Boolean* type is perhaps the simplest type and is common in most general purpose languages. The two values true and false can be ordered so that **false < true** (though not necessarily for all languages), but such comparisons (if defined for the type) would be unusual. The logical connectives **and, or**, and **not** may be used to form expressions, though **xor**[5] and others might also be provided. Boolean variables are most commonly used as flags such as endOfData or notFound.

It would seem natural to implement Boolean values as single bits, using 0 for false and 1 for true. Since many machines cannot address single bits, a byte or word

---

[3]EBCDIC (Extended Binary Coded Decimal Interchange Code) is used on IBM mainframes.

[4]In Unicode, niño, for example, can be a valid Java identifier.

[5]xor (exclusive or) is true if either operand is true, but not both.

may be allocated. In C, integer values are used, with false as 0 and true as any non-zero value.

A common cause of errors in programming is the expectation that a language will short-circuit some Boolean expressions. For example, consider the expressions:

```
1)  if (i = 0) or (a/i > 0) then ...
2)  while (i <= 100) and (a[i] > 0) do ...
```

Once the left operand is evaluated, it may appear that the right operand need not be. In the first example, **or** is true if either operand is true. Supposing that i is 0, since the left operand is true, it appears that it is not necessary to evaluate the right expression. A compiler might evaluate the right expression anyway, resulting in a division-by-zero error.

In the second example, **and** is false if either operand is false. If i reaches the value 101, the left operand is false, which might lead one to assume the right operand may not be evaluated. However, the array a may not be defined if the index is over 100, so evaluation of the right operand produces an error. To circumvent this problem, Ada provides the special Boolean operators **and then** and **or else** which give the desired short-circuited result. The code may be changed to:

```
while (i <= 100) and then (a[i] > 0) do ...
```

If i has the value 101, the failed evaluation of the left side prevents evaluation of the right. Java uses the operators | (or) and & (and) as the logical operators that evaluate both operands, while || and && perform shortcut evaluation of the operands.

Pointer

The *pointer* type is different from the preceding primitive types. Instead of containing a data object directly, it contains the location of an object. Hence pointer values are the memory addresses of other objects, much like the idea of indirect addressing used in assembly language. They may be called *reference* or *access* types in some languages.

For example, the memory location associated with an integer variable i may contain the value 12. If p is a pointer to an integer at address 3080, then p contains the address 3080, while location 3080 may contain an integer value 15, as shown in Figure 1.1.2.

In order to test whether or not a pointer variable p contains an address, its contents can be compared to a special pointer value **nil** or **null**, which cannot represent a valid address.

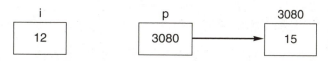

FIGURE 1.1.2
An integer variable versus a pointer to an integer

Pointer variables are normally associated with a single type.[6] In Pascal, for example, consider listing (1.1.1).

```
type                                                        (1.1.1)
  gradeRec = record
    letter: char;
    number: integer;
  end;
var
  p, q: ^integer;
  r: ^gradeRec;
```

This allocates sufficient storage for each variable p, q, and r to contain an address, as shown in Figure 1.1.3.

An address (or **nil**) can be stored in each during execution. The actual address contained in a pointer variable is not normally known by the user, but one can use it in assignments such as q := p, which copies the address found in p to q. Note that r also contains an address. It can point to a record, as shown in Figure 1.1.4.

In order to manipulate the contents of a cell at an address, we must *dereference* the pointer. Using Pascal notation for the example in Figure 1.1.2, p refers to address 3080. After dereferencing, p^ refers to the value 15, the contents of address 3080. Since r^ is of type gradeRec, r^.letter and r^.number would be used to specify the field entries. The values in Figure 1.1.4 could be assigned by the statements

```
r^.letter := 'B';
r^.number := 86;
```

Pointers are particularly interesting in that they provide a means of dynamic memory management in a special area of storage called the *heap*. The term heap indicates that we have a pool of memory in which space can be dynamically allocated and deallocated during execution. Space can be created when needed. When no longer needed, it may be returned to the heap for later use. It is important to note that the objects allocated here are commonly not associated with variables directly but are accessible only by pointers. If we work with objects (such as a stack or queue) in an array of fixed or static size, much of the array may be empty or, worse yet, the size allocated may turn out to be too small. With dynamic storage, use of storage from the heap can grow (and shrink) as needed. It may be possible

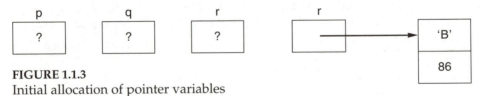

FIGURE 1.1.3
Initial allocation of pointer variables

FIGURE 1.1.4
r contains the address of a record

---

[6]This is not the case in PL/I, which simply permits declaring a variable of type POINTER.

for a program to run out of heap storage, however, if it makes heavy use of dynamic storage. In this case, it may be necessary to run the program again after making sure that a larger heap is available.

When a new object is created in the heap, storage is allocated for an object of the proper type, and the pointer to (address of) that object is returned. In Pascal this is accomplished by the procedure call new(p);. After the call, p contains the address of an object of the appropriate type, as shown in Figure 1.1.5. Assuming the declaration in listing (1.1.1), the object at the right in Figure 1.1.5 is of integer type.

Pascal provides the procedure dispose(p) to deallocate the storage at address p. Since several pointers may contain the same address, one must be careful not to deallocate one of them, otherwise *dangling references* are created. For example, suppose we start with the configuration in Figure 1.1.6.

If we now dispose(p), the location where 7 is stored may be reused for some other purpose. Since q still contains this address, it is now a dangling reference into the heap. The programmer must make sure there are no other references to an address before deallocation.

When changing the contents of a pointer by assignment or allocation, it is possible to lose access to the prior address stored there, despite the fact that it may contain useful data. This lost storage is called *garbage* because it is no longer accessible and has not been deallocated. For example, consider the initial configuration shown in Figure 1.1.7. If we apply the assignment p := q;, then the address where 4 was stored is no longer accessible.

As another approach to heap management, some languages (like LISP) provide a *garbage collector*, which keeps track of inaccessible storage and permits it to be reallocated. While an Ada compiler implementation may provide garbage collection, it is uncommon. Hence Ada includes a generic procedure called unchecked_deallocation to allow disposal of garbage.

FIGURE 1.1.5
new(p) allocates storage in the heap

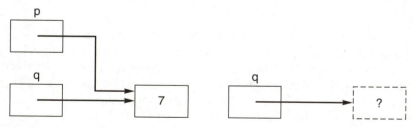

FIGURE 1.1.6
dispose(p) creates a dangling reference

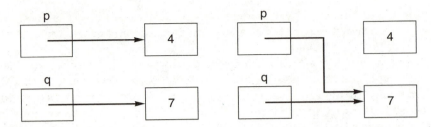

FIGURE 1.1.7
p := q; creates inaccessible garbage

EXERCISES 1.1

1. Decimal digits can be stored in four bits on a binary machine. Since the bit patterns 0000 to 1111 represent 0 to 15, we just use 0 to 9 for a decimal digit.
   a. What are advantages and disadvantages of using this BCD notation to represent integers?
   b. Are there any additional problems if we use such a representation for fixed point decimal numbers?
2. It is possible for a language to support "infinite" precision integers.
   a. How might such a type be stored?
   b. What problems and difficulties does this present?
3. ASCII and EBCDIC character codes have different ordering of characters. What problems does this create for a language?
4. What are the advantages and disadvantages of storing Booleans in bits instead of words?
5. If a language supports both **and** and the short-circuited **and then**, under what circumstances might they produce different results?
6. In C, a Boolean variable b is considered false if b = 0, and true in all other cases. Discuss the merits of this versus true = 1 and false = 0, or true = some special reserved value and false = some other special reserved value.
7. Pointers point to dynamic storage allocated in the heap.
   a. What are the advantages and disadvantages if a language does not support deallocation of heap storage?
   b. What are the advantages and disadvantages of garbage collection support?

1.2
VARIABLES

When writing in machine code, machine addresses are used to specify where items are to be stored. The programmer has to keep track of what type of object a storage cell contains. Extending this somewhat, a *variable* provides an abstraction for this notion. As we shall describe shortly, a variable is bound to a tuple[7] of attributes: (name, address, type, value). Other important concepts include the scope and the

---

[7]An *n*-tuple is an ordered set of *n* entries. Here, the attributes form a 4-tuple.

lifetime of the variable, as well as issues of the time of binding, scoping rules, and type checking.

Identifiers

Identifiers or *names* are not used for variables only. In a program, names may be assigned to such things as procedures, labels, types, and more.

While early languages permitted only single characters as names, most ALGOL-like languages permit some string of letters and digits. The string starts with a letter to prevent syntactic confusion, as, for example, between a name like 10x and the integer 10. Names in COBOL, early versions of FORTRAN (through FORTRAN-77), and PL/I were restricted to uppercase letters, but mixed case is normal for many languages. One must be careful to check language rules, however. For example, a FORTRAN-90 compiler may recognize lowercase letters, but is not required to, so continued use of uppercase is common.

Languages may place limits on the lengths of names or on the number of significant characters. In early C compilers, only the first eight were significant, so that dataQueue and dataQueue2 were not distinguished. ANSI C now specifies the first 31 to be significant. While some language specifications permit any name length, an implementation may force limitations.

Languages like C and Ada permit the use of the underscore character as well, and LISP permits the hyphen. Since a program can be more readable with meaningful names, multiple word identifiers are encouraged. In Pascal, one might mix cases to use names like dataQueue, while Ada programmers might use data_queue. When names are not case sensitive, then DataQueue, dataqueue, dataQueue, and DATAQUEUE would all refer to the same variable.

While style conventions for a programming language may be set by common usage, programmers are often guided by the standard reference manuals. In the Ada 83 standard, for example, identifiers were listed in uppercase (such as DATA_QUEUE), while the Ada 95 standard would use Data_Queue. As a result, books are starting to shift to this new style.

In C, however, names are case sensitive, so one must be careful with naming and perhaps adopt a convention of using only lowercase identifiers for variables and names beginning with an uppercase letter for procedures and functions. Any variation from the convention can cause bugs in programs. In Java, the convention is to start the names of classes (introduced in Chapter 2) with uppercase letters, while other identifiers start with lowercase, e.g., dataQueue. Normal practice for other languages vary, so it is important to check naming conventions when learning a new language.

Reserved Words and Keywords

Many languages use certain names as part of their syntax (such as **for**, **while**, **of**, **else**, **end**, etc.) or as special functions or operators (**mod**, **nil**, **not**, **sin**, and input/output routines like **read** or **print**). Any word whose meaning is predefined and cannot be redefined by the programmer is called a *reserved word*. When starting with a new language, it is not uncommon for a novice programmer to unintentionally use one of the reserved words as a variable name. Hopefully the compiler will recognize this error as a simple one and produce a clear error message. If the error message is misleading, the problem could be rather tricky for a novice to diagnose.

There are often a number of words which are not reserved but have a predefined meaning. These *keywords* may, in fact, be defined by the user for another meaning. In Pascal, for example, most of the predefined types (`integer`, `real`, `boolean`, etc.) and predefined functions (`trunc`, `sqrt`, `sin`, `ln`, etc.) are not reserved. In Ada, a number of such items are provided in the Standard package. If one does use a name like `integer` for a variable, however, then the predefined meaning may be unavailable, and the program may be more difficult to read. The same problem can arise in FORTRAN, in which no words are reserved.

Binding

The *binding* of a variable is the assignment to its attributes: name, address, type, and value. In order to properly understand the semantics of a language, one should know the *binding time* of these attributes, whether it is associated at compile, load, or run time. The program source code is converted into machine code at *compile time*. At *load time* the relocatable machine code addresses are assigned to real addresses. Associations that occur during execution are said to occur at *run time*.

A *static binding* is one that occurs prior to run time and remains fixed throughout execution. A *dynamic binding* is one that normally occurs or can change during run time.

Name Binding

Name binding generally occurs at compile time. If the language requires that variables be declared, binding can occur when the compiler sees the variable declaration.

Address Binding and Lifetime

As we will see later in this section when activation records are discussed, the *address binding* of global variables occurs at load time and is transparent to the user. Variables local to a procedure are commonly allocated space on the run-time stack, hence addresses are bound at the time of activation during run time. Since variables provide an abstract notion of memory locations, there is no need to know the absolute address. While this is a bit more complicated in a virtual memory machine[8], this is still consistent with the user's view.

It is commonly found that a language may permit two identifiers to be bound to the same address. Consider in Pascal, for example, a procedure with a formal parameter which is a **var** parameter. When the procedure is called, the formal parameter is then associated with the same address as the corresponding actual parameter.

---

[8]In a machine with virtual memory, only part of the program and data might be loaded into memory. The user views the program as a whole, while the system may load sections as needed.

To complicate things further, it is also possible for the same name to be bound to different addresses. Suppose a program has a global variable called i. A procedure may also declare i as a local variable. Despite the duplicate name, these are clearly declared as two different variables. In the case of a recursive procedure, however, a local variable is likely to be associated with a different address each time the procedure is called. We will clarify how this works in the discussion on activation records for procedure calls later in this section and in the discussion on recursion in section 2.2.

Data objects can be created and destroyed during execution. When we call a Pascal procedure, the formal parameters and local variables are allocated when the procedure is called and are deallocated when it completes. The period of time that the object is bound to an address is called its *lifetime*.

Value Binding

Value binding of variables generally occurs at run time, since values may change while executing an assignment or read statement, for example. Note that, as we saw in section 1.1, the actual storage required for a value may be different for different primitive types. In this sense, value is something of an abstraction of a memory cell: storage for an item, independent of what actual storage is needed.

If the language supports initialized variables, such as the following Ada-like notation:

```
var sum: integer :=0;
```

then the binding is still dynamic because the value can change. *Constants* may be handled differently if we have a syntax as simple as Pascal, so it may be possible to bind these at compile time. This is not always so with Ada constants, however, as some type issues may delay binding until run time.

Type Binding

Type binding is static in languages that require declaration of variables. Languages like Pascal, C, and Ada require explicit declarations. BASIC and FORTRAN, however, have some implicit typing. BASIC variable names like A are real, A% is integer, A$ is string. FORTRAN variables starting with I through N default to integer type, while others default to real.

APL, SNOBOL4, and SETL2 are among the languages that support dynamic type binding. In SETL2, for example, a program may contain statements like:

```
val := {1, 3, "hello", 6};

val := 7;
```

While initially containing a set, val is later bound to the integer 7. The type must then be bound when the value is bound—at run time.

Blocks and Scope

The binding of a variable name occurs when it is declared. The set of statements and expressions for which a variable is bound is called the *scope* of the variable. The scoping rules of a language specify which variables are *visible* in expressions or statements.

The collection of variables, functions, and procedures that are visible at any point during execution (along with the associated addresses) is called an *environment*. This includes the local identifiers, while the scoping rules determine the binding for the nonlocals.

In the pseudocode procedure shown in listing (1.2.1), the expressions between the **begin** and **end** are in the scope of l, i, sum, and size. They constitute the entire scope of l and i, but not of sum or size. Here l and i are bound variables, as they are bound to the particular values assigned to them in the procedure. sum and size are free in addList, hence their values must be obtained from some larger scope.

```
procedure addList (l: arrayType);                                    (1.2.1)
  var i: integer;
begin
  sum := 0;
  for i := 1 to size do
    sum := sum + l[i];
  end for;
  print ('The sum is: ', sum);
end procedure;
```

Procedures, of course, may have local variables, such as i above, as well as parameters, e.g., l. They may also have subprocedures, which are bound to the parent procedure, with free variables. By a *free variable*, we mean one that is not locally bound to the procedure in which it is used. The variable size above is free in addList. In many languages, bound variables include parameters and variables declared to be local to a procedure. Global variables are free in all but the main procedure. What happens to these free variables depends on the type of binding that occurs.

In the pseudocode of listing (1.2.2), v is bound to each block, program a and procedures b and c; thus it names a different variable in each. It is sometimes helpful to think of them as a.v, b.v, and c.v. x is free in b but bound in c. w is bound in program a, but is free in both b and c, and is thus a global variable. y is bound in procedure b, but free in c, while z is bound only in c.

```
program a;                                                           (1.2.2)
  var v, w, x, y: integer;

  procedure b;
    var v, y: integer;

    procedure c (v: integer);
      var x, z: integer;
      begin {c}
        ...
        b;
        ...
      end procedure;
    begin   {b}
      ...
    end procedure;
```

```
begin      {a}
   ...
   b;
   ...
end program;
```

Static Scoping

Languages based on ALGOL 60 use a method of *static scoping* or *lexical scoping*. In this case, a variable that is free in a procedure gets its value from the environment in which the procedure is defined, rather than from where the procedure is called. This means that the binding of a variable is determined by the structure of a program, not by what happens at run time.

It is often useful in this case to construct a *contour diagram* for the program. If a variable is free in a procedure, we look outward for the nearest enclosing block in which it is bound. For listing (1.2.2) we create the contour diagram shown in Figure 1.2.1.

If y occurs in procedure c, it would be bound to its value in procedure b, since this is the nearest enclosing environment in which y is bound. Now if, as in listing (1.2.2), procedure c calls procedure b, any reference to x during execution of b is a.x, not c.x, since a is an enclosing block, while c.x is not visible. Similarly, during execution of c, a reference to y would be b.y, not a.y, since b is the closer enclosing block. The name "lexical scoping" comes from the fact that we can determine the binding of a variable by looking at the source code to find the innermost environment or block in which the variable name is bound.

Blocks

A *block* is a contiguous section of code in which local variables can be declared. While this includes our program and procedures, some of the block-structured languages include a block construct that can be placed in the code, like the pseudocode in listing (1.2.3).

```
block b;                                          (1.2.3)
var i, j: integer;
begin
   ...
end block;
```

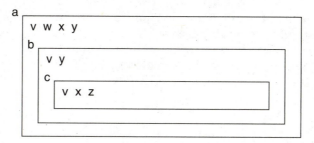

FIGURE 1.2.1
Contour diagram for static scoping

It would be common for such blocks to be used as the body of a **while** loop, for example, so the loop may have its own local variables. Similarly, they may be used as the body of the **then** or **else** clauses in an **if** statement. Such a construct was introduced in ALGOL 60 and is available in such languages as C and Ada.

While Pascal includes declarations within procedures, its compound statement structures don't permit such in-line declarations. As a child of ALGOL 60, it is nonetheless still considered a block-structured language. In some ways the distinction between blocks and compound statements can be blurred. Consider the pseudocode in listing (1.2.4), based on an example in the ALGOL 60 report [Naur, 1963].

```
block q;                                              (1.2.4)
var i, k: integer; w: real;
begin
  for i := 1 to m do
    for k := 1 to m do
      w := a[i,k];
      a[i,k] := a[k,i];
      a[k,i] := w;
    end for;
  end for;
end block;
```

Here i, k, and w are local to the block, while a and m are free. In ALGOL 60, local variables are visible throughout the block.

In Pascal, a subtle change was made. Since the control variables of a **for** loop (here i, k, and m) are intended to control the number of iterations and do nothing else, two rules were made: first, the body of the loop can contain no statement changing these variables, and second, they are completely undefined on exit from the loop.[9] In a sense, the loop **for** i then creates a block in which i has a new definition.

The designers of Ada took this notion one step further. In the Ada version of this code, the loop control variables need not be explicitly declared. When we use a loop **for** i, i is implicitly declared to be of an integer subtype in range 1 .. m on entrance to the loop, may not be altered in the body of the loop, and ceases to exist on execution of **end loop**.

Dynamic Scoping

By *dynamic scoping*, we mean that a free variable gets its value from the environment from which it is called, rather than from the environment in which it is defined. This should not be confused with dynamic variables, which are either pointer variables that can be allocated or destroyed in the heap (see section 1.1), or variables local to a procedure that are created when the scope of the procedure is entered and cease to exist when it is exited. Consider, for example, the pseudocode in listing (1.2.5).

---

[9]Since undefined, the value of the loop control variable outside the loop may vary from compiler to compiler.

```
program b;                                                    (1.2.5)
var a: integer;
procedure p1;
  begin
    print(a);
  end procedure;
procedure p2;
  var a: integer
  begin
    a := 0;
    p1;
  end procedure;
begin
  a := 7;
  p2;
end program;
```

What value of a will be printed? With static scoping, when p1 is called, it gets the value of a from the block containing p1, which is b, hence the value printed would be 7. With dynamic scoping, the call to p1 occurs in p2, so the value of a is taken from the environment of p2, and 0 would be printed.

It is interesting to note that static scoping is prevalent in programming languages. Exceptions include APL and some LISP dialects. John McCarthy [McCarthy, 1960 and 1965] designed LISP as a dynamically scoped language in order to make possible sharing of code with free variables. More recent versions, such as SCHEME [Steele, 1978] and Common LISP [Steele, 1984], use static scoping.

Activation Records

Implementation of the storage allocation for a procedure or function is commonly provided through an *activation record* or *frame*. Information needed by the procedure includes local variables and parameters, as well as how to return to the calling environment.

Figure 1.2.2 demonstrates the kind of information kept for each procedure. The dynamic link points to the activation record of the calling procedure. The static link

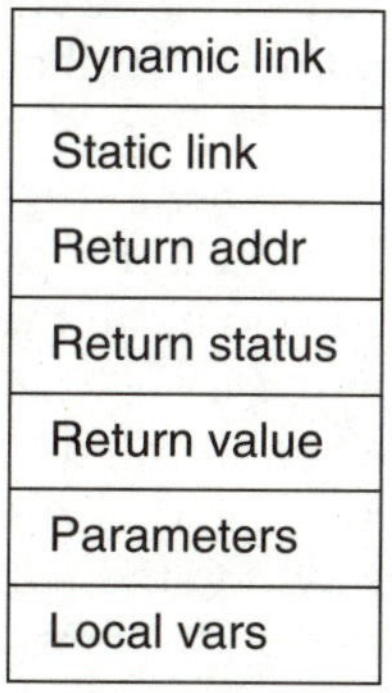

Dynamic link
Static link
Return addr
Return status
Return value
Parameters
Local vars

FIGURE 1.2.2
Information in an activation record

provides access to the lexically enclosing scope. The return address and prior machine status are needed to restore the calling environment upon exit. A function needs a place to store the return value. Storage is allocated for both formal parameters and local variables. It is also common to allocate room for temporary variables used for intermediate steps in calculations, the number of parameters, etc. For the current discussion of storage allocation and scoping, however, it is sufficient to consider a simplified activation record.

The stack is a natural place to maintain these records, so they are often called *stack frames*. When a procedure is called, its activation record is placed on the top of the stack and the proper links are set. To clarify this, consider the pseudocode in listing (1.2.6).

(1.2.6)

```
program a;
var v, w: integer;
procedure b(x: integer);
  var y: integer;
  procedure c;
    var z: integer
    begin {c}
      ...
    end procedure;
  begin {b}
    c;
  end procedure;
procedure d;
  var s, t: integer
  begin {d}
    ...
  end procedure;
begin {a}
  b;
  d;
end program;
```

Figure 1.2.3 demonstrates the activation record stack with the dynamic links and local variables as changes occur when we enter and exit procedures. Evaluation of the static links will be left as an exercise.

The activation record establishes the local environment of a block. With static scoping, the static links provide access to the environment of the enclosing blocks. For dynamic scoping, the dynamic links could be followed until an environment is found that includes the needed declaration.

This example also helps to clarify the difference between scope and lifetime. The variables are bound to addresses and are live while the appropriate activation record is on the stack. Imagine in listing (1.2.6) that we had a call from procedure d to procedure b. While the static scope of locals in b and d is separate because they are separate lexically, locals in d would still be live when it called b. Details of this will be left as an exercise.

Languages will vary in what information must be kept in the activation records. Without nesting of blocks in FORTRAN, the structure can be simpler. A language which supports recursion may need more information, as we shall see in section 2.2.

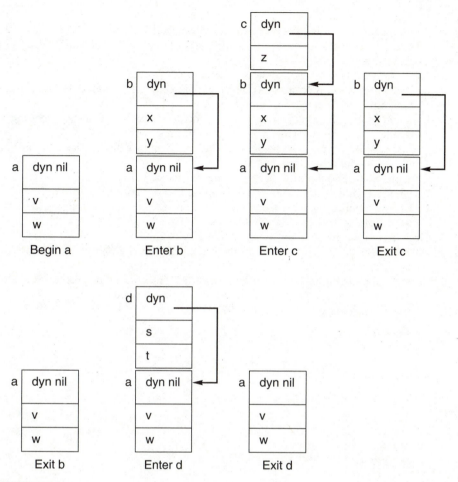

FIGURE 1.2.3
Activation records for listing (1.2.6)

While this was intended as a simple introduction to the general concept of activation records, other interesting points may arise. If a local is of an array type, for example, we might need to allocate room for the entire array in the activation record, resulting in a loss of efficiency. Instead of using static links forming a static chain, all the static links may be kept in a single array, called the *display*, for improved efficiency. Further details will be left to a course in compiler design.

EXERCISES 1.2
1. Uninitialized variables are those that have not been assigned any value. Left unrecognized, this can cause hard-to-find program errors. Discuss the merits of the following solutions:
    a. Forcing the programmer to assign initial values when a variable is created (APL).
    b. Initializing variables at compile time if the appropriate statement is encountered (FORTRAN).

c. Automatically initializing numeric variables to 0 (BASIC).

d. Initializing variables to some special indicator (SETL2).

e. Making initialization at the time of declaration easy, but not mandatory (Ada and C).

2. Now that you have seen the details of activation records,

a. Reread the section on address binding, regarding which variables are bound at load time and which at run time.

b. Review the definition of environment, considering each case of static scoping and dynamic scoping rules for visibility of nonlocals.

3. In Pascal, a procedure must be declared before it can be called, unless forward declaration is made. Why is this needed?

4. Consider static and dynamic scoping rules for the code in listing (1.2.5).

a. Draw a contour diagram for static scoping and confirm the output of 7.

b. Draw activation records, use the dynamic link for dynamic scoping, and confirm the output as 0.

5. Draw a contour diagram for the code in listing (1.2.6).

6. As in Figure 1.2.3, draw activation records for listing (1.2.6), but include both the dynamic and static links.

7. Suppose that listing (1.2.6) included a call from procedure d to procedure b. Draw the sequence of activation records, including both dynamic and static links.

8. Consider the pseudocode in listing (1.2.7).

```
program a;                                      (1.2.7)
const x = 1;
var z: integer;
procedure p(x: integer);
  var y: integer;
  begin {p}
    y := z * x;
    print(y);
  end procedure;
procedure q(x: integer);
  var z: integer;
  procedure r;
    var y: integer
    begin {r}
      y := z+1;
      p(y);
    end procedure;
  begin {q}
    z := 2;
    r;
  end procedure;
begin {a}
  z := 3;
  q(x);
end program;
```

a. Draw a contour diagram to determine static scoping.

b. Draw activation records for execution of this pseudocode, including both dynamic and static links.

c. Assuming static scoping, what value will be printed?

d. Assuming dynamic scoping, what value will be printed?

1.3
STRUCTURED DATA TYPES

While we have discussed primitive types in section 1.1, in application we find that the data is generally structured in some way. Most imperative languages provide some support for *structured types*. Users may be able to define their own types, and this can create more meaningful programs. Various types can be combined to create aggregate types, composed of elements of other types, such as arrays and records.

Most programming languages have at least one built-in type, although there are typeless languages, such as APL and MUMPS, where data objects can be coerced automatically from one type to another. Even here, the programmer is thinking and the program operating on some sort of structured type.

User-Defined Types

When a type consists of discrete values that have a unique predecessor and successor, it is referred to as an *ordinal type* or (in Ada) *discrete type*. This includes character, Boolean, and integer types. The real type is generally excluded—though there is an order, it is not composed of discrete values. Many languages permit the programmer to define new ordinal types, either by defining subranges of those previously defined or by enumeration.

Subrange Types

A *subrange type* is used to constrain the values of some parent type to be within a specified range. The parent type is limited to ordinal type in Pascal, while Ada permits subranges of fixed and floating point types. Since the operations are those defined on the base type, this does not actually create a new type. Most languages even permit operations, including assignments, to be performed between the base and subrange types.

```
type                                                          (1.3.1)
  monthRange = integer 1 .. 12;
  dayRange = integer 1 .. 31;
var
  month: monthRange;
  today, day: dayRange;
```

Subrange types are commonly used to make the code more readable. In the pseudocode in listing (1.3.1), the listed type name implies the use of variables of that type. While month and day could simply be of integer type, the subrange clarifies the intended use. If hour is another type, which happens to specify the range 1 .. 12, should assignments be permitted between the two types? This is an issue of type equivalence, which is discussed later in this section.

An added benefit of subrange types is the assistance available in error checking. If a variable is assigned a value outside the specified range during run time, a constraint error can help the programmer find the problem. Since this constant checking can mean longer run times, some compilers may offer a switch that turns range checking on or off (and may even have range checking off by default). It might be switched off after some preliminary debugging is completed, provided one is willing to risk errors in order to improve execution times.

Enumeration Types

In *enumeration types* one lists all the values that can be taken by that type. Consider the pseudocode example in listing (1.3.2).

(1.3.2)

```
type
    months = (Jan, Feb, Mar, Apr, May, Jun, Jul, Aug, Sep, Oct, Nov, Dec);
var
    month: months;
```

The values are called enumeration *literals,* shown here as identifiers. They cannot also be used for variable names. In many languages, the Boolean type is essentially a predefined enumeration type: `boolean = (false, true);`. Ada also permits characters to be used as character literals, hence the character type in Ada is also considered a predefined enumeration type.

The listing of the enumeration literals provides an ordering of the discrete values, hence they are also ordinal types. The code can include comparisons, such as `if` month <= Jun `then`, or loop constructs like `for` Month := Jan `to` Dec `do`. In order to step through the values, `pred` and `succ` functions return the predecessor or successor in the list, though an attempt to find `succ(Dec)` should cause an error condition.

The language design question that arises is that of repeated use of the same enumeration literals. While not permitted in Pascal or C, this is important in Ada, since the character types fall into this category. A pseudocode declaration such as:

```
type vowels = ('a', 'e', 'i', 'o', 'u');
```

includes the same character literals as those in the predefined character type. Hence Ada makes provisions for this overloading[10] of literals.

The user-defined enumeration types may well not be supported by the input/output routines. An attempt to `print(month)` could cause an error unless the language makes special provision for output of this type.

When programming in languages without enumeration types, it is common practice to simply use integers. If we define the identifiers Jan = 1, Feb = 2, etc., and `month` is of integer type, then `month := Jan` makes sense, as does `for` month := Jan `to` Dec `do`.

Aggregate Types

FORTRAN II had five simple data types: integer, real, double-precision real, complex, and logical. The single aggregate type was the array. Character strings were

---

[10]Overloading refers to the situation in which a single item has multiple meanings.

facilitated through a crippled Hollerith[11] type, which was really relegated to the integers. There were no other types, so users kept the "real meaning" of the data in their heads or described it through numerous comment lines.

Most newer languages (including FORTRAN 90) permit a number of *aggregate types*, formed from components of other types. These commonly include strings, arrays, records, and possibly others. These enable the user to combine various components in ways that make the structures more meaningful.

Arrays

An *array* is a collection of elements of homogeneous type. This type is usually bound statically with information provided in the type declaration. Entries are selected by an index or subscript which specifies its location within the array. In the pseudocode declaration,

```
type gradeList = array [1 .. 100] of integer;
```

each entry is of integer type, while the indices are integers in the range 1 to 100.

While some languages with declarations like the pseudocode,

```
var a: integer [100];
```

may limit the indices to integers starting at 0 or 1, it is now common to permit enumeration and character types, as in the examples in listing (1.3.3).

```
type                                                              (1.3.3)
    days = (Sun, Mon, Tue, Wed, Thu, Fri, Sat);
    weekSales = array [ days ] of real;
    grades = 'A' .. 'F';
    gradeCounts = array [ grades ] of integer;
    shoeSaleCounts = array [ 5 .. 15 ] of integer;
```

In the last example, if the store only carries shoe sizes 5 to 15, this integer subrange may make sense. In other cases, negative integers may be appropriate.

Specification of an array index permits the selection of an array entry. Languages generally use either a(i) or a[i] for notation. In early FORTRAN, the square bracket was not available on the keyboard, so the compiler had to differentiate between a function call with parameters and an array. When the size of the character set increased, the square bracket became available, so many languages adopted it for arrays. Ada shifted back to parentheses since it conforms more to mathematical usage. The readability of the code may suffer, however, if the usage is not obvious to the reader.

While the element type is generally bound statically, the approach to the number of entries varies. Since the chief design goal in Pascal was simplicity, the lower and upper bounds are constants, so array size can be determined statically.

In some cases, it might be useful to be able to designate the array size at run time. Suppose we have a routine that will sort an array with integer indices from 1 to 100. If it could be written to sort an array with any integer subrange, filling in

---

[11]This was named for Herman Hollerith, who developed the punch card in the nineteenth century.

the lower and upper bounds dynamically, it would make the code more reusable. Ada supports this with an *unconstrained array* type. In this case, the array type includes the type of the index, but the bounds are not assigned until run time. Note that, once the size is fixed (even at run time), the size does not change during its lifetime. This is still less than a truly dynamic scheme, such as supported in APL, which allows the array size to grow and shrink as needed.

If variable bounds are permitted, such as in the pseudocode,

```
type list: array [m .. n: integer] of integer;
```

then m and n may be filled in upon a procedure call if we have a variable declared such as:

```
var a: list[1 .. 100];
```

Dynamic arrays are available in Java using another approach. An array may declared by:

```
int a [] = new int [5];
```

As in C, the indices begin with 0. A multidimensional array can be declared as:

```
int a [] = new int [5][];
```

in which the dimension other than the first can be allocated later. As a result,

```
int oneDimDynamic = new int [1][];
```

gives you the effect of a 1-dimensional dynamic array.

Implementation of arrays requires both information about the type, kept in a descriptor, and storage allocation for the array entries. If we assume that the index of a 1-dimensional array is a subrange of the integers, then the descriptor must contain the range of index values (lower and upper bounds) and the storage required for each entry, as shown in Figure 1.3.1. This scheme permits random access of the array entries, since the address of the entry at the ith location of the array can be calculated by the formula,

```
ithAddrs = baseAddrs + (i - lb) * storagePerEntry
```

A similar setup is used for a 2-dimensional array, where there are two sets of indices. Since computer memory is linear, however, the entries must be stored in a single list. If the values are stored a row at a time, they are in *row major order*. In *column major order* they are stored by column.

These schemes provide an efficient way of selecting an array entry or of changing a value. A data structure, like a stack, can easily be created within such a fixed-size structure. Since insertion or deletion of entries at the front or in the middle is awkward, there are problems in using them for queues or other more dynamic abstract data types.

The set language SETL2 provides an interesting alternative in a tuple, which permits heterogeneous entry types and is dynamic in size. No predeclaration of tuple sizes is needed. It is much easier for the user to insert or delete sections and to create a queue, but the cost of this higher level programming capability is slower execution times, because the additional details must be handled by the compiler.

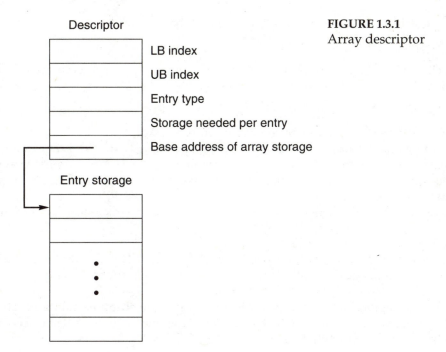

Descriptor

LB index

UB index

Entry type

Storage needed per entry

Base address of array storage

Entry storage

FIGURE 1.3.1
Array descriptor

Strings

A character *string* is composed of a sequence of characters. A number of languages, including Java, incorporate strings as a primitive type, and this is probably most convenient for the user. In Pascal, Ada, and C, however, the character is the primitive type, so strings must be stored as arrays of characters. In Pascal, they must be stored as packed arrays in order to permit lexical comparisons.

Several approaches can be taken to maintaining the length of a string. Three will be considered here. Pascal and Ada require a declaration of the size of string as in the pseudocode example,

```
lastNameType = string [1 .. 15];
```

hence use a *static string length*. This can be implemented as a contiguous block of storage for the number of characters specified. Strings must match exactly the size declared, so truncation or padding may be needed. If shorter strings are desired, the array may be partially filled, but the programmer must keep track of the number of characters used.

PL/I permits a *variable length scheme with a fixed maximum*. In this case, longer strings are truncated, and the compiler keeps track of the number of characters filled.

SNOBOL4 allows a *dynamic string length* (within certain memory limits). This is certainly more convenient to use, but more system overhead is required. Either a linked list of characters is needed, or strings would have to be stored in dynamic memory in the heap, which was described in section 1.1 under pointer types.

A variety of string-handling operations is often useful. When lexical ordering is supported by the relational operators, then 'ball' < 'balm' since 'l' < 'm'.

Substrings may be selected by predefined functions, such as:

```
substr(name, 1, 10)
```

which extracts the first 10 characters of name. Another approach is to use slices in which,

```
name [1 .. 10]
```

performs the same function. Slices are supported in Ada.

String *concatenation* forms a longer string by joining two strings. For example, 'program' + 'ming' forms the string 'programming'. When a language supports only static string lengths, some caution must be taken if the result is to be stored in a string variable.

Pattern matching functions are also very useful for string processing. For example,

```
pos( 'l', 'hello')
```

returns 3, the first position of the letter 'l' in the string 'hello'. SNOBOL4 is a string processing language that supports a variety of very powerful pattern matching operations.

Some languages, Java for example, do not include string-handling functions directly, but provide a package (like Java's java.lang) that includes a string class and methods for manipulating them.

Records

While entries in an array are homogeneous, a *record* is an aggregate structure in which the entries may be heterogeneous. The record structure was first introduced in COBOL and has been common in programming languages since then. It permits the grouping of information kept on a particular item. Consider the pseudocode example in listing (1.3.4).

```
type                                              (1.3.4)
  date = record
    month: 1 .. 12;
    day: 1 .. 31;
    year: integer;
  end record;
  employeeRec = record
    name: string [25];
    payRate: real;
    birthday: date;
  end record;
var
  employee: employeeRec;
```

In this case, the data on an employee is kept together, rather than in separate variables. The *components* or *fields* are specified using identifiers as field names. Within the employeeRec, the field for birthday is itself a record, demonstrating that multiple levels are possible.

Selection of a field in COBOL and ALGOL 68 is performed with a notation like name **of** employee, selecting the name field of the variable employee. In most Ada-like languages selection is done with a dot notation, such as `employee.name`. Similarly, `employee.birthday.year` specifies a multiple level reference. Since this fully specified notation can become cumbersome when coding, Pascal provides a **with** notation, in which the record is established so that only fields need be specified, as demonstrated in the pseudocode in listing (1.3.5).

```
with employee.birthday do
   month := 5;
   day := 12;
   year := 1971;
end with;
```
(1.3.5)

Use of **with** seems to work best with smaller sections of code, since references to field names buried in code may become less understandable. Caution must also be taken if nesting of **with**s is used. If we have `employee1` and `employee2`, a reference to the field `payRate` can be ambiguous unless `employee1.payRate` or `employee2.payRate` is specified.

Operations on records are generally limited. It is common to permit the assignment of full records of the same type, such as:

```
employee1 := employee2;
```

rather than requiring that each field be copied. Similarly, it may be possible to compare two records for equality in an **if** statement.

Storage allocation is generally made as a contiguous block for each field, as shown in Figure 1.3.2. Since the storage for each field is known, the offset to each component can easily be computed.

A single record is often less useful in programming than a collection of records, such as an array of records. In the latter case, `Employee[i].Name` could refer to the ith in a list of employees. It is also common that one of the fields be of a pointer type, so that linked lists of records may be created.

Union Types

If it is desired or necessary to store more than one type of value at the same location, it may be possible to use a *union type*. ALGOL 68 and C permit such union types in a manner similar to the pseudocode in listing (1.3.6).

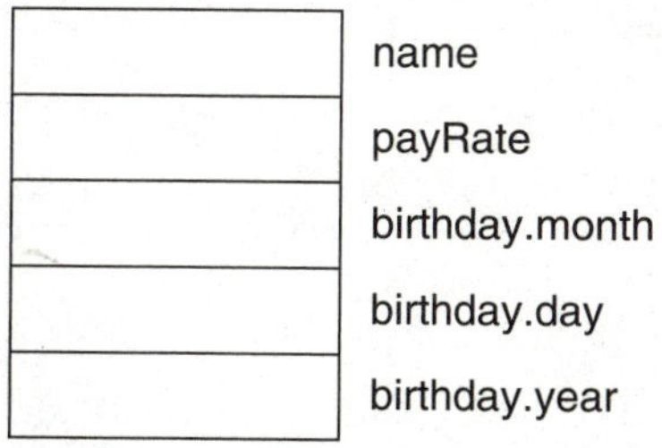

FIGURE 1.3.2
Storage allocation for a record

```
type                                                        (1.3.6)
  intReal = union
    i: integer;
    r: real;
  end union;
var
  x: intReal;
  y: real;
```

Unlike the record structure in which values of both types would be stored, here x can contain only a single value of either integer or real type. The identifiers i and r are used as *tags* or *discriminants*, indicating which variant is being used. Assignments such as:

```
y := x.r;
x.i := 7;
```

may be used, but caution must be taken to assure that the proper type value is being stored. After storing an integer value, a reference to x.r would be improper. Because of the use of tags, such constructs are called *discriminated unions*. In languages that permit tags to be omitted, they are known as *free unions*.

Starting with Pascal, it became common to form union types with variant records. The variant part may occur at the end of the record declaration. Consider the Pascal example in listing (1.3.7).

```
type                                                        (1.3.7)
  employeeRec = record
    name: string [25];
    case salaried: boolean of
      true: ( salary: real;
              unionMember: boolean);
      false: ( hourlyRate: real;
               hoursWorked: real)
  end; {record}
var
  employee: employeeRec;
```

The tag field salaried permits discrimination of the type of data kept on salaried employees from those of hourly employees, and code can take the form shown in listing (1.3.8).

```
if employee.salaried then                                   (1.3.8)
  begin
    monthlyPay := Salary / 12;
    if employee.unionMember then
      monthlyPay := (1 - 0.02) * monthlyPay
  end
else {hourly}
  monthlyPay := hoursWorked * hourlyRate
```

The storage allocated for a variant record must be sufficient for the largest of the records to be stored, and record descriptors for each of the variants must be maintained. Figure 1.3.3 demonstrates the allocation for listing (1.3.7).

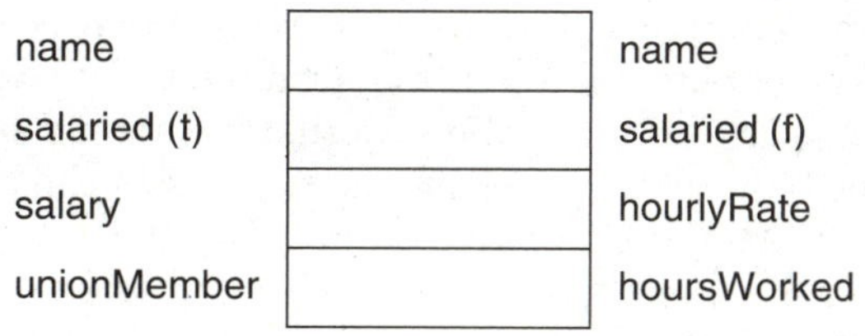

name		name
salaried (t)		salaried (f)
salary		hourlyRate
unionMember		hoursWorked

FIGURE 1.3.3
Overlaid allocation for variant record

The storage required for the Boolean field unionMember is less than that needed for the real field hoursWorked in this case, while salary and hourlyRate are both real. In other examples the forms of the variants can differ greatly. Note that, since the tag field can be changed without changing the data, the problem of ensuring that the value of the tag field matches the values stored still exists. Ada guards against this by requiring that a tag field can only be changed if all fields in the record are reassigned appropriately.

Another problem that occurs in Pascal is that free unions may be formed by omitting the tag field, such as in the example of listing (1.3.9).

```
type                                                           (1.3.9)
  employeeRec = record
    name: string [25];
    case boolean of
      true: ( salary: real;
               unionMember: boolean);
      false: ( hourlyRate: real;
                hoursWorked: real)
  end; {record}
```

Since there is no field for the tag, it is impossible to distinguish the variant type. This kind of structure may be used to trick the compiler into performing some type conversions that the language would not otherwise permit. In order to avoid the problems that occur in Pascal, the design of Ada's variant record construct prevents writing such code.

Sets

In the mathematical sense, a *set* is any unordered collection of distinct elements, unlike arrays, which are ordered. In the Pascal model, the elements must be of homogeneous type. This base type is limited to enumeration and subrange types, since they are finite in size. Consider the example in listing (1.3.10).

```
type                                                           (1.3.10)
  intSet = set of 1 .. 10;
var
  s: intSet
begin
  s := [1, 3, 5, 9];
  ...
end
```

Note that square brackets are used, since curly braces are used for comments.

The Pascal implementation uses a power set model. The *power set* of a set is the collection of all of its subsets, hence the idea that we should be able to construct any subset. Since the base set has 10 elements, any subset can be represented by a string of 10 bits, the 1/0 bit indicating whether or not the corresponding base element is in the subset. The set [1, 3, 5, 9] can then be represented as 1010100010, with only the 1st, 3rd, 5th, and 9th bits on from the range 1 .. 10. Limits on the size of the base set are implementation dependent and are often kept quite small so that the bit string fits in a machine word. This is a severe limitation on the use of sets.

Set operations include x **in** s, to test whether x is a member of the set s. Similarly, s1 <= s2 is true if s1 is a subset of s2. Operations for set union, intersection, and difference are available. The notation s + [x] forms a set whose elements are x and those of s.

The set language SETL2 provides a model closer to the mathematical one. Elements may be heterogeneous, there being no base set to limit size, and sets are dynamic in size, growing and shrinking as needed. The cost for this flexibility is generally slow execution speed.

Lists

The declarative languages LISP and PROLOG include a *list* type. The entries in lists can be either items (called atoms) or other lists. Consider the usual representation of a linked list, shown in Figure 1.3.4. In pseudocode, you might think of a declaration such as shown in listing (1.3.11).

```
type                                                          (1.3.11)
  listPtr = ^list;
  list = record
    data: <some type>;
    link: listPtr
  end;
```

Unlike LISP, this simple declaration restricts the entries to be of the same type.

If we use the LISP dot notation (a . b) to denote entries in the list, then the last entry is (en . nil), where nil represents the null pointer or empty list. The entire list can be expressed as:

```
(e1 . (e2 . ( ... (en . nil) ... )))
```

It is more convenient to write this as (e1 e2 ... en). In this notation the list (a b c) has three entries, as does (a (b c) d), the middle entry here being the list (b c). It is important to note the equivalances in listing (1.3.12).

```
(a) = (a . nil)                                               (1.3.12)
(a b) = (a . (b . nil))
```

FIGURE 1.3.4
Linked list representation

Operations on lists include the ability to construct and disassemble lists. The functions car and cdr[12] select the two components of a dotted pair (an entry and a list pointer). Considering listing (1.3.12), (car (a b)) = a, the atom, while (cdr (a b)) = (b), the list. Similarly, cons permits the joining of a pair, so (cons a (b c d)) = (a b c d). Further details will be provided in Chapter 8 on LISP.

Type Issues

A number of important type issues arise in language design. If a language requires type declarations, use of a variable must be consistent with its declared type. Further, when expressions involving some operator (such as +) are evaluated, the operand types must be consistent with those allowed for that operator.

Type Checking

Type checking is the process of evaluating expressions for *type compatibility*. For example, in the statements,

```
c := a + 3 * b;
p(t+1, 2.5, x);
```

b must be of a type that permits multiplication by an integer. Similarly, the operands for addition and assignment can be evaluated. The types of the actual parameters for the call to procedure p can be checked for compatibility with the types of the formal parameters.

In order to evaluate type compatibility, we must first see how languages treat *type equivalence*—under what circumstances two type names are considered the same type. Consider the pseudocode declarations in listing (1.3.13).

```
type                                              (1.3.13)
   month = 1 .. 12;
   hour  = 1 .. 12;
   array1 = array [1 .. 12] of integer;
   array2 = array [month] of integer;
   array3 = array [1 .. 12] of integer;
   array4 = array3;
var
   m:    month;
   h:    hour;
   a,b:  array1;
   c:    array3;
   d,e:  array [1 .. 12] of integer;
```

Since array1 through array4 all have the same structure, as formed by the primitive types, they have *structural equivalence*. In *name equivalence*, a language would require

---

[12]The functions car and cdr relate to the organization of the early IBM 704 machines on which LISP was run, with car standing for "contents of the address register," and cdr signifying the "contents of the decrement register." They are pronounced "kar" and "kudder."

that variables and operands must have the same type name; hence the example represents four different types.

Structural equivalence is supported in FORTRAN and ALGOL. In listing (1.3.13), however, month and hour are structurally equivalent, though assignments or operations between the types would certainly be confusing. Pascal compatibility rules don't fit strictly into either category. Name equivalence is required for parameter passing, but not in most other cases. In addition, Pascal supports *declaration equivalence*, in which array3 and array4 are considered compatible since array4 is a duplicate of the array3 declaration. Ada uses a form of name equivalence. In listing (1.3.13), variables a and b are compatible with each other, but not with c, d, or e. In fact, d and e are not even compatible with each other in Ada, since the notation is simply considered a shorthand for two separate declarations.

Since Ada supports unconstrained arrays, in which the lower and upper bounds are variable, the bounds cannot be part of such a type, though the type of the index would be. Considering a pseudocode declaration of

```
type list: array [m .. n: integer] of real;
```

the type list can only specify the type of the index (integer) and of the entries (real), not the bounds. In the Pascal syntax of [ANSI/IEEE-770x3.97, 1983], the bounds must be included.

As discussed in section 1.2, if variable types are declared, then type binding generally occurs at compile time. In this case, most type checking can be done statically. If the type information is maintained at run time, then dynamic type checking can occur. If object types can only be determined at run time and type checking is to be performed, it must be done dynamically. The next section on strong and weak typing will provide further information about this.

In order for mixed mode operands to be compatible, it may be necessary to perform a *type coercion*, in which the compiler provides an implicit conversion from an incompatible type to one that is. In the expression 3 * b, if b is real, then 3 may be implicitly converted to 3.0 to permit the operation. Other languages do not permit such mixed mode operations but provide functions to perform the needed conversion, such as float(3) * b.

Type checking of operands is complicated by the practice of *operator overloading*, the use of one operator for several operand types. In Pascal, for example, the + operator is used for both integer and real arithmetic, as well as set union. A further complication is the use of the - operator in both unary form (such as -a) and binary form (a - b). The = (test for equality) operator is often heavily overloaded and may be defined for aggregate types. Ada further complicates this by permitting additional overloading by the programmer. Given operators may defined on user-defined types or on different types of operands. Overloading of operators can make a program much more readable, however. Use of different operators for each type (such as +int, +real, +set) would be far more cumbersome.

Strong and Weak Typing

A language is said to be *strongly typed* if type rules are strictly enforced at both compile and run time. If type rules are not enforced, despite implicit or explicit type declarations, the language is considered *weakly typed*.

A useful definition of strong typing is due to Gehani [Feuer, 1982]:

1. Every object in the language belongs to exactly one type.
2. Type conversion occurs by converting a *value* from one type to another. Conversion does not occur by viewing the representation of a value as a different type.

While Pascal is generally considered to be strongly typed, there are certain exceptions. One of these is the variant record, discussed earlier in this section under union types. Consider the code in listing (1.3.14).

```
type                                                  (1.3.14)
  horrible = record
    case b: boolean of
      true: (int: integer);
      false: (c2: array [1 .. 2] of char)
  end;
var
  h: horrible;
begin
  h.int := 1;
  if (h.c2[1] = chr(0)) then
    ...
```

In this example, h will contain either an integer or array of two characters, but there is no way to tell at compile time which variant is active. The Pascal 83 Standard [ANSI/IEEE-770x3.97, 1983] states that the fragment of listing (1.3.14) should cause an error. The h.int variant would be activated at the statement h.int := 1; and the h.c2 variant would be completely undefined. An error should occur on encountering the inactive variant h.c2 in the **if** statement. Just what is meant by "completely undefined" and "cause an error," however, is left up to the compiler writer.

Given the Pascal 74 Standard or the lack of high-quality error detection in the compiler, the result would still be ambiguous. Assuming a 16-bit machine, integers are sometimes stored with the most significant 8 bits first and sometimes the last. Thus h.int could be represented (in sequential hexadecimal digits) as 00:01 or 01:00. Then, *if* the variant fields are overlaid, and *if* a character occupies 8 bits, the value of (H.c2[1] = chr(0)) will be true in the first integer storage case and false in the second. If either of the *if*s is not true, our result could be either true or false.

The Ada language, which is based on Pascal, resolved the variant problem by requiring discriminated, static unions only, so consistency can be checked at compile time. Our variant record of listing (1.3.14) would be declared in Ada as shown in listing (1.3.15).

```
type b: boolean;                                      (1.3.15)
type notSoHorrible(tag: b) is
  record
    case tag is
      when true => int: integer;
      when false => c2: array [1..2] of char
    end case;
  end record;
var
  h1: notSoHorrible(true);
  t: b;
  h2: notSoHorrible (T);
```

h1 would always have an int field, and never a c2 field. h2 could have either, but the entire record must be specified, as in:

```
h2 := (false, ('O','K')); or
h2 := (true, 35);
```

The C language was developed with different design goals than Pascal or Ada and is weakly typed. If asked to print the integer 67 in character format, the result will be the character 'B' because it has ASCII value 67. A comparison such as 8 < '8' is permitted, resulting in true because '8' has ASCII code 56. Pointer addresses can be treated as decimal numbers without explicit conversion. While variables have a declared type, they can be converted to another type almost without the programmer being aware of it. C provides overt machine access, but can lead to hard-to-find bugs.

EXERCISES 1.3

1. If you can't read or print entries of enumeration types, what are some advantages of using them?
2. Some languages support the character, and others the string, as the primitive type. What might be the reasoning and advantages behind each decision?
3. What are the advantages and disadvantages of having range checking off during execution for subrange types? Why might a compiler have this as a default setting?
4. What are the advantages and disadvantages of having Boolean as a predefined enumeration type? Is the implied ordering useful at all?
5. The BASIC language permits undeclared arrays of up to 10 elements. Why do you think the designers forced users to declare larger arrays but not small ones?
6. In an unconstrained array, the lower and upper bounds of the index need not be specified. What are advantages and disadvantages of this construct?
7. What is the exception in Pascal to the rule that all types must be declared before they are used?
8. Consider the following four assumptions:
   (1) Variant fields are overlaid;
   (2) A single character occupies 8 bits;
   (3) 16-bit integers are stored with the most significant digits first;
   (4) 16-bit integers are stored with the least significant digits first.
      Trace the fragment of listing (1.3.14) under assumptions:
      a. 1, 2, and 3.
      b. 1, 2, and 4.
      c. 1 and 3 with characters occupying 6 bits.
      d. 1 and 4 with characters occupying 6 bits.
      e. a through d without 1.
9. Explain how Ada's rules governing variant records would resolve 8a to 8e above.
10. Draw a linked list representation for the lists (in LISP notation):
    a. (a b c)   b. (a (b c) d)
11. What are advantages and disadvantages of a language supporting type coercion (between integers and reals) for numeric calculations such as 4 + 3.2?
12. What are some advantages and disadvantages of a language supporting type equivalence as
    a.   name equivalence   b. structural equivalence

1.4
SUMMARY

Primitive types in imperative languages generally include integer, real, character, and Boolean types. Pointer types provide access to dynamic storage.

Variables are bound to the attributes: name, address, type, and value. Binding may be static or dynamic, depending on the attribute and the language.

Variables may be declared as local in a block or free. Scoping rules, which may be static or dynamic, determine the visibility of the free variables. Activation records are a means of implementing procedure calls, and provide for storage of local variables as well as scoping information.

Structured types support ways of organizing data. User-defined types can make programs more readable, as well as provide better reliability.

Arrays and sets are collections of homogeneous data, while records permit collections of related nonhomogeneous types. A variety of string representations are possible, and a variety of string-handling operations can be very useful. Union types can be useful for storing different types of items, but can cause some language design problems. Lists are a basic aggregate type for languages supporting list processing. Storage allocation and implementation issues were addressed, since they may be important concerns in language design.

Type declarations may permit a language to perform type checking at compile time, while some type checking may occur dynamically. This may be complicated by operator overloading—the use of one operator with more than one operand type. Type compatibility of operands is an important consideration when evaluating expressions. The restrictions of a strongly typed language provide error detection and reliability, while a weakly typed language allows easy type conversions when desired.

1.5
NOTES ON REFERENCES

Implementation issues have been addressed only briefly here. Those wishing more details may want to refer to books on computer organization or compiler design.

Further information on the representation of numeric and alphanumeric data can be found in [Knuth, 1981]. He includes algorithms and analysis for single- and double-precision arithmetic. A readable introduction to various data representation is found in [Mano, 1982].

Details on blocks, scope, and the visibility of variables can be found in compiler design books such as [Aho, 1986]. In addition to symbol table information, activation records are further explained.

[Aho, 1986] also provides more details for implementation of arrays and records, but is rather technical.

CHAPTER 2
ABSTRACTION

2.0	**In this Chapter**	64	Exceptions	81
2.1	**Data Abstraction**	64	Exercises 2.2	82
	Data and the Store	65	**2.3** **Procedural Abstraction**	**83**
	Abstract Data Types	65	Procedures	84
	Data Independence and		Functions and Operators	85
	Information Hiding	66	Parameters	86
	Theoretical Considerations	67	Modules and ADTs	90
	Implementation Example	70	Classes of ADTs	91
	Generic Types	72	Objects	92
	Exercises 2.1	73	Concurrent Execution	93
2.2	**Control Abstraction**	**74**	Exercises 2.3	93
	Branching	74	**2.4** **Summary**	**94**
	Iteration	76	**2.5** **Notes on References**	**95**
	Recursion	78		

Abstraction

"Euclid alone has looked on beauty bare." To Edna St. Vincent Millay, Euclid's abstraction of plane geometry comprised "beauty bare," while others' more muddled views did not. Euclid perceived the bare bones of the plane and expressed them in nine general axioms and seven postulates. He showed that these are sufficient to describe the plane and its figures, and also that each axiom or postulate is necessary. Essential properties are lost if any are omitted. To abstract is to condense a larger object to its essential parts, ignoring details; to bare the underlying structure. When you write a paper, you might include a brief summary or abstract to let the potential readers know if they are interested in reading further. To abstract also means to find those essential parts of an example that must be shared by any other example considered similar. An abstract painting may have had all representations of visual reality removed except certain lines or colors to emphasize something particular.

Many computer scientists, including Edsgar Dijkstra, have noted that the amount of complexity the human mind can cope with at any one time is considerably less than that needed for writing even fairly simple software. Peter Denning [Denning, 1988] describes abstraction in computer science as "modeling potential implementations. These models suppress details while retaining essential features; they are amenable to analysis and provide means for calculating predictions of the model's behavior." For example, two implementations for a linear list are an array or a linked list. The abstraction is the same for both, a list including the usual operations for manipulating it.

Much of mathematics is concerned with abstract systems that help us organize our world and our thinking. The seven postulates of Euclidean geometry may have been the first such system you encountered. They define the essential features of a flat world without perspective, in terms of the two undefined notions, point and line. This system does not work very well when describing the geometry of the eye, where parallel train tracks appear to meet in the distance. For this we use a differ-ent set of axioms to define projective geometry. An even different system, spheri-cal geometry, is needed to model the globe.

Among programming languages, some systems work better for certain types of problems than do others. For programmers to be productive, the abstractions that have proved useful for applications need to be available in the languages they use. Abstractions in languages for programming computers are different from those in mathematical systems. We must consider the abstraction both in its relationship to problem solving and in its relationship to a physical machine. There is a certain "how to" about computing that may be missing in mathematics. We need to think about abstract machines as well as language paradigms. For our implemented list, an ab-stract machine might include consecutive storage locations with random access op-erations, or binary cells containing data in the first and the address of the succeeding cell in the second. Ideally, in an all-purpose programming language, all abstractions for all potential applications would be built-in for the programmer to use.

2.0
IN THIS CHAPTER

Barbara Liskov of MIT and her colleagues [Liskov, 1977; Zilles, 1986] have identified three sorts of abstraction supported by programming languages:

- Data abstraction
- Control abstraction
- Procedural abstraction

A data abstraction consists of a set of objects and a set of operations characterizing their behavior. Control abstraction defines a method for sequencing arbitrary ac-tions. Procedural abstraction specifies the action of a computation on a set of in-put objects and the output object(s) produced.

2.1
DATA ABSTRACTION

The crossword puzzle clue for "data" is something like "raw material for a com-puter." Older dictionaries define it as "collected facts used as a basis for inference," while newer ones include the notion of computation to be performed upon these facts. The *Random House Dictionary* defines data as "the plural of datum." In all these definitions, the emphasis is on individual items, which may be collected together in some way.

High level programming languages look at data according to what can be done to and with it. For each sort of data, certain operations apply either to select out parts or to put parts together. For example, if our data is composed of names, i.e., character strings, one selector might print out the last name of a string. A constructor could, when combined with a selector, append an appropriate address to a name, or could produce a list of all names where the last name begins with A. What is important to remember is that only certain selectors and constructors apply to certain types of data. It makes no sense to multiply two names together to construct a single object from two others, or to select out the first name of an integer.

Data and the Store

The *store*, which is the collection of data values at a particular moment in the execution of a program, is composed of bits, and can be thought of as a series of 0s and 1s. It may have no other defining characteristics.[1] High level programming languages were developed to help programmers solve problems correctly. Structured programming methods are intended to enhance both the reliability and understandability of programs. Very few programmers can assure themselves of the correctness of their programs if their only access to them is through pages and pages of bit strings. Grace Hopper, one of the developers of COBOL, reports that one of her supervisors would not let programmers use even assembly language, as it was felt that direct contact with the machine produced better programs. Current thinking has it that users will be able to employ computers more effectively if languages are available with built-in abstractions that are useful in their particular application areas. These abstractions include operations, data structures, and control structures.

Abstract Data Types

Integers are often built into a language. If the statement $n = 5 + 3$ occurs in a program where $=$ is the assignment operator, the contents of the storage location assigned to n will be thought of as the integer 8. On the other hand, if $n = $'O' + 'K', n will contain the string 'OK'. Each data type is recognized, not only by its data items, but by the operations associated with it. A set of data items is called a *data domain* (abbreviated, D).[2] One or more data domains with associated operations is called an *abstract data type (ADT)*.

As an example, the type integer in Pascal is described in listing (2.1.1).

```
D = {0, ±1, ±2, ..., ±maxint}                              (2.1.1)
Constant identifier: maxint (machine dependent)
Operations:
  Unary operators = {+, −}
  Binary operators = {+, −, *, div, mod}
```

---

[1]The store, of course, does have structure since it is organized into bytes, words, blocks, pages, etc. It also is addressed, and differentiates between registers, RAM, ROM, user-addressable, and nonaddressable sectors. Such organization need not concern anyone programming in a high level language.

[2]What we have called a data domain is sometimes called a data object. In this chapter, we will reserve the term *object* to refer to a "container for data," following [Liskov, 1986]. Among object-oriented languages, the term is used to refer to hierarchical modules containing abstract data types.

In LISP, the list is the basic built-in data type, and integers are described (in the SCHEME dialect) in listing (2.1.2).

```
D₁ = {0, ±1, ±2, ...}, D₂ = {#T, #F}
Constants: #T, #F (representing true and false)
Procedures:
    (* num1, num2) -> num
    (+ num1, num2) -> num
    (- num1, num2) -> num
    (abs num) -> num
    (integer? obj) returns #T if obj is an integer, #F otherwise.
    (zero? num) returns #T if num = 0, #F otherwise.
```

(2.1.2)

Underlying these descriptions is a common mathematical abstraction that defines integers and their properties, and underlying that is the abstraction for a ring,[3] which describes all structures with the same operations and behavior as the integers. The integers with their associated operations are expected to behave properly on any machine on which a program is run. Thus a further abstraction representing the integral properties of a CPU is needed to complete our abstract data type for integers. Actual compilers for particular computers represent implementations of these abstractions, as does the particular syntax used. A language standard, which specifies the necessary characteristics of any implementation of the language being considered, specifies some implementation details as well as syntax for data types.

Data Independence and Information Hiding

The approach to problem solving called *stepwise refinement* involves two activities: definition of the program modules needed to carry out the various activities involved in the solution, and defining data types, including their interaction with the solution activities. Consider the problem of laying out airplane routes. Some will be nonstop flights between cities, while others will involve one or more connecting flights. When we start on the program, the form of the data is rather vague, perhaps a list of cities and the number of daily flights desired between them. Fairly early in the problem-solving process, it will be obvious that we will be working with a graph, since connections between two cities go both ways, and any single city might be connected to more than one other city. However, we need not worry about how to represent the graph with the types available in the language we have chosen at this level. All we need to do is think of the graph in relation to the operations we desire. Consider, for example, those in listing (2.1.3).

```
connect(city1, city2, day, time)
disconnect(city1, city2, day, time)
distance(city1, city2)
listAllCities
whereICanGoFrom(city)
```

(2.1.3)

---

[3]A ring is a structure $R = \langle S, +, *, 0, 1 \rangle$, where S is a set. $+$ and $*$ are binary operations on S that have the same properties as integer addition and multiplication, e.g., $a + b = b + a$, $a + -a = 0$, $a * 1 = 1 * a = a$, and $a * (c + d) = a * c + a * d$, among others. For a complete definition, see any modern algebra text, e.g., [MacLane, 1968].

Each program module will know about the cities and the routes only through these known, but as yet unspecified, operations associated with the cities and the routes. *Data encapsulation* refers to the gathering of information about the types and operations of an abstract data type together into a single program unit.

If, after the data and its associated operations have been defined, it becomes necessary to change the representation of the data, including the graph of routes, nothing else in the program need be changed but these operations. This property is known as *data independence*, i.e., actual data is independent from its representation.

Programs written independently from the final data representations have many advantages. Among these is *information hiding*, which makes a program easier for the user to understand, makes programs portable between different languages and machines, and makes certain security measures practical. The principle of information hiding is to make visible all that is essential for the user to know, and to hide everything else. We will discuss this further in section 2.3 on procedural abstraction.

Theoretical Considerations

You may have wondered why this section on data abstraction began with a discussion of bits and machine storage of characters. This gets us back to the difference between mathematical and computer-related abstractions, where the actual machine is always lurking in the background. We need assurance that abstractions developed for an application can be implemented both in the high level language we are using and in its machine implementation through a compiler, in conformance with the common notions we had in mind. Just what sort of abstract machine represents our abstract data types, including their data domains and associated procedures? Before we can answer this question, we must be absolutely sure what is meant by abstract data types, which enable a programmer to postpone selection of actual data structures until all uses of the data are fully understood. They also facilitate program modification and maintenance to improve performance or accommodate new requirements.

Theoretical computer science employs the methods of mathematics to specify and prove semantic notions, the "meaning" of language constructs. Data abstraction can be defined briefly as the pair, [objects, operations]. Some discussions of abstract data types (ADTs) don't bother with objects at all. Any object that is subject to the various operations is acceptable. In this way of thinking, an ADT is described *entirely* by its operations. An ADT, when implemented on a (theoretical) computer, specifies what sorts of values a particular object or container for data can hold. The container for data, of course, must be specified eventually in terms of bits, bytes, and computer words.

The burden of this theoretical discussion is to investigate how we can make these notions precise, and prove that an implementation of a data type faithfully represents the abstract type. Two such approaches have been explored: the method of abstract models pioneered by C.A.R. Hoare [Hoare, 1972] and algebraic specification introduced by John Guttag [Guttag, 1977].

Abstract models. The method of *abstract models* embodies procedures plus conditions on the data on which they operate. These conditions can be of three kinds: preconditions, postconditions, and invariants. A precondition must be true before a procedure executes, a postcondition true when a procedure terminates, and an invariant true both upon entry and exit from a procedure. It is the job of either the programmer or the compiler writer to specify and prove these conditions when implementing a procedure. As you are asked to explore in exercise 2.1.2, it is not possible or even desirable for a high level language to include all the abstract data types a user might want. Thus verification of data types must be approached by both the language implementor and user.

This method was introduced by C.A.R. Hoare [Hoare, 1972], using the syntax of SIMULA [Dahl, 1966], the first class-based language. A class contains a data type, or types, plus a description of the associated operations. Consider the pseudocode example in listing (2.1.4).

```
specification SmallIntSets;                                    (2.1.4)

export
    initialize, size, insert, remove, isIn;

constant
    maxSize: integer;

type
    integer, boolean, smallIntSet;

function initialize(): smallIntSet;
function size(s: smallIntSet): integer;
function insert(s: smallIntSet; i: integer): smallIntSet;
function remove(s: smallIntSet; i: integer): smallIntSet;
function isIn(i: integer; s: smallIntSet): boolean;

end specification;
```

Those identifiers (types, procedures, etc.) which are to be visible outside of the specification are included in the export list.

An invariant for all five procedures (functions here) is:

$$i: 0 \quad size(s: smallIntSet) \quad maxSize$$

Thus for any parameter s, which represents a smallIntSet, size(s) must be between 0 and whatever value has been set for maxSize. For initialize, there are no preconditions, since initialize has no parameters. The post-condition that must be proved in addition to the invariant i is that for output s: s = {}.

For size, the invariant must hold and also the postcondition size(s) = |s|, where |s| is the cardinality of the set s.

For insert, the invariant i must hold for both input s1 and output s2, as well as the two postconditions shown in listing (2.1.5).

```
1)  if (i ∈ s1)                                                (2.1.5)
        then |s2| = |s1|
        else |s2| = |s1| + 1;
2)  s2 = s1 ∪ {i}
```

Notice how these conditions are expressed using the language of set theory. Notice also that two previously defined types, integer and boolean, are included in SmallIntSets. The properties of the integers and boolean values are inherited by smallIntSet, which enables us to compare size(s) to maxSize without specifically defining <.

The method of abstract models is actually more detailed than we have presented here. There are three levels of abstraction involved. The highest, or most abstract, level is the set T of all classes defined as data types. Second is the particular class or abstract type t, such as SmallIntSets. Included in the class t = SmallIntSets are a constant (maxSize); data types (integer with parameter i, smallIntSet with parameter s, and boolean with values true and false); and five procedures. At the lowest level are the implementations of the procedures and the data structure smallIntSet, and the specification of the data domains for integer and boolean. Hoare's method of abstract models provides mappings between each of these levels, which are formally proven to interpret the abstract data type (ADT) according to the invariants, preconditions, and postconditions.

Algebraic specification. The second method for formally proving that abstract data types actually do what we thought they would is due to John Guttag [Guttag, 1977]. An *algebraic specification* has two parts: a syntactic specification and a set of relations. An example of a specification for a queue is given in listing (2.1.6).

Syntax: (2.1.6)

newQueue ()	→ queue
add (queue, item)	→ queue
front (queue)	→ item
remove (queue)	→ queue
isEmpty (queue)	→ boolean

Relations

```
1)  isEmpty(newQueue()) = true
2)  isEmpty(add(q,item)) = false
3)  front(newQueue()) = error
4)  front(add(q,item)) = if isEmpty(q) then item
                         else front(q)
5)  remove(newQueue()) = error
6)  remove(add(q,item)) = if isEmpty(q) then newQueue()
                          else add(remove(q),item)
```

This specification would be written at the design phase, before even considering a computer language. The advantage to this system is that we do not need to use any metalanguage,[4] such as the language of set theory above, to talk about the procedures we are defining. The disadvantage is that we must convince ourselves or prove that the relations are consistent and sufficiently complete.

---

[4]A theoretical system S is written in a particular language L_s. When discussing S, we use L_s and the language of logic, the predicate calculus. This includes relations such as =, or, and &. If we use any other language L to discuss S, L is called a *metalanguage*, i.e., L discusses S.

When we say that relations 1 through 6 above are consistent, we mean that they do not contradict each other. That is, we cannot show that any relation (i) is false, given that the other five relations are true. To consider the specification complete, we must be sure that we have not missed any feature necessary to a queue. Boundary conditions, such as those causing errors above, are particularly easy to overlook.

In any implementation of an ADT for a queue, we would need to demonstrate that the relations above hold. In addition, each of the five procedures can be furnished with invariants, preconditions, and postconditions. There are two types: those inherent to the abstract data type itself and those depending on the particular implementation. For example, if we implement a queue as an array, a dependent precondition on add(q,item) would be that q was not already full. An inherent precondition on remove(q) would be that q not be empty.

Implementation Example

Zilles and his colleagues [Zilles, 1986] identify two requirements that must be satisfied by a language supporting data abstractions:

1. A linguistic construct is needed that permits a data abstraction to be implemented as a unit. The implementation involves selecting a representation for the data objects and defining an algorithm for each operation in terms of that representation.
2. The language must limit access to the representation to just the operations. This limitation is necessary to ensure that the operations completely characterize the behavior of the objects.

The first requirement means that the language itself must support some method for bundling data types and their associated operations into one class. The second facilitates verification of programs and data independence.

Let us assume that our pseudocode includes syntax for specification declarations following the pattern of listing (2.1.4). We will also assume that functions can return aggregate types. Then a partial implementation of listing (2.1.6) takes the form shown in listing (2.1.7).

```
specification ItemQueue;                                    (2.1.7)

import
    item;

export
    queue, newQueue, destroy, add, front, remove, isEmpty;

type
    queue,  item;

function newQueue(): queue;
    {effects: Returns a new queue with no elements in it.}

function destroy(var q: queue): queue;
    {effects: Deallocates storage for all nodes in the q.}
```

```
function add(var q: queue; i: item): queue;
  {modifies: q
   effects: adds i to the end of q}

function front(q: queue): item;
  {effects: returns the item at the front of the q.}

function remove(var q: queue): queue;
  {modifies: q
   effects: removes the first item from q, unless q is
            empty, in which case an error occurs.}

function isEmpty(q: queue): boolean;
  {effects: returns true if q is empty, false otherwise.}

end specification;

implementation ItemQueue;

type
  queue = ^queueNode
  queueNode = record
    element: item;
    next: queue
  end record; {queueNode}

function newQueue(): queue;
begin
  newQueue := nil;
end function; {NewQueue}


  . . .


end implementation;
```

If we can group data objects and their operations together, and if the implementation is hidden from the user, the structure supports abstract data types. Ideally, the only operations permitted on items of type queue are those defined in the specification, i.e., newQueue, destroy, add, front, remove, and isEmpty. In a program that uses the ADT ItemQueue in which **var** q: queue; has been declared, the statement q := **nil** should be illegal. The only assignments to q must be made through newQueue, destroy, add, or remove.

LAB 2.1: ABSTRACT DATA TYPES: ADA/PASCAL

Objectives (Labs can be found in the *Instructor's Manual*.)

1. To construct and use an abstract data type in a language with facilities for constructing modules.
2. To compile the package or module separately, if possible, and incorporate it in another program.
3. To investigate the security provisions in the language you are using by trying illegal operations on such things as private types.

Generic Types

One of the annoyances of a language like Pascal is the necessity for writing new procedures and functions for every data type. For example, if we want a swap procedure for each of `integer`, `real`, and `char` types, we would need three procedures, with procedure declarations shown in listing (2.1.8).

```
procedure swapInt(var n, m: integer);
procedure swapReal(var x, y: real);
procedure swapChar(var c1, c2: char);
```
(2.1.8)

It might be useful to have a single swap procedure name that will deal with all three (and perhaps more) parameter types.

A *generic type* can act as a template for items of different types by using a parameter in the type declaration. A generic facility is supported by Ada, Smalltalk, C++, and Object Pascal, among others.

In Pascal, any array type, such as:

```
type
  intlist = array [1 .. 100] of integer;
```

comes with standard array operations (such as indexing) no matter what the range or type of array entry. Ada permits the range to be left blank when declaring the base type, and the type is instantiated when the range is provided later. Consider the pseudocode declarations in listing (2.1.9).

```
type
  intlist = array [m .. n: integer] of integer;
var
  list: intlist [1 .. 100];
```
(2.1.9)

Here we have specified that the indices will be of integer subrange type, which is generic since the `m .. n` acts as a parameter list to be instantiated later. The inclusion of 1 .. 100 in the declaration for the variable `list` provides the needed range limits.

In our example in listing (2.1.7), we got a start on making an ADT `ItemQueue` general to whatever type `item` was wanted. We may wish to make `ItemQueue` a base type for a variety of `item` types by declaring it as a generic ADT. Suppose we change the definition of `ItemQueues` to the form shown in listing (2.1.10).

```
specification ItemQueue;

export
  queue, newQueue, destroy, add, front, remove, isEmpty;

type
  queue (generic type item);

  ...
end specification;
```
(2.1.10)

All we have done is move the declaration of item so that it appears as a parameter of the queue type in the specification and labeled it **generic**. We can now create and use an ItemQueue containing real items, as shown in listing (2.1.11).

```
type  specification
use ItemQueue;
type realQueue = new queue(real);
var
  Q: realQueue;
begin
  Q := newQueue();
  ...
end;
```

(2.1.11)

We could also declare other queues, as in listing (2.1.12).

```
type specification
use ItemQueue;
type charQueue = new queue(char);
var
  Q: charQueue;
begin
  Q := newQueue();
  ...
end;
```

(2.1.12)

. The **new** instances above are generic specifications. The generic facility need not be tied to these specifications, but is useful for declaring **new** instances of individual functions or procedures. With a generic specification, we of course get versions of each procedure and function specialized to the particular data type(s) we want to use. Think how nice it would be to program a swap procedure just once, and then declare new instances of it for pairs of values we want swapped!

EXERCISES 2.1

1. When modeling traffic crossing a bridge, an abstraction for a queue is needed. List as many abstractions as you can for the applications below.
   a. A grocery checkout counter
   b. A LIFO (Last In, First Out) accounting system; a FIFO (First In First Out) system
   c. Constructing a dictionary
   d. A word processing package
   e. An automatic theorem prover
   f. An airline reservations system
   g. A computerized fuel-injection system in an automobile
2. Give two reasons why an all-purpose language with all useful abstractions built-in is impractical.
3. Using manuals for two or more languages available to you:
   a. What data types are built-in?
   b. Write a description of one of these data types, including the data domain(s), associated constants, and operations, as in listings (2.1.1) and (2.1.2).
4. Define an abstract data type for pointers. Would you allow unlimited arithmetic operations, as in the C language? If not, which would you include?

5. Consider the specification of SmallIntSets in listing (2.1.4).
    a. Using a language familiar to you, suggest two different implementations of SmallIntSets.
    b. What are the preconditions and postconditions for remove and isIn?
    c. Choose one of your implementations from a above, and write procedures for size, insert, remove, and isIn.
    d. Specify SmallIntSets algebraically, as in listing (2.1.6).
6. Convince yourself that relations 1 through 6 of listing (2.1.6) describe a queue completely. You might find using an example queue helpful. Are there any other procedures you might want? If so, what additional relations are needed?
7. Check that the description of the abstract data type for queue of listing (2.1.7) satisfies the algebraic specification of listing (2.1.6).
8. Listing (2.1.7) includes a pseudocode implementation of the operation newQueue. Implement the other four operations on type queue in pseudocode.
9. Write a generic swap procedure in pseudocode and declare new versions of it for reals, integers, and characters (see listings (2.1.10) and (2.1.11)).

2.2
CONTROL ABSTRACTION

Most programs are constructed to transform or respond to data. We have looked briefly at data abstractions above, and will now consider mechanisms that allow us to move through a data structure, changing or maintaining values as we wish.

Branching

Ordinarily a program executes sequentially, beginning at the first statement and terminating at the last. Branching involves relocating program execution to a portion of our source code possibly different from the succeeding statement. Those who are familiar with an assembly language will recognize that branching can be implemented using a (conditional) branch statement or a jump statement. On most machines, a relocation from a branch statement is restricted to a small range of addresses and/or labels, while a jump permits relocation to any word.

Jumps are necessary to implement procedures, but have also been implemented directly in source code through the **goto** statement. Controversy still rages over the advisability of permitting **goto**s, beginning with Dijkstra's famous article, "Go to statement considered harmful" [Dijkstra, 1968b].

It may be helpful to remember that the first high level programming languages (e.g. FORTRAN) were written for particular machines, and started with an assembly language, which was then rewritten into something more like a conventional scientific language. Thus assembly constructs were gussied up to look like English. Such stylistic niceties are often called "syntactic sugar": they may not be necessary, but make the language more appealing to a programmer. Modern language designers often start with a language familiar to the community of end users, and worry about compilers and assemblers later. For example, the syntax of ALGOL and its successors, Pascal and Ada, is close to an algebraic language describing algorithms.[5]

The most common high level branch statements are the **if...then...(else)** and **case** statements. The first provides a two-way branch and the second a multiway branch.

When a language like Pascal or C does not require completing an **if** statement with **end if**, some problems may occur. Consider the pseudocode fragment in listing (2.2.1).

```
y := 1;                                          (2.2.1)
if y = 0 then x := 3
else x := 1;
print(x);               {1 will be printed}
z := y < 0;
if z then
 if y > -5 then x := 3
else x := 5;
print(z, x);            {false, 1 will be printed}
```

To see why the value of x remains 1 after the second **if** is executed, we should be aware that these language rules state that an **else** belongs with the nearest **if** that can accept it. The indenting shown in listing (2.2.2) illustrates its proper evaluation.

```
z := y < 0;                                      (2.2.2)
if z then           {this if has no else clause}
 if y > -5 then x := 3
 else x := 5;
```

Here z is assigned the Boolean value false, since the expression y < 0 is false. So the statement is: **if** false **then...**;. The problem of more **if**s than **else**s is called the "dangling else" problem.

Languages like Ada require the use of **end if**, which can help to avoid confusion. Using this construct, the statement above would be written in pseudocode as shown in listing (2.2.3).

```
if y < 0 then                                    (2.2.3)
 if y > -5 then x := 3;
 else x := 5;
 end if;
end if;
```

This clarifies which **if** statement has an **else** construct and which doesn't.

The case statement depends on a *discriminant* to select the appropriate case. The pseudocode example in listing (2.2.4) includes the discriminant today.

```
case today of                                    (2.2.4)
  Mon..Thu: work;
  Fri:      work;
            party;
  otherwise: relax;
end case;
```

---

[5]An algorithm is an orderly description of the steps necessary to solve a problem.

Multiway selection may also be supported by an extension of the `if` statement, such as:

```
if <condition> then <statement>
{elseif <condition> then <statement>}
[else <statement>]
end if;
```

The `if` and each `elseif` have a condition to be tested. Evaluation proceeds through each until a true condition is found, whence the corresponding result is returned. If all are false, the `else` branch applies. Consider the pseudocode function in listing (2.2.5).

```
function salesTax (state: string[2]; cost: real): real;      (2.2.5)
  var
    taxRate: real;
  begin
    if state = 'AZ' then taxRate := 0.05;
    elseif state = 'CA' then taxRate := 0.06;
    elseif state = 'CT' then taxRate := 0.075;
    elseif state = 'NJ' then taxRate := 0.06;
    else taxRate := 0;
    end if;
    salesTax := taxRate * cost;
  end function;
```

Then salesTax('CT', 100) = 7.5, salesTax('AZ', 100) = 6.0, and salesTax('VT', 100) = 0. The `else` statement will be executed if all the preceding conditional expressions are false.

It is common that the case discriminant must be of ordinal type (limited to integer, char, Boolean, enumeration, or subrange types). If a condition involves a test of real values, multiway selection can still be performed by the `elseif` construct, as the following example shows:

```
if numGrade >= 90 then grade := 'A';          (2.2.6)
elseif numGrade >= 80 then grade := 'B';
elseif numGrade >= 70 then grade := 'C';
elseif numGrade >= 60 then grade := 'D';
else grade := 'F';
end if;
```

If numGrade = 84.3, then the first test is false; the second test is true, so grade becomes 'B' and we exit the construct.

Iteration

By *iteration*, we mean the repetition (perhaps zero, one, or more times) of a statement or block of statements. This permits moving through all the elements of an aggregate in an orderly fashion, visiting each just once. For example, if silverware is a set of flatware, we might like to go through it all, counting the number of forks, knives, spoons, etc. We may not care exactly how this is accomplished, just what result is achieved.

The simplest iterator is a **for** statement. Consider listing (2.2.7).

```
sum := 0;
for i := 1 to 20 do
  sum := sum + i;
end for;
```
(2.2.7)

The loop iterates over the integers between 1 and 20, computing their sum as we go.

In executing the **for** statement, the following steps occur:

1. The loop control variable (lcv) i is initialized to the starting limit.
2. If the lcv is less than or equal to the ending limit, the loop body is executed, otherwise we exit the loop.
3. The lcv is incremented and control returns to step 2.

Note that in the case **for** i := 5 **to** 1 **do**, the test in step 2 is false, so the loop body is never executed. Many languages do provide a feature like **for** i := 5 **downto** 1 **do** to permit reversing order. Step sizes other than 1 may also be supported.

Since incrementation of the lcv is done automatically, it should not be modified within the body of a **for** loop, since doing so could jeopardize the test in step 2. In Pascal, the lcv is undefined upon exit, hence the programmer cannot rely on the lcv having any particular value upon loop termination.[6]

In the use of **for** i := 1 **to** n **do**, can n be changed within the loop body? This could cause a problem if the test in step 2 compares i with n each time before executing the loop. It is common that languages establish the ending limit once prior to the first execution and that comparisons are made to this fixed value, rather than the variable n. Another approach would be to calculate and fix the number of iterations before proceeding to the loop execution.

The loop of listing (2.2.7) can also be accomplished by a statement that repeats until some terminating condition is encountered, as shown in listing (2.2.8).

```
sum := 0; i := 1; delta := 1; max := 20;
repeat
  sum := sum + i;
  i := i + delta;
until i > max;
```
(2.2.8)

Since the test occurs at the end, however, such a construct requires that the loop body be executed at least once.

A **while** loop tests at the top of the loop rather than the bottom, as in listing (2.2.9).

```
sum := 0; i := 0; delta := 1; max := 20;
while i < max do
  begin
    i := i + delta;
    sum := sum + i;
  end while;
```
(2.2.9)

---

[6]In Turbo Pascal, the last value of the loop control variable remains after leaving the loop.

Since the test can initially be false, it permits zero loop iterations, when appropriate. If zero iterations should be able to occur in a section of code, the while construct should be used instead of the **repeat...until**.

Such systematic processing works well for data that is in some sort of linear order. **For** loops are commonly limited to ordinal types, so we could have:

```
for ch := 'a' to 'z' do    {character subrange}

for day := Mon to Fri do   {enumerated type}
```

Declarative programming deals with the "what are" of data rather than the "how to." A typical declarative query might be:

```
which(x: x lives-in Michigan).
```

The system would iterate through the database in question and respond with all individuals living in Michigan. How this iteration is accomplished will be explored in Part IV.

Recursion

Iteration may also describe the behavior of a procedure. In an iterative procedure, statements are executed sequentially, even though control may be transferred temporarily to another procedure or function. For such procedures, one enters its environment at the "top" and exits in exactly one place.

In *recursion*, one can create many different environments for a procedure or function. This is done when a procedure/function contains a call to itself (or to another procedure that eventually calls the original one), thus creating an additional invocation of its environment. For example, suppose a is an array of integer entries, then consider the pseudocode function in listing (2.2.10), which adds the first n entries of the array:

```
function sumArr(a: intArray; n: integer): integer;     (2.2.10)
  {a is the array name, sum from entry 1 to n}
  begin
    if n = 1 then
      sumArr := a[1];
    else
      sumArr := sumArr(a,n-1) + a[n];
    end if;
  end function;
```

An environment for sumArr will include three variable names: sumArr (for the return value), a, and n. Use of sumArr on the right side in the else clause invokes the recursive call to the function.

Figure 2.2.1 traces the call for sumArr([3,2,6], 3), where [3,2,6] is the notation for an array of the three entries shown.

There are four environments in the execution, labeled 0 through 3. Environment 0 is the calling environment, but each of 1 through 3 has the same three names

```
0)  sumArr([3,2,6],3)                              →  ?
        call sumArr([3,2,6],3)
1)      = sumArr([3,2,6],2) + a[3]                 →  ?
           call sumArr([3,2,6],2)
2)         = sumArr([3,2,6],1) + a[2]              →  ?
              call sumArr([3,2,6],1)
3)            = a[1] {since n = 1}                  →  ?
              = 3                                   →  3
              return
2)         = sumArr([3,2,6],1) + a[2]              →  ?
           = 3 + 2                                  →  ?
           = 5                                      →  5
           return
1)      = sumArr([3,2,6],2) + a[3]                 →  ?
        = 5 + 6                                     →  ?
        = 11                                        →  11
        return
0)  = sumArr([3,2,6],3)                             →  ?
    = 11                                            →  11
```

FIGURE 2.2.1
Evaluation of recursive function sumArr

(sumArr, A, and n), though their locations are different. We end up with three calls to sumArr, as shown by the sequence of activation records in Figure 2.2.2 (page 80).

As a second example, consider the function sumN in listing (2.2.11), which adds the values $(1 + \ldots + n) + t$, the sum of the first n integers plus some value t.

```
function sumN(n, t: integer): integer;        (2.2.11)
  {adds integers 1 .. n to the value t}
  begin
    if n = 1 then
      sumN := 1 + t;
    else
      sumN := sumN(n-1, n+t);
    end if;
  end function;
```

The recursive call takes advantage of the fact that $(1 + \ldots + n) + t = (1 + \ldots (n–1)) + (n + t)$. If we wish to add the integers from 1 to 3, the call would simply be the expression sumN(3,0). The reader will be asked to evaluate this call in exercise 2.2.4 by tracing the activation records, as was done in Figure 2.2.2.

We again have three calls to sumN. In this case, however, when we get to environment level 3, the function already takes on the value 6. We simply need to pass that value back through environments 2 and 1, to the calling environment. The alert reader may wonder why that value of 6 has to be passed all the way down the recursive stack. The answer, of course, is that it doesn't, so we could simply quit there. A function whose value becomes defined at the top of the recursive stack is called *tail recursive*. As we will see in Part IV, compilers or interpreters for newer versions

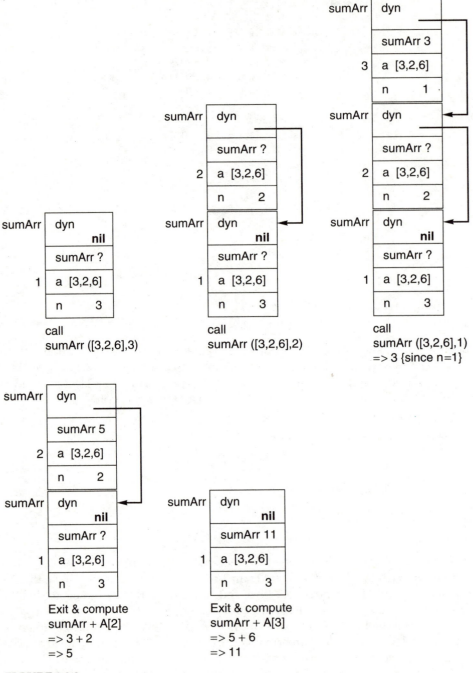

FIGURE 2.2.2
Activation records for a recursive call

of LISP, including SCHEME and COMMON LISP, have been optimized to terminate tail recursive functions at the top rather than the bottom of the stack.

Exceptions

An *exception* occurs when program execution is interrupted because some unusual event occurs. If a program is running in real time, it is particularly important that such events be handled appropriately. Our astronauts might not be very happy to see "ERROR 12, ARRAY SUBSCRIPT OUT OF RANGE, PROGRAM ABORTING" flash on their monitor when they are halfway to Mars. A banking program might include a special routine if a customer tried to deposit an unusually large amount, outside the declared range of the input variable.

An exception is *raised* when the unusual event occurs, and control is transferred to an *exception handler*. As examples, the exception could be raised by division by zero, arithmetic overflow, variable out of range, insufficient space for the stack, or errors in input data (such as 2t, when an integer value is expected). A language may also support user-defined exceptions.

The location of the exception handler is another important language issue. The code for the handler might be part of the block in which the exception occurs, or it could be placed in a structure like a procedure. In any case, the scoping rules for the handler must be specified.

After completing execution of the handler, to what point in the program does execution return? This is called the *continuation* of the exception. In the *resumption model*, control returns to the point of occurrence. In this case, we must know whether an expression, statement, or block is to be reevaluated or whether execution continues after the location of the exception. In the *termination model*, execution of the block in which the exception occurs is terminated. Exceptions not handled in a block can be *propagated dynamically* to the calling block by passing the information to its activation record. If the handler is local to a block, handlers are then required for each block. Since an exception may need to be treated differently, depending on where it occurs, this may be preferable to having one handler that attempts to deal with all occurrences.

The designers of PL/I pioneered the orderly management of unexpected program interrupts with *ON conditions*. The programmer can override whatever customary action would be taken by an operating system by writing:

```
ON <condition> ON-unit
```

For example, consider listing (2.2.12).

```
ON ZERODIVIDE X := -999;
ON ENDFILE(SYSIN)
  BEGIN
    PUT PAGE LIST('END OF LISTING');
    MOREDATA = 'NO';
  END;
```

(2.2.12)

The first would assign to X the value -999 whenever an attempt was made to divide by zero. In the second, a message is printed and the MOREDATA flag is set when the input is at end-of-file. One can also raise an exception oneself, e.g.:

```
IF DELTA < 0.001 THEN SIGNAL ZERODIVIDE;
```

Here the ZERODIVIDE routine would be invoked whenever the variable DELTA became less than 0.001, and X would then be assigned the value -999.

PL/I follows the resumption model, though just what happens after an exception occurs is treated somewhat inconsistently. In particular, just which X becomes -999 after an attempt to divide by zero? PL/I programmers also can disable exceptions, so that program execution will continue. Depending on the exception, only nonsense might be generated subsequently.

In Ada, the exception handler is part of a block specification, and users can define their own exceptions, as in the program fragment in listing (2.2.13).

```
    Invalid: exception;                              (2.2.13)
begin
    ...
    if Data < 0 then raise Invalid; end if;
    ...
exception
    when Constraint_Error =>
        Put("Error - data out of range");
    when Invalid =>
        Put("Error - negative value used");
    when others =>
        Put("Some other error occurred");
end;
```

Here Invalid is a user-defined exception that is raised in the **if** statement shown. Ada follows the termination model, so it exits the block upon completion of the handler. If no exception handler is provided, the exception is propagated dynamically to the calling block. For a user-defined exception, it should be declared in a larger block to ensure that it can be propagated.

EXERCISES 2.2

1. A case statement may be restricted to discriminants of ordinal type. If a language supports the **if...elseif...else...end if;** construct for multiway selection, why support both constructs?
2. Some authors advocate eliminating statements like the **repeat** of listing (2.2.8), which iterate at least once, in favor of the **while** that tests before entering the loop. What is your opinion? In particular, what if there is a test condition, such as reaching the end of an input file, or data elements being in a certain range?
3. Trace the activation records as in Figure 2.2.2 for the evaluation of factorial(4) for the pseudocode function in listing (2.2.14).

```
    function factorial(n: integer): integer;        (2.2.14)
      begin
        if n = 1 then
            factorial := 1;
```

```
    else
      factorial := n * factorial(n - 1);
    end if;
  end function;
```

4. Trace the activation records as in Figure 2.2.2 for tail recursive function call sumN(3,0) of listing (2.2.11). Note the difference between its execution and that of sumArr of listing (2.2.10).

5. If an exception (such as division by zero) may occur in more than one place in a program, might they need to be handled differently or can one global handler deal with all occurrences?

2.3
PROCEDURAL ABSTRACTION

In section 2.1 on abstract data types, we found that an ADT contains both a data type and its associated operations. In this section, we will begin by looking at an operation or process to be done. In Parnas's terms [Parnas, 1972], we look from the viewpoint of a subprogram module as a "responsibility assignment." Such a subprogram would have its own name and might contain declarations, procedures, and functions. A language may even support separate compilation of some type of subprograms.

A program will generally have the following sections:

1. Input data
2. Process data
3. Output results

The program could be decomposed into three parts, one responsible for each of the three activities. This is a *procedural abstraction,* since we do not care how each part gets done, just how they interface with one another. These three parts could be procedures, but they could also be more. A subprogram module could include abstract data types as well as other functions and procedures. We can think of a such a subprogram module as a "black box." Known inputs enter the box, and verifiable results come out. The details of what goes on in the box, however, are hidden.

Parnas states the benefits of modular programming as:

1. Managerial—Development time should be shortened because separate groups would work on each module with little need for communication.
2. Product flexibility—It should be possible to make drastic changes to one module without a need to change others.
3. Comprehensibility—It should be possible to study the system one module at a time. The whole system can therefore be better designed because it is better understood.

A procedural abstraction for simplifying a program is achieved by specifying a process or function to be performed. For example, a publisher may use a large program to transform text supplied by an author into a book. One subprogram module might receive text at a certain stage in the process and produce an index. Here the function could be

```
indexModule(textFiles) => index
```

We must, of course, carefully specify requirements on the `textFiles`, and also describe what the output will be. Although users need not be concerned with what happens inside `indexModule`, the form of `textFiles` must be specified completely and well, so a possibly naive user can prepare `textFiles` for `indexModule` to work properly.

The variable `index` may not be the final product. There may be other modules, such as:

```
moduleAssemble(textFiles, index) => galleys
```

The `textFiles` here might be subject to different requirements than when used as input to the `indexModule`. So why not use a different name, such as `indexedTextFiles`, to make the distinction clear? This might be a good idea, but certainly isn't necessary. The key point is that the description of `textFiles` is in the *interface* between whichever modules it is coming from and going into. In a different interface, the description may be entirely different. We are quite comfortable with this notion when considering procedures. For example, `findThirdLetter(x)` certainly expects a different input x than would `squareRoot(x)`.

If we modify the `textFiles` while constructing the index, our function `indexModule` would produce a pair, rather than a single output, i.e.,

```
indexModule2(textFiles) => (newTextFiles,index)
```

In an ideal system, modularization would be completely orthogonal (i.e., independent; see section 0.4), with no restrictions on either input or output.

Procedures

Before looking further at aggregates or collections of declarations and/or procedures and functions, as we would need for abstract data types, we will consider the procedures themselves. Certainly Parnas's definition of a subprogram module as a responsibility assignment will include procedures.

Abelson and the Sussmans define a procedure as "a pattern for the local evolution of a computational process" [Abelson, 1985]. By local, they mean that a procedure carries out its responsibility assignment in an environment separate from the rest of the program; and that a procedure is a pattern, allowing its work to be performed on various actual objects in similar ways, depending on the objects present.

A procedure is an abstraction in two senses. First, by parameterization, where we abstract from the identity of various data instances. Here actual data values are unimportant; our concern is with the number and types of the data items. The second sense is abstraction by specification. We specify the behavior of a procedure only by what results the user can expect. Just how these results are accomplished is irrelevant. This is the black box described previously, where the "how" details are hidden from the user. These two abstractions working together allow procedures to be separated from the rest of a program (enhancing understandability and correctness) and modified individually, without changing parts of a system that call them.

Functions and Operators

Functions are procedures of a special type that return a value (or, in some languages, multiple values). The specification must indicate the type of the value to be returned. A language may place some limits on this return type. In Pascal, for example, the result must be of ordinal, real, or pointer type. Aggregate types such as arrays and records are not permitted. This may severely restrict the flexibility of the use of functions.

While a function appears in notation to be similar to a procedure, a function is a block that represents an abstraction of an expression. As such, functions may be used in code as expressions, as in listing (2.3.1).

```
z := f(x) + f(y);                                        (2.3.1)
if empty(stack) then ...
print (f(x), z);
```

Here they are used as operands of arithmetic operators, in a conditional expression that returns a Boolean result, and as parameters of other functions and procedures, among others.

Listing (2.2.10) demonstrated one way of specifying the value to be returned in a Pascal-like style: use of the function name on the left side of an assignment statement, such as:

```
sumArr := a[1];
```

In the associated activation records in Figure 2.2.2, we see that storage for the return value sumArr is provided. Another common approach for the syntax of a return value is by means of a return statement, as in Ada. The example above might be written:

```
return (a[1]);
```

It is important to note that, in order to be true to the mathematical notion of functions, the only effect should be the production of the result. It should have no other *side effects*, i.e., changes in either its calling parameters or other variables in an enclosing scope.

We could avoid functions altogether by using procedures that return a value through a parameter. This, however, makes the usual mathematical notion of function composition hard to express. Functional languages, such as Pure LISP, avoid procedures entirely, working only with functions. Similarly, C and C++ use only functions, while a procedure is essentially a function that returns the special type **void**. For our present purposes, we will use the word "procedure" to include both procedures and functions.

Some languages also support user-defined *operators*. Consider, for example, the pseudocode definition in listing (2.3.2).

```
operator max(a, b: integer): integer;                    (2.3.2)
  begin
    if a >= b then max := a;
    else max := b;
    end if;
  end operator;
```

The definition is very close to that of a function, but notational usage in a program may be different. Since max has two operands, it is a binary operator and may be used with *infix* notation, in which the operator appears between the two operands. Hence it is used as m := x max y; instead of m := max(x, y);. If x = 3 and y = 5, then m will contain the result of 3 max 5 = 5.

A unary operator would have one operand. Supposing that a is of an array type, we might have m := max a;, where the largest of the array entries is placed in m. Here max is used in *prefix* notation. C and C++ also have some *postfix* operators, used as i++ and i--, for example.

When defining an operator, its operator precedence must be clear. For example, in m := x max y + 2;, is max or + to be applied first? The language may provide syntax that permits setting the precedence.

Some languages, such as Ada, limit operator definitions to permitting the programmer to redefine existing operators for different operand types. In this case, the operator is simply defined as a function. If we consider a complex number c to be a pair [a, b] of real numbers (representing a + bi), we might define in Ada,

```
function "+"(C1, C2: Complex) return Complex is
  ...
```

This operator overloading (see section 1.3) can be particularly useful when defining ADTs, since the common notation of existing operators can be defined for new data types. In this case, the operator precedence is the same as the predefined operator.

Parameters

Parameters are associated with procedures, specifying the form or pattern of data objects with which they will work. For example,

```
squareRoot(x: in real; y: out real);
```

has two real-numbered *formal parameters*, x and y. The pseudocode modifiers **in** and **out** follow Ada syntax. An **in** parameter must be supplied a value at the time of a procedure call, whereas the procedure itself will provide a value for an **out** parameter. A value can be both received and returned through an **in out** parameter (again using Ada syntax).

When the calling module calls squareRoot(2, result), 2 and result will take the place of x and y, and are called *actual parameters*. The procedure squareRoot gets the value 2 from x and places its result in the data container named result. In order to return a value through an **out** or **in out** parameter, it must be possible to store the result in the actual parameter. This commonly means that the corresponding actual parameter must be a variable, array entry, etc., of compatible type, not a literal value.

When a procedure is called, control is transferred to the environment of the procedure, which may or may not have portions in common with the calling environment. If communication is desired between the caller and the callee, arrangements must be made for passing values back and forth through the procedure's parameters.

As discussed in section 1.2, variables that are not bound locally must be declared in some other environment and be visible by the applicable scoping rules. Changes in these nonlocal variables, or side effects, are generally discouraged, because they may hide the communication between caller and callee, which might properly be done through parameters.

Value parameters. A *value parameter* is one into which the value of the actual parameter is copied into the location identified with the name of the corresponding formal parameter. In many languages, this is the default parameter passing mode, the mode used if none is explicitly given. Value parameters provide a model for **in** parameters, since they come into a procedure, but provide no new outgoing information. These value parameters are often associated closely with functions, in which only one value is to be computed and returned, all other parameters remaining unchanged in the calling environment.

One disadvantage is that, if the parameter is of a large aggregate type, sufficient space must be made for the copy passed to the formal parameter. The time needed for the transfer may also be costly.

Reference parameters. A *reference parameter* behaves somewhat like a global variable, in that any changes to a formal parameter result in changes to the corresponding actual parameter as well. This provides a model for an **in out** parameter. This is accomplished by passing to the procedure the address of the actual parameter, rather than its value. Such an address is called a *reference to a variable,* hence the term, reference parameter.

For parameters of aggregate type, reference parameters can be more efficient than value parameters. Since the entire aggregate is not copied, only its address, there is both storage and time savings. If a reference parameter is used in place of a value parameter in order to achieve these savings, and only **in** passing is intended, one must be careful that inadvertent changes to the actual parameter do not occur.

Since the address of the actual parameter is passed to the formal parameter, *aliasing* can occur—we can have more than one name for the same location. This can make the program more difficult to understand. Consider the procedure,

```
procedure p(x: in out integer);
```

in which x is implemented as a reference parameter. If there is a call p(a), and if a is visible within p, then a and x are aliases.

While this may not seem a problem, suppose we extend the declaration to:

```
procedure p(x, y: in out integer);
```

A call to p(a, a) associates both x and y to the same address, hence x and y become aliases, and the effect of the procedure may be obscured.

In the fifties, FORTRAN was the only high level language that was widely available. Its only parameter passing mode was by reference. Thus any parameter could be passed **in out**. A procedure ADDONETO(X) could result in the value of X being increased by one. Contrary to most programmers' intentions, however, ADDONETO(2) might result in the constant 2 being increased to 3, depending on the implementation. A reference to the location of a constant need be no different than a reference to the location assigned to a variable. This could not happen if the 2 were passed by value, since 2 would be copied into ADDONETO's formal parameter.

Result parameters. A *result parameter* is one that does not receive a value upon entry to its procedure, but is assigned a value during the procedure's execution, which is subsequently available to the calling module. This provides a model for **out** parameters. This generally requires local storage for the parameter, and result parameters are copied back to the actual parameter upon exit. Thus we have the same storage and transfer disadvantages as for value parameters.

The address for the return value can be set either at the time of call or just before returning from the procedure. Unfortunately, different answers may result. Consider the call p(a[i]). Suppose i changes from 1 to 2 within the procedure body. The time of address binding determines whether the result in the formal parameter gets copied back to a[1] or a[2].

Value-result parameters. A *value-result parameter* behaves like a value parameter up until control returns to the calling environment. As part of this transfer of control, the new value, or result, computed for that parameter in the environment of the procedure, is copied back into the actual parameter. This provides another model for **in out** parameters.

As with result parameters, the time of address binding for the return result is important. Aho, et al. [Aho, 1986] assume the convention of fixing the return address at the time of call, so that the value received and that returned refer to the same location.

Even under this assumption, however, different results can occur between reference and value-result implementations of **in out** parameters. Consider the pseudocode example in listing (2.3.3).

```
program inoutparms;                                                    (2.3.3)
var a: integer;
procedure p(x: in out integer);
  begin
    x := 5;
    a := 2;
    end procedure;
  begin
    a := 1;
    p(a);
    print(a);
end program;
```

As a reference parameter, x and a refer to the same address, hence the value 2 is printed. For value-result, x is changed to 5 within the procedure, and this value is passed back to actual parameter a upon completion, hence 5 is printed.

The Ada 83 standard [ANSI-1815A, 1983] specifies that scalar **in out** parameters are to be implemented as value-result, but that composite types may be implemented by the compiler builder as either reference or value-result. However, a program must produce the same result to be considered valid.

Name parameters. When using a *name parameter*, the name of the actual parameter is passed, rather than an address or copy. Hence pass-by-name means that the name of an actual parameter is textually substituted for the formal parameter in the body (between the **begin** and the **end**) of a procedure to which it is passed. Consider the pseudocode example in listing (2.3.4).

```
procedure increment(name x: real; in d: real);          (2.3.4)
begin
   x := x + d;
end procedure;
```

A call of increment(a, .01); would result in:

```
procedure increment(name x: real; in d: real);
begin
   a := a + d;
end procedure;
```

and it would execute a := a + .01.

Pass-by-name is powerful, because functions and procedures can be passed as well as simple and structured variables. The usual example demonstrating this power is that of listing (2.3.5).

```
function SIGMA(name i: integer; in l, u: integer;          (2.3.5)
               name x: real): real;
var s: real;
begin   .
   s:= 0;
   for i := l to u do
      s := s + x;
   end for;
   SIGMA := s;
end function;
```

A call to SIGMA(i,1,m,SIGMA(j,1,n,a[i,j])) computes:

$$\sum_{i=1}^{m} \sum_{j=1}^{n} a[i,j]$$

This is a facility afforded by few languages, but implemented in ALGOL 60.

Pass-by-name can yield some unexpected results, however. You will be asked to explore some of these dangers in exercise 2.3.7.

Procedures as parameters. Some languages permit the passing of procedures or functions as parameters. In this case the actual parameter is the name of a procedure, while the formal parameter indicates it to be a procedure and specifies its parameter types.

(2.3.6)

```
program procparam;
var a, b: integer;
procedure p(x: integer; procedure r(z: integer));
    var b: integer;
    begin
    ...; r(x); ...;
    end procedure;
procedure s(y: integer);
    begin
    ...
    end procedure;
begin
    a := 0; b := 1;
    p(a,s);
    ...;
end program;
```

In the example in listing (2.3.6), the declaration of p indicates that the procedure parameter r should have a single integer parameter. This permits some static type checking within p. In the call p(a,s), we pass the procedure parameter s, but not its actual parameters, since they are not yet known. However, the compiler can statically compare the parameter list of s to that of the actual procedure parameter r.

An additional point of consideration is the treatment of nonlocal variables. Suppose that the body of s included a reference to a variable b, which is nonlocal to s. It makes sense to treat the call r(x) as though s(x) appeared in its place. In static scoping, then, b (within the body of s) would refer to the declaration in the main program. In order to accomplish this, the call p(a,s) would send a pair (CP, EP), the code pointer to the procedure, and an environment pointer to its activation record, which determines the proper reference.

Object-oriented languages also permit the passing of procedures that are members of objects. We will defer this discussion to Chapter 4.

LAB 2.2: PARAMETER-PASSING METHODS: PASCAL

Objectives (Labs can be found in the *Instructor's Manual.*)

1. To investigate the parameter-passing mechanisms, particularly as implemented in compilers.
2. To investigate the problems that arise from global variables and various parameter-passing techniques.

Modules and ADTs

The term *modularization* is used to describe several different notions. As we noted earlier, a subprogram module can be thought of as a "responsibility assignment" that performs a particular function. The term *module* has come to mean more than this. Recalling from section 2.1, in order to provide abstract data types, program units are needed that support the data types and operations on them. In this light, we will consider a *module* to be a named program unit which supports:

1. Encapsulation
2. Data independence
3. Information hiding

Data encapsulation is the grouping of the data types and operations into the same program unit. Since the module specification does not specify the representation, it provides data independence. And, since the users can be given access to only what they need to know, information hiding is supported.

Languages supporting modularization provide for two sorts of modules: *definition modules,* which formally describe the interfaces to the module, and *implementation modules,* which can be hidden from the user and which implement the definition faithfully. We saw an example of this in our ADT example in listing (2.1.7), which includes both a specification and implementation for an ItemQueue.

An important modular notion is the extent of information hiding realized. Just which variables, constants, types, procedures, and functions are accessible inside and outside a particular module? Those that are listed to be visible outside the module in which they are defined are said to be *exported* from a module, and those to be used, but defined and implemented in other modules, are *imported* into a module. The use of such import and export lists provides a means for making accessible to the user only those types and procedures that define the ADT.

Different languages have given different names to their modules, and the notion of a module differs among them. The designer of Pascal, Niklaus Wirth, promoted the concept of the module, from which the name of the language Modula (and Modula-2) derives. Borland's Turbo Pascal provides a Pascal enhancement called a Unit, which provides for separate modules. Ada builds on Modula in defining its modules, called packages, which will be described in Chapter 3.

Another useful notion of modules is the use of independent program sections, each module being independent of all others. Such independence aids in proving programs to be correct. If each module does what it is supposed to do, and the module interfaces are correct, a program should produce the desired result, given appropriate input. As programs and systems have become more complex, modularization has become a necessity for understanding a system design, getting a large program completed in a reasonable amount of time, and demonstrating that it works properly.

One advantage of modularization is that self-contained program parts can be tested independently. Separate programming teams can write modules, compile, and debug them, without communicating with the rest of the project team. This, of course, requires very specific design criteria so that everything will fit together when the time comes for assembling the entire program.

Classes of ADTs

In discussing modules above, we saw that the notion of ADTs was feasible because of the ability to form collections of data types and related procedures. However, our example of ItemQueue of listing (2.1.7) depended on the specification of the type of item.

Classes can represent collections of ADTs, as they provide templates for ADTs, as discussed in section 2.1 under "Generic Types." For example, realQueue = **new** Queue(Real) and intQueue = **new** Queue(Integer) may be two instances of an ADT for a class of ItemQueues. These instances can be *dynamic*, i.e., constructed and destroyed during run time. Further details and examples will be presented in the discussion of object-based languages in Chapter 4.

Objects

Wegner describes an object as a group of procedures that share a state [Wegner, 1988]. Consider again our ADT for an ItemQueue in listing (2.1.7). If q is of type queue, then add(q,5) results in a state change for the object q. If we consider that q is defined and can change only through the defined operations, then we can view the object as really the pair [object, operations].

A language can be considered object-oriented if it supports:

- Data abstraction
- Information hiding
- Polymorphism
- Inheritance

Data abstraction refers to the ability to encapsulate both the data type and the operations to be performed, thus providing information hiding. Hence, encapsulation by an object includes data private to an object, data shared with other objects, global data shared by all objects, and a set of *messages*, or protocol, to which an object responds.

Polymorphism, meaning "many forms," refers to the ability of different objects to respond to the same message differently. For example, while 'A' and 3 are different objects, we may apply the message successor to each. Then successor('A') and successor(3) elicit different responses, 'B' and 4, as appropriate to the object.

The operations defined for an object are known as *methods*. When an object receives a message, the associated method is selected and applied. The state of an object will persist between invocations of methods. We can view a message as the name of a method.

While methods sound much like procedures, there are differences. In order to support polymorphism, we need to be able to send the same message to different objects. Procedures are generally defined by the number and type of their parameters. In our example above, the message successor must be defined for both character and integer objects. To provide this, a language would have to support some overloading of method names, providing definitions of one procedure name for different parameter types.

Objects may be organized into a hierarchy of classes. A language supports *inheritance* if subobjects inherit the attributes of a parent object. Further details will be left to Chapter 4.

Concurrent Execution

If modules are independent of each other, they can run concurrently if multiple processors are available. Concurrency demands time synchronization as well as the specification of a data interface. One module may have to wait for another to complete before proceeding further.

A further complication arises when modules are not completely independent, but share data. If you work on a network, you may have experienced delays when using the same software as other users. Networks can provide for copying a particular compiler or editor into a user's individual workspace, in which case no sharing occurs. Other systems maintain only one copy of such software on the file server and users access it by some sort of time-sharing method. Here the user is probably not changing the shared data, which may be a compiler, editor, or other utility, only using it, so many synchronization problems do not apply. We will discuss concurrent execution in Chapter 5.

EXERCISES 2.3

1. Suppose a language provided only procedures and no functions. How would you implement a procedure to compute the length of the hypotenuse of a triangle if procedures square(x, y) and squareroot(x, y) were provided? What methods of parameter passing should be used for x and for y?
2. Why does the Pascal language provide procedures in addition to functions?
3. Create a unary operator max, using pseudocode notation as in listing (2.3.2), whose operand is an array of 10 integer entries. The result should be the largest of the 10 entries.
4. a. Why would an array passed by value-result require more memory than the same array passed by reference?
   b. In real-time programming, which are more desirable, value-result or reference parameters? Can you think of situations where your answer would differ?
5. If a reference parameter behaves somewhat like a global variable, what advantages are there in passing by reference instead of using global variables?
6. Consider the procedure in listing (2.3.7).

```
procedure p(in out x, y: integer);                    (2.3.7)
begin
   x := 5; y := 2;
end procedure;
```

Suppose parameters are passed by value-result. A call of p(a,a) can produce ambiguous results, hence is called a *collision*. What is the problem here?

7. Consider the procedure in listing (2.3.8), intended to exchange the values of two integer variables, x and y.

```
procedure swap(x, y: integer);                        (2.3.8)
var temp: integer;
begin
   temp = x; x := y; y := temp;
end procedure;
```

Suppose i = 1, a[1] = 2, and a[2] = 3 when we call swap(a[i], i). What are the values of i, a[1] and a[2] upon completion of the swap procedure if:

a. x and y are passed by value?
b. x is passed by value, and y by reference?
c. x and y are passed by reference?
d. x and y are passed by name?
e. Repeat a through d if the call is swap(i, a[i]).

8. How would you compute the triple sum of all the elements of a 3-dimensional matrix a[i,j,k] using the ALGOL 60 procedure SIGMA of listing (2.3.5) and call by name?

2.4
SUMMARY

We have looked in this chapter at abstractions, which raise a programming language above the level of the machine. These are grouped into three categories: data, control, and procedural abstraction.

The principle methods of abstracting data from the underlying bits and bytes are through simple data types such as integers, reals, and characters; through structured data types such as records, arrays, lists, and sets, as introduced in Chapter 1; and through abstract data types, where data is packaged with and defined by its associated operations. Differences among languages reflect the level of abstraction and whether typing is enforced or not. We also looked at two methods for proving theoretically that an implementation of a data type faithfully represents an abstract type: abstract models and algebraic specification.

Control abstraction involves run-time movement through a program. Methods for two-way or multiway branching, iteration, and recursion were examined in several languages.

Procedural abstraction involves the assignment of individual tasks to procedures and their interfaces. Here we considered modules, including data and associated procedures. One of the important advantages of modularization is information hiding, so that users know everything they need, but nothing more. Such hiding promotes understanding by removing unnecessary details, and facilitates program revision and security. Modularization also fosters top-down program development, which may be done by independent members of a team, and concurrency, where more than one module may execute at the same time.

This ends our consideration of preliminary concepts. In succeeding chapters, we will see how these abstractions have been implemented in various languages. In Part II, we will look at imperative languages, considering block structure, objects, and concurrency. Part IV deals with imperative languages designed on the basis of functions, mathematical logic, or the foundations for designing and maintaining databases.

2.5
NOTES ON REFERENCES

Hoare's introductory article on abstract models [Hoare, 1972] is rather tough going for those unfamiliar with the notation of mathematical logic and formal proof theory. A more accessible treatment is contained in [Zilles, 1986], Chapter 4. An earlier article by Liskov and Zilles [Liskov, 1975] discusses the purposes of formal specification techniques, criteria for evaluating such techniques, and the methods of both abstract models and algebraic specification. The article is well written and accessible to undergraduates. It could provide the basis for a good seminar report. John Guttag has developed a system for aiding in the automatic generation of algebraic specifications. References to this work can be found in [Guttag, 1977].

Some of the vagaries of pass-by-name are documented in [Knuth, 1967]. Insecurities and ambiguities in the construct were so extensive that pass-by-name has not been implemented in most modern languages.

PART II

Imperative Languages

In the next three chapters we will consider the imperative languages, where an *imperative* is a command—in this case, to a computer to do something. Variables represent memory locations in the central processing unit (CPU) of a computer, and an imperative language provides commands for sequentially storing or changing the values at these locations. By sequential execution, we mean that the commands are given and carried out one after another in time. For example,

```
var Name: string;
Name := "Jack";
Name := Name + " the Ripper";
```

provides four commands. First, to find a storage location and identify it with the variable Name; second, to store the value "Jack" at that location; third, to concatenate " the Ripper" onto the value of Name; and finally, to replace "Jack" with the concatenated string at the location identified with Name.

In Chapter 3, we will look at procedural languages, which facilitate the organization of a program into separate blocks or procedures, each of which carries out a specific task. Chapter 4 considers languages that support object-oriented programming (OOP), where procedures and data are collected into meaningful modules called objects. In Chapter 5 we will look at some languages that support parallel execution, where multiple CPUs run simultaneously, working on different parts of a problem at the same time.

CHAPTER 3
BLOCK STRUCTURE

3.0	**In this Chapter**	**100**
3.1	**ALGOL 60**	**100**
Historical Vignette: Design by		
	Committee	100
Concepts from ALGOL 60		103
	Block Structure	103
	Explicit Type Declarations for	
	Variables and Procedures	104
	Scope Rules for Local Variables	104
	Nested if…then…else Expres-	
	sions and Statements	105
	Call-by-Value and Call-by-Name	106
	Recursive Subroutines	107
	Arrays with Dynamic Bounds	107
Trouble Spots in ALGOL 60		108
Language Specification		109
Exercises 3.1		110
3.2	**ALGOL 68**	**111**
3.3	**Pascal**	**113**
Historical Vignette: Pascal and		
	Modula-2: Niklaus Wirth	113
Philosophy and Structure		114
	Strong Data Typing	115
Exercises 3.3		117
3.4	**Ada**	**117**

Historical Vignette: Ada		118
Program Organization		120
Types		122
The Generic Facility		127
Exceptions		128
The Ada Programming Support		
	Environment (APSE)	129
Exercises 3.4		131
3.5	**C**	**132**
Historical Vignette: The Dynamic		
	Duo, Dennis Ritchie and	
	Kenneth Thompson	132
Data Types in C		134
	Type Conversions and Casts	136
C Operators		137
	An Example of Low Level Bit	
	Operations	139
	Arrays, Pointers, and the Comma	
	Operator	142
C and UNIX		143
The C Standard		143
Advantages and Disadvantages		144
Exercises 3.5		144
3.6	**Summary**	**145**
3.7	**Notes on References**	**146**

Block Structure

The block-structured paradigm is characterized by

- Nested blocks
- Procedures
- Recursion

A block is a contiguous section of code in which variables can be localized. Thus any information that is to be used exclusively within a block, and need not be known by surrounding blocks, can be hidden.

This characteristic is advantageous for several reasons. First, it localizes changes that might be made in the future. Local variables can affect performance only in the block(s) in which they are visible. Second, when proving correctness, assumptions can be made at the beginning and end of a block. If the structure of the block can be used to show that the end assumptions necessarily follow from those at the beginning and the operations performed within the block, complex proofs are made easier. Third, an individual or a group of programmers need not concern themselves with conflicting names for any variables local to a block. Finally, block structure facilitates program organization if a block embodies a single concept. The structure of ALGOL 60 was a start in this direction.

Once blocks have been implemented, procedures follow naturally as named blocks that can be called from other parts of a program, and that facilitate explicit information exchange between the calling and the called blocks through parameters. As we saw in Chapter 1, the implementation model for blocks is the stack. Only one block can be active at any one time, and its allocated storage occupies the top of the run-time stack. When a block terminates, its memory allocation will be popped, and memory for the calling block reactivated. We saw in Chapter 2 that the stack implementation supports recursion, as successive invocations of a recursive procedure can be pushed onto the run-time stack and popped in reverse order, passing values back down the stack.

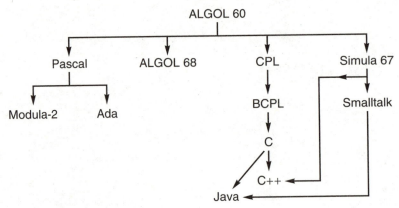

FIGURE 3.0.1
Lineage of ALGOL-like languages[1]

ALGOL's blocks were a good start, but not enough to insure local modification and correctness for large complex systems. The first paper outlining the needs for more explicit information hiding and connections between modules was [Parnas, 1971]. He proposed that systems designers should control the distribution of design information, since "a good programmer makes use of the usable information given him," and somebody has to be in charge. In the descendants of blocks, modules and objects, explicit control of information has been implemented. Data, procedures, or entire modules can be visible or invisible to a user or programmer using, but unable to modify, hidden features.

3.0
IN THIS CHAPTER

The lineage of ALGOL-like languages is demonstrated in Figure 3.0.1.

In this chapter, we will discuss the branches for ALGOL 68, Pascal-Ada, and CPL-BCPL-C. The Simula-Smalltalk-C++/Java branch will be considered in Chapter 4.

3.1
ALGOL 60

HISTORICAL VIGNETTE

Design by Committee

It is commonly accepted that nothing good can come from a committee. Since many are involved, compromise is inevitable, so better results are more likely from an

---

[1]Figure 3.0.1 indicates the major influences of ALGOL on subsequent languages. There are many variations on this diagram, e.g., see [Sammet, 1969], [Baron, 1986], [Sethi, 1989], or [Sebesta, 1993].

individual's efforts. If one were to take a superficial look at ALGOL's (ALGOrithmic Language) history, one might conclude that this opinion is valid. ALGOL failed to come even close to its goal of becoming a universal programming language. Looked at differently, it is a success story in which the main character, ALGOL, became one of the most important conceptual milestones in the history of computer science.

The story began in 1957. FORTRAN had just entered the computer scene, and a programming revolution was underway. New languages were surfacing everywhere. Many users' groups in the United States began to see that the situation was getting out of hand. If a programmer moved, it was almost inevitable that he or she would have to learn a new programming language. Time and resources were being wasted. The groups asked the Association for Computing Machinery (ACM) to come up with a solution. A German organization, the Society for Applied Mathematics and Mechanics (GAMM), was struggling with the same problem, so in May, 1958, ACM and GAMM joined forces. A joint committee met in Zürich to develop a universal programming language.

FORTRAN's close ties to IBM and its products would have made its choice seem like "the U.S. Department of Transportation endorsing United Airlines or Ford Escorts™" [Baron, 1986]. Thus this initial committee of eight embarked on the design of an entirely new programming language.

After eight days of work, the group completed a rough draft of the ALGOL language, originally known as IAL (International Algebraic Language). Although the draft was put together quickly, all did not run smoothly at committee meetings. At one point, a meeting came to a complete deadlock over decimal points. Americans use a period, while Europeans use a comma. One committee member pounded the table, vowing "never (to) use a period for a decimal point." This conflict was resolved by the decision that ALGOL would be represented at three levels: as a reference language, a hardware language, and a publication language. This gave everyone the freedom to represent decimal points however they liked in the publication language.

The product of the committee's work, the ALGOL 58 report, set forth the objectives of the new language:

- The new language should be as close as possible to standard mathematical notation and be readable with little further explanation.
- It should be possible to use it for the description of computing processes and publications.
- It should be mechanically translatable into machine programs.

This report generated considerable interest, and IBM considered abandoning FORTRAN in favor of ALGOL.

It is interesting that, as Baron noted, "many of the European framers of the language . . . recognized 'Algol'[2] as the name of the second-brightest star in the

---

[2]In most circles, the rule on capitalization for the names of programming languages is that all letters are capitalized if the name is an acronym, e.g., ALGOL, standing for "ALGOrithmic Language," and only the first letter is capitalized for proper names, e.g., Pascal. We have followed this custom except for nonconforming quotations, including this reference to the star, Algol. We have not used hyphens in ALGOL 60 and ALGOL 68, as they are not used in the original reports. They are often used in the literature, however. Modula-2 was hyphenated in Wirth's writings, and the hyphen is only occasionally omitted.

constellation Perseus. The amount of light emanating from Algol changes: for roughly every 69 hours, the star is eclipsed by a large dark body, its partner star, which is about six million miles away. Yet Algol always manages to regain its brilliance. The double meaning was not lost on the Europeans: The ALGOL language was not to be eclipsed by FORTRAN" [Baron, 1986]. But ALGOL *was* eclipsed when IBM made the decision to stick with FORTRAN. ALGOL was still a rough draft so that programmers could make suggestions about its final form, while FORTRAN was complete and debugged.

In January 1959, thirteen members of ACM and GAMM met in Paris for six days to transform ALGOL 58 into a complete language, ALGOL 60. The resulting report was unique in that the language's syntax was described in the new Backus-Naur form (BNF), developed by committee members John Backus and Peter Naur. Semantics were described in clear, unambiguous English, which resulted in a very readable report [Naur, 1963]. "The brevity and elegance of this report contributed significantly to ALGOL's reputation as a simple, elegant language" [MacLennan, 1987].

ALGOL 60 proved to be a major breakthrough in computer science. The European passion for orderliness influenced its metamorphosis into the first structured, second-generation programming language. Important language constructs were introduced [Wegner, 1976], such as:

- Block structure
- Explicit type declarations for variables
- Scope rules for local variables
- Dynamic, as opposed to static, lifetimes for variables
- Nested if-then-else expressions and statements
- Call-by-value and call-by-name for procedure parameters
- Recursive subroutines
- Arrays with dynamic bounds

These new constructs led directly to the development of Pascal, Modula-2, and Ada. The BNF notation, first used in the ALGOL 60 report, made the development of a formal theory of programming languages possible, which facilitates successful compiler design. Thus ALGOL, a commercial failure, is considered a scientific triumph.

IBM wasn't solely responsible for ALGOL's downfall in the marketplace. For one thing, ALGOL 60 had no input/output statements. This seemingly major flaw was intended by its designers to make ALGOL machine independent, as is fitting for a truly universal language. Instead, a library of I/O routines was to be provided, specific to each implementation. This notion of separating I/O from the language specification is continued in Ada, but Ada includes a standard library. Eventually, this I/O situation was corrected in ALGOL 68, but it was too late. That the ALGOL 68 report was generally considered to be unreadable didn't help matters. The designers of ALGOL 68 strove to provide language constructs of maximal generality and flexibility. These constructs proved, however, to be too complex to be readily learned by an applications programmer.

ALGOL 68's future is bleak. Its users are almost extinct in the United States, and they are an endangered species in Europe as well. But ALGOL 60's successors, Pascal, Modula-2, and Ada, are successful both commercially and scientifically. And the C programming language is also thriving.

Concepts from ALGOL 60

ALGOL has had such a large influence on programming languages that the term "ALGOL-like" is used widely to describe languages with the following six features [Horowitz, 1984]:

1. It is an algorithmic language, i.e., it facilitates the step-by-step solution of problems, including loops.
2. The algorithm is conveyed to the computer as a sequence of changes to the store (memory).
3. The basic units of computation are the block and the procedure.
4. Variables are typed, and types are checked at compile and/or run time.
5. It uses the lexical (static) scoping rule, i.e., the environment of a procedure is that in which it is defined.
6. It is designed to be compiled, rather than interpreted.

Although many of these ideas were mentioned in Chapters 1 and 2, we will examine them further in the sections that follow.

Block Structure

While blocks were introduced in Chapter 1 using pseudocode in listing (1.2.4), let us consider the ALGOL 60 version, shown in listing (3.1.1).

```
Q:  begin integer i, k ; real w ;                              (3.1.1)
        for i := 1 step 1 until m do
        for k := i+1 step 1 until m do
        begin w := A[i,k] ;
              A[i,k] := A[k,i];
              A[k,i] := w
        end for i and k
    end block Q
```

According to the scoping rules, local variables i, k, and w are visible throughout the block, while we look to enclosing blocks for declarations of nonlocal variables such as A and m.

ALGOL 60 defines a block as either labeled or unlabeled. As labeled, Q may be accessed from outside via a statement such as **go to** Q. An unlabeled block could be the same if the two references to the label Q were deleted.

In PL/I and Ada, both labeled and unlabeled blocks have been implemented, while in Pascal, local variables may be declared only in procedures or functions.

Explicit Type Declarations for Variables and Procedures

FORTRAN provides for declaring variables, but allows the implicit declaration of integers and reals. Unless otherwise declared, any FORTRAN variable beginning with I, J, K, L, M, or N is an integer, and all others are real. ALGOL 60 has three simple variable types: **integer**, **real**, and **boolean**, and all variables must be explicitly declared. A **boolean** variable may have the value **true** or **false**. Characters and strings are not typed, but can be passed by name as an actual parameter. The only structured type in ALGOL 60 is the **array**, which is an ordered set of elements of the same type. For example, **integer array** A[1:20] describes a 1-dimensional array of 20 integers. The statement,

```
integer array B[if c<0 then 2 else 1:20]
```

declares an array B similar to A, unless the variable c has a value less than 0, in which case B has only 19 storage locations, indexed from 2 to 20. We will discuss arrays with dynamic bounds further below. ALGOL 68 added the **record** and **character** types, among others, where a **record** is a template for an aggregate containing items of possibly different types.

Any ALGOL 60 type declaration can be preceded by the designation **own**, e.g., **own integer array** A[5:100]. In this case, on exit from the block in which A is declared, its value will be retained and may be accessed upon reentry to the block. Local variables and their values in Pascal, Modula, and Ada are destroyed upon exit from the block in which they are declared. In C, however, the notion of "own" variables has been implemented. A C variable declared to be **static** will retain its values for the life of the program, whereas **auto**matic variables (the default storage class) are destroyed on exit from their defining block.

Scope Rules for Local Variables

Storage for ALGOL variables declared local to a block is not allocated until entry to the block, and is deallocated upon exit from the block. There are, however, certain exceptions to this rule. The first is for **own** variables, as noted above. The second is in execution of the **switch** statement, which is ALGOL's case statement. It is really a disguised "go to" statement. An example of a **switch** statement is:

```
switch S := S1, S2, Q[m], if v > -5 then S3 else S4;                    (3.1.2)
```

Each of the four expressions on the right-hand side of the statement evaluates to a label. If S = 3, then control will be switched to the statement labeled by the value of the third expression, Q[m]. ALGOL allows this label to refer to a line of code outside the block in which the **switch** statement occurs. The ALGOL 60 report states that in such a case, "conflicts between the identifiers for the quantities in this expression and the identifiers whose declarations are valid at the place of the switch designator will be avoided through suitable systematic changes of the latter identifiers" [Naur, 1963]. This means that if m = 5 in the block B2, where the **switch** statement is encountered, and the value of Q[5] is a label in block B, outside B2, the name of the variable m may be changed in B if its value or type differs from that of m in B2. (See exercise 3.1.3 for a further exploration of this situation.)

The rather baroque **switch** statement of ALGOL 60 is similar to FORTRAN's computed **GO TO**, where **GO TO**(L_1, ..., L_n) S switches execution to the statement labeled L_i, if the value of S = i. Since FORTRAN has no nested blocks, a **GO TO** is quite straight-forward, and execution continues at the statement labeled appropriately. In block-structured languages, however, variables must be deallocated upon exit from a block, so the rules become quite strict. In Pascal, a **goto** can only reference a statement in the block in which the label is declared. One may not transfer into a compound statement, such as a **for**, **if**, or **case** statement, as the control variable(s) would not be active. In Ada, the rules are somewhat more complex, to accommodate packages and tasks. As a general rule, Ada **goto**s may transfer into the same lexical level.

Because of resulting program disorganization and subsequent errors, **goto**s are generally discouraged but allowed for special uses, such as block or program termination upon error. Transfer is not permitted into a contained block, and if execution is transferred to a surrounding block, the block where the **goto** occurs and all intermediate blocks must be deactivated during the transfer. In Figure 3.1.1, if control is transferred from block S to the statement labeled 1 in block P, blocks S, R, and Q must be deactivated during the transfer.

Nested if...then...else Expressions and Statements

ALGOL was the first language that permitted nested statements as well as blocks. A statement

```
if A then S1 else S2
```

has no restrictions on statements S1 and S2; either can be an **if...then...else** to any level of nesting. The ALGOL 60 Report gives the following as an example of a valid ALGOL statement:

```
if if if a then b else c then d else f then g else h<k
```

Can you sort this out? Which variables necessarily represent Boolean expressions?

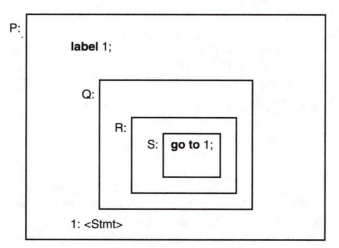

FIGURE 3.1.1
Effect of **go to** on block activations

Call-by-Value and Call-by-Name

Parameters in ALGOL 60 are name parameters by default, though specifications permit the use of value parameters. Consider the function in listing (3.1.3).

```
procedure Increment(u, inc); value u, inc; real u, inc;            (3.1.3)
begin u := u + inc; end;
```

The call may be Increment(x + y, z). Here the actual parameters x + y and z are passed by value to the formal parameters u and inc. Upon entry to the procedure block for Increment, storage is allocated for two real numbers, and the values of x + y and z are stored at locations for u and inc, respectively. None of the variables x, y, or z are changed by the Increment procedure. There is no link between the actual and the formal parameters after the initial copying of the actuals into the formals.

In contrast, consider listing (3.1.4).

```
procedure Increment2(u, inc); real u, inc;                          (3.1.4)
begin u := u + inc; end;
```

Here the parameters are passed by name, the ALGOL 60 default. The effect is that the call Increment2(x, z) is replaced *in the environment of the caller* by the body of Increment2, with the name x substituted for the formal parameter u, and z for inc, i.e.,

```
begin x := x + z end;
```

Here the value of x is changed.

If the call were Increment2(x, y+z), the substitution would be,

```
begin x := x + thunk; end;
```

The *thunk* provides an address of code for the expression y + z. Whenever the thunk is encountered, control switches to that address, y + z is calculated, and its value returned in place of the thunk.

Call-by-name is very powerful, as we have seen in section 2.3. As another example, consider the ALGOL procedure Integral in listing (3.1.5).

```
real procedure Integral (func, low, high, interval);              (3.1.5)
real procedure func; real low, high, interval;
begin integer i, n; real LastInterval;
  n := entier (high - low);        comment: entier ≡ truncate;
  Integral := 0;
  for i:= 1 step 1 until n do
    Integral := func (low + i*interval/2) * interval;
  LastInterval := high - (low + n*interval);
  Integral := func (LastInterval/2) * LastInterval;
end;
```

Suppose the call was Integral(sqrt, 0, 10, 0.001). Each time func is encountered, control will transfer to code for the sqrt function (via a thunk), where the appropriate value will be computed and returned to Integral.

All is not well, however, with call-by-name. We considered a simple swap procedure in exercise 2.3.6, where you found (hopefully) that, using name parameters, a call to swap(I, A[I]) did not necessarily switch the two parameters. Because of irregularities such as this, call-by-name has essentially disappeared from modern imperative languages. The mechanism is, however, employed in the functional languages SCHEME and ML to **force** evaluation of an expression that was previously **delay**ed. We will discuss this use further in Chapter 8.

Recursive Subroutines

Though the report makes no explicit mention of recursion, it is allowed by what the report doesn't say. Listing (3.1.6) shows how a procedure is defined in the BNF of the report.

```
<procedure declaration> ::=                                    (3.1.6)
    procedure <procedure heading><procedure body> |
    <type> procedure <procedure heading><procedure body>.
<procedure body> ::= <statement> | <code>
```

The term code refers to non-ALGOL procedures. The designers envisioned FORTRAN or assembly language procedures being imported into an ALGOL program. Just how this was to be done was left to the hardware and/or publication languages and was not specified in the report, which considered only the reference language.

The definition of the procedure body specifies that it be a statement or code, but does not put any restrictions on the statement. One sort of statement is a procedure call, so a call to P, within the procedure P, is quite all right. PL/I, which was being developed about the same time, also allows recursive procedures, but only if they are declared to be so, e.g., a recursive version of the factorial function is declared in PL/I as:

```
Factorial: procedure (n) recursive;
```

but in ALGOL as:

```
integer procedure Factorial (n);
```

It is left to the ALGOL compiler writer to recognize that Factorial is indeed recursive and to implement it properly.

Arrays with Dynamic Bounds

In a language such as Pascal, the size or dimension of an array must be declared before a program is compiled.[3] Thus its storage can be allocated before the program is run. A second advantage is that the index type need only be checked once. If its maximum value is within the array bounds, no further checks need be done. Checking a simple index type for its maximum may be faster than other more complex tests. In a situation where the size of an array depends on some value computed by the program, the array is sometimes declared to be of some maximum estimated size, and then only partially filled.

---

[3]The ISO Standard Pascal Level 0 excludes dynamic array types, but the disputed Level 1 extension includes conformant array parameters, which allow array parameters with read-only upper and lower bounds [Cooper, 1983].

ALGOL 60, PL/I, and Ada prescribe arrays with *dynamic bounds.* These bounds can be computed at run time, but must be known before the array is used. Storage is then found for the entire array, just as it is for dynamic variables. ALGOL 68 calls for arrays with *flexible bounds,* which may change after the array has been created and storage allocated for it. APL is even less demanding, and any variable can have an array of any size as its value, simply by assigning an array to it.

Trouble Spots in ALGOL 60

In 1967, the *Communications of the ACM* published an article by Donald Knuth [Knuth, 1967], collecting all the ambiguities and errors noticed in the ALGOL 60 report. By an "ambiguity," Knuth means that a number of knowledgeable people find different meaning in a part of the report. An "error" constitutes an ambiguity on which nearly everyone is agreed on the correction needed. We mention some of them here, as various remedies will be seen in the successors to ALGOL 60.

First, we will consider a few of the nine ambiguities.

1. If side effects are allowable, then the order of computation must be specified. (A function has a side effect if in addition to computing a value, changes are made to other nonlocal variables.) Knuth gives the example in listing (3.1.7), which we leave to exercise 3.1.8 for the reader to find the 11 possible answers.

(3.1.7)

```
begin
    integer procedure f(x,y); value y,x; integer y,x;
        a := f := x + 1;

    integer procedure g(x); integer x;
        x := g := a + 2;

    a := 0;
    outreal⁴ (1, a + f(a, g(a))/g(a))
end;
```

Notice that each of the procedures f and g has a side effect. Procedure f increases the value of the global variable a by 1, and g increases it by 2. Notice also that x and y are value parameters in procedure f, but name parameters in g. One of the outputs is 4½, which occurs if the order of computation is as follows:

1. g(a) is computed first as the denominator of a fraction.
2. f(a, g(a)), the numerator, is computed second.
3. The **value** parameters in f are computed with a first, and g(a) second.
4. a + f(a,g(a))/g(a) is computed and output last.

---

[4] outreal (1,...) indicates that an output procedure should be supplied by the compiler writer for output onto device number 1. It is an expression of the reference language, and may be different in any particular publication language for ALGOL 60.

2. Allowability of a **go to** statement within a procedure. Gotos violate the principle of one-entry/one-exit in a procedure, which makes debugging difficult. The idea of a procedure embodies the transfer of control from a calling routine to a callee. The callee is entered at the top, and when exited, returns to the statement immediately following that from which it was called. Gotos allow return to (almost) anywhere.[5]

3. To what extent do variable types have to be specified, and what automatic type changes may occur? For example, if x and y are integers, is x := x/y always allowed? If so, is x rounded? truncated?

4. own variables are a disaster.

5. No precision is specified for real numbers. In particular, when can two reals be considered equal?

Among the corrections, only three will be mentioned here.

1. Division by zero should result in an error.

2. The report suggests that "certain identifiers should be reserved for the standard functions of analysis." It goes on to suggest, but does not specify, that these might include abs, sign, sqrt, sin, cos, and arctan. Knuth suggests that this would cause confusion, unless the list is strictly adhered to and not added to, in all implementations.

3. Call-by-name should be restricted (recall exercise 2.3.6).

Language Specification

ALGOL 60 was the first language to have a complete defining description, as detailed in the "Report on the Algorithmic Language ALGOL 60" [Naur, 1963]. Any compiler written for ALGOL had to implement faithfully each language element as defined. The report consists of five chapters totaling seventeen pages:

1. Structure of the Language
2. Basic Symbols, Identifiers, Numbers, and Strings
3. Expressions
4. Statements
5. Declarations

The report was written in the *reference language*. *Publication languages* were also to be permitted, which might differ from country to country, but "correspondence with the reference representation must be secured." The intention for different publication languages is to ease communication between computer professionals so a more natural language style is allowed.

---

[5]R.L. Clark [Clark, 1973] suggested that the "go-to" problem was really a "come-from" problem. If a program contains several statements of the form **go to** L, and if an error occurs at or subsequent to the statement labeled L, we may not know where to search for the error, since we won't know where we "came from."

Closely related to publication languages are *hardware representations*, which relate to individual machines. For example, the reference language defines:

<relational operator> ::= < | | = | | > |

Most keyboards are not equipped to handle , , or . The particular substitutions can be listed for a hardware representation, but their meaning must conform with the usual mathematical notions represented in the reference.

One of the greatest contributions of the report is the use of Backus-Naur (Backus-Normal) Form, or BNF, to define the reference language. In the fifties, the linguist Noam Chomsky [Chomsky, 1965] was attempting to develop a mathematical theory of natural languages, i.e., those in everyday use for communication between people. Although his four types do not include all spoken or written languages, the hierarchy has been very useful for formal and programming languages. Although Backus's work proceeded independently from that of Chomsky, it was quickly recognized that BNF notation was equivalent to Chomsky's type 2, or context-free, grammars. Both use recursive definitions to identify valid units of a language.

BNF was introduced in Chapter 0. We will look at formal languages and their relationship to theoretical machines further in Chapter 6.

EXERCISES 3.1

1. Discuss the advantages and disadvantages of the **own** designation in ALGOL 60. What would a programmer have to consider about an **own** variable on the first entry into the block where it is declared? on subsequent entries?

2. ALGOL allows arrays with dynamic bounds. If **own array** A[1:100] is declared in a procedure P, what happens to the retained values if P initializes all 100 elements of A, and then changes the bounds of A to, say, 1:50? What is available on the second invocation? (Don't panic! This is a compiler writer's problem and various solutions are acceptable.)

3. Trace the value of the variables B.m and B2.m in the ALGOL 60 code in listing (3.1.8), following the semantics of the report. (Here B.m refers to m in block B, and B2.m to the m in block B2.)

```
B: begin integer array Q[1..20]; real m, r;                        (3.1.8)
       Q[2] := 1;
     m := 3.1416; r := 2.0;
  1:   begin print (m*2*r); end;


  B2: begin integer m;
         m := 2; S := 3;
         switch S := S1, S2, Q[m], if v>-5 then S3 else S4
       end;
  end;
```

4. Can you see why a call of Increment2(x + y, z), using the declaration in listing (3.1.4), is not allowed in ALGOL 60?

5. In numerical computations, it is quite common to sum the elements of an array, $\Sigma A[i]$ (i=j to n). Pass-by-name accomplishes this quite neatly using a technique called Jensen's Device, as shown in listing (3.1.9).

```
real procedure Sigma(A, i, low, high);                              (3.1.9)
value low, high; real A; integer i, low, high;
begin real sum;
  for i := low step 1 until high do
    sum := sum + A;
  Sigma := sum
end;
```

    a. Why are `low` and `high` value parameters?

    b. Trace the call `total := Sigma(A[k], k, 1, 20)`. Be careful to substitute correctly for the name parameters `A` and `i`.

    c. Why did we need to pass explicitly to the index variable `i`?

6. Why can't arrays expand and contract? For example, what is wrong with connecting two portions of an array of size n with a pointer from the first i elements to the last $(n - i)$?

7. APL is usually interpreted, rather than compiled. Why would this make it easier to assign arrays to any variable?

8. Since the ALGOL 60 report does not specify in which order computations must proceed, or in which order parameters labeled **value** are to be evaluated, there are 11 possible values printed on output device 1, at execution of the statement `outreal(1, a + f(a,g(a))/g(a))`, discussed above.

    a. Find as many as you can.

    b. It is hard to imagine a real-life example of a function such as `f(a,g(a))/g(a)`. Why do you think Donald Knuth paid any attention to it?

9. Different programming languages use different strategies on identifiers with special meanings. For example, in FORTRAN it is perfectly valid to say if = 2. Supposedly, a compiler should be able to figure out whether "if" is part of an **if...then** statement or a variable name. ALGOL did not specify any reserved words, but suggested that certain familiar functions should be provided. Discuss the pros and cons of:

    a. No reserved words

    b. As few reserved words as possible

    c. A rich list of special functions, named by reserved words (ALGOL 68 had over 100)

    d. A rich list of defined functions, which could be redefined by the user (PL/I's solution)

    e. A small list of reserved words plus a list of defined functions and procedures that can be redefined by the user (Pascal's solution)

3.2
ALGOL 68

ALGOL 68 was the first language to be completely described in a formal grammar, a W-grammar, sometimes called a vW-grammar.[6] In BNF, which was used for the ALGOL 60 report, the authors were able to describe syntax, but not the semantics

---

[6]The vW-grammar, named after its inventor A. van Wijngaarden, is *context sensitive,* while BNF is *context free.* For example, the FORTRAN statement IF (IF = 1) X = 2 is sensitive to the context in which the IF is used, the first IF being a conditional, and the second a variable name. We will discuss these differences in Part III.

of the language. Even though a language is completely expressible in the W-grammar, readers found it extremely hard to understand. This obscurity[7] is often cited as one of the reasons for ALGOL 68's demise.

The defining feature of ALGOL 68 is its orthogonality. "An orthogonal language has a small number of basic constructions and rules for combining them in regular and systematic ways. A very deliberate attempt is made to eliminate arbitrary restrictions" [Tanenbaum, 1976]. For example, a function maps parameters onto a single result. In orthogonal ALGOL, each parameter and the functional result can be of any type, whereas only scalar or pointer values can be returned by a Pascal or PL/I function. Arbitrary rules and restrictions are eliminated in ALGOL 68, reducing program errors and programmer frustration.

Procedures in ALGOL 68 are of mode[8] **proc**. Since parameters of any mode can be either passed to a procedure or returned as a functional value, procedures can also. It would seem impractical to transfer a procedure as a segment of code into or out of another procedure, thus the facility is usually implemented by passing a pointer. A pointer, or reference, to the code segment becomes the actual parameter or functional value. Tanenbaum [Tanenbaum, 1976] provides the elementary example shown in listing (3.2.1) to produce a sum of functional values, f(1) + f(2) + ... + f(n), for an arbitrary function f.

```
proc sum = (int n, proc (real) real f) real:            (3.2.1)
begin real sum := 0;
    for i to n do sum := sum+f(i) od;
    sum
end
```

A call to sum might be sum(100, sin), which would yield sin(1) + sin(2) + ... + sin(100). Notice that the counter i of the **for** loop defaults to integer mode, starting at 1. Since sin requires a real parameter, i is automatically transformed into a real, for use with f(i).

This notion of procedures as first-class objects was present in LISP and being experimented with in SIMULA, the first of the object-oriented languages. Procedure passing survived in Pascal only in limited form.

Another of the genuine achievements of ALGOL 68 was its use of operators. An *operator* is a symbol representing a procedure or function, such as the arithmetic binary operators, + and ∗, or the unary, −. 2 + 3, 5 ∗ 6, and −2, are familiar to us all. One operator may have *precedence* over another, so that 2 + 3 ∗ 5 evaluates to 17 rather than 25. Not only can one define new operators in ALGOL 68, but define and redefine precedence as well. Thus if one wants 2 + 3 ∗ 5 = 25, as on some simple hand-held calculators where ∗ does not have precedence over +, one can have it in ALGOL 68. The orthogonal principle dictates that we can redefine built-in precedence in ALGOL, since we can define precedence for user-defined operators. The

---

[7]Programmers were not expected to learn ALGOL 68 using the definition, and several tutorials were written for them, e.g., [Tanenbaum, 1976].

[8]Types in Algol 68 are called *modes*. Many common notions were renamed to warn the user that the ideas were somewhat different than in other languages.

designers of Ada included user-defined operators, as have those defining declarative languages such as PROLOG and LISP. A C++ user may redefine an existing operator, but may not redefine its precedence.

Although ALGOL 68 gained little popularity in the United States, many of its pioneering features have been used in other languages.

3.3
PASCAL

In contrast to the much more complicated ALGOL 68, ALGOL 60 influenced a much simpler language, designed for teaching good programming principles and style. This is the Pascal language.

HISTORICAL VIGNETTE

Pascal and Modula-2: Niklaus Wirth

Complexity has and will maintain a strong fascination for many people. It is true that we live in a complex world and strive to solve inherently complex problems, which often do require complex mechanisms. However, this should not diminish our desire for *elegant*[9] solutions, which convince by their clarity and effectiveness. Simple, elegant solutions are more effective, but they are *harder* to find than complex ones, and they require more time, which we often believe to be unaffordable. (Niklaus Wirth, Turing Award Lecture, 1984) [Wirth, 1985].

During the mid- to late sixties, ALGOL was the focus of much attention in the world of computer programming. Niklaus Wirth was in the midst of it all, working on improved versions of ALGOL 60 at the ETH laboratory in Zurich. The need for a successor to ALGOL had become apparent after the release of the Revised Report. Although it contained many brilliant conceptual ideas, the language lacked such practical capabilities as character variables and I/O. Wirth and Tony Hoare, of Oxford University, but both at Stanford University at the time, suggested to the ALGOL committee several modest but important improvements to ALGOL 60. The ideas were rejected and the successor became the overly complex ALGOL 68.

Wirth, refusing to be daunted by a closed-minded committee, developed his own successor to ALGOL 60, called ALGOL-W. During the next four years, with the help of three assistants, he developed a successor to that language, which came to be known as Pascal, after Blaise Pascal, the French mathematician, scientist, and religious writer.

---

[9]In mathematics, *elegant* is often used to describe a theory or construct that is parsimonious. That is, it contains everything that is necessary, but excludes any unneeded adornments. Fred Astaire is elegant, whereas Liberace is not.

Pascal is in many ways an elegant version of ALGOL 60. "Like ALGOL 60, the standard Pascal language contains all the code necessary for implementation on computers" [Baron, 1986]. It is both beautiful and practical. Wirth had designed Pascal with the following two goals in mind [Cooper, 1983]:

1. To provide a teaching language that would bring out concepts common to all languages while avoiding inconsistencies and unnecessary detail
2. To define a truly standard language that would be cheap and easy to implement on any computer

These goals have been realized. Many universities and colleges teach Pascal as a first programming language, and it has been the language used for the AP Computer Science Exam for high school students (though they are switching to C++). That Pascal is a structured language has a lot to do with its popularity in the world of education. According to Wirth, programs are designed "according to the same principles as electronic circuits, that is, clearly subdivided into parts with only a few wires going across the boundaries" [Wirth, 1985]. He believes that students should program this way, *especially* in the beginning of their education, because "the language in which the student is taught to express his ideas profoundly influences his habits of thought and invention" [Jensen, 1974].

An important milestone in the history of Pascal occurred when Kenneth Bowles developed a Pascal compiler and operating system for use on mini- and microcomputers, including a text editor, assembler, and linker. This system is UCSD (University of California at San Diego) Pascal and was distributed to educational institutions as well as industry. Since 1984, interpreted versions and the fast Turbo Pascal have added to its popularity. Wirth, however, has moved on to newer interests, in particular, concurrent programming.

Niklaus Wirth's tenacious adherence to an elegant and strict programming discipline has made him one of the major architects of computer science. In his 1984 Turing Award Lecture he stated, "The subject [computer languages] seemed to consist of 1 percent science and 99 percent sorcery, and this tilt had to be changed." Wirth's commitment to this change has molded the conceptual framework of computer science and will continue to influence it for years to come.

Philosophy and Structure

Wirth's purposes in designing Pascal [Wirth, 1971] were to:

1. Allow the systematic and precise expression of programming concepts and structure
2. Allow systematic program development
3. Demonstrate that a language with a rich set of flexible data and program structuring facilities can be implemented efficiently
4. Demonstrate that the use of a machine-independent language with flexible data and program structures for compiler writing leads to an increase in the compiler's readability, verifiability, and consequently its reliability, without loss of efficiency

5. Help gain more insight into methods of organizing large programs and managing software projects
6. Have extensive error-checking facilities and thus be a good vehicle for teaching programming

Thus Pascal was not envisioned as a production language, but as an experimental and teaching language. The DOD's selection of Pascal as the basis for Ada gives evidence to Wirth's attaining his goals.

A Pascal program is block-structured, with nesting allowed to any depth, but in a special way. Its form is:

```
program name(list of file identifiers);                    (3.3.1)
    label declarations
    constant declarations
    type declarations
    variable definitions
    procedure and function definitions
    program body enclosed by begin...end.
```

The list of procedure and function definitions may be long indeed, separating the main program's variable list from its body. One might need to look back several pages of source code to find just what the range of indexType is, or whether x is real or integer valued. Local blocks encapsulating a section of related code are not a part of Pascal. Each block must be either a procedure, function, the main program block, or a statement block, such as a **for** or **while** construction. This structure is simple, but encourages global variables or variables with unnecessarily large scope.

Strong Data Typing

Pascal insists (up to a point) on strongly typed data, in which type rules are strictly enforced (see section 1.3). Every variable, every constant, and every procedure or function must be declared before it is used. Strong typing helps avoid programming errors and also eases the compiler writer's job.

Pascal's types adhere to the definition of strong typing, with two exceptions. Variant records may include free unions in the variant part, and procedures passed as parameters are not typed objects. We have already looked at the problem of Pascal's variant records in listing (1.3.14) of section 1.3. An example of Pascal's procedure-passing facilities is shown in listing (3.3.2).

```
function realFunctionSum (a, b: integer;                   (3.3.2)
                    function f (i: integer): real): real;
var
    j: integer;
    sum: real;

begin
    sum := 0;
    for j := a to b do
        sum := sum + f(j);
    realFunctionSum := sum
end;
```

The parameters of the function f above are typed, but functions themselves are not types. If we wished to sum an integer-valued function, we would have to define a different function, `integerFunctionSum`, with the parameter,

```
function g(k: integer): integer;
```

Ada has broadened the notion of performing the same operations on objects of different types by providing *generic* procedures and functions.

Regularity in a language means that there are no exceptions to rules. Consider again the form of Pascal's variant record:

```
<record name> = record                                        (3.3.3)
  <fixed field list>
  case <variant-tag-selector> of
      <tag1> : <field list>;
          ...
      <tagn> : <field list>
end;
```

One irregular feature of Pascal is the termination of both the **record** and **case** constructs by the single **end**. One would expect (and, in fact, one may use) two **end**s, one for each. A regular language is easier for programmers to remember and thus fosters efficient programming.

There are practical situations where everything you need cannot be listed previously. One of these is in a linked list, where the "links" both point to and are part of records, as shown in listing (3.3.4).

```
type                                                          (3.3.4)
  link = ^listNode;
  listNode = record
    item: itemType;
    next: link
  end;
```

This irregular feature with `listNode` referenced before it is defined appears to be unavoidable. Ada cleans this up a bit by writing the declaration shown in listing (3.3.5).

```
type List_Node;       --Incomplete declaration              (3.3.5)
type Link is access List_Node;
type List_Node is
  record
      Item: Item_Type;
      Next: Link;
  end record;
```

Requiring the incomplete declaration of `List_Node` allows the Ada rule that any data type mentioned must have been previously defined without exception. As long as we're looking at an Ada fragment, there are a few other things to notice as well. First, the keyword **is** is just a nicety (syntactic sugar) for =, which can be used interchangeably with **is** or **are**. The **end record**; is also optional; a plain **end;** will suffice.

However, the semicolons mark a change from Pascal, where they are used to *separate* statements. An Ada statement always ends with ;. One of the motivations for this change from the Pascal rule that semicolons be used to separate statements was the common Pascal programmer error of placing a ; before an `else` in an `if...then...else` statement. We should be very clear here about the difference between separating and ending statements. For example, an `if...then...else` statement is defined as:

```
if <expression> then <statement1> else <statement2>
```

No separation of statements is needed if both statement1 and statement2 are single statements because the `else` separates them. However, if we use semicolons to terminate statements, statement1 and statement2 will each end with ;. The Ada designers also thought it closer to natural language, where statements represent sentences and should have some sort of punctuation.

As discussed in Chapter 0, orthogonality means the ability to combine independent language features freely. Obviously, Pascal functions are not orthogonal, since only scalar or pointer values may be returned. There are also limitations on parameters, with files always being passed by reference. What's more, the default parameter-passing method is *by value* in Pascal, so `procedure p(f: fileType);` will cause an error, while `procedure p(var f: fileType);` will not.

EXERCISES 3.3

1. As a teaching language, Pascal was missing some features common in production languages. For example, there was no built-in string type (though it was often supported in implementations).
   a. Why might a string type be absent?
   b. Name some other common production language features that were missing.
2. Use of a ; before an `else` in an `if...then...else` statement was a problem, but could be placed before an **end**. Why didn't this cause a problem too?

3.4
.ADA

Ada was designed at the behest of the United States Department of Defense (DOD) as a "common language for programming large scale and real-time systems" [ANSI-1815A, 1983]. It is a strongly typed algorithmic language with the usual control structures for iteration, recursion, branching, procedures, and functions. It also provides for modularity, where data types and procedures can be packaged and compiled separately. To facilitate real-time programming, Ada provides for modeling parallel tasks and handling exceptions without stopping program execution.

The DOD was concerned about program portability and supported the development of a standard language definition of Ada 83 [ANSI-1815A, 1983], which has since been followed by Ada 95 [ANSI/ISO-8652, 1995]. Ada was written with "three overriding concerns: program reliability and maintenance, programming as a human activity, and efficiency" [ANSI/ISO-8652, 1995].

HISTORICAL VIGNETTE

Ada

In the mid-seventies the DOD, which is not known for its budgetary restraint, was spending approximately $3 billion a year on software. We're all used to seeing such huge figures attached to the military, but in this case the cost was a bit too steep. Something had to be done to lower the software price tag. A large part of the problem was the fact that more than 450 different programming languages or incompatible dialects of the same language were being used by the military. This created problems of limited portability from machine to machine, limited reusability of procedures in subsequent programs, and general confusion. The time had come to find a standard language in which *all* programs for the department would be written.

Since about 56 percent of the software purchased was used for embedded or mission-critical computer applications, it was decided that this standard language should be geared toward those applications. "Much of the computer programming done by the U.S. military is used for controlling military hardware—tanks, airplanes, nuclear bombs. To control such hardware, a computer program must operate in "real-time," that is, while the tank is rolling or the plane is flying. A navy fighter pilot can't wait for results to be returned from the computer center the next day" [Baron, 1986]. Embedded real-time systems are embedded within a larger mechanical system, such as a robot or a pilotless plane.

In 1975, the DOD set up the Higher-Order Language Working Group (HOLWG) to find a standard language for embedded computer applications. HOLWG's first step was to develop a set of requirements for this language with input from the Army, Navy, Air Force, universities, and industry. From 1975 to 1979, as the set of requirements evolved and grew, the name given to the set changed from Strawman (1975), to Woodenman (1975), to Tinman (1976), to Ironman (1978), to Steelman (1979). This final Steelman set contains close to 100 requirements. These constrained the language "to have language constructs with specified characteristics in areas such as data types, control structures, modules, tasks, and exceptions. Certain global requirements on 'readability,' 'no excessive generality,' 'simplicity,' and 'verifiability' were also included" [Wegner, 1980].

The next step taken by HOLWG was to study existing languages to see if any met the set of requirements. After an intensive study of the 26 existing candidate languages, it was decided that none filled all the requirements, and that a new state-of-the-art language would have to be developed. HOLWG recommended that one of ALGOL 68, Pascal, or PL/I should be used as a foundation for the design.

An international language design competition was held. Seventeen groups sent proposals, but only four were chosen for further development. These were funded for six months to produce a preliminary language design. Each group was given the name of a color to preserve anonymity and insure fair evaluations. These groups were CII Honeywell Bull (Green), Intermetrics (Red), Softech (Blue), and SRI International (Yellow). It is interesting that each of these groups chose Pascal as a base for their language design. At the end of six months, the Red and Green groups were chosen as finalists and given an additional year for development.

In 1979, the Green team was chosen winner. This team, led by Jean Ichbiah, renamed the Green language "Ada." The name honors Augusta Ada Byron, the Countess of Lovelace and daughter of the English poet, Lord Byron. "She was the assistant, associate, and supporter of Charles Babbage, the mathematician and inventor of a calculating machine called the Analytical Engine. With the help of Babbage, she wrote a nearly complete program to compute the Bernoulli numbers, *circa* 1830. Because of this effort, the Countess may be said to have been the world's first computer programmer" [Gehani, 1994].

Jean Ichbiah's team completed the design of Ada in September of 1980, only after considering 7000-plus comments and suggestions from language design experts in more than 15 nations. In January 1983, Ada became a military and American national standard. Beginning in 1984, all embedded military software had to be programmed in Ada.

Even though a standard language had been developed, the problem of too many languages was not solved. The DOD realized that if subsets and supersets of Ada developed and were allowed to retain the Ada name, the portability problem would return. To insure that this would not happen, the DOD took "the unprecedented action of registering the name 'Ada' as a trademark. This provided the ability to control the use of this name and to guarantee that anything called 'Ada' was the standard language. That is, subsets and supersets of Ada could not legally be called 'Ada'" [MacLennan, 1987]. In addition to this trademark, the DOD set up the Ada Compiler Validation project to develop a set of standard tests to determine if a compiler does in fact implement the standard language. This process includes over 2500 tests. DOD has since dropped its trademark, although both defense and NATO contracts specify the use of validated Ada compilers.

Although designed for embedded processes, Ada is not restricted to these applications. Ichbiah sees a potential use for Ada in both business and education. Because of its rich general-purpose features, Ada has become more popular and is being used as the beginning programming language at a number of colleges and universities.

Ada has its problems and its critics. Although it is based on the small language Pascal, Ada is huge. It is over three times the size of Pascal. This size has been cited as Ada's biggest flaw. A real-time language should be close to 100 percent reliable. Can a complex language like Ada meet this criterion? Tony Hoare, one of Ada's critics, states passionately, "Do not allow this language in its present style to be used in applications where reliability is critical, i.e., nuclear power stations, cruise missiles, early warning systems, anti-ballistic missile defense systems. The next rocket to go astray as a result of a programming language error may not be an exploratory space rocket on a harmless trip to Venus: it may be a nuclear warhead exploding over one of our own cities. An unreliable programming language constitutes a far greater risk to our environment and to our society than unsafe cars, toxic pesticides, or accidents at nuclear power stations" [Baron, 1986].

The revised version of the Ada 83 standard is termed Ada 95 [ANSI/ISO-8652, 1995]. It was initially named Ada 9X because it was due in the 1990s, though the last digit of the year was unknown at the time of development. Aside from correcting minor errors, several enhancements are included, particularly in the areas of object oriented programming and in parallel and distributed processing. It was considered important to maintain upward compatibility, so that existing software and tools wouldn't become obsolete. The needs of information systems software are very different from those of real-time systems, however. It is hoped that various additions to the language may provide for the specific needs of different users.

Program Organization

An Ada program is composed of one or more *program units*, which can be compiled separately. A unit may be a subprogram, a package, a task, or a generic unit. Each unit will ordinarily have a *specification* and a *body*. The specification is public information needed to execute the unit, while the body may be hidden from the user and contains executable statements.

A subprogram may be either a **procedure** or a **function**. A program needs a main procedure to run, which will call other program units. For example, suppose we wished to print out the date, using a main procedure called Print_Date, as shown in listing (3.4.1).

```
with Calendar, Integer_IO, Text_IO;                         (3.4.1)
procedure Print_Date is
   use Calendar, Integer_IO, Text_IO;
   Today: Time;
begin
   Today := Clock;
   Text_IO.Put("The date is: ");
   Integer_IO.Put(Month(Today)); Text_IO.Put("/");
   Integer_IO.Put(Day(Today)); Text_IO.Put("/");
   Integer_IO.Put(Year(Today));
end;
```

Three predefined packages are used with this procedure unit: Calendar, Integer_IO, and Text_IO. The type Time is declared in the package Calendar. Part of the specification for Calendar is shown in listing (3.4.2).

```
package Calendar is                                          (3.4.2)
   type Time is private;

   subtype Year_Number   is Integer   range 1901 .. 2099;
   subtype Month_Number  is Integer   range 1 .. 12;
   subtype Day_Number    is Integer   range 1 .. 31;
   subtype Day_Duration  is Duration  range 0.0 .. 86_400.0;

   function Clock return Time;

   function Year    (Date: Time) return Year_Number;
   function Month   (Date: Time) return Month_Number;
   function Day     (Date: Time) return Day_Number;
   function Seconds (Date: Time) return Day_Duration;
```

```
function Time_Of (Year    : Year_Number;
                  Month   : Month_Number;
                  Day     : Day_Number;
                  Seconds : Day_Duration) return Time;

Time_Error: exception;  --can be raised by Time_Of;

private
    --implementation dependent specification of the type for Time
end;
```

This specification would be followed by an implementation-dependent package body defining each function in the specification, as outlined in listing (3.4.3). Notice that a group of related types and functions are packaged together in Calendar. Since Time is a private type, it can be accessed only through the functions Clock, Year, Month, Day, Seconds, and Time_Of. It is through *private types* that Ada supports abstract data types.

The *limited private type* is even more restrictive than the private type. Values may be assigned to private types, and variables may be tested for equality and inequality. If a variable is declared to be limited private, even these operations must be explicitly defined.

```
package body is Calendar                                      (3.4.3)

function Clock return Time is
begin ... end;

function Year (Date: Time) return Year_Number is
begin ... end;
...
end Calendar;
```

We leave the discussion of tasks until Chapter 5, where we will combine a consideration of distributed and concurrent programming paradigms.

Ada is block-structured, with blocks being statements formed as in listing (3.4.4).

```
declare                                                       (3.4.4)
    --type and variable declarations here
begin
    --statements go here
end;
```

As in ALGOL, blocks can be nested to any level. Thus variables declared in an outer block can be made invisible in an inner block if redeclared, as shown in Figure 3.4.1.

There is a difference between scope and visibility. A variable exists throughout its scope, but may not be accessible, i.e., visible. Although the outer N is invisible in Block2, it does not cease to exist. Thus Block2 is within the scope of the outer N. In fact, Ada allows reference to the invisible outer N in the inner block, by using Block1.N. An undiscriminated use of N in Block2 has the same result as using Block2.N.

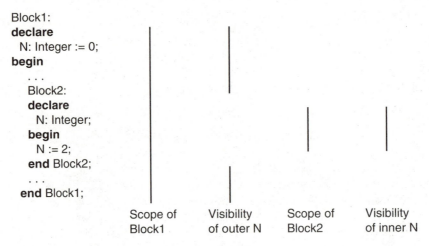

```
Block1:
declare
  N: Integer := 0;
begin

   . . .

  Block2:
  declare
    N: Integer;
  begin
   N := 2;
  end Block2;

   . . .

 end Block1;
```

Scope of   Visibility   Scope of   Visibility
Block1   of outer N   Block2   of inner N

FIGURE 3.4.1
Scope and visibility for Ada blocks

Blocks serve purposes other than organizing program units. In addition to controlling visibility, they provide for levels of control. One may leave a block or a loop using a **goto** statement, or leave a loop to the immediately surrounding block using an **exit**. Neither may be used to leave a subprogram, but as many **returns** as wanted may be included in either a function or procedure. The **goto** is somewhat restricted, but was included to ease the translation of programs from other languages into Ada or the automatic generation of Ada programs. **goto**s are very noticeable in Ada programs, as labels are set off by brackets, e.g., <<LabelX>>. Procedures and functions behave like blocks with their own scopes.

Packages and tasks interact differently. A package is a passive unit that is realized (called *elaborated* in Ada) in the scope where it is declared. Tasks depend on the block or subprogram in which they execute and must all be completed before the unit on which they depend is executed.

Types

Ada has both scalar and structured types as shown in Figure 3.4.2. Among the reals, there are two types: Float, which can specify relative precision; and Fixed, for situations requiring absolute precision. Relative accuracy is defined in terms of significant digits, that is, 3.46 has the same relative accuracy as 0.000346 or 3,460,000,000,000, three significant digits. Declarations for floating-type reals are demonstrated in listing (3.4.5).

```
type Area_Measure is digits 7;
type Person_Height is digits 4 range 0.5 .. 9.0;
```
                                                                    (3.4.5)

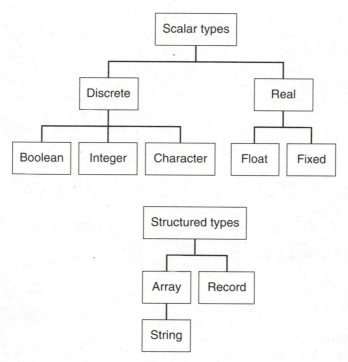

FIGURE 3.4.2
Ada scalar and structured types

in which the variables have seven and four significant digits, respectively. Fixed reals are declared using the reserved word **delta**, which indicates the allowed range of error.

```
type Money is delta 0.005 range -1000.0 .. 10_000.0;
```

Computation with fixed reals is slower than with floating types, but necessary in some situations.

Not all of Ada's types are built directly into the language. Types Boolean, Integer, Float, Character, Natural, Positive, and String are defined along with operations on them in a package specification called Standard, which is implementation dependent but required as part of any Ada compiler. Standard is always available throughout the scope of any program.

Ada also has three anonymous types: *universal-integer*, *universal-float*, and *universal-fixed*. Literals and constants are of universal type, such as:

```
PI: constant := 3.141_592_65;
```

If N is of float type **digits** 7, then the assignment N := 2.0 + PI; will convert both the literal 2.0 and the constant PI from universal types to **digits** 7, and N = 5.141593. (Notice that the result is rounded, rather than truncated.) Automatic conversions are not allowed in Ada, thus the expression 3.6 + 5 would have to be written either 3.6 + Float(5) or Integer(3.6) + 5. In the first case, the result would be 8.6, and in the second, 9. However, universal-integers and universal-reals may be combined for the operations ∗ and /, with a result of universal-real. The result of either ∗ or / operating on two fixed types returns a universal-fixed value, with implementation-dependent accuracy, **delta**.

Ada includes a number of useful operators, called *attributes*, for scalars. If P is of type Person Height, as declared in listing (3.4.5), attribute P'First is 0.5, P'Last is 9.0, and P'Digits is 4. No set type is provided in Ada (see Figure 3.4.2), but built-in operators on arrays make the implementation easy, as shown in listing (3.4.6).

```
type Set        is array (Positive range <>) of Boolean;            (3.4.6)
subtype Color is Set (1..3);
Red             : constant Color := (T,F,F);
Yellow          : constant Color := (F,T,F);
Blue            : constant Color := (F,F,T);
Orange          : constant Color := (T,T,F);
Purple          : constant Color := (T,F,T);
Green           : constant Color := (F,T,T);
White           : constant Color := (F,F,F);
Black           : constant Color := (T,T,T);


C               : Color;
```

The <>, called *box*, indicates that the range will be filled in later. If we assign C := Red **and** Yellow;, the resulting color is C = White. If we assign C := Red **or** Yellow;, we get C = Orange. Similarly, **not** Green = Red and Orange **xor** Yellow = Red, while Orange **xor** Blue = Black. **or** represents set union; **and** is set intersection; and **xor** is set symmetric difference: elements which are in one, but not both, sets.

String is a pre-defined array type:

```
array (Positive range <>) of Character;
```

String may be used only for constants and determines the length of a constant string upon assignment. Both String and Positive are types defined in the package Standard. In addition to the required package Standard, a valid Ada implementation must also provide Library units Calendar, IO_Exceptions, Direct_IO, Low_Level_IO, Sequential_IO, System, Text_IO, Unchecked_Conversion and Unchecked_Deallocation.

Ada's records are much like Pascal records, with a few bells and whistles added. As in Pascal, a record may have only one variant part, which must be the last component, as shown in listing (3.4.7).

```
type Device is (Printer, Disk, Drum);                               (3.4.7)
type State  is (Open, Closed);

type Peripheral (Unit: Device := Disk) is   --Disk is the default
  record
    Status: State;
    case Unit is                            --variant component
      when Printer =>
        Line_Count: Integer range 1 .. Page_Size;
```

```
      when others =>
         Cylinder: Cylinder_Index;
         Track   : Track_Number;
      end case;
   end record;
```

Peripheral is a *discriminated record*, with three possible subtypes depending on the discriminant Unit: Peripheral(Printer), Peripheral(Disk), or Peripheral(Drum). All subtypes have the component Status in common. Disk and Drum also have Cylinder and Track in common, while Printer has a Line_Count component. If a variable is declared to be of type Peripheral, with no discriminant, Disk is the default Unit value.

Ada arrays and records can also be assigned as *aggregates*. For our Set type of listing (3.4.6), we could give initial values using:

```
S: Set := (F,F,F);                                                  (3.4.8)
S: Set := (1 .. 3 => F);
```

For Peripheral in listing (3.4.7), we could have aggregate assignments such as shown in listing (3.4.9).

```
P: Peripheral := (Printer,Open,1);                                  (3.4.9)
P: Peripheral := (Disk, Open, 1, 0);
P: Peripheral := (Drum, Closed, 0, 0);
```

A 3 x 3-dimensional array could be declared in any of the ways shown in listing (3.4.10).

```
A: array (0..2,0..2) of Real := ((0.0,0.0,0.0),                    (3.4.10)
                                 (0.0,0.0,0.0),
                                 (0.0,0.0,0.0));

A: array (0..2,0..2) of Real := (0..2 => (0.0,0.0,0.0));

A: array (0..2,0..2) of Real := (0..2 =>
                                 (0..2 => 0.0));
```

Slices of 1-dimensional arrays can also be assigned, as in:

```
B: array (0..2) of Integer := (3, 4, 5);                           (3.4.11)
C := B(1..2);
```

Here B'First = 0, while C'First = 1. But B'Last = C'Last = 2, where First and Last are array attributes. The result is shown in Figure 3.4.3. To avoid errors, Ada programs usually iterate over arrays from First to Last, rather than from 1 to N.

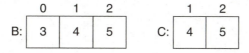

FIGURE 3.4.3
Ada slice

As mentioned in section 1.3, Ada supports an unconstrained array type, which permits array bounds to be designated at run time. In the declaration,

```
type List is array (Integer range <>) of Integer;
```

the bounds of box <> must be filled in when we declare items of type List, such as:

```
L: List(1 .. 10);
```

It is also possible to create subtypes of type List, which may then be used in declarations:

```
subtype List_10 is List(1 .. 10);                                    (3.4.12)
L: List_10;
```

In addition to scalar and structured types, Ada provides an **access** type for storage location addresses. As with Pascal's pointer type, an access type must access storage for a distinct type, as shown in listing (3.4.13).

```
type Node;                                                           (3.4.13)
type List is access Node;
type Node is
  record
    Item: String(1..20);
    Next: List;
  end record;

Grocery_List, Jobs_List, Name_List, Temp: List;
```

Grocery List, Jobs List and Name List will all have the initial value **null**. This is the *only* situation where Ada assigns initial values to variables without an explicit programmed assignment. Access types provide for dynamic allocation using the function **new**. Thus, Grocery List := **new** List'("eggs"); will allocate a new storage location accessed by Grocer List, with Grocery List.Item = "eggs". We could have written Grocery List := **new** List'("eggs",**null**); with the same effect. Do you see why? Examples of this notation are included in the Ada statements shown in listing (3.4.14).

```
declare Prior, Temp, Bought: List;                                   (3.4.14)
        Grocery    : String(1..Length);
        L          : Length;
begin
  Grocery_List := new List'("");
  Prior := Grocery_List;
  Get_Line (Grocery, L);                      --L counts the length of Grocery
  while (Grocery /= "That's all") loop        --Make Grocery list
    Temp := new List'(Grocery);
    Prior.Next := Temp;
    Prior := Temp;
    Get_Line (Grocery, L);
  end loop;
  Prior := Grocery_List;
  Temp := Grocery_List.Next;
  while Temp /= null loop                      --empty list or end of list
    if Store_Has(Temp.Item) then
      Buy(Temp.Item);
      Bought := Temp;
```

```
      Temp := Temp.Next;
      Prior.Next := Bought.Next;
      Bought := null;
   else
      Prior := Prior.Next;
      Temp := Temp.Next;
   end if;
end loop;
```

In listing (3.4.14), the nodes for the entire original grocery list are still allocated, even though after we Buy an item, access to it is set to **null**.

Although not required, some Ada compilers include a garbage collector, which periodically returns storage to which there is no access to the available storage pool. For the braver programmer, Ada provides a generic procedure called unchecked_deallocation, which can return storage to the heap, similar to Pascal's dispose procedure. However, the programmer who does this has no Ada guarantees against dangling pointers, as we described in section 1.1, and is thus on his or her own.

Ada 95 has included features to support object-oriented programming. Since that is the paradigm described in Chapter 4, those language features will be described there.

The Generic Facility

The thesaurus included with a popular word processor lists "common," "general," and "universal" as synonyms for generic. We have already seen the flavor of Ada's generic facilities in the use of <>, or box, for array bounds. We defined Set in listing (3.4.6) as a general array type, with indices to be determined as the need arose. String is also a predefined generic array type:

```
subtype Positive is Integer range 1 .. Integer'Last;          (3.4.15)
type String is array(Positive range <>) of Character;
```

In Ada, when we use the reserved word **generic**, we mean that the **type**, **procedure**, or **package**, rather than the **range**, is yet to be determined. We could have specified Sets generically, as shown in listing (3.4.16).[10]

```
generic                                                       (3.4.16)
   type Base is (<>);
package Sets is
   type Set is array (Base) of Boolean;
   type Elements is array (Natural range <>) of Base;
   function Create_Set (A: Elements) return Set;
   function "*" (A, B: Set) return Set;    --intersection
   function "+" (A, B: Set) return Set;    --union
end Sets;

package body Sets is
   --define all the functions here
end Sets;
```

---

[10]A fuller version of a generic set definition can be found in [Barnes, 1996].

Ada is a strongly typed language, so a generic unit is not compiled when first encountered, but when instantiated. For our example above, we might instantiate Color as shown in listing (3.4.17).

```
type Primary is (R, Y, B);                                    (3.4.17)
package Color is new Sets (Base => Primary);
E: Elements;
C, Red, Yellow, Blue, Orange, Purple, Green, White, Black: Set;
```

It is this reserved word **new** that triggers the compilation of the generic unit, with the type Primary filling in for <>. Since Elements are arrays of type Primary, they take the form (R), (R, Y), etc. We can assign colors as in listing (3.4.18).

```
E := (R); Red := Make_Set (E);                                (3.4.18)
Yellow := Make_Set ((Y));
Orange := Make_Set ((R, Y));
White := Make_Set (());
Black := Make_Set ((R, Y, B));
```

The other colors could be assigned similarly. Applying the operators, Red + Yellow = Orange and Orange * Red = Red.

The generic facility allows for the reuse of software and for restricting visibility of program parts when combined with [**limited**] **private** declarations.

Exceptions

As discussed in section 2.2, an exception is an unexpected event in program execution that would ordinarily cause an error. An exception handler is a program unit that is invoked only if the exception occurs.

Ada has five predefined exceptions:

```
Constraint_Error
Numeric_Error
Program_Error
Storage_Error
Tasking_Error
```

The first occurs if constraints are violated, such as exceeding array bounds or using the wrong variant component of a variant record. Numeric errors are such things as attempting to divide by zero or the inability of the system to deliver a sufficiently accurate value for a fixed type. Program errors occur when trying to call subprograms that have not been elaborated, and storage errors occur when memory is exhausted. Tasks may be executing concurrently. The most common error here occurs when two or more tasks attempt unsuccessfully to communicate. We'll discuss more of this in Chapter 6.

The designers of Ada extended the exception utility in two ways. First, one can define, raise, and handle one's own exceptions. Second, exceptions may be propagated up through the dynamic chain of execution until a handler is found. These are demonstrated in listing (3.4.19).

```
Block1:                                            (3.4.19)
declare
   M: Integer;
   function F return Integer is
    E: exception;
    N: Integer;
   begin
     ...
     raise E;                 --exception occurs here
     ...
     return N;
   end F;
begin                         --Block1
  M := F;                     --call F
  ...                         --continue
  exception                   --exception handler here
    when E =>
      begin
        Put("Trouble with E!");
        return 0;
      end exception;
end Block1;
```

Block1 begins executing by calling the function F, where an exception E is raised. Exceptions may be raised by the program itself as well as occur automatically. Since F has no exception handler for E, F is terminated and control returns to Block1. Since E was propagated to Block1, its exception handler deals with the exception. Notice that the handler includes a **return** statement so that M will have a value, and execution can continue at the code marked --continue. Of course, the handler could have been included at the end of the function F itself, where it would always be handled in the same way. In this example, it is handled as specified by Block1, since F was called from Block1. If called from a different environment, handling might have been different.

The Ada Programming Support Environment (APSE)

In addition to the successive language requirements documents—Strawman, Woodenman, Tinman, Ironman, and Steelman, the DOD published Stoneman in 1980, which specified requirements for an Ada programming support environment (APSE). It was the purpose of the APSE to "support the development and maintenance of Ada applications software throughout its life cycle, with particular emphasis on software for embedded computer applications" [Booch, 1986].

The most common model for this cycle is the *waterfall model* shown in Figure 3.4.4, which was first presented by [Royce, 1987]. Each phase may involve different personnel, programming and debugging tools, machinery, etc. It was the desire of the DOD to standardize all these activities as much as possible to reduce costs and improve portability of both programs and programmers.

Figure 3.4.5 illustrates the various parts of the APSE. The innermost ring, past the host operating system, is the KAPSE, or kernel APSE. KAPSE interfaces with the host machine and will differ from machine to machine. Theoretically, a new KAPSE will be all that is needed to transport software to a different machine. The

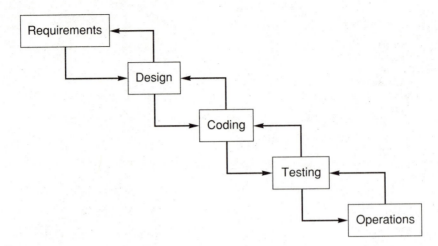

FIGURE 3.4.4
Waterfall model for software life cycle

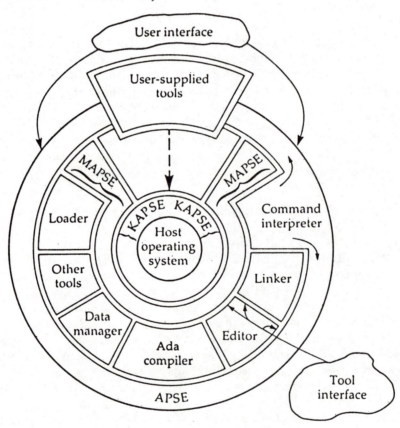

FIGURE 3.4.5
Reproduced with permission from Wolf, M. I., Babich, W., Simpson, R., Tholl, R., and Weissman, L. (1981). The Ada language system. *Computer* 14 (6). © IEEE.

MAPSE is the minimum APSE, which provides common tools, including an editor, compiler, linker, peripheral interfaces, and various tools for run-time analysis. Any Ada system must provide these tools. The full APSE is not defined precisely, but will include tools for managing databases, interfacing with graphics displays, and maintaining software, among others.

EXERCISES 3.4

1. The Standard package requirements suggest that additional real types be provided, such as Short_Float and Long_Float. Many implementors also provide a type Real. If you were writing an Ada compiler, what would you suggest for type Real? Why?
2. Why does the result of multiplication or division of two fixed reals result in a universal-fixed value, rather than a value of the same type as one of the operands?
3. Ada allows overloading of operators for various types. We could define set intersection using "*" as shown in listing (3.4.20).

```
function "*" (A, B: Color) return Color is                          (3.4.20)
begin
    return A and B;
end "*";
```

   How could you define a set difference operator in Ada using **not**, **and**, **or**, and **xor**? (e.g., {1, 2, 3} – {2} = {1, 3}).
4. Describe the differences between and rationales for the three different ways of interrupting sequential execution: exit, goto, and return. How do these processes differ from an exception?
5. Suppose we wanted to redefine sets as linked lists rather than as arrays. Why would we be better served having chosen a limited private type for a set, rather than a private type?
6. Following the declarations of listing (3.4.14), we can create the first node of Grocery_List with the statement Grocery_List := **new** List'("");. Suppose Node had been declared as in listing (3.4.21).

```
type Node is                                                        (3.4.21)
  record
    Item: String(1 .. 4);
    Next: List;
  end record;
```

   We could have assigned Grocery_List := **new** List;, followed by Grocery_List.Item := "";. Why would this method of assignment have been invalid with Item declared String?
7. Can you think of an example where the short-circuit form **or else** works better than the usual **or**, where both expressions are always evaluated? When using A **or else** B, B is not evaluated if A evaluates to True.
8. Consider the recursive program in listing (3.4.22), where an exception is raised [ANSI-1815A, 1983]:

```
function Factorial(N: Positive) return Float is                     (3.4.22)
begin
  if N = 0 then return 1.0;
    else return Float(N) * Factorial(N-1);
  end if;
```

```
exception
   when Numeric_Error => return Float'Safe_Large;
end Factorial;
```

If the call is Factorial(100), and Float'Safe Large = 2^{31} = 2 147 483 648.0, how many times will Numeric Error be raised? What value will finally be returned?

9. A portable program is one that can run on various machines. What is meant by a portable programmer?

LAB 3.1: BLOCKS: ADA/PASCAL

Objectives (Labs can be found in the *Instructor's Manual.*)

1. To explore the different blocks available, not including modules or packages (named, unnamed, block statements, procedures, functions, and system supplied).
2. To try out different schemes of local/global variables in nested blocks.
3. To trace a simple recursive procedure or function that employs both local and global variables.
4. To observe and handle exceptions occurring in an inner block, but propagated to the outer block if possible. (In Pascal, this will be an implementation-dependent interrupt handler.)

3.5
C

As we saw in Figure 3.0.1, C has a different lineage from other ALGOL-like languages. Here we will look more closely at the CPL-BCPL-C branch. C++ and Java will be discussed in Chapter 4.

Combined Programming Language (CPL) was devised in the decade following the ALGOL 60 Report to provide a language closer to computing hardware. It was intended to be a means for solving *all* types of problems: numeric, nonnumeric, and systems. In contrast to the Pascal principles intended to encourage reliable structured programs, CPL was intended to allow as wide a range of applications as possible. Its successor C was kept small and flexible so that it could run on a variety of machines, with unimplemented features such as I/O and string processing developed easily on-site. While ALGOL-like languages are strongly typed, C comes from the typeless language BCPL, where the store is viewed as bit strings, rather than as integers, reals, characters, etc.

HISTORICAL VIGNETTE

The Dynamic Duo, Dennis Ritchie and Kenneth Thompson

C (along with its extension C++) has become one of the most popular programming languages around town. It is famous for its amazing duality. It is both a high level programming language and a low level one. It is also both special and general purpose. Unlike some before him, such as the creators of ALGOL, Dennis Ritchie did not set out to develop a popular programming language. He wanted to design a better operating system.

Back in the sixties, Ritchie was a Harvard physics major. After completing his undergraduate work, he specialized in the study of mathematics, like most computer science pioneers. In 1968, he went to work for Bell Labs (now Lucent Technology) and was teamed up with Ken Thompson. Thompson, who had grown up with ham radios and chess, received his undergraduate and graduate degrees in electrical engineering from the University of California at Berkeley. The two were given a compelling task: to think about interesting problems in computer science. The duo began to think about OS (operating systems).

At that time, scientists at Bell were experimenting with an operating system called MULTiplexed Information and Computing Service (MULTICS). This multiuser, time-share system became the instant friend of programmers who were used to doing things the hard way. Instead of giving a stack of punch cards to an operator and waiting an hour or more for a printout of results, MULTICS allowed users to type commands at a keyboard and get an instant response. There was, however, one big problem: MULTICS was very expensive to run. Everyone was using it, and that cost money. Bell Labs, to the dismay of many, decided to abandon MULTICS. But Ritchie and Thompson couldn't get used to doing things the old way again. They decided to design a system just for themselves and their fellow programmers at the lab. This operating system would soon be known to the world as UNIX, a takeoff on the MULTICS name.

Thompson, excited about the new project, turned in a proposal to his superiors. After the MULTICS financial disaster, they were wary of OS projects, and he was turned down. Refusing to be discouraged, he found a discarded, obsolete DEC PDP-7 and began work with Dennis Ritchie. The work was not easy, but the two soon had a complete OS on their hands. They knew it was unlikely that their work would be usable by others "as long as it ran only on an antiquated computer of which only a few existed" [Slater, 1987]. To get his hands on an up-to-date computer, Thompson sent in a proposal to develop an editing system for office tasks. It was approved, and Ritchie and Thompson had a PDP-11 to work with. In 1971, UNIX was completed, and its use inside Bell Labs began to grow, starting with the patent department. Problems developed, however. UNIX had been written in assembly language, which meant that it was not portable to machines other than the PDP-11.

In the sixties there were two types of languages. Low level assembly languages allowed a programmer to control a particular computer, since he or she could manipulate individual bits of the store. High level languages were easier to use and were implemented on a variety of hardware. A programmer need not worry about messy low level details and could concentrate on good algorithm design. A joint committee from the University of London Computer Unit and the University Mathematical Laboratory at Cambridge decided to design a language that was both high and low level. It would be high enough so it wouldn't be tied to a particular computer, but low enough to allow the manipulation of specific bits. The resulting language was called Combined Programming Language (CPL). It was never popular, since it was a very large and difficult language, but a pared-down version, Basic CPL (BCPL) attracted some users.

Back at Bell Labs, Thompson created an even smaller version of BCPL, called B (perhaps symbolizing that he only needed part of BCPL). Ritchie later transformed B into C by restoring some of the CPL features, such as rich data typing. UNIX was then rewritten in C. The resulting portability made UNIX a computer industry standard in the mid-eighties. Ritchie refuses to solve the mystery of C's name. He leaves it for us to decide "whether he was following Thompson in pulling out the next letter in the name BCPL or taking C as the next letter in the alphabet following B" [Baron, 1986].

C, like its ancestor CPL, is both low and high level. It is a special-purpose language designed for systems programming, i.e., UNIX, and general-purpose as well. Ritchie states that "C is a general-purpose programming language . . . . Although it has been called a 'systems programming language' because it is useful for writing operating systems, it has been used equally well to write major numerical, text-processing, and database programs" [Kernighan, 1978].

C is known as a programmer's language, written by a programmer for programmers. This is apparent when you look at some of C's characteristics, which are short instead of pretty. For example, instead of **begin...end**, brackets {...} are used. This makes for faster programming, but it also makes less readable code. Another example of C's orientation toward experienced programmers is its permissive data typing. If you make mistakes, you won't get neat error messages. You'll probably have to hunt down your own errors—no small challenge. Later versions, however, do include a "lint" program that does error checking.

Ritchie and Thompson have collaborated on several editions of the ever-evolving UNIX. Considering their past successes, the two were given almost unlimited freedom at Bell Labs. One can't help but wonder what they'll come up with next.

Data Types in C

C has two numeric types, **int** and **float**. A real can be **double** or **long double**, and an **int** may be **short**, **long**, or **unsigned**. There is a character type **char**, but no Boolean type. In C, any nonzero value is considered to be true and 0 false. Since C is close to the machine, certain nonprinting character constants are available, such as \n for a newline and \b for backspace.

Types derived from the simple types above are:

Arrays: `<element type> <array name>[size]`
Example: `char name[25]`

Pointers: `<type referenced> *<pointer name>`
Example: `int *pn`

Structures: `struct [<structure name>]{<field list>}`
Example: `typedef struct {int day, month, year;} date;`
or: `struct hire_date {int day, month, year;};`

Using the **typedef** for date, we can then declare: date hire_date; and assign its fields as follows:

```
hire_date.day = 25;
hire_date.month = 9;
(&hire_date) -> year = 1990;
```

Note here the combination (&...)->. -> is a special symbol meaning "the field of the structure (union) pointed to by the variable on the left." Parentheses are needed around (&hire_date) because -> has precedence over &.

Unions: **union** [<union name>]{list of variants}
Unions are always discriminated, so no ambiguities can occur. For example:

```
typedef union {int iarg; float farg;} numeric_const;
numeric_const pi, zero;
(&pi) -> farg = 3.141592; zero.iarg = 0;
```

Unions and structures are declared similarly, but in a **struct** (C's record), storage is allocated for all fields, whereas in a **union**, storage is allocated for the largest variant, and only one is assigned to a union variable. Pascal's variant record can be created in C if desired, since a union can be a field of a record (and vice versa).

Functions: <value type> <function name>(parameter list)
```
        parameter definitions;
        {
          local declarations;
          statements;
        }
```

A functional value may be of any type except another function or an array. In functions returning integers, the value type may be omitted. A function returning no value is of **void** type. For example:

```
void swap(px,py)
        float *px; float *py;
        {...}
```

One important difference between C and Pascal functions is that no type checking occurs on either the number or type of parameters when a function is called, if the function is defined as above in the so-called *classic* style. More modern versions of C include a *modern* style, where parameter type information is included in the parameter list, and type checking can occur. For example:

```
void swap(float *px, float *py)
          {...}
```

Another difference is that parameters are always passed by value, except for arrays. f(a) will pass a pointer to the first element of the array a, a[0]. Reference calls are quite easily achieved by passing addresses.

C is commonly organized into modules of three types: manifest constants (macros), external variables (array and string initializations), and function definitions. These can be organized for separate compilation but may also reside in the same file. When a program is organized into several separate modules, it is important that they have identical declarations for common items. To maintain this consistency, such declarations are generally placed in a header file (say prog.h), which marks as **extern** those items to be referenced by another module. The other modules can gain access to those declarations by including in the beginning:

```
#include <prog.h>
```

Implementations of C also provide for obtaining extra memory when needed, using the function **calloc**(n,s), where n is the number of items of size s to be allocated. **calloc** returns a pointer to the first word of extra memory. This can also be released using **free**(*ptr), where ptr points to the beginning of the storage to be released.

Type Conversions and Casts

C allows a small number of automatic type conversions. As Kernighan and Ritchie say, "The only conversions that happen automatically are those that make sense" [Kernighan, 1978]. **char**s and **int**s may be interchanged freely, with characters being converted to their ASCII valued **int**. The value of the expression,

```
(c + 'a' - 'A')
```

is a lowercase character if c contains an uppercase character. **float** and **int** types may be combined, as in farg+iarg, with the **int** converted to **float**. In general, the conversion always is to the "higher type."

Any unstructured type may be converted to any other through the use of a *cast*. If n is an **int**, we can explicitly convert it to **float** by **(float)** n. The C terminology is that n is cast to **float**. In practice, casting pointers from one pointer type to another does not always work, although any pointer type p can be cast to **(char)** p. Casting is handy when calling functions, where parameters may be of a different type. For example, sqrt((**double**) n) will convert n to a **double** before sending it to the sqrt function. We could, of course, have used a three-statement block,

```
{double x; x = n; sqrt(x);}
```

to achieve almost the same effect. In the first call to sqrt, n will remain a **double**, while in the block it remains an **int**.

The integer types are very flexible in C, and can be used for arithmetic, logical, or bitwise variables. As was mentioned before, any nonzero numeric value (integer or real) is true while 0 is false. Since C is based on expressions, the statement in listing (3.5.1) is perfectly valid.

```
if (m -= 1){                                                    (3.5.1)
  /* execute if m decremented by 1 is not 0 */
  statement_m1;
  if ( m -= 1)
    statement_m2;
}
else
  statement_m3;
```

Note the use of the expression (m -= 1) where we would anticipate a Boolean expression. C is a lean language, carrying no extra baggage. There are no predefined constants true and false. If one wants this feature, a macro can be defined at the beginning of a program (or placed in a header file):

```
#define false 0
#define true 1
```

C relations return values of 1 or 0, so the usual Boolean expressions, such as (x < y), will evaluate to 1 if true and 0 if false.

C Operators

One useful notion made operationally explicit in C is that of left and right values (l- and r-values). When we make an assignment b = a, a and b are treated differently. A value is computed for a, and then an address is located for b. Finally, the value of a is copied into the storage location for b. Here b (or any other identifier for that matter) is an l-value, since the expression refers to an object that can be examined or modified, while other expressions are considered r-values. An expression such as 2 * x + 5 can have a right value, but not a left value. C has two operators that extend this: the address operator & may be applied to an l-value (or to a function designator) and returns a pointer to its operand; and the indirection operator *, which is applied to a pointer and produces an r-value (or a function designator, if the pointer points to a function).

Consider the assignments shown in Figure 3.5.1. In the second, the address of a is placed into b. In the third, we take the contents of b, then treat it as an address to get the contents 5. The last assignment might seem a bit odd. *a selects the right

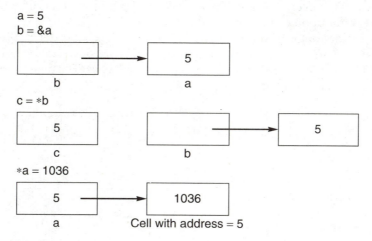

FIGURE 3.5.1
l-values and r-values in C

value associated with a, but a is on the left, so this value is an address. The value 1036 is stored in a cell with address stored at the location associated with a.

C has, in addition to * and &, the four arithmetic operators: +, *, −, /; and arithmetic comparators: <, >, ==, <=, >=, != ("not ="). It also has two shift operators, left shift << and right shift >>. 12 << 3 yields 96, and 26 >> 2 is 6 (see Figure 3.5.2).

While its typeless predecessor BCPL is statement-oriented, C is an expression language. A valid expression, such as x + y, always has a value. Assignment is treated as an operator =, with the expression (x = 3 + 5) having the value 8. As a side effect, x is assigned the value 8. This also permits us to write assignments such as x = y = 0, since the value of (y = 0) is again 0, allowing that value to be placed in x. Consider a C program block to count the number of characters of input, as shown in listing (3.5.2).

```
{                                                    (3.5.2)
  n = 0;
  while ((c = getchar ()) != EOF)
    c != \0 || c != \n ? ++n : n;
}
```

Let's look at the two lines in the **while** statement. Remember that in an expression language, every expression yields a value. First, assignment of a character to c and comparison to EOF can all be done in the same expression. The value of the expression is either true or false, but the variable c is assigned a value in any case as a side effect. The second expression is a conditional, signaled by ?. The expression (e ? a : b) yields the value a if e is true, otherwise b. First, we compare c to \0 (null character) and to \n (newline). If it is not equal (!=) to either, the value of the conditional expression is n+1 (++n). If it equals one or the other, the value is n. The ; is used to turn the expression into a statement. In expression languages, statements have no value, only side effects. The value of the expression is no longer needed, so it is thrown away. However, the side effect of increasing n has still occurred, so n has the desired count upon completion of the loop.

The operators of C are shown in Table 3.5.1, grouped in order of precedence, with those listed first taking precedence over those lower down in the figure. Since C is a typed language, usage is restricted to particular types. The new "comma" operator will be discussed later in this section.

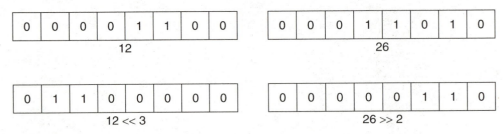

FIGURE 3.5.2
C shift operators

TABLE 3.5.1
Operators of the C language

Primary		Relational	
()	parentheses	x<y (>,<=,>=)	x less than y, etc. 0 if false, 1
x[y]	value of yth element of array x		otherwise
x->y	value of y field of structure pointed to	**Equality**	
	by x	x==y (x!=y)	x equal (not equal) y
x.y	value of y field of structure x		

Unary		Bitwise (in order of precedence)	
!x	not x; !x = 0 if x is nonzero, 1	x&y	bitwise and of x and y, 1&1=1, else 0
	otherwise	x^y	bitwise xor of x and y, 1^0=0^1=1,
~x	1s complement of x. 0s become 1s		else 0
	and 1s become 0s.	x|y	bitwise or of x and y, 0|0=0, else 1
++x (--x)	x is incremented (decremented)	**Logical (in order of precedence)**	
	before use	x&&y	1 if both x and y are nonzero, else 0
x++ (x--)	x is incremented (decremented)	x||y	1 if x or y are nonzero, else 0
	after use		
-x	arithmetic negation of x	**Conditional**	
*x	value at address x	x?y:z	y if x is nonzero, z otherwise
&x	address of x		
sizeof x	# bytes in x	**Assignment**	

Multiplication			
x*y (x/y)	product (quotient) of x and y	x=y	x gets the value of y
x%y	x MOD y	x*op*=y	x gets the value of x*op*y, where *op* may
			be +, −, *, /, %, >>, <<, &, ^, or |.

Addition		Comma	
x+y (x-y)	sum (difference) of x and y	x,y	x, then y, are evaluated, expression
Shift			gets value of y
x<<y (x>>y)	x gets left (right) shifted y places		

C has an **if** and an **if...else** statement, as well as **repeat, while, do...while...,
switch,** and **for** statements. An example of a C **for** statement is shown in listing (3.5.3).

$$\textbf{for } (i=0; \ i<5; \ i++) \ x=i; \tag{3.5.3}$$

The first expression gives a 0 start for the loop, it terminates when i==5, and i is
incremented by 1 *after* it is used (i++). x will be assigned successively: 0, 1, 2, 3, and 4.

An Example of Low-Level Bit Operations

In this section, we will include an example of a simple database program that
gives a little of the flavor of bit manipulations. Let us assume that student records
for a small college are stored on disk, in records defined by listing (3.5.4).

```
#define Ln 35                                                           (3.5.4)
typedef struct {
    char name[Ln+1];       /* student name */
    long ID;               /* student ID */
    char year;             /* year in school: 1 .. 4 */
    char gender;           /* gender: 'M' or 'F' */
    } std_type;
```

When the records are read from disk and placed into memory, the name and ID will have the same format, but we will use low level operations to pack both the year and gender into a single field. The packed records will have the form shown in listing (3.5.5), and we form our student database st_db as a global array of such records.

```
typedef struct {                                                        (3.5.5)
    char name[Ln];
    long ID;
    char year_gender;      /* year 0 .. 3; 1(male), 0(female) */
    } packed_std_type;
extern packed_std_type st_db[];
```

First we look at the functions pack and unpack, which convert standard records to packed ones, and vice versa. These are shown in listing (3.5.6), in which line numbers are added to aid discussion.

```
1)  void pack(packed_std_type *packed_std, std_type *std)               (3.5.6)
2)  {   int is_male = std->gender == 'M' ? 1 : 0;
3)      strncpy(packed_std->name, std->name, sizeof packed_std->name);
4)      packed_std->ID = std->ID;
5)      packed_std->year_gender = (is_male<<2)|(std->year-1);
    }

6)  void unpack(std_type *std, packed_std_type *packed_std)
7)  {   strncpy(std->name, packed_std->name, sizeof packed_std->name);
8)      std->ID = packed_std->ID;
9)      std->year = ((packed_std->year_gender) & 3) + 1; /*unpack year_gender*/
10)     std->gender = (packed_std->year_gender>>2) == 1 ? 'M' : 'F';
    }
```

Consider a standard record of a male (gender = 'M') Junior (year = 3). In that case, is_male gets the value 1 (true). In lines 3 and 4, the name and ID are copied to the packed record. In line 5, year-1 shifts the values 1 .. 4 to the range 0 .. 3, so that it will fit within two bits. By shifting is_male left two places, the 1 (male) bit is placed into the third position from the right. Applying the | (bitwise or) operator then packs both information into the year_gender field, as shown in Figure 3.5.3.

When a record is unpacked, applying the & (bitwise and) operator with the value 3 = 0000 0000 0000 0011 in line 9 will mask out all but the right two bits. Adding 1 then shifts the two-bit values 0 .. 3 back to the original range 1 .. 4. Then the >> (right shift) operator puts the gender bit back into the rightmost bit.

Once a database st_db of packed records is stored into memory, functions will be needed to add, delete, and edit records (among others). Consider the form of the add function shown in listing (3.5.7).

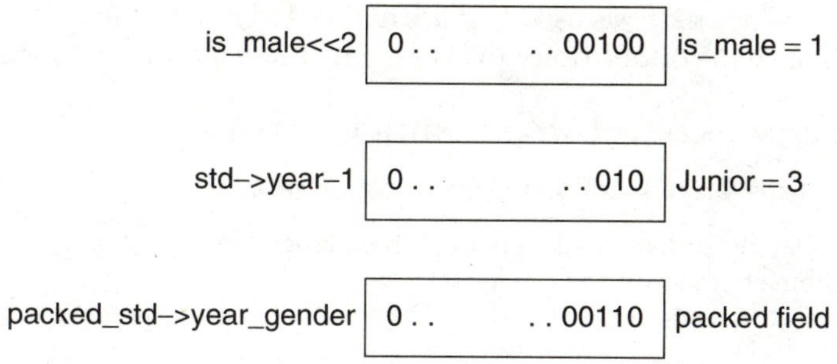

is_male<<2 | 0 . .   . . 00100 | is_male = 1

std->year–1 | 0 . .   . . 010 | Junior = 3

packed_std->year_gender | 0 . .   . . 00110 | packed field

FIGURE 3.5.3
Packing the year_gender field

```
/* Add a student to the data base */                              (3.5.7)
/* RETURNS: 0 if couldn't be done, else 1 */
int add()
{       int location;
        packed_std_type packed_std;
        std_type std;

        if (current_size == MAX_db) /* if data base is full */
        {       printf("Data base is full\n");
                return 0;
        }

        if (getID(&std.ID) <= 0) /* gets & checks for valid ID */
                return 0;
        if (find(std.ID, &location)) /* get insert location */
        {       printf("Cannot add; student already exists.\n");
                return 0;
        }

        if (getinput(&std) == 0) /* get name, year, & gender */
                return 0;

        pack(&packed_std, &std);
        /* make room for the new student */
        memmove(&st_db[location+1], &st_db[location],
                    (current_size-location)*sizeof(st_db[0]));
        /* insert new student */
        memcpy(&st_db[location], &packed_std, sizeof(st_db[location]));
        ++current_size;
        return 1;
}
```

No parameters are listed, since st_db is global. Upon the call to find, the intended insert location is determined. Here getID gets the student ID number and checks for validity, and getinput gets the remaining fields. After packing the record, a memmove is performed, which moves all the records from location to the end up one record. Then, finally, a memcpy is used to place the packed record into the database st_db. Students will have the opportunity to investigate this example further in Lab 3.2.

LAB 3.2: COMBINING LOW AND HIGH LEVEL FEATURES: C

Objectives (Labs can be found in the *Instructor's Manual*.)

1. To familiarize students with syntax of the C language.
2. To combine both low and high level features of C.
3. To illustrate the space savings gained by the use of low level features.

Arrays, Pointers, and the Comma Operator

Since C does not allow nested procedures, and all parameters except arrays are passed by value, compilation and execution are fast. Programs tend to be composed of lots of little functions. When an array is passed as a parameter, it is this pointer that is passed; the array is not copied. A straightforward example, similar to one from *The C Puzzle Book* [Feuer, 1989] is shown in listing (3.5.8).

```
int a[]={0,1,2,3};          /* array with elements, 0-3    */      (3.5.8)
int *p[]={a,a+1,a+2,a+3};  /* array with pointer elements */
int **pp=p;
main(){
  printf("a=%p, *a=%d, p=%p, *p=%p, **pp=%d\n", a,*a,p,*p,**p);
                          /* "..." is a format directive */
}
```

The printout is a = <address of a>, *a = 0, p = <address of p>, *p = <address of a>, **pp = 0. Do you see why? Although somewhat inconsistent, it helps to remember that the array a is &a[0], the address of the 0th element of the array a, and that a[0] is *a, the value of the 0th element (see Figure 3.5.4).

C also supports pointer arithmetic. Using the variables of Figure 3.5.4, pp-p==0, since the array variable p is a pointer to the array. Also, ++pp-p==1, since ++pp makes pp point to the second element of the array p, p[1]. Thus the value of pp is p+1, and pp-p == (p+1)-p == 1.

Most of C's expressions and statements are direct carry-overs from BCPL. One operator, however, is new to C: the , (comma) operator. (a,b) is an expression that evaluates a and has the value of b. It is particularly useful for initialization, e.g.,

```
for(s=0,i=1;i<=10;s+=i,i++);                                        (3.5.9)
```

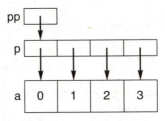

FIGURE 3.5.4
Identifiers in listing (3.5.8)

will end with s==55, the sum of the first 10 integers. There are two uses of , here: first, in the initialization part, s=0, i=1; and second, in the reinitialization part, s += i, i++. The **for** loop evaluates s, but uses the value of the expression i during each iteration.

LAB 3.3: FUN WITH C TRICKS: C

Objectives (Labs can be found in the *Instructor's Manual.*)

1. To demonstrate the effects of C's weak typing.
2. To pipe output from one C program into a second.

C and UNIX

As we have seen, C is intimately related to the UNIX operating system, which is written almost entirely in C. UNIX is composed of a kernel, one or more shells, and a large set of service routines. The kernel is small, about 10,000 lines of code, which creates a virtual machine that:

1. Schedules, coordinates, and manages process execution
2. Provides system services such as I/O
3. Handles machine-dependent hardware operations [Silvester, 1983]

All but the set of machine primitives tailored to the particular computer on which UNIX is running are written in C. The user rarely sees the kernel, but interacts with the set of procedures comprising one of the shells.

A UNIX system provides a variety of utilities such as editors, debuggers, and preprocessors as well as compilers for BASIC, FORTRAN, RATFOR, Pascal (at least in the Berkeley version), C, and Assembler. Source code in any of these languages is first translated into C intermediate code before being translated into Assembler, relocatable object, and finally executable machine-language code. Since all programs are first translated into C, new compilers are particularly easy to write. All one need do is design a translator into C, with no writing of Assembler code. This translator also enables the mixing of code written in different source languages and interfacing with applications such as databases, spreadsheets, and graphics programs.

The C Standard

The de facto standard for C has been Kernighan and Ritchie's book [Kernighan, 1978]. There is now, however, a standard from Technical Committee X3J11 of the American National Standards Institute [ANSI/ISO-9899, 1990]. All C compilers will now be expected to conform. When adopted by the International Standards Organization (ISO), it was basically identical to the ANSI standard. Since there was some weakness in the provision for locale-dependent features (e.g., comma or period for decimal point, month/day/year versus day/month/year, or a different alphabetic sequence), the ISO adopted an Amendment 1 in 1994 [ANSI/ISO-9899, 1994], which is now part of the standard.

Committee X3J11 was guided by several principles, the most important being, "Don't make presently working code obsolete." That is, programs written in correct Kernighan/Ritchie code should still compile and run. Others advocate both portability and system-dependent C. The committee tried to preserve C pretty much as it exists, and not "fix" it.

Advantages and Disadvantages

The main disadvantage of C is the difficulty of debugging programs due to automatic type coercions, pointer arithmetic, and side effects within expressions. It also fosters a terse programming style that is sometimes hard for anyone but the program designer to read. Thus it is often not the preferred language for business or scientific applications.

Its closeness to the machine, however, makes it ideal for writing operating systems and compilers. It is also very flexible for interactive programming, due to the variety of I/O facilities.

EXERCISES 3.5
1. What are the values of 114 >> 3? 96 << 2? 8 >> 4? What is the relationship between >> and division by powers of 2? between << and multiplication?
2. What values will x be assigned if we change the loop of listing (3.5.3) to **for** (i=0; i<5; ++i) x=i;?
3. Pascal allows automatic conversion of integers to floating types, but not characters to integers. Neither Modula-2 nor Ada allow either, and C allows both. How do Pascal, Modula-2, and Ada handle an expression like (r+i), where r is real and i an integer?
4. Why can one always cast a pointer to be a pointer to a character, but possibly not a pointer to an **int** or **float**?
5. Consider the following values of m on entry to the code of listing (3.5.1). Which statement(s) will be executed? (== is a C comparator, while = is the assignment operator.)
   a. m==3   b. m==2   c. m==1   d. m==0
   Now, remove the block delimiters { and }, and answer a through d again.
6. What will be the bit pattern of the packed year_gender field for a female Sophomore, following the example of Figure 3.5.4?
7. Suppose the packed year_gender field has the bit pattern 0000 0000 0000 0100. Follow listing (3.5.6) to find the unpacked year and gender fields.
8. Suppose we reverse the last two expressions in the loop of listing (3.5.9) to: **for**(s=0,i=1; i<=10; i++,s+=i);. What value will s have upon completion of the loop?
9. Discuss the different collating sequences, other than the U.S. 26-letter alphabet and period for decimal, that might be used in non-American standard versions of C.

LAB 3.4: IDE TOOLS: PASCAL/C

Objectives (Labs can be found in the *Instructor's Manual*.)

1. To investigate the programming tools provided with the version of Pascal or C available, especially string and graphics packages, editor, debugger, tracer, and browser.
2. To use and evaluate these tools for their intended purposes.

LAB 3.5: APSE TOOLS: ADA

Objectives (Labs can be found in the *Instructor's Manual.*)

1. To investigate the various tools provided with the Ada package being used.
2. To become familiar with the packages provided from the APSE. In particular, to look at the various I/O packages included in the implementation being used.

3.6
SUMMARY

In this chapter, we have considered block-structured languages, which implement nested blocks and (recursive) procedures, beginning with ALGOL in 1957. We followed this development through its orthogonal cousin, ALGOL 68; through its simplification, Pascal, on to Ada. This line of languages was also syntactically defined carefully through a formalization called the Backus-Naur Form (BNF).

We also looked at the development of C from ALGOL 60, through CPL, BCPL, and B. As rules became stricter and the languages higher level in the first group, things were relaxed in C so that a programmer could manipulate a machine's store directly.

Procedures may have formal parameters to which the values of actual parameters are passed. In Chapter 2, we considered five parameter passing mechanisms: by value, reference, result, value-result, and name. Pascal implements the first two under programmer control, C passes all parameters except arrays by value, and Ada provides **in** and **out**, which behave like value or value-result parameters respectively, but may be implemented differently, depending on the compiler writer. Ada's support of **in out** parameters was discussed further in Section 2.3.

Functions are procedures returning a single value. This value has been restricted to particular types by some languages. ALGOL 68 was the first to allow functions with values of any type. Ada also includes this feature and enforces value parameters.

Strong typing, where the values of a variable remain true to type throughout its usage, has been enforced in Pascal and in Ada, but not in C. Free unions in Pascal are an exception to this notion, but resulting difficulties have been minimized in both C and Ada through insistence on discriminated unions only. The notion of generic functions and procedures, where types of both parameters and functional values can vary depending on use, has been provided in Ada.

The block-structured languages we looked at also provide for dynamic variables in two ways. First are local variables, which are created on entry and destroyed on exit from a block. The second sort are reference variables, which hold addresses of storage locations. These are called pointers in Pascal and C and **access** variables in Ada. Structures (records) can be defined recursively in Pascal, Ada, and C by including a pointer to a similar structure as one of the fields. If p is a pointer to such a structure, storage can be located for a new instance through the functions **new** (Pascal, Ada) or **alloc** (C). Pascal and C also provide the functions **dispose** and **free**, respectively, to release previously allocated storage.

Programmer control over exceptions was first introduced in PL/I and expanded in Ada. PL/I also includes arrays of bits, which have been exploited more fully in C.

Both Ada and Modula-2 have provided higher level modules, where variables and procedures can be grouped in self-contained units. In Ada, these are packages, and in Modula-2, modules. Ada 95 support for object-oriented programming will be described in Chapter 4. Ada also includes tasks to implement concurrency. Modula-2 has implemented co-routines, and UNIX has fork and join operations to implement concurrent C programs. We will look at these further in Chapter 5.

3.7
NOTES ON REFERENCES

To achieve a thorough understanding of block-structured procedural languages, one would do well to look at ALGOL 60 and ALGOL 68. [Naur, 1963] provides a good discussion and the entire 17-page report. [Tanenbaum, 1976] is a tutorial on ALGOL 68. [Branquart, 1971] provides a readable discussion of ALGOL semantics. Reading these three articles plus Knuth's summary of still ambiguous issues in ALGOL 60 [Knuth, 1967] would also give a reader a good idea of how hard it is to be precise.

Among the survey books, [Baron, 1986] describes programming languages to laypersons in a superficial, but interesting and competent way. More technical histories are [Sammet, 1969] and [Wexelblat, 1981]. [Horowitz, 1987] is a collection of important and easily read papers, originally written for publications as disparate as the *IBM Journal of Research and Development* and *BYTE Magazine*. This collection had been revised every two years since 1983, but a call to the publishers found no new edition planned since 1987.

The [Feuer, 1982] paper in the *Computing Surveys* series from ACM compares Pascal and C, while [Smedema, 1983] considers Pascal, Modula, Chill, and Ada.

Three ANSI (American National Standards Institute) documents were mentioned in this chapter: [ANSI-1815A, 1983], which defines Ada 83, [ANSI/ISO-8652, 1995], which describes Ada 95, and [ANSI/ISO-9899, 1990], the standard for C. Pascal also has an American standard, [ANSI/IEEE-770X3.79, 1983]. This was devised jointly by Committee X3J9 of ANSI and Project P770 of the Institute of Electrical and Electronics Engineers (IEEE). A Pascal international standard, [ISO-DP7185, 1980], differs somewhat from 770X3.97. Programs following the American standard will run in ISO Pascal, but the ANSI/IEEE standard does not include the *conformant array* of DP 7185. In ISO Pascal,

```
procedure Process(A: array [start..finish] of SomeType);
```

is perfectly valid, with start and finish conforming to the bounds of the actual parameter passed to the parameter A in Process.

The Standard documents, which are very terse, are unsuitable for learning a language. The Ada "bible" is [Booch, 1986]. Pascal manuals abound, with [Cooper, 1983] describing the standard to experienced programmers. [Kernighan, 1978] has been updated to include ANSI C and is still the most widely used C manual. [Plauger, 1996] includes information about the 1994 Amendment 1 to the C Standard. New books that include both C and C++, such as [Stoustrup, 1991] and [Deitel, 1994], are now becoming available.

CHAPTER 4
LANGUAGES FOR OBJECT-ORIENTED PROGRAMMING (OOP)

4.0	**In this Chapter**	**150**
4.1	**Programming with Objects**	**150**
	Messages, Methods, and Encapsulation	153
	Early Notions of Objects in Simula	155
	Objects in Ada 83 and Ada 95	158
	Exercises 4.1	162
4.2	**Classes and Polymorphism**	**162**
	Generic Procedures and Packages in Ada	163
	Classes in Object Pascal	165
	Classes in C++	171
	Implementation of Inherited Classes	173
	Exercises 4.2	175
4.3	**Smalltalk**	**175**
	Historical Vignette: Smalltalk: Alan Kay	176
4.4	**Inheritance and Object-Orientation**	**177**
	Types and Subtypes in Inheritance Hierarchies	180
	Multiple Inheritance	181
	Language Exemplars	185
	More Object Pascal	186
	Inheritance in C++	189
	Dynamic Binding	193
	Exercises 4.4	196
4.5	**Java**	**196**
	Java Language Constructs	198
	Object, the Superclass of All Other Classes	198
	An Elementary Java Class	200
	The Java Application Programming Interfaces (APIs)	200
	Compiling and Running a Java Program	202
	HotJava and Applets	202
	Program Types	203
	Differences Between Java, C, and C++	203
	Exercises 4.5	205
4.6	**Summary**	**206**
4.7	**Notes on References**	**206**

Languages for Object-Oriented Programming (OOP)

In dividing programming languages into two paradigms, imperative and declarative, each with three subparadigms, *object-oriented* languages have been placed in the imperative paradigm, since it was in the imperative language Simula that these notions began. An object is defined as "a group of procedures that share a state" [Wegner, 1988]. Recall that a program written in an imperative language involves a sequence of state transition commands. Informally, an object is an item or thing with its associated, well-defined behaviors.

We will define an *object* as a collection of data, called its *state,* and the procedures capable of altering that state. If an object is a simple robot consisting of a movable arm and a gripper, its state will include its position in the room where it is located, the angle of the arm, and whether its gripper is open or closed. A robot object must have a name, to distinguish it from other robots.

The collection of all robots is called a *class*. You can think of a class as a type, although some languages make a distinction, with types being used for data and classes for object definitions. We will define a class as a collection of objects sharing the same *attributes,* where an attribute is the type of a data member or a method for manipulating that data. An attribute of an object may be another object as well as data or a method.

Everything in Smalltalk is an object, with the class **object** being the *superclass* of all other objects, i.e., all objects have the attributes of **object**, plus, possibly, others. Objects have associated *operations* and *values.* For example, if Queue is the class of all queue objects, as discussed in section 2.1, and an object named q is in the class, then the operations on q include newQueue, add(q, i), front(q), remove(q), and isEmpty(q).

q might have a default state, representing the empty queue. Otherwise, the state of q will include the list of items that have been added to q, so that the relations of Listing (2.1.6) hold. In the language of objects, newQueue is a *constructor* that brings the object q into being. A *destructor,* which destroys an object, is often included in the operations of an object as well.

Blair asserts that there is no real consensus on what is meant by an object-oriented system, and proposes that the key feature of anything called an object is that it be *encapsulated.*"An object is encapsulated if the notions of an operation set and a data set are incorporated in a single entity (i.e., the object). Furthermore, clients should be restricted to accessing the object only through the well-defined, external, operational interface" [Blair, 1989].

This seems similar to an abstract data type (ADT), which we discussed in Chapter 2, and indeed, an ADT can be implemented as an object. We will consider other attributes of objects and their usefulness in what follows.

4.0
IN THIS CHAPTER

An object-*based* language supports:

- Information hiding (encapsulation)
- Data abstraction (the encapsulation of state with operations)
- Message passing (polymorphism)

A language that is object-*oriented* also implements:

- Inheritance, including dynamic binding

Inheritance, the organization of objects into a hierarchy of classes where an object may be given the properties of its parent class without redeclaration, is the distinguishing feature of the object-oriented approach. This includes dynamic binding, where data types and/or procedures may be bound to names at run time. We will discuss this feature in section 4.4.

As language examples, we will consider Ada, Object Pascal, C++, and the new language from Sun Microsystems, Java™. Although the notion of state, which is just another name for the store of an individual object, is not a focus of declarative languages, objected-orientation has made an impact there as well as in imperative languages. We will leave discussion of the SCHEME Object-Oriented System (SCOOPS) and the Common LISP Object System (CLOS) for Chapter 8, which introduces functional languages as part of the declarative paradigm.

4.1
PROGRAMMING WITH OBJECTS

In the real world, an object is a dynamic entity. It may change, but still remain the same object. A very complex object is a human being. A somewhat simpler object is a checkbook. It may (or may not, depending on how careful its owner is) represent the state of a bank account. It may balance or not, yet it is still the same checkbook. There are many checkbooks, with any instance representing an object in the class of all checkbooks.[1] Sending a message to a checkbook to Draw itself makes no sense, but asking it to CheckBalance or to process a $500 transaction does.

   An object-oriented programmer approaches a problem by dividing it into interacting agents, called objects, which can do things and interact with other agents. When using a top-down style, one proceeds algorithmically, delegating responsibility for each step to a procedure. The process of visiting an ATM (automatic teller machine) to either deposit or withdraw funds is shown algorithmically in Figure 4.1.1 and in an object-oriented style in Figure 4.1.2.

   Figure 4.1.1 represents a typical top-down algorithm, with the main procedure or "driver" being decomposed into three subprocedures: two for input, Get User ID and Get Transaction; and one for output, Put$$. This third procedure is decomposed into two, which do the main work of the problem; Adjust Bank Balance and Put Receipt. Adjust Bank Balance is further decomposed into two tasks, Send Bank Statement and Balance Checkbook.

   A problem can be decomposed algorithmically or in an object-oriented manner, but one cannot mix the two approaches. They are entirely different. Objects are independent of each other, thus easier to verify, port (move to a different machine), and maintain than interdependent procedures. They also facilitate the reuse of tested code without recompiling it. Robert Moskowitz claims that the provision of preprogrammed and user-modifiable objects "allows users who understand very little about computers to grasp and manipulate computer features, functions, and operations as easily as they grasp and manipulate tangible objects in the real world" [Moskowitz, 1989].

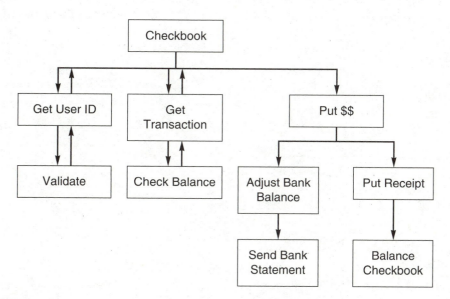

FIGURE 4.1.1
Algorithmic analysis of Checkbook program

---

[1]Booch [Booch, 1994] considers the terms *instance* and *object* to be interchangeable. Not all authors agree, however. In Object Pascal, an **object** is a template for particular instances.

There are many definitions for the word "object," other than CLU's "container for data." Perhaps the simplest is that of [Cox, 1984], in which "objects are private data and the operations supported on that data." Objects communicate by passing messages, which are "request[s] for an object to perform one of its operations." A *message* is nothing more than a call to a procedure, called a *method*, which belongs to an object and may be hidden from the user. Thus a message must reference a particular object as well as the name of the method being invoked. In this chapter, when we refer to an object, we will mean the pair (data, methods), not just the data container. Data can be viewed as data types, variables, or values (state), depending on the context.[2]

In our checkbook example of Figure 4.1.2, there are four objects: ATM, CheckBook, BankAccount, and User. Communication from a User to the ATM, as indicated by arrows, is through the messages ID and Transaction. The ATM can respond by sending Money or a printed Receipt. The object ATM is thought of as an active entity including data, and also capable of sending messages, receipts, or money, whereas algorithms manipulate passive data. A User object asks an ATM object to respond to a request. The ATM has its own data or can request it from another object, and can respond to the request. The message Transaction(Withdraw, BookOfJane, 500.00), should result in Jane having $500 cash (Money) discharged from the ATM and $500 subtracted from her current account balance, through a method belonging to BankAccount. AccountBalance (which does not appear in Figure 4.1.2) could be data probably belonging to BankAccount, but User need not know this. If there had been a rash of thefts at that ATM recently, the bank might

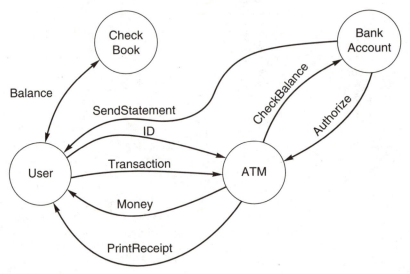

FIGURE 4.1.2
Object-oriented decomposition of Checkbook problem

[2]Terminology varies from author to author and from language to language. C++ uses the term *member function* to indicate a method, while Ada does not change the usual procedure and function declarations when dealing with objects.

want Jane's name recorded on a list of users of the ATM. This could be accomplished by rewriting and reinstalling the method Transaction at headquarters, with Users being unaware of the change. Client programs (those that use objects) are unaffected by changes to the implementation of the class of objects.

Notice that many of the procedures listed in Figure 4.1.1 are not mentioned in Figure 4.1.2. These procedures would be methods internal to the object in which they function. For example, PrintReceipt would be a method used in the ATM object, and SendStatement would belong to BankAccount.

Messages, Methods, and Encapsulation

Message passing provides a means for objects to communicate with a client program and with each other. A message is sent to an object, where a method for responding is selected from those available. A method in one object cannot invoke a method in another object, like a procedure calling another procedure. A method in ATM cannot directly access a method in BankAccount, but must send a message to BankAccount (e.g., OK?) which will respond using its own methods (e.g., Authorize).

Just as a data type is a template for variables, a class is a template for objects. We will discuss this further in section 4.2. Suppose we declare in C++ syntax the classes Square and Triangle as shown in Listings (4.1.1) and (4.1.2).

```
#typedef int numSides;                                                 (4.1.1)
#typedef int sideLength;
#include <math.h>                                      //for sqrt function

class Square
{
 public:  //these methods can be accessed from anyplace in a program
    Square(sideLength side): s(side), n(4) {};          //constructor
      sideLength getSide(){return s;}
      sideLength perimeter(){return n * s;}
      double area(){return (double) s * s;}
 private: //can only be accessed through methods of a Square object
      sideLength s;
      const numSides n;
};
```

```
class Triangle                                                         (4.1.2)
{
 public:
    Triangle(sideLength side): s(side), n(3) {};        //constructor
      sideLength getSide(){return s;}
      sideLength perimeter(){return n * s;}
      double area(){return sqrt(3.0) * getSide() * getSide() /4.0;}
 private:
      sideLength s;
      const numSides n;
};
```

The public parts of both the Square and Triangle classes list declarations for methods (called member functions in C++), while the private sections contain variables for data. These member data and methods are the object's attributes. A procedure is controlled by the types of its parameters, whereas a method can also use information contained in its object's member data (state) and call methods either public or private to the object. For either a square or a triangle, private data includes its sideLength s and the number of sides n. Neither Square nor Triangle has private member functions nor public data, although other objects may well have one or both.

A user needs to choose a side length for each object. A Square square1 is constructed in C++ syntax with a side of length 5, by the declaration Square square1(5);. In C++, objects are created when declared. Thus an object constructor is a method having the same name as the class of objects to be constructed.

square1.perimeter() will invoke a method for computing the perimeter of square1, while square1.area() activates the method for computing the area. Since both n and s are hidden from a client (**private**), we also include a public method getSide among the public attributes of Square to enable a client's access to s. This provides read-only access to s from outside a Square.

The set of values of an object's member data, or the object's state, persists between invocations of methods. This means that if a particular object triangle1 of class Triangle has a side length of 1 and 3 sides, these values will remain as long as triangle1 remains in the active environment of the running program. This is not true of a procedure's local constants and variables. Methods can also access global data. These globals may be available to several procedures or methods and are not part of any object's state.

Data can be encapsulated along with associated operations in a module (Modula-2), data type (CLU), or package (Ada). So how does encapsulation, in the object-oriented sense, differ from what we have seen? One way is that an object may include persistent data and several data types with their associated operations. Figures 4.1.3 and 4.1.4 below may help make the difference between methods and procedures clear. In Figure 4.1.3, we are using the procedure perimeter to compute the perimeter of a regular triangle with side of length s. It acts on whatever operand it is presented with, in this case s = 3.

The message/object model of Figure 4.1.4 assumes a layer of structure, the object, between the message and the data. The message perimeter can be sent to an object, which will behave according to its own method for handling the message. In Figure 4.1.4, square1 represents an active object with both of its data attributes, n and s, having values. Objects of type Triangle or Square each have three methods: perimeter, area, and getSide. Each message can be meaningful to a variety of different objects, so sending a message must include naming the receiving object. You may have noticed that the Triangle and Square classes repeat data and method

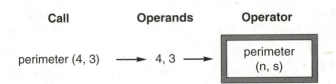

FIGURE 4.1.3
The operator/operand model

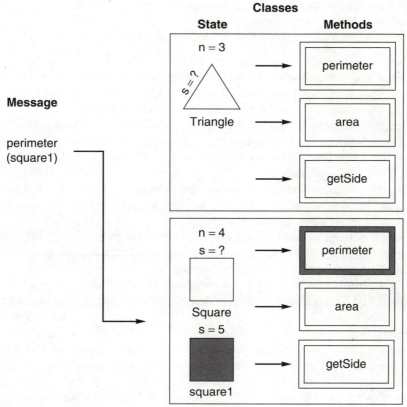

FIGURE 4.1.4
The message/object model

definitions. We will be able to eliminate these redundancies as shown in Figure 4.4.1 when we examine classes and inheritance.

The term "message" is somewhat misleading, but so well established in object-oriented literature that it is likely to remain. A message suggests that objects are acting independently and concurrently, and indeed, *actor* languages, such as Pract and Acore [Agha, 1987], make these assumptions. In the languages we will consider here, a method is a function or procedure that has state and is associated with a class of objects. A message is the name of a method and initiates a call to a method.

Early Notions of Objects in Simula

Simula originated at the Norwegian Computing Center in 1961, in the hands of Kristen Nygaard and Ole-Johan Dahl. Its purposes were to describe systems and to program simulations [Nygaard, 1981]. Its development was motivated by the desire to:

- Express processes that are permanent and active
- Create and destroy such processes as needed

- Extend an existing language to include processes
- Provide for processes to run concurrently
- Group processes subject to the same procedures into classes

Procedural languages separate a problem into passive data and unconnected procedures which manipulate it and which are activated only when needed. *Processes* (or objects, as they were later called) would contain any procedures related to their data, so that they could manipulate themselves as needed.

A system, such as airport departures, was thought of as consisting of components of two different kinds: permanent active objects and passive objectives, acted upon by the active ones. Passengers are examples of the first type, "grabbing and holding the passive counter clerks, fee collectors, etc." [Nygaard, 1981]. In Figure 4.1.5, there are four passengers, P_i, and three clerks, C_j. Passenger P_0 is about to switch from the line waiting for clerk C_1 to clerk C_0's shorter line. Abstract objects were thought of as nodes in a network.

Later work suggests that objects are better thought of as of one kind, which are sometimes active and sometimes passive, and that interacting processes form a better notion for objects than does a network.

At first, Simula was to be a preprocessor to ALGOL 60, with Simula code translated into ALGOL. This idea of objects being implemented on top of existing languages has been used in a preprocessor to Ada (InnovAda [Simonian, 1988]) and in extensions to Pascal (Object Pascal [Tesler, 1985]) and to C (C++ [Stroustrup, 1986]).

Simula's processes (objects) are dynamic, that is, they can be created when needed and later destroyed. Procedures (methods) in a process differ from the usual procedure block. They may run quasi-concurrently[3] and contain statements requesting time delays. Simula's early operator **pause**(<boolean expression>), which

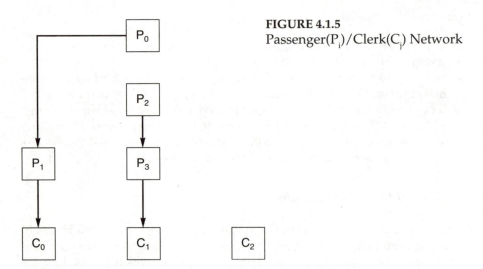

FIGURE 4.1.5
Passenger(P_i)/Clerk(C_j) Network

---

[3]Two or more procedures are quasi-concurrent if they can be active at the same time, and one is not a subprocedure of the other. Quasi-concurrency may be implemented through some form of single CPU time-sharing, or through multiple CPUs running in parallel.

requested suspension of a currently active process until the Boolean expression became true, caused so much trouble that it was abandoned in later versions of Simula for the four directives **passivate**, **activate**, **hold**, and **cancel**.

Simula I's successor, Simula 67, has classes of objects as its basic concept. Dahl and Nygaard had been working on a simulation of a bridge with a toll booth and a queue of trucks, buses, and cars. They noticed that a process for a truck included many of the same procedures as that for a bus or car. They developed an object class that included all the queue operations, made Vehicle[4] a subclass of Queue, and Truck and Bus subclasses of Vehicle. Although vehicle objects contain all the attributes of Queue objects, while Queues do not contain all those of Vehicles, the object literature calls a class higher in the hierarchy a superclass and those derived from the superclass subclasses. Thus a Queue is a superclass of the subclasses Vehicle, Truck, and Bus as in Figure 4.1.6. Queue is also called the *base class* of Vehicle, and Vehicle the base class for Bus and Truck, where a base class for a class is immediately above it in the class hierarchy.

The concept of classes of processes leans heavily on Hoare's notion of classes of records, with procedure as well as data fields. Each subobject *inherits* the procedures

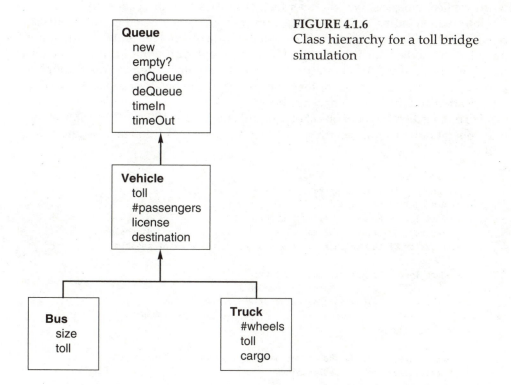

FIGURE 4.1.6
Class hierarchy for a toll bridge simulation

---

[4]Dahl and Nygaard labeled the class we have called Queue, link, and labeled Vehicle, car. We have taken the liberty of renaming them to conform more to American usage of the terms.

of the superclass. In Figure 4.1.6, Truck inherits all the procedures of Queue and all those of Vehicle, with the exception of toll, which is redefined for each of Bus and Truck.

Objects in Ada 83 and Ada 95

Two of the major goals in developing object-oriented software are cost reduction and security. The development of objects as reusable software units aids in the first, while information hiding promotes the second. When objects are created and destroyed dynamically, security requires special machine architectures. The design specifications for Ada 83 did not require object-orientation, but that all type checking and allocation (binding) of storage for procedures be done at compile time. This is called static binding. Thus we did not find dynamic binding and inheritance in Ada 83 (see section 4.4). By the time the revised standard for Ada 95 [ANSI-1815A, 1983] appeared, experience with both other object-oriented languages and with Ada suggested that security and reliability issues, important for Department of Defense applications, would not be compromised by adding inheritance and dynamic binding to the language. Dynamic binding was defined in section 1.2, but it has an extended meaning when applied to objects. We will defer further discussion until section 4.4.

Information hiding and data abstraction are both implemented in Ada 83. It also provides for a hidden state in an object. Thus an Ada object's procedures can rightly be called methods, which we shall do here, although you will not find any mention of methods in the Ada literature. An object is implemented in Ada through a **package**. If you recall from Chapter 3, an Ada package has two parts, the visible specification and the hidden package body.

Let us consider the robot object of Buzzard and Mudge [Buzzard, 1985]. We will only look at outlines for declaring the objects in listing (4.1.3), leaving details for Lab 4.1.

```
package Robot is                                                    (4.1.3)
   type RobotArm is limited private;
   type ArmModel is (ASEA,PUMA);
   type Position is array (1..4,1..4) of Float;
   --stores the location of the RobotArm in 3-space plus the 3-dimensional
   --orientation of the gripper relative to the coordinates of the arm

   procedure InitializeArm (x: out RobotArm;
                            Kind: in ArmModel);
   --places initial values in the fields of Robot-Arm for its
   --position in 3-space, status of its gripper as open or closed,
   --and what kind it is

   procedure Move (x: in out RobotArm; Destination: in Position);
   --Relocates the Robot to Destination

   procedure Open (x: in out RobotArm);
   --Opens the gripper

   procedure Close(x: in out RobotArm);
```

```
function GetPosition(x: RobotArm) return Position;
--Returns the Robot's current position

private     --Not visible outside the package
  type RobotArm is record
    Pos: Position;     -- Robot position in 3-space
    Open: Boolean;     -- True if gripper is open
    Kind: ArmModel;    -- Arm model type
  end record;
end Robot;
```

A Robot consists of a single arm that can Open or Close its gripper. A robot object will have values for Pos, Open, and Kind, as its state. Its methods to alter the state are InitializeArm, Move, Open, Close, and GetPosition. We will assume along with Buzzard and Mudge that the only two kinds supported by this package are the ASEA and the PUMA, although more may be added. This specification may be all a user will see and can be compiled separately from either its body or a program using the **package**.

That RobotArm is **limited private** does not mean that the user cannot see the structure of its type. The record field names—Pos for Position, Open for the boolean indicating whether the gripper is open or shut, and Kind indicating the robot's model—would be listed in the specification, but a user would have no access to them except through the four procedures InitializeArm, Move, Open, Close, and the function GetPosition listed above. The state of this simple robot indicates where it is, whether its gripper is open or shut, and its model. You will be asked in the second part of Lab 4.1 to add methods for rotating the gripper as well. The state of the gripper's orientation will be kept in a 3 x 3 submatrix of Pos.

In the object-oriented extension to Turbo Pascal, the declaration would be as shown in listing (4.1.4).

```
unit Robot;                                          (4.1.4)

interface

type
  ArmModel = (ASEA,PUMA);
  Position = array [1..4,1..4] of real;
  Arm = record
    Pos: Position;
    Open: boolean;
    Kind: ArmModel;
  end;

  RobotArm = object
    A: Arm;
    procedure Init(Kind: ArmModel);
    procedure Move(Destination: Position);
    procedure Open;
    procedure Close;
    function GetPosition: Position;
  end;

implementation
...
end;
```

The declaration for an object looks very much like a record declaration, and indeed it is. A Pascal object *is* a record, with procedures and functions as well as data allowed as fields. Each of the procedures in the object RobotArm operates implicitly on the Arm field, A. If we declare:

```
MyASEARobot: RobotArm;
```

we can initialize it using MyASEARobot.Init(ASEA); move it with MyASEARobot.Move(...); etc. Although these are called procedures in Pascal syntax, they are really methods. They can only be used with variables of type Arm, which have not been declared as part of an object of type RobotArm, and they can only be activated through the object's name, in this case, MyASEARobot.

Object Pascal has no facilities for restricting access to RobotArm. A user can assign values to the fields of a variable of type Arm without using any of the object's methods. The implementors assumed that those programming in an object-oriented style would discipline themselves to use instances of objects only through the methods included in the object definition. The inclusion of an Init method encourages this.

In C++ we might declare a Robot:

```
#include <string.h>          // headers for              (4.1.5)
#include <iostream.h>        // library modules for I/O
enum boolean {false, true};  // false = 0, true = 1
enum armModel {ASEA, PUMA} ; // enumeration type

struct armPosition() {
    armPosition();                    //constructor
  private:
    float pos [4][4];
  friend ostream & operator << (ostream& s, const armPosition& pos);
  friend istream & operator >> (istream& s, armPosition& pos);
};

class Robot {
  public:
    Robot(armModel kindIn);           //constructor
    Robot& move(armPosition& destination);
    Robot& closeGripper();
    Robot& openGripper();
    armPosition getPosition();

  private:
    armPosition position;
    armModel kind;
    boolean open;
};
```

These declarations would be stored in a header file, robot.h, and also included in the file robot.cpp,[5] which contains definitions for the methods move, closeGripper, and

---

[5]Both C and C++ programs almost always separate function declarations from definitions. ANSI Standard C++ puts declarations in header files with the .h extension. The extension for function definitions source code depends on the implementation, here it is .cpp.

openGripper, as well as for the constructors Robot and armPosition. The declarations of listing (4.1.5) describe objects that will be members of the **class** Robot. A **class** is an object template having both member data variables and member functions. One of the data members of the **class** is a **struct** called position of type armPosition. A **struct** is C++ notation for a record. We will look at this **struct** in more detail below.

C++ has three levels of member protection. **public** items of **struct**s or **class**es are known to clients and inherited by public substructures. **protected** items are not known to clients, but are known in substructures. **private** items, the most restricted, are known only within the **class** or **struct** in which they are declared and by **friend**s of that **struct** or class. In C++, the only difference between a **struct** and a **class** is that the default protection in a **struct** is **public**, and in a **class** it is **private**.

The message to construct a PUMA robot pointed to by r1 would be:

Robot* r1 = **new** Robot(PUMA);   (4.1.6)

If we do not want a dynamically constructed robot, we could declare one using:

Robot r2(PUMA);   (4.1.7)

The constructor Robot(armModel kindIn) is called automatically when r1 is declared as in listing (4.1.6), or r2 in listing (4.1.7). The definition of the constructor function will be found in the C++ robot.cpp file. Construction of the robot allocates memory and initializes member data. As in the Ada and Object Pascal declarations, details can be found in the C++ version of Lab 4.1.

The **struct** armPosition contains a constructor of its own, which will be called automatically when memory is allocated for the private member, position, of Robot. The body of the constructor will be defined in the file robot.cpp. A **friend** is not a member of a **class** or **struct**, but has access to its private members. The **class**es istream and ostream are external classes for input and output that are declared in the file iostream.h. **class** istream has an operator >>, which is overloaded here to have direct access to the private member pos of armPosition. Similarly, ostream has an operator <<, which is overloaded to output items of type armPosition. We will discuss overloading below when we consider another characteristic of object-oriented languages, polymorphism. If getPosition is appropriately defined in robot.cpp, we could print the robot's position to the terminal (cout) in one statement, as in listing (4.1.8).

cout << r.getPosition();   (4.1.8)

In both cases, armPosition& pos means that values for pos are accessed by reference. These **friend**s serve as go-betweens for iostream and armPosition.

LAB 4.1: OBJECTS, ENCAPSULATION, AND METHODS: OBJECT PASCAL/ADA/C++

Objectives (Labs can be found in the *Instructor's Manual*.)

1. To complete the Robot package, unit, or class through suitable definitions for the associated procedures in Ada, Object Pascal, and/or C++.

2. To consider the differences between the object implementation and an implementation using data types and procedures. Students should pay particular attention to the languages in which they do *not* program.

EXERCISES 4.1

1. Describe what is meant by:
   a. Information hiding (encapsulation)
   b. Data abstraction (the encapsulation of state with operations)
   c. Message passing
   d. Inheritance
2. Procedures have local variables and constants. What is the difference between these local entities and the data private to an object?
3. Name two ways that messages differ from procedures or functions.
4. Why is it advantageous to enforce accessing an object only through its methods?
5. What meaning can you give to the position of the passenger object, P_0, in Figure 4.1.5? Why couldn't a clerk object, such as C_1, be "out of line"?
6. a. In the interface for the Robot unit of listing (4.1.4), what represents the state of an object of type RobotArm?
   b. What corresponds to the Pascal **interface** in Ada? to the Pascal **implementation**?
   c. An Ada package specification can be compiled separately from the package body, where procedures are implemented. One advantage of this is that a main program using a package only needs the specification to compile properly, so work on a client program can proceed while a package is being completed. Object Pascal does not have this facility. The interface and the implementation may be compiled separately from another program, but not from each other. How could you achieve the advantage stated above of Ada's separate compilation using Pascal?
7. a. If you wanted to put the robot of listing (4.1.4) to work and you already felt competent in moving it around, orienting it, and opening or closing its gripper, what other objects might you define so that it could actually pick up things?
   b. How would the objects communicate with each other?

4.2
CLASSES AND POLYMORPHISM

We have given a good bit of consideration to modules, i.e., collections of related data types, data, and procedures. We have also discussed languages that are strongly typed, where each variable is of exactly one type. A class is a description for objects yet to be instantiated, just as a type is a description for variables yet to be declared. For our purposes here, you will not be wrong to think of a class as an abstract type for an object containing data and methods. The class concept differs from that of a module in that it allows the existence of subclasses containing common attributes. We will consider subclasses in section 4.4 below.

The class notion comes from mathematical logic. A class is a set, but more tightly structured. Georg Cantor's notion of a set as a collection of objects sharing certain attributes led to a number of paradoxes. A paradox is a statement that is both true and false. A definition attributed to Bertrand Russell leading to a paradox is the set

A={x | x ∉ x}. Mathematics, above all else, is assumed to be consistent and not lead to paradox. Thus it was realized that some sets are not valid. The theory of classes was developed to build sets that would eliminate at least the known paradoxes.

In object-oriented languages, a class is a collection of objects, where any object of the class includes the same methods and variables but may include different data values. In the type declarations above, **type** RobotArm (listing (4.1.3)), RobotArm = object (listing (4.1.4)), and **class** Robot (listing (4.1.5)) are descriptions of what a RobotArm (in Ada or in Pascal) or Robot (in C++) will be like when instantiated. Thus a class is a template or descriptor for specific objects in the class. The C++ keyword **template** has a specific meaning, which is described in the C++ MiniManual. Also see listing (4.2.15) below. If Russell's paradox were true in classes of objects, the theory would be inconsistent. Thus no object-oriented system permits a class that has itself as a member.

You are now familiar with an object, as encapsulated data and methods, and with a class of objects, all of which have the same attributes. Square in listing (4.1.1) and Circle in listing (4.1.2) are the C++ implementations of two classes. We have also looked at how objects communicate with each other through messages. As we have seen, a message may be interpreted differently if received by different objects, such as square1 or triangle1. The message draw, which may invoke different methods, is called polymorphic ("many forms"). You are already familiar with functions that do different things when confronted with different data types. One example supported by most languages is the arithmetic operator +. (1.5 + 3.246) is handled differently from (1 + 3) or from (1.5 + 3). Thus, + is a polymorphic or generic operator. In object terms, + is a message, and there are different methods for computing the sum in each of the three expressions. 1.5 and 3.246 are state values of real objects, which include a method +. Similarly, 1 and 3 are state values of integer objects, including +. The 1.5 and 3 of the third expression are instances of mixed objects, also including a + operator. To keep everything transparent, a language could designate the three different pluses as real.+, int.+, and mixed.+, instead of asking the system to choose the right + by checking the arguments in the expression. That would be a procedural way to approach the problem. When a language token representing an operator, e.g., +, has different meanings depending on the context, it is said to be overloaded. It also exhibits polymorphism, meaning that the definition for the operator + has a different form, depending on the data being acted upon.

Generic Procedures and Packages in Ada

Ada 83 and Ada 95 provide for generic or polymorphic procedures and functions as well as generic packages. Let us look at procedures first, as they are somewhat simpler than packages. Squaring an item is a good candidate, as the process applies to several types of objects. Squaring X is X * X, where * may be interpreted differently for integers, reals, complex numbers, or vectors. A generic Ada subprogram begins with the reserved word **generic**, as shown in listing (4.2.1).

```
generic                                                          (4.2.1)
   type Item is private;
   with function "*" (x, y: Item) return Item is <>;
function Squaring (x: Item) return Item;
```

Squaring has two generic parameters, which must be supplied before an actual function is instantiated. The first is the type of the Item to be squared, and the second is the multiplication function, *. The box <> indicates that * will be matched with a previously defined function when Squaring is instantiated, as shown in listing (4.2.2).

```
function Squaring(x: Item) is                                    (4.2.2)
begin
   return x * x;
end;
```

When an Ada compiler encounters a generic subprogram body, it elaborates it, which, for generics, has no other effect than establishing that the body can be used by other program units to obtain instances (see listing (4.2.3)).

```
type Vector is array (Integer range <>) of Real;                (4.2.3)
function CrossProduct (u,v: Vector) return Real is
begin...end;

function Square is new Squaring(Item => Vector, "*" => CrossProduct);
function; Square is new Squaring (Integer);   --"*" of listing (4.2.2)
                                              --used by default
function Square is new Squaring (Real);
```

Squaring would now contain the elements Square(Integer), Square(Real), and Square(Vector). Note that the instantiation of Square(Vector) assumes the existence of the function CrossProduct. The instantiations of listing (4.2.3) can occur only in a program's declarative section, where procedure and function declarations are permissible. Ada allows the overloading of procedure names, as can be seen from the three different uses of Square above. Since Squaring names a **generic** (polymorphic) function, to avoid ambiguities, it may not be overloaded.

Generic packages are declared and instantiated similarly. An abbreviated example for a generic stack package is shown in listing (4.2.4), and a package body, Stack, is shown in listing (4.2.5).

```
generic                                                          (4.2.4)
   Size: Positive := 100;
   type Item is private;
package Stack is
   procedure Push (I: in Item);
   procedure Pop  (I: out Item);
   Overflow, Underflow: exception;
end Stack;
```

```
package body Stack is                                            (4.2.5)

   type Table is array (Positive range <>) of Item;
   MyStack: Table(1..Size);
   Index: Natural := 0;
```

```
    procedure Push(E in Item) is
    begin...end Push;

    procedure Pop(E out ITEM) is
    begin...end Pop;

  end Stack;
```

Recall that a package body may be hidden from the user. Stack above is an example of an ADT, with the type of MyStack known only in the (hidden) package body. Notice also that Index is initialized in the declaration to 0. Stacks could be instantiated using:

```
package IntStack25 is new Stack(Size => 25,                       (4.2.6)
Item => Integer);
package IntStack is new Stack(Item => Integer);
   --uses the default value of 100 for Size
package RealStack50 is new Stack(50, Real);
```

The designers of Ada had security as one of their primary goals, so a compiled generic package specification may not be used by another program until the package body has also been compiled. Ada requires all types to be established before run time, thus any vagaries of a generic package must be resolved before being incorporated in another program unit. To bring IntStack into a procedure, we would use a **with** clause to attach the package to a client program, as shown in listing (4.2.7).

```
with IntStack;   --IntStack specification made visible              (4.2.7)

procedure SomeSubprogram is
--declarations

begin...end SomeProgram;
```

In the Pascal language, **with** allows us to omit qualifications to records. In Ada, this is accomplished with a **use** clause. We may use Push or Pop rather than IntStack.Push and IntStack.Pop by preceding the code with **use** IntStack;.

Classes in Object Pascal

Object Pascal provides for classes[6] of dynamic objects. For the examples in this book, we have used the object-oriented extension to Turbo Pascal. Objects are *first-class entities,* that is, they can be passed to procedures as parameters and returned as functional values. This is accomplished through pointers to objects, called *references.* In Object Pascal, all access to an object is through references, while in Turbo Pascal 7.0, objects may be passed as objects or as references to objects. An entity of type

---

[6]Some authors have criticized Pascal because it does not enforce information hiding (encapsulation). An object's data can be accessed directly, as well as through its methods. A second complaint is that objects are not automatically constructed upon variable declaration. The user must call a separate procedure, called a **constructor**.

object may not be returned by a function, but a reference to an object may. This should not come as a surprise, because pointers, but not structured types, may be functional values in Pascal.

A Turbo Pascal declaration for a stack might be as shown in listing (4.2.8). It provides for stacks with elements of a single type, in this case, integers.

```pascal
unit Stacks;                                               (4.2.8)

interface                         {visible}

const
    MaxSize = 1000;
type
    Item  = integer;
    Range = 1..MaxSize;
    Table = array [Range] of Item;

    Stack = object
        MyStack      : Table;
        Index, Size  : Range;

        procedure Init(S: Range);
        procedure Push(E: Item);
        procedure Pop(var E: Item);
    end;

implementation                    {hidden}
{-------------------------------------------------------}
{              Stack's method implementations           }
{-------------------------------------------------------}

procedure Stack.Init(S: Range);
begin
    Size  := S;
    Index := 0;
end;

procedure Stack.Push(E: Item);
begin
    if Index >= Size
        then writeln('Error: Stack Full')
        else begin
            Index := Index + 1;
            MyStack[Index] := E
        end
end;

procedure Stack.Pop(var E: Item);
begin
    if Index = 0
        then writeln('Error: Stack empty.')
        else begin
            E := MyStack[Index];
            Index := Index - 1
        end;
end;
```

Object Pascal also provides for generic objects through its inheritance and virtual facilities. To see how this is done, first we must provide a template for Items to be stack elements, as shown in listing (4.2.9).

```
unit Items;                                                        (4.2.9)

interface

  type
    ItemPtr = ^Item;
    Item = object
      procedure Display; virtual;
    end;

    RealPtr = ^RealItem;
    RealItem = object(Item)
      R : real;
      constructor Init(X: real);
      constructor CueR;              {Requests value of R from user}
      procedure Display; virtual;
    end;

    IntPtr = ^IntItem;
    IntItem = object(Item)
      I : integer;
      constructor Init(J: integer);
      constructor CueI;              {Requests value of I from user}
      procedure  Display; virtual;
    end;

implementation
   . . .
```

There are a number of things to notice here. RealItem and IntItem are of type **object**(Item). Thus objects of type RealItem or IntItem inherit the method Display from the object Item. Each object class except Item has a **constructor**, which is needed for calling virtual methods. **virtual** is Object and Turbo Pascal's reserved word indicating that a message is polymorphic. There may be different methods for processing objects of different types, but the message is the same. We will consider what the **constructor** does in Figure 4.2.1.

A RealItem object is of type Item, as is an IntItem. Each has a Virtual Method Table (VMT), which includes the address of the **constructor** for the object, called Init, as well as addresses for any virtual methods, e.g., a Display method for each subobject. When confronted with a call to Display, the Object Pascal compiler checks to see what type object is involved in the Display and then selects the appropriate method.[7] Item is a class that has no **constructors**. Thus there can be no instances of type Item. Such a class is called an *abstract class* and serves as a base class for RealItem and IntItem.

Notice how different this is from Ada's generics. Polymorphic Ada packages are declared at compile time, using the **new** function. There was no hierarchy of packages

---

[7]The method Display is included in the object Item even though we cannot construct an Item instance. This is needed because the two descendents have methods called Display.

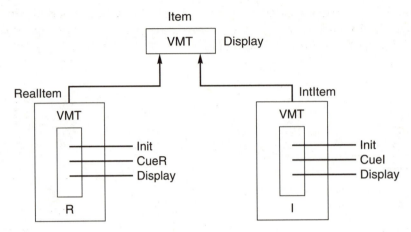

FIGURE 4.2.1
Hierarchy of Item objects

in Ada 83, and pointers to packages could not be passed as parameters. We will see, however, an example of the addition of subtypes to Ada 95 in listing (4.4.1).

When we use **new** with an object in Pascal, we will be creating a pointer to a new object. The object itself, however, will not exist until the **constructor** is called. Recall that a new Pascal record pointer is created pointing to a new empty record when **new**(RecordPtr) is called, but does not initialize it. **new**(ObjectPtr) also reserves space, but a **constructor** must be called as well, to set up the VMT and to initialize any variables contained in the object. Item's method implementations are shown in listing (4.2.10).

```
implementation                                              (4.2.10)

     {------------------------------------------------------}
     {  Item's method implementations                       }
     {------------------------------------------------------}

     procedure Item.Display;
     begin end;

     {------------------------------------------------------}
     {  RealItem's method implementations                   }
     {------------------------------------------------------}

     constructor RealItem.Init(X: real);
     begin
       R := X
     end;

     constructor RealItem.CueR;
     begin
       write('Enter a single real and press return:  ');
       readln(X)
     end;
```

```
procedure RealItem.Display;
begin
  writeln(R:5:2)
end;

{-------------------------------------------------------}
{  IntItem's method implementations                     }
{-------------------------------------------------------}

constructor IntItem.Init(J: integer);
begin
  I := J
end;

constructor IntItem.CueI;
begin
  write('Enter a single integer and press return:  ');
  readln(I)
end;

procedure IntItem.Display;
begin
  writeln(I:5)
end;

end.
```

We are now ready to see how Items can be incorporated into a Stack, as shown in listing (4.2.11).

```
unit Stacks;                                              (4.2.11)

interface

  uses Items;

  const
    MaxSize = 100;

  type
    Range = 0..MaxSize;
    Stack = record
      Table: array[Range] of ItemPtr;   {ItemPtr is declared in Items}
      Max: integer
    end;

  var
    Index: Range;
    procedure Init(M: Range; var S: Stack);
    procedure Push(var S: Stack; E: ItemPtr);
    procedure Pop (var S: Stack; var E: ItemPtr);

implementation

procedure Init(M: Range; var S: Stack);
var I: Range;
```

```
begin
  S.Max:= M;
  Index:= 0;
end;

procedure Push(var S: Stack; E: ItemPtr);
begin
  with S do begin
    If Index = Max
      then writeln('Error: Stack Full')
      else begin
        Index := Index + 1;
        Table[Index] := E
      end
  end
end;

procedure Pop(var S: Stack; var E: ItemPtr);
begin
  if Index = 0
    then  writeln('Error: Stack Empty')
    else begin
      E := S.Table[Index];
      Index := Index - 1
    end
end

end.
```

Stacks contains no objects other than those imported from Items. It does make sense to include Stacks in a **unit** to encapsulate stack data and procedures. We should mention that Pascal units do not enforce information hiding of ADTs or objects. One can access a stack directly, rather than only through Init, Push, and Pop.

And finally, listing (4.2.12) shows a Pascal program using both real and integer stacks.

```
program StackDemo;                                    (4.2.12)

uses Stacks, Items;

var
  RealStack      : Stack;
  IntStack       : Stack;
  AReal          : RealPtr;
  AnInt          : IntPtr;
  ItemP          : ItemPtr;

begin

{A RealStack example}

  Stacks.Init(10, RealStack);
  new(AReal, CueR);
  Push(RealStack, AReal);
  new(AReal, CueR);
  Push(RealStack, AReal);
  Pop(RealStack, ItemP);
```

```
    ItemP^.Display;
    Pop(RealStack, ItemP);
    ItemP^.Display;

{An IntegerStack example}

    Stacks.Init(5, IntStack);
    new(AnInt, CueI);
    {... with appropriate changes}
  end.
```

This is not really a very object-oriented way to implement a stack unit, since Stack itself is not an object. We'll see how to implement a Stack object in section 4.4, after we have discussed inheritance.

Classes in C++

As an example of classes in C++, we will use code for Figure 4.4.1, which appears in section 4.4. We have already seen an example of declarations for C++ classes in listing (4.1.5) and will now look at another class, Polygon, which includes the subclasses Square and Triangle. Polygon has four methods: one to compute the perimeter of a regular polygonal object, another to compute its area, and two to make the number of sides and the side length visible to a client. Square and Triangle will use the same perimeter method, but have more efficient area methods. Thus the class Polygon supports polymorphism, since its methods are different but appropriate for three different sorts of objects.

```
#include <math.h>                                              (4.2.13)
#define PI 3.1415926536
typedef int numSides;              //number of sides
typedef int sideLength;            //side length

class Polygon {
  numSides n;                      //private
  sideLength s;

 protected:                 //may be used by Polygon and any subclasses
    double sqr(sideLength) const{return ((double)t)*t;}

 public:
    Polygon (numSides m, sideLength t) : n(m), s(t) {};
    sideLength perimeter () const {return n * s;}
    virtual double area() {
      return n * sqr(s)/4.0/tan((double)(n-2)/(2*n)*PI);}
    sideLength getSide() const {return s;}
    numSides getNumSides() const {return n;}
    virtual ~Polygon(){};

};
```

```
class Square: public Polygon {
   public:
      Square (sideLength side): Polygon(4,s){};     //constructor
      double area() const {                          //redefined area function
         return sqr(getSide());}
      ~Square(){};                                   //destructor
};


class Triangle: public Polygon {
   public:
         Triangle(sideLength side): Polygon(3,s){};  //constructor
         double area();                              //redefined area function
      ~Triangle(){};                                 //destructor
};
```

There are a few new C++ constructs to notice in listing (4.2.13) that were not in listing (4.1.5). First is the designation **virtual** preceding the member function (method) declaration area. Any function can be redefined in a derived class (subclass) if desired, but a virtual function is one that is available to any derived class within an object hierarchy, whether or not it has been redefined within that class, and that is available for dynamic binding, if necessary. We will discuss binding times in section 4.4. A function (and also the class in which it is declared) is *pure* **virtual** if it is declared, and defined as 0 in a superclass. It cannot be called, of course, until it is redefined, which would necessarily be in a class derived from the superclass.

We have also added a **protected** section, containing one function, sqr. sqr is called from area in either Polygon or Square, but not from outside the classes. Both the Square and Triangle classes have access to all the nonprivate declarations and methods of their superclass Polygon, including perimeter. As discussed in section 4.1, properties declared **private** are accessible only within the object in which they are declared, while **protected** properties are also accessible to subclasses of the object where they are declared. Thus if we need the value of the private attribute s for a Square or Triangle object, we must get it by sending the message getSide().

If we had declared area as in listing (4.2.14), area would have been a pure **virtual** member function, which cannot be called until redefined in a subclass.

```
virtual double area() = 0;                                                (4.2.14)
```

The assignment of 0 to area() indicates that it is a null function at that point and will be dynamically bound to a definition when an object in one of the subclasses defining it is created. Any class containing a pure virtual member function is also virtual, so there can be no objects of type Polygon. A virtual class is also called an abstract class and serves as a parent class for object members of its subclasses. We will discuss virtual classes and functions further when we consider dynamic binding. area is defined as an in-line function in the class Square, and left to be defined elsewhere in Triangle.

Now let's look at listing (4.2.15) to see how a generic stack can be declared in C++ to accomplish the same job we addressed in Object Pascal in listings (4.2.11) and (4.2.12)).

```
//intstack.h                                                    (4.2.15)
//Define generic class Stack using an array of size 10
template <class T> class Stack {
    public:
        Stack(unsigned int sizeIn = 10):
                top(0), size(sizeIn), items(new T [size]) {};
        ~Stack() {delete [] items;};
        void push(const T &item);
        T pop();
        int isEmpty() const {return top == 0;}
    private:
        const unsigned int size;
        T *items;
        unsigned int top;
};


//stack.cpp
//definitions for the methods push and pop
template <class T> void Stack<T>::push(const T &item) {
    if (top >= size)
    {
        cerr << "Stack full\n";
        exit(EXIT_FAILURE);
    };
    items[top++] = item;
};


template <class T> T Stack<T>::pop() {
    if (isEmpty()) {
        cerr << "Tried to pop an empty Stack\n";
        exit(EXIT_FAILURE);
    };
    return items[--top];
};
```

Here we have used the C++ **template** construct, where a separate copy of the **template** code is made for each object using Stack. A stack of integers would be declared by **typedef** Stack<int> IntStack;, and a stack of reals by **typedef** Stack<**double**> RealStack;. At this point, the template would be copied with **int** or **double** substituted for T, wherever it occurs.

Implementation of Inherited Classes

In C++, most implementations use a *v-table* to locate code for methods. It is defined for each object when it is created and contains a list of pointers to virtual functions. Thus the v-table for a triangle object (Figure 4.4.1) would list the address where code for the function area can be found. Since area is an in-line function in the Square class (listing (4.2.13)), no entry in the v-table would be needed as it would be treated as a macro and expanded in-line when encountered. Here the trade-off is speed over space. The v-table is similar to Pascal's VMT, as mentioned above.

Smalltalk utilizes a message dictionary for method look-up. When a message is sent to a Smalltalk object, the object looks up the message in its dictionary. If the method is found, it is invoked. If not, search continues up the inheritance hierarchy until a method for carrying out the message is found. This can make Smalltalk run slowly, as method look-up takes an average of 1.5 times as long as it takes for a subprogram call [Booch, 1994].

In Ada 95, inheritance is implemented through **tagged** records. The declaration:

```
package Polygons is
  type Polygon is tagged
    record
      S : Float;
      N : Integer;
    end record;

    function Perimeter(P: in Polygon) return Float;
    function Area(P: in Polygon) return Float is abstract;
end Polygons;
```

provides a base class for the derived classes, Triangle and Square. The designation **tagged** announces that the Polygon class can be extended and that the type of instances of the Polygon type can be distinguished through the hidden tag at run time. The Area function is declared to be **abstract**, enforcing redefinition in each derived class. In this case, the derived classes are Square and Triangle.

A Square class is defined as:

```
type Square is new Polygon with
  record
    N := 4;
  end record;
function Area(Sq: in Square) return Float;
```

In Ada terminology, Square is called a type extension of Polygon. Square is a **public** extension, but could be declared to be **private** as well. Which version of the methods, Perimeter or Area, to be called is determined either statically (at compile time) or dynamically (at run time) through the controlling tag. In the dynamic case, a message *dispatches* to the body of the method through dynamic links into the **new** code accessed via a dynamic tag, which is a hidden attribute of the Square type.

LAB 4.2: POLYMORPHISM: OBJECT PASCAL/ADA/C++

Objectives (Labs can be found in the *Instructor's Manual*.)

1. To use the mechanisms available (packages, units, classes, objects) to encapsulate an ADT. In doing this lab, information hiding should be emphasized, even though the language may not enforce it.
2. To program a method already named in another object so that it acts differently on the new object. Overloading and/or virtual methods will be exemplified.

EXERCISES 4.2

1. Explain the differences between the notions of polymorphism and classes.
2. Why would the following C++ class definition be illegal?

```
class Robot
{
  public:
    Robot(ArmModel kindIn);                         //constructor
    Robot& move(const ArmPosition & destination);
    Robot& close();
    Robot& open();
    armPosition getPosition();

  private:
      ArmPosition position;
      ArmModel kind;
      Boolean open;
      Robot babyRobot;
};
```

3. Write generic declarations and a function body for Vector and CrossProduct of listing (4.2.3), so that Square will take vectors of any type, not just real vectors. Be careful about the sequence of instantiations.
4. Complete the coding for Push and Pop of the Stack package of listing (4.2.5).
5. In Object Pascal, a **constructor** is needed to set up the VMT for an object. Suppose we have three instances of an object of type RealItem. Will each contain a table of pointers to the two functions Init(X) and Display? If not, what will the VMT for an instance contain? If so, will these tables be identical or different?
6. Finish the IntStack example of listing (4.2.12).
7. In the StackDemo program of listing (4.2.12), why did we have to qualify Stacks.Init, RealItem.Init, and IntItem.Init, but not Push or Pop?

4.3
SMALLTALK

At first glance, "Smalltalk" seems like a strange name for any programming language. In society, "small talk" is the stuff of most gatherings. The word brings to mind conversation that is open to anyone. It can be understood and engaged in by people from various backgrounds and intellectual orientations, since it deals with subjects that are universally understood and agreed upon, such as the weather. Small talk is comfortable and easy with its traditional format. It doesn't delve into details. It skates along the surface of ideas. When Alan Kay developed Smalltalk as a language and philosophy of programming, his aim was to take the idea of "small talk" and bring it into the world of computing. This vignette will acquaint the reader with some of the Alan Kay's motivation in designing Smalltalk, the first language to be developed entirely in the OOP style.

HISTORICAL VIGNETTE

Smalltalk: Alan Kay

The story of Smalltalk™, the computer language, begins when Alan Kay was in graduate school at the University of Utah in the late sixties. He was a man with a vision, which was to develop a notebook-sized portable computer that would have the capability of holding thousands of pages of information and execute millions of instructions per second. It would be programmed in a language nonspecialists could understand, utilize, and learn from—unlike other programming languages of the sixties, which were geared toward specialists and applications that would not be used by nonspecialists. The computer would have high-quality graphics that could make it more user friendly. It would have a keyboard, a CRT, and a mouse that would make it possible for areas of the screen to double as a keyboard.

As Baron observed, "To appreciate how radical the hardware component of this vision was at the time, consider the state of computing in the 1960s. The personal computer had not yet been heard of. Keyboards and CRTs were still novelties in a world of punched cards, and the graphics capabilities of most mainframe computers were limited to printing pictures of Snoopy out of X's" [Baron, 1986]. Kay envisioned the use of his computer and language as a tool that could reshape education with its ability to help students understand concepts and create new ones. This educational view was as radical as Kay's hardware visions. In the sixties, the only projected educational computer use involved drill and practice exercises.

Kay began working on a programming language called FLEX, a "flexible, extensible language." He incorporated ideas from the recently developed LOGO of Seymour Papert and his colleagues at MIT. It was being used to teach programming concepts to children. Like LOGO, FLEX maintained an open, interactive dialogue between the user and the machine and allowed the user to create new discussions whenever needed.

After earning advanced degrees at the University of Utah, Kay went to work for the Xerox Palo Alto Research Center (PARC). There he continued working toward his vision. He organized the Learning Research Group to work to develop his computer, called the "Dynabook," since it was based on the dynamic retrieval of information. Its software was named Smalltalk. An entire system was developed incorporating the special hardware and software. The first version of Smalltalk was completed and implemented in 1972. 1973 saw an Interim Dynabook completed for purposes of research. Smalltalk-72 and this Dynabook were used experimentally with over 250 children, aged 6 to 15, and 50 adults. Experience with Smalltalk has led to several revisions, including Smalltalk-74, -76, -78, and -80. Work is proceeding now on a Smalltalk ANSI standard. Along with the attention being paid to OOP in general, interest in Smalltalk has increased.

Smalltalk is intended as a language for everybody. There is a problem, however. It is very different from most other computer languages. It is a nightmare for lazy programmers, since learning a language based on unique concepts is harder than learning a language similar to others one knows. Kaeler comments, "As a language,

Smalltalk offers a uniform and powerful metaphor: procedures and data that belong together are packaged in an 'object.' An object interacts with the rest of the system by singling out another object and sending it a message. Smalltalk's combination of good editors, a natural modularization of code, and a language based on a powerful idea forms a system that is at its best during construction and evolution of a large application program" [Kaeler, 1986].

In 1980, the Xerox corporation began distributing Smalltalk-80. Companies chosen to review the language were Apple Computer, Digital Equipment Corporation, Hewlett Packard, and Tektronix. Xerox wanted to expand both the communities of Smalltalk programmers and researchers, influence hardware designers to improve Smalltalk performance, and establish a standard for Smalltalk as an object-oriented, graphics-based programming language [Krasner, 1983].

By 1982, the review process was complete and it became possible to publish material about the Smalltalk system. In return for their help, the companies involved were given the right to use Smalltalk-80 in their research and hardware development projects. When Alan Kay left Xerox in the early eighties to work for Apple, he renamed his research group the Software Concepts Group, reflecting a change from the original educational focus.

Smalltalk as a production language never took off, but it has influenced other systems. The Apple Macintosh® mouse-controlled system of icons and overlapping windows was first pioneered by Kay for Smalltalk. Unlike conversational small talk, the Smalltalk System has proven to be anything but trivial.

4.4
INHERITANCE AND OBJECT-ORIENTATION

Object-oriented languages support objects, classes of objects, and the inheritance of attributes by a subclass from a class higher in the hierarchy. Smalltalk is a pure object-oriented language, where everything is an object descended from an abstract class called **Object**. **Object** has no instance variables, but does have 66 methods, which are inherited by all other objects. These define default methods for displaying, copying, and comparing objects and reporting errors.

We have already seen in listing (4.2.13) an example of inheritance in the declarations of our C++ classes, Square and Triangle, which inherit the functions perimeter, getSide, and getNumSides, and the two data members s and n, from the class Polygon.

Figure 4.4.1 shows the message perimeter being sent to the object square2 in class Polygon, which responds with its method for computing perimeter. square2 has previously been initialized with a side length s = 3. All Squares have the same number of sides, n = 4. Since the object in question, square2, is a Square, the message perimeter should be answered according to a method defined in class Square. The perimeter method is an attribute of a Square, not because it was declared there, but because it is inherited from the superclass Polygon. When an object receives a message, it checks to see if there is a method for answering the message. If there is not, it checks

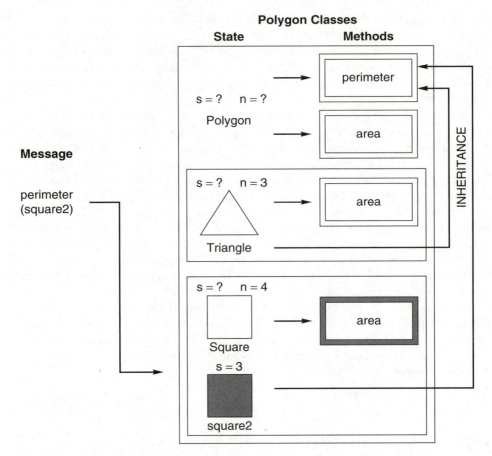

FIGURE 4.4.1
The message/object model including methods inherited from the Polygon class

up the class inheritance hierarchy via pointers as far as necessary to find one. In Figure 4.4.1, there is only one superclass to Square, and it is here in Polygon that the perimeter method is found.

In our C++ code, there are constructor and destructor methods, which we have omitted in the figure. Constructors and destructors are not inherited, as are other member functions, so they must be provided in each subclass. The definition:

```
Square (sideLength side): Polygon(4,side){};          //constructor
```

indicates that the constructor for Polygon is to be called to fill in the value 4 for n and the client-supplied value side for s. Here, a square is considered a polygon with four sides. It inherits all the attributes of a polygon and provides its own method for computing area. For details, see the C++ *MiniManual*.

When discussing inheritance and the hierarchy of object types, an animal example is often used, as in Figure 4.4.2. The tree structure for object inheritance is

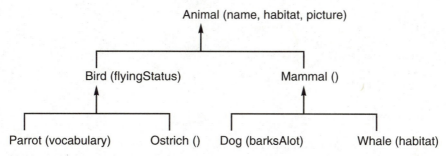

FIGURE 4.4.2
Hierarchy of animal objects [Digitalk, 1986]

similar to that used for classification systems in the natural sciences and with which most users are familiar. This structure demonstrates the *isA* and *hasA* relations. A Bird isA Animal, that hasA flyingStatus of true or false. Since a Bird isA Animal it also hasA habitat. It inherits this attribute from the class Animal. Attributes can be of three kinds:

1. Redefined—An attribute that has the same name as one in a superclass, but is defined in a subclass. Habitat is redefined in the Whale class. The default habitat might be the constant, "land," while the redefined whale habitat could be one of the seven seas.
2. Specific—An attribute that is defined in only one subclass. FlyingStatus, vocabulary, and barksALot are specific to Bird, Parrot, and Dog respectively. Note that flyingStatus is inherited by both Parrot and Ostrich because they are Birds.
3. Inherited—An object possesses an attribute that is defined only in one of its superclasses. Name and picture are inherited throughout the hierarchy. FlyingStatus is inherited, but only in subclasses of Bird.

The attributes listed here are instance variables, but methods may also be inherited, redefined, or specific. In our `Item` example of listings (4.2.10) through (4.2.12), `Display` is redefined in each subclass, while the constructors and variables are specific.

   The object-oriented programming style involves being well-acquainted with classes that are already available, and then extending them to create other classes and objects specialized to the programming task at hand. Smalltalk-80 (from ParcPlace Systems) is shipped with over 240 classes, while Smalltalk/V (from Digitalk) includes 110. Objective-C (Stepstone) includes 20. The original C++ provided none, but the new ANSI standard prescribes 43. Java defines 251 classes organized into 8 packages.

   Ada 83 lacked inheritance and dynamic binding of objects and was not considered an object-oriented language. In Ada 95, however, inheritance has been implemented using *tagged types*. Only records and private types can be tagged. As suggested, such types will be discriminated by having an associated tag. As a very simple example, we will return to our geometric figures [Ada 9x, 1993].

```
type Shape is tagged with null record;                          (4.4.1)
function Size (S: in Shape) return Float is <>;

type Rectangle is new Shape with
   record
      Length: Float;
      Width: Float;
   end record;

function Size (R: in Rectangle) return Float is
begin
   return R.Length * R.Width;
end Size;

type Cuboid is new Rectangle with
   record
      Height: Float;
   end record;
```

In listing (4.4.1), Shape is an abstract type, containing an empty record. Size is an abstract subprogram, which has no **body**, as indicated by the box <>. The subclasses Rectangle and Cuboid will each define Size as appropriate. Size(S: Shape) is Ada's notation for what we called a virtual method in Object Pascal.

In the function Size(R: Rectangle), R is the tag on both R.Length and R.Width. Since Cuboid is a **new** Rectangle, it inherits Length, Width, and the function Size from the class Rectangle. It also has Height. If we want to redefine Size to something more appropriate for a Cuboid, we could redefine it as shown in listing (4.4.2).

```
function Size (C: in Cuboid) return Float is                     (4.4.2)
begin
   return Size(Rectangle (C)) * C.Height;
end  Size;
```

Notice that the Cuboid C of listing (4.4.2) is converted to its parent type Rectangle when computing Size(Rectangle (C)).

Types and Subtypes in Inheritance Hierarchies

Let's refer once more to the hierarchy of animal objects in Figure 4.4.2. Suppose we declare in C++ a particular object salty to be a Parrot. Then salty isA Parrot. It also isA Bird and isA Animal.

```
// Allocate memory for a Parrot object, salty                   (4.4.3)
Parrot salty;

// Declare a and b to be of type Bird and Animal, respectively.
Animal a;
Bird b;
```

We can then make the assignments:

```
a = salty; b = salty; a = b;
```
(4.4.4)

But the reverse,

```
salty = a; salty = b; b = a;
```
(4.4.5)

should signal errors. This is known as the *subtype principle,* which states that an object of a subtype may be used anywhere its supertype is legal. Assumed is that an object of a supertype may not be used anywhere that a subtype is legal. In listing (4.4.4), we assume that a and b are legal supertypes, so the subobjects, salty and b, may be used as well.

The situation with pointers to objects is somewhat different. Suppose we make the following C++ declarations:

```
Parrot *saltyPtr; Bird *bPtr; Animal *aPtr;
```
(4.4.6)

Memory is allocated for three pointers. Memory for the Animal, Bird, and Parrot objects can be allocated using the **new** operator.

```
new aPtr; new bPtr; new saltyPtr;
```

The following assignments will then be legal:

```
aPtr = saltyPtr; aPtr = bPtr; bPtr = saltyPtr;
```
(4.4.7)

However, only those members of saltyPtr* that are also members of a* can be accessed through aPtr. That is, a pointer to a base class can access only the members of the derived class that are also members of the base class. If we wish a pointer to a base class to access all members of the derived class, an explicit conversion must be made if the base class is **virtual**, as shown in listing (4.4.8).

```
saltyPtr = dynamic_cast <Parrot*> (aPtr);
```
(4.4.8)

The following are illegal:

```
saltyPtr = aPtr; bPtr = aPtr; saltyPtr = bPtr;
```
(4.4.9)

The assignments of listing (4.4.7) assume that the derived classes, Bird and Parrot, have **public** base classes.

If the base class is **private** in the derived class, as in listing (4.4.10), aPtr = bPtr would not be legal, since the public members of Animal are not public in Bird.

```
class Animal {/*...*/};
class Bird: Animal {/*name, habitat, picture are not public members of Bird */}
```
(4.4.10)

Multiple Inheritance

So far we have seen classes providing for tree-structured inheritance, with descendents exhibiting an isA relationship with a parent. Some objects could rightly inherit from multiple parents, e.g., a Book isA Novel and a Book isA Story make good sense, so Book might inherit attributes and methods from both Novel and Story. The inheritance structure would be as shown in Figure 4.4.3.

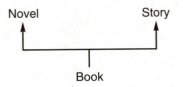

FIGURE 4.4.3
Multiple inheritance

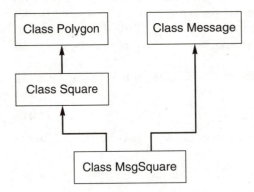

FIGURE 4.4.4
MsgSquare inheriting from Square and from Message

The Eiffel language [Meyer, 1988], the Common Lisp Object System (CLOS), and Version 2.0 and higher of C++ all support multiple inheritance. One must be conceptually careful when designing classes that inherit from multiple parents. First of all, the <descendent> isA <parent> relation should be maintained. isA restricts its descendents to be of the same object type as each of their parents, while a descendent may extend the parent type to include new variables and methods. These notions must be preserved to keep designs understandable and clean.

One potential problem for a descendent object is name clashes among methods. What if Novel and Story each have a method ListPlot? This must be handled in the descendent, but is not difficult. Eiffel solves it by introducing a **rename** operator as shown in listing (4.4.11).

```
class Book export...inherit                          (4.4.11)
   Novel;
   Story
     rename ListPlot as StoryLine
     ...
end                    --class Book
```

Let's look at an addition to the declarations for our C++ Square class so that we can write messages inside squares, as shown in Figure 4.4.4.

A C++ program using MsgSquare is shown in listing (4.4.12).

```
#include <graphics.h>     //Graphics library declarations⁸      (4.4.12)
#include <string.h>       //String library functions
#include <conio.h>        //for Console I/O
```

---

[8]Libraries are supplied with Turbo C++®. The Message class is adapted from a similar one found in [TurboC++, 1992].

```
#include <math.h>
#define PI 3.1415926536
typedef int sideLength;
typedef int numSides;

class Polygon{
    numSides n;
    sideLength s;
  public:
    Polygon (numSides m, sideLength t): n(m), s(t){};
    //other declarations as in listing (4.2.13)
    virtual void show(){};
    ~Polygon(){};                          //destructor
};

class Square: public Polygon{
  public:
    Square (sideLength s): Polygon(4,s){};   //constructor
      //other declarations
    void show(){};                         //method to draw a square
    ~Square(){};                           //destructor
};

class Message{
    char *msg;                             //message to be displayed
    int font;                              //graphics font declared in graph.h
    int field;                             //size of field for message
    int x, y;                              //location of message
  public:
    Message(int startX, int startY, int msgFont, int fieldSize, char *text):
        msg(text), font(msgFont), field(fieldSize), x(startX), y(startY){};
            //constructor
    void show(){};                         //show message
};

class MsgSquare: Square, Message{          //inherits from both Square and Message
  public:
    MsgSquare(sideLength side, int x, int y, int font, int size, char *m):
        Square(side), Message(x, y, font, size, m){};   //constructor
    void MsgSquare::show(){
    Square::show();                        //draw the square
      Message::show();                     //show the message
    };
};

main(){
  initgraph(...);                          //Initialize graphics driver
  MsgSquare mSquare (5, 10, 20, GOTHIC_FONT, 5, "HI!");
      //declare a square with side = 5 and message starting at (10,20)
  mSquare.show();
  return 0;
};
```

Notice that the class MsgSquare of listing (4.4.12) inherits both from Square and from Message. When mSquare is constructed, it uses Square's constructor to establish the sideLength which, in turn, uses that of Polygon to set the number of sides. It also uses the constructor from Message to locate where the message and square are to be, the font, field size, and the message itself. When the message mSquare.show is sent, the method of MsgSquare is invoked. It calls those of Message and Square, using the scope resolution operator :: to decide which show method to use. We have left Square :: show and Message :: show with empty definitions here, as they require familiarity with the graphics classes.

Shopiro [Shopiro, 1989] discusses implemented, multiply-inheriting classes from the iostream library, which supplies I/O utilities. Ten interconnected classes have been designed to specialize the base classes shown in Figure 4.4.5 to files. This provides a good example of using inheritance to restrict general I/O to files and to extend classes by providing specialized methods for files.

iostream inherits from both istream, containing input methods, and from ostream, which has output methods, as shown in Figure 4.4.5. It has no variables or functions at all, but inherits all its attributes from ios :: istream or from ios :: ostream. ios is an abstract class, containing only virtual methods, which are implemented in one of istream or ostream. streambuf is also a class, to which *streambuf points. Most of the real I/O work is included in streambuf or in other specialized classes. ios decides whether input or output is being done and makes the connection to streambuf through a pointer, bp. istream contains an input function bp–>get(), and ostream has an output method bp–>put(c).

So what is the advantage of being able to think of an iostream as either an input stream or an output stream? Before multiple inheritance, there was only one kind of C++ stream. It was only at run time that an inappropriate operation, such as trying to write to an input stream, would be caught. Multiple inheritance allows

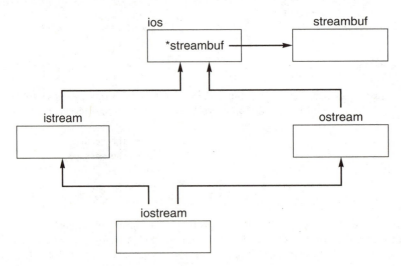

FIGURE 4.4.5
Multiple inheritance in C++

the two kinds of streams to be separated into istreams and ostreams. This could have been done without multiple inheritance only by copying over shared code for the two different stream types.

When these objects are specialized to files, however, the real utility surfaces, since there is more common code, as Figure 4.4.6 shows. Shopiro says that the C++ code implementing the objects of Figures 4.4.5 and 4.4.6 "is not quite a practical example of multiple inheritance in C++, because the facility it describes is too simple to be useful" [Shopiro, 1989]. Object-oriented programmers be warned!

Language Exemplars

We are now ready to look at what are known as object-oriented languages, those supporting information hiding, data abstraction, message passing, and inheritance. Objects + classes + inheritance = object-orientation.

From Shopiro's comment above, it might seem that object-oriented programming isn't worth the trouble. It is inheritance that belies this conclusion. Even though tricky to write, classes are reusable. Once they have been verified, creating

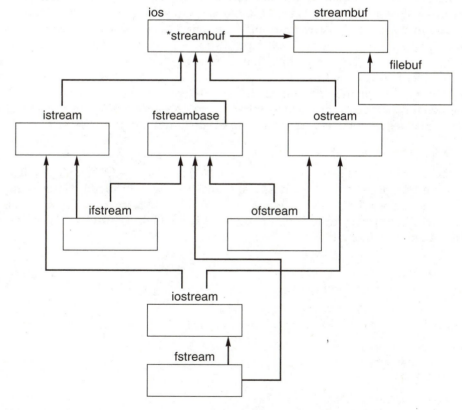

FIGURE 4.4.6
Specialization of ios to files

new classes and objects through inheritance should be easier than starting from scratch each time.

Learning an object-oriented language won't be a short task, however, because one must learn and understand class libraries in order to choose which ones to build on effectively. OOP languages are either pure, such as Smalltalk, or hybrid, like C++ and Object Pascal. The hybrid languages have been built on top of existing languages and attract a coterie of programmers experienced in using the base language. Habits die slowly, and object-oriented programmers will realize little improvement in productivity if they merely throw a few objects into a block-structured program. One must learn to think in terms of objects rather than procedures.

OOP has some efficiency disadvantages. Classes use extra space to keep the Virtual Method Tables (VMTs). Pointers from object instances into the VMT must also be maintained. Accessing methods through at least two pointers makes OOP programs run somewhat slower than their procedural counterparts. Researchers have also noticed something called the "Yo-Yo effect," where execution involving an object that inherits methods from ancestor classes keeps bouncing up and down the class hierarchy to find which method to use.

As an elementary example, consider the object hierarchy of Figure 4.4.4 and listing (4.4.12). Here, each object class has a method called by the message show. If an object of type MsgSquare is sent the message to show itself, the version of show defined in the class MsgSquare first calls that defined in Message followed by that in Square. This involves following the pointer from MsgSquare to Message, back to MsgSquare, back up to Square, which may or may not (depending on the implementation) refer to Polygon, which directs us back to Square, since show as defined in Polygon is **virtual**. Implementation is finally referred back to MsgSquare to terminate. This behavior suggests short ancestor trees or some sort of optimization, so that the whole tree need not be traversed each time a distant method is accessed.

More Object Pascal

Let's rewrite the Stacks unit of listing (4.2.11) more in the OOP style. We'll start at the very beginning and let a Stack class inherit some of its methods from a more general List class. The object-oriented programming style includes reusing classes that have already been tested and debugged. Listing (4.4.13) provides a Pascal List class called, obviously, List.

```
uses                                                      (4.4.13)
  Items;

type

NodePtr = ^Node;
Node = record
  Item: ItemPtr;
  Next: NodePtr
end;

ListPtr = ^List;
List    = object
  Nodes: NodePtr;
  constructor Init;
```

```
  destructor Done: virtual;
  procedure AddAtFront(I: ItemPtr);
  procedure AddAtRear(I: ItemPtr);
  procedure AddAfter(I, Loc: ItemPtr); {Adds I after node pointed to by Loc}
  procedure DeleteFromFront;
  procedure DeleteFromRear;
  procedure DeleteAfter(Loc: ItemPtr); {Deletes node after one pointed to by Loc}
  procedure Report;
end;

var
  ItemList: List;
```

A List, then, is a list of pointers to nodes. In this case, each node contains two pointers, one to the Item on the list and the second to Next, as shown in Figure 4.4.7.

As we have seen, Item objects can be polymorphic, thus the List above, pointed to by Nodes, can include Items, RealItems, and IntItems, or any other sort of items if we wish to create more descendents of Item.

We have already seen **constructor**s, but a **destructor** is new. It does as the name suggests, destroy an existing object after we are through with it. Just as **new** was extended to initialize objects, as in **new**(RealItem, CueR), **dispose** can be used with **dispose**(ItemList, Done). A destructor cleans up any pointer fields in an object and any pointers inherited from ancestor objects. It also disposes of the VMT pointers and calls **dispose** to release storage occupied by the object. Implementation for a List **destructor** in Pascal 7.0 is shown in listing (4.4.14).

```
  destructor List.Done;                                          (4.4.14)
  var
    N: NodePtr;
  begin
    while Nodes <> nil do begin
      N := Nodes;
      dispose (N^.Item, Done);
      Nodes:= N^.Next;
      dispose (N);
    end
  end;
```

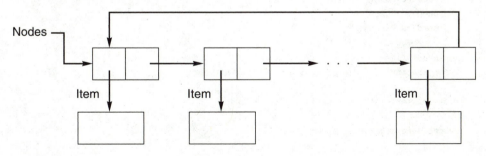

FIGURE 4.4.7
A circular List of pointers to objects

In the second line of the **while** statement, we call **dispose**(N^.Item, Done). This Done refers to a **destructor**, Item.Done, not to List.Done, so we must add it to the Item **object**. In this case, the **destructor** need do nothing but the invisible operations of eliminating VMT pointers (see listing (4.4.15)).

```
type                                                          (4.4.15)
  ItemPtr = ^Item;
  Item = object
    procedure Display; virtual;
    destructor Done;
  end;

  destructor Item.Done;
  begin...end;
```

List.Add adds a new Item to the front of the List, while List.Report takes care of output of Items. These will be left for Lab 4.3.

The List class is a template for Items of any type object. A client program must have access only to the type of Node:

```
Node = record                                                 (4.4.16)
  Item: ItemPtr;
  Next: NodePtr
end;
```

We may not wish to change this record, so we can name an abstract class heading the objects we want to incorporate on our list Item. The other alternative is to change the first field of Node to SomeOtherItem : SomeOtherPtr, which might require making changes to List methods. Pointing to SomeOtherItem with a pointer called ItemPtr is probably the most flexible we can be.

And finally, our stack object is shown in listing (4.4.17).

```
uses List;                                                    (4.4.17)
StackPtr = ^Stack;
Stack    = object(List)
  constructor InitStack;
  destructor Done;
  procedure Push(Item: ItemPtr);
  procedure Pop;
  procedure Report;

implementation
  constructor Stack.InitStack; begin List.Init end;

  destructor List.Done; begin List.Done end;

  procedure Stack.Push(Item: ItemPtr);
  begin
    List.AddAtFront(Item)
  end;
```

```
procedure Stack.Pop;
begin
  List.DeleteFromFront
end;

procedure Stack.Report;
  ...
end;

var
  S: Stack;
```

Inheritance in C++

C++, like Object Pascal, is built on an existing language. That is, any C programs, after minor changes, should run on a C++ compiler. With a few exceptions, C is a subset of C++. One of the goals in writing C++ was efficiency. In part, C was written to eliminate the need for assembly language code. Bit manipulations are included right in the language, providing for fast translation and compilation and the elimination of calls to assembly language procedures. C++ programs, though they include higher level features than C, can use the same run-time library developed for C.

C++ adds the **class** type to C's simple and derived types. Continuing with our stack example, we will look at a declaration for a linked list in C++, which serves as an abstract class [Stroustrup, 1986]. First, we need to define an item type, a node class for objects holding an item, and a pointer to the next link (listing (4.4.18)). As in our Pascal implementation, the first link field is a pointer to some object to be defined later.

```
typedef void* itemPtr;                                      (4.4.18)
class Node {
friend class List;           // have access to itemPtr's private members
friend class ListIterator;
public
  Node* next;
  itemPtr  e;
  Node(itemPtr a, Node* p) {e = a; next = p;  };
};
```

void serves as the base type for a pointer. Thus **void*** itemPtr declares itemPtr to be a pointer to any type we may want to use later. Pointing to a nonspecified type through **void*** is idiomatic to C++ and may lead to errors; thus it is not supported by languages such as Ada or Smalltalk. next points to a Node. The function Node is the constructor for an object of type Node and assigns a to the instance variable e, and p to the node pointer next. When a variable is declared to be of type Node, the constructor is called automatically.

```
double* x;         //x holds a pointer to a real
node a(x, 0);⁹
```

---

[9]In C, the token 0 is used for the null pointer as well as the number zero. Its use is determined by the context.

This initializes a to:

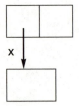

So far nothing looks different from our Pascal implementation but, and this is important, the data fields e and next and the Node constructor are not public information. e and next are known only through their **friend**s, List and ListIterator. The constructor is called upon declaration of a Node variable.

Listing (4.4.19) shows declarations for a class of linked-list objects, while listing (4.4.20) defines the functions.

```
//List.h                                                          (4.4.19)

typedef void *itemPtr;

class Node {
    friend class List;
    friend class ListIterator;
    Node *next;
    itemPtr e;
    Node(itemPtr a, Node *p): next(p), e(a) {};
};

class List {
    friend class ListIterator;
    Node *last;
    public:
        void insert(itemPtr a);
        void append(itemPtr a);
        itemPtr get();
        List(): last(0) {};
        List(itemPtr a): last(new Node(a,0)) {last->next = last;}
};

class ListIterator  {}; //Needs to be defined to get around the list
                        //We leave these definitions as an exercise


//List.cpp                                                        (4.4.20)

inline void List  :: insert(itemPtr a) {last->next = new Node(a,last->next); }
void List :: append(itemPtr a)
{
    last->next = new Node(a, last->next);
    last = last->next;
}
```

```
itemPtr List :: get()
{
    if (last == 0){
        cerr << "Tried to remove an item from an empty list";
        return 0;
    }
    Node *head = last->next;
    itemPtr ret = head->e;
    if (last == head) last = 0;
    else last->next = head->next;
    delete head;
    return ret;
}
```

The List class, as shown in listing (4.4.20), is not very useful as is, because all we can do with it is make linked lists of void pointers. It does, however, provide a reusable parent class for other useful structures. The C++ style includes combining many small files into the input for other programs. Thus we will store list declarations in a file, "list.h". We will **include** it in any programs requiring its methods. Listing (4.4.21) shows the derived **class** Stack and the **struct** realStack, derived from Stack.

```
//Stacks.h                                                (4.4.21)

#include "list.h"

class Stack: private List {
    public:
        Stack(): List() {}
        Stack(itemPtr a): List(a) {}
        void push(itemPtr a)      {insert(a); }
        itemPtr pop()             {return get(); }
};

struct realStack: private List {
    public:
        Stack myStack;
        realStack(): myStack() {}
        realStack(double *r): myStack((itemPtr) r) {}
        void push(double *a)  {myStack.push((itemPtr) a); }
        double* pop() {return (double*) myStack.pop();}
};
```

Stack is a subclass derived from List (Stack: **private** List). Here, all the attributes of List are **private** in Stack. The code:

```
{realStack rs; {rs.push(1.0); rs.push(2.0); } };
```

will produce the stack of Figure 4.4.8.[10]

---

[10]Keeping a list as a circular list enables easy access to either the front or the rear node. For details, see [Stroustrup, 1986].

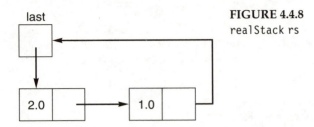

FIGURE 4.4.8
realStack rs

Note that the **class** List has **public** methods, which are thus available to any clients. However, clients of Stack or realStack will find the methods of List **private** (**class** Stack: **private** List). List's methods are only available through using either the **class** Stack or realStack. The auxiliary variable myStack was declared in realStack to facilitate using Stack's constructors. To return the correct type value from a realStack, the return type in pop was cast to **double** using (**double**∗).

Multiple inheritance in C++. Although the first versions of C++ did not support multiple inheritance, Versions 2.0 and higher do. Earlier problems involved storage for pointers to virtual functions, i.e., those that were eligible for late binding. C++ uses an implementation similar to Pascal's VMT to store pointers to its virtual functions. Consider the four classes A, B, C, and D of listing (4.4.22).

```
class A {                                          (4.4.22)
  int h;
public:
  virtual f1();
  virtual f2();
};

class B {
  int i;
public:
  virtual f2();
  virtual f3();
};

class C: public A {
  int j;
public:
  f2();
  f4();
};

class D: public A, public B {
  int k;
public:
  f2();
  f4();
};
```

In the Tau Metric C++ compiler [Ball, 1989], a class derived from only one ancestor would use only one virtual table. For example, **class** C: A would be stored as in Figure 4.4.9.

If we want **class** D to inherit from both A and B, two virtual tables are used, the first for D : A and the second for D : B, as shown in Figure 4.4.10. Inheritance from more than two classes can be handled similarly, with an additional virtual table added for each new ancestor class.

Dynamic Binding

By now the notion of late binding shouldn't be too mystifying. When a source file is parsed and compiled, machine code for a static procedure is stored beginning at a particular memory address. Procedure calls found within the program are replaced with transfer instructions to that address, as discussed in section 1.2. The call is *bound* to that beginning address. This is called early binding, because the call is bound at the earliest possible time. In contrast, a procedure call, such as ItemP^.Display (see listing (4.2.10)), cannot be bound at compile time, because it will not be known until run time whether ItemP is pointing to an Item, a RealItem, or an IntItem. Thus the location where code for Display (the server) is to be found must be bound late to the calling program or client.

If a parent object has many descendents, and it is not known which descendents will be constructed during a program run, there are going to be many virtual procedures and functions that are never called. There are, however, optimized

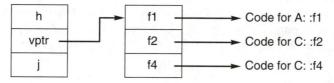

FIGURE 4.4.9
class C derived from **class** A

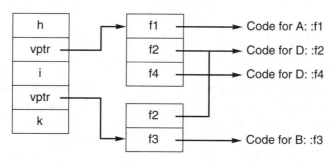

FIGURE 4.4.10
class D derived from **class** A and **class** B

object-oriented compilers that remove procedures that are never called by the program, generating code only for those that will potentially be used.

If a language includes objects that may be created at run time, including information about their data types, it supports dynamic binding.

As defined in the C++ code of listing (4.2.13), if a pentagon with sides of length 3 of type `Polygon` is declared (`Polygon polygon1(5,3);`) and sent the message `polygon1.area()`, the method for defining `area` included in the **class** `Polygon` will be used, and the location for code for that `area` method bound statically to the call. But suppose that we are using polygons, squares, and triangles to decorate students' homework papers. Poor papers get triangles, better ones get squares, and the truly outstanding homeworks get a polygon. Which to use will not be known until the papers are turned in, evaluated, and the grade is submitted to the program producing the merit decorations. If we add a virtual `show` method to the polygon hierarchy, it will be quite possible to decide which figure to draw at the time the grade is determined, as shown in listing (4.4.23).

```
Polygon* p;                                                   (4.4.23)
char x;
cout << "Which figure do you want drawn? Enter P, S, or T: ";
cin >> x;
switch (x) {
  case 'P': Polygon polygon1;   p = &polygon1; break;
  case 'S': Square square1;     p = &square1;  break;
  case 'T': Triangle triangle1; p = &triangle1;
};
p->show;
```

A language such as Ada 83, in which all data types must be determined at compile time, is statically bound. Ada 95 includes the notion of *class-wide types*. Referring to listing (4.4.1) on page 180, `Shape'Class` is the type of Shapes, Rectangles, and Cuboids. An Ada procedure applicable to any object in the class could be as in listing (4.4.24).

```
procedure ProcessShapes(A: Shape'Class) is                    (4.4.24)
   S: Float;
...
begin
   ...
   S := Size(A);   --dispatch according to tag
   ...
end ProcessShapes;
```

When `ProcessShapes` is compiled, there is no way to know whether it will be sent a `Rectangle` or a `Cuboid`. When the parameter `A` takes on a value at run time, it will be tagged, so that the correct function body can be bound to `Size`. This is called *dynamic dispatch* or *dynamic method look up* in Ada 95. The decision to lookup a particular method is made during run time, at which time the call site is bound to the address of code for the method chosen, and control is dispatched or routed to that memory location.

To make the notion of dynamic binding in Object Pascal concrete, let's add another sort of `Item` to the `Items` class of listing (4.2.11), as in listing (4.4.25).

```
uses List;                                                          (4.4.25)

  TrianglePtr = ^TriangleItem;
  TriangleItem = object(Item)
    T: Triangle;              {assume type Triangle has been defined previously}
    constructor Init(T: Triangle);
    constructor CueT;
    procedure   Display; virtual;
  end;
```

Then our list shown in Figure 4.4.7 could include Items of type IntItem, RealItem, and TriangleItem. Suppose we have constructed such a list, called MyList. Each item object contains a Display procedure, which will, of course, be different for a triangle than for either an integer or a real number. We can Display each Item on MyList through the call TraverseAndDisplay(MyList), as defined in listing (4.4.26).

```
procedure TraverseAndDisplay;                                        (4.4.26)
var
  N: NodePtr;
begin
  while Nodes <> nil do begin
    N := Nodes;
    Items(Item).Display;
    Nodes := N^.Next;
  end
end;
```

If Object Pascal were statically bound, the location of each Display procedure would be bound at compile time to the name Display. This, of course, cannot happen if the types of the nodes of MyList are unknown until run time. Thus, just which Display procedure is to be invoked is determined dynamically at run time.

We have already seen a C++ example calling for dynamic binding in listings (4.4.20) and (4.4.21). The type for an Item is not known until a variable is declared to be of type realStack, which can occur anywhere in a C++ program. **class** Stack could also be compiled separately from **struct** realStack. Thus the definitions for both push and pop cannot be bound until run time, when the sort of Items to be pushed or popped are known. The keyword **virtual** signals that the function or procedure name that follows is to be bound to a definition at run time.

LAB 4.3: CLASSES AND INHERITANCE: OBJECT PASCAL/C++

Objectives (Labs can be found in the *Instructor's Manual*.)

1. To complete the declarations for a List object, incorporating pointers to other objects.
2. To write some of the List utilities, such as DeleteFromFront, DeleteFromEnd, DeleteAfter, DeleteBefore, AddAfter, AddBefore, etc.
3. To complete the implementation of a stack of objects.
4. To sketch the implementation of a queue of objects.
5. To see how inheritance contributes to the value of reusable code.

EXERCISES 4.4

1. Redraw Figure 4.4.1 so that it conforms to the structure for Item, RealItem, and IntItem objects of listing (4.2.9). Label each class and method with its message name.

2. Consider each of the variables and methods defined for the classes Item, RealItem, and IntItem of listing (4.2.9) and classify each as inherited, redefined, or specific.

3. Does the class IntegerArray satisfy the isA relationship with both its superclasses, Integer and Array?

4. Connect the entities (Figure 4.4.1) of the left-hand list below with those of the right-hand list by the isA and/or hasA relationship.

	perimeter
triangle	sideLength
polygon	NoOfSides
square	polygon
	area

5. Write C++ code for the functions needed in the ListIterator class of listing (4.4.19). These should include at least findNode, findAfter, findBefore, and any others you think might be useful.

6. In the C++ code of listing (4.4.21), why are there parentheses around (itemPtr) in the definitions of push and pop?

7. Redraw the diagrams of Figure 4.4.9 to represent class c: b, and Figure 4.4.10 to represent class c: b, a.

8. Suppose we change the declaration for a List in listing (4.4.13) to List = **object**(RealItem);, deleting **uses** Items;, and declare the following variables:

```
R: RealItem; L: List; RPtr: ^RealItem; LPtr: ^List; Data: real;
```

Which statements are legal and which are not?

a. L := R;	d. L.CueR;	g. R := RPtr^.Item;
b. R := L;	e. LPtr^.CueR;	h. Data := RPtr^.R;
c. R.CueR;	f. RPtr^.CueR;	i. Data := LPtr^.R;

4.5
JAVA

The newest OOP language is Java™ from Sun Microsystems of Mountain View, California. As the people at Sun claim, it is a "simple, object-oriented, distributed, interpreted, robust, secure, architecture-neutral, portable, high-performance, multithreaded, dynamic, buzzword-compliant, general-purpose programming language" [Sun, 1995]. Java supports programming for the Internet in the form of platform-independent Java *applets*. Applets are Java applications that are loaded and run in the Java run-time environment. Thus Java includes two separate products: Java itself, which is a full-fledged, object-oriented programming language, and HotJava™, a browser for the World Wide Web (WWW) that enables users of the Web to download applets written in Java and run them on their own system. Any applet-enabled browser, such as Netscape, can download and run applets as well as HotJava.

The buzzwords on which Sun's White Paper is based are listed below. They provide a fairly good description of just what Java is.

Simple. The syntax of Java is as close to that of C as possible so C programmers can master it quickly. Since C++ is an extension to C, some features unnecessary to OOP have remained, causing confusion. Thus C++'s operator overloading, multiple inheritance, and extensive automatic conversions have been omitted from Java. Most importantly, Java does not include pointers, which probably are the cause of most bugs in C or C++ programs. Since C arrays are accessed through pointers and C strings are character arrays, the provision of both was needed in Java. This is accomplished through the provision of both a string and an array object.

Object-oriented. The object-oriented facilities of Java are essentially those of C++, i.e., data and methods encapsulated in a module called an object, classes of objects, inheritance, and interfaces between objects through methods. Java has the advantage of being developed as an object-oriented language, so it is not burdened with structures, implemented in a prior language, that are no longer needed, as is C++ which grew out of C. Thus you will see no **struct**s (C records) in Java and no **template**s (C++ methods for creating polymorphic classes).

Distributed. Java has an extensive library of routines for coping easily with the protocols: TCP/IP (Transmission Control Protocol/Internet Protocol), HTTP (HyperText Transfer Protocol), and FTP (File Transfer Protocol). Java applications can open and access objects across the Internet via URLs (Uniform Resource Locators) with the same ease that programmers are used to when accessing a local file system [Sun, 1995].

Robust. Some of the lax compile-time checking inherited by C++ from C has been tightened up in Java. Java implements true arrays, rather than arrays manipulated through pointer arithmetic, where subscript checking is impossible. Casting of pointers to integers has also been eliminated.

Secure. Since Java applets were designed to function over the Internet, with many users accessing the same files, concerns for virus- and tamper-free systems were addressed through public-key encryption. Applets are restricted in just what they can do, e.g., they cannot write to or delete a client's files. The philosophy behind implementing Java for the Internet is to trust no one.

Architecture neutral. The Java compiler generates an object file of byte code instructions that have nothing to do with a particular computer. These files can run on any system enabled with the Java run-time system, be it an IBM PC or Apple Macintosh.

Portable. The Java system is written in Java itself, and the run-time system is written in ANSI C. Simple data types are implemented uniformly across all platforms, i.e., **int**s are 32 bits and **long**s are 64 bits. The downside of this is that Java won't run on a machine supporting only 16-bit words.

Interpreted. The Java compiler, `javac`, generates byte code, rather than machine code, that can be executed directly on any machine to which the Java interpreter has been ported. Java source code (`<fileName>.java`) that has been compiled into byte code (`<fileName>.class`) is then run by the Java interpreter (`java <fileName>`).

High performance. If higher performance is desired, the interpreted byte codes can be translated at run time into machine code for the particular CPU on which Java is running. Tests at Sun show that byte codes converted to machine code compare favorably in performance with C/C++ code.

Multithreaded. A set of synchronization primitives based on monitors, which will be discussed in Chapter 5, are integrated into Java. This enables Java applications to run concurrently, limited only by the capabilities of the underlying operating system.

Dynamic. Java includes interface concepts from Objective-C similar to classes, where an interface is a listing of methods that an object responds to. These interfaces can be multi-inherited, unlike Java-derived classes, which can only inherit from a single base class. One can look up a Java class given a string containing its name and have its definition dynamically linked into the run-time system.

Java Language Constructs

While Java's control structures are much like those in C, its data structures and modules are not. Java, like Smalltalk, considers almost everything to be an object. Simple numeric, character, and Boolean types are the only exceptions.

Object, the Superclass of All Other Classes

A class, `Object`, the superclass of all other objects, is included in the implementation-dependent package `java.lang`, described in listing (4.5.1). `Object` has no data fields, but includes the following methods, which are inherited by any other object:

```
public class Object {                                          (4.5.1)
    public Object();    //constructor

    // public instance methods
    public boolean equals(Object.obj);
        /* should be redefined in derived classes to test equality
           of objects, where o1.equals(o2) means the values of all
           the fields of o1 are the same as those in o2  */
    public final Class getClass();
    public int hashCode();    // provides a hash code when storing an object in a hash table
    public String toString();//converts an Object to a string

    // public methods for synchronization of threads
    public final void notify();    // throws IllegalMonitorState exception
    public final void notifyAll();
```

```
    public final void wait(long timeout);
    public final void wait(long timeout, int nanos);
    public final void wait();


    // protected instance methods
    protected Object clone();          // makes a copy of an Object
    protected void copy(Object src);   // copies src into the current object (this)
    protected finalize();              // releases system resources other than memory
}
```

A number of things are worth commenting on regarding the **class** Object. First, Java is case sensitive, and all the reserved words (here in bold type) are lowercase. The Java convention is that the names of classes begin with capital letters, while the first letter of names of methods or variables are lowercase. Thus the method getClass() returns a class definition object of type **Class**, not a **class**. The object stores information about the class name, superclass name, interfaces, and other information about an object, sending the message getClass(). If an object named triangle1 of type Triangle sends the message triangle1.getClass().getName(), the string "Triangle" is returned.

Next are the method modifiers **public** and **protected**. Java has five security levels, as shown in Table 4.5.1, in contrast to the three in C++. The additional two, **default** and **private protected**, are needed because collections of related classes reside in **package**s.

The **default** level allows accessibility between classes within a package, but not between packages. A **protected** class loosens up inheritance between subclasses in different packages, but not accessibility. The methods clone and copy are **protected**, because objects can only be copied into other objects of the same type. If they were in different packages, they would necessarily be of different types.

A **final** method is one that cannot be redefined in a subclass, thus all the methods in the **class** Object for synchronization of concurrent processes (threads) are **final**. A running subobject cannot terminate or wait without all its superobjects terminating or waiting as well.

TABLE 4.5.1
Security levels of Java classes, data fields, or methods [Flanagan, 1996]

Situation	public	default	protected	private protected	private
Accessible to:					
Nonsubclass from same package?	Yes	Yes	Yes	No	No
Subclass from same package?	Yes	Yes	Yes	No	No
Nonsubclass from different package?	Yes	No	No	No	No
Subclass from different package?	Yes	No	No	No	No
Inherited by:					
Subclass in same package?	Yes	Yes	Yes	Yes	No
Subclass in different package?	Yes	No	Yes	Yes	No

The **class** Object is a member of the **package** java.lang, which provides the basic functions needed by programmers at the lowest level. We will discuss the standard packages below.

An Elementary Java Class

Since almost every Java entity is a class, let us consider the Polygon class defined in listing (4.5.2) following the hierarchy of Table 4.5.1.

```
public abstract class Polygon(int n, int s) {                          (4.5.2)
  int n;
  int s;
  int perimeter() {return (this.n * this.s);};
  abstract double area();
}

public final class Triangle(int sideLngth) extends Polygon {
  int n = 3;
  super(int n, int this.sideLngth);  //constructor
  double area() {
    return (Math.sqrt(3) * Math.sqr(this.sideLngth)/4.0;
}
public final class Square(sideLngth) extends Polygon {
  int n = 3;
  super(this.n, this.sideLngth);  //constructor
  int area() {
    return this.sideLngth * this.sideLngth;
}
```

Polygon is an **abstract** class because it has an **abstract** (as yet undefined) method area. Both Triangle and Square are **final**, so neither can have any subclasses. Note also that Java has a **this** modifier, which refers to the object calling the method.

The Java Application Programming Interfaces (APIs)

Just as Ada includes no implementation-dependent features in its official language specification, neither does Java, where platform independence is a key feature. Sun has, however, as have the developers of Ada, provided interfaces (APIs) to standard packages of utilities. A user will be provided with an appropriate set of APIs upon acquiring a Java Development Kit (JDK) for the operating system on which it is to be installed. Each API includes an interface to the OS, a collection of Java classes, and a collection of exceptions that may be raised when one of these classes is active.

One package is java.lang, which was mentioned above as including the superclass Object. Some of the classes included are: java.lang.Class, java.lang.Compiler, java.lang.Math (a library of standard mathematical functions), java.lang.Ref (used by Java's garbage collector), java.lang.SecurityManager, java.lang.String (for constant text strings), and java.lang.StringBuffer (support for mutable strings).

Type *wrappers,* which are classes, hold information about the basic types, which are not. java.lang.Number is an **abstract** class that is the superclass of the type wrappers java.lang.Integer (for 32-bit integers), java.lang.Long (64-bit integers), java.lang.Float, and java.lang.Double. The two other wrappers in java.lang.* are java.lang.Boolean and java.lang.Character. A variable could be declared **boolean** b1; or Boolean b2;, but not both. A Boolean value can be either TRUE or FALSE, while a **boolean** value is either **true** or **false**. The Boolean class provides methods useful for working with logic-valued data, such as toString(), which converts a Boolean value to a string so it can be printed.

The package can be imported into an application by including in your source code the statement shown in listing (4.5.3).

```
import java.lang.*;                                              (4.5.3)
```

Exceptions such as ArithmeticException, ArrayIndexOutOfBoundsException, IOException, and FileNotFoundException are found in this package.

The java.util API includes objects such as Date and Linker. java.io manages stream I/O and random access files.

java.awt (Abstract Window Toolkit) includes over 60 classes and interfaces for creating graphical user interfaces (GUIs). We will use the java.awt.graphics subclass in Lab 4.4 to create an application with animation, and combine it with the java.applet class to make our application into an applet, which we can transfer to the World Wide Web.

APIs for HotJava are java.browser, java.browser.audio, java.net (for interacting with the Internet), java.net.ftp (for interacting with FTP), java.net.nntp (for accessing network news groups), java.net.www.html (for managing HTML documents), and java.net.www.http (for managing the HyperText Transfer Protocol (HTTP) on the World Wide Web).

Each of these packages is imported into an application by including the statement in listing (4.5.4):

```
import <PackageName>.*;                                          (4.5.4)
```

in the source code.

Users can write interfaces as well. These interfaces provide collections of method declarations with unimplemented bodies. For example, consider the interface shown in listing (4.5.5).

```
public interface PolygonGraphMethods {                           (4.5.5)
  public void setColor();
  public void setLocation(int x, int y);
  public void Draw(DrawWindow dw);
}
```

A class SquarePicture should inherit methods from both Square and from PolygonGraphMethods, but Java does not allow multiple inheritance. So we implement SquarePicture as a subclass of Square as in listing (4.5.6).

```
public class SquarePicture extends Square                        (4.5.6)
                           implements PolygonMethods{
// definitions for setColor, setLocation, and Draw go here
}
```

Compiling and Running a Java Program

Each class is compiled separately and must be located in the proper directory so a
Java application can find the code. Source code for the class Polygon would be located
in java\polygon\Polygon.java. Square and Triangle would be located in
java\polygon\square\Square.java and in java\polygon\triangle\Triangle.java.
Source code for SquarePicture is in java\polygon\square\SquarePicture.java. (In
UNIX, the directory separators would be / instead of \). Notice that the file extensions are four characters long, which can be supported by operating systems such as
Windows NT, Windows 95, and UNIX. When these files are compiled into platform-
independent byte code, the files are stored in the same directories in *.class files. One
can place multiple classes in a single *.java file, but each class will be compiled into
a separate *.class file. java\polygon\square\SquarePicture is compiled through:

```
javac SquarePicture.java
```

which creates the java\polygon\square\SquarePicture.class file.

To run a Java application, a **main** method is needed. One possible such method
to be included among the methods of SquarePicture is shown in listing (4.5.7).

```
import java.awt      // for Color                                    (4.5.7)
public static void main (String argv[]) {
    SquarePicture sp = new SquarePicture(10);
    System.out.println("The area is: " + sp.area());
    System.out.print("and the perimeter is: " + sp.perimeter());
    sp.color = Color.red;
    sp.setLocation(100,50);
    sp.draw();
}
```

The method **main**() returns nothing (**void**), and is **static**, i.e., accessible throughout the class and independent of any instance such as sp above. The only argument
to **main**() is an array of strings, argv[], which are any directives included in the interpreter command line. Note that the Java compiler is javac and the interpreter is
java. To run the Java program above after compiling it into byte code with javac,
we use the command line java SquarePicture.

One useful directive in this application that would eliminate the need to qualify
instance variables and methods is shown in listing (4.5.8).

```
-classpath java SquarePicture                                        (4.5.8)
```

One must be sure, however, that there are no name conflicts between packages
when using -classpath. Other directives facilitate debugging, execution reporting
style, size of the heap, etc. The **main** method is run by using the command java
java\polygon\square\SquarePicture.

HotJava and Applets

One of the design goals for Java was to create applications that can be shipped over
the Internet and run on a client's machine, accessing remote as well as local files.
As discussed above, these applications are called applets. Applications such as the

Web browser, HotJava, can be Java-enabled by giving them access to the Java run-time interpreter. A simple applet, which is presented in almost every reference, including [Gosling, 1996] and [Flanagan, 1996], is shown in listing (4.5.9)

```
import java.applet.*      // base class for applets            (4.5.9)
import java.awt.*         // abstract windowing toolkit: includes graphics

public class EasyApplet extends Applet {
   public void paint(Graphics g) {
        g.DrawString("Hello World", 25, 50);
   }
}
```

Since `EasyApplet` is to be called from an HTML file that references it, we need that as well. Code for the HTML file is shown in listing (4.5.10).

```
<APPLET code="EasyApplet.class" width=150 height=100>            (4.5.10)
</APPLET>
```

A browser such as HotJava that understands the `<APPLET>` tag can call `EasyApplet`. A browser that is not Java-enabled will just ignore the `<APPLET>` tag. We will investigate HTML files in Lab 4.5, and create and run an applet in Lab 4.6.

Program Types

Java has four program types:

- Applications
- Applets
- Content handlers
- Protocol handlers

Content handlers are found in classes of the `java.net.*` package. The `java.net.URL` allows the data found at a URL (Uniform Resource Locator) to be downloaded to the user's system. Using this interface, a sequence of pages can be loaded automatically, giving the effect of a movie. `java.net.SocketImpl` provides methods for implementing net communication through sockets. When used with `java.net.DatagramSocket`, unreliable datagram packets can be sent and received over the network.

Protocol handlers for HTTP, FTP, and Gopher are included in the HotJava Web browser, which was written as a Java application. As new protocols become available, users can write their own handlers.

Handlers are put in the java\classes\net\www* directory, with content handlers in the \content* subdirectory and protocol handlers in the \protocol* subdirectory.

Differences Between Java, C, and C++

Java has no preprocessor (cpp) as does C, which is capable of macro substitution (**#define** PI 3.14159), conditional compilation (**#ifdef** CYBER **#define** BYTESIZ 10 **#else** **#define** BYTESIZ 8 **#endif**), and the inclusion of named files (**#include** <polygon.h>).

There are no Java global variables, but one can define a class-wide **static** variable, which persists through various instances of a class. Constants are created by declaring a variable to be **static final** and then assigning it a value. Named files are **import**ed into a class. Java does not require conditional compilation because it is platform independent.

Java has no macro facility, which was thought unnecessary by its designers, given the advanced state of compiler technology.

Java adds **boolean** and **byte** to its simple data types. Java arrays and classes are reference types in that they are passed by reference, but one cannot manipulate their addresses (by using the & operator) nor dereference them through -> and ∗, as in C. Simple types are passed by value. Since references to variables cannot be manipulated, Java has no pointer type. In C, the null pointer is 0. In Java, **null** is the default value for reference types, i.e., classes or arrays. It can be assigned to any variable of either of these types.

Strings in Java are of two classes: constant text strings (java.lang.String) and mutable strings (java.lang.StringBuffer). Constant strings behave almost like simple types and are passed by value, whereas strings of class StringBuffer are passed by reference.

Java does not support the C &, ∗, or **sizeof**, since it does not include a pointer type. It does, however, add some new operators, shown in listing (4.5.11).

+	String concatenation	(4.5.11)
o **instanceof** C	Returns **true** if object o, is an instance of class C	
>>>	Right shift with 0 for the sign extension	
&	Bitwise AND for integers; AND for **boolean** types	
|	Bitwise OR for integers; OR for **boolean** types	
&&	Shortcut AND (does not evaluate second argument if first is **false**)	
||	Shortcut OR (does not evaluate second argument if first is **true**)	

The Java **for** statement is somewhat different from that in C, in that it allows the declaration of local loop variables in the initialization section. It does not allow the C comma (,) operator in the test section of a **for**, but does in the initialization and the increment sections, as in listing (4.5.12).

```
for (int i=0, String s="count";int j=s.length;       (4.5.12)
    i<j;
    i++, s=s.substring(0,j-i);) {
      System.out.println(s);
      System.out.print(" Still counting! ");
      System.out.print(j-i, " characters to go!");
    }
```

Output would be:

```
count Still counting! 5 characters to go!
coun Still counting! 4 characters to go!
cou Still counting! 3 characters to go!
co Still counting! 2 characters to go!
c Still counting! 1 characters to go!
```

C++ has several features not supported in Java. These include:

- Multiple inheritance
- Templates to implement polymorphism
- User overloading of operators
- The definition of conversion functions that automatically determine a constructor when a class variable is assigned a value

In addition, C++ objects are manipulated by value, while Java objects are manipulated by reference [Flanagan, 1996].

LAB 4.4: OBJECTS AND OBJECT-ORIENTED PROGRAMMING: JAVA

Objectives (Labs can be found in the *Instructor's Manual.*)

1. To complete a Java application exhibiting object-oriented techniques.
2. To use the java.awt class to implement a simple automated application.

LAB 4.5: HTML TO BE USED ON THE WORLD WIDE WEB WITH JAVA

Objectives (Labs can be found in the *Instructor's Manual.*)

1. To provide the student with experience in building a simple HTML application.

LAB 4.6: AN APPLET: JAVA

Objectives (Labs can be found in the *Instructor's Manual.*)

1. To use the HTML techniques explored in Lab 4.5 and the Java application of Lab 4.4 to build a HotJava applet.
2. The student will play the role of the server, using the World Wide Web intermediary to ship it to clients.

EXERCISES 4.5

1. Why do you think each of the buzzwords describing Java was adopted as a design goal?
2. a. The methods of listing (4.5.2) have no security level modifiers attached. What is the security level?
   b. Given your answer to a, how should the three classes defined be packaged: in the same or in different packages?
3. Java does not provide for multiple inheritance except as shown in listing (4.5.6). It does, however, allow the importing of multiple **interface**s through the inclusion of multiple statements of the form shown in listing (4.5.4). If a method Draw occurred in more than one of the imported packages, how would you differentiate between them in code for a Java application?
4. What is the difference between redefining a method, M(), in a subclass where M() has already been defined in a superclass, and defining a method in a subclass that had been declared **abstract** in a superclass? When would you want to use each?
5. Java includes no templates for implementing polymorphic classes, as does C++. However, it does include a generic Stack class (in the package java.util.Stack) which **extend**s the generic class Vector (java.util.Vector).
   a. What type would you guess is used for the generic element of a vector?
   b. Vector inherits from both Object and from Cloneable. How could Vector be declared to achieve this?

4.6
SUMMARY

In this chapter, we have looked at object-based and object-oriented languages, both of which support objects encapsulating data, with state and operations on that data called methods. Objects communicate with each other through message passing, where a message is the name of an object's method. Inheritance implies a hierarchy of classes, with objects in a subclass inheriting methods and/or data from a superclass. Inheritance can be single or multiple, in which case a subclass may inherit from more than one superclass. In addition, object-oriented languages support dynamic binding, where an object and its methods can be created or destroyed at run time, and a message need not be bound to a method until run time, when the object to which it is being directed is determined.

Ada 83 is an object-based language, while Ada 95, Object Pascal, C++, and Java are object-oriented. The first object-oriented languages were Simula and Smalltalk. Smalltalk is a pure object language, where every data type or aggregate is an object, as is also the case in the newest object-oriented language, Java. Objects have been added to existing imperative languages in the case of Simula, Ada 95, Object Pascal, and C++. Both Smalltalk and Java were designed as object-oriented languages and are thus somewhat simpler and cleaner than the others.

Programming with objects involves quite a different style from top-down procedural methods. Here a problem is envisioned as a collection of interacting objects. One of the aims of object-oriented programming is to maintain libraries of tested reusable objects, with specifications that can be easily understood by clients and combined into applications that meet their particular needs.

4.7
NOTES ON REFERENCES

A good, although brief, summary of object-oriented languages is [Saunders, 1989]. He discusses and provides vendors for 16 languages categorized by type as Actor, concurrent, distributed, frame-based, hybrid (C or LISP-based), logical, Smalltalk-based, ideological extensions, and miscellaneous. Ada 83 and other object-based languages are not included.

Several newsletters and magazines are attempting to publish the latest information in this rapidly developing field. Four of these are *The Journal of Object-Oriented Programming (JOOP)*, which publishes 10 issues a year, *Hotline on Object-Oriented Technology (HOOT)*, a monthly, the *C++ Report*, 10 issues a year, and *Java Report*, the newest bimonthly. JOOP contains articles plus regular columns on the Eiffel, Smalltalk, Actor, Common LISP Object System (CLOS), Objective-C, and C++ languages.

Creating reusable classes that are practical and useful is hard work. [Johnson, 1988] follows a discussion of object-oriented toolkits and libraries with 13 good programming practice rules.

[Krasner, 1983] presents a good collection of papers describing the background of Smalltalk-80, experiences with implementing it for various computers, test results, and proposals for future development.

An in-depth understanding of object-oriented design can be obtained by reading Grady Booch's book [Booch, 1994]. Some consider it the "bible" on the concepts and applications of object-orientation.

[Sun, 1995] provides information about the Java language. It is available over the Internet through java@java.sun.com or through the World Wide Web through http://java.sun.com. Another source for information on Java is SunSITE at the University of North Carolina (http://sunsite.unc.edu/pub/languages/java). It is easy to find your way to tutorials, source code, downloadable code, etc., through hypertext transfers, since both sites are well indexed. Another Web source that provides example applets you can run is http://www.gamelan.com/.

Java has captured the imagination of the computer world, and publishers have rushed to print with books and manuals to acquaint users with this new language. We looked at several that were available as of April, 1996, and found [Flanagan, 1996], from O'Reilly & Associates, Inc., to be the most helpful and well organized.

CHAPTER 5
LANGUAGE CONSTRUCTS FOR PARALLEL PROCESSING

5.0	**In this Chapter**	**209**	
5.1	**The Paradigm**	**210**	
5.2	**Multiple Processes**	**212**	
5.3	**Synchronization of**		
	Cooperating Processes	**213**	
	Semaphores	215	
	Monitors	218	
	Rendezvous	219	
	Message Passing	219	
	Exercises 5.3	221	
5.4	**Some Synchronization**		
	Solutions	**221**	
	Semaphores in ALGOL 68, C,		
	and Pascal S	221	
	ALGOL 68	221	
	C	222	

Pascal S	223
Monitor and Process Types in	
Concurrent Pascal	225
The Rendezvous in Ada and	
Concurrent C	226
Ada	226
Concurrent C	230
Message Passing in Occam	232
Exercises 5.4	235
5.5 Tuples and Objects	**235**
The Tuple-Space of Linda	235
Objects As Units of Parallelism	239
5.6 Managing Partial Failure	**240**
5.7 Summary	**241**
5.8 Notes on References	**242**

208

CHAPTER 5

Language Constructs for Parallel Processing

If we divide a job up between two or more workers, it usually gets done faster, and sometimes better. But too many cooks really can spoil the broth. Joint projects take coordination. In this chapter, we will look at languages that support more than one processor working on a problem. The processors may work independently and then communicate partial results to each other, or they may all work on the same project. The work may be done simultaneously or alternately.

5.0
IN THIS CHAPTER

In this chapter we will look at:

- Shared memory models with synchronization through semaphores or monitors
- Message passing
- Processes accessing a common associative memory called tuple space

The modules written to run in parallel are called processes, which run, at least potentially, on separate processors. We will see examples of processes written in:

- Pascal S
- Concurrent C
- Ada
- Occam
- C-Linda

Labs in all but Concurrent C will let you fill in the details on programs implementing the producer-consumer problem, in which items are concurrently produced and consumed as they become available. The term *parallel* implies the positions of multiple processors, while *concurrent* suggests that processes are running at the same time. The terms are often interchangeable.

5.1
THE PARADIGM

Whatever the system, three issues distinguish concurrent from sequential programming [Bal, 1989]:

1. The use of multiple processors
2. Cooperation among the processors
3. The potential for partial failure, i.e., one or more processes may fail without jeopardizing the entire project

Figure 5.1.1 illustrates the two models for parallel processing. Labels have been intentionally omitted from the figure, since there is no unanimity in the literature for naming what each of the two diagrams represent. All agree, however, that both involve two or more CPUs that communicate with each other. The top diagram shows each with its own memory and a communication channel between them. Here memory as well as CPUs are distributed. The bottom diagram shows no communication channel, but shared memory. Only the CPUs are distributed.

Bal, Steiner, and Tanenbaum [Bal, 1989] call the top system *distributed,* and the bottom not, while Shatz and Wang [Shatz, 1989] consider them both to be distributed, since more than one communicating CPU is involved and work can be distributed over them. To complicate matters further, Shatz and Wang consider the top system to be *loosely coupled* and the bottom *tightly coupled.* Bal and his colleagues call only the top configuration coupled. To them, a loosely coupled system is one where the cooperating CPUs are physically far apart and communication may be unreliable. If the communication channel is a network, this is called a *wide area network* or WAN. The tightly coupled system is a *local area network* or LAN.

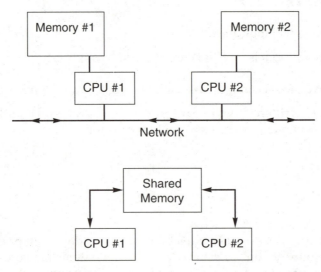

FIGURE 5.1.1
Physical models for parallel processing

In this chapter, we will look at both situations and not worry too much about the names. Where memory is unshared, CPUs communicate by sending and receiving messages. When shared, each cooperating CPU can initialize and/or update the same memory locations. A third configuration for multiprocessors provides for both message passing and memory sharing. In Figure 5.1.2, shared memory is represented by a dashed-line box to indicate logical memory. It may physically be Memory #1, Memory #2, or some third block of Memory. When many processors are involved, sometimes thousands, a great variety of architectures is possible. The IEEE Computer Society has provided a very brief tutorial, with several diagrams and guides to further reading in the February 1990 issue of *Computer* [Duncan, 1990].

Distributed systems are advantageous because:

- They can speed up programs by running different processes in parallel.
- They can enhance reliability if two or more processors duplicate each other's jobs.
- They provide a natural avenue for system growth when additional processors are added.
- They facilitate naturally distributed tasks, such as electronic mail.

A word needs to be said about *processes* and *processors*. So far we have talked about CPUs or physical processors, hardware items you can touch and see. In this sense, a process is a single sequential procedure running on a single physical processor. Processors can also be logical, however. On a single machine, processes can execute alternately and one at a time, sharing the same CPU. This is sometimes called *time-sharing*. In a multiple-CPU architecture, a compiler could distribute the processes to different CPUs. This might well be an operating system function, with the user unaware whether processes are running in parallel or alternately. Some authors reserve the term *multiprocessing* for processes running in parallel, and use *multiprogramming* to include either parallel or alternating execution of processes. In most cases, a program would be the same whether execution was through time-sharing of a single processor or concurrent using several processors.

Whether processes share memory or not, or are loosely or tightly coupled, the probability that one or more processors will fail adds up when several are running at a time. The further apart the processors are physically also contributes to system failure. Thus languages in this paradigm will include some mechanism for continuation of the still working processors and/or recovery from partial failure. How do we raise and handle exceptions among cooperating processes? We will address each of these issues below.

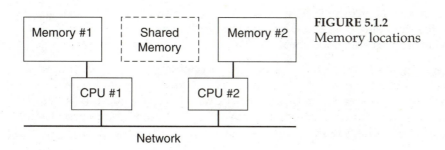

FIGURE 5.1.2
Memory locations

5.2
MULTIPLE PROCESSES

A *process* is an abstract data type that can, although need not, run in parallel with another process. A *process unit* is the language construct capable of encapsulating a process. These units may also be called *units of parallelism*. In Modula-2, the unit is a co-routine; in Ada, a task; and in Concurrent Pascal, a process. The Occam language allows individual statements to serve as process units. A sequence of Occam statements preceded by **PAR** will execute in parallel. For example,

```
PAR i = 0 FOR 100
   A[i] := 0
```

will initialize an entire array to 0 simultaneously. This may or may not save time, depending on how quickly the operating system can switch execution to the 100 separate processors. Objects can also serve as process units in languages that support them, such as Concurrent Smalltalk or Emerald. Functional languages use expressions as process units, while logic-based languages use clauses. In some, although not all, of the literature, any unit of parallelism is called a process. We will observe this definition here.

ALGOL 68 includes the notion of *collateral clauses*, such as:

```
begin x := 3, y := 2, z := "bird" end;
```

ALGOL statements are separated by semicolons, but in the collateral clause, by commas. These can be executed in any order. As with most parallel execution schemes, which gets done first is not specified.

Collateral clauses do not communicate with each other. If we write:

```
x := 0;
begin x := 3, x := x + 1, z := "bird" end;
```

the value of x will be indeterminate after the collateral clause has executed, since we don't know which goes first. Is $x = 3$, or is $x = 4$? It is even possible that $x = 1$. Let's see how this could be. To facilitate discussion, we will call $x := 3$ clause c_1, $x := x + 1$ clause c_2, and $z := "bird"$ clause c_3. If c_1 completes before c_2 starts to execute, then c_2 will be $x := 3 + 1$, or 4. If c_1 executes after c_2 has completed, x will be 3. Now suppose the clauses are executing concurrently and sharing the memory location for x. Execution of an assignment statement on a machine with registers usually involves three steps:

1. Load current value of x into a register r.
2. Perform the right-side operation, leaving the result in r.
3. Store value of r in the location for x.

We will assume that c_1 and c_2 have associated registers r_1 and r_2. Now suppose c_1 starts executing and stores 0 in r_1. Then $x = r_1 = 0$. c_2 is also running, with $x = r_2 = 0$. Now if c_1 completes, so that $x = r_1 = 3$, c_2 will not know about it. It has already performed the "read the value of x into r_2" operation, and proceeds to increment r_2. The final "store r_2 into x" will leave $x = 1$. (See Figure 5.2.1.)

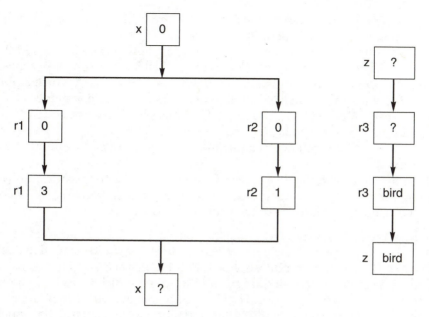

FIGURE 5.2.1

Without some method for synchronization, we may make no assumptions about how concurrent processes will be interleaved. By interleaving, we mean that one process runs for a while, then another and another before returning to complete the first process. Eventually, all interleaved processes terminate. Several issues arise here. Our three collateral clauses illustrate who gets access to a shared resource, for how long, and when.

Communication between processes can be handled either through message passing or through data sharing. Message passing tends to be more reliable, but experience shows that the programs are harder to write than those for shared memories.

We will look at the synchronization of shared resources first. What follows makes little reference to existing languages, but discusses three synchronization mechanisms: semaphores, monitors, and rendezvous. We will discuss their implementations in section 5.4.

5.3
SYNCHRONIZATION OF COOPERATING PROCESSES

Two or more running processes may communicate partial results before continuing or may share resources. Resource sharing involves each process gaining access to the same memory locations, but only one at a time. Processes run at different speeds, so there is no guarantee that one process will have its results computed or relinquish shared resources by the time a second needs them. Thus the processes need to be synchronized in some fashion.

The Dining Philosophers, illustrated in Figure 5.3.1, is a famous example of potential problems with cooperating processes.

The five philosophers sit around a table with a bowl of rice in the middle and five chopsticks. Each alternately thinks or eats, and all five perform one of these two actions concurrently. Thus there are five processes, P_i (i=0..4), in which a philosopher eats or thinks alternately. Each does at most one of these activities at a time. In order to eat, a philosopher P_i must stop thinking, signal Hungry, and pick up two chopsticks, one from his right (C_i) and one from his left ($C_{(i+1) \bmod 5}$). These are the shared resources. How can we schedule their actions so no one is without thoughts and no one starves?

Five problems should be avoided when scheduling cooperating processes. These problems are busy waiting, alternation, starvation, unfairness, and deadlock. We will describe each in terms of the Dining Philosophers.

Busy Waiting. One way to schedule the philosophers is to set up and test shared variables, and test them repeatedly. For example, we could set up five Booleans H_i (i=0..4), one for each philosopher. If P_2 is hungry and sets $H_2 = $ true, then P_1 would be required to relinquish C_2 and P_3 to relinquish C_3 to P_2, in a reasonable amount of time. This could easily be implemented using counters to monitor how long a particular philosopher had monopolized a particular chopstick. It is the repeated testing of the H_i variables that is called *busy waiting*. While a philosopher waits for two chopsticks, processes for eating philosophers are busily testing to see if a neighbor has signaled Hungry.

Alternation. A simple solution would be to let P_0 and P_2 eat for a specified period of time, then P_1 and P_3, then P_4 and P_1, etc. However, the notion of concurrency includes response to random requests within a reasonable amount of time, not rigid scheduling of access. Each philosopher should be able to think when there is something to think about and eat only when hungry.

Starvation. One possible scheme for scheduling the philosophers' eating is to let each check on the availability of the necessary chopsticks and eat only when both are available. Suppose P_0 picks up C_0 and C_1. Then P_1 and P_4 must keep on thinking, whether or not they have anything interesting to think about. P_2 could eat, however. P_0 and P_2 will finish eating eventually, but we still may

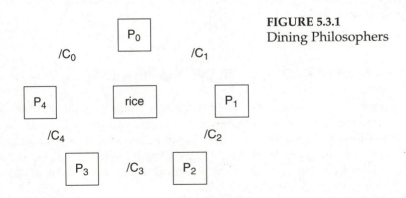

FIGURE 5.3.1
Dining Philosophers

starve out one of the others. Only two can eat at a time, but the presence of five philosophers requires something more sophisticated than checking to see if both chopsticks are available.

Unfairness. Unfairness results when one or more of the philosophers have to wait an unreasonable length of time to either think or eat. Somehow, the average waiting time should be the same for all five. One unfair, but easy, solution would be to let philosophers eat (whether they want to or not) in the order: $P_0 P_2, P_1 P_3, P_4 P_1$, and then start over. P_1 would get fat, or have to pass up some of his turns.

Deadlock. Deadlock is a situation where two or more processes are waiting for events that will never happen. If each of our philosophers picks up the left chopstick and waits to eat until the right one is available, all will starve. The situation is *deadlocked* because eating cannot proceed for anyone. Since each has indicated hunger, thinking will also cease, since it was to alternate with eating for each philosopher.

In all synchronization schemes for cooperating processes involving shared resources, provision must be made for *mutual exclusion.* A philosopher who is using a chopstick must be able to prevent his neighbor from grabbing it until he has finished eating. This is accomplished in code through the use of a *critical section* (CS). A process executing code in the CS will have exclusive access to shared resources until exiting the CS. What is more, once the critical code has been entered, it cannot be interrupted by a competing process until the CS is exited.

In some problems, multiple shared resources may be grouped into *data regions*, with only one process allowed into a region at a time. Do not confuse data regions, which are collections of data, with critical sections, which are portions of code.[1] We will not discuss data regions further, but will look later at a less expensive solution called a *monitor*.

Semaphores

One way to manage CSs and eliminate busy waiting is the *semaphore,* first implemented in ALGOL 68. A semaphore acts very much like its namesake on the railroad. When it is down, execution is halted, and when it is up, a process may proceed. The actual workings of a semaphore, including its list of waiting processes, is usually implemented deep down in an operating system, with users accessing it through its two operations, wait and signal.

A semaphore is a nonnegative, integer-valued variable S on which two operations are defined, Wait and Signal.[2] S is initialized to 1 (up) so that some process can proceed.

---

[1]The reader should be warned that in some of the literature, a critical section of code is called a *critical region.*

[2]The Wait procedure was originally called P [Dijkstra, 1968a], the first letter of the Dutch word *passeren,* "to pass." Signal is V, standing for *vrygeven,* "to release."

```
Wait(S)                                                         (5.3.1)
begin
  if S = up
    then S := down;  {Block other processes and enter the CS}
    else {put the calling process on the wait queue}
end {Wait};

Signal(S)
begin
  if {1 or more processes are waiting on S}
    then {let 1 proceed into the CS}
    else S := up
end {Signal};
```

For the five chopsticks, we would need a semaphore S_i for each. If P_i got hungry, he would execute Wait(S_i) and Wait($S_{(i+1) \bmod 5}$). If both chopsticks were available (S_i = up, and $S_{(i+1) \bmod 5}$ = up), he could enter a CS and start eating immediately. Otherwise, he will wait until the processes using the chopsticks signal their availability.

For simplicity, we will consider the binary semaphore S, which takes on only values of 0 (down) or 1 (up), and two processes, Process1 and Process2. If a process executes a Wait(S) and finds the semaphore up, S is first put down to block other processes. Process1 then executes its critical code, and executes a Signal(S), putting the semaphore back up. Two processes, P1 and P2, wishing to execute code that modifies shared variables, could be scheduled using:

```
var S : semaphore;                                             (5.3.2)

process P1:
  loop {forever}
    Wait (S);
      {CS for P1}
    Signal (S);
    {Other noncritical code}
  end {loop}
end {P1};

process P2:
  loop {forever}
    Wait (S);
      {CS for P2}
    Signal (S);
    {Other noncritical code}
  end {loop}
end {P1};
```

Note that if **process** P1 grabs its CS first, and **process** P2 executes Wait (S), execution of **process** P2 will be suspended until **process** P1 executes its Signal (S). Busy waiting is eliminated using semaphores, since a waiting process is picked off the waitqueue when the shared resources become available. The Wait procedure "puts a process to sleep" if another process is using the shared resources, while Signal "wakes up a sleeping process" if there are any.

A semaphore can be used for a single purpose. S enforces mutual exclusion. Another could be used for time coordination. The producer-consumer problem is one in which goods are produced and consumed concurrently. A consumer cannot acquire a resource until it has been produced, and consumers compete for the available resources. The simplest example involves a single producer and one or more consumers, with the producer producing a new resource only when the resource bin is empty, and a consumer consuming when it is full. The producer-consumer relationship requires synchronization. This requires two semaphores: `full` initialized to down and `empty` initialized to up.

```
full  := down;      {Nothing available to consume}                 (5.3.3)
empty := up;        {Go ahead and produce something}
```

```
            Producer: loop {forever}
                         Wait (empty);
                            Produce something;
                         Signal (full);
                      end loop;
```

```
Consumer1: loop {forever}          Consumer2: loop {forever}
              Wait (full);                       Wait (full);
                 Consume resource;                  Consume resource;
              Signal (empty);                     Signal (empty);
           end loop;                           end loop;
```

Since `empty` starts up, indicating that the resource bin is empty, the producer can begin producing. The two Consumers will have to wait until the bin is full (`full` = up) to start consuming. Since both Consumers are waiting for the same `full` signal, some sort of synchronization is needed.

We have assumed in both examples that a semaphore can take on one of only two values, up or down. This need not be the case. With minor variations, a semaphore can have any positive value. Our consumers would wait for `full` > 0. With `full` initialized to 0, and `empty` to 1, `Wait` and `Signal` would look like:

```
Wait(S: Semaphore)                                                 (5.3.4)
begin
   if S > 0
     then S := S-1; {Block other processes and enter the CS}
     else {put the calling process to sleep on the wait queue}
end {Wait};

Signal(S: Semaphore)
begin
   if {1 or more processes are waiting on S}
     then {wake up 1 process and let it proceed into the CS}
     else S := S + 1;
end {Signal};
```

Semaphores cannot assure fairness or prevent starvation. In exercise 5.3.2, you will be asked to solve the Dining Philosophers problem using semaphores. Unfortunately, we cannot assure that a philosopher will surrender his two chopsticks once he starts eating. Semaphores cannot eliminate greed!

Monitors

A *monitor* is an interface between concurrent user processes and provides:

- A set of procedures callable by users
- A mechanism for scheduling calls to these procedures if other concurrently executing processes request usage before the procedure has terminated
- A mechanism for suspending a calling procedure until a resource is available (`delay`) and then reawakening the process (`continue`)

A monitor has no access to nonlocal variables and can communicate with other monitors only by calling procedures in them. Thus a monitor serves as a third-party policeman between two or more cooperating processes.

A monitor can be considered as an abstract data type that includes a shared data structure and all the operations various (concurrent) processes can perform on it. These operations determine an initialization operation, access rights, and synchronizing operations. Concurrent processes $P_1, \ldots, P_n$ must be prevented from accessing the same data item simultaneously.

Other monitor functions must avoid mindless alternation of processes or starvation, where one or more processes run indefinitely while another is never activated. Other synchronization operations must prevent deadlock, where all processes are suspended, waiting for some event which never happens.

A monitor has the form shown in listing (5.3.5).

```
monitor <MonitorName>                                          (5.3.5)

    var <permanent variable declarations>

    procedure <operation1> (<parameter-list1>)
    ...
    procedure <operationN> (<parameter-listN>)

begin
  <initialization code for permanent variables>
end;
```

The permanent variables are maintained from invocation to invocation of the monitor. Thus a monitor, like an object, has a state. Processes can call a monitor's operations just like one would make a procedure call. Permanent variables can be accessed only through these calls.

Two operations, in addition to those defined in the monitor, are associated with each monitor. These are `delay` and `continue`, which are analogous to the semaphore's Wait and Signal. A monitor also has a queue in which to store requests for access. Thus execution of a `delay` enqueues a process, and `continue` dequeues the first waiting process and allows it to enter the monitor.

A monitor can be viewed as a module [Parnas, 1972], with most details hidden from the user. Its implementation will also be hidden in the operating system, so users will behave as if each were the only process running. An early use of monitors was in one of the BASIC time-share systems. Interactive BASIC users do not run in parallel, but one at a time, sharing a single CPU. Their processes are suspended or allowed to run using monitor operations associated with two queues, one for suspended processes and another for terminated processes. They are also included in Concurrent Pascal and in Modula.

Ben-Ari [Ben-Ari, 1982] proves that monitors can be replaced by semaphores, except for the First-In–First-Out (FIFO) assumption on the monitor queues. When using semaphores, what process goes next will be random rather than ordered. But the choice of using a monitor or semaphore generally depends on what is available to the programmer. The main benefit of monitors is in the clarity and reliability of the system using them, not their operation.

Rendezvous

The *rendezvous* includes synchronization, communication, and execution of a block of code in one of two or more concurrently running processes. It coordinates what have been called *remote procedure calls* (RPCs), i.e., a procedure running on a remote processor calling a procedure located on a different processor. The calling procedure or function is a *client* of the accepting procedure or function, which is called the *server*. Each kind of rendezvous in a server process is called a *transaction*. This word is suggestive of what actually happens. A client sends a message to a server requesting service of some sort and is blocked from further execution until the service has been performed. A rendezvous can be implemented with or without shared memory.

The rendezvous differs from a monitor in two fundamental ways. First, it is not a separate module coordinating running processes, but is achieved through the processes themselves. One process (the client) initiates a call, and another (the server) accepts it. The call is processed by the server, which receives any parameters transmitted by the call and returns parameter values to the client.

The second way in which it differs is that a process (called a **task** in Ada) can include several **entry**s, which other processes can call. Each **entry** maintains its own request queue, whereas a monitor has only one queue. A process gaining access to a monitor can call any of its procedures, whereas a process requesting a rendezvous must get in the queue for each entry it needs.

In addition to the production language Ada, rendezvous are implemented in CSP (Communicating Sequential Processes), an experimental language to explore concurrent programming facilities, and in Concurrent C.

Message Passing

Passing messages involves two issues: how sources and destinations are designated and how processes are synchronized.

A source and a destination define a *communications channel.* The simplest designation is *direct naming,* i.e., send data to a receiver or receive data from a sender, where "receiver" and "sender" are the names of processes. When multiple processes are sending or receiving messages, buffering may be necessary to hold a message until a receiving process is ready for it. Such a buffer is often called a *mailbox.* In the particular case where there is only one receiver but many senders, the mailbox is called a *port.* A particular program may involve several ports, but a receive statement will designate a single port. The idea here is that all requests for a particular service go into a single mailbox, or port. Another channel notion is that of a *pipe,* where output from one process is piped as input into another. Both processes can be running concurrently, with the second process receiving input from the pipeline as it is produced by the first process. Pipes, however, flow only one way. We have already looked at the rendezvous notion, where messages can be sent in any direction.

Synchronization of message passing differs from that for shared resources since no critical sections or regions need be maintained. Still, a process receiving a message must be ready to receive it, or the sending process must wait until the receiver is ready to process it. Waiting is usually managed by a queue or queues.

There are four basic message passing models:

Point-to-Point. The simplest message passing technique involves one process sending a message to another, which receives it. Some languages, such as SR and Concurrent C, provide for conditional receipt. For example, a request in Concurrent C to open a file, if it isn't locked, can be coded as follows [Bal, 1989]:

```
accept open(f) suchthat not_locked(f)
    {
    ... open process coded here...
    }
```

If the file f is locked, the request will not be accepted. Point-to-point schemes are *symmetric* if both the calling and receiving processes name each other. The schema above is *asymmetric* because the receiver does not name the sender. In this case, a sender requesting that a file be opened is willing for it to be opened by any process capable of doing so.

Point-to-point messages can be passed *synchronously* or *asynchronously.* In synchronous passing, the sending process is blocked until the receiver is ready to accept it. If passing is asynchronous, the sender continues to execute even though its message has not been accepted. In a synchronous system, there can be only one message pending from any process, while there may be several as yet to be answered messages from an asynchronous sender. Occam, the assembly language for transputers and a descendent of CSP, passes messages synchronously, while NIL (Network Implementation Language) is implemented asynchronously.

Rendezvous. We have already discussed rendezvous, based on the three concepts: **entry** declarations, **entry** calls, and **accept** statements. The rendezvous is fully synchronous, involving only two processes: the sender, which is suspended until accepted, and the receiver.

Remote Procedure Calls (RPCs). RPCs are much like the processes used to accomplish rendezvous. They are intended, however, to have exactly the same meanings as regular procedures. When this can be achieved, it permits the coding of concurrent processes in traditional procedural languages and allows conventional programs to be ported into the synchronizing system. RPCs have been considered for use with Modula-2 and implemented in the V operating system and in Concurrent CLU.

One-to-Many Message Passing. One-to-many message passing is also called *broadcasting*, as it behaves much like a radio station, where all receivers hear the same message. One type is *unbuffered*, so that a message sent can be picked up only by those processes ready to receive it. If messages are *buffered*, they can remain in the buffer indefinitely so that processes can receive them at any time. One language implementing one-to-many message passing is Broadcasting Sequential Processes (BSP), another descendent of CSP.

EXERCISES 5.3
1. A cafeteria line is a good application for parallel processing. Customers are joining the line at the same time as others are leaving it. This situation typifies a producer-consumer problem, where one cannot "consume" an item until it has been "produced," but consumers and producers can work in parallel. Write an informal algorithm to simulate a cafeteria line, with two processes, MakeLunch and BuyLunch, operating in parallel. Test it out with some simulated customers. Try to avoid:
   • Starvation: A buyer waits forever while lunches get made.
   • Alternation: A second lunch does not get made until the first one is sold.
   • Deadlock: A lunch preparer waits for a signal to make another lunch, while a buyer waits for a signal to buy one.
2. Use five binary semaphores, $Chopstick_0$ to $Chopstick_4$, and write Philosopher Processes P_i that will run in parallel to implement the Dining Philosophers problem. The critical section will include the statement Eat and should be surrounded by Wait and Signal operations. Initially, each $Chopstick_i$ should be set **up** to indicate its availability.
3. To what does a process have access when it "enters a monitor"?

5.4
SOME SYNCHRONIZATION SOLUTIONS

Various solutions to either CPU sharing or parallel execution have been implemented. We will look at some of these below.

Semaphores in ALGOL 68, C, and Pascal S

ALGOL 68

ALGOL 68 was the first language with a built-in semaphore, and its two operations, **up** and **down**. ALGOL's **sema** mode (type) provides for several processes to execute in parallel, with a counter keeping track of how long to wait for communication from another process. Thus ALGOL 68 provides the possibility of avoiding deadlock from greedy processes. When the counter reaches some preassigned limit, a running process that had executed a **down** on a particular semaphore will be forced to execute an **up**, which will allow the next waiting process to access shared resources.

C

C running under the UNIX operating system has a semaphore and its operations provided in a library in three system files, with headers sys/types.h, sys/ipc.h, and sys/sem.h. Two of the operations are:

```
sem1 = semget(...), which creates a semaphore named sem1
semctl(sem1,...,val), which resets sem1 to val
```

The operations semaphore_send and semaphore_wait, implementing Signal and Wait, are accessed using semop. For example, semop(semaphore_send,...) will execute a signal.

Semaphores written in C can be used with UNIX's fork, execl, and wait operations. C (and UNIX) manage memory in various ways. fork, execl, and wait allow a running (*parent*) program to be suspended while another program executes and uses the same memory locations. A call to fork produces a new copy of the parent program, and execl(child_name,a1,a2,...,an,0) allows a new program called child_name to run in place of this copy. wait forces the parent to remain suspended until the child completes. A user can command UNIX to run two or more programs "simultaneously" using UNIX's & operator.

```
$ payroll hours employee payment & ed
```

will start payroll executing, but allow the editor to interrupt it if necessary. If more than one processor is available, these operators can administer parallel processing.

A child can run concurrently with its parent, and can fork to its own child as well, as shown in Figure 5.4.1. A call to fork with no parameters creates a new copy of its parent process (process1), which runs concurrently with the parent. A subsequent call to execl(p2,a_1,...,a_n,0) replaces the copy of process1 with p2 and starts

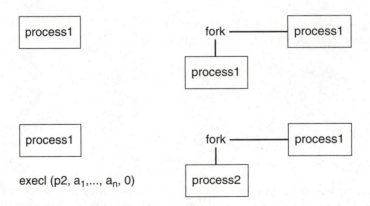

FIGURE 5.4.1
UNIX fork and execl operations to start two processes running concurrently

process p2 running concurrently with the parent, process1. Here p2 is a pointer to a character string naming process2, and $a_1, \ldots, a_n$ are pointers to the names of process2's arguments.

There is (theoretically) no limit to the number of processes that can be running concurrently on multiple processors or swapped in and out on a single processor. In the latter case, UNIX overlays a parent's memory with that needed by the child. Thus large programs can be run "in relatively limited memory, provided that it is possible to subdivide the program text and data in such a way that each and every executable [process] fits within the memory limitations of the machine" [Silvester, 1984] (see Figure 5.4.2).

A pipe can be established through the shell so that output from one program is piped directly as input into another. For example,

```
$ payroll | lpr
```

will pipe the output of the payroll program directly to the line printer. It accomplishes the same thing as the three commands:

```
$ payroll>scratch_file /* output of payroll to scratch_file   */

$ lpr<scratch_file     /* send scratch_file to the line printer */

$ rm scratch_file      /* remove scratch_file from the system */
```

Similarly,

```
$ payroll | sort | lpr
```

will pipe payroll output to the sort program, and sort will pipe it to lpr, for a sorted listing. All three programs would start executing simultaneously, with possible pauses for output from another.

Pascal S

Pascal S stands for Sequential Pascal, and is an interpreter that can be implemented as an augmented subset of Pascal. The Pascal program pascals compiles Pascal S into pseudocode, called P-code, and then proceeds to read in and interpret a

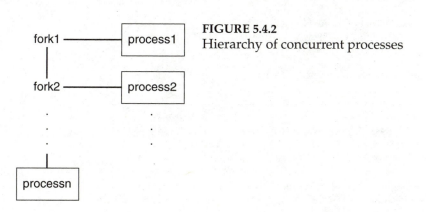

FIGURE 5.4.2
Hierarchy of concurrent processes

program written in Pascal S. Niklaus Wirth authored both Pascal and Pascal S, which was subsequently modified by M. Ben-Ari at Tel Aviv University. "Concurrent" processes are interleaved rather than run concurrently. Pascal was envisioned as a teaching rather than a production language, as is Pascal S. Anyone with a single processor capable of running Pascal can run Pascal S, but expect it to be inefficient in running time.

Concurrent processes P1, P2, .., Pn, are signalled by:

```
cobegin P1; P2;..; Pn coend;
```

Wirth describes this statement as follows: "The **cobegin** statement is a signal to the system that the enclosed procedures are not to be executed but are to be marked for concurrent execution. When the **coend** statement is reached, the execution of the main program is suspended and the concurrent processes are executed. The interleaving of the executions of these processes is not predictable and may change from one run to another. When all concurrent processes have terminated, then the main program is resumed at the statement following the **coend**" [Ben-Ari, 1982].

The Pascal S program in listing (5.4.1) is a solution to the Dining Philosophers problem, with one variation. The chopstick semaphore is up (1) if a chopstick is available, and down (0) if a philosopher is holding it. The hungry semaphore is up (1 thinking 4) if four or fewer philosophers ar e hungry, and down (room = 0) if there are five. This assures (via the pigeonhole principle)[3] that at least one philosopher will have access to two chopsticks. In this case, the number of hungry philosophers represents the number of holes, and the number of chopsticks represents five pigeons. The semaphore notHungry works as follows: when a Philosopher procedure starts, the philosopher first waits for notHungry to take on a value from 1 to 4, indicating that from zero to four philosophers are not hungry, and thus not interested in eating. This provides at least a chance that there might be two chopsticks available. When this occurs, wait(notHungry) executes by decreasing notHungry by 1. When he also finds his two adjacent chopsticks available (C[i]=1 and C[(i+1)mod 5]=1), he proceeds to eat, after which he signals that the two chopsticks are available for another philosopher and that he is no longer hungry (notHungry := (notHungry + 1) mod 5).

```
program DiningPhilosophers;                              (5.4.1)[4]
const SomeBigNumber = maxint;
var
    C: array[0..4] of {binary} semaphore;
    notHungry : semaphore;     {Assumes values 0..4.}
    i : integer;

procedure Philosopher(i : integer);
begin
    for j := 1 to SomeBigNumber do
        think;
      wait(notHungry);
```

---

[3]The pigeonhole principle states that if there are n holes and n+1 pigeons, at least one hole must accommodate two or more pigeons.

[4]From [Ben-Ari, 1982] with modifications.

```
            wait(C[i]);
            wait(C(i+1) mod 5]);
            eat;
            signal(C[i];
            signal(C[(i+1) mod 5]);
            signal(notHungry)
        end {for};
end; {P}
```

```
begin {main}
    notHungry := 4; {all 5 philosophers are notHungry}
    for i := 0 to 4 do C[i] := 1; {all chopsticks available}
    cobegin
        Philosopher(0);
        Philosopher(1);
        Philosopher(2);
        Philosopher(3);
        Philosopher(4);
    coend
end.
```

Monitor and Process Types in Concurrent Pascal

Recall that a buffer is an area of storage on a disk used to store input and output data temporarily. It can also be implemented in Concurrent Pascal using a monitor.

There are two ways to enter the buffer, Send and Receive. Send sends a page to the buffer from a calling process, and Receive returns a page to a process from the buffer. In the DiskBuffer monitor, the entries are procedures and are called from some process, which controls an input or output device. These controllers cannot access a VirtualDisk directly, only through a monitor procedure labeled Entry. Coordination of possibly concurrently running processes calling Send and Receive is accomplished within the monitor.

```
type DiskBuffer =                                              (5.4.2)[5]
    monitor(ConsoleAccess, DiskAccess: Resource;
        Base, Limit: integer);
var                         {shared data}
    disk: VirtualDisk; Sender, Receiver : queue;
    Head, Tail, Length : integer;
```

```
procedure entry Send(Block: Page);
{sends a page from a calling procedure to the disk buffer}
begin
    if Length = Limit then delay(sender); {buffer full, wait}
    disk.write(Base + Tail, Block);
    Tail:= (Tail + 1) mod Limit;
    Length:= Length + 1;
    continue(Receiver)
{transfers control to Receive if there is something in its queue, Receiver}
end;
```

---

[5][Brinch Hansen, 1978]

```
procedure entry Receive(var Block: Page);
{returns a page to the calling process}
begin
...
end;

begin
    init disk(ConsoleAccess, DiskAccess);
    {initialization operation not described here}
    Head:= 0;  Tail:= 0;  Length:= 0;
end.
```

Looking at the code in listing (5.4.2) from the top down, we first see that `DiskBuffer` is to be a **monitor** type with four parameters. The first two, `ConsoleAccess` and `DiskAccess`, will be variables of a system-dependent type, `Resource`. The second two provide for a base address where the `DiskBuffer` starts and a `Limit`, which fixes its size. The `VirtualDisk` type is a Concurrent Pascal class, which includes both data and associated operations. Two of these operations are `disk.write` and `disk.read`. Our buffer data will be of this class.

Concurrent Pascal includes a built-in type, `queue`. A queue can be associated with a monitor to manage multiple processes waiting for a mutually requested resource. A calling process, if not delayed in the `queue`, will have exclusive access to the shared variables `disk`, `Head`, `Tail`, and `Length` from the **begin** of the entry called until reaching the **continue** statement. `Head` is initialized to 0, the relative address of the start of the buffer. `Tail`, which is the relative address of the end (in pages) of the buffer, is also initialized to 0, indicating an empty buffer.

The `Send` procedure includes three statements that must be executed before a calling process, which has successfully gained entry to `Send` without being delayed, gives up shared data to a process entering the `Receive` procedure. These write to the buffer and increment `Tail` and `Length`.

Although the `DiskBuffer` monitor does not provide for it, Concurrent Pascal monitors can include calls to other monitors.

The Rendezvous in Ada and Concurrent C

Ada

Ada's program unit with potential for running in parallel with other units is called a **task**. It is syntactically similar to a **package**, having a specification and a body.

```
task T is          --specification                              (5.4.3)⁶
...
end T;

task body T is     -- body
...
end T;
```

Let's look at a simple example of tasks that might run concurrently. Suppose we're planning a party.

```
procedure Plan_Party is                                              (5.4.4)
   task Invitations;

   task body Invitations is
   begin
      Write_Invitations;
      Mail_Them;
   end Invitations;

   task Clean;

   task body Clean is
   begin
      Clean_House;
   end Clean;

begin
   Prepare_Food;
end Plan_Party;
```

Plan_Party is the parent unit for the two tasks Invitations and Clean. When **procedure** Plan_Party is running, and the **begin** for this parent unit is reached, the two local tasks automatically start running as well. The **end** for Plan_Party cannot be executed until all local tasks have terminated. In the schema above, the three procedures, Invitations, Clean, and Prepare_Food, run concurrently, but in no particular order. There is no communication between them. Depending on the compiler and on the hardware, these three procedures could run in parallel or on a single processor using some sort of time-sharing.

Now let's fancy up the party a bit, so the tasks can communicate with each other. In Ada, this is accomplished by one task (the callee), **accept**ing an **entry** into it when called by another task. An **entry** is a procedure call, but what gets done is determined by the task accepting the call (see listing (5.4.5)).

```
procedure Plan_Party is                                              (5.4.5)
   type Name_List is array (integer range <>) of String(1..50);
   task Invitations is
      entry Guest_List(Names: in Name_List);
   end Invitations;

   task body Invitations is
      Guests: Name_List;
   begin
      accept Guest_List(Names: in Name_List) do
         Guests:= Names;
      end Guest_List;
      Write_Invitations;
      Mail_Them;
   end Invitations;
```

```
    task Clean;

    task body Clean is
    begin
        Clean_House;
    end Clean;

    G: Name_List;

begin
    Prepare_Food;
    Read_List(G);
    Invitations.Guest_List(G);
end Plan_Party;
```

Here, Plan_Party is the caller to Invitations. Since all three tasks, Plan_Party, Invitations, and Clean, begin simultaneously, Invitations must wait to **accept** the **entry** Guest_List until it is sent by the main procedure. What happens during the **accept...do...end;** is rendezvous.

A simple but practical tasking example is that of an input/output buffer for a single character, as shown in listing (5.4.6).

```
task Char_Buffer is                                            (5.4.6)
    entry Read  (C: out Character);    --Read from buffer
    entry Write (C: in Character);     --Write to buffer
end Char_Buffer;

task body Char_Buffer is
    Full: Booolean := False;
    Ch: Character;
    loop
        select
            when Full =>
                accept Read(C: out Character) do
                    C := Ch;
                end Read;
                Full := False;
            or
                when not Full =>
                accept Write(C: in Character) do
                    Ch := C;
                end Write;
                Full := True;
            or terminate;
        end select;
    end loop;
end Char_Buffer;
```

As usual, there are a number of things to notice here. First of all, Char_Buffer. Read(...) and Char_Buffer.Write(...) will be called by other tasks. Each entry has an associated queue, so if several tasks are trying to Read or Write simultaneously, the calls will be queued and processed in First-In–First-Out (FIFO) order. We must, of course, have something in a buffer before it can be Read from. Thus **accept** Read is guarded by the **when** Full expression. The **select** statement means that either of the **accept** statements may be chosen in no particular order. In particular, if the buffer is empty and Full = False, the Char_Buffer task may **select** a call from the Write queue before accepting a Read.

Another way to handle a read/write character buffer might be to set up Read_Char and Write_Char as two tasks and start them running simultaneously, as shown in listing (5.4.7).

```
procedure Buffer_Tasks;                                      (5.4.7)
   Full: boolean := False;
   pragma Shared (Full);
   Ch: Character;
   pragma Shared(Ch);

   task Read_Char is
      entry Read(C: out Character);
   end Read_Char;

   task Write_Char is
      entry Write(C: in Character);
   end Write_Char;

   task body Read_Char is
   begin
      loop
         when Full =>
            accept Read(C: out Character) do
               C := Ch;
               Full := False;
            end Read;
      end loop;
   end Read_Char;

   task body Write_Char is
   begin
      loop
         accept Write(C: in Character) do
            Ch := C;
            Full := True;
         end Write;
      end loop;
   end Write_Char;

begin
   --Set both Read_Char and Write_Char running
   ...
end Buffer_Tasks;
```

An Ada **pragma** is a compiler directive. The Shared **pragma**, to implement memory sharing, guarantees two things. First, if a shared variable, such as Ch or Full above, is read in a critical section (CS) in a task, it will not be updated by any other task until the CS is exited. In listing (5.4.7), such a CS occurs for Ch between **accept** Read and its **end**. Second, if a shared variable is updated in a CS, it will not be either read or updated by any other task until the CS is exited. This occurs between **accept** Write and its **end** for Ch, and in both **accept** statements for Full.

Ada implements neither semaphores nor monitors, so these must be programmed in if we wish to avoid the synchronization problems discussed in section 5.3. Only simple or **access** (pointer) variables may be declared Shared, so we must devise other means for protecting structured data. We will address this in Lab 5.1, where we will construct a read/write buffer larger than a single character.

Ada's tasks may be dynamic as well as static. That is, they can be created or destroyed as a program runs. Suppose we wished to create Char_Buffer tasks as needed in a program, and also wanted the capability of having more than one such buffer at a time. To achieve this, we would add the reserved word **type** to the task declaration, and then create **access** type values pointing to the tasks, as shown in listing (5.4.8).

```
task type Char_Buffer is                                    (5.4.8)
   entry Read  (C: out Character);
   entry Write (C: in Character);
end Char_Buffer;

type Buffer_Ptr is access Char_Buffer;
P, Q: Buffer_Ptr;

begin
   ...
   P := new Buffer_Ptr;
   Q := new Buffer_Ptr;
   ...
   P := null;
   Q := null;
   ...
end;
```

Ada does not destroy dynamically created objects through a procedure like **dispose**. This was a Pascal design decision to eliminate dangling pointers that point to nonexistent data objects. In Ada, assigning an **access** variable the value **null** makes objects inaccessible. Their storage locations will be released when program execution exits the scope of the objects.

Concurrent C

The C language has no constructs for concurrent processing, although we saw above how concurrently running procedures could be implemented using directives to the UNIX operating system. Concurrent C was developed to provide a **process** type and its associated operations as concurrent language features. It does not implement memory-sharing, but employs synchronous message passing with running of the client program blocked until service has been received. It differs from Ada in several ways, of which we will mention four here. First, C's transactions are similar to function calls, whereas in Ada they are like procedures. This means that a call can appear anywhere that a function would be appropriate, whereas in Ada, a call is always a statement. C provides for user-specified process priorities, while in Ada they are always processed in FIFO order. C allows a transaction call with parameters so that only those calls meeting certain criteria are served. In Ada, when a main block with tasks is entered, its tasks are activated as well and terminated when the block is exited. In Concurrent C, one must activate each process, e.g.,

```
process buffer b;
b = create buffer(128);
```

It can also be terminated via c_abort(b);. Other more subtle differences can be found in [Gehani, 1986].

Concurrent C has a type, **process**, which requires a specification (**spec**) and a **body** part. The **spec** is visible to other processes, while the **body** is not. A server process includes an **accept** statement to receive transaction (**trans**) calls. Let's look at the Dining Philosophers implemented in Concurrent C, as shown in listing (5.4.9).

```
process spec Chopstick()                                               (5.4.9)[7]
{
 trans void pick_up();
 trans void put_down();
};

process spec Philosopher(
            int id, process Chopstick left, process Chopstick right);

#define LIFE_LIMIT 100000

process body Philosopher(id, left, right)
{
  int times_eaten;
  for (times_eaten = 0; times_eaten != LIFE_LIMIT; times_eaten++)
    { /* think, then enter dining room */
      /* pick up Chopsticks*/
         right.pick_up();
         left.pick_up();
      /*eat */
         printf("Philosopher %d: *burp*\n", id);
      /*put down Chopsticks */
         left.put_down();
         right.put_down();
      /*get up and leave dining room */
    }
```

---

[7]Dining Philosophers in Concurrent C. Reproduced with permission from N.H. Gehani and W.D. Roome, *Concurrent C*, © 1986 by John Wiley & Sons.

```
process body Chopstick()
{
  for(;;)                      /*forever */
    select
    {
      accept pick_up();
      accept put_down();
    or
      terminate;
    }
}

main()
{
  process Chopstick f[5];      /*array of five chopsticks */
  int j;

  /*first create the chopsticks, then create the Philosophers */
  for (j = 0; j < 5; j++)
    f[j] = create Chopstick();
  for (j = 0; j < 5; j++)
    create Philosopher(j, f[j], f[(j+1) %8 5]);
}
```

Each philosopher exists only until he has eaten 100,000 times. The chopsticks go on forever. However, once all the philosophers have terminated, the chopsticks have nothing else to do, and so the **or** option of the **select** statement is chosen and each chopstick terminates. Then, since all the processes have completed, the Concurrent C program main can also terminate.

LAB 5.1: SIMULATION OF PARALLEL PROCESSING: ADA

Objectives (Labs can be found in the *Instructor's Manual.*)

1. To experiment with different methods of synchronizing a buffer implemented through tasks.
2. To see what happens when the buffer is accessed by only one outside task or by several.
3. To devise a synchronization scheme for two client tasks using the buffer so that string code from the two clients does not intermix.

Message Passing in Occam

In Occam, messages are sent through channels that are visible to both the calling and the accepting processes. Associated with each channel is a protocol, which describes the type of data that can be sent through each channel. A channel and the

---

[8]Remember that % is the mod operator in C.

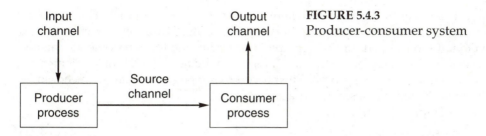

FIGURE 5.4.3
Producer-consumer system

two processes it connects are established when the program declaring them is compiled, and neither the processes nor the channel can be allocated at run time. A message is output to the channel by one process and input to the other process from the channel. To synchronize channel communication, the first process to undertake either input or output upon a channel must wait until the other process is ready for either output from or input to the channel. Any further operations by a process are suspended during a wait. If bidirectional communication is desired, i.e., data is input to Process2 from Process1's output, and data from Process2's subsequent output input to Process1, then two channels must be established.

The producer-consumer problem consists of one or more producers and one or more consumers working concurrently with a consumption possible only if an item has been produced and is available. The simplest version is where one producer produces items for a single consumer, as shown in Figure 5.4.3.

The producer must not output an item until the consumer is ready to input and process it. An Occam outline of the problem is:

```
{{{F OCCEXAMP.OCC                                                    (5.4.10)

--file occexamp.occ
#INCLUDE "hostio.inc"
PROC prodcon (CHAN OF SP fs, ts, [] INT memory)⁹
  #USE "hostio.lib"
  CHAN OF BYTE input, output, source

  ...   PROC producer

  ...   PROC consumer

  ...   PROC interface

  PAR
    interface (fs, ts, input, output)
    producer(input, source)
    consumer(output, source)
  :

}}}
```

---

[9] fs and ts are channels from and to the host file server, as described in the "Occam 2 Toolset User Manual," which is part of the CSA Transputer Education Kit. The channel type is indicated by the key words **CHAN OF**. The SP protocol used by the host file's channels is defined in "hostio.inc".

The curly brackets indicate a *fold,* where program text can be hidden. Here we used the Occam 2 toolset, which runs on the CSA Transputer Education Kit and includes the Origami folding editor. In a complete program, the folds become comments, preceded by "---", replacing the "...". Folds can be nested. Occam is oriented toward screen use, so if the program text becomes too large for a single screen, some of it can be folded into a smaller space.

The complete program is:

(5.4.11)

```
--file occexamp.occ
#INCLUDE "hostio.inc"
PROC prodcon (CHAN OF fs, ts SP, [] INT memory)
  #USE "hostio.lib"
  CHAN OF BYTE input, output, source

  --{{{  PROC producer
  PROC producer(CHAN OF BYTE input, source.ch)
    BYTE x:
    WHILE TRUE
      SEQ                              -- process sequentially
        input ? x
        source.ch ! x
  :
  --}}}

  --{{{  PROC consumer
  PROC consumer(CHAN OF BYTE output, destination.ch)
    BYTE y:
    WHILE TRUE
      SEQ
        destination.ch ? y
        output ! y
  :
  --}}}

  --{{{  PROC interface
  PROC interface(CHAN OF fs,ts, SP,CHAN OF BYTE to.prod,from.cons)
    BOOL done:
    BYTE ch1, ch2, result:
    VAL end IS '**':
    SEQ
      so.write.nl(fs,ts)               -- newline
      done := FALSE
      WHILE NOT done
        SEQ
          so.getkey(fs, ts ch1, result)  -- wait for a key, no echo
          to.prod ! ch1                  -- send to producer
          from.cons ? ch2                -- echo it on the screen
          IF
            ch2 = end
              done := TRUE
            TRUE
              SKIP[10]
```

---

[10]Occam requires an "else" statement for each **IF**. Here the dummy statement **SKIP** is used.

```
    so.exit(fs, ts, sps.success)
  :
--}}}

PAR
  interface (fs, ts, input, output)
  producer(input, source)
  consumer(output, source)
:
```

EXERCISES 5.4

1. a. Trace the Dining Philosophers in Pascal S (listing (5.4.1)) a few times to convince yourself that it really does work. Remember that the order in which the five `Philosopher(i)` procedures are called is indeterminate.

   b. Remove the `notHungry` loop (`wait(notHungry)..signal(notHungry)`) and trace the program again. Is it possible for a philosopher to starve without the room semaphore?

2. If `Head` is the relative address of the `DiskBuffer` of listing (5.4.2), what is the variable `Base`?

3. Complete the **entry** `Receive` for the `DiskBuffer` monitor of listing (5.4.2).

4. Why is it necessary to include a **terminate** clause in the `Char_Buffer` task of listing (5.4.6), and why is it not listed as an **entry**?

5. What would happen if we left the updating of `Full` outside the **accept** statements in the second buffer implementation of listing (5.4.7), as we did in the first Ada fragment of listing (5.4.6)?

6. Write code for an Ada task with two entries to implement Dijkstra's binary semaphore (listing (5.3.1)).

7. The Dining Philosophers program of listing (5.4.9) can lead to deadlock. When will this happen? Suggest how to avoid this problem. Notice also that output from the Philosophers processes can get mixed up if more than one tries to access standard output at the same time. How might this be resolved?

5.5
TUPLES AND OBJECTS

There are units of parallelism other than the the synchronized processes we have seen. Versions of the objects of Chapter 4 can also execute concurrently. Here methods act as processes running in parallel. A radically different paradigm called *tuple space* can also be used. Tuple space is a shared data space that is owned by none of the processes. Tuples containing both data and processes are extracted from and restored to the space as needed. We will consider these next.

The Tuple Space of Linda

Not all processes communicate through message passing or through shared memory locations. Both of these suffer from some degree of unreliability due to the necessity of programmer-managed synchronization. Linda,[11] developed at Yale University, is a language for parallel processing that implements tuple space. It acts like an associative memory, associating a base address with a key in a fast store. Messages can, but need not, be passed using tuples. Linda itself is not a fully developed production-quality language, but has been embedded in several languages, including Ada and C. In what follows, we will use the C-Linda syntax.

A tuple is an ordered collection of data items, e.g., ("hello world", 22, 2.17). Tuple space is the collection of tuples placed in tuple space using the operators **out** and **eval**. There are four operations on tuples: **out**(t), **in**(T), **rd**(T), **eval**(t); and two predicates, **inp**() and **rdp**().

out(t) evaluates the tuple t and places it in tuple space. For example, **out**("hello world", 22, 2.17) creates a tuple and places it in tuple space.

in(T) matches the template (description) T with a tuple in tuple space if there is one, and removes it from tuple space. If no matching tuple is found, the calling process suspends until one is available. If more than one is found matching T, one is chosen arbitrarily to be removed. For example, **in**("hello world", ?i, ?f) removes a tuple with the first coordinate "hello world", second, any integer, and third, a float, assuming that i and f have previously been declared to be integer and float.

rd(T) functions much as **in**, but the matched tuple remains in tuple space. A copy of the matched tuple is returned. **rd** lets tuple space function as read-only memory, which can be shared by any number of running processes. If no matching tuple is found, the calling process blocks.

eval(t) is similar to **out**, except that the tuple is evaluated after, rather than before, being placed in tuple space. **eval** creates a new, active tuple (a new process); for example, **eval**(45, SomeFunction(x)) creates a new process, which runs in parallel with the process that called **eval**. The tuple (45, SomeFunction(x)) is active as long as SomeFunction is running, and passive when SomeFunction terminates.

The two predicate operations (returning either true or false) are **inp**() and **rdp**(). They behave just like **in** and **rd**, but do not block the calling process. If no match is found, false (0 in C-Linda) is returned and processing can continue.

The idea, put simply, is that a process wishing to alter data will remove a tuple from tuple space using an **in**, process the data, and then return it to tuple space using **out**. Any other process will be unable to access that tuple until it is returned. Messages can also be sent using **out** and received using **in**.

Implementations of Linda include a preprocessor that uses queues and semaphores, among other techniques, to speed up tuple searches. A Linda Kernel is included in the QIX operating system, developed to implement parallel processing. Its originators claim it to be more efficient than UNIX, while maintaining considerable compatibility with it. They also claim that it makes writing parallel programs easier and that they are independent of the particular architecture being used.

---

[11]The name "Linda" is an in-joke. Ada was named after Ada Lovelace, reputedly the first female computer programmer, who worked with Charles Babbage on his analytical engine. At the time the Linda language was being developed, there was a female porn star named Linda Lovelace. So, with youthful good humor and in an attempt to keep languages "all in the family," David Gelerntner named his new language after the modern Lovelace—Linda.

David Gelernter, Linda's originator [Markoff, 1992], believes that parallel processing using an ordinary network of workstations, or even PCs, will characterize the modern office of the future. At least one Wall Street firm is conducting its daily trading activity using Linda on a network and also using idle CPU cycles from various machines throughout the day to generate large mathematical models of financial systems.

Linda processes are loosely coupled, i.e., without shared memory, allowing the programmer to ignore many of the synchronization problems that occur in shared memory systems. A simple C-Linda program for simulating a ping-pong game with two players, which demonstrates process communication, is shown in listing (5.5.1).

```
/* PING_PONG.CL - Two communicating processes */                    (5.5.1)[12]

#define NUM_PING_PONGS 1000

real_main()
{
    int ping(), pong();         /* the two cooperating processes */

    eval(ping());               /* places ping in tuple space and
                                   forks a new process to perform
                                   the evaluation */

    eval(pong())
}
ping()                          /* definition of ping */
{
    int i;
    for (i = 0; i < NUM_PING_PONGS; ++)
    { out("ping");              /* evaluate and then return ping to
                                   tuple space */
      in("pong");               /* remove pong from tuple space */
    }
}
pong()
{
    int i;
    for (i = 0; i < NUM_PING_PONGS; ++)
    { in("ping");               /* remove ping from tuple space */
      out("pong");              /* evaluate and then return pong to
                                   tuple space */
    }
}
```

This program does nothing but switch control back and forth between ping and pong. Both processes start executing simultaneously, with ping being evaluated after pong removes it from tuple space. After executing, ping removes pong from tuple space, which can then be evaluated when the pong process reaches **out**("pong"). If we added

---

[12]Taken from the C-Linda Reference Manual®, Scientific Computing Associates, New Haven, CT.

a little C graphics to each process after each **out**, we could see the "ball" go back and forth on the screen. Perhaps ping could send the ball from left to right and pong from right to left.

C-Linda also has a facility for timing modules. This acts like a stopwatch and is useful for collecting statistics on parallel execution and speed-up factors. There are also several levels of tuple tracing that can be switched on or off.

A data structure, such as an array, can be distributed to several tuples, e.g., each row or element could occupy a separate tuple. A program could then be written with a single master and as many workers as there were array tuples, all running simultaneously, to process the array. The loops of listing (5.5.2) compute the "fives" times table row, m = [0,5,10,15,20,25,30,35,40,45].

(5.5.2)

```
#define FALSE 0
#define TRUE  1

int dim = 9;
int workers = #processors available
int *m[dim];
int worker();

for (i = 0; i <= dim; ++i)
    out("fivesrow", i, FALSE, m[i]);   /*distribute array in ten tuples*/

/*start workers*/
for (i = 0; i <= dim; ++i){
    eval("function", i, worker());
}

worker(){
    int i, *p;
    in("fivesrow",?i, FALSE, ?p); /*grab any unprocessed tuple available*/
    *p = i * 5;                   /*compute value for *p[i]*/
    out("fivesrow",i, TRUE, p)    /*put it back in tuple space*/
}
```

The declarations are C-code. The first loop distributes the array element locations to separate tuples. FALSE indicates that the element value has not yet been computed. Note that ?i is converted to i and ?p to p after p is evaluated and assigned to m[i]. Each of the worker processes started by the second loop evaluates any unprocessed tuple in the distributed array. If there are fewer processors than the number dim of tuples to be processed, each processor will have to evaluate the worker function more than once. Before processing, the third tuple t is ("fivesrow", 3, 0, p), where p points to the fourth element of the array m[3]. After **out**(t), *p = 15, and the tuple is ("fivesrow", 3, 1, p).

In Lab 5.2, you will be asked to finish the producer-consumer program for two producers and one consumer, involving communication among three processes running in parallel.

LAB 5.2: PRODUCERS-CONSUMERS: PASCAL S/OCCAM 2/C-LINDA

Objectives (Labs can be found in the *Instructor's Manual.*)

1. To see three cooperating processes as implemented in a concurrent language.
2. To experiment with different solutions to the producer-consumer problem using concurrency.
3. To try a different sort of solution—the tuple space of Linda.

You will be asked to program two Producer processes and a Consumer process in the languages selected by your instructor.

Objects As Units of Parallelism

Object-based or object-oriented programming is the hottest area in both programming language research and applications for the nineties. Thus, using objects as units of parallelism has received a fair amount of attention. Objects may be considered as "independent abstract machines that interact in response to messages" [Caromel, 1989]. But most attempts to implement concurrently executing objects do not include asynchronous, randomly timed message passing. Remote procedure calls, where one object calls a procedure in another object and waits for a reply, is the preferred method. This is so in languages like Concurrent Smalltalk, ABCL/1, and Orient85. Emerald, developed at the University of Washington, also supports concurrent processes. It is not object-oriented, but object-based, as inheritance is not supported.

Caromel [Caromel, 1989, 1993] proposes a model for parallel object-oriented languages that fosters the strengths of objects—reusability, extendibility, and highly readable programs. Experimentation with this model is currently being pursued in Nancy, France, using the object language Eiffel. This implementation employs an object called PROCESS, with two methods, Create and Live. Create allows the creation of an instance of a PROCESS object, which proceeds to execute its Live routine. When this routine completes, the PROCESS dies. Eiffel supports multiple inheritance, where a single object can inherit from more than one superclass, thus any appropriate object could become a PROCESS by inheriting the PROCESS methods.

Another similar, but somewhat different, extension of Eiffel [Karaorman, 1993] allows any object to inherit from the class CONCURRENCY, which inherits from ICP, the UNIX System Interprocess Communication Primitives. CONCURRENCY requires any class inheriting from it to provide its own scheduler.

The focus of object-oriented concurrency is to model situations where objects act together, rather than to speed up program execution. This is a new and growing area of research, including efforts to combine Concurrent C with its object-oriented cousin C++ as a single extension to C.

5.6
MANAGING PARTIAL FAILURE

When messages are passed, several things can go wrong:

1. The message can be lost by the network.
2. The reply can be lost.
3. The server can crash before sending the reply.

One way to handle these situations is for the client to declare a pause for a specified period of time. If the desired reply is not received when the time expires, it is assumed that one of the three problems above occurred and remedial action is taken. This could be as simple as resending the request. In a situation like the second, however, this may not be appropriate. Processes often exhibit persistence, where state values are maintained from invocation to invocation. For example, suppose the server incremented a counter N and remembered it. Resending a request would result in N being increased twice, even though only one reply was returned. One possible solution to this problem is to make the server atomic, that is, all or nothing. Either it replies successfully, or the previous state is restored.

Ada tasks are quite unrestricted, which can lead to both sequencing and deadness errors. A sequencing error occurs when tasks communicate in an unanticipated order. A task is dead when it cannot proceed further. One particular possibility is *circular deadlock,* as shown in Figure 5.6.1, where each task has called the next in the circle, which cannot accept it until it rendezvous with the one ahead.

Concurrently running tasks are particularly hard to debug because they may run differently each time they are invoked. Debugging tools that are being developed are based on run-time monitoring, where a sequence of program "snapshots" are taken to pinpoint the states of selected running processes when one went dead.

Because of the inconsistencies that occur from one run to the next, an axiomatic proof system is particularly appropriate for validating concurrent processes.

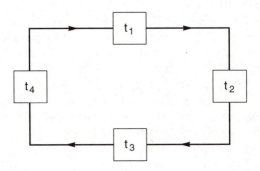

FIGURE 5.6.1
Circular deadlock

5.7
SUMMARY

Distributed programming includes several models. All involve the use of multiple processors, cooperation among the processors, and handling the failure of one or more concurrently running processes while others continue. There are four main models:

1. Those based on shared memory
2. Those based on asynchronous (nonblocking) message passing
3. Those based on synchronous (blocking) message passing
4. A combination of message passing and shared memory

Ada implements the fourth model, while Concurrent C implements the third. No matter which model is chosen, cooperating processes must be synchronized if information is to be exchanged. Early mechanisms for synchronization were the semaphore and monitor. A semaphore controls access to a critical section of code. A process that begins executing this critical code cannot be interrupted until it has completed execution of that code. Monitors contain shared variables and any operations allowed on them. They communicate with other monitors and can also be accessed by cooperating processes.

The rendezvous is a third mechanism for synchronizing processes. It is based on the client/server model, where a client requests service and then waits until it has been provided. Occam also implements the rendezvous, but here it is called message passing. Ada's processing units, called tasks, can be created and destroyed at run time, while those in Occam, called processes, are static, as are its communication channels.

Several languages have been developed to experiment with concurrency on a single processor. This is sometimes called multiprogramming. Processes are thought of as operating concurrently, but are actually implemented through being swapped in and out of a single CPU. ALGOL 68, C, Modula-2, Pascal S, and Concurrent Pascal are examples of such languages.

A fifth model for concurrency is the tuple space of Linda. Here processes and their associated variables are created and destroyed as tuples in a memory associated with, but separate from, the RAM of each process. Linda's creators find this model easier to imagine than message passing and shared memories. Linda has been implemented as a preprocessor to either C or Ada.

Not all theorists agree that procedurally oriented languages provide the best vehicle for implementing concurrency. The VonNeumann bottleneck, where only one word is transferred in or out of memory at each processor cycle, still causes problems. We will look at notions for parallel processing using functions in Chapter 8, after the reader is more familiar with functional languages themselves. Processing logical clauses in parallel will be considered in Chapter 7.

5.8
NOTES ON REFERENCES

[Wegner, 1983] provides a good discussion of the differences between monitors and the rendezvous concept. He uses Ada and CSP as examples of languages implementing rendezvous. They implement a monitor in Ada using the monitor definition of Brinch Hansen [Brinch Hansen, 1978].

[Barnes, 1994, 1996] is a quite literate introduction to Ada and Ada95 written by John Barnes, one of the key members of the Ada design team. His special concerns included tasking.

A nice presentation of Concurrent C, with lots of elementary example programs, is [Gehani, 1986]. It describes a version implemented under UNIX for a single processor. At the time the paper was written, a version for distributed systems was under development at Bell Labs.

An "Implementation Kit" for Pascal S is contained in Appendix A of [Ben-Ari, 1982]. The Kit provides all the Pascal program code needed to implement a Pascal S interpreter running as a Pascal program. The second edition of this book [Ben-Ari, 1990], which is divided into three parts, makes no reference to Pascal S. Part I considers shared memory systems, semaphores, and monitors. Part II deals with message passing and looks at the languages Ada, Occam, and Linda. Part III discusses implementation issues, with special attention given to real-time systems, where response time may be an issue.

[Kerridge, 1987] is a good tutorial on Occam that provides a number of elementary programs as well as a discussion of how Occam works with transputers.

For brief discussions of Linda, the reader is referred to [Leler, 1990], [Markoff, 1992], or to [Carriero, 1989]. The second paper compares Linda to message-passing, object-oriented, logic, and functional models for concurrent programming.

Four good tutorials on parallel programming stand out, three from the ACM and the fourth from the IEEE. These are [Brinch Hansen, 1978], [Andrews, 1983], [Bal, 1989], and [Shatz, 1989]. Included in Shatz is a good discussion of debugging Ada tasks.

The September 1993 issue of the *Communications of the ACM* is devoted to concurrent object-oriented programming. It includes [Caromel, 1993] and [Karaorman, 1993], as well as articles on operating systems supporting concurrency, and a concurrent successor to Trellis/Owl called DOWL.

PART III

Formal Languages and Automata

This section contains one chapter, in which we will begin looking at languages in a more theoretical way. We also include topics on the practical application of these theoretical concepts to programming languages and compiler design.

Chomsky's hierarchy of formal language types provides the structure for the material, from Type 3 (the most restrictive) to Type 0, which includes all the other types. We look particularly at Type 3, regular grammars, because of their common use in compilers in recognizing the tokens, or program elements, of a language. Type 2, context-free grammars, are often used to describe how these tokens are combined to form valid language constructs. Techniques used give some insight into the parsing of a program, and the understanding of its semantics (meaning).

CHAPTER 6
FORMAL LANGUAGES

6.0	**In this Chapter**	**245**
6.1	**Formal Languages**	**246**
	Formal Languages Defined	247
	The Chomsky Hierarchy of Formal	
	Languages	249
	Historical Vignette: Language	
	Classifications: Noam Chomsky	250
	Type 3: Regular Grammars	251
	Type 2: Context-Free Grammars	252
	Type 1: Context-Sensitive	
	Grammars	253
	Linear-Bounded Automata (LBAs)	254
	Historical Vignette: Alan Turing:	
	What Machines Can't Do	256
	Type 0: Unrestricted Grammars	258
	Exercises 6.1	260
6.2	**Regular Grammars**	**260**
	Regular Expressions	261
	Finite Automata (FAs, NFAs	
	and DFAs)	262

	Applications	265
	Exercises 6.2	266
6.3	**Context-Free Grammars (CFGs)**	**267**
	Push-Down Automata (PDAs)	268
	Parse Trees	272
	Ambiguous Grammars	272
	Applications	274
	Normal Forms	275
	Chomsky Normal Form (CNF)	275
	Backus Normal Form (BNF)	275
	Syntax Diagrams	277
	Exercises 6.3	278
6.4	**Grammars for Natural**	
	Languages	**279**
	Exercises 6.4	281
6.5	**Summary**	**281**
6.6	**Notes on References**	**282**

CHAPTER 6

Formal Languages

Chapter 2 dealt with abstraction, the distillation of a language construct to its stripped-down essential form. It is in this spirit that we will study formal languages. As you may remember, we looked at three aspects of abstraction: data, control, and modularization. Here we will not consider language constructs, but syntax, the written form a language may take. We will mention semantics, the intended meaning of syntax, only briefly, leaving a fuller treatment for a later course.

The purpose of a language is to communicate, either with other people, a computer, or some other entity. The party receiving our communication must understand it as well as the writer. Computer languages are no exception to this requirement. Both other people and a computer must understand the language in which the programmer writes. Since a machine is involved, programming languages must be very precise. They must conform to fixed rules. Here we will study the rules and symbols of the formal languages suitable for communicating with computers.

This chapter is intended for those students who do not plan to include a full course in Compiler Design or Computation Theory in their undergraduate course of study. Rather than address the question of which programming language is best for performing a particular task, we will deal with what characteristics any computer language must have to be recognized by a computer, how formal languages are constructed, and how machines are built to recognize these languages.

6.0
IN THIS CHAPTER

We begin by looking at formal ways of specifying a grammar. There are four recognized types of formal languages (plus some subtypes), each of which can achieve different things and is useful for different tasks. Following Chomsky's hierarchy, we begin with the most restrictive, Type 3, proceed through Types 2 and 1, and end with Type 0, which includes all the others. We will describe as briefly as possible three aspects of each type:

- What differentiates the type from the next higher type
- The form of grammar rules for languages of the type
- The theoretical machine that recognizes valid words of the type

Following that, we will take a closer look at Type 3, regular grammars, and the related regular expressions, since they are of practical use in defining the tokens of a language. Then we consider Type 2, context-free grammars, and their use in recognizing legal phrases in the grammar. Finally, we will take a brief look at grammars for natural languages.

6.1
FORMAL LANGUAGES

The *lexical* structure of a language is the form of its *tokens*.[1] *Syntax* describes the statements that will be accepted as correct by a compiler or interpreter for the language. Syntax, or precisely what constitutes a valid statement, is defined by a grammar which generates a formal language. A *formal language* is the set of syntactically correct statements.

A *grammar* consists of a finite list of symbols, called an alphabet, a finite list of rules for forming words from the alphabet, and possibly another set of rules for forming statements from words. As an example, consider the mini-language Beach-Fun.

Alphabet:	Nouns: {Joe, Jane}
	Verbs: {swims, sails}
	Alphabet = Nouns ∪ Verbs ∪ {' ', .}[2]
Rule:	S is a statement of Beach-Fun if S is of the form N V., where N ∈ Nouns, followed by a space, followed by V ∈ Verbs, followed by a period.

The language Beach-Fun is then the four statements {Joe swims., Jane swims., Joe sails., Jane sails.}

A computer, although essentially composed of binary strings and operations on them, can also be thought of as a *virtual machine*, behaving as if it had been designed to recognize exactly one language, and to perform the instructions encoded in that language. For example, a block-structured language is implemented as a single stack, while concurrent imperative languages require several stacks with associated queues. The virtual machine for the first behaves like a stack, while that for the second operates as cooperating stacks with associated queues. In this chapter,

---

[1]A token is a valid string in a language, such as an identifier, an assignment indicator (:=), a reserved word (e.g., **if**), a comparator (e.g., <), etc.

[2]' ' indicates a space. The quotation marks are not elements of the alphabet.

we will look at the most basic of these virtual machines and comment on their essential links to language types.

When we speak of a formal language, we mean the form or syntax of valid words in the language. We are not concerned with what it means, i.e., its *semantics*. If "work" and "house" are valid words, and one of the word formation rules says that the concatenation of two words is also a word, then "workhouse," "housework," "househouse," and "workwork" are all valid words. The first two are meaningful in English, although their semantics are different, but the last two make no English sense. No matter! In a formal language with a concatenation rule, all four are equally valid. Numbers are not as ambiguous as English words. If 3 and 17 are words in a language with a concatenation rule, then 317, 173, 33, and 1717 are also.

The formal rules for generating and recognizing computer languages are syntactic rather than semantic, with the semantics described in some natural language, in our case, English. The syntax for the string 5 + 3 * 5 is that the symbol 5 is followed by a space, then the symbols +, space, 3, space, *, space, and 5. Its semantics capture some common rules of natural number arithmetic. The semantics of valid strings will not be of concern here, although much of language theory addresses the notion that proper syntax captures intuitive meanings, and that statements that are inexpressible may well be meaningless.

Formal languages are useful in writing standard descriptions, analyzing languages for correctness, and building parser-generators as part of a compiler. As its first task, a compiler must parse source code into finer grained parts, e.g., statements into expressions, expressions into words, words into tokens. If the language follows formal, unwavering rules, this can be automated without difficulty. Different levels of analysis apply, from the recognition of syntax errors to the determination of which programs generate infinite loops and which always terminate with correct solutions to the problem at hand. Formal languages and the theoretical machines that recognize them are useful throughout, from language element recognition to the higher levels of proving program correctness.

Formal Languages Defined

To define a formal language L, we will need two things:

1. An alphabet Σ of individual symbols.
2. A set of rules to determine which strings or words[3] from Σ are valid in L. We will denote the set of rules by the letter P, as each will be given in the form $\alpha \to \beta$, called a production.

Taken together, the alphabet and the rules for forming valid words are called a *grammar over* Σ. Hence a grammar can be considered a pair or 2-tuple (Σ, P). If G is a grammar (Σ, P), generating a language L, L is written L(G).

---

[3]A word in a language L(G) includes only symbols from Σ, including the empty word ε. ε is neither a terminal nor a nonterminal symbol. A string may include any symbol.

For example, the language L(B), generated by the grammar B = (Σ, P) in listing (6.1.1), is all possible nonnegative binary decimals less than 1, correct to two places. L(B) = {0.00, 0.01, 0.10, 0.11}, where

$$\Sigma = \{0, ., 1\} \tag{6.1.1}$$

P = {R1: $S_0 \rightarrow 0S_1$
    R2: $S_1 \rightarrow .S_2$
    R3: $S_2 \rightarrow 0S_3$
    R4: $S_2 \rightarrow 1S_3$
    R5: $S_3 \rightarrow 0$
    R6: $S_3 \rightarrow 1$

Rules written in the form $\alpha \rightarrow \beta$ are called *productions*, because a new string is "produced" from an old one by replacing the substring on the right by the one on the left. For example, the string 0.11 can be produced from $0.1S_3$ by replacing the substring S_3 by 1, using production rule R6.

When generating a word for inclusion in L(B), we always start at S_0, the *start symbol*. The initial string generated when producing a word is the single symbol S_0. S_0 is not in the alphabet Σ of *terminal symbols*, and is called a *nonterminal*. It will have to be eliminated by applying some rule if a valid string of L(B) is to be produced. In the grammar B of listing (6.1.1), the set of nonterminals is N = $\{S_0, S_1, S_2, S_3\}$.

Application of rule R1 involves replacing S_0 with $0S_1$. Applying other rules involves replacing, in the string generated so far, an occurrence of one of the nonterminals S_i by x, if $S_i \rightarrow x$ is a rule. If $S_i \rightarrow x$ and $S_i \rightarrow y$ are both rules, either may be applied. For example, S_3 may be replaced with either a 0 or a 1. A *derivation* of the string 0.01, representing the binary decimal for ¼, is:

  R1   R2   R3   R6
$S_0 \rightarrow 0S_1 \rightarrow 0.S_2 \rightarrow 0.0S_3 \rightarrow 0.01$

A *production system* is a grammar G, where the rules are given in the form of productions. G = $(\Sigma, N, P, Start)$ is a 4-tuple that includes a set of terminal symbols, Σ; a set of nonterminals, N; a set of production rules, P; and a start symbol, Start $\in \Sigma \cup N$. In the grammar above, $\Sigma = \{0, 1, .\}$, N = $\{S_0, S_1, S_2, S_3\}$, and Start = S_0. G is called a *phrase-structured grammar* if every production is of the form $s_i \rightarrow s_j$, where s_i and s_j are strings from $(\Sigma \cup N)$ and s_i contains at least one nonterminal. (Most authors use capital letters for nonterminals and lowercase or digits for terminals, but this is merely convention.)

You may be surprised to discover that there are only four types of formal languages, depending on what sort of production rules are used. That communication at its fundamental level is not as various as one might think has attracted the attention of investigators in diverse fields. Languages of each form have definitive properties. In fact, the relationship between language and theoretical machine is one-to-one. A language of a particular type is recognized by a particular machine. The opposite holds as well. But more on that later. First we need to see what sorts of formal languages there are.

The Chomsky Hierarchy of Formal Languages

Various researchers have worked on the forms of decidable[4] rules to generate languages of particular types, raising several questions. Just what restrictions are essential and which can be eased? With a given class of rules, what sorts of problems can be solved? Given a language, which machines can recognize properly formed strings and reject those that are invalid? For that matter, what is a machine? For what sorts of languages will a machine always be successful in recognizing valid strings? Can a machine recognize potentially infinite strings?[5] For what applications are particular languages best suited?

Although investigators worked independently on formal language theory, their various formulations fell into the same four distinct classes, starting with sets of fairly unrestricted rules through those that were increasingly more rigid. Only later was it recognized that each of these formulations was equivalent to the same four language classes. Machines that recognize languages formed using unrestricted rules can generate solutions to a large class of problems, but no machine can decide whether it can or cannot solve any arbitrary problem. Machines recognizing languages based on stricter rule classes can guarantee the generation of solutions, but to a limited class of problems.

We will look at the formal language types described by the linguist Noam Chomsky. As shown in Figure 6.1.1, these languages form a hierarchy in that any Type 3 language is also Type 2, any Type 2 language is also Type 1, and those of Type 1

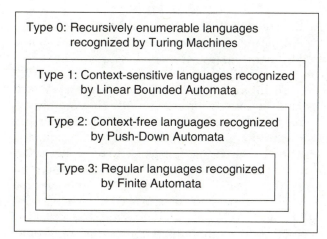

FIGURE 6.1.1
The Chomsky hierarchy

---

[4]A rule is *decidable* if there is an effective decision procedure to generate a yes or no in a finite number of steps.

[5]A string is *potentially infinite* if we do not know its length, e.g., a string of the form a^n is potentially infinite if we do not know the value of n. For any fixed value of n, we can generate a string that is longer.

are also Type 0. Type 0, the most general, includes all the other three types. As we will see, each language type is associated with a particular computing machine.

Phrase-structured grammars are assigned to the Chomsky hierarchy on the basis of the forms of the productions. But first, let's look at just who Noam Chomsky is.

HISTORICAL VIGNETTE

Language Classifications: Noam Chomsky

We've all heard of the romance languages, but rarely do we hear of an individual who has had a lifetime romance *with* languages. Noam Chomsky is such an individual.

His deep interest in the study of linguistics began when he was only 10 years old. He was fascinated with the proofs he read in his father's edition of a thirteenth-century grammar. These were informally written and did not conform to the traditional structural school of linguistics. Chomsky's informal introduction to the study of languages colored his future work in that field. One can't help but wonder whether he would have become the revolutionary linguist that he did if his first introduction to the field had been more traditional.

In 1945, Chomsky entered the University of Pennsylvania where he majored in linguistics. Here his lifelong interest in political change began to surface. He was particularly attentive to developments leading to the establishment of the state of Israel.

In 1951, he received an M.A. degree from the University of Pennsylvania with a thesis called "Morphonemics of Modern Hebrew," based on efforts to develop a system of rules that could be used to characterize every sentence structure in a language. He received a Ph.D. in linguistics in 1955.

At first Chomsky had a very difficult time publishing any of his work, which was too revolutionary for the established linguistic community. He not only exposed the inadequacy of structuralist grammars, but he criticized more modern linguistic practice as well. The structuralist school contended that language is primarily behavioristic, depending on an individual's response to his or her external environment. Chomsky felt that the structural explanation did not take account of linguistic creativity in humans. About behaviorism, he said, "Skinnerian-type training is appropriate only for industrial-type workers who need to develop complex technical skills. Is growing up and learning no more than the shaping of behaviors? If that's what education is all about, authoritarian figures shaping people, then maybe we don't need it" [*Newsweek*, August 26, 1968]. He also felt that modern linguistics "has not explicitly recognized the necessity for supplementing a 'particular grammar' of a language by a universal grammar if it is to achieve descriptive adequacy. It has, in fact, characteristically rejected the study of universal grammar as misguided, and . . . it has not attempted to deal with the creative aspect of language use. It thus suggests no way to overcome the fundamental descriptive inadequacy of structuralist grammars" [Chomsky, 1965].

To support his theories, Chomsky relied heavily on mathematics, and published his first book in 1957. By then he was a professor of linguistics at MIT. In *Cartesian Linguistics* [Chomsky, 1966], he divides the study of linguistics into three main categories:

1. Investigations that focus directly on the nature of language, including descriptions of syntax, semantics, phonology (the study of sounds), and their evolution
2. Studies dealing with the use of language and the abilities and mental organization that it presupposes, such as the language learning processes of both children and adults and language as used in literature
3. Background sociological studies placing the various approaches to the study of language in appropriate historical and intellectual settings

Although considered a genius in the linguistics field, Chomsky never minimized its difficulties. He once claimed, "It may be beyond the limits of human intelligence to understand how human intelligence works" [*Time*, February 16, 1968].

Chomsky's political interests resurfaced around 1965 when he began protesting the Vietnam War. He became a leader in peace organizations such as Resist, a national draft-resistance movement. He taught undergraduate courses dealing with political change and published widely on his pacifist views. Once again, he was openly challenging the authorities. Israel Shenker wrote in the *New York Times* (October 27, 1968), "In his twenties, Noam Chomsky revolutionized linguistics. In his thirties, he has been trying to revolutionize society." His writings continue to the present. *The Culture of Terrorism* [Chomsky, 1988] protests U.S. policies in areas such as Central America and Iran. He states, "Even in a largely depoliticized society such as the United States, with no political parties or opposition press beyond the narrow spectrum of the business-dominated consensus, it is possible for popular action to have a significant impact on policy, though indirectly. That was an important lesson for the Indochina wars. It is underscored, once again, by the experience of the 1980s with regard to Central America. And it should be remembered for the future" [Chomsky, 1988].

His present-day influence continues in fields other than linguistics and political activism. His legacies are very apparent in computer science. His development of a mathematical theory of natural languages and description of four different classes of languages have made the analysis of the syntax and grammar of programming languages possible. "This has had important practical benefits since it has permitted the development of automatic parser-generators, thus automating what had been one of the more difficult parts of compiler writing" [MacLennan, 1987].

Type 3: Regular Grammars

A phrase-structured grammar G = (Σ, N, P, Start) is a *regular grammar* if its productions are of the form:

$$A \rightarrow a, \text{ or } A \rightarrow aB, \text{ where } A,B \in N, \text{ and } a \in \Sigma. \tag{6.1.2}$$

That is, the first symbol on each right-hand side must be a terminal, and may be followed by a nonterminal.

Consider, for example, the following rules for creating a Pascal identifier I:

$$I \rightarrow a\,|\,...\,|\,z\,|\,aL\,|\,...\,|\,zL\,|\,aD\,|\,...\,|\,zD \qquad (6.1.3)$$
$$L \rightarrow aL\,|\,...\,|\,zL\,|\,aD\,|\,...\,|\,zD\,|\,a\,|\,...\,|\,z$$
$$D \rightarrow 0L\,|\,...\,|\,9L\,|\,0D\,|\,...\,|\,9D\,|\,0\,|\,...\,|\,9$$

Here | means OR, permitting a shorthand for a number of rules. Then I is either a letter or a letter followed by a finite sequence of letters and/or digits.

Such grammars can be recognized by finite automata (FA), sometimes referred to as finite-state automata (FSA). Beginning at the start state S_0, as each new symbol is read, there is a transition to another (or perhaps the same) state. Within a finite number of steps, a string must be determined valid or invalid.

Regular grammars are often used in the *lexical analysis* phase of a compiler, sometimes called the *scanner*, in which valid tokens of a language are accepted. Because of this important application, we will look more closely at regular grammars and finite automata in section 6.2.

Type 2: Context-Free Grammars

The next type, which is less restrictive than Type 3, is Type 2. Type 2 languages, which are also called *context-free*, are especially important in computer science because all but a few features of high level programming languages can be written using them. As before, we will characterize these languages by describing context-free grammars (CFGs) that generate valid strings, and the theoretical machines that recognize them.

A phrase-structured grammar, $G = (\Sigma, N, P, \text{Start})$, is *context-free* if productions are of the form:

$$A \rightarrow s, \quad \text{where } A \in N, \text{ the set of nonterminals,} \qquad (6.1.4)$$
$$\text{and s is any string from } \Sigma \cup N$$

Regular grammars are, of course, context-free since strings of the form 'a' or 'aB' are candidates for s of the right side. Context-free grammars may be written using productions of forms different from (6.1.4), but such a grammar can always be shown to be equivalent to one of type (6.1.4).

CFGs are called context-free because replacements can be made wherever they occur, and not in the context of other surrounding symbols. For example, a context-free rule might allow the replacement of "the" with "this" in any English sentence, i.e., "The dog barked" → "This dog barked." A context-sensitive rule might be to replace "the" with "an" if the following word begins with a vowel, otherwise replace it with "a". "The dog barked" → A dog barked," while "The otter barked" → "An otter barked." Here the context of the replacement is the word following the article to be replaced.

As regular grammars are recognized by FAs, a CFG can be recognized by a push-down automaton (PDA). As the name implies, aside from the input string, a stack can be used for a PDA. These are often used in a compiler in the parser, which takes tokens of the grammar as input and recognizes whether the program is in proper syntax. In this case, when the form of the right-hand side of a rule is on the stack, we may pop those entries, then push the resulting left-hand nonterminal onto the stack. We will look more closely at CFGs, PDAs, and parsing in section 6.3.

Type 1: Context-Sensitive Grammars

There are languages that are not context-free. One of the simplest words that cannot be generated by a CFG is $a^n b^n c^n$, for arbitrary but fixed n. The proof is beyond the scope of this brief introduction, but can be found in [Cohen, 1991]. Productions $\alpha \to \beta$ for context-sensitive grammars (CSGs) are like those for context-free languages except that:

1. The left side α can contain more than one symbol as long as at least one is a nonterminal.
2. The length of α is less than or equal to the length of β.

The second rule ensures that there are no empty productions, those in which the right side is the empty string ε. The reader can refer to the issue of erasing rules in exercise 6.1.3. This last restriction prevents dead ends, where what is to be replaced, α, may become longer than the word so far generated. A CSG grammar for words of the form $a^n b^n c^n$ is:

1. $S \ \ \to aSBC$
2. $S \ \ \to aBC$
3. $CB \to BC$
4. $aB \to ab$
5. $bB \to bb$
6. $bC \to bc$
7. $cC \to cc$

and the production of $a^3 b^3 c^3$ is:

$$S \xrightarrow{1} aSBC \xrightarrow{1} aaSBCBC \xrightarrow{2} aaaBCBCBC \xrightarrow{3} aaaBBCCBC \xrightarrow{3} \ldots \xrightarrow{3}$$

$$aaaBBBCCC \xrightarrow{4} aaabBBCCC \xrightarrow{5} \ldots \xrightarrow{5} aaabbbCCC \xrightarrow{6} aaabbbcCC \xrightarrow{7} \ldots$$

$$\xrightarrow{7} aaabbbccc$$

The only difference between these production rules and those for a CFG is the presence of two symbols on the left sides of rules 3–7 above. These provide the *contexts*. B may be changed to b when preceded by a (rule 4) or when preceded by b (rule 5).

Type 1 grammars being used for natural language processing are sometimes called *restricted phrase-structured grammars*. A typical phrase-structured rule is: $S \to$ NP VP, where S denotes a sentence, NP a noun phrase, and VP a verb phrase. Restrictions other than those listed above for context-sensitive grammars are included, to eliminate features not occurring in natural languages. Examples of such undesirable constructs are NP $\to$ NP S, or VP $\to$ V VP, where V indicates a verb. With context-sensitive rules, strings of the form NP NC VP can be replaced by NP PP VP_2 VP, where PP is a personal pronoun. For example, if NP is "The tiger" and VP is "ate the lady," NP PP VP_2 VP could be replaced by something like "The tiger, who was behind the first door, ate the lady."

Context-sensitive grammars may be recognized by a linear-bounded automaton, which is a Turing Machine (TM) with a finite tape. We include a short introduction to TMs below, since some readers may not have a course in Computation Theory in their undergraduate curriculum.

Linear-Bounded Automata (LBAs)

Given a language L, a *recognizer* is a program that is used to determine whether or not a given string S is a valid string in the language. Consider again the language L defined in listing (6.1.1), which determines certain binary decimal numbers. A recognizer should tell us that $0.01 \in L$ and that $1.01 \notin L$.

A recognizer for a context-sensitive language is a deterministic Turing Machine (TM) with a finite tape, called a *linear-bounded automaton* or LBA. It requires only one tape, whereas the PDA, which recognizes context-free languages, uses two. A TM requires six things [Cohen, 1991]:

1. An alphabet, Σ, of input symbols.
2. A tape divided into cells, labeled 1, 2, 3, ...
3. A read/write head that can move left or right one cell, read what it finds, and write or erase this information. We do not allow the head to go left from cell 1, since there are no cells preceding it.
4. An alphabet, Γ, of characters that can be written onto the tape. Γ may include Σ, but need not.
5. A finite set, S, of states, including Start and Halt.
6. A set of rules called a *program*, P. Each rule is of the form, (state$_1$, read-char, write-char, direction, state$_2$). If the current state of the TM is state$_1$, the head reads the value of read-char in cell$_1$, and writes a value from write-char to the same cell and moves either right or left. The new state is then state$_2$.

Let's look at a fairly extensive example of an LBA, LBA(AnBnCn) = (Σ, Γ, S, S_0, S_5, P), to recognize strings of the form $a^n b^n c^n$. The input language $\Sigma = \{a\ b\ c\ \#\}$. Here # marks the end of the input. $\Gamma = \{A\ B\ C\ T\}$. T is a temporary symbol used to replace B's. The string 'aabbcc' will be transformed into 'aabbcc' $\rightarrow$ 'AATTcc' $\rightarrow$ AABBCC. The T's take care of context; the extra transformation is needed because the b's are in between a's and c's. The LBA tape is initialized to the input string, and starts processing in state S_0. It will have recognized a correct string when all the lowercase letters have been changed to uppercase, the end symbol # has been reached, and the machine is in S_5.

States are:

S_0: When the read-write head, *, is at cell$_i$ and the machine is in S_0, all cells before cell$_i$ are correct and need no further processing.

S_1: An a has just been changed to an A, and we are looking right for a b to match it.

S_2: A b has just been changed to a T, and we are looking left for the next a to change.

S_3: A T has just been changed to a B, and we are looking right for a c to match it.

S_4: A c has just been changed to a C, and we are looking left for the next T to change.

S_5: HALT

Figure 6.1.2 shows the processing of 'aabbcc'. The * shows the position of the read-write head.

We have seen the execution of a successful program, so now it's time to see the program itself, as shown in listing (6.1.5). Each instruction applies to the (current

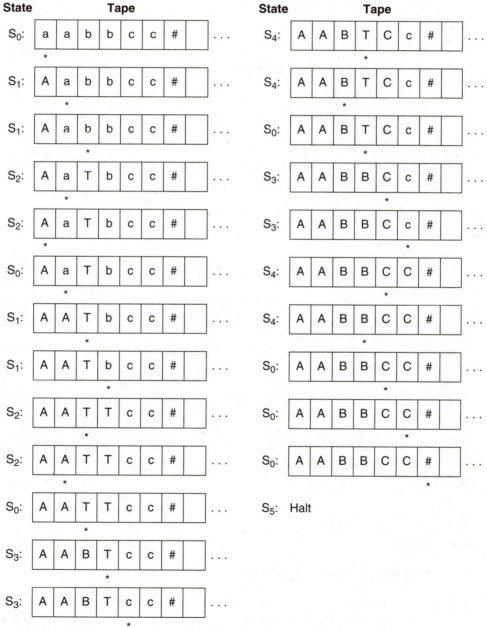

FIGURE 6.1.2
Recognizing aabbcc in LBA(AnBnCn)

state, reads, writes, moves, and new state), giving us the needed details to be used for the state changes described above. In the first rule, for example, if we are in state S_0 and read an a, we write an A, move right, and switch to state S_1. In exercise 6.1.4, the reader will be asked to follow the sequence of instructions used in the execution shown in Figure 6.1.2.

$(S_0 \text{ a A R } S_1)$ {Start processing here}   (6.1.5)
$(S_0 \text{ T B R } S_4)$
$(S_0 \text{ C C R } S_0)$ {Looking for # to HALT}
$(S_0 \text{ # # R } S_5)$ HALT
$(S_1 \text{ a a R } S_1)$ {Looking forward for a b to match an A}
$(S_1 \text{ T T R } S_1)$
$(S_1 \text{ b T L } S_2)$
$(S_2 \text{ T T L } S_2)$ {Looking back for the next a}
$(S_2 \text{ a a L } S_2)$
$(S_2 \text{ A A R } S_0)$
$(S_3 \text{ T T R } S_3)$ {Looking forward for a c to match a B}
$(S_3 \text{ C C R } S_3)$
$(S_3 \text{ c C L } S_4)$
$(S_4 \text{ C C L } S_4)$ {Looking back for next T}
$(S_4 \text{ T T L } S_4)$
$(S_4 \text{ B B R } S_0)$

The last rule $(S_4 \text{ B B R } S_0)$ is similar to others, where the symbol read, in this case B, is the same as the one written, indicating that the cell being scanned remains unchanged when we move to the next cell and state. Some descriptions of Turing Machines offer the option of moving without writing. We chose to rewrite a symbol just to make the presentation easier.

A deterministic linear-bound automaton (LBA) is a Turing Machine that halts in a finite amount of time and that is deterministic, i.e., for each pair of instructions, IN_1 and IN_2, if $IN_1 = (S_1 \text{ X Y Z } S_2)$ and $IN_2 = (S_3 \text{ A B C } S_4)$ and if $S_1 = S_3$, X=A, Y=B, and Z=C, then $S_2 = S_4$. This means that the next step is always completely determined by the state and the input. If we input a string, the TM can decide whether it is a legal string or not in an amount of time proportional to the length of the string. Of course, it will take longer to process $a^{2346}b^{2346}c^{2346}$ than $a^2b^2c^2$, but some function of the TM will tell us how much longer it will take. Our final group of languages will not have these guarantees.

HISTORICAL VIGNETTE

Alan Turing: What Machines Can't Do

The title of Andrew Hodges' biography of Alan Turing [Hodges, 1983], *Alan Turing: The Enigma,* is a pun. Enigma, meaning a mystery or perplexing problem, is also the name of an ingenious machine used to generate German codes during World

War II. Turing was a mathematical genius who cracked the Enigma code in 1942, was convicted of "gross indecency" (a euphemism for homosexuality) in 1952, and committed suicide by eating an apple dipped in cyanide in 1954. It is of such stuff that legends are made, and, indeed, Hodges' book was made into a successful Broadway play in 1988.

Alan Turing was born in 1912, to parents in the Indian Civil Service of Great Britain. In 1933, he entered Cambridge University to read mathematics. These were heady times, as two important questions about the nature of mathematics, whether it is complete and/or consistent, had been answered negatively, while a third remained open.

In 1931, Kurt Gödel had shown that any worthwhile mathematical system could not be complete without being inconsistent. A complete system is one in which any true statement can be proved, while a consistent one is one in which no false statement can be proved. In 1931, Gödel had shown that any mathematical system complex enough to include multiplication and division contains true statements that make the system inconsistent if proven. One such statement that can be expressed in the Theory of Integer Arithmetic (IA) is,

G: "The formula G is not demonstrable."   (6.1.6)

The formula G thus says *of itself* that it is not demonstrable, i.e., provable within IA. If a proof is provided, the statement is false, making the theory inconsistent, and if the statement is true, no proof can be found, so the theory would be incomplete. Such statements are called "self-referent" because they talk about themselves. The formula G itself is:

G: (x) ~Dem(x,sub(n,13,n))   (6.1.7)

Just how formula (6.1.7) expresses (6.1.6) is beyond the scope of this book. The interested reader is referred to [Nagel, 1958].

In 1933, a still open question was whether there could be any "mechanical" method to determine which statements are decidable or not, i.e., can it be decided in advance which sorts of problems will lead to answers and which will lead to endless indecisive computing. A "mechanical" method is one that follows rules, but may or may not be realized in a physical machine.

Alan Turing chose to address this problem of decidability. First, he had to make precise just what is meant by a "machine." This resulted in a theoretical machine that could be expected to solve any problem that any other machine, or human being, following specified rules, could solve. He was able to find seven questions such a machine cannot answer.

1. Given an arbitrary problem-solving machine M and an arbitrary problem P, can M solve P?
2. Given a particular machine M, can M solve an arbitrary problem P?
3. Given M, can it recognize a nonproblem when it sees it?
4. Given M, can it solve any problems at all?
5. Given M, can it solve all problems?

6. Given two machines, M_1 and M_2, can they solve the same problems?
7. Given a Turing Machine TM, is the language TM accepts regular? context-free? decidable?

World War II interrupted Turing's theoretical studies, when he was assigned to the Government Code and Cypher School (GCCS) at Bletchley Park, just half-way between Oxford and Cambridge Universities. The Germans were using a machine with four rotors to generate codes for transmissions to, among other things, submarines. With 26 characters, and four rotors, a code could have 26 x 26 x 26 x 26 = 456,976 different configurations, and the Germans changed the code daily. By 1940, the British had designs for the Enigma machine, obtained by Polish agents, but determining just what the state of the rotors was remained a problem. What was needed was a machine to analyze Enigma codes and decipher them quickly. Turing's interests in number theory, mathematical logic, and probability theory, plus the engineering necessary to build a practical machine paid off.

In 1942, GCCS built a machine, called a "Bombe" because of its loud ticking, capable of deciphering Enigma codes. Alan Turing was the brains behind this endeavor. It is not an overstatement to say that this effort changed the course of the war. As a result, the British were able to determine the exact location of every German submarine in the various seas.

After the war, Turing returned to his investigation of the capabilities of the Turing Machine at the National Physical Laboratory and at the University of Manchester. His promising career came crashing down with his conviction in 1952. His death in 1954 was assumed by most to be a suicide, but sloppy police work was never able to eliminate the possibility of an accident. Some commentators feel this was subterfuge, intended by Turing to spare his family the ignominy of a suicide. They were free to believe what they wanted.

In his brief life, Alan Turing dealt with some of the most profound questions presented by computers. Can a machine be as "intelligent" as a human? Is free will compatible with a mechanistic view of the world? Are emotion and reason the same or different? Can machines understand human experiences? love? frustration? suffering? despair? He also tried to combine mathematics, philosophy, and engineering—scoffed at during his lifetime, but taken seriously now, 42 years after his death.

Type 0: Unrestricted Grammars

Type 0 grammars are constructed with no restrictions on replacement rules, except that a nonterminal must appear in the string on the left side. The languages generated are called Type 0 languages or, more commonly, *recursively enumerable* (r.e.).

Type 0 productions are the same as those for Type 1 languages, except that rule 2, that the left side must be no longer than the right, is eliminated. Thus a Type 0 grammar is:

1. An alphabet Σ of terminal symbols
2. An alphabet Γ of nonterminals, including a start symbol

3. A set of production rules $\alpha \to \beta$, where α and β are strings from $\Sigma \cup \Gamma$, α contains at least one nonterminal, and there are no restrictions on β

Recognizers for Type 0 languages are Turing Machines, which were introduced earlier, but in this case the tape may be infinite, though the number of states is finite.

A detailed example of a Type 0 language that is not also Type 1 is beyond the scope of this brief introduction, but there are such. Consider the regular language CWL (Code Word Language), generated by the regular grammar in listing (6.1.8).

$$\begin{aligned} S &\to aS \mid aB \\ B &\to bC \\ C &\to aC \mid aD \\ D &\to bE \\ E &\to aF \mid bF \\ F &\to aG \mid bG \\ G &\to aH \mid bH \\ H &\to aI \mid bI \\ I &\to a \mid b \end{aligned}$$
$$(6.1.8)$$

Cohen [Cohen, 1991] presents a TM = $(\Sigma, \Gamma, S, S_1, S_2, P)$, recognizing words of CWL as shown in listing (6.1.9).

$$\Sigma = \{a, b, \Delta\}, \Gamma = \{b\}, S = \{S_1, S_2, S_3\}$$
$$(6.1.9)$$
P:
(S_1, b, b, R, S_1)
(S_1, a, b, R, S_3)
(S_3, a, b, L, S_3)
(S_3, Δ, b, L, S_2)

Nothing new here! Since regular languages (Type 3) are also Type 0, they can be recognized by TMs. In fact, the TM of listing 6.1.9 is an LBA. So CLW is not the Type 0 language we are seeking, that is, a language that is not also Type 1.

Cohen then codes the four instructions of listing (6.1.9) into strings of a's and b's. One one-word code for the entire TM of four instructions is the string in listing (6.1.10):

ababababbabaaabaaabbaaabaaabaaabaaaabaabbaaba
$\qquad$ (6.1.10)

In fact, any TM over $\Sigma = \{a, b\}$ can be coded into a string from CLW! Strings from CLW can also be decoded into TMs, some legal and some not. (For example, a resulting TM may have duplicate rules.) The language MATHISON (Alan Turing's middle name) is then defined:

MATHISON = {all words in CWL that *are* accepted by their $\qquad$ (6.1.11)
$\qquad$ corresponding TM }

We leave it as an exercise to show that the string of listing (6.1.10), encoding the TM of listing (6.1.9), is accepted by TM(CWL).

Cohen provides a proof that MATHISON is recursively enumerable (Type 0), but we shall not, for we are getting in way over our heads here. Languages more general than those of Type 1 are strange and wonderful creations, of interest theoretically, but not for defining programming languages.

EXERCISES 6.1

1. Construct a production system P to generate strings from $\Sigma = \{1,0\}$,
   a. ending in 0 (even numbers).
   b. ending in 1 (odd numbers).
   c. strings with any combination of 0s and 1s of length exactly 8.
2. Construct production systems to generate strings over $\Sigma = \{a, b\}$ of the form:
   a. $a^n, n = 0, 1, \ldots$.
   b. $a^n b^n, n = 0, 1, \ldots$.
   c. $a^n b^n c^n, n = 0, 1, \ldots, 4$
   d. $a^n b^n c^n, n = 0, 1, \ldots$ (hard)
   You will notice differences in the form of the production rules in a, b, c, and in d.
3. Rules containing ε are called erasing rules. The symbol ε is the Greek letter epsilon, and represents the empty string, a word with no characters at all. ε is neither a terminal nor a nonterminal. But some way is needed to represent nothing, so ε is used. If $A \rightarrow \varepsilon$ is a rule, the nonterminal A can be erased. If $S_0 \rightarrow \varepsilon$ is a rule, the language generated contains the null string. What language does the following system generate?

   R1: $S \rightarrow aSb$
   R2: $S \rightarrow \varepsilon$

4. Using the program of listing (6.1.5), follow the sequence of instructions used in the execution shown in Figure 6.1.2, which recognizes the string 'aabbcc'.
5. Let $|a|$, $|b|$, and $|c|$ indicate the number of a's, b's, or c's in an input string. Using the TM LBA(AnBnCn) described in the subsection on linear-bounded automata, try test strings to show that:
   a. The TM halts in S_0 if $|a| = 0$.
   b. The TM halts in S_2 if $|a| > 0$, and $|b| = 0$.
   c. If $|a| > 0$ and $|b| > 0$, it halts in S_4 if $|a| < |b|$, and in S_2 if $|a| > |b|$.
   d. If $0 > |a| = |b|$, the TM halts in S_1 if $|c| > |a|$, and in S_4 if $|c| < |a|$.
6. What words are generated by the grammar of listing 6.1.8?
7. Show that the string of listing (6.1.10), encoding the TM of listing (6.1.9), is accepted by TM(CWL).
8. A code word for the one-line TM (S_1, b, b, R, S_2) is abaababb.
   a. Show that the code string is not accepted by the TM.
   b. What words does the TM accept?

6.2
REGULAR GRAMMARS

As we discussed in section 6.1, a phrase-structured grammar $G = (\Sigma, N, P, Start)$ is a regular grammar if its productions are of the form:

$$A \rightarrow a, \text{ or } A \rightarrow aB, \text{ where } A, B \in N, \text{ and } a \in \Sigma \qquad (6.2.1)$$

It is not necessary, however, that rules be in the form of listing (6.2.1) for a grammar to be regular. If rules are in the form of (6.2.1), the resulting grammar is guaranteed to be regular, but there are other systems for equivalent grammars. In Chomsky's formulation, the grammar, $B' = (\Sigma, N, P', S_0)$ of listing (6.2.2) generates the language L(B'). L(B') is the same language as L(B) that we looked at in listing

(6.1.1). Two grammars, B and B' over Σ, are said to be equivalent (=) if they generate the same language, here $L(B') = L(B)$. The productions P' are:

P': R1': $S_0 \rightarrow S_1 S_2$ (6.2.2)
     R2': $S_1 \rightarrow 0$
     R3': $S_2 \rightarrow S_3 S_4$
     R4': $S_3 \rightarrow .$
     R5': $S_4 \rightarrow S_1 S_1$
     R6': $S_5 \rightarrow 1$
     R7': $S_4 \rightarrow S_1 S_5$
     R8': $S_4 \rightarrow S_5 S_1$
     R9': $S_4 \rightarrow S_5 S_5$

Notice that R1', R3', R5', and R7' through R9' are not of the two forms specified in (6.2.1). But more on this later in the discussion of normal forms in section 6.3.

Regular Expressions

Regular grammars can also be built from *regular expressions*, rather than using production systems. Recall from Chapter 0 that tokens are constants, special symbols, reserved words, and identifiers. The form of these tokens is often rather simple, so it is useful to use a regular grammar in accepting these tokens. Regular expressions involve a notation that is especially nice for defining them, or generally for defining valid strings in a regular grammar.

Consider, for example, a Pascal identifier, which may be defined as follows:

ident → letter (letter | digit)*
letter → A |...|Z|a|...|z
digit → 0|...|9

It starts with a letter, then is followed by (concatenated with) a sequence of letters and digits. Here the | is alternation, meaning "or, but not both." The parentheses are used in grouping, and the Kleene star * indicates zero or more repetitions.

We define a *regular expression* e over an alphabet Σ as follows:

1. ε (the null string) is a regular expression.
2. If $x \in \Sigma$, then x is a regular expression.
3. If e_1 is a regular expression, then so is (e_1).
4. If e_1 and e_2 are regular expressions, then so are $e_1 e_2$, $e_1 | e_2$, and e_1^*.

That ε is a regular expression needs no explanation. Rule 2 says that each symbol of Σ is a regular expression. Note that regular expressions are closed under three operations: concatenation (no symbol between), alternation (|), and Kleene star (*). The parentheses of rule 3 need a little explanation. These are not symbols in Σ, but they may be used freely to make expressions clear. Symbols such as (,), |, and *, that may be used in expressions but are not part of the language itself, are called *meta symbols*.[6]

---

[6]In some texts, symbols of Σ are written in boldface to separate them from metasymbols, e.g., (**x**)(**yy**).

Within an expression, * has highest precedence, then concatenation, then alternation. Hence, in the example ab | cd*, the Kleene star is applied only to d, and the alternatives are ab and cd* (i.e., c, cd, cdd, cddd, etc.). The reader should confirm that strings like abd and acdd are not valid, but would be valid in a(b | c)d*. As another example, strings of a's and b's that contain at least one 'a' would be represented by (a | b)*a(a | b)*.

With regular expressions defined, we are ready to list the rules of a regular grammar, used to build a regular language L from a regular expression e. We will write L(e) to indicate the language L defined by e.

1. If e = x, then L(x) = {x}. That is, the only word in the language L is x. L(ε) = {ε}.
2. If L(e_1) = L_1, and L(e_2) = L_2, then
   a. L(e_1 e_2) = L_1L_2
   b. L(e_1 | e_2) = L_1 | L_2
   c. L(e_1*) = L_1*

Some examples are in order. Suppose L_1 = {x} and L_2 = {y}, where e_1 = x and e_2 = y. That is, each language has exactly one word in it. Then:

1. L(xy) = {xy}, a single word, xy
2. L(x | y) = {x} | {y} = {x, y}
3. L(x*) = L* = {ε, x, xx, xxx, . . .}
4. L(x*y) = L(x*)L(y) = {y, xy, xxy, xxxy, . . .}

To be a little more practical, consider the language B, of binary decimals including 0 but less than 1, correct to two places. The alphabet, Σ = {., 0, 1}. B = {0.00, 0.01, 0.10, 0.11}. B can be constructed from the two languages:

$$L_1 = \{0.\} \quad \text{and} \quad L_2 = \{00, 01, 10, 11\}$$
$$= L(0.) \qquad\qquad = L((0 \mid 1)(0 \mid 1))$$
$$\qquad\qquad\qquad = L((0 \mid 1)^2)$$

Then B = L((0.)(0 | 1)^2) = L_1L_2. B is generated by the regular expression 0 . (0 | 1)^2.

Finite Automata (FAs, NFAs, and DFAs)

Now that we have seen how to generate a regular language, we are faced with the opposite problem. Given the regular grammar B in listing (6.1.1) and a string from its alphabet, how can we recognize whether that particular string is a word of L(B) or not? We want a machine that will accept valid words and reject invalid strings. For regular languages, such a machine is called a *finite automaton* (FA). The machine must operate automatically and either recognize or reject an input string in a finite number of steps. Given a string to process, it proceeds mechanically symbol by symbol to either accept or reject the string as a word of the language for which the automaton was built. It will process one symbol at a time from left to right.

If a word is processed beginning at the start arrow pointing to the start state S_0, it is said to be *recognized* or *accepted* by the FA if processing terminates at a terminal or Final node, shown in Figure 6.2.1 as the double-boxed node F. Words that are not recognized are said to be rejected or to fail. The directed graph below, called a *transition diagram,* represents an FA for the language L(B). The S_i and F are called *states.* S_0 is the *start state,* and F, a terminal or *final state.* An FA must have exactly one start state, but may have no, one, or several final states.

To recognize the string s = '0.01', processing would start at S_0, at the left end of s. Since the first symbol read is 0, the machine would change to state S_1, where the second symbol, ".", is read. The FA would then change to state S_2, where 0 is read, and then to S_3, where 1 is read. The FA would then change to state F and stop, since it has reached the end of the input string. Since F is a terminal state, s has been recognized.

Formally, a finite automaton is a 5-tuple (S, Σ, T, Start, FS) with:

1. A set of States S = {S_0, S_1, . . ., S_{n-1}}. In Figure 6.2.1, S = {S_0, S_1, S_2, S_3, F}.
2. An alphabet Σ. In our case, Σ = {0, ., 1}.
3. A set of transitions T. In Figure 2.1.1, transitions are represented by arrows, e.g., a transition is made from state S_1 to S_2 if processing is in state S_1 and "." is recognized in the string being processed.
4. Start is the starting state. In Figure 6.2.1, Start = S_0.
5. A subset of the S_i (possibly empty) is designated as terminal, stopping, or final states FS. Here, FS = {F}.

An FA is finite because both the alphabet and the number of states are finite. An FA is in state S_0 if processing has just begun or if there is some transition looping back to S_0. The FA makes a transition to state S_i upon reading a symbol x. The FA is then in state S_i. The set of transitions can also be represented as a transition table. One is free to use whichever is the clearest. The transition table for the FA of Figure 6.2.1 is shown in Figure 6.2.2.

A table such as that of Figure 6.2.2 can be constructed from a regular grammar G = (S, Σ, T, Start, FS) as follows:

1. If m is the number of elements in Σ, and n is the number of nonterminals (S_0–S_{n-1}) used in T, construct an n x m table with rows labeled S_i (0 ≤ i ≤ n–1). If there are any productions of the form N → t, add a row labeled F. Row F is marked with * to indicate that it is a terminal state. Columns are labeled with the m terminal symbols of Σ.

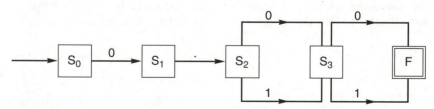

FIGURE 6.2.1
Transition diagram for L(B) including states

Inputs

States	0	1	.
S_0	S_1	–	–
S_1	–	–	S_2
S_2	S_3	S_3	–
S_3	F	F	–
*F	–	–	–

FIGURE 6.2.2
Transition table for the language B

2. For each rule of the form $S_i \rightarrow tS_j$, enter the transition from S_i to S_j by writing "S_j" in Table(S_i,t).
3. For each rule of the form $N \rightarrow t$, write "F" in Table(N,t).
4. Mark all other cells of Table with "-", representing the absence of a transition.

The nonterminals of the grammar, with the possible addition of F, become the states for the FA.

Similarly, a production system for a regular grammar can be constructed from a transition table, T-Table(X,y), as follows:

1. For each entry S_j in T-Table(S_i,t), write the rule $S_i \rightarrow tS_j$.
2. For each entry F in T-Table(S_i,t), write the rule $S_i \rightarrow t$.

If there is exactly one transition possible from each state, given a possible input symbol, an FA is called *deterministic* or a DFA. If multiple choices are offered from a state S_i for some symbol t, the FA is called *nondeterministic*, or an NFA. In this case, if the FA is in state S_i and t is read from the input string, what should be done is not determined.

Figure 6.2.3 represents an NFA, because there are two transition choices from S_0 upon recognizing the letter b, resulting in either state S_0 or S_1. As a result, it is more convenient to display the table entry as the set $\{S_0,S_1\}$. Correspondingly, all other table entries indicate the set of resulting states. Can you figure out what language this NFA recognizes?

The transitions $S_0 \xrightarrow{a} S_0$ and $S_0 \xrightarrow{b} S_0$ are called *loops*. One can go around zero or more times generating repeated a's or b's. The relationship to regular expressions may now have become clearer. The regular expressions (a | b)* b are represented by Figure 6.2.3. Alternation is indicated by multiple branches from S_0 to another state (in this case, back to S_0). Concatenation is indicated by the sequence of states from S_0 to S_1. The Kleene star results in a loop from a state back to itself.

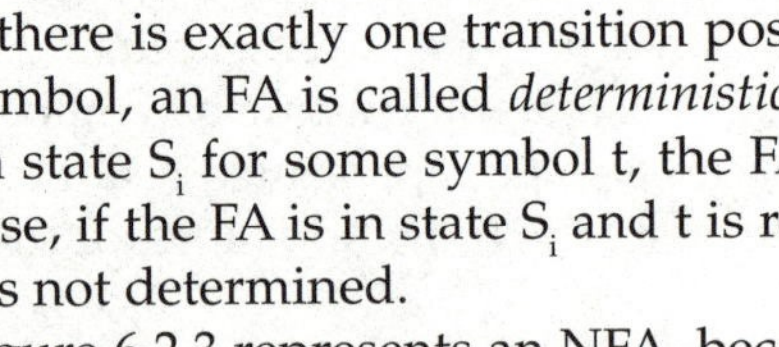

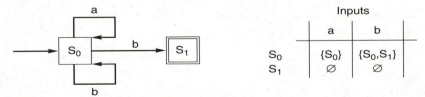

FIGURE 6.2.3
Transition diagram and table for an NFA

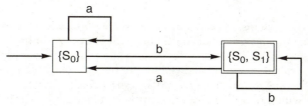

FIGURE 6.2.4
DFA equivalent to the NFA of Figure 6.2.3

Work by Kleene and others has shown that any language that can be recognized by a NFA can also be recognized by a (probably more complicated) DFA. A mechanical method for producing the DFA in Figure 6.2.4 from the NFA of Figure 6.2.3 is left for the exercises.

When processing has progressed to the termination state $\{S_0, S_1\}$, it may either stop, loop through zero or more b's, or return to $\{S_0\}$ if an a is read. The DFA recognizes infinitely many words since one can go around the loops any number of times. An important result of Automata Theory is that any language recognized by an FA, hence the language recognized by the FAs of Figures 6.2.3 and 6.2.4, is regular. It has also been shown that any language with a finite number of words can be recognized by a finite automaton. The converse is, of course, not true, as exemplified by the DFA of Figure 6.2.4. We refer the interested reader to [Cohen, 1991].

Applications

We have considered a group of languages, called regular, that are generated by regular grammars and whose words can be recognized by DFAs (NFAs). We saw an example of how to construct an FA from the regular grammar B, and a grammar from an FA expressed in the table of Figure 6.2.2.

Since a language with a finite number of words can be generated from a regular grammar, text processors can be written using DFAs. Compilation of a language involves several steps, the first of which, as mentioned earlier, is lexical analysis (scanning) or the recognition of valid tokens and symbols. A special language called LEX [Lesk, 1975] has been implemented to produce a DFA from source code. Some compilers also use a DFA to implement the first pass over source code. For an example of how LEX produces a DFA scanner for FORTRAN arithmetic statements, see [Aho, 1986].

LAB 6.1: REGULAR EXPRESSIONS: grep

Objectives (Labs can be found in the *Instructor's Manual*.)

1. To use the utility grep or egrep to investigate the form and notation of regular expressions.
2. To rewrite a regular expression as a finite automaton (FA).
3. To create a transition diagram and transition table for the FA generated in 2 above.

EXERCISES 6.2

1. Which of the systems you constructed in exercise 6.1.2 above are regular?
2. Construct a regular grammar to generate words over {a, b} that contain the string 'abab'.
3. Why is the rule S → aSb not allowed for producing a regular language?
4. Suppose the language with words $a^n b^n$ is restricted to n < 1000. Call it L_{1000}. Since any language with a finite number of words is regular, L_{1000} is regular. How could we construct production rules to generate words of L_{1000} and an FA for recognizing these words?
5. Is the grammar B' of listing (6.2.2) a phrase-structured grammar?
6. Construct a transition table and an FA for a language L with two symbols, Σ = {a b}, where L contains words that contain a string of at least two a's. Some words of L are aa, aaab, abba, baa, and bbaaaaa.
7. You probably built an NFA for exercise 6. If so, construct the equivalent DFA. There is an automatic way to do this. We demonstrate the method by example, using the grammar and NFA of Figure 6.2.3, which we include below.

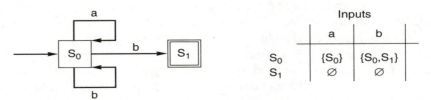

Step 1: Let S = {S_0, S_1} be the states of the NFA in Figure 6.2.3, and let P(S) = {$\emptyset$,{S_0},{S_1},{S_0,S_1}} be the powerset of S. Let P(S) be the set of states for the related DFA in Figure 6.2.4.

Step 2: We construct transitions from P(S) by:

- {S_0} is the start state, where S_0 was the start state for the NFA.
- $\emptyset \rightarrow \emptyset$ for any input.
- $S_i \rightarrow \emptyset$ for input x, if there is no transition in the NFA from S_i for x.
- $P_i \rightarrow P_j$ for input x, if $P_j = \bigcup_{S_i \in P_i} T(S_i,x)$ such that there is a state, S_i in P_i, and there is a transition in the NFA, $S_i \rightarrow T(S_i,x)$, the transition table entry set for state S_i and input x.
- Mark any state terminal (*) that contains a state that was terminal in the NFA.

Proof that this process always produces a DFA from an NFA for a finite number of inputs can be found in [Johnsonbaugh, 1993]. The resulting transition table is:

	Inputs	
States	a	b
$\emptyset$	$\emptyset$	$\emptyset$
{S_0}	{S_0}	{S_0, S_1}
*{S_1}	$\emptyset$	$\emptyset$
*{S_0, S_1}	{S_0}	{S_0, S_1}

The DFA shown at the top of the next page represents this table.

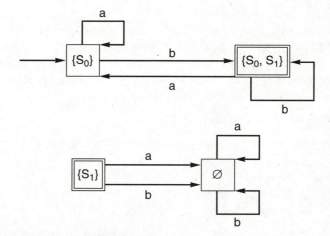

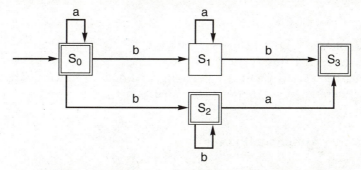

The transitions from $\{S_1\}$ and $\emptyset$ can be eliminated, since one cannot reach them from the start $\{S_0\}$, and we are left with the diagram of Figure 6.2.4.

8. Construct a DFA from the following NFA:

9. Construct production systems for your languages of exercises 6, 7, and 8.
10. Write a grammar to generate words containing a single vowel with a single consonant on each side, or the single consonant on the right followed by an s. You may limit your consonants to {b, d, m, n} to simplify matters. Some words in the language generated would be "bed," "beds," "dad," "man," "muns," etc.
11. Write a grammar, transition table, and FA to generate words with any number of a's, and exactly three b's.

6.3
CONTEXT-FREE GRAMMARS (CFGS)

There are languages that cannot be recognized by FAs and are not regular. One of the simplest of these is the language:

$$LN = \{a^n b^n : n = 1, 2, ...\} = \{ab\ aabb\ aaabbb\ ...\} \tag{6.3.1}$$

The proof that LN is not regular uses the fact that if it were, there would be a finite automaton that recognizes legal and rejects illegal strings, and that the existence of such an FA leads to a contradiction. The proof can be found in [Cohen, 1991]. Thus there are languages of type other than Chomsky's Type 3.

Recall from section 6.1 that for CFGs the left side must be a nonterminal, while the right side may be any string of terminals and nonterminals. As an example, we will look at the CFG for LN. Here $\Sigma = \{a,b\}$, $N = \{S\}$, and the start symbol is S. Production rules for strings of the form $a^n b^n$ are

$$P = \{R1: S \rightarrow aSb, R2: S \rightarrow \varepsilon\}$$

As we have seen in notation previously, these two rules can be combined into $S \rightarrow aSb \mid \varepsilon$.

We can produce the word $a^2 b^2$ using the derivation:

$$\begin{array}{ccc} R1 & R1 & R2 \\ S \rightarrow aSb & \rightarrow aaSbb & \rightarrow aabb \end{array}$$

where the final production erases the S. Notice that since $S \rightarrow \varepsilon$ is a valid production, the empty string ε is in the language LN. Erasing can lead to trouble, so various strategies have been developed to eliminate erasing rules. Here, we could have used, instead of the rules in P:

$$P2 = \{S \rightarrow aSb \mid ab\} \tag{6.3.2}$$

Let's denote LN' = L(P2). The productions of P2 do not produce the language LN = L(P), since $\varepsilon \in$ LN, but $\varepsilon \notin$ LN'.

It has been shown that any language that does not include the empty word ε can be generated by a grammar with no erasing rules.

Push-Down Automata (PDAs)

Just as the words of a regular language can be recognized by a finite automaton (FA), words of a context-free language are recognized by a *push-down automaton* (PDA). The converses are also true—any language recognized by an FA (or PDA) is regular (or context-free).

A PDA is composed of two tapes (possibly infinitely long). The first is an input tape containing the word to be recognized. We have added the symbol # at the end of the input tape to signify the end of the particular input we are trying to recognize. The second tape functions as a push-down stack, initially containing the start symbol S and the termination symbol #. Let's see how this works in Figure 6.3.1, when recognizing $a^2 b^2$ from our language LN' of listing (6.3.2). The action is to stack the a's, and pop them off as we find corresponding b's. The * below the data tape marks the position pointer for the symbol to be read next. Why don't we need a position pointer for the stack?

A PDA can be defined as a set of rules for two tapes, one containing an input string and one to be used as a stack. A rule is of the form:

$$[r, s_1] \rightarrow [x, s_2], \tag{6.3.3}$$

where r is a single character read from the input tape, s_1 lists what is on the top of the stack, and s_2 replaces s_1 on the stack. The read-pointer advances one character

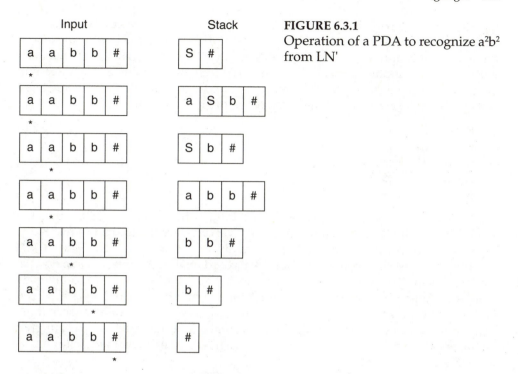

Input   Stack

FIGURE 6.3.1
Operation of a PDA to recognize a^2b^2 from LN'

Success!

if x is > in the right-hand side of the rule, or remains at the character last read if x is –. We are not confined to considering only one symbol from the stack, but may pop as many as are needed. For example, the rule [a,S] → [–,aSb] means that if a has been read on the input tape, the read-pointer remains where it is, S is popped from the stack, and aSb is pushed on. For clarity, σ may be used to represent arbitrary input tape elements. PDA rules are thus somewhat like production rules, in that the left side represents the current states of the two tapes, while the right side shows the states after appropriate actions are taken.

Production rules for a CFG can be used to construct PDA rules using the Nonselective Top-to-Bottom (NTB) Algorithm of Griffiths and Petrick [Griffiths, 1965] shown in listing (6.3.4).

NTB: CFG condition	**PDA rule**	(6.3.4)
1. $A \rightarrow s_1 s_2 \ldots s_n$	$(\sigma, A) \rightarrow (-, s_1 s_2 \ldots s_n)$	
2. $a \in \Sigma$	$(a, a) \rightarrow (>, \varepsilon)$	

NTB says (1) to replace on the stack a left-hand side of a CFG production with its right-hand side, or (2) to pop a terminal symbol found on both tapes from the stack and advance the read-pointer.

Rules for the PDA of LN' in listing (6.3.2) are shown in listing (6.3.5). The first rule was described above. The second rule says, "If S is on the top of the stack, pop S, and then push ab onto the Stack." The third rule is, "If you read an a on the input

tape and see an a on the stack, pop the a from the stack and advance the read-pointer."
The fourth rule is similar to the third, with b in place of a, and the fifth rule lets us
know when the input string has been recognized by the PDA. The stack is initialized
with S#, and the input tape with the string to be recognized followed by #. Reading
of the input string begins at the front of the tape and is from left to right. Follow these
rules through the execution of the PDA shown in Figure 6.3.1 for a^2b^2.

$$R1: [\sigma, S] \rightarrow [-, aSb] \qquad (6.3.5)$$
$$R2: [\sigma, S] \rightarrow [-, ab]$$
$$R3: [a, a] \rightarrow [>, \varepsilon]$$
$$R4: [b, b] \rightarrow [>, \varepsilon]$$
$$R5: [\#, \#] \rightarrow Success!$$

Notice that R1 and R2 are nondeterministic. Either can be used to replace S on the
stack. This is why the algorithm is nonselective: there are no guidelines for choosing which PDA rule to use if two or more apply.

Why can this PDA recognize strings that could not be recognized by an FA? We
explore this for fixed n in exercises 6.3.1 and 2. An FA has no ability to count on its
own. If a string a^nb^n is submitted to an FA for recognition, where a loop has been
built-in to recognize the a's, the FA cannot remember how many a's it has seen (how
many times it has gone around the loop), so that a loop recognizing b's could not
be traversed an equal number of times. As we have seen above, the stack can perform this counting function.

More formally, a PDA is a 6-tuple $(\Sigma^*, N \cup \Sigma^*, Start, \#, \{>, -\}, R)$, where:

1. Σ^* is $\Sigma \cup \{\#\}$, the set of input tape symbols.
2. $N \cup \Sigma^*$ is the stack symbols.
3. Start is the start symbol.
4. # is the termination symbol.
5. $\{>, -\}$ indicate movement of the read-pointer.
6. R is the set of PDA rules.

As a more practical example in programming languages, let's consider a
simplified version of a Pascal arithmetic expression. The grammar is ArithExp = $(\Sigma$,
N, P, Start), where $\Sigma = \{0, 1, +, *, (,)\}$, N = {EXP, FAC, TERM}, the start symbol is
EXP, and production rules are:

$$P: \quad R1: EXP \rightarrow TERM \mid EXP + TERM \qquad (6.3.6)$$
$$R2: TERM \rightarrow FAC \mid TERM * FAC$$
$$R3: FAC \rightarrow 0 \mid 1 \mid (EXP)$$

Three valid words from L(ArithExp) are 1*0, 1+0+1, and (1+1)*0.

Using the NTB algorithm of listing (6.3.4), a PDA to recognize L(ArithExp) has:

$$\Sigma^* = \{0,1,+,*,(,),\#\} \qquad (6.3.7)$$
$$N \cup \Sigma^* = \{0,1,+,*,(,),\#,FAC,TERM,EXP\}$$
$$Start = EXP$$
$$R: \quad AE1a-b: [\sigma, EXP] \quad \rightarrow [-, TERM] \mid [-, EXP + TERM]$$
$$AE2a-b: [\sigma, TERM] \rightarrow [-, FAC] \quad \mid [-, TERM * FAC]$$

$$\text{AE3a–c:} \quad [\sigma, \text{FAC}] \quad \rightarrow [-, 0] \quad | \ [-, 1] \ | \ [-, (\text{ EXP })]$$
$$\text{AE4a–f:} \quad [0, 0] \ | \ [1, 1] \ | \ [+, +] \ | \ [*, *] \ | \ [(, (] \ | \ [),)]$$
$$\rightarrow [>, \varepsilon]$$
$$\text{AE5:} \qquad [\#, \#] \qquad \rightarrow \text{Success}$$

Spaces between stack elements are for readability, and the | (or) is to save space. The first two rules, AE1a–b and AE2a–b, represent two rules each, AE3a–c represents three rules, and AE4a–f represents six rules. Note that rules AE1–AE3 are nondeterministic.

Now let's look at the operation of the PDA of listing (6.3.7) on the input string $(1 + 1) * 0$. This is shown in Table 6.3.1.

TABLE 6.3.1
Recognition of $(1 + 1) * 0$ by PDA(ArithExp)

Input	Stack	Rule to be applied
(1+1)*0# *	EXP #	AE1a
(1+1)*0# *	TERM #	AE2b
(1+1)*0# *	TERM * FAC #	AE2a
(1+1)*0# *	FAC * FAC #	AE3c
(1+1)*0# *	(EXP) * FAC #	AE4e
(1+1)*0# *	EXP) * FAC)	AE1b
(1+1)*0# *	EXP + TERM) * FAC) #	AE1a
(1+1)*0# *	TERM + TERM) * FAC) #	AE2a
(1+1)*0# *	FAC + TERM) * FAC) #	AE3b
(1+1)*0# *	1 + TERM) * FAC #	AE4b
(1+1)*0# *	+ TERM) * FAC #	AE4c
(1+1)*0# *	TERM) * FAC #	AE2a
(1+1)*0# *	FAC) * FAC #	AE3b
(1+1)*0# *	1) * FAC #	AE4b
(1+1)*0# *	) * FAC #	AE4f
(1+1)*0# *	* FAC #	AE4d
(1+1)*0# *	FAC #	AE3a
(1+1)*0# *	0 #	AE4a
(1+1)*0# *	#	AE5
Success!		

The reader who worked through Table 6.3.1 will have realized that the indeterminism of rules AE1–AE3 is a serious disadvantage, and that the PDA may well take many wrong paths before recognizing a valid string. Griffiths and Petrick present a selective top-to-bottom algorithm that uses an automatically generated precedence matrix to aid in the selection of which PDA rule to choose when more than one applies. Other algorithms are also given, and efficiency measures reported. Some of these are bottom-to-top, the stack initialized to #, and success reported when the input string is exhausted and the stack contains only the start and termination symbols. In a top-to-bottom PDA, we would work up through FACtors, TERMs and EXPressions until an input string was recognized as a single EXPression.

Cohen [Cohen, 1991] provides an extensive treatment of PDAs, relating them to flowcharts rather than rule pairs.

Parse Trees

Parsing, or recognizing words, is often thought of as a tree. Branches of the tree reflect which production rules were applied in recognizing the string. The parse of a^2b^2 in Figure 6.3.1 can be depicted by the *parse tree* shown in Figure 6.3.2.

The first row indicates application of S → aSb, and the second of S → ab. An inorder traversal (left-root-right) of the tree results in aabb as the resulting order of the terminals, as desired.

Similarly, the parse tree for (1 + 1) * 0, following the PDA(ArithExp) execution shown in Table 6.3.1, is shown in Figure 6.3.3. When a compiler performs the steps of syntax analysis on a program, one common method involves creating such a parse tree. Such a tree also indicates something about the semantics. It implies *operator precedence*—that the + operator and the evaluation of the expression within the parentheses comes first, and that the multiplication comes later. Hence, clearly the value of the expression is 0.

In addition, what about the question of associativity of operators? Let's look at the parse tree for 0 + 1 + 1, as shown in Figure 6.3.4. Note that it is implied that the left + operator will be applied first, with the right + to be applied later. As a result, + will be left associative. Hence, it evaluates as (0 + 1) + 1. It will be left as an exercise to show that * is also left-associative in ArithExp.

Ambiguous Grammars

Suppose that, instead of using the rules for LN' in listing (6.3.2), we generate strings of $\{a^nb^n\}$ using the rules in listing (6.3.8).

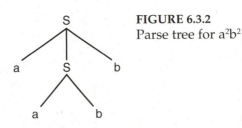

FIGURE 6.3.2
Parse tree for a^2b^2

$$S \rightarrow aS_2 \mid S_1b$$
$$S_1 \rightarrow a \mid aS_1b$$
$$S_2 \rightarrow b \mid aS_2b$$

(6.3.8)

The language generated is the same as that of LN', but two different trees represent parses of a^2b^2, as shown in Figure 6.3.5. When one or more strings produce two different parse trees, the grammar is said to be *ambiguous*.

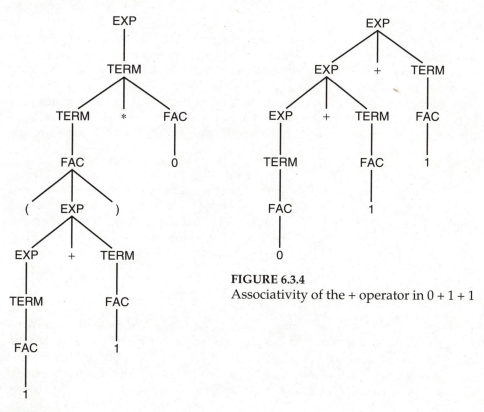

FIGURE 6.3.4
Associativity of the + operator in $0 + 1 + 1$

FIGURE 6.3.3
Parse tree in ArithExp for $(1 + 1) * 0$

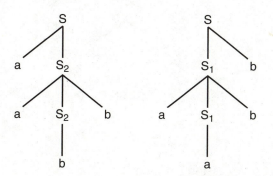

FIGURE 6.3.5
Two parses for a^2b^2 in an ambiguous grammar

Consider again our ArithExp grammar of listing (6.3.6). Suppose we try to simplify the productions to the form shown in listing (6.3.9).

EXP   → TERM   (6.3.9)
TERM → 0 | 1 | TERM + TERM | TERM * TERM

Unfortunately, now two parse trees are produced for 1 + 1 * 0 using these unparenthesized rules, as shown in Figure 6.3.6. If we evaluate the expression of the left tree using ordinary base 2 arithmetic and an inorder traversal of the tree, we would get 1. The result for the right tree is 0.

Programs have semantics as well as syntax, and the meaning of a statement (in this case, the value of the expression) must be unambiguous. There are two common ways to make an arithmetic expression unambiguous: insistence on full parentheses in the language syntax, or using an *operator precedence* that is built into the language. An expression is parsed for syntax and then evaluated in order (from left to right), with operations being performed in the order of their precedence, with those highest in the hierarchy being executed first. In Ada, the hierarchy from highest to lowest is:

** | **abs** | **not**	(exponentiation, absolute value, logical not)
* | / | **mod** | **rem**	(multiplication, division, mod, remainder)
+ | –	(unary plus or minus)
+ | – | &	(addition, subtraction, concatenation of arrays)
= | /= | < | <= | > | >=	(relational operators)
and | **or** | **xor**	(logical binary operators)

Applications

Context-free grammars have many practical uses, as much of the syntax of programming languages can be specified using them. The first to use CFGs for the language defininition was Algol 60, followed by FORTRAN, Pascal, BASIC, PL/I, and finally, Ada, among others. Each of these languages has non-context-free constructs, however. One of these is that in typed languages, a variable type must be declared before it

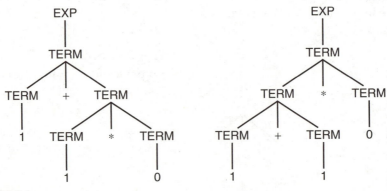

FIGURE 6.3.6
Two parses for 1 + 1 * 0 in an ambiguous expression language

is used in a program. The BNF description usually lists a variable declaration section as optional, to include (sub)programs with no variables. An official language description will include some other method than BNF for describing such features. Compilers are particularly amenable to CFGs with their implementations as stacks, so as much of a language as possible is defined using a CFG.

Normal Forms

Normal forms are methods of language description following certain rules. One of their important uses is in constructing proofs about language properties. For many languages, we may assume that they are specified in normal form and confine our proof to these constructs. Normal forms may not be particularly easy to read or to understand, but they are easier to analyze than more casual language descriptions.

Any context-free language can be described by any of the normal forms below.

Chomsky Normal Form (CNF)

A grammar is said to be in Chomsky Normal Form if all its production rules are of one of two forms:

1. $N_1 \rightarrow N_2 N_3$, where N_i is a nonterminal
2. $N \rightarrow t$, where N is a nonterminal and t is a single terminal

Let's write our CFG for LN' in CNF. Remember from listing (6.3.5) that LN' is the language of words of the form $a^n b^n$, and its context-free grammar is the two rules (1) $S \rightarrow aSb$ and (2) $S \rightarrow ab$. An equivalent CNF for this grammar is:

C1) $S \rightarrow AC$
C2) $C \rightarrow SB$
C3) $S \rightarrow AB$
C4) $A \rightarrow a$
C5) $B \rightarrow b$

And a derivation of $a^3 b^3$ is:

$$
\begin{array}{cccccccc}
\text{C1} & \text{C2} & \text{C1} & \text{C2} & \text{C3} & \text{C4} & \text{C4} \\
S \rightarrow AC & \rightarrow ASB & \rightarrow AACB & \rightarrow AASBB & \rightarrow AAABBB & \rightarrow aAABBB & \rightarrow \ldots
\end{array}
$$

$$
\begin{array}{c}
\text{C5} \\
\rightarrow aaabbb
\end{array}
$$

The notation above an arrow indicates which rule was used to produce the right side from the left.

CNF makes language analysis particularly easy, because you only have to worry about words produced through productions of two kinds. The two-rule CFG for LN' was rewritten into five CNF rules. This commonly occurs, so CNF grammars tend to be very long.

Backus-Normal Form (BNF)

A more readable normal form is Backus Normal Form (BNF). BNF is also called Backus-Naur Form, recognizing the contributions of Peter Naur as the editor of the ALGOL 60 Report, which was written in BNF.

BNF, as described in Chapter 0, is a metalanguage used to describe production systems to generate context-free languages. Each language generated using BNF includes a set of terminals, a set of nonterminals, and a list of productions. BNF terminals are indicated variously in different language references. We will use a boldface lowercase string. As shown below, nonterminals are enclosed in angle brackets. The metasymbols of BNF (as used in this text and in the MiniManuals) are shown in listing (6.3.10).

Symbol	Meaning	(6.3.10)
::=	is defined to be	
|	alternatively	
<something>	nonterminal	
something	terminal	

As time has passed, BNF has been extended to EBNF to make language descriptions more readable by replacing some recursive definitions with iterative ones, as shown in listing (6.3.11).

Symbol	Meaning	(6.3.11)
[something]	zero or one occurrence of something, i.e., optional	
{something}	zero or more occurrences of something	
(this | that)	grouping; either of this or that	

We refer the reader to Chapter 0, BNF and EBNF, for examples of the use of each of these symbols.

A recursive BNF definition for a Pascal identifier is:

<identifier> ::= <letter> | <identifier><letter> | <identifier><digit>

In EBNF we could write nonrecursively:

<identifier> ::= <letter> | <letter>{letter | digit}

The Ada EBNF definition for an **if** statement is shown in listing (6.3.12):[7]

```
if_statement ::=                                              (6.3.12)
   if condition then sequence_of_statements
   {elseif condition then sequence_of_statements}
   [else sequence_of_statements]
   end if;
```

In CNF, it gets quite long. We could start out as in listing (6.3.13):

$$IS \rightarrow I\,TP \qquad\qquad (6.3.13)$$
$$I \rightarrow \mathbf{if}$$
$$TP \rightarrow C\,TS$$
etc.

---

[7]In the Ada Language Reference Manual, terminals are written in lowercase boldface, and nonterminals in plain face.

Let's look at LN' = {$a^n b^n$ | n = 1, 2...} of listing (6.3.2), defined in BNF.

<AnBn> ::= **ab** | **a**<AnBn>**b**

Notice the recursive use of <AnBn>. To derive $a^3 b^3$, we would use the definition three times:

<AnBn> → **a**<AnBn>**b** → **aa**<AnBn>**bb** → **aaabbb**

with the final substitution for <AnBn> being the terminal **ab**.

BNF has an advantage other than making definitions precise and aiding in language analysis. It imposes a structure on words that aid in constructing a recognizer, as shown in Figure 6.3.7. Methods for traversing trees are well-developed. To recognize $a^3 b^3$, we could traverse the tree from the bottom aaabbb up to the top <AnBn>, or from the top down.

LAB 6.2: EBNF: PAPER AND PENCIL

Objectives (Labs can be found in the *Instructor's Manual*.)

1. To use EBNF form as a language generator, employing EBNF definitions for an existing language such as Pascal or Ada.
2. To rewrite the EBNF definitions as a context-free grammar.
3. To build a push-down automaton (PDA) to recognize the language fragments generated by problem 1 above.
4. To program problem 3, if the instructor wishes it and there is time.

Syntax Diagrams

Normal forms can still be hard to read and understand for those untrained in mathematical logic. *Syntax diagrams* equivalent to the forms can be used by even novice programmers. A syntax diagram for $a^n b^n$ is shown in Figure 6.3.8. Notice the

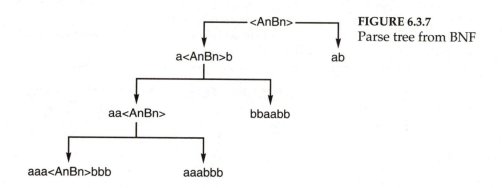

FIGURE 6.3.7
Parse tree from BNF

AnBn

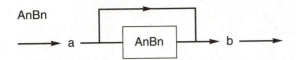

FIGURE 6.3.8
Syntax diagram for $a^n b^n$

recursion here. We are defining AnBn, as listed in the heading to the diagram, and AnBn occurs in the diagram itself. It's not hard to see that AnBn is taking the place of the start symbol S of the production rule $S \rightarrow ab \mid aSb$.

EXERCISES 6.3
1. Strings of the form $a^n b^n$ (e.g., $a^2 b^2$, $a^3 b^3$, etc.) cannot be generated from a context-free grammar (CFG). See if you can figure out why by attempting the NFA.
2. a. Design an FA to recognize strings of the form $a^n b^n$ (n 3). Will this method work for any strings $a^n b^n$ where (n k) for fixed k?
   b. Why won't the method work for arbitrary n?
3. a. Let A = (Σ, N, P, S) where Σ = {0,1,2,3,4,5,6,7,8,9,+,–,=,X}, N = {NUM, VAR, NEGNUM}. Write context-free rules to produce words that are addition expressions such as X = –2 + 6. (Notice that we are using the – symbol in two ways: a unary –, as in –2, and a binary –, as in 5 – 2. Spaces are for ease of reading, but you need not include them in your rules.)
   b. Could the same language be produced using a regular grammar? Why or why not?
   c. Rewrite your grammar to include spaces so that X = 2 + 6 is a legal word.
4. a. Extend your grammar of exercise 3a to include numbers of any length, such as – 1230, 546682, etc. Be careful to eliminate leading 0s, i.e., your grammar shouldn't produce 0053 as a NUM.
   b. Do you think this language could be produced from a regular grammar? Is this answer different from 3b? Why or why not?
5. Extend your grammar of exercise 4 to include sums of more than two numbers. Try this in two ways, with and without parentheses.
6. Extend the grammar of exercise 5 to include multiplication. Two words produced could be X = 4 + (2 * 3), and X = (4 + 2) * 3.
7. Consider the following context-free grammar to generate English sentences.

({the, a, man, boy, ball, hit, saw, said, believed}, {S, NP, VP, DET, N, VT, VS}, P, S),
P:

S $\rightarrow$ NP VP	DET $\rightarrow$ the $\mid$ a
NP $\rightarrow$ DET N	N $\rightarrow$ man $\mid$ boy $\mid$ ball
VP $\rightarrow$ VT NP	VT $\rightarrow$ hit $\mid$ saw
VP $\rightarrow$ VS S	VS $\rightarrow$ said $\mid$ believed

Is "The ball believed the man hit the boy" a valid sentence? If so, rewrite the CFG to eliminate it.

8. Consider the grammar G1 = ({a, b, c, d}, {S, A, B}, P, S):

   P: 1. S → AB   4. B → bc
       2. A → a   5. B → Bd
       3. A → ABb

   a. Show that abcd ∈ L(G1).
   b. Prove that G1 is context-free.
   c. Construct a PDA = (Σ^*, N ∪ Σ^*, Start, #, {>,-}, R), that recognizes words from L(G1) using the NTB algorithm of listing (6.3.4).
   d. Show that the PDA you constructed in 8c recognizes abcd.
9. Show that $1 + 1 * 0$ ∈ L(ArithExp) using the PDA of listing (6.3.7).
10. Verify that multiplication $*$ is left-associative for the grammar ArithExp of listing (6.3.6).
11. Suppose that we replaced the production rules of ArithExp of listing (6.3.6) with:

    P': 1. EXP   → TERM | TERM + TERM
         2. TERM → FAC | FAC $*$ FAC
         3. FAC   → 0 | 1 | (EXP)

    Call this grammar ArithExp2. Using parse trees:
    a. Is $(1 + 1) * 0$ in L(ArithExp2)?
    b. Does $(1 + 1) * 0$ evaluate the same way as in ArithExp?
    c. Is $0 + 1 + 1$ in L(ArithExp2)?
    d. Is $0 + (1 + 1)$ in L(ArithExp2)?
12. Finish the CNF definition of listing (6.3.13) for an Ada if_statement. For the sake of brevity, omit CNF definitions for conditions and for a sequence_of_statements.
13. Construct a syntax diagram for an Ada if_statement. The EBNF is shown in listing (6.3.12).

6.4
GRAMMARS FOR NATURAL LANGUAGES

Human beings communicate in natural languages, but few natural languages can be characterized precisely enough to define a grammar that generates all valid sentences. Arbitrary statements cannot always be parsed either, to facilitate understanding. However, in addition to phrase-structured grammars, both context-free and context-sensitive techniques have proven useful in understanding natural languages in some fairly restricted settings. It is the ambiguousness of unrestricted everyday language that hinders the development of practical speech-recognition devices.

Closely related to the finite automata (FAs) we described as recognizers for regular languages are *recursive transition networks* (RTNs). These can be used as context-free language generators equivalent to CFGs. They differ from FAs in that they allow arc labels that refer to other networks. For example, the CFG to generate strings of the form $a^n b^n$ is: S → ab | aSb. An equivalent RTN is shown in Figure 6.4.1.

The difference here from an NFA is that the arc labeled S occurs in the middle of the RTN. It means that the entire S network is to be inserted for the label S. You will be asked to investigate a related NFA in exercise 6.4.2 on page 281.

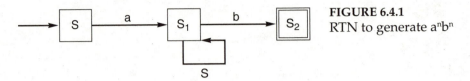

FIGURE 6.4.1
RTN to generate $a^n b^n$

A simple CFG for generating English sentences is the following:

S $\leftarrow$ NP VP	NOUN $\leftarrow$ cat(s) | rat(s) | dog(s)
VP $\leftarrow$ VERB NP	ART $\quad \leftarrow$ the | a
NP $\leftarrow$ NOUN	VERB $\leftarrow$ ate | meowed
NP $\leftarrow$ ART NOUN	

where S stands for sentence, VP for verb phrase, NP for noun phrase, and ART for article. Sentences such as "The cat ate a rat" can be generated with it, but so can "A cats ate a rats" or "Cats meowed dogs." A good bit more information is needed to generate meaningful sentences. Augmented RTNs can be of help here. Notice that the arrows in the grammar rules are reversed from what we have seen before. This suggests bottom-up sentence parsing, which is one of the first steps in understanding natural language (see Figure 6.4.2).

One method that has proved useful in automatic language understanding is the *augmented transition network* (ATN). Here the RTN is augmented by tests on each arc, which guarantee agreement between nouns and adjectives, subjects and verbs, verbs and auxiliaries, etc. A transition network must also be augmented to handle verb complements, such as adverbial and infinitive phrases.

ATNs can be used to generate and recognize grammatically correct sentences, but meaning is another complex activity. Consider the various meanings of "broke":

1. Alex broke the glass with a rock.
2. The rock broke the glass.
3. The glass broke.

Add an adverb to number 1: "Alex intentionally broke the glass." Does "The rock intentionally broke the glass" or "The glass intentionally broke" make sense? Only animate entities should have "intention." Semantic networks have been developed

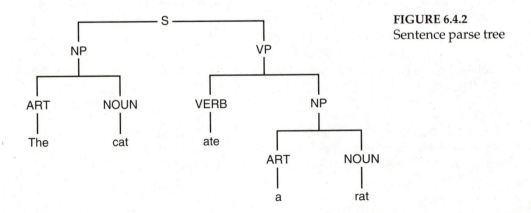

FIGURE 6.4.2
Sentence parse tree

to deal with questions such as these and many others. We will deal with some of these sorts of relationships when we discuss declarative languages in Part VI.

EXERCISES 6.4

1. Below are three ambiguous English phrases. Can you find at least two meanings for each? Do the two meanings parse differently?
   a. "I hate visiting relatives."
   b. "5 * 3 + 2"
   c. "Here's to my last wife!"
2. Parse the three sentences using the verb "broke" (discussed on the previous page) in a manner similar to that of Figure 6.4.2.
3. What is the language recognized by the NFA shown in the figure below? How does it differ from the RTN of Figure 6.4.1? What type language is recognized?

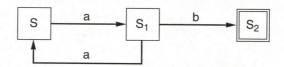

6.5 SUMMARY

We have looked at four formal language types. Grammars to generate languages of Chomsky Types 0 to 3 are called phrase-structured. A grammar to generate a language is a system $G = (\Sigma, N, P, Start)$, where Σ is the set of terminal symbols from which strings are constructed, N is a set of nonterminals, S is a symbol of N called the start symbol, and P is a set of production rules of the form $\alpha \to \beta$, where α (or part of it) is to be replaced by β (or part of it).

Type 0 is the most general, and includes all the others. Productions for these grammars are unrestricted, except that if $\alpha \to \beta$ is a production, α must contain at least one nonterminal. Type 0 languages are also called recursively enumerable (r.e.), which means that there is some function $f(n)$ from the natural numbers to the alphabet Σ, which will generate valid strings. Strings may be infinite in length. It is widely held by mathematicians that any function that can be effectively computed is r.e. Strings of Type 0 languages can be recognized by Turing Machines (TMs).

Type 1 languages are generated by context-sensitive grammars (CSGs). Productions are restricted in that the length of α must be less than or equal to the length of β. They can be recognized by linear-bounded automata (LBAs), which will halt in time proportional to the length of an input string.

Context-free grammars (CFGs) are of Chomsky Type 2. They can be generated using production rules with a single nonterminal on the left side. Context-free languages are recognized by push-down automata (PDAs). These are the most important for the construction of parsers for compilers, since many computer languages can be almost completely defined by a context-free grammar. Although we have not discussed it here, the construction of parse trees from PDAs is straightforward. Backus Normal Forms (BNFs) and their extensions are equivalent to context-free grammars. BNF and EBNF (Extended BNF) are widely used to specify context-free language rules. The Ada and Pascal Standards are written in EBNF, with those portions that are not context-free described in ordinary English.

Regular languages are context-free, but can be generated by production rules of the form $N \rightarrow t$, or $N_1 \rightarrow tN_2$, where N_i is a nonterminal. Any language with a finite number of words is regular, and can be recognized by a finite automaton (FA). Some parsers are based on FAs for first-pass checking for valid tokens, PDAs for second-pass checking of statement syntax, and some other process for statements that are neither regular nor context-free.

6.6
NOTES ON REFERENCES

Treatment of formal languages has been very brief here. A course in theoretical computer science would consider proofs of much that we have mentioned. We have referred to Daniel Cohen's readable elementary text [Cohen, 1991]. It would be a good choice to add to your library. Lewis and Papadimitriou's text [Lewis, 1981] has long provided a somewhat more advanced handling. Hopcroft and Ullman [Hopcroft, 1979] also provides a good treatment. The classic book on recursive function theory is [Rogers, 1967].

Those interested in the practical use of these techniques in programming languages would benefit from a book on compiler design. Aho, Sethi, and Ullman [Aho, 1986] is the standard in this area. Pittman and Peters [Pittman, 1992] is particularly readable and gives a nice treatment of scanners and parsers.

Turing Machines are considered in many mathematical logic texts, e.g., [Mendelson, 1979]. Using Turing Machines to build context-free recognizers continues to receive attention. See [Griffiths, 1965] for earlier work, and [Graham, 1980] for something more recent. Both articles contain extensive bibliographies. Hodges' [Hodges, 1983] biography of Alan Turing is notable in its combination of sensitive commentary on a troubled life with correct scientific exposition. For a brief but meritorious review of Hodges, see [Hofstadter, 1985b].

A well-written little book for nonspecialists is *Gödel's Proof* [Nagel, 1958]. As a note on the inside cover says, "In 1931 Kurt Gödel published a revolutionary paper—one that challenged certain basic assumptions underlying much traditional research in mathematics and logic. Today his exploration of *terra incognita* has been recognized as one of the major contributions to modern scientific thought. . . . It offers any educated person with a taste for logic and philosophy the chance to satisfy his or her intellectual curiosity about a previously inaccessible subject."

Natural language understanding is often the purview of linguists. A good place to get started in the literature is through the Synthese Language Library published by D. Reidel. One collection surveying current trends is Volume 15, *The Nature of Syntactic Representation* [Jacobson, 1982].

Declarative Languages

Unlike an imperative language, which allows one to write a sequence of commands to a computer, a declarative language facilitates the writing of declarations, or truths. In contrast to the four commands, shown in the Part II opening page, used to store "Jack the Ripper" at a particular memory location, the single declaration,

```
(cons 'Jack (list 'the 'Ripper))
```

states that the **cons** function constructs an expression from the literal 'Jack and a list, '(the Ripper), produced by the **list** function. Where the result is stored in memory is left up to the particular language being used.

Declarative languages are considered to be higher level than imperative languages, because a declarative programmer works with concepts rather than with storage locations of the machine itself.

In Chapter 7 we will look at languages based on logic, while Chapter 8 considers those rooted in the mathematical notion of a function, which operates on its arguments to produce a single value. In the example above, the arguments are 'Jack and '(the Ripper), and the value produced by the **cons** function is '(Jack the Ripper). Chapter 9 briefly considers languages for databases, based on the manipulation of ordered tuples, called relations.

CHAPTER 7
LOGIC PROGRAMMING

7.0	**In this Chapter**	**285**
7.1	**Formal Logical Systems**	**286**
Historical Vignette: Aristotle		286
Proofs		288
Resolution		288
Unification		293
Searching		294
Backtracking		295
Facts, Goals, and Conditions		296
Backward and Forward Chaining		297
Representing Negative Facts		298
Exercises 7.1		299
7.2	**PROLOG**	**301**
Historical Vignette: PROLOG:		
Colmerauer and Roussel		301
Conversing in PROLOG: Facts,		
Rules, and Queries		302

Syntax		303
Data Structures		304
Built-In Operators and Functors		306
Control		308
PROLOG Implementations		312
A Theoretical Machine		312
Parallel Architectures		315
Garbage Collection		316
Types and Modules		316
Applications		317
Artificial Intelligence		317
Relational Databases		317
The Fifth Generation		317
Strengths and Weaknesses		318
Exercises 7.2		319
7.3	**Summary**	**321**
7.4	**Notes on References**	**322**

Logic Programming

Logic is the science of reasoning, and as such includes formal methodologies that have been found useful for solving problems other than those resolved by intuition, leaps of faith, or compromise. Such nonlogical methods are used to arrive at workable solutions to many social problems, but often cannot be translated into algorithms usable for computer programs.

During the first quarter of the twentieth century, it was believed that all of mathematics as well as formal verbal reasoning could be expressed in a formal system of logic. Bertrand Russell and David Hilbert worked independently to show that this was so, but both researchers were eventually disappointed. Nonetheless, a logical system includes enough of mathematics to make it a reasonable theoretical basis for a programming language.

7.0
IN THIS CHAPTER

We will assume that the reader of this chapter knows something about the calculus of statements, sometimes called the propositional calculus, and also the predicate calculus, which includes quantified variables in propositions. If not, Appendix A contains enough material on these calculi for understanding the material that follows.

The main topics in the chapter include:

- Proof by the method of resolution
- Unification of variables
- Managing a database search through backtracking
- Reasoning through backward or forward chaining
- The PROLOG language
- Artificial intelligence using PROLOG

- Relational databases in PROLOG
- PROLOG Implementations

7.1
FORMAL LOGICAL SYSTEMS

The first known logical system, attributed to Aristotle during the fourth century B.C., included laws of deduction based on statements of four possible forms. "All students work hard" and "Some students eat a lot" are examples of two of the forms. The deduction rules then allow us to state that "Some who eat a lot work hard."

HISTORICAL VIGNETTE

Aristotle

He was the student of Plato, tutor to Alexander the Great, and a prolific author who wrote on virtually every field of study known in his time. His works dealt with such diverse topics as logic, politics, economics, biology, physics, meteorology, ethics, psychology, and theology. His name is Aristotle, and he was one of the greatest philosophers of the ancient Greek world.

Aristotle was born in the Ionian colony at Stagira in Macedonia in 384 B.C. Randall notes that "all the major Greek philosophers, with the exception of Socrates and Plato, had been Ionians" [Randall, 1960]. Although Aristotle's father is listed as Nicomachus, physician to King Amyntas, it was rumored that his real begetter was the god of healing and medicine and that his grandfather was Apollo, god of reason and light [Randall, 1960].

Aristotle was sent at age 17 to Athens to study at the Academy. There he was trained in philosophy by Plato and quickly established himself as "the mind of the school" and "the reader." He disagreed with some of Plato's doctrines, but was influenced greatly by Plato's work, especially during his early years. His writings during this period reflect Plato's own on such topics as the immortality of the soul, rhetoric, justice, and the idea of pure good.

However, Aristotle was sharply critical of the instructor Isocrates. "He shared Plato's contempt for Isocrates's poverty of thought and for his elevation of oratorical success over the pursuit of truth" [Ross, 1923]. This criticism made him the enemy of the Isocratean school.

When Plato died in 348–7 B.C., he left the direction of the Academy to his nephew, Speusippus, even though he considered Aristotle to be his best student. Some say this is why Aristotle left the Academy. Others claim it was because of Speusippus's stressing of mathematics, while still others hypothesize that Aristotle had not been fully accepted socially.

Aristotle spent several years studying plants and animals along the coast of Asia Minor before travelling to Macedonia to assume the post of tutor to King Philip's 13-year-old son Alexander. When the boy became king, Aristotle returned to Athens to establish his own school in the Lyceum. The school was called "The Peripatetic" because Aristotle often walked and talked with his students in the Lyceum gardens. Mornings were devoted to logic, and afternoons given to rhetoric, politics, and ethics. Aristotle stated that logic, originally called analytics, is "not a substantive science, but a part of the general culture which everyone should undergo before he studies science; and which alone will enable him to know for what sorts of proposition he should demand proof and what sorts of proof he should demand for them" [Ross, 1922].

Aristotle's inspiration to develop logic was a desire to lay down the mathematical pattern present in all sciences. He defined science as "a series of incontestably true statements for which it can be maintained that they fall into two classes. To the first class belong the basic principles or axioms, i.e., the remarkable propositions whose truth is so evident that they are neither capable of nor in need of proof. To the second class belong the propositions or theorems, i.e., the propositions whose truth can be demonstrated on the basis of the truth of the axioms" [Scholz, 1961]. The model for these propositions was Greek geometry. Aristotle's greatest work in the field of logic is the *Organon*, which is comprised of several volumes. The main body of the work deals with different types of statements and their logical properties and relationships.

When Alexander died in 323 B.C., anti-Macedonian feelings were widespread. Aristotle's Macedonian connections, along with the enmity of the Isocrateans, made him a likely scapegoat. He retired to Chalcis where he died the following year at the age of 62. He has been remembered not only for his intellectual genius, but also for his kind and affectionate nature.

Aristotle's rules of deduction were found to be inadequate for many statements, and a somewhat different logical system was formalized later. It is known as the propositional calculus (PC) because it provides rules for calculating the truth values of propositions, which are simply declarative sentences or statements. In this system, any proposition must be assigned the value TRUE or FALSE. There are no MAYBEs.

For example, from the two propositions,

p: Brutus killed Caesar.
q: Cassius killed Caesar.

we can construct the proposition,

r: p or q

expressing the notion that either Brutus or Cassius killed Caesar, or possibly both. Then the truth value of r would be calculated in PC as TRUE (Value(r) = TRUE, if either Value(p) = TRUE or Value(q) = TRUE).

Proofs

A theory is a set of axioms, assumptions, and theses or theorems provable from them. We review the logical axioms and the theories of the propositional and predicate calculi in Appendix A. Logical axioms are usually assumed without restatement for a theory. Sometimes assumptions are also called axioms, as in Peano's axioms for the theory of whole number arithmetic. A statement that is expressible in a theory is called a hypothesis until it is proven true, when it is renamed a thesis of the theory.

There are several methods of proof. Some start with axioms and assumptions that are assumed true for the situation at hand, and proceed through repeated use of rules of inference to other theses, which are then TRUE given the assumptions. In the predicate calculus (PC), using the logical axioms of *Principia Mathematica* (PM), there are two rules of inference, *modus ponens* and *uniform replacement*. Modus ponens states that if the two statements, a and p, are TRUE, where p is "if a is TRUE, then b follows," then b is TRUE. Uniform replacement requires that if in a statement s we replace a free variable X with something else, say Y, then all free occurrences of X in s must also be replaced with Y. Again, the reader is referred to Appendix A for explanations of these rules.

Other methods start with the hypothesis to be proved and proceed backwards to axioms and assumptions. Another method is proof by *contradiction*, where the hypothesis p to be proved is assumed false. The axioms of PC assure us that if p is FALSE, then not(p) is TRUE. A chain of inference proceeds from not(p) until a contradiction is reached. A statement is contradictory if it can be proven to be both TRUE and FALSE, in which case a contradiction has been shown. Since a theory is assumed to be consistent, i.e., contradiction-free, and since the assumption of not(p) leads to a contradiction, p must be TRUE. There is, however, another method that is better suited to computer solution.

Resolution

In 1965, J. Alan Robinson published an article in the *Journal of the Association for Computing Machinery* demonstrating a new principle called *resolution*, which is a single process including no axioms other than logical rules, and which is a complete and consistent first-order logical system. The order of a system depends on what substitutions are allowed for variables. "X killed Caesar" is a first-order statement if only constants (individuals) or expressions that evaluate to constants, and not other statements, may be substituted for X. Resolution bears similarities to the *reductio* method of proof by contradiction in Appendix A.

In its simplest form, resolution works like this: Suppose we are interested in p or q: "Brutus killed Caesar or Cassius killed Caesar." This statement can be *resolved* to p: "Brutus killed Caesar" if we also have the fact ¬q[1]: "¬Cassius killed Caesar." p: "Brutus killed Caesar" is called the *resolvent*. This resolution can be written symbolically in three equivalent ways as shown in listing (7.1.1).

---

[1]We use the abbreviation "¬p" to represent not(p).

$$p \text{ or } q \qquad\qquad \neg q \rightarrow p \qquad\qquad (p \text{ or } q) \text{ and } \neg p \qquad\qquad (7.1.1)$$
$$\frac{\neg p}{q} \qquad\qquad \frac{\neg p}{q} \qquad\qquad\qquad q$$

We say that q is a logical consequence of facts $p_1, p_2, \ldots, p_n$ if whenever all of the p_i are interpreted as TRUE, so is q. This is nothing more than modus ponens.

The theorem applicable to resolution as used for logic programming is:

Resolution theorem: q is a logical consequence of $p_1, p_2, \ldots, p_n$, if ($\neg q$ and p_1 and p_2 and ... and p_n) is FALSE.

In the notation of listing (7.1.1), and using the "or" form of ($\neg q$ and p_1 and p_2 and ... and p_n), q is TRUE if the derivation of listing (7.1.2) holds.

$$q \text{ or } \neg p_1 \text{ or } \neg p_2 \text{ or } \ldots \text{ or } \neg p_n \qquad\qquad (7.1.2)$$
$$\frac{\neg q}{\text{FALSE}}$$

For example, suppose we want to prove that q: "Harry is Larry's brother" is a consequence of:

p_1: Joe is Harry's father.
p_2: Mary is Harry's mother.
p_3: Joe is Larry's father.
p_4: Mary is Larry's mother.
p_5: Two boys are brothers if they have the same mother and the same father.

Formally, we want to prove that $q \leftarrow p_1 \& p_2 \& p_3 \& p_4 \& p_5$,[2] and then use modus ponens to derive q from the assumption of the truth of $p_1 \& p_2 \& p_3 \& p_4 \& p_5$.

The resolution theorem suggests that our strategy is to show that:

$$\neg q \& p_1 \& p_2 \& p_3 \& p_4 \& p_5 \qquad\qquad (7.1.3)$$

is FALSE, i.e., we will assume they are not brothers.

This is easy to do if we rewrite p_5 by substituting Harry and Larry for the two boys. Then we have:

p_5':   Harry and Larry are brothers if they have the same mother and father.

That they have the same mother and father is shown using p_1 through p_4. So we have $q \leftarrow p_1 \& p_2 \& p_3 \& p_4 \& p_5'$.

The resolution theorem says that:

$$p_1 \& p_2 \& p_3 \& p_4 \& p_5' \qquad \text{theses} \qquad\qquad (7.1.4)$$
$$\frac{\neg q}{\text{FALSE}} \qquad\qquad \text{assumption}$$
$$\text{contradiction}$$
$$q \qquad\qquad \text{resolution}$$

---

[2]Writing the implication arrows backwards has become customary in logic programming to emphasize the goal of a proof, i.e., that which is to be proved on the left by implication from premises on the right. Thus A ← B & C, should be read, "A is true if both B and C are true."

A statement such as (7.1.3) can be written in the or, or disjunctive normal form, as we explore in exercise A.2 of Appendix A. Thus $q \leftarrow p_1 \& p_2 \& p_3 \& p_4 \& p_5'$ can be written equivalently as:

$$q \text{ or } \neg p_1 \text{ or } \neg p_2 \text{ or } \neg p_3 \text{ or } \neg p_4 \text{ or } \neg p_5' \qquad (7.1.5)$$

This last statement, which contains six disjuncts, only one of which is positive, is called a *Horn Clause*. If in addition we allow the universal quantifier FORALL, statements are said to be in extended Horn Clause form. It is the resolution of extended Horn Clauses that forms the basis for pure logic programming, of which PROLOG is an enhanced implementation.

Resolution need not be confined to finding a single disjunct or fact as shown in listing (7.1.2). The general resolution principle states that:

$$\begin{array}{l} \text{S1 or q or S2} \\ \underline{\text{S3 or } \neg q \text{ or S4}} \qquad \text{resolves to:} \\ \text{S1 or S2 or S3 or S4,} \qquad \text{for any S1, S2, S3, and S4.} \end{array} \qquad (7.1.6)$$

As an example, suppose we have in our database the inferences:

$$\begin{array}{l} \text{in\_jail} \leftarrow \text{committed\_crime \& got\_caught.} \\ \neg\text{in\_jail} \leftarrow \neg\text{got\_caught.} \end{array} \qquad (7.1.7)$$

These can be written as the Horn Clauses:

$$\begin{array}{l} \text{C1:in\_jail or } \neg\text{committed\_crime or } \neg\text{got\_caught.} \\ \text{C2:} \neg\text{in\_jail or got\_caught.} \end{array} \qquad (7.1.8)$$

Using the resolution principle of listing (7.1.6) twice, C1 and C2 resolve to the clause C3:

$$\begin{array}{l} \text{C1:in\_jail or } \neg\text{committed\_crime or } \neg\text{got\_caught.} \\ \underline{\text{C2:} \neg\text{in\_jail or got\_caught.}} \\ \text{C3:} \neg\text{committed\_crime or } \neg\text{got\_caught or got\_caught.} \end{array} \qquad (7.1.9)$$

C3 adds no new information because it is always TRUE (why?), so we do not add it to the database. Suppose we add C4:committed_crime, C5:got_caught, and C6:¬in_jail to the database.

$$\begin{array}{l} \text{C1:in\_jail or } \neg\text{committed\_crime or } \neg\text{got\_caught.} \\ \underline{\text{C4:committed\_crime.}} \\ \\ \text{C7:in\_jail or } \neg\text{got\_caught.} \\ \underline{\text{C5:got\_caught.}} \\ \\ \text{C8:in\_jail.} \\ \underline{\text{C6:} \neg\text{in\_jail.}} \\ \\ \text{FALSE} \end{array} \qquad (7.1.10)$$

Our database is now:

C1:in_jail or ¬committed_crime or ¬got_caught.   (7.1.11)
C2:¬in_jail or got_caught.
C7:in_jail or ¬got_caught.
C4:committed_crime.
C5:got_caught.
C6:¬in_jail.
C8:in_jail.

Listing (7.1.11) shows an inconsistent database. (It is obvious here that the inconsistency is the inclusion of the two clauses, C6 and C8. No one can be both in jail and not in jail at the same time.) Listing (7.1.10) shows its resolution to FALSE. Resolution is *refutation complete,* which means that FALSE will always be derivable from an inconsistent database. Resolution is also *correct,* which means that FALSE will only be derived from an inconsistent database. These properties lead to a process of *querying* the database. Suppose we submit the query, committed_crime? This is equivalent to temporarily adding the clause ¬committed_crime to the database. This resolves to listing (7.1.12):

committed_crime   (7.1.12)
¬committed_crime
FALSE

Thus we are looking for an empty (FALSE) derivation from a consistent database to answer a query. When we query the database committed_crime?, the resolution strategy is to temporarily add ¬committed_crime to the database. If the database then becomes inconsistent—which it will if committed_crime is derivable from the original, consistent database since resolution is complete—we know it was made so by this addition, since resolution is also correct.

Our resolution strategy is to search through a database, looking for two Horn Clauses, one of which contains a disjunct d and the other contains ¬d. Remember that:

d

¬d   resolves to

FALSE

We are only able to derive FALSE if the database is inconsistent. If we know (or assume) that our database was consistent, and that by adding the clause ¬d it becomes inconsistent, we can conclude that the clause d must have been TRUE in the first place. This follows by the *principle of excluded middle,* which you are asked to prove in exercise A.5 of Appendix A. This principle says that if d is a clause, then it must be either TRUE or FALSE, with no MAYBEs. Furthermore, it can't be both TRUE and FALSE.

Let's look at an example due to Doug DeGroot [DeGroot, 1984], of a database of Horn Clauses and their resolution with a query to that database. For ease of understanding, we will first write the database clauses in "&/←" form. The database is our theory, and we will assume that each clause or statement in it is TRUE.

C1: happy(tom) ← watching(tom,football) & has(tom,supplies)   (7.1.13)
C2: has(tom,supplies) ← has(tom,beer) & has(tom,pretzels)
C3: watching(tom,football) ← is_on(tv) & playing(cowboys)
C4: is_on(tv)
C5: playing(cowboys)
C6: has(tom,beer)
C7: has(tom,pretzels)

If we wish to find out if Tom is happy, we have to show that happy(tom) is a logical consequence of C1 through C7. We know from the resolution theorem that if C8 is ¬happy(tom), and that C1 & C2 & . . . & C7 & C8 resolves to FALSE, then the query happy(tom) is TRUE. We thus add to our database the negation of the query (C8) and resolve the database. At each step in the resolution chain, the two statements that were resolved are listed to the right of the resolvent, which is then added to the database, e.g., C8 and C1' were resolved to produce C9. C1' through C4' are Horn Clauses equivalent to C1 through C4.

C8: ¬happy(tom)   (7.1.14)
C1': happy(tom) or ¬watching(tom,football) or ¬has(tom,supplies)
C2': has(tom,supplies) or ¬has(tom,beer) or¬has(tom,pretzels)
C3': watching(tom,football) or ¬is_on(tv) or ¬playing(cowboys)
C4': is_on(tv)
C5: playing(cowboys)
C6: has(tom,beer)
C7: has(tom,pretzels)
C9: ¬watching(football,tom) or ¬has(tom,supplies)   C8, C1'
C10: ¬has(tom,supplies) or ¬is_on(tv) or ¬playing(cowboys)   C9, C3'
C11: ¬is_on(tv) or ¬playing(cowboys) or ¬has(tom,beer) or
     ¬has(tom,pretzels)   C10, C2'
C12: ¬playing(cowboys) or ¬has(tom,beer) or ¬has(tom,pretzels)   C11, C4'
C13: ¬has(tom,beer) or ¬has(tom,pretzels)   C12, C5
C14: ¬has(tom,pretzels)   C13, C6
     FALSE   C14, C7

Let's look at the first resolution, following listing (7.1.6).

C8: ¬happy(tom)
C1':   happy(tom) or ¬watching(tom,football) or ¬has(tom,supplies)

C9:   ¬watching(tom,football) or ¬has(tom,supplies)

The second resolution is:

C9: ¬watching(tom,football) or ¬has(tom,supplies)
C3':   watching(tom,football) or ¬is_on(tv) or ¬playing(cowboys)

C10: ¬has(tom,supplies) or ¬is_on(tv) or ¬playing(cowboys)

Third is:

C10: ¬has(tom,supplies) or ¬is_on(tv) or ¬playing(cowboys)
C2':   has(tom,supplies) or ¬has(tom,beer) or¬has(tom,pretzels)
_____
C11: ¬is_on(tv) or ¬playing(cowboys) or ¬has(tom,beer) or ¬has(tom,pretzels)

Fourth is:

C11: ¬is_on(tv)or ¬playing(cowboys) or ¬has(tom,beer) or ¬has(tom,pretzels)
C4':   is_on(tv)
_____
C12: ¬playing(cowboys) or ¬has(tom,beer) or ¬has(tom,pretzels)

Fifth is:

C12: ¬playing(cowboys) or ¬has(tom,beer) or ¬has(tom,pretzels)
C5:   playing(cowboys)
_____
C13: ¬has(tom,beer) or ¬has(tom,pretzels)

Sixth is:

C13: ¬has(tom,beer) or ¬has(tom,pretzels)
C6:   has(tom,beer)
_____
C14: ¬has(tom,pretzels)

And finally, we have two clauses, one of which negates the other:

C14: ¬has(tom,pretzels)
C7:   has(tom,pretzels)
_____
FALSE

Since we have derived FALSE from ¬happy(tom) and C1 through C7, we may conclude that Tom is indeed happy following listing (7.1.14). An interactive PROLOG interpreter would announce SUCCESS! or something like it upon reaching the contradiction. Notice the order in which the resolution chain proceeds. First, the negation of the query is resolved with the first clause on the list. If this is not possible, resolving ¬QUERY (C8), with C2, C3, etc., would be tried in order. In each step after the first, resolution of the new clause, called the resolvent, is attempted with the next clause down the list.

Unification

Just as we wished to extend the propositional to the predicate calculus to include general formulas containing variables and quantifiers, proofs by resolution should apply to such statements as well. This requires a process known as *unification.*

Suppose we change the first clause C1 of our Happy Database to:

D1: happy(X) ← watching(X, football) & has(X, supplies)

This new statement suggests that anyone, not just Tom, who is watching football and has supplies is happy. A first step in resolving D1, C2 through C7, with the negated query ¬happy(tom)?, is to *unify* the query with D1. We need to find substitutions (bindings) for any variables in the two expressions, which will make them look alike except for sign. If we substitute "tom" for X in D1, the two expressions match. The substitution must be uniform, resulting in:

D8: happy(tom) ← watching(tom, football) & has(tom,supplies)

D8 and D1 are unified by the substitution sets {}[3] and {X/tom}.

Let's rewrite our conditions for happiness again, adding a few more choices. We have not rewritten our statements as Horn Clauses here, leaving that as an exercise.

E1: happy(X) ← watching(X,football) & has(X,Y)   (7.1.15)
E2: has(X,supplies) ← has(X,Y) & has(X,Z)
E3: has(X,beer)
E4: has(X,pretzels)
E5: watching(X,football) ← is_on(tv) & playing(Y)
E6: is_on(tv)
E7: playing(cowboys)

The unification and resolution, if queried with happy(tom)?, would proceed as shown in listing (7.1.16) (as before, explanations are found in the right-hand column):

E8:	¬happy(tom)	(7.1.16)
E9:	¬watching(tom,football) or ¬has(tom,Y)	{X/tom} in E1
E10:	¬has(tom,Y) or ¬is_on(tv) or ¬playing(Y1)	{Y/Y1}[4] in E9,{X/tom} in E5
E11:	¬has(tom,Y) or ¬playing(Y1)	E10,E6
E12:	¬has(tom,Y) or ¬has(tom,Y2) or ¬playing(Y1)	{Y/supplies} in E11, {X/tom} in E2
E13:	¬playing(Y1)	{Y/beer,Y2/beer} in E12,E3
E14:	¬playing(cowboys)	{Y1/cowboys} in E13 in E7
FALSE		

In this resolution, we never used the clause has(X,pretzels), because we substituted "beer" for both X and Y in E12. For Tom, beer seems to be enough. You'll be given a chance to think about this in exercise 7.1.6.

Searching

Proof through resolution involves searching through a database of clauses for unifiable terms and for resolvable clauses. In our examples so far we started at the

---

[3]The query ¬happy(tom)? has no free variables, and is called a *ground clause*. Its replacement set when unifying it with D1 is {}. D1 has one free variable X, replaced by tom, so its replacement set is {X/tom}, read "X is replaced by tom."

[4]Y1 must be substituted for Y in E9 because it may not represent the same value as the Y in D5.

top of the clause list and successfully matched the query with the first clause, and so on down the list until FALSE was obtained. Things don't always work out so well. Suppose we add the clause C0 to the front of C1 through C7 of the Happy Database of listig (7.1.13), where C0 is:

C0: happy(tom) ← watching(tom,football) & has(tom,dinner)

An attempt to resolve the query happy(Tom)? is:

(7.1.17)

C15: ¬watching(tom,football) or ¬has(tom,dinner)	C8, C0
C16: ¬has(tom,dinner) or ¬is_on(tv) or ¬playing(cowboys)	C15, C3
C17: ¬has(tom,dinner) or ¬playing(cowboys)	C16, C4
C18: ¬has(tom,dinner)	C17, C5
FAIL	

Our failure certainly can't mean that we proved Tom to be unhappy. We already know that the query is resolvable with C1 through C7, so it should surely resolve with C0 through C7. We need to undo the resolutions done already, and start over trying to resolve C8 with C1 instead of C0. This is accomplished through a technique called *backtracking*, which is discussed in the next section.

It is important to understand the difference between a resolution chain that leads to a contradiction, i.e., FALSE, and one that FAILs. Since we are looking for a contradiction to the negation of our query, a final resolution to FALSE means that we have proved that the query is in fact TRUE, and may be added to the database without inconsistency. If the inquiry FAILs, it means that, given the facts in the database, we can neither prove the query TRUE or FALSE. Thus the database is incomplete. We may add either the query that failed or its negation to the database if we wish, without introducing a contradiction.

Backtracking

The situation of our example can be drawn as a tree, as shown in Figure 7.1.1. We delete C18 and backtrack to C17. Since C17 could resolve with no clause other than C5, we delete them and look at C16, our nearest choice point. We are ready to choose a clause different from C4 to resolve with C16. The only other clause possible is C5, which also FAILs. There are no other choices at C16, so we delete the left branch below C16 and again backtrack to the nearest choice point up the tree, C8. Our next choice for resolution with C8 would be C1, which we know results in success.

A situation related to the lack of pretzels to go with Tom's beer occurs if we query D1 through D7 with the query, has(tom, X)?, and expect as a solution a list of all the things Tom has. Our resolution tree would be that shown in Figure 7.1.2.

Unifications occur from left to right in the order represented in Figure 7.1.2, assuming we examine clauses in order from the top of the list to the bottom. This was Robinson's assumption in presenting the resolution method, but other optimizations are possible. See, for example, [Genesereth, 1985]. Notice also that has(tom,supplies) is used three separate times when backtracking, and that has(tom,beer) is repeated four times. Finding all solutions that apply is not usually automatic, however. One has to use a special predicate, usually called "findall," e.g., findall(X: has(tom, X)).

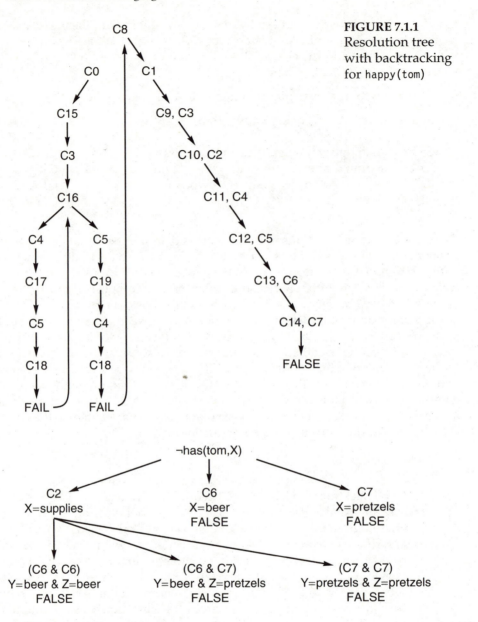

FIGURE 7.1.1
Resolution tree
with backtracking
for happy(tom)

FIGURE 7.1.2
Unification and resolution for has(tom,X)?

Facts, Goals, and Conditions

As we noted above, statements can be written as conditionals in the form "if A then B" or "B if A," where B is a single statement or clause, and A is zero or more clauses. If A has no clauses, then B is a *fact*, i.e., true under any conditions whatsoever.

These facts are called proper axioms in logic and function in the same way as the logical axioms of Appendix A. If A contains one or more clauses, then B is called the *goal,* and the conditions of A, *subgoals.* As we move through a resolution chain, each subgoal becomes a goal. When all these subgoals have been resolved with the facts, the principle goal B has been proved.

Backward and Forward Chaining

When we begin a resolution chain with a goal B, as in demonstrating the goal happy(tom), we chain backward from the goal to the facts. As with proof by contradiction, we start with what is to be proved contradictory, rather than with what is known, i.e., the axioms or facts. When there is only one or possibly a few choices for clauses to resolve with a goal, backward chaining is effective. However, if there are many choices (two or three are shown at some of the decision points in Figures 7.1.1 and 7.1.2), backward chaining can become inefficient because of all the backtracking necessary to undo fruitless resolution paths.

For certain problems, forward chaining from facts and rules to the main goal is more efficient. If there are more facts than rules, forward chaining will probably do better. That is, if we chain from the smaller to the larger (easier to find) set of statements, we may encounter fewer wrong paths. Another situation where forward chaining proves preferable is when there are fewer choices at each decision point when reasoning from the facts. This, of course, may be hard to know in advance. Forward chaining may also be more effective when a user wants to see a justification for each step in a proof, and naturally thinks from the known to the unknown.

Satisfying the goal happy(tom) would proceed as follows. First, we would rearrange the order of the database of listing (7.1.13) so that facts precede rules, as in listing (7.1.18).

C4: is_on(tv)	(7.1.18)
C5: playing(cowboys)	
C6: has(tom,beer)	
C7: has(tom,pretzels)	
C1: happy(tom) ← watching(tom,football) & has(tom,supplies)	
C2: has(tom,supplies) ← has(tom,beer) & has(tom,pretzels)	
C3: watching(tom,football) ← is_on(tv) & playing(cowboys)	

Then we query and resolve the database as in listing (7.1.19).

C8: ¬happy(tom)		(7.1.19)
C9: watching(tom, football)	C4, C5, C3	
C10: has(tom,supplies)	C6, C7, C2	
C11: happy(tom)	C9, C10, C1	
FALSE	C8, C11	

Note the order of the resolutions. C9 is resolved first, because C4 and C5 come first in the database of listing (7.1.18).

The language PROLOG, which we will discuss in section 7.2, uses resolution with backward chaining as its problem-solving strategy. Other languages, such as OPS-5, rely on forward chaining. PROLOG itself can be used, however, to implement an interpreter that uses forward rather than backward chaining [Malpas, 1987, Section 5.3].

Representing Negative Facts

Negative statements have often caused trouble to logicians and mathematicians. In formal logic, if p is false, then ¬p is true. This is not quite the case in PROLOG, where the success of a query (its negation resolving to FALSE) and failure (its negation leading to FAIL) are not mutually exclusive, i.e., (not FAIL) is not the same as SUCCESS. When a failure occurs, all variables are unbound, since the bindings did not work out. Suppose eats_hot_fudge_twice_every_day(sally) and not(eats_hot_fudge_twice_every_day(olaf)) are both facts in our database. Then,

```
eats_hot_fudge_twice_every_day(sally).
not(not(eats_hot_fudge_twice_every_day(sally))).
```
(7.1.20)[5]
(7.1.21)

resolve to the same thing. When attempting to resolve (7.1.21), the first not is encountered, and an attempt is made to show that not(eats_hot_fudge_twice_every_day(sally)) succeeds. It resolves to FALSE with the database, so does not succeed. The second not results in an attempt to show that (7.1.20) succeeds, which it does. Thus not(eats_hot_fudge_twice_every_day(sally)) FAILs, and (7.1.21) succeeds.

Now suppose we replace sally with X.

```
eats_hot_fudge_twice_every_day(X).
not(not(eats_hot_fudge_twice_every_day(X))).
```
(7.1.22)
(7.1.23)

When we try to show (7.1.23), we follow the same resolution chain as we did with (7.1.21). When (7.1.20) succeeds, X is instantiated with sally, so X=sally. The result for not(eats_hot_fudge_twice_every_day(sally)) FAILs. In addition, X loses its value of sally. Listing (7.1.23) succeeds, but X=sally is not returned, as X is now an uninstantiated variable. One feature of PROLOG is that when a new fact is added to a database, values of any formerly free variables are fixed and may not be replaced. Thus if a query FAILs, any unifications that have occurred are undone.

```
not(eats_hot_fudge_twice_every_day(mohammed)).
```
(7.1.24)

If the clause of listing (7.1.24) is a fact, during backtracking PROLOG would find it and instantiate X with mohammed. This binding would again be lost when the second not is tested. Thus double negation has little use. not(p) can only succeed or fail. If p has any free variables, they will not be instantiated, even though they were unified with appropriate values during the course of the resolution chain.

LAB 7.1: LANGUAGE INTRODUCTION: PROLOG

Objectives (Labs can be found in the *Instructor's Manual*.)

1. To become acquainted with entering and executing PROLOG programs.
2. To use some of the tools provided with the PROLOG you are using, particularly EDIT, TRACE, and DEBUG.

---

[5]Notice that we have switched to our font for code to inform the reader that what is being looked at is PROLOG code. Notice also that clauses are terminated with periods.

3. To see in action the way your PROLOG backtracks.
4. To gain some experience with the differences order has when entering the various instances of a relation.

EXERCISES 7.1

1. Recalling that r ← p & q ≡ r or ¬p or ¬q, resolve the following:

   a. r ← p & q   b. q or r
      ¬r   ¬q or ¬r

   c. s ← p & q & r   d. s or ¬p or ¬q or ¬r
      p   p
      q   q

2. Consider the clauses below, and use resolution to answer the queries following:

   C1: in_jail(mary) ← committed(mary,crime) & caught(cop,mary)
   C2: caught(cop,mary) ← saw(cop,crime)
   C3: saw(cop,crime) ← on_duty(cop)
   C4: committed(mary,crime) ← took(mary,wallet) & belongs_to(wallet,jane)
   C5: took(mary,wallet) ← had(mary,opportunity)
   C6: on_duty(cop)
   C7: had(mary,opportunity)
   C8: belongs_to(wallet,jane)

   Query 1, C9: committed(mary,crime)?
   Query 2, C10: in_jail(mary)?

3. Suppose that in a resolution chain, the first predicate to the right of a "←" must be resolved before trying to match any of those further to the right. For example, in exercise 2 above, when ¬Q2 is resolved with C1 to ¬committed(mary,crime) or ¬caught(cop,mary), the next resolution would necessarily involve the committed predicate, even if an instance of "caught" were encountered earlier on the list. Which method would make a more efficient algorithm: (1) Resolve the rightmost predicate first, or (2) check all predicates in a clause, and resolve with the first match you find on the list? Might this depend on the length of the clause list? Redo the happy(tom)? query, following each matching strategy. Does it make any difference?

4. Unify the following terms, or state why they cannot be unified:

   a. a(X,3); a(2,3)
   b. a(X,3); a(Y,Y)
   c. mother(rhea,X); mother(Y,jupiter)
   d. father(saturn,X); father(Y,Y)
   e. son(jupiter,saturn); son(Y,Y)
   f. p(X,Y); p(Z,Z)

5. Write an algorithm for a function unify(Term1,Term2), which returns Term3 or FAIL. A term is defined recursively:

   i. If C is a constant then C is a term.
   ii. If X is a variable, then X is a term.
   iii. If p_N is an n-place predicate symbol, and $t_1, \ldots, t_N$ are terms, then $p_N(t_1, \ldots, t_N)$ is a term.

6. The unification and resolution of E1 through E13 of listing (7.1.16) assumed that we used E3 twice, once to unify and resolve with has(tom,Y) and then to unify and resolve with has(tom,Z). Suppose we desired the process to continue as shown at the top of the following page.

E12: ¬has(tom,Y) or ¬has(tom,X) or ¬playing(Z)
E13: ¬has(tom,X) or ¬playing(Z)   {Y/beer} in E3,E12
E14: ¬playing(Z)   {X/pretzels} in E13,E4
     FALSE   {Z/cowboys} in E14,E7

  a. Suggest two ways to disallow the substitution of "beer" for both X and Y in E12. One way could modify E2 and the other could modify the search rule for resolution clauses.

  b. If one always tries to unify and resolve a clause with E2 before trying E3 or E4, what would happen when querying E1 through E7 with ¬happy(tom)? How could you prevent this?

7. Listing (7.1.6) provides the resolution rule for two clauses in what is called disjunctive normal form. That is, the only logical connectives are "or" and "not." The resolution examples we have seen involved clauses written in the form $A \leftarrow B_1 \& \ldots \& B_n$.

  a. Prove that a clause in the $A \leftarrow B_1 \& \ldots \& B_n$ form is a Horn Clause as defined in listing (7.1.5).

  b. State a resolution rule equivalent to listing (7.1.6) for Horn Clauses in the $A \leftarrow B_1 \& \ldots \& B_n$ form, which does not first translate clauses into "or" form.

  c. Using your rule from b, suggest a clause form for a query to clauses in $A \leftarrow B_1 \& \ldots \& B_n$ form.

8. Consider the set of rules and facts below.

C1: North-of(X1, X2) ← Location(X1, Y1, Z1) & Location(X2, Y2, Z2) & Less(Y2, Y1)
C2: Location(NewYork, 41, 74)
C3: Location(Chicago, 42, 88)
C4: Location(Tokyo, 35, 140)
C5: Location(Oslo, 60, 11)
C6: Location(Quito, 0, 80)
C7: Location(Cairo, 30, 30)

  a. Construct a resolution tree such as those in Figures 7.1.1 and 7.1.2, starting with the query,

    Q: North-of(Chicago, NewYork)?

  b. Now construct a tree starting with the query,

    Q': North-of(X, NewYork).

Be sure you backtrack to explore *all* the possible substitutions for X.

9. Using the rule p ← q & r, which can be written as an equivalent Horn Clause, p or ¬q or ¬r, rewrite the clauses of listing (7.1.15) as Horn Clauses.

10. Construct a resolution chain for happy(tom), using clauses C0 through C7 of the sections "Resolution" and "Searching," but chain forward from the facts C4 through C7, rather than backwards as in the examples shown.

11. a. Why would forward chaining be preferable when trying to determine a travel route from home to an unknown destination (the goals)?

  b. Suppose facts determine which words are verbs, nouns, adjectives, etc., and rules describe what comprises an English sentence. For simple sentences, the following three rules suffice:

    R1: Sentence(NP, VP) ← NounPhrase(NP) & VerbPhrase(VP)

R2:   NounPhrase(A, N) ← Article(A) & Noun(N)
R3:   VerbPhrase(V, NP) ← Verb(V) & NounPhrase(NP)

If our goal is to parse a given sentence, would forward or backward chaining be preferable? Try a few sentences to see which seems more natural.

c. In a medical diagnosis problem, the facts are symptoms, and the goal is to match these symptoms with a disease. Would forward or backward chaining be more reasonable here?

d. In a game of tic-tac-toe, the goals are winning configurations of the 3 x 3 grid. How many are there for a single player? (Be careful about this calculation; remember that a configuration involves all nine squares, not just the winning row, column, or diagonal.) How many total configurations are there? (A blank grid is one!) Would forward or backward chaining find a winning solution more easily? Why? Does it matter?

7.2
PROLOG

HISTORICAL VIGNETTE

PROLOG: Colmerauer and Roussel

A look at the history of PROLOG is another look at the history of logic itself, and its future. Originally developed by Alain Colmerauer, Philippe Roussel, and their colleagues of the Greupe d'Intelligence Artificielle (University of Marseille) to be a theorem-proving language, PROLOG has entered the fourth generation as a good language for database management, and into the fifth in the field of artificial intelligence.

PROLOG's beginnings date back 22 centuries to Aristotle's traditional logic. One of the problems of that system is that it is entirely static. A statement can have only one value, True or False, and once established can never be changed. The first dissatisfactions surfaced during the nineteenth century, when DeMorgan, an English mathematician, began the development of a formal system, more representative of mathematical reasoning than natural language. Gottlob Frege's contributions in the latter half of the century firmly established symbolic logic as a branch of mathematics, only sometimes tied to philosophy.

During the sixties, there was great interest in automatic theorem proving. Robert Kowalski, working at the University of Edinburgh, concentrated on logic programming, the use of computers to make controlled logical inferences.

Colmerauer and Roussel, a Canadian student, developed with others the first logic programming language. They called it PROLOG, an abbreviation for *programmation en logique,* following a suggestion of Roussel's wife, Jacqueline.

Given the close ties to mathematical logic and theorem proving, it may seem surprising that PROLOG is known as an artificial intelligence language. Yet logic was originally designed for clarifying ordinary discourse, not for investigating mathematics. There was little interest in PROLOG in either the United States or in Europe until the early eighties, when Japan's Institute for New Generation Technology announced plans to produce a fifth generation of computer hardware that would accept natural-language input and process large quantities of information. Their chosen language was PROLOG. At first scientists in the U.S. laughed at Japan's move, quickly assuming that a big mistake was being made, but the laughter died down as reports of Japan's success with its fifth-generation projects began to spread. The nineties have seen Japan still interested in becoming the hub of a worldwide information network. PROLOG remains a powerful tool for system development, with the final product, however, implemented in C or C++.

Today PROLOG is used in the U.S. as well as in Japan for theorem proving, relational database design, software engineering, natural-language processing, knowledge representation in artificial intelligence, and expert systems programming. Perhaps PROLOG's most important feature is that it is a step towards nonprocedural programming, where less programming is involved as more gets done automatically. The user can concentrate more on what needs to be done than on how to do it.

The future of both PROLOG and logic programming is unclear. PROLOG is to logic programming what FORTRAN was to modern computer programming, a beginning. The Japanese have developed a new logic programming language called KL, replacing PROLOG applications. For the present, most PROLOG programmers are computer enthusiasts who want to learn more about AI programming. Several versions are available for microcomputers. Perhaps PROLOG will be left behind as a production language and remain as an AI teaching tool as newer languages are developed.

Conversing in PROLOG: Facts, Rules, and Queries

PROLOG has been described as relational [Malpas, 1987], descriptive [Genesereth, 1985], and declarative. Both the relational and descriptive views consider the organization of the database, or set of PROLOG facts and rules, assumed to be true for the application at hand. PROLOG is considered declarative in that one describes to it what one wants to accomplish, e.g., "sort([5,3,7,2],Answer)!", with little regard to the procedure for accomplishing the sorting task, which returns "Answer = [2,3,5,7]". Of course, we must describe further just what is meant by "sort," if it is not predefined in the implementation.

PROLOG is also called a language for programming in logic [Calingaert, 1988; Ghezzi, 1987]. This last may be the most accurate classification, but PROLOG itself is only logic-based, and does not produce all the proofs possible from methods using the full power of the predicate calculus.

PROLOG comes in several dialects. The original version of Colmerauer and Roussel is Edinburgh syntax, also called DEC-10® PROLOG, due to its early implementation on DEC-10 computers running on the TOPS-10 operating system. Micro-PROLOG, another dialect, is available for microcomputers, although "Core PROLOG," a subset of the DEC-10 version, appears to have become the de facto standard for micros, minis, and mainframes. We will use the Core PROLOG syntax, since it is widely available for both 32-bit and 16-bit machines, although learning PROLOG on one's own is still most easily accomplished using Clark and McCabe's manual for micro-PROLOG [Clark, 1984].

The main difference between Edinburgh and micro-PROLOG is in the form of a clause.

```
happy(tom) :- watching(tom,football),has(tom,supplies).
```

is an Edinburgh clause, while

```
((happy tom)(watching tom football)(has tom supplies)).
```

is the same clause in micro-PROLOG syntax. Each means that Tom [is] happy [if] Tom [is] watching football [and] Tom has supplies.

There are some differences in the evaluation of arithmetic and some other expressions as well. Once you have mastered one, it is not hard to shift to the other dialect. Either syntax is fairly easy to learn. Writing efficient PROLOG programs, however, requires a fairly sophisticated understanding of both logic and the execution of an abstract PROLOG machine.

Syntax

A PROLOG program is a list of statements, called facts and rules, that is entered through a query. The general form of a statement is: HEAD :- BODY., where HEAD is a single *structure,* and BODY is comprised of zero or more structures, called subgoals, separated by commas meaning "and" or semicolons meaning "or." A fact is a statement with no body, while a rule contains both a head and a body. A query is a fact preceded by ?-, and returns either TRUE or FALSE. A query, fact, or rule is terminated by a period. If a query that contains variables succeeds, constant values for the variables are printed that make the query true.

The form of a structure is that of a PROLOG fact, functor(term$_1$, . . ., term$_n$). A *term* may be either a constant, variable, or structure. Functors are predicate symbols, operators, or relation names. A predicate can take on the values TRUE or FALSE. =<(2,4) is TRUE, whereas =<(4,2) is FALSE. Here[6] =< is a functor and 2 and 4 are constant terms. An operator is a functor written in infix rather than prefix form, e.g., 2 =< 4. Some operators built into PROLOG are those for integer arithmetic, e.g., X+Y and X+Y*Z. A PROLOG user may declare functors to be operators by specifying the functor name, precedence, and type, where types may be infix (X+Y), prefix (–2) or postfix (5!), where '!' is the factorial operator. Precedence and associativity must also be specified for operators. Those for arithmetic obey the standard rules, e.g., * precedes +, and operators associate left to right, e.g., $2 + 3 + 4 \equiv (2 + 3) + 4$.

A constant is thought of as naming a specific object or relation and is either an *atom* or an integer. A constant atom is a string of letters and digits beginning with

---

[6]PROLOG manuals tend to surround signs used as operators or functors with single quotes. The full designation is '=<'/2, signifying that =< requires two arguments.

a lowercase letter and containing no signs other than the underscore. john_alden, x, y, and map2 are all constants, but 2X, Mary, and gambier-ohio are not. However, any character may be used to form a constant between single quotes. Thus 'Gambier-Ohio' is a constant.

An atom may also be composed entirely of signs, but these are reserved for special purposes. Two of these special atoms are :-, which means "if" and ?-, which signals a query. The signs are: {+ - * \ / ^ < > ~ : . ? @ # $ &}. A relation-name is also an atom, e.g., the < in <(2, 4), or the has in has(tom,beer).

A variable is any string beginning with either a capital letter or the underscore. Who, Salary_Amt, X, and _2_brothers are variables, while Last-Name and 2ndBase are not. PROLOG also has a special anonymous variable, '_'. The query, ?- has(tom,_)., succeeds if any atom satisfying the has relationship, with tom as the first term, unifies with the _ variable. has(tom,_) either succeeds or fails, but we won't know just what it is that tom has, even though, as we saw in the section "Resolution," beer, pretzels, and supplies satisfy the has relation for tom. The anonymous variable _ must be unified when resolving has(tom,_), but its values will be discarded.

Data Structures

The only data structure built into PROLOG is a list, implemented as the functor '.'/2. The period is overloaded, and is here a functor name, where we used it previously to terminate a clause. The 2 represents its *arity*, or the number of terms expected as arguments. When using any functor, the arity is omitted. The two arguments to the period are the head and the tail. .(broccoli,[]) is a list with a single element, broccoli. The [] is a special symbol representing the empty list, which marks the end of any list. .(broccoli,.(potatoes,.(milk,[]))) is a three-element list. For convenience, PROLOG allows writing this same list as [broccoli,potatoes,milk] or as [broccoli|[potatoes,milk]]. Here the operator '|'/2 is used to append the second argument, which must be a list, to the first element, which is the head of the list. A list of indeterminate length can be written as [broccoli|X], where X is a variable representing the tail of the list.

The following is a PROLOG program to append two lists.

```
append([],L,L).                                          (7.2.1)
append([X|L1],L2,Y) :- append(L1,L2,L3), Y = [X|L3].
```

Listing (7.2.1) contains two predicates: a fact and a rule. The rule is recursive in append, since append appears on both the left and the right side of the rule. As we saw before, PROLOG examines clauses in a database from top to bottom, so the nonrecursive relation that will stop the recursion is listed first.

Now suppose we query, ?- append([1,2],[3],Y). PROLOG will return:

```
Y = [1,2,3].
No.
```

The No indicates that there are no solutions other than those listed. If we name the program's clauses of listing (7.2.1) C1 and C2 :- C3, C4, and name the query Q, our resolution proceeds as shown in Figure 7.2.1.

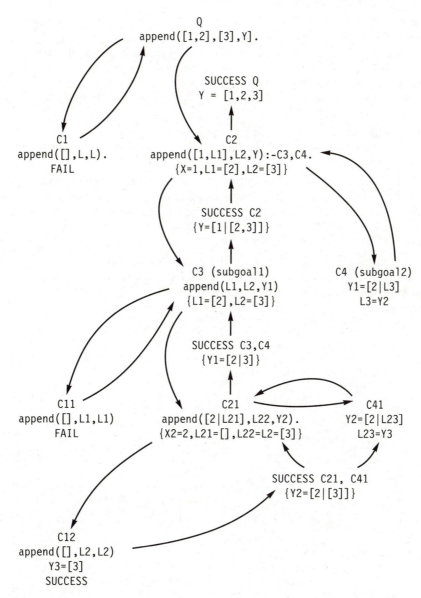

FIGURE 7.2.1
Resolution chain for `?-append([1,2],[3],Y).`

There were only three calls to C1 and two to C2, so the recursion was short in this example. Had L1 and L2 been longer, there would have been many recursive calls back and forth to C1, C2, C3, and C4. Recursion is usually implemented using a stack with unresolved clauses pushed on, and popped off when either success or failure occurs.

The action of the recursive stack is as shown in Figure 7.2.2. Each "push" represents an attempt to unify a clause (downward arrow), and a "pop" corresponds to backtracking (upward arrow) in the tree of Figure 7.2.1. Notice that the append procedure (listing (7.2.1)) lists as its first clause append([],L,L). This clause is used at the bottom of the recursion, before backtracking up the recursive stack to unify uninstantiated variables. Omission of a recursion-terminating clause at the beginning of a recursive procedure leads to infinite loops. PROLOG doesn't care, but you'll probably get a "no space left" notice after such a procedure runs for a while. Try reversing the order of the two clauses and see what happens with your PROLOG version.

Core PROLOG has no built-in structures for arrays, sets, or strings, but some implementations are extended to include strings and string-manipulation operators. Several contain extensions for writing top-down parsers.

Built-In Operators and Functors

In addition to the **not** predicate (which was mentioned before in the section "Representing Negative Facts" and will also be discussed again later in this chapter) and arithmetic operators, PROLOG provides several comparators, operators for control of execution and debugging and for determining types. We will look briefly at a few of these here.

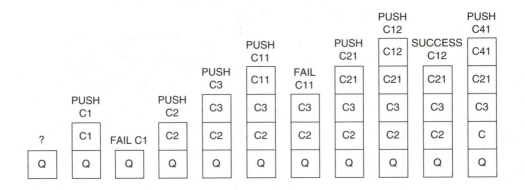

FIGURE 7.2.2
Recursive stack for resolution of Figure 7.2.1

PROLOG does not include equality in the usual sense. If the term X = Y is encountered, PROLOG attempts to unify the X with the Y. Thus butter = butter succeeds, and butter = guns fails. butter = W succeeds as does X = Y. As a side effect, W will have the value butter and Y the same value as X, or the variable X itself if X is uninstantiated. A variable is said to be instantiated if it has been assigned a value. In Figure 7.2.1, X was instantiated with the value 1, L1 with [2], L2 with [3], and (eventually) Y with [1,2,3]. The only way an instantiation of a particular variable can be changed is if the predicate containing it fails. If a predicate fails, PROLOG undoes its variable bindings and searches for a different way to unify and/or resolve it. This process is called backtracking, which we have already discussed.

The operator '=='/2 is PROLOG's comparator. X==Y will not try to unify Y with X. Thus if either X or Y is an uninstantiated variable, X==Y will fail. However, if we follow X=Y by X==Y, both X=Y and X==Y succeed.

```
X = cat.          X now has the value, 'cat'.                      (7.2.2)

?-X==Y.           since Y is uninstantiated.

no

?-X=Y.            Y now also has the value, 'cat'.

yes

?-X==Y.

yes
```

Two structures are equivalent (==) if they have the same functor and number of arguments, and all the arguments are equal (==).

One very useful operator is '=..'/2, called *univ*. If we query:

```
?-append([1,2], [3], Y) =.. L.
```

PROLOG will return:

```
L = [append, [1,2], [3], Y].
```

Similarly, ?-T =.. [append, [1,2], [3], Y]. returns T = append([1,2], [3], Y).

Such switching between lists and terms allows the modifying of programs while they are running, since terms can easily be added to or deleted from lists. Thus programs can be made to learn while they execute. One use of univ is in constructing the function mapcar, which is one of the functions built into LISP (see "Functions as First-Class Objects" in section 8.1). Notice that we have added comments, preceded by % for clarity in listing (7.2.3).[7]

---

[7]The functors foo and foobar have been used traditionally by programmers as in-jokes. foo stands for "fouled up," and foobar is for "fouled up beyond all repair." You will see these acronyms scattered through many texts and papers. See [Raymond, 1993] for further discussion.

```
mapcar(_,[],[]).                                              (7.2.3)
mapcar(Foo,[X|Args],[Y|Answers]) :-

        Foobar =.. [Foo,X,Y],          % Foobar is Foo(X,Y)
        call(Foobar),                  % Y is Foo(X).
        mapcar(Foo,Args,Answers).
```

The application of mapcar(func,L1,L2). will return as L2, the result of applying func successively to the elements of L1. Here func is a function name, L1 is a list, and L2 is a variable identifier.

```
?-mapcar(upper_case, [a,b,c,d], X).
```

will return X = ['A','B','C','D'], assuming upper_case has been appropriately defined. The elements of the list X are uppercase(a), uppercase(b), uppercase(c), and uppercase(d).

Terms can be tested for type using the predicates 'var'/1, 'nonvar'/1, 'integer'/1, and 'atom'/1. atom(X) is true for noninteger constants.

Arithmetic. If PROLOG encounters X = 1+2, it will try to unify X with the term 1+2. To have X assigned the value 3, we must use 'is'/2. X **is** 1+2, performs the desired arithmetic and instantiates X to 3. If we want to evaluate and test arithmetic equality, we query ?- X =:= 1+2. The operator '=\='/2 tests arithmetic inequality. '<'/2, '>'/2,'=>'/2, and '=<'/2, behave as one might expect. (Notice the '=<' rather than the usual '<='.)

Only integers are built into PROLOG. Real number arithmetic is not supported, although floating point capabilities are an extension in some versions.

?-X is 5/2 will normally return X = 2. However, where floating point numbers are supported, '/'/2 may mean real number division and '//'/2 integer division.

Input/Output. I/O is usually the most nonstandard part of a programming language, as it is often tailored to a particular platform. In addition to '**get0**'/1 and '**put**'/1 for characters, and '**read**'/1 and '**write**'/1 for terms, PROLOG has various predicates for file control. Although there can be only one current input stream, and one current output stream, each can be changed through '**see**'/1 or '**tell**'/1. Most implementations also provide some version of '**consult**'/1, which allows various files to be consulted as needed.

Control

Because PROLOG performs exhaustive depth-first searches when trying to unify its variables, program execution can be very inefficient in both speed of execution and use of memory. Thus it is up to the programmer to write procedures that minimize both search time and memory usage.

Tail recursion. Tail recursion was mentioned in section 2.2, "Recursion." The append procedure of listing (7.2.1) is not tail recursive.

However,

```
append2([],L,L).                                              (7.2.4)
append2([X|L1],L2,[X|L3]) :- append2(L1,L2,L3).
```

is. Let's follow through ?-append2([1,2],[3]) using Figures 7.2.3 and 7.2.4. The operation of the stack for append2 of Figure 7.2.3 is shown in Figure 7.2.4.

Notice that in the transitions from the fourth to the fifth, from the seventh to the eighth, and from the eighth to the ninth stacks, C2, C21, and C22 need not be maintained, as any instantiated variables have been copied to the unification sets (marked by {...}) for C21, C22, and C12 respectively. Thus the memory requirements are as shown in Figure 7.2.5.

A tail recursive subgoal can be recognized by its form at the time it is called, and some PROLOG implementations automatically apply tail recursive optimization, as shown above. A tail recursive procedure saves stack space, since intermediate results

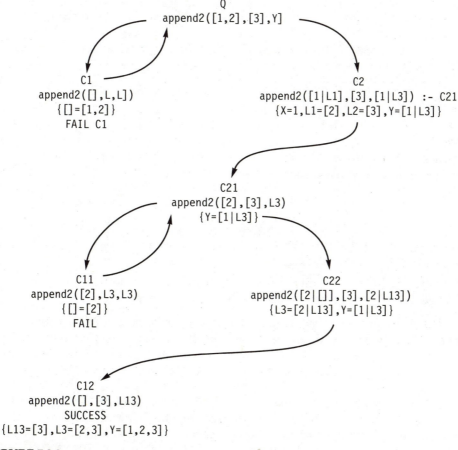

FIGURE 7.2.3
Resolution Tree for append2([1,2],[3]),Y).

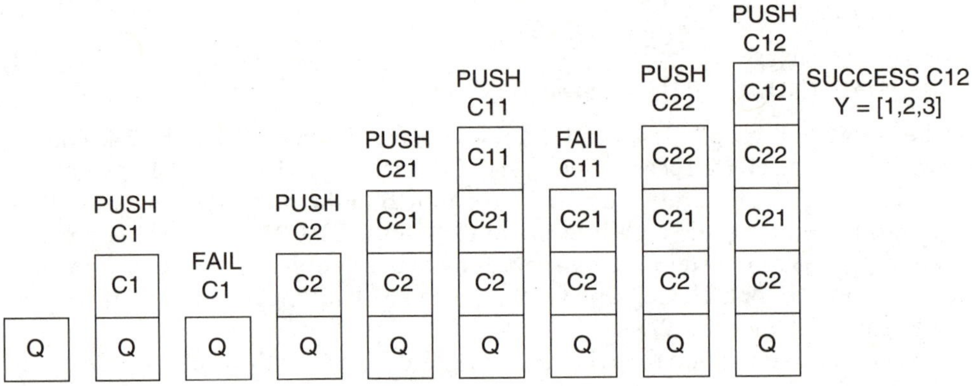

Figure 7.2.4 (tail recursive stack):

```
                                                              PUSH
                                                              C12
                                          PUSH      PUSH     ┌────┐ SUCCESS C12
                                          C11       C22      │C12 │ Y = [1,2,3]
                               PUSH      ┌────┐ FAIL┌────┐   ├────┤
                               C21       │C11 │ C11 │C22 │   │C22 │
                    PUSH      ┌────┐     ├────┤     ├────┤   ├────┤
          PUSH      C2        │C21 │     │C21 │     │C21 │   │C21 │
          C1       ┌────┐     ├────┤     ├────┤     ├────┤   ├────┤
 ┌────┐  ┌────┐ FAIL│ C2 │    │ C2 │     │ C2 │     │ C2 │   │ C2 │
 │ C1 │  │ C1 │ C1  ├────┤    ├────┤     ├────┤     ├────┤   ├────┤
┌┴────┴┐┌┴────┴┐┌────┴────┴┐  │    │ ... │    │     │    │   │    │
│  Q   ││  Q   ││    Q     │  │ Q  │     │ Q  │     │ Q  │   │ Q  │
└──────┘└──────┘└──────────┘  └────┘     └────┘     └────┘   └────┘
```

FIGURE 7.2.4
Tail recursive stack for Figure 7.2.3

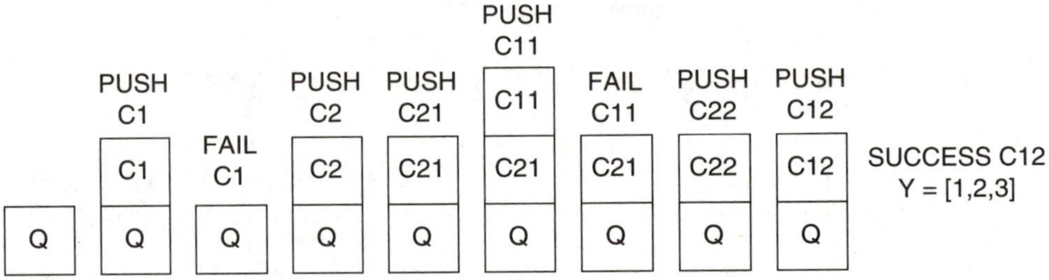

Figure 7.2.5 (optimized tail recursive stack):

```
                                   PUSH
                                   C11
          PUSH          PUSH  PUSH ┌────┐ FAIL  PUSH  PUSH
          C1            C2    C21  │C11 │ C11   C22   C12
 ┌────┐  ┌────┐ FAIL   ┌────┐┌────┐├────┤┌────┐┌────┐┌────┐ SUCCESS C12
 │ C1 │  │ C1 │ C1     │ C2 ││C21 ││C21 ││C21 ││C22 ││C12 │ Y = [1,2,3]
┌┴────┴┐┌┴────┴┐┌──────┴────┴┴────┴┴────┴┴────┴┴────┴┴────┴┐
│  Q   ││  Q   ││  Q    Q     Q     Q     Q     Q     Q    │
└──────┘└──────┘└──────────────────────────────────────────┘
```

FIGURE 7.2.5
Optimized tail recursive stack for Figure 7.2.4

need not be saved on the recursive stack. Note that the partial value for Y was carried along through the subgoals in Figure 7.2.3. Such a recursive (sub)goal is characterized by the following:

1. At the time it is called, all previous subgoals have been determined.
2. There are no further subgoals after the recursive subgoal.

The append procedure of listing (7.2.1) is not tail recursive, because when the call to the subgoal C3 is called the first time, there is still a subgoal C4 remaining to be satisfied. When writing a rule, it is guaranteed to be tail recursive if it is of the form:

$$R(t_1, \ldots, t_n) :\text{-} C_1, C_2, \ldots, C_m, R(t_1', \ldots, t_n').$$

where each of the C_i are subgoals satisfied by a *single* solution, or if C_m is a cut !, which cuts off backtracking. We will discuss the effect of the predicate cut in the next section. If there are no C_i, as in the append2 procedure, the condition is, of course, satisfied. For examples of how to change procedures into equivalent tail recursive ones, see [Clark, 1984].

A form of recursion always to be avoided is left recursion. Consider the following rule and fact:

```
R: ancestor(X,Z) :- ancestor(X,Y) & ancestor(Y,Z).
F: ancestor(gaston,ferdinand).
```

If we query, Q: ?-ancestor(gaston,A). to find gaston's ancestors, PROLOG will match Q with the head of R, using the unification set {X=gaston, Z=A}, and activate the first subgoal, ancestor(gaston,Y1). {Y1=A} will unify this subgoal, which again matches the head of R. A new subgoal, ancestor(gaston,Y2), will be activated, which will match R, and so on. This infinite circling through R will continue until a "no space left" error appears. Our problem is that we keep recursing from the right to the left of R, with identical goals to be satisfied, and never reach the fact F. In this example, left recursion can be recognized by the appearance of identical clauses (except for variable names) on both the left and the right sides of the rule R.

Cut, **fail**, *and* **not**. The built-in predicate cut ('!'/0) always succeeds, and prevents reevaluation of any clauses that precede it. If your PROLOG version does not provide tail recursive optimization, you can do some of the job using cut. PROLOG searches for all possible solutions to a query. If you know there is only one, cutting off further search after the single solution has been found saves both time and space.

Since append2 stops when the first clause succeeds, we will place a cut there. append3 is identical to append2, except for the added cut.

```
append3([],L,L) :- !.                                    (7.2.5)
append3([X|L1],L2,[X|L3]) :- append2(L1,L2,L3).
```

PROLOG will stop the search the first time it satisfies append3([],L,L). Such a one-solution procedure would be useful if we were always to use it with two ground clause lists as the first two arguments, as in ?-append3([1,2,3],[4,5,6],L). However, if we want to find all possible sublists, as in:

```
?-append3(X,Y,[1,2,3,4,5,6]).                            (7.2.6)
```

PROLOG would return only one answer, X = []; Y = [1,2,3,4,5,6]. The cut would prevent any further search.

The predicate **fail** is one that always fails. Suppose we want to determine whether an individual is a British citizen—not an easy task in a colonial nation. An individual, such as Guy Burgess,[8] who has renounced his citizenship in the United Kingdom, is clearly not a British citizen. Thus we might have a rule:

```
citizen(X) :- renounced(X,UK), !, fail.                  (7.2.7)
citizen(X) :- born_in(X,UK);...
```

where the ... indicates all the myriad conditions allowing citizenship. Then ?-citizen(Burgess). would return **fail**.

---

[8]Guy Burgess was a British citizen who spied for the Soviet Union during World War II, and later defected to that country.

We need the cut here to prevent any further search for a rule that would give citizenship to Burgess, but we also need the **fail** to return a negative answer to our query.

The cut/**fail** combination can always be replaced by the use of **not**. Our definition above would be:

```
citizen(X) :- not(renounced(X,UK)).
citizen(X) :- born_in(X,UK);...
```
(7.2.8)

In more complicated definitions, using **not** may require deeply nested parentheses, which makes a program less readable to some.

Programs that modify themselves. PROLOG has predicates that can delete or add clauses to the database while a program is running. Below is a program that queries a user about drug allergies and adds the information to the database.

```
drug(penicillin).
drug(sulfadiazine).
drug(aspirin).
drug(carbromal).

drug_quiz :- write('Please enter your last name: '),
            read(Patient),
            write('After each drug is listed, answer yes'),
            write(' or no if you are allergic to it or not.'),nl,
            drug(DrugName), write(DrugName),nl,
            read(yes),assert(allergic(Patient,DrugName)),
            fail.
```
(7.2.9)

The **fail** is used here to force PROLOG to backtrack through all the drugs in the database to check other drug allergies. The nl causes a carriage return in the output stream.

PROLOG can also add to or delete from the database facts and/or rules while a program is running using the predicates **assert**, **retract**, and **abolish**. **assert**(C1) adds clause C1 to the database, **retract**(C2) removes clause C2, and **abolish**(N/A) removes all clauses with predicate name N and arity A from the database. We will leave examples of the usage of these predicates for the PROLOG MiniManual and the Labs.

PROLOG Implementations

A Theoretical Machine

The execution of a PROLOG program can be described by the theoretical machine of Figure 7.2.6. Colmerauer [Colmerauer, 1985] calls it "the PROLOG Clock," since its main function is to keep track of time.

A computer clock, not to be confused with a real-time clock (RTC), which measures the time of day, counts execution cycles. Here the clock value is that of the variable i above and starts at 0. The PROLOG clock has the ability to run backward as well as forward, thus it is two clocks in one. The outer circle represents the forward-running clock, and the inner circle, the one that backs up. The C_i are *constraints*

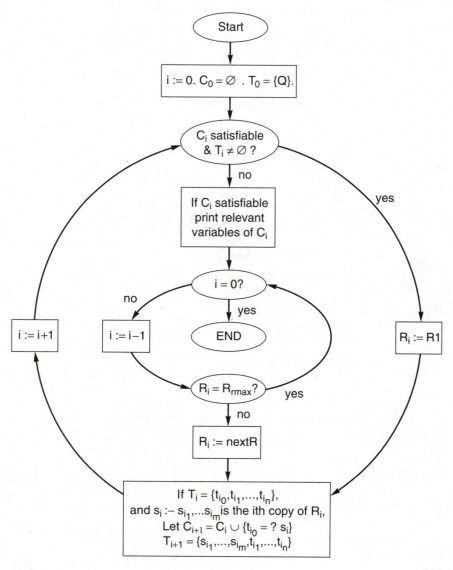

FIGURE 7.2.6
The PROLOG Clock

and represent attempts to match PROLOG terms T_i with others in the database. R_i represents the rule we are testing for a match at clock=i, and the s_{ij} and t_{ik} are the terms still to be matched at succeeding times.

Let's follow through the execution of `?-append(A,B,[1,2])`. at the various clock times i as shown in listing (7.2.10).

```
R1: append([],L,L).                                          (7.2.10)
R2: append([X|L1],L2,[X|L3]).
i := 0
C₀ = ∅
T₀ = {append(A1,B1,[1,2])}
R₀ := R1
C₁ = {append(A1,B1,[1,2]) =? append([],L1,L1)}
T₁ = ∅

i := 1
A1=[], B1=L1, L1=[1,2]
print answer1:    A = [], B = [1,2]

i := 0
R₀ := R2;
C₁ = {append(A2,B2,[1,2]) =? append([X1|L11],L21,[X1|L31])}
T₁ = {append(L11,L21,L31)}

i := 1
A2=[1|L11], 1=X1, B2=L21, [2]=L31
R₁ := R1
C₂ = C₁ ∪ {append(L11,L21,[2]) =? append([],L2,L2)
T₂ = ∅

i := 2
L11=[], L21=[2], [2]=L2
print answer2:    A = [1], B = [2]

i := 1
R₁ := R2
C₂ = {C₁ ∪ {append(L12,L22,[2]) =? append([X2|L13],L23,[X2|L33]}
T₂ = {append(L13,L23,L33)}

i := 2
L12=[2], L22=L23, 2=X2, []=L33
R₂ := R1
C₃ = C₂ ∪ {append(L13,L23,[]) =? append([],L3,L3)}
T₃ = ∅

i := 3
L13=[], L23=[], []=L3
print answer3:    A = [1,2], B = []

i := 2
R₂ := R2
C₃ = C₂ ∪ {{append(L14, L24,[]) =? append([X3|L15],L25,[X3|L35])}
T₃ = {append(L15,L25,L35)}

i := 3
dead end

i := 2
i := 1
i := 0
end
```

Other theoretical machines have been devised to interpret or compile PROLOG programs, but Colmerauer's PROLOG Clock was the first and is still commonly used.

Parallel Architectures

PROLOG is admirably organized for parallel processing. If a rule is t0 :- t1, t2, . . ., tn with goal t0, and we have n-processors available, why not resolve all n subgoals simultaneously? This sort of parallel execution is called *and parallelism*, because in a clause such as A :- B, C, we will attempt to prove B and C concurrently in order to prove A. Unfortunately, PROLOG programs work from left to right, and often the order of the terms is important. For example, suppose we define a descendent relation as in listing (7.2.11).

```
R1: descendent(Y,X) :- parent-of (X,Y).                    (7.2.11)
R2: descendent(Y,X) :- parent-of(X,Z), descendent(Y,Z).
```

This works just fine, but now consider:

```
R2': descendent(Y,X) :- descendent(Y,Z), parent-of(X,Z).
```

R2' contains the same information as R2, but reverses the order of the two subgoals. As we saw in the section "Tail Recursion," R2' is left-recursive and will produce an infinite loop. The resolution of descendent(Y,Z) requires that parent-of(X,Z) already be resolved.

And parallelism requires that subgoals be independent of each other, or that some other method of avoiding variable clashes be devised. For example, in Concurrent PROLOG, the clause A :- B(X), C(X?) restricts assigning X a value in B(X). C(X?) may only read X, not write to it. There is, however, a hidden advantage in assignment restrictions. A variable can be used as a communication channel with processes such as C(X?) waiting until X has received a value.

Or parallelism, which eliminates backtracking, is substantially easier. If we look again at listing (7.2.10), and if all the processing at a given time occurs in parallel (i.e., the assignment, i := i–1 of the inner clock never happens), we would have an example of or parallelism. And parallelism involves concurrent processing across different time levels. Or parallelism works concurrently on clauses such as:

```
A :- B.
A :- C.
```

Here we can prove A true by either proving B or C. Thus we work concurrently on both B and C, stopping when either B or C is resolved. The proof of A is thus indeterminate. When PROLOG announces that A is true, we may not know or care whether B or C is also true. "Don't know" nondeterminism is a feature of closed systems, where only successful resolutions are visible to the user. PROLOG is often implemented as a reactive system, where the user can see partial results as a computation progresses. This requires "don't care" nondeterminism, also called *indeterminism*. A subgoal may fail, but the application doesn't care as long as the primary goal can be shown.

The development of parallel processors, and compilers to take advantage of them, is receiving much research attention at this time. For example, see [ProcSLP,

1986]. A good exposition of the complexities of parallel execution using Parlog86 can be found in [Ringwood, 1988].

Garbage Collection

Parallel execution can speed up processing, but PROLOG programs still consume large amounts of memory. To keep variables separated, each time a rule is invoked, its variables must be given new names. When a particular resolution has completed, these variables may still exist. Reclaiming storage locations that are no longer needed through a memory reorganization is known as garbage collection. The theoretical machine of Figure 7.2.6 is a simplified form of an actual PROLOG compiler. The *Warren Abstract Machine* (WAM) [Warren, 1988] is one widely accepted basis for implementations. Data is kept in three areas: the code area containing the program, the control area made up of machine registers, and three stacks. The first stack, which may or may not be recursive, keeps track of the chain of clauses called and simple variables, the second contains structure and list variables, while the third, called the trail, refers to variables that have to be undone during backtracking. Various methods for garbage collection during execution of the WAM have been proposed, e.g., see [Appleby, 1988].

Types and Modules

Besides space and time inefficiencies, PROLOG has other shortcomings [Genesereth, 1985]. One of these is that the logic used relies on complete (closed world) systems and is not well suited for applications that generalize knowledge beyond the database, reason from analogies, or make deductions from uncertain data. The ability to write, debug, and maintain large programs is also limited due to a lack of data typing and modularity, although modules are supported in some implementations. When we speak of data typing, we don't mean just integer, real, or character, but the ability of the user to define and maintain abstract data types, along with their associated operations. Object-oriented extensions, such as IPW in IBM PROLOG, have been implemented for this purpose.

Goguen and Meseguer [Goguen, 1984] have suggested a revision and extension of PROLOG, called Eqlog. It includes genuine equality, as in $3 + 4 * 5 = 23$; user-defined types, called *sorts;* modules, such as integer sets with definitions for membership and union; and a mechanism for defining generic modules. We won't discuss just what a generic module is here, but give Goguen's example for a quasi-ordered set instead. (A quasi-ordering is reflexive and transitive, but not every two elements need be comparable.)

```
theory QUOSET is                                        (7.2.12)
sorts elt
preds _=<_ : elt,elt
vars A,B,C : elt
axioms
   A =< A.
   A =< C :- A =< B, B =< C
endtheory QUOSET
```

A user can then ask to have an Eqlog object, X, "certified" as being of generic sort QUOSET. If such certification is successful, X must be quasi-ordered. A module, including predicate, function, and variable definitions, and a group of axioms using sort QUOSET could be:

```
module INTSORT[T::QUOSET] using INTSET = SET[INT]
...
endmodule INTSORT
```
(7.2.13)

Applications

Artificial Intelligence

Artificial intelligence is a loosely defined term encompassing activities, carried on by computers, that are ordinarily thought to require some sort of human intelligence. These include understanding written and spoken natural language, learning new information, recalling previously learned facts, scientific analysis, planning and problem solving, and various physical feats, such as navigating a room without bumping into the furniture. PROLOG is being used in all these areas.

Another area is the so-called expert system. For some systems, such as MYCIN, which is used to diagnose and recommend therapy for infectious diseases, a trained knowledge engineer extracts information from medical experts and then incorporates it into a computer program which would provide the combined wisdom of the experts. MYCIN was not written in PROLOG, but in LISP, which is generally acknowledged to be harder to learn. Some developers believe that knowledge engineers will no longer be needed when user interfaces to expert systems, called *shells*, become easier to use.

Relational Databases

Without question, the most prevalent use of computers is in the construction and maintenance of databases. Every enterprise with more than a very few employees has to keep records for payroll and tax purposes. Every manufacturing or retailing business must provide for inventory control. The amount of data kept by local, state, and federal governments is monumental, including information on health, crime, taxes, etc. Thus it is not surprising that developing new and better ways to manage this information has been, and will continue to be, an area of interest.

Once a database is established, it is quite difficult to reorganize or shift to a new and better database manager. The relational database, with its theoretical basis in the relational algebra (operations for manipulating relations), has become the style of most promise. PROLOG, which is itself based on the relation concept, is thus an ideal language for these applications.

The Fifth Generation

During the eighties, the adoption of PROLOG by the Japanese as the core language for its fifth generation effort spurred interest from industry and universities alike. Japan planned to package and sell knowledge as other nations marketed wine or clothing. To do this, their computers needed to be intelligent, i.e., able to "learn, associate, make inferences, make decisions, and otherwise behave in ways we have always considered the exclusive province of human reason" [Feigenbaum, 1983]. According to the Japanese researcher Ichikawa, quoting Shigeru Watanabe, "AI is a technology which analyzes knowledge and judgement used by human beings, and attempts to utilize them on the computer" [Ichikawa, 1991].

The Japanese envisaged a computer system using PROLOG as its core language. PROLOG was to be built into the hardware itself. Although present plans do not envisage PROLOG machines per se, the Fifth Generation Project, budgeted at about 50.5 billion yen ($472 million) from fiscal 1982 to fiscal 1991, included the development of the PROLOG-like parallel logical programming language KL-1. It includes some operating system functions as well as modularity and concurrent processing. As an experiment, 64 computers were connected in parallel under the operating system PIMOS (Parallel Inference Machine Operating System) running KL-1. Time efficiencies were measured at 5–8 mega LIPS (logical inferences per second). The target for this project was the development of knowledge information processing capabilities. Research and development are continuing, with a new goal of connecting 1000 parallel inference computers, with inference speed of 200 mega LIPS. The Japanese have also developed a PROLOG-based language called Extended Self-Contained PROLOG (ESP) for programming many fifth-generation projects on PCs and workstations. ESP runs under UNIX.

Applications range from resource exploration, through medical diagnosis and library functions, to weapons systems. Research areas are roughly organized under problem solving and inference, knowledge-based, human-machine interface, development support, and basic applications systems. An amazing feature of the Japanese effort was its ten-year implementation plan, with interindustrial, university, and governmental cooperation.

The use of special machines for artificial intelligence projects is decreasing in Japan, with almost half being carried out on personal computers. LISP is the language used for about 35 percent of AI projects, 33 percent of C, and a mere 5 percent of PROLOG. The most active AI applications area is the development of expert systems.

LAB 7.2: CANNIBALS AND MISSIONARIES: PROLOG

Objectives (Labs can be found in the *Instructor's Manual.*)

1. To see examples of well-written and well-documented PROLOG programs.
2. To see an appropriate example of a program that solves an interesting, nondeterministic problem.
3. To see a good use of relation addition and/or removal through the use of **assert** and **retract**.
4. To observe the flexibility and utility of PROLOG lists.

Strengths and Weaknesses

PROLOG has several features whose combination is unique from those encountered in other languages [Cohen, 1985]. These are:

1. Each parameter to a procedure can be either input or output at each invocation, as the user wishes.
2. Procedures may return results with unbound variables, thus presenting partial or generic solutions to a problem.
3. Multiple solutions may be found using built-in backtracking.

Cohen also lauds the logic base of PROLOG in the interests of effective problem specification, the potential for parallel processing, and the conciseness of PROLOG programs—estimated at 5–10 times smaller than those written in a procedural language.

There are, however, recognized shortcomings, other than those mentioned in [Goguen, 1984; Cohen, 1985; Feigenbaum, 1983]. It is not very easy for the uninitiated to read or write information using the first-order predicate calculus (PC). But once that is done, PROLOG takes over and makes inferences on its own. Some see this, too, as a serious flaw, since experienced programmers can improve the efficiency of program execution if they can control the method of solution. As it now exists, PROLOG has no mechanism for specifying parallel execution, no block structure, no methodology for documentation, and no type checking.

EXERCISES 7.2

(If possible, it is best to do most of these exercises at a terminal. However, think each one through first and then see what actually happens.)

1. Read "PROLOG Dialects: a *deja vu* of BASICs" [Sosnowski, 1987], and compare the merits of Edinburgh, Turbo, and micro-PROLOG.
2. What answers would you expect to the queries:
   a. `?-append2(X,[2],[1,2]).`
   b. `?-append2(X,Y,[1,2]).`
   c. Try the query of listing (7.2.6) using append2 both with and without cut.
   d. Consider `?-append2(comanche,[],Z).` Could you fix this up so PROLOG won't accept this input?
3. Write a PROLOG query to append the address, state, and zip code to the name "Donald Trump."
4. Consider a PROLOG procedure to reverse a list:

```
reverse([],[]).
reverse([X|Y],Z) :- reverse(Y,Z1),
                    append2(Z1,[X],Z).
```

   a. Construct a resolution tree for `?-reverse([1,2],Z)`.
   b. Construct stacks for X, Y, and Z. Is this procedure tail recursive?
5. Now consider a different procedure to reverse a list:

```
reverse2(L1,L2) :- reverse3(L1,[],L2).
reverse3([],L1,L1).
reverse3([X|L1],L2,L3) :-
              reverse3(L1,[X|L2],L3).
```

   (reverse3 is introduced for the sole purpose of making the call more natural. The second variable of reverse3 is used to accumulate partial results.)
   a. Trace the execution of `?-reverse2([1,2],R)`.
   b. Is this procedure tail recursive?

6. The query ?-findall(X,p(X),List). will return the List of all values satisfying p(X). What value would you expect PROLOG to return for List if p(X) is has(tom,X) (from the database in the section "Resolution" in section 7.1)?

7. A PROLOG function for computing N! is:

```
factorial(0,1).
factorial(N,M) :- N1 is N - 1,
                  factorial(N1,M1),
                  M is N * M1.
```

   a. Build the resolution tree and stack for ?-factorial(3,X).
   b. Is this procedure tail recursive?
   c. If your answer to b is no, can you write a procedure factorial2(N,M) that is tail recursive?

8. The Fibonacci series is {1,1,2,3,5, . . .}, where each term after the 0th and the 1st is the sum of the two previous terms, i.e., Fib(i) = Fib(i–1) + Fib(i–2). A PROLOG procedure for Fib is:

```
Fib(0,1).
Fib(1,1).
Fib(N,M) :- N1 is N - 1, N2 is N - 2,
            Fib(N1,M1),Fib(N2,M2),
            M is M1+M2.
```

   This procedure is not tail recursive. Can you make a new procedure Fib2(N,X,M), which uses X to store partial results and which is tail recursive?

9. Write in PROLOG what might be a definition for the '='/2 predicate. Must it be recursive? Why?

10. What might happen if we allow the substitution {Y/f(Y)} in a PROLOG implementation? Consider the query ?-Y=f(Y). Try this query, using any functor for f, with your version of PROLOG and see what happens.

11. Why is the list ['A','B','C','D'] returned when using mapcar (listing (7.2.3)) with the functor upper_case, instead of [A,B,C,D]?

12. Read "The British Nationality Act As a Logic Program" [Sergot, 1986] and write a review and/or report to your class on this very interesting use of PROLOG to sort out a complicated bit of British law.

13. Consider the following set of gardening facts:

```
flower(phlox).      type(phlox,perennial).
flower(petunia).    type(petunia,annual).
flower(rose).       type(rose,bush).
flower(daisy).      type(daisy,perennial).
                    type(daisy,annual).
```

   a. Use your PROLOG **debug** and/or **trace** utilities to trace the execution of ?-perennial_garden(X)., if perennial_garden is the rule: perennial_garden(F) :- flower(F),type(F,perennial).
   b. Add a cut to the rule in a, and trace again.
   c. Which rule could produce a list for the entire perennial garden? Which is faster?

14. Consider the following definition using cut [Clocksin, 1984]:

```
number_of_parents(adam,0) :- !.
number_of_parents(eve,0) :- !.
number_of_parents(X,2).
```

a. What will be the response of PROLOG to:

```
?-number_of_parents(betty,N).
?-number_of_parents(X,Y).
?-number_of_parents(eve,2).
```

b. Clocksin and Mellish fix this up as:

```
number_of_parents(adam,N) :- !, N = 0.
number_of_parents(eve,N) :- !, N = 0.
number_of_parents(X,2).
```

Can you think of another way to do this, by modifying the last clause, rather than the first two?

c. Will either of these work properly for:

```
?-number_of_parents(X,Y).
```

15. Rewrite the following rule using cut/**fail** to an equivalent rule using **not**.

```
marriageable(X,Y) :- (first_cousins(X,Y);
                      same_sex(X,Y);
                      siblings(X,Y)),
                     !,fail.
marriageable(X,Y) :- !.
```

16. Consider the following Hamburger database:

```
condiment(ketchup).     veggies(onion).
condiment(mustard).     veggies(lettuce).
cheese(cheddar).        cheese(swiss).
cheeseburger :- condiment(X), veggies(Y), cheese(Z).
```

Trace the execution of ?-cheeseburger. through the PROLOG clock of Figure 7.2.5.

17. Program the append procedure in a procedural language you know, such as Pascal, C, Ada, or FORTRAN. Comment on the differences between this program and the PROLOG one regarding:
   a. ease of programming   c. versatility
   b. speed of execution   d. I/O differences

18. The Cannibals and Missionaries problem involves three missionaries, three cannibals, one boat, and one river. The problem is to get all six across the river, with there never being more cannibals than missionaries on either side. The boat holds only two people. Look at the Eqlog solution to this problem in [Goguen, 1984, pp. 204–206] and trace its execution.

7.3
SUMMARY

The foundation for logic programming is the predicate calculus, an extension of the logical systems of Aristotle. Aristotelian logic is used to find new information from a given database following rules of deduction. One of these rules is called reductio ad absurdum, where we assume that a statement to be proved is false, and derive a contradiction. A version of the reductio method of proof called resolution is the basis for the logic programming language, PROLOG. The Resolution Theorem states that:

q is a logical consequence of $p_1, p_2, \ldots, p_n$ if $(\neg q \ \& \ p_1 \ \& \ p_2 \ \& \ldots \& \ p_n)$ is FALSE.

q :- $p_1, p_2, \ldots, p_n$ (meaning that the truth of p_1 and $p_2 \ldots$ and p_n implies the truth of q as well) is resolved in PROLOG by first proving all the subgoals p_1 through p_n, and then deriving a contradiction from the inclusion of not(q). If goals include variables, e.g., $p_i(x)$ and $p_j(y)$, substitutions are sought to unify the two goals, making both true. This might be substituting z for both x and y, $(p_i(z)$ and $p_j(z))$, and finally KingTut for z $(p_i(KingTut)$ and $p_j(KingTut))$.

PROLOG, which exists in several dialects, is logic-based and includes facts, rules, and queries. Rules produce derivations of new facts from old ones, while a query asks whether a given statement is true or false according to the existing facts, e.g., `?-(which(x (lives_in(Montana, x))))`. would check the two-place `lives_in` relation to see which people (values of x) in the database live in Montana.

Backtracking is the method of undoing the trail of a derivation which has led to a dead end before reaching a solution, and trying another path. Backtracking can also be used to find more than one solution to a query.

Backtracking is the natural method for backward chaining, i.e., reasoning from a goal backwards through rules to the underlying facts. This involves proving the right sides of rules first. Forward chaining is also possible in PROLOG, where we start with the goal and explore all possible rules or facts that could lead to it. This involves reasoning from the right sides of rules. In general, we try to move from the smaller to the larger (easier to find) set of states. For example, if there are many theorems and only a few axioms, we reason from the axioms to the theorems, i.e., backwards to the goal theorem.

PROLOG, as it exists, is inefficient in both time and storage usage, but is the first fully functional logic-based language, with others being developed rapidly. Some of these include facilities for parallel execution. PROLOG formed the early basis for Japan's Fifth Generation Project to mechanize and disseminate information rapidly.

PROLOG is used for artificial intelligence, especially where formal reasoning, such as in proving theorems, is needed. It is also a natural for relational databases, since each fact is expressed as a relation in a database.

PROLOG has been implemented in various ways, one of the most commonly used being the Warren Abstract Machine (WAM), which works like a clock running forward (establishing new facts) and backward (backtracking and undoing fruitless derivation paths.)

7.4
NOTES ON REFERENCES

J. Alan Robinson writes beautifully while explaining basic theory. His original presentation [Robinson, 1965] of resolution is quite comprehensible. For his view of the future, see [Robinson, 1983]. An extended discussion on the relationship of logic to programming can be found in Hoare and Shepherdson [Hoare, 1985].

Several journals are either devoted to or regularly publish articles on PROLOG. A guide to these can be found in [Cohen, 1988], and [Poe, 1984]. Also check issues of *PROLOG Digest* for current controversies.

The January, 1988 issue of the *Communications of the Association for Computing Machinery (CACM)* contains good historical articles on PROLOG [Cohen, 1988]; [Kowalski, 1988]. An earlier issue (December, 1985) is also devoted to PROLOG. For a good introduction to the underlying ideas, application areas, and a manual of DEC-10 PROLOG itself, see [Malpas, 1987]. Clocksin and Mellish [Clocksin, 1984] and Clark and McCabe [Clark, 1984] are the standard beginners' references to Edinburgh- and micro-PROLOG respectively, and are often included with a compiler or interpreter purchase.

The Warren Abstract Machine (WAM) is not the only model for PROLOG compilation. PROLOG has been compiled into intermediate languages which are known to be reasonably efficient and are implemented on a large number of machines. Work has been done using Pascal and C, among others [Weiner, 1988].

Expert systems are only one application of what are generally called rule-based systems or RBSs. For an overview, see [Hayes-Roth, 1985]. If you're not familiar with the series *Computing Surveys*, now is the time to become so. These quarterlies are written for students and provide surveys of important research areas, or tutorials. For an excellent treatment of logic and databases in this series, see [Gallaire, 1984].

The *ACM Computing Surveys* special issue on programming language paradigms [Wegner, 1989] discusses parallelism in logic programming in two articles. The first [Bal, 1989] is easy to understand and discusses both and and or parallelism in the context of concurrency in general. The second [Shapiro, 1989] is devoted entirely to logic parallelism, and is hard to read, but thorough. He includes a discussion of the current implementations: GHC, Parlog, FGHC, P-PROLOG, ALPS, FCP, Concurrent PROLOG, and CP.

8.0	**In this Chapter**	**327**
8.1	**Features of Functional**	
	Languages	**327**
	Composition of Functions	327
	Functions As First-Class Objects	328
	No Side Effects	329
	Clean Semantics	329
8.2	**LISP**	**330**
	Historical Vignette: LISP:	
	John McCarthy	330
	The LISP Language (SCHEME Dialect)	332
	Data Types	332
	Method for Storing Data	334
	Built-In Functions	336
	Functional Forms	338
	apply, eval, and Arithmetic	
	Operators	339
	Recursion and Control	341
	Side Effects	342
	A Self-Modifying Function	344
	Other Nonfunctional Features	347
	Iteration	347
	Vectors and Strings	348
	Objects and Packages	348

	Dialects	352
	Common LISP	352
	Exercises 8.2	353
8.3	**Implementing Functional**	
	Languages	**354**
	Lazy Versus Strict Evaluation	356
	Scope and Bindings	357
	The funarg Problems	358
	Garbage Collection	361
	Exercises 8.3	362
8.4	**Supporting Parallelism with**	
	Functions	**362**
8.5	**Other Functional Languages**	**364**
	APL	364
	ML	364
	Data Types	365
	Polymorphic Data Types	368
	Modules	368
	Exceptions	369
	Semantic Definition of ML	369
	Others	373
	Exercises 8.5	373
8.6	**Summary**	**373**
8.7	**Notes on References**	**374**

Functional (Applicative) Programming

A function is an "association of a certain object (or objects)[1] from one set (the range) with each object from another set (the domain). E.g., a function might be defined as having its value as a person's age when the person is specified—it would then be said that a person's age is a function of the person, and that the domain of this function is the set of all human beings, and the range is the set of all integers which are ages of persons presently living" [Glenn, 1959]. A function is thus an expression and its associated values, where the expression provides a method or rule for making the association between domain and range values. Functions may, but need not have, names. If age is the name of a function, then age(Amalia) = 7 is one way of indicating that the value of the age expression, age(Amalia), when associated with Amalia, is 7. Another syntax, which is common to most LISPs, one of the functional languages to be considered in this chapter, is (age Amalia), which evaluates to 7. A third form is that used by PROLOG, (age Amalia 7). However it is written, the age function when applied to the parameter Amalia returns the value 7.

The word *applicative* includes the notion of some sort of process or rule to construct the value of a function from the values of parameters presented to it. A function can usually be applied to different parameter values in different invocations. In defining a function as a parametrized expression that returns a single value, it is implied that there is some, possibly quite complicated, method for arriving at the single value given particular parameter values. A functional expression, when *applied* to a set of parameters, returns the value of the expression.

---

[1] One of the distinguishing features of a function is that it is *single-valued*, i.e., for each domain value, there is exactly one associated range value. A function can be multiple-valued and still meet this requirement if we put objects in a single tuple, e.g., $(obj_1, obj_2, ..., obj_n)$. The range would then be a set of tuples of objects from another set. The values of a function need not include every element of its range set, but each domain element must be associated with some value in the range.

The distinguishing features of the functional paradigm are that:

- Programs are constructed as the composition of functions.
- Functions are supported as first-class objects.
- There are no side effects (well, maybe a few).
- A clean, simple semantics is possible.

Control is usually achieved through recursion rather than the loop mechanisms commonly used in imperative languages.

Among the advantages of functional languages is simplicity.[2] In a procedural language, a main block might comprise three procedure calls:

```
begin
   GetData(...);
   ProcessData(...);
   OutputResults(...);
end.
```

In a functional language, this is accomplished with a single expression

```
(print(process-data(get-data(...)))).
```
(8.1.1)

Here the value of the expression `get-data(...)` is used as input to the function `process-data`. The `print` function then takes the value of `process-data` as its argument.[3] Using a function as an argument to another function, or as the value of a variable, is what makes functions *first-class*. They can be used anyplace any other object can, in particular, as the value of a variable. Perhaps the most striking feature of functions being first-class objects and programs being functions is that programs can be treated as data and modified at run time.

Functional language advocates claim that programs can be written quickly, are closer to traditional mathematical notation, are easier to verify, and can be executed more easily on parallel architectures than in traditional imperative languages [Hudak, 1989].

The first functional language LISP (for LISt Processing), was implemented in the fifties by John McCarthy. His original description of LISP [McCarthy, 1960], including a motivating preface and a description of an interpreter for the IBM 704, needed only 12 pages. More important than an economical language manual, however, is that the semantics or meanings of legal expressions are very simple. Thus proofs of correctness are quite possible for many programs. The notation for LISP is based on the theory of functions, as written in the lambda calculus (λ-calculus) of Alonzo Church [Church, 1941], which is discussed in Appendix B.

Just as PROLOG, the logic-based programming language of Chapter 7, makes some practical accommodations to the predicate calculus, implemented functional languages do not follow the lambda calculus exactly. A functional programmer will find some nonfunctional features in the language being used, as well as the availability of some side effects, e.g., input and output.

---

[2] Here we use the word "simplicity" in its mathematical sense as parsimony or elegance, not easiness. A single expression is considered simpler than a block containing three statements.

[3] In functional terms, a parameter is called an argument to a function.

8.0
IN THIS CHAPTER

We will discuss the primary features of the functional paradigm as listed above.

In his work, Church showed that all that is needed theoretically to express all the provable parts of mathematics is the lambda calculus. Thus a programming language that implements most of the lambda calculus can be quite powerful. There are practical considerations that must be considered when transforming a mathematical theory into a language that can be interpreted to control a digital computer. Thus LISP has, in addition to notational rules, or syntax:

• A method for storing data
• A set of built-in functions
• A set of functional forms
• Operators for applying a function to parameters and for evaluating the results

As an example, we will look at the SCHEME dialect of typeless LISP. We will also take a brief look at a more modern functional language, ML (an acronym for Meta Language[4]) which is strongly typed.

8.1
FEATURES OF FUNCTIONAL LANGUAGES

Composition of Functions

We discussed relations in the last chapter, as ordered tuples. A function can also be thought of as a special sort of relation, $f = (x_1, x_2, \ldots, x_n, y)$ where the last coordinate, y, called its value, is uniquely determined by the values of $x_1, x_2, \ldots x_n$. A functional relation is often written $f(x_1, x_2, \ldots, x_n) = y$, where the x_i are called the arguments of and y the value of f, when applied to $x_1, x_2, \ldots, x_n$. Here the x_i are the independent variables of f, and y the dependent variable, since its value depends on the values of the x_i. A function may also be considered as an expression $f(x_1, x_2, \ldots, x_n)$, which can be evaluated. We are quite used to expressions such as print(x1 + x2), where 8 is printed if x1 = 5 and x2 = 3.

In PROLOG, M + N = S would be represented as the relation (SUM M N S), which is true only if S = M + N. SCHEME uses the expression (+ m n), with the value of m + n being returned. As a relation, PROLOG's (SUM 2 N 6) makes sense since N can be assigned the value 4, but as a function it does not. The SUM relation can be used for both addition and subtraction, but the rule for a function can perform only one task, and return only one value. We would need a second function to compute (- 6 2) and return the value 4. Note also here the distinction between a relation and a function. A relation is an ordered association of elements often listed as a tuple,

---

[4]A metalanguage is a language used to discuss some other language or symbolic system. ML is used to discuss the theory of functions in the context of a computer programming language.

while a function returns a value, given an ordered tuple or argument list of elements. As noted above, however, a function can be implemented as a special sort of relation, with one coordinate (usually the last) being reserved for the functional value.

The expressive power of the functional paradigm comes from composing two or more functions. (+ (* w x)(- y z)) represents the composition of the * and - functions with +. Since the evaluation of a function involves first evaluating each of its arguments, both the values of (* w x) and of (- y z) would be returned to the + function, which would then invoke the + rule. Such a function is composed of the three functions, *, -, and +.

There are three reasons why attention is being paid to functional programming [Eisenbach, 1987]. First, functional notation is concise, allowing shorter, more elegant programs to be written. Secondly, mathematical function theory is well developed, allowing programmers to write programs that look like specifications with automatic transformation systems that convert the specifications into efficiently running programs. Finally, functional programs can run in parallel on multiprocessors. The two arguments to our function above, (+ (* w x)(- y z)), which are function calls to * and -, could be evaluated in parallel, and then returned to +.

Functions As First-Class Objects

A function is first-order if it takes *individuals* as arguments, i.e., such things as numbers, strings, records, etc., and returns an individual value. In functional terms, an individual is a function of order 0. There are two steps in evaluating a function such as $f(x)$. First, a suitable value must be substituted for x, e.g., the substitution of 2 for x yields $f(2)$. Next, $f(2)$ is evaluated according to some defining rule for f. If $f(x)$ is the rule $x + 3$, then f, when applied to 2, evaluates to 5, i.e., $f(2) = 5$.

If a domain D and a range R are sets of individuals, a function from D into R is said to be *first-order*, e.g., if both D and R are sets of integers, $x \in D$, and $y \in R$, then (+ x y) is first-order. A *higher-order* function can take other functions, as well as individuals, as arguments and return either functions or individuals as values. A second-order function can take first-order functions as arguments and return first-order functions or individuals as values. In general, a function of order n may have functions of order n–1 or lower as arguments and return them as well. Functions of order n are important to function theory, as they provide the structure for recursive proofs about functions. A function that can have functions of any order as arguments and return functions of any order is called *first-class*. LISP functions are potentially first-class, accepting functions of any order as arguments and returning functions of any order as values. We looked at a first-class function mapcar in Chapter 7. (mapcar fun lis), when supplied with the arguments fun = '+' and lis = ((1,1),(1,2),(1,3)), returns the list (2, 3, 4). mapcar applies the + function successively to each element of lis and returns a list of these values.

One of the interesting things about LISP is its view of data as the value of an expression. If (print(process-data(get-data(...)))) is a program, it can be considered as an executable bit of code, and this code can be considered as data itself. If we name the program (define do-the-job(print(process-data(get-data(...))))), then do-the-job has the value (print(process-data(get-data(...)))), which can be viewed as either an executable function or as a list of strings enclosed in parentheses. These strings can be changed by other functions, as we will see below.

No Side Effects

As noted in Chapter 2, a function (f x y z) is said to have a side effect if the values of x, y, and/or z change in the calling environment during application of the function to its arguments, or if some other action, such as printing, occurs while evaluating f. Most imperative languages implement the passing of parameters by value or by reference. A memory location associated with an actual parameter in the environment from which a procedure or function call is made is not changed if the call is by value. Thus a function defined with all value parameters, and where no assignments are made to global variables, has no side effects. But it is often the side effect we are after when we pass a parameter by reference. A procedure in an imperative language called GetData(x,y,z) will most likely be used to provide values for x, y, and z, and to communicate this information to other parts of the program. We are assured that variable arguments to a function with no side effects have the same values upon exit from a function that they did upon entry. So how do these arguments get any values at all? In a purely functional language, the answer is that they are the values of other functions. Put differently, a functional GetData would be something like (GetData Getx, Gety, Getz), where Getx, Gety, and Getz are functions returning values. Most LISP implementations incorporate some side effects and built-in data types. These have been included to facilitate easily readable code and efficient implementations.

Clean Semantics

Some of the features of a language that make it useful and reliable are that it means what it says, it is not ambiguous, and the results of a program can be verified. In a functional language, f(3) will always return the same result, while in an imperative language, such as Pascal, this may not be the case. Consider the Pascal function:

```
function f(I : integer):integer;                                    (8.1.2)
begin
   Count := Count + I;
   f := Count
end;
```

If Count is a suitably initialized global variable, f(3) will return a different result each time it is called! This is only a simple example of the difficulties that may be encountered when trying to prove what an imperative program's semantics are.

There is no point in reinventing the wheel if one is available and suitable for the task at hand, so the authors of functional languages used the mathematical theory of Alonzo Church, called the lambda calculus, enhanced by the calculus of combinators of Haskell B. Curry and R. Feys. One can code a program and often prove it correct using the same notation in which these two theories are written.[5] A computer scientist can rely on the mathematical work already done using these theories to develop sound algorithms for specific tasks. We have included a brief look at the lambda calculus in Appendix B for the reader who is interested.

8.2
LISP

HISTORICAL VIGNETTE

LISP: John McCarthy

Artificial intelligence (AI) is the part of computer science concerned with designing intelligent computer systems, that is, systems that exhibit the characteristics we associate with intelligence in human behavior—understanding language, learning, reasoning, solving problems and so on [Jackson, 1986].

LISP is a programming language with a purpose. It was developed specifically for AI programming in the late fifties by John McCarthy, then a professor at Dartmouth. The seeds of LISP were sown in McCarthy's mind back in the summer of 1956 when he attended the first major workshop on AI at Dartmouth. He realized that existing languages would not meet the needs of AI programmers. Languages such as FORTRAN deal with numbers. An AI language, if it were to truly mimic the human brain, would need to encode words and concepts.

McCarthy worked to develop LISP for the next two years. The language is a combination of four elements: two existing languages, mathematics, and the last from McCarthy himself. LISP borrowed algebraic syntax from FORTRAN and methods of symbol manipulation from IPL (Information Processing Language). In mathematics, McCarthy found two equivalent systems, Kleene's recursive function theory and the lambda calculus, a convenient notation for LISP's anonymous functions. The inventor of the lambda calculus, Alonzo Church, had been McCarthy's thesis advisor at Princeton. Although the lambda calculus influenced McCarthy, it was not followed slavishly. The last elements are his own: the use of lists to represent information, the representation of programs as data, and the creation of garbage collection to round up and make available memory locations that are no longer needed.

Like FORTRAN, the first implementation of LISP was for the IBM 704. It had only a few primitives and used punched cards in batch mode. An interactive LISP system developed in 1960 has the honor of being one of the earliest examples of interactive computing. Still, the growth of LISP usage was slow. AI was a relatively new field which needed large computers with massive memories.

---

[5]Not all programs can be proved correct or incorrect, no matter what method you use. A result known as the halting problem shows that if there was a function H(f), that returned TRUE if f was a function that terminated and returned a value, and FALSE if f was going to run forever, then H would lead to a paradox in function theory.

Interest in AI grew with interest in LISP, which became the primary experimental AI language. "It is a characteristic of artificial intelligence applications that the problem is not well understood. Indeed, often one goal of the research is to understand the problem better . . . . LISP is very [well] suited to this kind of problem" [MacLennan, 1987]. LISP is good for ambiguous problems because of its dynamic type system and flexible data structures, which encourage an experimental approach to problem solving.

Of course, not every aspect of the LISP picture has been rosy. Early systems were all interpreted, rather than compiled, making programs run very slowly. Today, most LISP systems provide compilers with speed optimizers, but its reputation as a slow language remains. Also, LISP makes much use of recursion, which many programmers find difficult to grasp. And finally, LISP programs require very large central memories to run. Thus the development of better garbage collectors remains an active area of research.

AI can be divided into three areas: natural language processing, robotics, and knowledge engineering. It is in the second and third areas where LISP excels. "Knowledge engineering focuses on both the development of software for expert systems and on the analysis of ways in which human experts solve problems. Knowledge engineers interact with human experts to help them describe their knowledge and inference strategies in terms that will allow the knowledge to be encoded. Thus, a knowledge engineer combines a large measure of cognitive psychology with symbolic programming techniques to develop expert systems" [Harmon, 1985].

Expert systems focus on two types of knowledge. The first, *public knowledge,* is the sort found in textbooks. A human expert in a field has a firm grasp of factual information. Expert systems can surpass human experts in retrieving pertinent information, given an adequate database. The second is *private knowledge,* which might be called intuition or common sense. "This private knowledge consists largely of rules of thumb that have come to be called *heuristics.* Heuristics enable the human expert to make educated guesses when necessary, to recognize promising approaches to problems, and to deal effectively with errorful or incomplete data. Elucidating and reproducing such knowledge is the central task in building expert systems" [Hayes-Roth, 1983]. When it comes to private knowledge, humans usually beat the machines.

Examples of expert systems written in LISP and in use today are DENDRAL, MACSYMA, EXPERT, and MYCIN. DENDRAL is used to analyze mass spectgraphic, nuclear, magnetic resonance, and chemical experimental data to infer the plausible structure of an unknown compound. MACSYMA performs differential and integral calculus symbolically and excels at simplifying symbolic expressions. EXPERT is used to build consultation models in endocrinology, ophthalmology, and rheumatology. MYCIN diagnoses infectious blood diseases and prescribes treatment.

Interest in LISP has slowed as the programming community has focused more on object-oriented techniques. In the late eighties, an attempt was made to standardize a merged Common LISP and SCHEME. The effort to merge the two languages failed, but the IEEE did produce a standard for SCHEME in 1989. The Common LISP draft document, produced by the IEEE working group X3J13 in 1992, is over 1000 pages long—a far cry from McCarthy's original 12 pages.

The LISP Language (SCHEME Dialect)

Data Types

LISP has one simple data type, the *atom*, which is a number or a string beginning with a letter, called a *literal atom*. Numbers evaluate to themselves and use the built-in hardware for integer and real arithmetic. A literal atom a may have a value and be evaluated, or may remain unevaluated. A literal atom also has an associated property list, **proplist**, which is originally an empty list (). Properties can be added to the **proplist** of an atom using (**putprop** <name> <value> <property>), or removed using (**remprop** <name> <property>). (**getprop** <name> <property>) returns the value of a property of the atom <name>.

SCHEME Expression	Value	(8.2.1)
(**proplist** 'blue-whale)	()	
(**define** sea 'ocean)	unspecified value	
(**putprop** 'blue-whale 'krill 'eats)	unspecified value	
(**putprop** 'blue-whale sea 'dwells-in)	unspecified value	
(**proplist** 'blue-whale)	(DWELLS-IN OCEAN, EATS KRILL)	
(**getprop** 'blue-whale 'dwells-in)	OCEAN	
(**remprop** 'blue-whale 'dwells-in)	unspecified value	
(**proplist** 'blue-whale)	(EATS KRILL)	

After the first six expressions of listing (8.2.1) are evaluated, the atom blue-whale would be represented in memory as diagrammed in Figure 8.2.1.

The name blue-whale would also be an entry in a table called the *object list*, which is similar to a symbol table. The entry in this object list under blue-whale is the pointer to the structure of Figure 8.2.1. The atom nil represents the end of a list. The structure of Figure 8.2.1 represents the list (blue-whale, **proplist**), where **proplist** is ((eats krill) (dwells-in ocean)).

LISP's structured type is the list, which may be empty or contain ordered objects, (obj$_1$ obj$_2$ ... obj$_n$). Some LISPs, such as Common LISP, also include arrays using a particular machine's array facilities.

We have already seen abstract data types in Chapters 2 and 3. This binding of operations to data can also be implemented in functional languages. What is needed are functions called *constructors*, which construct instances of a particular compound data type, and *selectors*, which select out features of the aggregate. As an example, complex numbers can be represented in two ways, *rectangular* (RealPart, ImaginaryPart) form, or *polar* (Magnitude, Angle) form, as shown in Figure 8.2.2.

A constructor function returns a complex number, and the complex arithmetic operators return complex numbers, regardless of the form. Such operators must be generic functions that can perform the desired operation correctly, regardless of the parameter types.

LISP, including the SCHEME dialect that we will look at below, is not strongly typed, but we can construct two different forms of complex number through user-defined functions called, possibly, rectangular and polar. The programmer must watch for type mismatches, because the system does not do so. In SCHEME, we can define the function rectangular(r, i) = (r, i). Given two real numbers r and i as

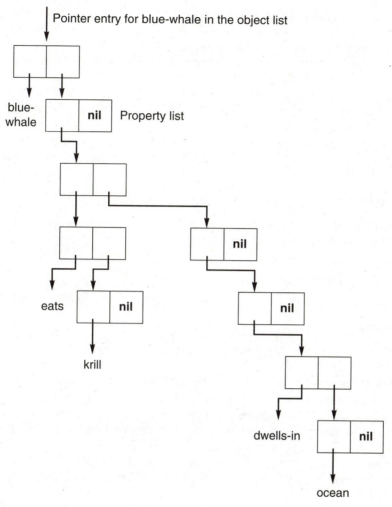

FIGURE 8.2.1
Representation in memory for the atom, `blue-whale`

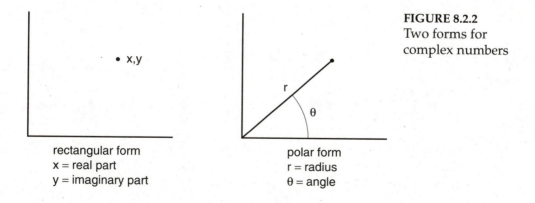

rectangular form
x = real part
y = imaginary part

polar form
r = radius
θ = angle

FIGURE 8.2.2
Two forms for
complex numbers

arguments, rectangular returns a two-element list containing r as the real and i as the imaginary parts of a complex number. Similarly, polar(m, θ) could return a list with m as magnitude and θ as angle. Functions for complex arithmetic can then be defined that take as arguments two-element lists of reals and that convert complex numbers from one form to another.

It is worth noting that in the LISP language, the pair (1.0, 0.0) could represent a complex number in either rectangular or polar form, since it matches the complex pattern for either representation: a two-element list of real numbers. LISP does not return a type along with a list value. It is up to the programmer to do any type checking that is necessary. This invitation to program bugs has been remedied in the functional language, ML, which we will discuss briefly at the end of the chapter.

Method for Storing Data

McCarthy's original syntax for LISP was the S-expression (or sexpr), standing for "symbolic expression." An S-expression is defined recursively as:

1. An atomic symbol is an S-expression.
2. If e_1 and e_2 are S-expressions, then so is $(e_1 \cdot e_2)$.

This last expression is called a *dotted pair*. A list can be implemented as:

$$(e_1 \cdot (e_2 \cdot (\cdots (e_n \cdot \mathbf{nil})))) \tag{8.2.2}$$

where **nil** is an atomic symbol for the empty list. In most LISPs, the list of listing (8.2.2) is abbreviated $(e_1\ e_2 \ldots e_n)$.

Data storage was implemented on the IBM 704 as atomic cells or as cons ("construction") cells for dotted pairs as shown in Figure 8.2.3. The identifiers **car** and **cdr** are related to the IBM 704, where a word of memory included the contents of the **address register** (**car**) and the contents of the **decrement register** (**cdr**). The names continue to be used today to indicate the head and the tail of a list, where (**car** l) returns the first element of the list l, and (**cdr** l) returns all of the list except its first element. If l = (a b c) is a list, (**car** l) is a and (**cdr** l) is (b c). (b c) is called the *tail* of l.

car   cdr

FIGURE 8.2.3
The binary or cons cell for a dotted pair

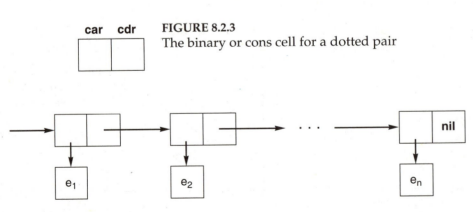

FIGURE 8.2.4
List implemented as dotted pairs. The e_i may be either cons cells or atoms.

A list is then as shown in Figure 8.2.4. In Figure 8.2.4, the head, or **car**, of the list is e_1, and the tail is the rest of the list, which is located at the address contained in the **cdr** of the first cons cell.

Lists as data structures. Lists are amazingly flexible for developing data structures. An ordered binary tree shown in Figure 8.2.5 is (((0) 1 (2)) 3 ((4) 5 (6))) in list form. Notice that each subtree is itself a list. The left subtree appears to the left of the root node, and the right to the right.

We have seen a variety of data structures, which will all be expressed as lists in LISP. For example, a 1-dimensional array is just a simple list, and an $n \times m$ array of two dimensions is a list of lists, $(ROW_1\ ROW_2 \ldots ROW_n)$, where each ROW is an m-dimensional list. A 3-dimensional array is $(A_1\ A_2 \ldots A_p)$, where each A_i is a 2-dimensional array, etc. Suppose A = ((1 2 3)(4 5 6)(7 8 9)) represents a 3×3 array. SCHEME (and most other LISPs) have special functions to quickly find individual elements. (**car** A) is the list (1 2 3). But suppose we want A[1,1] = 1 or (**car** (**car** A)). This is abbreviated (**caar** A). A[2,1] = 4 is (**car**(**car**(**cdr** A))) or (**caadr** A), and A[3,1] = 7 is (**caaddr** A), or (**car**(**car**(**cdr** (**cdr** A)))), which is (**car**(**car**(**cdr** ((4 5 6) (7 8 9)))))), which is (**car**(**car** ((7 8 9)))), or (**car** (7 8 9)) = 7. All these abbreviations start with c, end in r, and have as many a's or d's as we need **car**s or **cdr**s.[6] Get it?

Lists as programs. A LISP *form* is an S-expression that is meant to be evaluated. The number 2 is a form that evaluates to 2. (+ 3 5) is a form that evaluates to 8, as is ((**lambda** (x) (+ 3 x)) 5). ((**lambda** (x) (+ 3 x)) 5) is called a *lambda expression*, with the word **lambda** preceding the argument list, in this case, (x). Suppose we use (**define** plus3 (lambda (x) (+ 3 x))). When plus3 is applied to the value 5, using ((plus3 x) 5), it has the same effect as (**lambda** (x) (+ 3 x)) 5), but also names the function so defined. Forms such as (+ 3 x) are built into the SCHEME system. Each form could be considered to be a program.

In practice, a program is saved for repeated use and contains a collection of function definitions. One function call starts things off. For example, the program for the SCHEME Help facility begins with the definition (slightly modified here) of a function to access the various aspects of the facility.

```
(define help                                            (8.2.3)
   (lambda subject
      (if (null? subject)
      (show-help-topics)
      (fetch-help (car subject))))
))
```

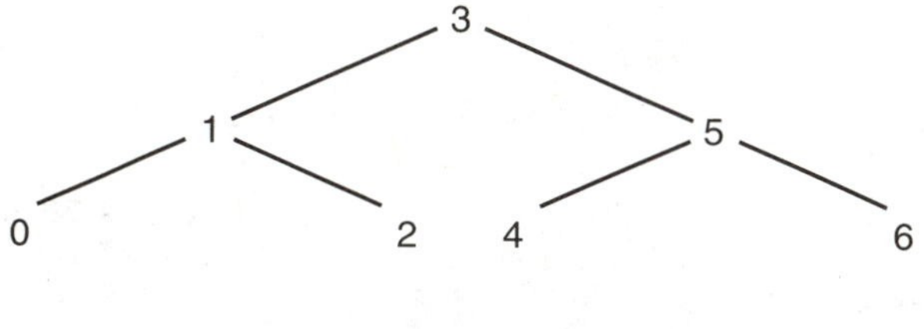

FIGURE 8.2.5
Binary search tree

---

[6]Most LISPs limit the length of a c . . . r operator. In PC-SCHEME, it is c**xxxx**r, where each x may be **d** or **r**.

(**if** <condition> <if-part> <else-part>) is a special form taking three arguments. If <condition> is true, the <if-part> is evaluated, otherwise the <else-part> is evaluated. There are two auxiliary functions to help, show-help-topics and fetch-help. These invoke still other functions, which invoke others, etc. help accepts either zero or one argument, subject. If there are no arguments, show-help-topics is called. If subject is a list, as in (help (editor)), fetch-help is called with the first element of subject as argument; in this case, help on using the editor would be exhibited.

When help is loaded, evaluation puts the body of each of the Help system functions in the current environment and makes them available to respond to function calls from the terminal. The Help facility is composed of 22 defined functions, with initial access through the function call (help).[7]

A SCHEME program could also include other expressions to be evaluated. For example, we could end the help file with the function call (help). Then loading the file would result in the help topics being listed automatically. Probably not a good idea, but possible.

Data abstractions, although not built into SCHEME, can be implemented by choosing suggestive names for functions. For example, an implementation for an ADT for rational numbers in the SCHEME dialect of LISP could be defined with the eight functions shown in listing (8.2.4) [Abelson, 1985]:

make-rat (n d)	returns (n·d)	(8.2.4)
numer (x)	returns n, where x is (n·d)	
denom (x)	returns d, where x is (n·d)	
+rat (x y)	returns x + y, where x and y are rationals	
-rat (x y)	returns x − y, where x and y are rationals	
*rat (x y)	returns x * y, where x and y are rationals	
/rat (x y)	returns x / y, where x and y are rationals	
=rat (x y)	returns true if x = y, otherwise false, where x, y are rationals.	

One aspect of LISP, not shared by other languages, is that programs (S-expressions) and data are indistinguishable. Just as a program can modify the values of variables, so can it modify other programs or even itself. Function definitions, environments,[8] programs, and files are all first-class LISP objects which can be passed to functions and returned as values.

Built-In Functions

There were only six functions built into McCarthy's original LISP: **cons**, **cond**, **car**, **cdr**, **eq**, and **atom**.[9] Most LISPs in use today provide others, including arithmetic operators, input, and output. All the atoms, functions, and forms of early LISPs are

---

[7] A function usually has arguments, as in the call (+ 1 2). If there are no arguments, as in help, the call (help) still requires parentheses.

[8] An environment is a sequence of tables containing variable bindings. It is similar to the bindings in nested blocks in a language such as Pascal. In SCHEME, an environment can be returned as the value of the special form, make-environment.

[9] In the original LISP, atoms were written in uppercase, e.g., **CAR**, because early computers did not recognize lowercase characters. We have not done so here, as the practice has largely been abandoned.

included in newer versions, but many more have been added for programmer convenience.

(**cons** a b) returns the dotted pair (a · b). If lyst is a list, (**cons** 'head lyst) returns a new list, with head added to lyst as the first element, as shown in Figures 8.2.6 and 8.2.7.

(**car** lyst) returns the first element of lyst, and (**cdr** lyst) returns everything on lyst but the first element, as discussed in the section "Method for Storing Data." Thus if lyst is (a b c), (**car** lyst) returns a, (**cdr** lyst) returns (b c), and (**cons** 'head lyst) returns (head a b c). (**cons** 9 ()) evaluates to (9 · **nil**), which is abbreviated (9), the list with a single element, 9.

Notice that in Figure 8.2.7, the list produced by the **cons** operation has no name. Such niceties as naming functions have been added to all LISP implementations. These are nonfunctional features, however. In a purely functional language, values are not assigned to storage locations. If we want to build the list (1 2 3) and then find its first element, we could achieve this in a functional manner using (**car** (**cons** (1 (**cons** 2 (**cons** 3 **nil**)))))). If (1 2 3) had the name 11, we could use (**car** 11). We will consider naming atoms and S-expressions in the section "Side Effects."

(**eq** A B) tests whether the atoms A and B are the same or not. (**atom** A) returns #T (true) if A is an atom, and otherwise #F (false). In some LISPS, #T, #F, and **nil** are self-evaluating constants, as are the numbers. In SCHEME, #T, #F, and **nil** are ordinary symbols, which are bound in the global environment to appropriate values. **nil** represents the empty list, although () may be used as well. Not all LISPs use #T and #F, but may use t and f, true and false, or TRUE and FALSE.

Control is provided through the *conditional expression* **cond**. We will discuss **cond** in more detail in the section "Recursion and Control," but will mention it briefly here as we can't get very far in LISP without it. The form of the **cond** <expression> is shown in listing (8.2.5).

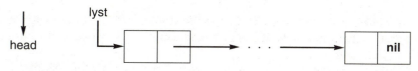

FIGURE 8.2.6
head and lyst before the **cons** operation

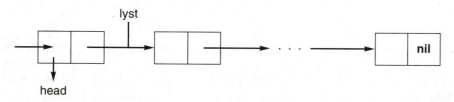

FIGURE 8.2.7
After the **cons** operation

$$(\textbf{cond} \;\; (<c_1> \; <e_1>) \qquad\qquad\qquad\qquad\qquad (8.2.5)$$
$$(<c_2> \; <e_2>)$$
$$\cdots$$
$$(<c_n> \; <e_n>)$$
$$)$$

Execution starts at the top, evaluating the c_i, or *guards*, until one evaluates to true. The value of the corresponding e_i is returned. If none of the c_i are true, the **cond** returns a value of false (**nil** or **#F**). A **cond** expression returning the absolute value of its argument is:

$$(\textbf{cond} \;\; ((> \; x \; 0) \; x) \qquad\qquad\qquad\qquad\qquad (8.2.6)$$
$$((\textbf{eq} \; x \; 0) \; 0)$$
$$(\text{\#T} \; (- \; x))$$
$$)$$

The last S-expression, (#T (- x)), is evaluated only if the first two guards, (> x 0) and (**eq** x 0), are false (#F). Its guard #T is always true.

Functional Forms

There is only one functional form built into the original LISP, the lambda expression, (**lambda** (<formal parameters>) <body>), which comes from Church's lambda calculus as discussed in Appendix B. (**lambda** (x y) (* x y)) represents a function of two variables, which returns their product. ((**lambda** (x y) (* x y)) 2 3) returns 6, after binding 2 to x, and 3 to y, and then applying the multiplication operator to 2 and 3. The scope of x and y is the lambda expression.

To implement recursion, LISP uses a labeled lambda expression.

```
(label (factorial (lambda(n)                              (8.2.7)
        (cond ((eq n 0) 1)
              (#T (* n (factorial (- n 1))))
        )
)))
```

label does not bind a function definition to the atom factorial, but does give a temporary name to the function so it can be called recursively as in the third line of the expression in listing (8.2.7).

In SCHEME, we can bind the atom factorial to its definition using:

```
(define factorial (lambda(n)                              (8.2.8)
        (cond ((eq n 0) 1)
              (#T (* n (factorial (- n 1))))
        )
))
```

In listing (8.2.8), factorial is bound to its lambda definition, and can then be called repeatedly. (**define** <identifier> <S-expression>) is a SCHEME special form that serves the purpose of **label** in the earlier LISP to implement the recursion of the last line. In addition, as a side effect, it binds <identifier> to <S-expression>.

As an example of a functional form constructed in LISP using a lambda expression, we will consider the mapcar function described previously in the section

"Functions As First-Class Objects." In mathematics, a map is a set of ordered pairs (x, y), with x "mapped" onto its value y. (mapcar func lyst) repeatedly maps the **car** of the list lyst onto a functional value. If lyst has 25 elements, $e_1, \ldots, e_{25}$, (mapcar fun lyst), will return another list of 25 values, (fun(e1),...,fun(e25)). For example, add1 is a function of one variable that adds 1 to its argument. (mapcar add1 (1 2 3)) returns the list (2 3 4).

mapcar can be defined using SCHEME syntax as shown in listing (8.2.9) below.

```
(define mapcar (lambda(fun lyst)                              (8.2.9)
    (cond ((null? lyst) nil)
          (#T (cons (fun (car lyst))
                    (mapcar fun (cdr lyst))
              )   )
    )
))
```

Suppose we evaluate the expression (mapcar **(lambda** (x) (* x x)) (1 2 3)), where **(lambda** (x) (* x x)) is the form matching the parameter, fun, and (1 2 3) matches lyst. ((**lambda** (x) (* x x)) 2) evaluates to 4 since 2 is substituted for x before the multiplication takes place. The recursion is as shown in listing (8.2.10).

```
(cons ((lambda (x) (* x x)) 1)                               (8.2.10)
    (mapcar ((lambda (x) (* x x)) (2 3))
          (cons ((lambda (x) (* x x)) 2)
              (mapcar ((lambda (x) (* x x)) (3))
                  (cons ((lambda (x) (* x x)) 3)
                      (mapcar ((lambda (x) (* x x)) ())
                          (null? ()) nil)
                  (9)
          (4 9)
    (1 4 9)
```

Notice that the recursion repeatedly calls mapcar until the null list is encountered at line 7, at which time the whole chain can unwind, constructing the list of values. This is often called "consing up a list." This behavior causes problems for the beginning LISP programmer, who sometimes creates infinite recursive calls.

apply, eval, **and Arithmetic Operators**

McCarthy used the five basic functions to define apply, eval, and evalquote, which in effect built an interpreter for LISP. The first two are built into most modern LISPs. This is another example of an interpreter or compiler written in the language it is to translate to machine code. We already looked at another, the C language.

apply takes two inputs, evaluates each of its arguments, and then applies the first, which is a function, to the second, which is a list of arguments. (apply **car** (quote ((a b c))))[10] returns a, the first element of the list (a b c), i.e., applies the function **car** to the single argument (a b c).

---

[10]The function (quote ((a b c))), which can also be written '((abc)), returns ((a b c)) with a, b, and c unevaluated.

`eval` takes an expression and an environment, e, as values. Suppose that the values a, b, and c in environment e are 1, 2, and 3, respectively. (eval (**car** '(a b c)) returns the value of a, 1. eval includes a call to `apply` after evaluating a, b, and c. Thus (eval (**car** '(a b c)) invokes (apply **car** (quote ((1 2 3)))) after evaluating a, b, and c. You will see an application of both eval and apply in the section, "A Self-Modifying Function."

Just to warn the user of various LISP dialects, we have been writing our LISP functions as S-expressions, surrounded by parentheses, e.g., (**cons** a (b c)). When using some interpreters, this could be entered in more functional notation as **cons** (a (b c)). That is, f(x y) instead of (f x y). This practice has been largely abandoned, as it is inconsistent with most LISP syntax. However, you may see **cons** (a (b c)), (**cons** a (b c)), (**cons** a, (b, c)), **cons** (a; (b; c)), or other variations in different interpreters or compilers.

No arithmetic functions were built into early LISP, although both integer and real arithmetic operators are built into SCHEME and most other modern LISPs. Originally these, as well as everything else, had to be built by the programmer. For example, suppose the nonnegative integers are defined using the zero and a successor function succ as:

```
(define zero nil)
(define (succ n)(cons n n))
```

Then the numbers 0, 1, 2 and 3 are: **nil**, (**nil**), ((**nil**), **nil**), and (((**nil**), **nil**),(**nil**),**nil**).

In exercise 7.2.3, you will be asked to write the function pred (predecessor), where (pred n) returns the number before n if n is not 0, and (pred 0) returns an error.

```
(define plus (lambda (num1 num2)                    (8.2.11)
        (cond ((zero? num1) num2)
              (#T (plus (pred num1)(succ num2)))
        )
))
```

In listing (8.2.11), if num1 is 0, then the value of num2 is returned. Otherwise, we proceed to the second alternative, e2 = (plus (pred num1)(succ num2)). Let's evaluate (plus 2 3).

```
(zero? 2) = #F                                      (8.2.12)
#T (plus 1 4)
   (zero? 1) = #F
  #T (plus 0 5)
     (zero? 0) return 5
```

In SCHEME, the **if** special form is an abbreviated **cond**:

$$(\textbf{if } e_1 \ c_1 \ c_2) \equiv (\textbf{cond } (e_1 \ c_1) \qquad\qquad (8.2.13)$$
$$(\textbf{\#T } c_2))$$

In practice, a LISP program is a collection of function definitions, with one of them providing access into the program by calling others, which call others, etc.

Recursion and Control

As we saw in Chapter 2, control abstractions are branches, iterators, and procedures. In LISP, the **cond** expression, as defined in listing (8.2.5), controls branching, with (**cond** (boolean_1 exp_1) (boolean_2 exp_2) ... (boolean_N exp_N)) implementing both **if...then...else**s and case statements.

Procedural control in SCHEME, as in all LISPs, is through function calls, which are usually recursive. Each call sets up a new set of bindings, called an environment or frame, with the results from the bottom frame of a recursion being passed all the way back up to the top, as a value for the original function. Using that old standby factorial, let's once again see how this works, implementing its definition as:

$$\text{factorial (n)} \equiv \quad \textbf{if } (n = 0) \textbf{ then } 1 \qquad\qquad (8.2.14)$$
$$\textbf{else } (n * \text{factorial}(n - 1))$$

We defined factorial in listing (8.2.8), but will redefine it here in SCHEME code, which is slightly different, as shown in listing (8.2.15).

```
(define factorial                                    (8.2.15)
  (lambda (n)
    (if(zero? n)
    1
    (* n (factorial(- n 1)))
)))
```

A call to (factorial 3) will produce four nested environments before arriving at any value, and partial results must be passed all the way back to factorial. In listing (8.2.16) below, which shows the recursive action, we will use subscripts to indicate environments.

$$(\text{factorial}_1\ 3) \Rightarrow (* 3\ (\text{factorial}\ 2)) \qquad\qquad (8.2.16)$$
$$(\text{factorial}_2\ 2) \qquad \Rightarrow (* 2\ (\text{factorial}\ 1))$$
$$(\text{factorial}_3\ 1) \qquad\qquad \Rightarrow (* 1\ (\text{factorial}\ 0))$$
$$(\text{factorial}_4\ 0) \qquad\qquad \Rightarrow 1$$
$$(\text{factorial}_3\ 1) \qquad\qquad \Rightarrow (* 1\ 1) = 1$$
$$(\text{factorial}_2\ 2) \qquad \Rightarrow (* 2\ 1) = 2$$
$$(\text{factorial}_1\ 3) \Rightarrow (* 3\ 2) = 6$$

A more efficient computation is $N * (N–1) * (N–2) * ... * 1$. We can accomplish this in SCHEME using a frame for the function helper as shown in listing (8.2.17), which contains the temporary variables a, acting as an accumulator for the partial sums, and i, counting down to 0.

```
(define factorial2                                   (8.2.17)
  (lambda(n)
    (define helper
      (lambda (i a)
        (if (zero? i)
        a
        (helper (- i 1) (* a i))
    ))
    (helper n 1)
))
```

Here a call to factorial2(3) would first define helper and then call (helper 3 1), which would recursively multiply 3∗2∗1, returning 6.

This can also be implemented without the use of helper with SCHEME'S **let**, which initializes i to n and a to 1 as in listing (8.2.18).

```
(define factorial3
  (lambda (n)
    (let f ((i n) (a 1))
      (if (zero? i)
      a
      (f (- i 1)(* a i)))
)))
```
(8.2.18)

Here the action is:

```
(factorial3 3) ⇒ ?
   (f₁ 3 1)     ⇒ (f 2 3)
       (f₂ 2 3)      ⇒ (f 1 6)
           (f₃ 1 6)       ⇒ (f 0 6)
               (f₄ 0 6)        ⇒ 6
           (f₃ 1 6)       ⇒ 6
       (f₂ 2 3)      ⇒ 6
   (f₁ 3 1)     ⇒ 6
   factorial3  ⇒ 6
```
(8.2.19)

Notice that the final value, 6, is obtained at the bottom of the recursion, in environment$_4$. This behavior is tail recursive, as was mentioned in the previous chapter. Thus an optimal implementation for factorial would be:

```
(factorial3 3) ⇒ ?
   (f₁ 3 1)     ⇒ (f 2 3)
       (f₂ 2 3)      ⇒ (f 1 6)
           (f₃ 1 6)       ⇒ (f 0 6)
               (f₄ 0 6)        ⇒ 6
(factorial3 3) ⇒ 6
```
(8.2.20)

Interpreters for SCHEME, as well as Common LISP, are built to recognize tail recursive calls and evaluate them iteratively, as was done in listing (8.2.20), even though the function itself is recursive.

Side Effects

In SCHEME, built-in functions that produce side effects end with ! so they are obvious. As an example, consider the append function, which is definable in all LISP systems and **cons**tructs a new list from its two arguments. (append (mary hada) (little lamb)) returns as its value the new list, (mary hada little lamb). append has no side effects. In SCHEME, one can also define a function append!, which returns the same value as append, but has the side effect of altering the first list, (mary hada). Perhaps some diagrams will make the difference clear. Figure 8.2.8 shows the original two lists before application of either append or append!. For the expression (append l1 l2) in Figure 8.2.9, l1 has been copied over, and the original l1 has not been altered.

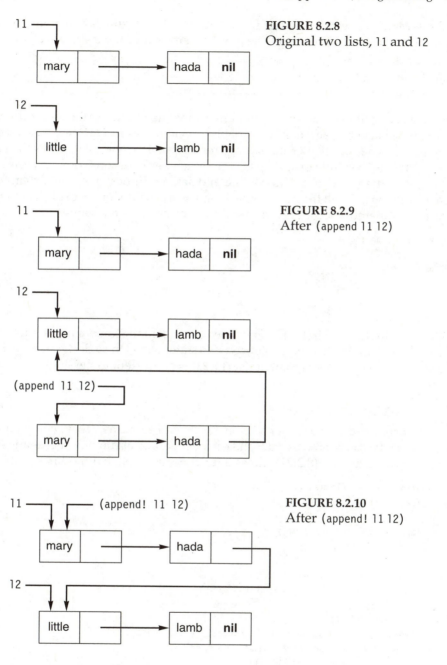

FIGURE 8.2.8
Original two lists, l1 and l2

FIGURE 8.2.9
After (append l1 l2)

FIGURE 8.2.10
After (append! l1 l2)

As shown in Figure 8.2.10, after an append!, the first list, l1, has been altered so that its last **cdr** cell points to l2. Not only does this save space, but also the time required to copy over l1. We have, however, violated the no-side-effects rule of the lambda calculus. Altering list structures requires two primitive functions, **set-car!**

and **set-cdr!**. To effect the change from Figure 8.2.8 to Figure 8.2.10 would require a call to **set-cdr!**, which changes the pointer in the **cdr** of the last cons cell of 11

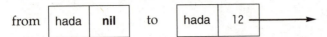

define was mentioned as a special binding form when defining the mapcar function above. It can also be used to bind variables to values, as in (**define** x 2). **define** accomplishes two tasks. It allocates storage for a variable x, and assigns 2 as the value of x. To change the value of x, we use **set!**, which performs only one task, the reassignment of the value of x. Thus **define** and **set!** are imperative rather than functional mappings. Recall that imperative languages provide for the explicit assigning of values to memory locations. (**define** x 2) is the same as the sequence:

```
var x: <type>;

begin
...
   x := 2;
...
```

with two differences. First, LISP is typeless, so x contains only a pointer to a storage location; and second, we don't need two statements, one a declaration in a special section and one an assignment. (**set!** x 23) is equivalent to the single statement, x := 23.

A Self-Modifying Function

We mentioned in the earlier section, "Lists As Programs," that code for a LISP function can be considered as data, and can be modified at run time just as any other data object can. Listing (8.2.21) shows a function, courses, that modifies itself.

```
(define courses (lambda ()                                    (8.2.21)
;;Makes calling courses1 easier.

  (apply (eval courses1) nil)
))

(define courses1 '(lambda ()
;; Function that gets modified at run time

  (let ((course '()))
    (display "What course will you study? ")(set! course (read))
    (cond ((eq? course 'none) 'must-be-summer)
          ((eq? course 'calculus)
           (set! courses1 (no-more-school-subj courses1))
           (courses))
          (#T (apply (eval school) course))
))))
```

```
(define school '(lambda(subj)
    (write subj)(writeln " is a school subject")(courses)
))

(define (college subj)
    (write subj)(writeln " is a college subject")(courses)
)

(define no-more-school-subj (lambda (p)
;; 1) deletes the second conditional pair from p
;; 2) redefines the list for the function, school, to the empty list
;; 3) substitutes college in the final (#T ...) expression of the cond in p

  (let((new-func
        (delete-one '((eq? course 'calculus)
                       (set! courses1 (no-more-school-subj courses1))
                       (courses))
                  p)))
    (write 'calculus)(writeln " is a college course")
    (set! school '())
    (subst 'college 'school new-func)
)))
```

This function is a cleaned-up version of a similar program first programmed by Laurent Siklóssy, and published in 1976 [Siklóssy, 1976]. A sample run for courses is contained in listing (8.2.22). User responses are in italics.

```
[1] (courses)                                                           (8.2.22)
What course will you study? algebra
ALGEBRA is a school subject
What course will you study? calculus*
CALCULUS is a college course
What course will you study? algebra
ALGEBRA is a college course
What course will you study? none
MUST-BE-SUMMER
[2]
```

When the user responds with a course to be studied, it is assumed that it is a school subject until the user response is "calculus." Those ready for calculus will study college courses from then on, and the system so responds. Entering "none" when asked What course will you study? stops the recursion, and the program ends.

After the user has entered "calculus" at the * in listing (8.2.22), the function courses1 of listing (8.2.21) will be altered to be:

```
'(lambda ()                                                             (8.2.23)
;; Function that gets modified at run time

  (let ((course '()))
    (display "What course will you study? ")(set! course (read))
    (cond ((eq? course 'none) 'must-be-summer)
          (#T (apply (eval college) course))
)))
```

and the function school will be '(), the empty list.

A few comments are in order.

1. There are two utility functions called in no-more-school-subj, (subst new old lis) and (delete-one expr lis), which will be left as exercises. The first substitutes all occurrences of new for old in lis, and the second deletes the first occurrence of expr in lis.

2. The definition for courses1 is "quoted" (is preceded by a single quote mark). If we ask to see it in SCHEME:

[1] courses1

the list (LAMBDA ()... (#T (apply (eval school) course))) will be returned as its value. Notice that courses1 returns the value (in this case, code) for courses1. If we then ask:

[2] (eval courses1)

#<PROCEDURE> will be returned, indicating that courses1 is the name of a procedure.

Courses1 has a list as its value which, when **eval**uated, turns into a procedure that can be **apply**'d to an argument list. In this case, the argument list is empty.

(**apply** (eval courses1))

Notice also that the definition of the function courses is not quoted, and that it can be applied without using the apply operator by calling (courses). This is just a SCHEME shortcut, which was not a part of the original LISP.

3. The first time the value of course is equal to the atom 'calculus, the two expressions that follow the predicate, (eq? course 'calculus) are evaluated.

First, the value of courses1 is **set!** to the value of (no-more-school-subj courses1), i.e., the list new-func, which is the value of the last expression in no-more-school-subj, (subst 'college 'school new-func). Second, courses is called again. no-more-school-subj modifies the definition of courses1. To do this, we must treat courses1 as a list, not as a procedure. new-func is the old definition for courses1 changed in two ways. First, using a call to delete-one, it has deleted the conditional expression:

```
((eq? course 'calculus)                                    (8.2.24)
 (set! courses1 (no-more-school-subj courses1 course))
 (courses))
```

And second, by calling (subst 'college 'school new-func), it has changed the identifier 'school to 'college. Thus when courses1 is called again, the expression:

```
(#T (apply (eval school) course))
```

will have been replaced by:

```
(#T (apply (eval college) course))
```

no-more-school-subj also changes the definition of the function school to the empty list, '(). If called, school would do nothing.

The next time courses1 is called from courses, the modifications will take effect.

LAB 8.1: GETTING ACQUAINTED WITH LISP: SCHEME

Objectives (Labs can be found in the *Instructor's Manual*.)

1. To familiarize students with the SCHEME (or other LISP) system they have available, including the Help facility.
2. To enter and execute simple SCHEME expressions interactively, noticing how both errors and successful evaluations are reported.
3. To use the SCHEME editor, Edwin, to enter and save a short program.
4. To run a program that produces an infinite loop and interrupt execution.
5. To write, save, and execute a simple recursive program, directing output to a printer.

LAB 8.2: A PALINDROME FUNCTION: SCHEME

Objectives

1. To design, write, save, and execute a larger SCHEME program involving several functions.
2. To design, write, save, and execute a SCHEME program dealing with file input and/ or output as well as screen I/O.

Other Nonfunctional Features

The lambda calculus as discussed in Appendix B is rather sparse, using only variables, parentheses, commas, and the special symbol λ, plus four formation and three transformation rules. Thus designers of languages based on it insert abbreviations instead of all those parentheses. Purely functional lambda calculus programming is also slow, relying on recursion and taking no advantage of space- or time-saving economies.

Iteration

Recursion is the means by which LISP travels over a data structure. Pure LISP provides no iterators. SCHEME has the special form, **do. do** specifies a set of variables to be bound, how they are initialized at the start, and how they are to be updated at each iteration. When a termination condition is met, the loop exits with a specified value.

```
(do ((i 0)(+ i 1)                                          (8.2.25)
    (sum 0 (+ sum i)))
   ((= i 10) sum))
```

As an example, the **do** loop of listing (8.2.25) sums the numbers 0 through 10, returning 55. Both sum and i are local to the **do** expression, and each is initialized to 0. At each iteration, i is increased by 1, (+ i 1), and then sum is increased by i, (+ sum i). The termination condition is (= i 10). The value of sum is returned when the condition becomes true.

LAB 8.3: PROGRAMMING USING LOOPS: SCHEME

Objective (Labs can be found in the *Instructor's Manual*.)

1. To use SCHEME's iterative **do** loop.

LAB 8.4: TRACING AND DEBUGGING: SCHEME

Objectives

1. To investigate SCHEME's tools.
2. When presented with a buggy program, to use the various tools to find and eliminate the bugs.
3. To monitor execution of a program with and without the PCS-DEBUGGER-MODE on.

Vectors and Strings

One disadvantage of the list is that it can only be accessed from the front. To get to the nth element, we have to **cdr** down n–1 times and then take the **car** of the remaining list. More modern LISPs have added other data types, in particular vectors and strings. In SCHEME, a vector is like a fixed-length array, with indices starting at 0. It is like a list, however, in that its elements can be of any type. One can access a particular element using the function **vector-ref** and modify it using **vector-set!**.

SCHEME strings are of specified length and are created using **make-string**. Individual characters can be modified with **string-set!**, or accessed with **string-ref**. These functions are nonfunctional, in that they directly reference and modify memory locations. They were included in the language in the interest of time efficiency.

SCHEME also includes a **list-ref** function that finds the nth element of a list. It behaves semantically like **vector-ref**, but is implemented differently. **vector-ref** calculates the address of the desired item and returns the element at that address, whereas **list-ref** uses n–1 **cdr** operations to find the nth element.

Objects and Packages

LISP has been extended to support object-oriented programming, notably through the languages Flavors [Moon, 1986] and LOOPS [Bobrow, 1983].

Recall from Chapter 4 that an object-oriented language supports:

- Information hiding (encapsulation)
- Data abstraction (the encapsulation of state with operations)
- Message passing (polymorphism)
- Inheritance

SCHEME also has an object-oriented extension, SCOOPS. In this section, we will look at an example of a SCOOPS object hierarchy. SCOOPS is implemented entirely through SCHEME *macros*. A macro is an S-expression beginning with the atom **macro**, followed by a name which will be the keyword of a new special form. When the SCHEME interpreter encounters a macro expression, its *expansion* is copied directly into the SCHEME program, where it is evaluated. Just how an expression is expanded depends on the interpreter or compiler. One method is to translate it into lambda expressions, including an expansion for each recursive call, if there are any. The user will not be aware of this expansion when running SCOOPS, but the expansions may appear in a printout of a program that has been run. In any case, once defined, macros will behave like any other special form.

As an example of a SCHEME macro, consider listing (8.2.26).

```
(macro sqr (lambda(sexpr)                                         (8.2.26)
   (list '* (cadr sexpr) (cadr sexpr)) ))
```

When the expression containing the keyword sqr is encountered, e.g., (sqr 3), the expression is replaced by the expansion of the macro. In this case, the expansion is the list (* 3 3), which is then evaluated.

Let's define a function implementing the Pythagorean rule and see how it works.

```
(define Pythagorean (lambda (a b)                                    (8.2.27)
  (sqrt (+ (sqr a)(sqr b))) ))
```

A call to Pythagorean and the resulting evaluations are:

$\Rightarrow$ (Pythagorean 3 4)   (8.2.28)
(sqrt (+ (apply(* a a) 3)
         (apply(* b b) 4)))

(sqrt (+ 9 16))
(sqrt 25)

$\Rightarrow$ 5.

When you run SCHEME, you will not be aware of the substitution of (* a a) and (* b b) for (sqr a) and (sqr b). The actual text of the macro is substituted when the keyword is encountered, and then evaluated. A macro is not called as a function is.

SCOOPS implements classes, instances of classes or objects, class variables, instance variables, methods, and *mixins*. Mixins are superclasses inherited by a class being defined. SCOOPS includes macros to define the keywords **define-class**, **classvars**, **instvars**, **define-method**, **make-instance**, and **mixins**. The first three implement information hiding and data abstraction; **define-method** defines classes, **make-instance** creates objects, and **mixins** implements inheritance.

Let's define the three SCOOPS classes, point, line, and rectangle, with line inheriting from point, and rectangle inheriting from both, as shown in Figure 8.2.11.

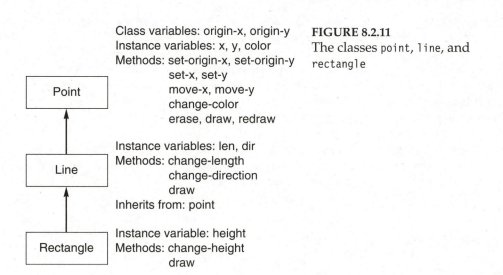

Class variables: origin-x, origin-y
Instance variables: x, y, color
Methods: set-origin-x, set-origin-y
         set-x, set-y
         move-x, move-y
         change-color
         erase, draw, redraw

Instance variables: len, dir
Methods: change-length
         change-direction
         draw
Inherits from: point

Instance variable: height
Methods: change-height
         draw

FIGURE 8.2.11
The classes point, line, and rectangle

Listing (8.2.29) shows the SCHEME definitions for the three classes.

```
(define-class point                                        (8.2.29)
   (classvars (origin-x 0)
              (origin-y 0))
   (instvars (x      (active 0    () move-x))
             (y      (active 0    () move-y))
             (color (active 'yellow () change-color)))
   (options settable-variables
            inittable-variables))

(compile-class point)

(define-class line
   (instvars (len (active 50 () change-length))
             (dir (active 0  () change-direction)))
   (mixins point)
   (options settable-variables))

(compile-class line)

(define-class rectangle
   (instvars (height (active 60 () change-height))
   (mixins line)
   (options settable-variables))

(compile-class rectangle)
```

The meanings of the new atoms, **classvars**, **instvars**, active, settable, and inittable, will be given below. The inheritance hierarchy is set up by calls to the function **compile-class**. line inherits from point, and rectangle from line, because of the order in which **compile-class** is called. Three objects, p1, l1, and r1, are created through:

```
(define p1 (make-instance point))
(define l1 (make-instance line))
(define r1 (make-instance rectangle))
```

The local state for p1 will have the values x = 0 and y = 0. Because a point is inittable, we can (define p2 (**make-instance** point) 3 42) with initial values x = 3 and y = 42. An instance of an object (also called an object) can also share a state with all instances of its class. This is accomplished through **classvars**. Any point has origin-x and origin-y with initial values of 0. Because point **classvars** are settable, four methods are defined automatically: set-origin-x, set-origin-y, set-x, and set-y. If we wished all points to be relative to an origin other than (0,0), we could set-origin-x and set-origin-y to the desired values.

The methods move-x and move-y are yet to be defined. x and y are active variables, which means that whenever either is accessed, nothing happens, but when a value is changed, move-x or move-y is automatically invoked.

```
(define-method (point draw) ()                             (8.2.30)
   (draw-point x y))

(define-method (point erase) ()
   (set-pen-color! 'black)
   (draw))
```

```
(define-method (point redraw) ()
   (set-pen-color! color)
   (draw))

(define-method (point move-x)(new-x)
               (erase)
               (set! x new-x)
               (redraw)
               new-x
)
```

A line has the two automatically defined methods, set-len and set-dir, which invoke change-length and change-direction when invoked. line inherits all the methods of listing (8.2.30), except for draw, which will be redefined as **define-method** (line draw). We do not have to redefine redraw for line, and if a line instance is sent the message draw, it will call line's draw method, not that for point. Thus draw is a polymorphic function, responding with a procedure appropriate to the receiver of its message.

If we want to draw p1, we call (**send** p1 (draw)). The rest of the methods for point and those for line and rectangle will not be given here, but can be found in the PC SCHEME demonstration file, SCPSDEMO.S [TI, 1987].

SCOOPS supports multiple, as well as single, inheritance, as shown in Figure 8.2.12. Here the class polygon inherits from both circle and line, with yet another redefinition of draw. If draw had not been redefined, polygon would inherit whichever draw method is found first among the **mixins**. The hierarchy is searched depth-first from the top for methods. Here point is at the top. This depends on the order in which classes were compiled. In this case, circle's draw method would be used, because it was compiled into the hierarchy closer to the compilation of polygon than was that for line.

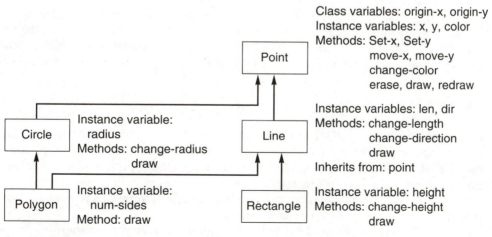

FIGURE 8.2.12
A multiple-inheritance hierarchy

LAB 8.5: PROGRAMMING IN SCOOPS: SCHEME

Objectives (Labs can be found in the *Instructor's Manual*.)

1. To run an interactive SCOOPS demo program, sending messages from object to object.
2. To define and include new classes as mixins.
3. To modify given classes to serve different purposes.

Dialects

SCHEME was developed as part of research and teaching efforts at the MIT Artificial Intelligence Laboratory in 1975. In 1981, a SCHEME chip was built that incorporated an innovative compiler. The language was further developed for special courses at Yale and at the University of Indiana, and language variants or dialects began to confuse users. A student who learned SCHEME at, say, Indiana and then went to MIT for graduate work might not even be able to read programs written there. Thus SCHEME's originators, Guy Steele and Gerald Sussman, along with a baker's dozen of assistants, took on the task of defining the language [Rees, 1987]. SCHEME was the first LISP to be lexically scoped, which means that the scope of a variable is the S-expression in which it is declared; the first to treat procedures as first-class objects; and the first to rely solely on procedure calls to express iteration, rather than relying on nonfunctional loops and goto's. It also incorporates first-class escape procedures. Some of these features have been incorporated into the production language, Common LISP. There have been many other dialects of LISP, where features were added when problems became apparent. SCHEME started over from the beginning, using the definition of Pure LISP, overcoming many of previous LISP's shortcomings.

The most common experimental LISPs used during the seventies were MacLISP (MIT) and its West Coast cousins, Franz LISP (University of California at Berkeley) and UCI-LISP (University of California at Irvine). InterLISP is a commercial product from Bolt, Beranek, and Newman, Inc., and Xerox. Zeta LISP was also developed at MIT to take advantage of a special LISP machine. These different locations were all research organizations, so the languages changed to fit particular interests of the researchers involved. One could usually, with some effort, rewrite programs from one dialect into another, but not always. This is fine if programs rarely travel off-location.

Common LISP

Common LISP [Steele, 1984] is a large commercial product, incorporating all the features anyone might want. As Guy Steele, one of its 63 developers, puts it, "Common LISP is to LISP as PL/I was to FORTRAN and COBOL," that is, the sort of language where you go down the hall and ask someone how to do what you want to do, rather than try to find what is needed in the huge manual. It's not usually the best choice for one's first LISP encounter.

By 1980, LISP implementations had begun to diverge due to their environments—Zeta LISP and Spice LISP for personal computers, NIL for commercial timeshared computers, and S-1 for supercomputers. Common LISP is intended to be compatible with Zeta LISP, MacLISP, and InterLISP, in that order. That is, a program written in the Common LISP core should run in any of the other systems, with non-Common LISP features considered as extensions. Common LISP also has extensions, such as an implementation of packages, but these are not part of the core.

Common LISP is intended to be portable, eliminating features that cannot be implemented on a large number of machines. Efforts have been made to make it consistent, expressive, efficient, and powerful. It is also intended to be stable so that later implementations will be extensions to an unchanging core.

One real plus for Common LISP has been the Department of Defense's interest in it, or some extension of it, as the basis for a very high level language for developing prototypes [Gabriel, 1989]. If, as has been suggested, the DOD accepts programs written only in Ada or in Common LISP, these languages will surely prosper, as the DOD is the United States' largest software consumer.

Although the core for Common LISP is a small language, it incorporates many extensions. One of these is packages, which we looked at in Ada. LISP packages were first developed for Zeta LISP and incorporated into Common LISP. A LISP package is essentially a name space. If NewAdd is a function in package1 and also in package2, a name conflict will not occur. One can think of NewAdd as package1.NewAdd and package2.NewAdd (much as in Ada). Packages must be manipulated with care to avoid subtle bugs, but they do provide modularization, and a basis for implementing objects, which allows several programmers to work on a large system without stepping on each other's turf.

EXERCISES 8.2

1. Consider the mapcar function of listing (8.2.9). Suppose 11 is a circular list where the last cons cell points to the beginning of the list. Show how (mapcar sqrt 11) will work if 11 is:

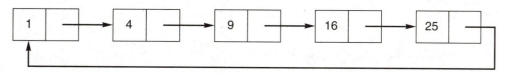

2. a. Draw figures similar to that of Figure 8.2.5 for the lists:

    1) (((J) I) M (M (Y)))   2) (((My) Dog) has (fleas))

   b. The trees of Figure 8.2.5 and the two above are listed in in order. What would the list representation be for the same lists if traversed in preorder? postorder?

3. a. Write the predecessor function for nonnegative integers as used in listing (8.2.11).
   b. Following the pattern of listing (8.2.11), write a LISP function for times.

4. a. Why does passing all parameters by value prevent side effects?
   b. Why do read and print functions produce side effects?

5. What c . . . r abbreviations would we use to find the second elements of each of the rows in A = ((1 2 3)(4 5 6)(7 8 9))?

6. How could we implement a stack as a list, and how would its operations be written in LISP?

7. Define a SCHEME function (subst new old lis) that substitutes all occurrences of old in lis with new. You may find it easier if you let subst call a helper function (subst2 new '() lis). subst2 splits the list into a front and rear portion and appends them together after a substitution has been made. The parameter portion of the definition is:

(**define** (subst2 new old front rear)...)

8. Define a SCHEME function (delete-one expr lis) that deletes the first occurrence of expr from lis.

(delete '(a b) '(a b (c d (a b)) (a b))

should return (A B (C D) (A B)). As in exercise 7, you may want to use a helper function, (delete-one2 item front rear).

8.3
IMPLEMENTING FUNCTIONAL LANGUAGES

Portable compilers for functional languages are easy to implement, since programs can be translated into a language intermediate to the machine code, as in Figure 8.3.1. Thus any compiler can be built if the second step, translation from the intermediate code, has been specified for a particular machine. How one translates a higher level functional language into the intermediate code is beyond the scope of this book, and the reader is referred to [Peyton Jones, 1987].

As we saw above, LISP is based on the S-expression and implemented through dotted pairs. The dotted pair implementation of Figure 8.2.3 does not take typing into account, and LISP is indeed typeless. However, some implementations append a third cell onto each binary pair with the (implied) type of the element (see Figure 8.3.2).

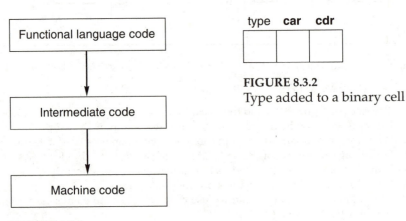

FIGURE 8.3.2
Type added to a binary cell

FIGURE 8.3.1
A possible compilation schema for
functional code

The entry in the type cell will be a code for a number (N); built-in function (P); application of a function (@); a structure, such as a non-empty list, called a cons cell (:); or a lambda abstraction, (λ). In addition, some languages, notably SKIM (1980) and NORMA (1985), add to each dotted pair a bit that marks it as a pointer or data cell (see Figure 8.3.3).

A possible graph for (+ 2 4) is shown in Figure 8.3.4. Its representation as cons cells is depicted in Figure 8.3.5.

As can be seen from the figures, LISP data, including function definitions, is usually referenced through pointers. Thus storage is in the heap, rather than through activation records, and referenced from an object list of literal atoms and their associated pointers, rather than through a symbol table and associated memory locations.

The object list is visible to a LISP programmer and varies widely from implementation to implementation. In SCHEME, three procedures, object-hash, object-unhash, and gc (garbage collection), allow a user to associate an object with a unique integer, based on a hashing function. The SCHEME object list is thus an *object-hash table*.[11] Objects that are no longer referenced are removed from the object-hash table

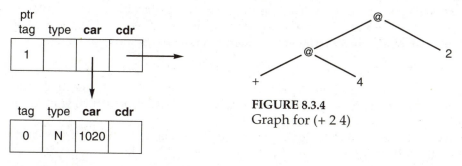

FIGURE 8.3.4
Graph for (+ 2 4)

FIGURE 8.3.3
Typed cons cell tagged as data

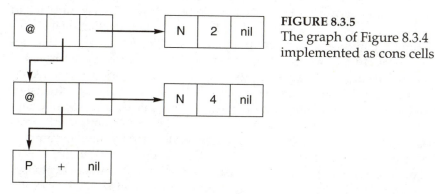

FIGURE 8.3.5
The graph of Figure 8.3.4
implemented as cons cells

---

[11]The object-hash table is indexed by addresses for objects. A hash function, h(object identifier) = address associates an object with its memory address.

during garbage collection, which can be user controlled by calling gc or automatic. gc will be discussed later in the section on garbage collection. (object-hash <obj>) assigns an integer to <obj> and records the relationship in the object-hash table. Objects that are identical (in the sense of **eq?**) are assigned the same integer. (object-unhash <int>) returns the object associated with <int>, provided some other reference to the object exists. If no association exists, **#F** is returned. An object with no reference other than the integer associated with it in the object-hash table is removed from the table during garbage collection.

Lazy Versus Strict Evaluation

We have already mentioned lazy evaluation as the computing of argument values only if needed. For example, in the expression (IF p THEN q ELSE s), q need only be evaluated if p is TRUE. Similarly, s is evaluated only if p is FALSE. In a strict evaluation, p, q, and s would all be evaluated before executing the conditional expression. Lazy evaluation also involves evaluating an expression as few times as necessary. For example, ((lambda (x) (+x x)) 2*10) reduces to (+ (2*10) (2*10)) assuming normal order (left to right) reduction. To complete the computation, (+ 20 (2*10)) → (+ 20 20) → 40, would involve two computations of 2*10. If we used applicative order reduction, where the innermost reduction is made first, we would have:

$$((lambda\ (x)\ (+\ x\ x))\ 2*10) \rightarrow ((lambda\ (x)\ (+\ x\ x))\ 20) \rightarrow (+\ 20\ 20) \rightarrow 40$$

eliminating one computation. As is mentioned in Appendix B, applicative order reductions do not guarantee reaching a normal form that cannot be further reduced, if there is one. As usual, everything has its price.

Lazy evaluation is implemented in many functional languages. A simple example is the following. Suppose a function f is defined as follows:

$$(define\ (f\ x\ p1\ p2)(if\ (>\ x\ 0)\ p1\ p2))$$

The arguments p1 and p2 need not be evaluated until the truth or falsity of the predicate, (> x 0), has been determined. Evaluation could be lazy, i.e., delayed until it had been determined which of p1 or p2 was needed. The case for lazy evaluation includes more than eliminating unnecessary computations. Another advantage is that potentially infinite data structures can be implemented, with only that portion needed being evaluated. The argument against lazy evaluation is execution speed. Determining just which computations can be either avoided or postponed is expensive, and involves the efficient implementation of thunks, which we discussed in Chapter 3. Functional languages like ML and Hope have made a compromise, with strict evaluation being the norm unless lazy evaluation is called for by the programmer. SCHEME has two built-in operators, (**delay** <exp>) and (**force** <exp>), to implement lazy evaluation. A **delay**ed expression is set aside (as in a thunk) and not evaluated until a **force** is executed. What SCHEME's **delay** and **force** do, as in other lazy evaluation schemes, is to decouple execution from the apparent structure of a program.

Another method for speeding up lazy evaluation is through graph reduction with normal evaluation, rather than the usual string reduction used with the lambda calculus. Our example above, if reduced through graphical methods, would yield the result shown in Figure 8.3.6 [Hudak, 1989].

Note that this takes the same number of steps as applicative order reduction, where the (2∗10) was evaluated first, but is otherwise a normal order resolution.

Scope and Bindings

LISP looks like the lambda calculus, as described in Appendix B, and allows lambda expressions to represent unnamed functions. A lambda expression like `((lambda(x)(+ x x))(∗ 2 10))` can never be used again since there is no name to reference it. To save computing an expression more than once, we can use a **let** clause, as shown in listing (8.3.1).

```
(let ((f ((lambda(x)(+ x x))(∗ 2 10))))
    <body involving f>...
)
```
(8.3.1)

The value of the lambda expression, 2∗10 + 2∗10 = 40, will be used as the value of f throughout the **let** expression, i.e., wherever f occurs in <body involving f> . . . . The **let** above is thus an easy-to-read and efficient way to evaluate and retain the value of a lambda expression.

We could also accomplish this using two **let** expressions, with the second within the scope of the first, as shown in listing (8.3.2).

```
(let ((x (∗ 2 10)))
    (let ((y (lambda(x)(+ x x)))
        <exp involving y>...)))
```
(8.3.2)

A **let** also allows the assignment of several variables, as in listing (8.3.3):

```
(let ((y (lambda(x)(+ x x))(∗ 2 10)))
    (w 22)
    (z (- 16 3))
    <expression involving y, w and z>))
```
(8.3.3)

In this **let** expression, w will be assigned 22 and z, 13. This behavior conforms to the evaluative independence of functional arguments. w, y, and z are all parameters to the

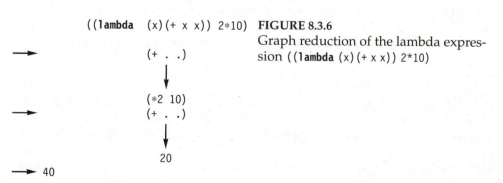

FIGURE 8.3.6
Graph reduction of the lambda expression ((lambda (x)(+ x x)) 2∗10)

let, and we may make no assumption about which gets evaluated first. If <expression> is (+ y w z), the **let** above is equivalent to the lambda calculus expression:

```
(λz.λw.λy.<exp involving z, w, & y>)(λx.(+ x x)(* 2 10) 22 (- 16 3)).
```

Which is easier to read is a matter of taste.

SCHEME allows the use of **let**∗ to assure an ordered evaluation so that previously assigned variables may be used in succeeding expressions, as in listing (8.3.4).

```
(let* ((x (* 2 10))
       (y (lambda(x)(+ x x)))
       <exp> ...)
```
(8.3.4)

This is equivalent to the two **let**s of listing (8.3.2).

letrec (recursive **let**) can be used in place of **let**∗, and is more powerful. The example of listing (8.3.5) shows the definition of two mutually recursive functions, even? and odd?, both of which recurse down to 0, followed by a function call to even?.

```
(letrec ((even? (lambda(n)
                 (if (zero? n)
                 #T
                 (odd? (- n 1)))
         ))
         (odd?   (lambda(n)
                 (if (zero? n)
                 #F
                 (even? (- n 1)))
         )))
 (even? 88))
```
(8.3.5)

The environment of the **letrec** is extended to bind the first lambda expression to the name even? and the second to odd?. The expression (even? 88) is then evaluated and returns a value of #T for the **letrec**. If this expression had been (even? x), #T or #F would have been returned depending on the value of x in the environment surrounding the **letrec**. Mutually recursive functions are not allowed in **let** or **let**∗ expressions.

As we have seen, variables can be either free or bound in a lambda expression. It is how the free variables are bound to values that is of concern to us here.

Dynamic scope can lead to errors, as keeping track of variable names and environments can become hopelessly confusing to a programmer. It also violates the "black box" notion for a procedure, that we do not meddle with its internal workings, and are guaranteed correct results if we pass appropriate actual parameters. We will look at two of these problems, the so-called *funarg problems*.

The funarg Problems

LISP was the first language to treat functions as first-class objects that can be passed to or returned as values of other functions. For example, the LISP function (mapcar func args), as defined in listing (8.2.9), produces a list of values for func(arg) when the name of a function is passed to func, and a list of arguments to args. There are no problems with the argument func since mapcar does not involve free variables.

There are, however, two problems discussed in the LISP literature when free variables are present, the *downward funarg problem* and the *upward funarg problem*. The downward problem is when a procedure captures free variables from another environment. The following example is from Abelson and Sussman [Abelson, 1985] and exhibits the downward funarg problem. First, we define a

function sum that returns $\sum_{x=a}^{b} f(x)$ when a and b are passed the

upper and lower limits for x, term is passed the function f, and next is passed a function for incrementing x.

```
(define (sum term a next b)                              (8.3.6)¹²
    (if > (a b)
    0
    (+ (term a)
       (sum term (next a) next b))))
```

If (sqr x) is defined to return the square of x, a call of (sum sqr 1 1+ 3) will return $1^2 + 2^2 + 3^2 = 14$. Next, we define a more specialized function, sum-powers, that returns $\sum_{x=a}^{b} x^n$.

```
(define (sum-powers a b n)                               (8.3.7)
    (define (nth-power x)
    · (expt x n))
    (sum nth-power a 1+ b))
```

A call of (sum-powers 1 3 2) will return the same sum of 14 that was returned from (sum sqr 1 1+ 3). Here 1+ is a function that increases its single argument by 1, and (expt x n), as defined in listing (8.3.1), returns x^n. Figure 8.3.8 shows the environments and bindings during the first step of the recursion, when a=1 and b=3. Here everything works as envisioned, returning the correct value of 14.

Now suppose sum had been defined using n as a variable name instead of next.

```
(define (sum term a n b)                                 (8.3.8)
    (if (> a b)
    0
    (+ (term a)
       (sum term (n a) n b))))
```

The situation is as in Figure 8.3.8, with nth-power's free variable n referring to the n of sum, since that is where nth-power is called. This should cause an error, since (2 a), when substituted for (n a), is not a function call (see Figure 8.3.8).

The upward problem occurs when a procedure is returned as a value and loses the bindings of its free variables. Listing (8.3.9) illustrates the problem [Abelson, 1985].

```
(define (make-adder increment)                           (8.3.9)
    (lambda (x) (+ x increment)))
```

---

¹²In defining SCHEME functions up until now, we have used lambda expressions such as (**define** sum (**lambda** (term a next b) ...)). A SCHEME alternative is (**define** (sum term a next b) ...).

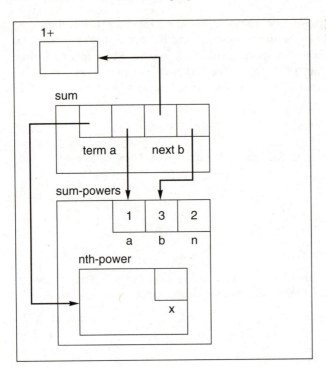

FIGURE 8.3.7
Bindings for (sum-powers 1 3 2)

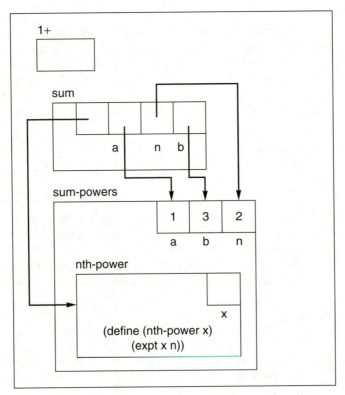

FIGURE 8.3.8
The variable next of
Figure 8.3.7 renamed n

(**let** ((add3 (make-adder 3))) ...) will bind the function name add3 to (**lambda** (x) (+ x 3)). A subsequent call of (add3 4), within the scope of the **let** expression, will return 7. However, if we try to evaluate make-adder directly, as in ((make-adder 3) 4) in a dynamically scoped LISP, the 3 will get lost if there is already a variable named increment in the calling environment. This time, the existing variable will "capture" make-adder's increment and substitute its value for the intended 3.

Garbage Collection

Functional languages require more storage than those that are block-structured for several reasons. Primarily, these are the extra storage needed for the graph reduction method of implementation and passing of functions.

As was illustrated in Figure 8.3.5, the graph reduction of the expression (+ 2 4) required five cells for its implementation. If the expression was (+ x y), additional cells would be created to implement the evaluation of x and y, to which other references might already be pointing, as shown in Figure 8.3.9. Such cells are created dynamically as expressions are encountered, so some way needs to be included in a compiler for a functional language to return them to available storage when they are no longer needed. Cells that cannot be accessed from a program because there are no active references (pointers) to them are called garbage.

In a language like Pascal, storage is divided into a heap and a stack. Allocation of storage from the heap is accomplished using the **new** procedure, and returned using **dispose**. Local variables and links to the calling procedure are automatically popped from the stack when a procedure terminates. This may not be so in a functional language, where functions may be passed as values of parameters, because references to a function's local variables may persist even after the function itself has terminated. Thus all storage is located in a heap with no automatic deallocation of unneeded cells.

Methods to collect and return unreferenced cells are called garbage collection. It can be time consuming, so much work has gone into implementing efficient collectors. One method, called *mark-scan*, runs automatically when storage is about to run out. Each cell must contain an extra bit for marking. During the mark phase,

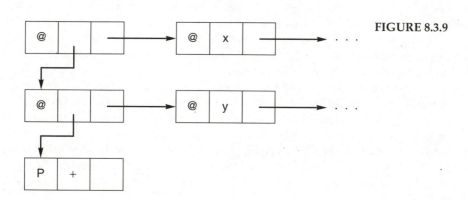

FIGURE 8.3.9

the entire graph structure is traversed, marking each cell that is encountered. If a cell remains unmarked, it is not referenced in the present structure, and is thus garbage. In the scan phase, all unmarked cells are returned to storage.

Other well-known methods are *copying* and *reference counting.* A copying procedure divides the available memory into two sections called from-space and to-space. A running program allocates memory in from-space. When the copying algorithm is invoked, the entire structure is traversed, but not marked in the mark phase of mark-scan. During the traversal, each cell is copied from from-space to to-space. What is inaccessible remains in from-space and is thus garbage. When the copying is finished, from-space and to-space are exchanged.

A reference-counting method requires an extra count field in each cell to count references to the cell. When a cell is created, the count is set to 1. If it is further referenced, count is increased by 1 and when dereferenced, it is decreased by 1. When the count reaches 0, the cell is returned to available storage.

We will not discuss the merits of the various methods here, but refer the interested reader to [Peyton Jones, 1987].

EXERCISES 8.3
1. Evaluate the following expressions using:
   - Normal evaluation (left to right)
   - Applicative evaluation (innermost expression first)
   - Lazy evaluation
   - Graph reduction

   Keep track of the number of substitutions.
   a. `(lambda (x)(lambda (y)(+ y y) x) 3*20)`
   b. `(lambda (x)(lambda (y) x))(lambda (x) x)(lambda (s)(s s))(lambda (s) s))`
2. How would a language like Pascal view the scope illustrated in Figure 8.3.7?
3. Draw an environment diagram for the function of listing (8.3.9), including the call to ((make-adder 3) 4) from another environment containing a variable increment = 25. What is the result of this call?

8.4
SUPPORTING PARALLELISM WITH FUNCTIONS

Pure functional languages, where side effects are not allowed, have been thought to be naturals for parallel processing. A function $f(e_1, e_2, ..., e_n)$ could be processed by assigning each of its n parameters to a different processor and returning their values to the processor working on f. Research has proceeded along the lines of automatic detection and assignment of parallel processes by a compiler. There would be no need for compound **PAR** statements as in Occam (see Chapter 5) to indicate that a sequence of statements was to be executed in parallel. The compiler would figure out which functional parameters could be evaluated simultaneously.

In section 8.3, "Implementing Functional Languages," we discussed lazy versus strict evaluation and provided a brief example of lazy evaluation using graph reduction. Graph reduction is the main method for introducing parallelism into functional language processing, where strict evaluation is (at least initially) assumed.

Suppose we have a function $(+\ e_1\ e_2)$. The + is strict (not lazy), because both its arguments must be evaluated. Its graph is shown in Figure 8.4.1. The @s mark nodes in the graph. A compiler detecting nodes that are candidates for initiating parallel processes would find the two nodes that are marked in Figure 8.4.1 with #. There should be no problems evaluating e_1 and e_2 concurrently, since they can't affect each other or any global variables.

Conditionals are expressions where lazy evaluation would be appropriate. (if test-exp then-exp else-exp) is the if-then-else statement in SCHEME. There are three expressions, all of which could be evaluated in parallel, only one of which, test-exp, is strict. A conservative compiler would evaluate only test-exp, and then one of then-exp or else-exp. A speculative compiler would evaluate all three in parallel, and use what is needed. There are several issues here. Not all the expressions may terminate, so that speculative parallel processing might unnecessarily use up CPU time. Some SCHEMEs do start processing all three expressions, but kill those which eventually become unneeded.

Although functional languages are usually made concurrent by the compiler rather than the programmer, the same issues that we saw in Chapter 5 are involved. Should we distribute expressions at every possible node, or only major program segments?[13] Which expressions should be assigned to which processors? Should memory be distributed or shared?

The advantages claimed for the functional approach, with parallelism detected by a smart compiler, are based on programmers needing only to produce mathematical expressions, rather than worry about parallelism. The programs produced are completely portable from machine to machine, more conducive to formal verification than traditional imperative programs, and easier to debug. Programs are also shorter and more elegant, thus easier to understand by those comfortable with mathematical methods. D.A. Turner writes that a basic difficulty of programming languages that are not functional is that "they are very long winded, in terms of the amount one has to write to achieve a given effect" [Turner, 1982].

The problem is that the programmer has no control over the granularity (see footnote 13) of the parallelism. Programmers often experiment with different versions of a program to make it more efficient. Usually, coarse-grained parallelism runs faster than fine-grained, as the expense of synchronization is minimized. A smart compiler

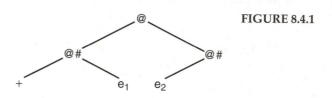

FIGURE 8.4.1

---

[13]Just how much gets done by each of the processors working in parallel is called *granularity*. Fine-grained parallelism partitions an expression into many small segments to be evaluated in parallel, while a coarse grain assigns larger program segments to fewer processors.

364 PART IV: Declarative Languages

cannot decide on a program-by-program basis whether it is more advantageous to divide a function up into many small expressions, assigning each to a different processor, or to assign fewer but larger program segments to fewer processors.

There are several experimental programs to develop parallel graph reduction. One is the Rediflow project at the University of Utah, which distributes memory over a collection of processor/memory/switch units called Xputers. A function graph is distributed over all the Xputers involved. Another is ALICE (Applicative Language Idealized Computing Engine) at Imperial College, London. Here the entire graph is held in shared memory, although processors also have individual memories. A group at Yale is working on the DAPS project (Distributed Applicative Parallel Systems), and a group at University College, London, is developing GRIP (Graph Reduction in Parallel). References to these systems can be found in [Peyton Jones, 1987].

8.5
OTHER FUNCTIONAL LANGUAGES

APL

APL is not a purely functional language, but is an example of a language with functional features that is not built on the lambda calculus. Just as LISP's primary data structure is the list, APL's is the array. It has influenced other functional languages, notably FP [Backus, 1978], where the primary data structure is the sequence. FAC [Tu, 1986], the Functional Array Calculator of Tu and Perlis, is based directly on APL, but includes infinite as well as finite arrays. FAC relies heavily on lazy evaluation to achieve this.

ML

John Backus's FP was one of the first functional languages other than LISP. Backus, the designer of FORTRAN, wrote an eloquent treatise on the advantages of functional programming in his 1978 Turing Award Lecture [Backus, 1978]. In it he discussed the inadequacy of imperative languages for the computing needs of the future. The essential problem is that program execution proceeds by altering the store, one computer word at a time. There is no provision for multiple concurrent actions in any single instant of time. FP is not based on the lambda calculus, but on a few rules for combining functional forms. Backus felt the power of the lambda calculus to express all computable functions was broader than necessary and could easily lead to chaos.

At the same time that FP was being developed in the U.S., ML appeared in the United Kingdom. ML stands for Meta Language, which means a language that speaks about another language, in this case, mathematics. Unlike LISP, ML is strongly typed, although a user need not always declare types, because the compiler can sometimes determine them by inference.

Standard ML is primarily a functional language, but also has powerful features of imperative languages, including an exception-handling mechanism. Functional languages have the reputation of being slow to execute, but writers of compilers for ML have taken advantage of recent advances in pattern matching to improve its efficiency. Its advantages over LISP are:

- Concrete, union, and recursive data types
- Polymorphic data types and functions
- Parametric modules
- Exceptions
- Two-phase program execution: a static phase where program soundness is checked, and a dynamic phase in which the program can run without further checking
- A semantic definition developed right along with ML's syntactic definition

Data Types

In Figure 8.2.2, we considered two representations for complex numbers, and we mentioned two functions, rectangular and polar, in SCHEME. ML has reserved words, **datatype** and **con** (constructor), to define these. Rectangular and polar complex numbers can be constructed as:

```
- datatype RECT = Rect of real * real;    (* user input *)
> datatype RECT = Rect of real * real     (* ML response *)
  con Rect = fn : real * real -> RECT     (* constructor function *)

- datatype POLAR = Polar of real * real;
> datatype POLAR = Polar of real * real
  con Polar = fn : real * real -> POLAR
```
(8.5.1)

When the lines beginning with the "-" prompt execute, RECT or POLAR is bound to a datatype composed of two numbers of the built-in type, real. Notice that RECT is a datatype, while Rect is a function returning a RECT. When RECT is declared at the "-" prompt, Rect is automatically defined. An object of either type can be constructed from two reals by the appropriate constructor function, Rect or Polar. The symbol ">" indicates that this binding has taken place. If we subsequently enter:

```
- Polar (1.0, 0.5);          (* input *)
  Polar (1.0, 0.5) : POLAR   (* ML response *)
```
(8.5.2)

the ML response is the complex number with radius = 1, angle $\theta = 0.5$ radians, and also its type, POLAR. A polar value can be assigned to the variable, x, using:

```
val x = Polar (1.0, 0.5);
```
(8.5.3)

A rectangular type RECT can be defined similarly. A conversion function can then be defined as:

```
- fun to-polar (Rect (x,y)) =
              Polar(sqrt (x * x + y * y),arctan (y/x));
> val to-polar = fn : RECT -> POLAR
```
(8.5.4)

Notice that parentheses are being used in three ways in listing (8.5.4). The first set, (Rect (x, y)), binds the type Rect with parameters (x,y) to the function to-polar being defined. (x, y) determines a pair, and (x * x + y * y) and (y/x) call for arithmetic computation. The definition of to-rect will be left as an exercise. Once we can convert easily from rectangular to polar coordinates and back, definition of complex arithmetic is straightforward.

```
- fun plus-rect ((x1,y1),(x2,y2)) : Rect =                              (8.5.5)
              Rect(x1 + x2, y1 + y2);
- fun plus-polar ((r1,a1),(r2,a2)) : Polar =
              to-polar(plus-rect(to-rect((r1,a1)),to-rect(r2,a2));
```

We can put these together in a union type, COMPLEX.

```
- datatype COMPLEX = Polar | Rect;                                     (8.5.6)
> datatype COMPLEX = Polar | Rect
con Polar = fn : POLAR -> COMPLEX
con Rect  = fn : RECT ->  COMPLEX;
```

Arithmetic functions could be defined on complex types, e.g.:

```
- fun plus-complex (Rect (r1, r2))  = Complex(plus-rect (r1, r2)))      (8.5.7)
   | plus-complex (Polar (p1, p2)) = Complex(plus-polar (p1, p2)));
> val plus-complex = fn : COMPLEX -> COMPLEX
```

complex is thus a polymorphic type, and plus-complex a polymorphic function, because the function allows parameters of either Rect or Polar type.

ML defines a list, which is enclosed in square brackets, as an ordered sequence of data objects, all of which are of the same type, unlike LISP, where list items can be of any sort. If we want to combine objects of different types, we must use fixed length tuples, enclosed in parentheses. The list:

```
- [6,1,2,3];                                                           (8.5.8)
  [6,1,2,3] : int list
```

which is of type int list, differs from:

```
- (6,1,2,3)                                                            (8.5.9)
  (6,1,2,3) : int * int * int * int
```

which is a tuple of fixed length 4, and of type int * int * int * int. The type int * int is a pair, with standard functions, **fun** fst (x,_) = x (as defined in listing (8.5.10)), **fun** snd (_, y) = y; **fun** pair x y = (x, y);, and **fun** swap (x, y) = (y, x);.

(sqr, 3) is a tuple of length 2, of type fn * int, and is not allowed as a list. Why? If we were interested in the first element of (sqr, 3), we could define a function fst:

```
- fun fst (x, y) = x;                                                  (8.5.10)
> val fst = fn : 'a * 'b -> 'a
```

The 'a * 'b -> 'a indicates that x and y can be of any type, and that the value returned will be of the same type as that of the first coordinate, x, of the argument pair. snd can be defined similarly.

```
- fst (sqr, 3);                                                    (8.5.11)
  sqr : fn

- snd (sqr, 3);
  3 : int
```

If we wanted to apply sqr to the integer 3, we could enter:

```
- fst (sqr, 3) snd (sqr, 3);                                       (8.5.12)
> 9
```

ML also provides for unnamed or named tuples, usually called records.

```
- {name = "Boole", alive = false};                                (8.5.13)
> {name = "Boole", alive = false} : {name : string, alive : bool}

- type MORTALITY = {name : string, alive : bool};
> type MORTALITY = {name : string, alive : bool}

- val x = Mortality {name = "McCarthy", alive = true};
```

Recall that one of our first LISP recursive functions computed the factorial function using the algorithm:

$$\text{factorial } (n) \equiv \text{if } (n = 0) \text{ then } 1$$
$$\text{else } (n * \text{factorial}(n - 1))$$

In ML this is defined as:

```
- fun factorial 0 = 1                                              (8.5.14)
  | factorial n = n * factorial (n - 1);
> val factorial = fn : int -> int
```

Notice here that no types are mentioned for either the parameters to, or value returned from, factorial. ML has a "smart interpreter" that implies datatypes when possible.

Data types can also be defined recursively, as those for natural numbers and stacks show in listing (8.5.15).

```
- datatype NAT = Zero | Succ¹⁴ of NAT;                             (8.5.15)
> datatype NAT = Zero | Succ of Nat
        con Zero : NAT
        con Succ = fn : NAT -> NAT

- datatype 'a STACK = Empty | Push of 'a * 'a STACK;
> datatype 'a STACK = Empty | Push of 'a * 'a STACK
        con Empty : STACK
        con Push  'a * 'a STACK -> STACK
```

---

[14]succ or pred can be defined in ML as add 1 or subtract 1. add (x y) is defined as x + y, that is, int ->
int -> int (x -> y -> x+y). add 1 adds 1 to whatever argument is provided. succ 10 returns 11, and pred 10
returns 9.

A stack is exactly the same as a list of type 'a. 'a can be matched with any type, but all stack elements must be of that same type, just as in an ML list.

One of the characteristics of functional languages is the support of higher-order functions. ML functions *always* take exactly one argument. Multiple parameters are passed as a tuple, e.g., add (x y); not (add x y;). We can, however, write *partially applicable* functions, which take one argument after the other, returning a function as the partial result.

```
- fun add x = fn y : int  -> x + y;
> val add = fn : int -> int -> int
```

This is shorthand for add = **fn** : int -> (**fn** : int -> int). y is returned as the identity function, and then x is added to it. Such a function is called a *curried function*, after the logician Haskell B. Curry. In ML, the curried function add can be defined:

```
- fun add x y : int = x + y;
```

This saves a bit of coding. More importantly, there is a large body of research using curried functions, which supports the search for powerful means of abstraction. The curried function does not, as it appears, take two arguments, but returns y as the value of the partially applied identity function first, and then adds x to it.

Polymorphic Data Types

We have already seen examples of polymorphic functions in fst and snd, which returned the first and second members of a pair, no matter what the type. When defining fst, ML returned

```
> val fst = fn : 'a * 'b -> 'a
```

The notation 'a * 'b -> 'a indicates that a and b are *polytypes*, i.e., each can be any type whatsoever. Such functions can be written by the user to eliminate the need to write a separate version of a particular function for each type involved.

Modules

The principle concepts for ML modules are *structures, signatures,* and *functors,* which have no parallel in most other programming languages. A structure results from executing a declaration and encapsulating its environment. A simple structure from the *Commentary on Standard ML* [Milner, 1991] is as in listing (8.5.16).

```
structure lamp =                                    (8.5.16)
  struct
    datatype bulb = ON | OFF
    fun switch(ON) = OFF | switch(OFF) = ON
  end
```

Later in a program, one can make a lamp available for use, using:

```
open lamp
```

The signature APPLIANCE summarizes the contents of the lamp structure, and is an abstract description for all things that have at least a bulb and a switch as defined in listing (8.5.17).

```
signature APPLIANCE                                               (8.5.17)
  sig
    type bulb
    val switch : bulb -> bulb
  end
```

This opens up possibilities for information hiding, since ML allows a structure to be viewed only through its signature.

A functor is a mapping from one structure to another. If ML were perfectly orthogonal, we would not need functors, since functions themselves could map structures onto structures. This is not, however, the case. A functor can be thought of as a special sort of function with domain and range the set of structures. An ML function signalled by the keyword **fun** cannot map structures. Functors can also have signatures, so their inner workings can be hidden.

Exceptions

An exception packet, [e], contains either an exception name, en, or an exception name paired with a value, (en, v). When an exception is constructed, it is assigned a new, unique name. The raising of exceptions is an imperative feature of ML, in that the order in which evaluations have been made is of importance, i.e., *when* the exception occurs makes a difference in the resulting state. In a pure functional language, the order of evaluation is unimportant, but when exceptions are raised, the system must know which evaluations have already been made at the time a sequence of computations is aborted.

A simple exception that returns 0 on an attempt to divide by 0 is shown in listing (8.5.18).

```
exception div0 :int * int                                         (8.5.18)
handle div0  with (x, 0) -> 0
             | (x, y) -> x div y
```

Notice in listing (8.5.19) the difference in the ML responses to div and div0. div is built into ML to perform integer division and has its own built-in exception handler, while we declared a different one for div0.

```
- 5 div 0                                                         (8.5.19)
Failure : div

- 5 div0 0
0 : int
```

In either case, ML will ask for new user input after the exception has been raised.

Semantic Definition of ML

ML is unusual in that its semantics and syntax were, and still are, being developed formally and simultaneously. We have seen EBNF used to define the syntax of a language, and now it is time to have a brief look at how one would go about defining language semantics at the same time. In an appendix to *The Definition of Standard ML* [Milner, 1990], the authors claim that one of the most striking phases in the development of ML has been the interaction between design and semantic description. In the opinion of those involved, this has led to a high degree of confidence in both the language and the semantic method.

ML was originally developed as a language for proving theorems and has since been used in developing executable prototypes for hardware design, as well as for more general purposes. The original, intended use influenced choosing the functional style for ML itself and a denotational method, called *Natural Semantics*, for describing its meaning. The semantic method is based on assertions about evaluation of the following form:

$$B \vdash P \Rightarrow M$$

which says, "Against the background B, the phrase P evaluates to the meaning M." The purpose of the semantic definition of ML is to prove which assertions of this form are true about ML and which are not.

Perhaps an example from the *Commentary on Standard ML* [Milner, 1991] will provide some of the flavor of this effort. Let s represent a state (mem, ens), where mem is its memory component, and ens is the set of names for exceptions. Let A represent a semantic object. A semantic object describes the meaning of a syntactic object and is either static or dynamic, simple or compound. Simple static semantic objects are in listing (8.5.20).

- Type variables $\alpha \in$ TyVar   (8.5.20)
- Type names $t \in$ TyName
- Structure names $m \in$ StrName

Subsequently, in the semantic definition, whenever α occurs, it represents a type variable. TyVar is the set of all type variables.

Simple dynamic objects are as in listing (8.5.21).

- Addresses $a \in$ Addr   (8.5.21)
- Exception names $en \in$ ExName
- Basic values $b \in$ BasVal
- Special values $sv \in$ SVal
- Failure   {FAIL}

Compound objects are built from simpler ones by union, e.g., {x} $\cup$ {y} = {x, y}; Cartesian product, {x} $\times$ {y} = {(x,y)}; finite subset, {x, y} $\subset$ {x, y, z}; or finite map, x –> int. Then the sentence,

$$s,A \vdash phrase \Rightarrow A', s'$$

means that, when the background state s and semantic object A are subject to an ML phrase, A is transformed into object A', and s into state s'. An ML phrase is an instance of one of the 16 Core Phrase Classes (expressions or value bindings) or of the Module Phrase Classes (signature expressions, datatype descriptions, or functor declarations).

The *Definition of Standard ML* [Milner, 1990] is composed of semantic object definitions as above and a set of 196 inference rules and theorems proved about them. As an example, let's look at the syntactical definition of listing (8.5.22) for a record type (called a type row in the ML Core), followed by its semantic definition in listing (8.5.23).

	`{ [patrow] }`	record	(8.5.22)

patrow	::=	`...`	wildcard
		`lab = pat <, patrow>`	pattern row

pat	::=	`atpat`	atomic pattern
		`longcon atpat`	value constructor, e.g., A.x
		`longexcon atpat`	exception constructor
		`pat₁ con pat₂`	infixed value construction
		`pat₁ excon pat₂`	infixed exception construction
		`pat : ty`	typed
		`var [:ty] `**as**` pat`	

atpat	::=	`_`	wildcard
		`scon`	special constant
		`var`	variable
		`longcon`	constant
		`longexcon`	exception constant
		`{ [patrow] }`	record
		`( pat )`	

`tyrow`	::=	`lab`[15]` : ty <, tyrow>`	record type expression

ty	::=	`tyvar`	type variable
		`{ [tyrow] }`	record type expression
		`tyseq`[16]` longtycon`[17]	type construction
		`ty → ty'`	function type expression (Right associative)
		`( ty )`	

1. $\rho \in$ RecType $=$ Lab $\rightarrow$ Type   (8.5.23)
2. $\tau \in$ Type $=$ TyVar $\cup$ RecType $\cup$ FunType $\cup$ ConsType
3. VE $\in$ VarEnv $=$ (Var $\cup$ Con $\cup$ ExCon)
4. Con   Value constructor
5. ExCon   Exception constructor

In listing (8.5.23), 1 means that ρ stands for a record type identifier of the form label $\rightarrow$ type. In 2, τ represents any type variable. A value constructor 4 is a function such as (two $\leftarrow$ (succ(succ(zero)))), where zero $\in$ SCon, the set of special constants. An exception constructor dynamically constructs an exception, including its name, when certain conditions are met.

---

[15]lab $\in$ Lab, the set of record labels.

[16]tyseq = ty (singleton sequence) | (empty sequence)

[17]tycon is an identifier used as a type constructor; longtycon is a discriminated tycon such as YourModule.MyType.

Now let's look at the two inference rules dealing with pattern rows, listing (8.5.24).

Rule 40: (8.5.24)

$$C \vdash \dots \Rightarrow (\{\},\rho)$$

Rule 41(a):

$$\frac{C \vdash \text{pat} \Rightarrow (VE, \tau)}{C \vdash \text{lab} = \text{pat} \Rightarrow (VE \ \{\text{lab} \vdash \tau\}}$$

Rule 41(b):

$$\frac{C \vdash \text{pat} \Rightarrow (VE, \tau), C \vdash \text{patrow} \Rightarrow (VE', \rho), \text{lab} \neq \text{Dom } \rho}{C \vdash \text{lab} = \text{pat}, \text{patrow} \Rightarrow (VE \cup VE', \{\text{lab} \vdash \tau\}, \rho)}$$

Rule 40 says that, in any situation (no premises) and any context C, it is a theorem that a wildcard for a pattern row, ..., produces a state with an empty variable environment {}, and some nameless record type variable ρ.

Rule 41(a) shows that if a pattern phrase "pat" produces a state with the variable environment VE and the type variable τ, then in the same context C, the phrase "lab = pat" will also produce the state VE and, in addition, the binding "lab $\vdash \tau$." Remember that "lab" is a record label.

Rule 41(b) indicates that a label can identify a compound pattern "patrow," composed of a pattern "pat" and a pattern "row." "lab" will be bound to both the pattern and the pattern row. General formation rules assure that the environments VE and VE' are disjoint.

Theorem (Determinacy)
Let the two sentences

$$s, A \vdash \text{phrase} \Rightarrow A', s'; s, A \vdash \text{phrase} \Rightarrow A'', s''$$

both be inferred. Then (A", s") only differs from (A', s') by a one-to-one change of addresses and exception names, which do not occur in (s, A).

Proof: The proof is a long induction on the various semantic objects and phrases that can occur (we will show an example of one of these below). But first, one needs to prove an auxiliary theorem, called a Lemma in mathematics.

Lemma: If s, A $\vdash$ phrase $\Rightarrow$ s', and A' can be inferred, and we change the addresses and exception names occurring in (s, A), the sentence can still be inferred if we make the same changes in (s',A').

This theorem says that if the same ML phrase is applied to the same semantic object A, its evaluation will always be the same (determined) except, possibly, for memory addresses where values are stored, or the names of exceptions. This second difference is because, when an exception is constructed, it is assigned a new, unique name. These names may differ from one run to another.

And now for our example of part of the proof. Suppose the phrase is the expression x + y, the state s is {{5 $\vdash$ x, 6 $\vdash$ y, }, {}}, and A is the type variable name, int. Then s' will be {{5 $\vdash$ x, 6 $\vdash$ y, 11 $\vdash$ a1}, {}}, where a1 is a register for the computation of phrase. s" might be {{5 $\vdash$ x, 6 $\vdash$ y, 11 $\vdash$ a2}, {}}, since register addresses are determined when needed. An exception may be raised if either x or y is not of type int. The exception name en can be bound to the variable where the exception was raised. If in one run no exception was raised, and in a second run, the name en was generated, the semantic object A' would reflect this fact, while A would not.

This very brief look at a semantic proof of ML constructs may be heavy going for readers not used to formal proofs. We include it to indicate the flavor of ML's two-part definition.

Others

Among the lambda calculus-based languages are SASL, KRC, Haskell, and Miranda, which is perhaps the only commercially marketed functional language. The reader is directed to [Hudak, 1989] for a summary of the features of these languages and an extensive bibliography.

EXERCISES 8.5
1. Write an ML definition for the function to-rect, which converts a complex number of type Polar to a number of type Rect (see listing (8.5.4)). sin x and cos x are standard ML functions.
2. Write definitions for times-rect, minus-rect, div-rect, times-polar, minus-polar, and div-polar similar to that for plus-rect of listing (8.5.5).
3. Write an ML polymorphic function, swap (x, y) = (y, x).

8.6
SUMMARY

Functional languages are based on the notion of mathematical functions, which, given a list of actual parameters, return a single value according to some rule. Pure functional languages allow no side effects, i.e., the values of parameters are never changed during a function call. Parameters are thus never passed by reference, name, or value-return, only by value.

Functional languages form a good basis for parallel execution, since a program is nothing more than a single function $p(a_1, a_2, \ldots, a_n)$, where each parameter a_i is also a function, returning a value to p. Each of the a_i can be assigned to a different processor and evaluated independently of other a_i.

The first, and still most common functional language, is LISP, based on the lambda calculus of Alonzo Church.

Simplicity of definition can lead to complicated expressions involving deeply nested parentheses. Thus LISP implementations such as Franz LISP, Zeta LISP, InterLISP, and Common LISP provide many extensions and abbreviations. The SCHEME dialect is closer to the lambda calculus than these others. SASL, KRC, Haskell, and Miranda are other languages that are based on the lambda calculus.

ML and Miranda have added data typing to the functional style. They have more imperative features than does LISP, but the programmer is able to catch errors more easily, and more efficient interpreters can be built. ML is particularly noteworthy in that its semantics have been formalized as the language was developed.

A second group of functional languages is based more on common mathematical notation than on the lambda calculus. The pioneer of these is APL. Its fundamental data type is the array, with its associated operations, rather than the list. The most promising successor to APL is the language FP.

Advocates of the functional style claim that it produces shorter programs that are easier to debug and verify than do procedural languages. Mathematics and its methods of proof have been around for centuries. Functional languages, which build directly on this experience, can take advantage of this large body of research.

8.7
NOTES ON REFERENCES

Douglas Hofstadter wrote a delightful series of three articles on LISP for *Scientific American,* when he was writing the "Metamagical Themas" column. These are reproduced in [Hofstadter, 1985a] and provide a pleasant romp through such LISP functions as HOTPO followed by TATO. The final column presents a solution to the Towers of Hanoi problem. Another "painless" introduction to LISP is *The Little LISPer* [Friedman, 1987], which includes many diagrams and humorous programs.

There are several SCHEME manuals, including [Dybvig, 1987]. The Reference Manual and Tutorial [TI, 1987] are quite adequate if one is using PC SCHEME. The 40-page report, put out by MIT defines the language [Rees, 1987]. Abelson, Sussman, and Sussman [Abelson, 1985] is a remarkable first course in programming, using SCHEME throughout. It reportedly works well for MIT freshmen, but is tough going for most other beginners.

The Fall 1989 volume of *Computing Surveys* [March, 1989] is devoted to programming language paradigms. The article by Paul Hudak [Hudak, 1989] provides a good, although not elementary, discussion of the history and possible future of functional languages.

An interesting book from Colorado State University by Robert Mueller and Rex Page is *Symbolic Computing with Lisp and Prolog* [Mueller, 1990]. The authors discuss declarative programming through typical applications, with solutions in either LISP, PROLOG, or both. It is quite suitable for self-study.

ML is presented in two companion volumes, *The Definition of Standard ML* [Milner, 1990] and *Commentary on Standard ML* [Milner, 1991]. A simple text is [Wikström, 1987]. It does not, however, include some of the more interesting features of ML such as modules.

CHAPTER 9
LANGUAGES FOR DATABASES

9.0	**In this Chapter**	**378**
9.1	**Hierarchical and Network Models**	**378**
Exercises 9.1		379
9.2	**The Relational Model**	**380**
Manipulating Relational Databases		381
	The Relational Algebra	382
	The Relational Calculus	384
SQL		385

Logic-Based Systems Using PROLOG		389
Exercises 9.2		389
9.3	**Semantic Data Models**	**390**
Exercises 9.3		392
9.4	**Object-Oriented Database Model**	**392**
9.5	**Summary**	**393**
9.6	**Notes on References**	**394**

CHAPTER 9

Languages for Databases

A database is a more or less permanent file that has structure. In its simplest form, it is a file of records or *entities,* such as a library card catalog. It is *persistent* in that both its entities and the relationships between them are preserved from one usage to the next. Almost all languages support persistence in the form of files, but very little structure remains off-line after a program has terminated. Pascal, for one, does support files of typed data in its **file of** declaration, but not relationships between the data objects.

Languages for manipulating databases must support a description of these relationships and entities and also means for changing both. These are sometimes called *data system languages,* or DSLs. DSLs often support two sublanguages, the *data definition language,* or DDL, and the data manipulation language, or DML. The DDL describes the structure and relationships between data entities, while the DML supports (at least) operations to lookup, insert, delete, and modify data. In addition, sometimes the DML has as a subset a query language, which is user friendly, screen-oriented, interactive, and relatively easy to use. Both the DDL and the DML may be embedded in a host language, such as Pascal (Pascal/R), COBOL (SQL), or FORTRAN (DL/I).

A database can be viewed in several ways, as seen in Figure 9.0.1. At the lowest level is the *physical view,* which describes the actual physical disks or drums where data is stored. At the next higher level of abstraction is the *storage view,* which gives structure to the physical data itself. The most common storage structure for large databases is the B-tree (height-balanced tree), with indexes, indexes to indexes, etc. Database administrators and programmers, but not the user, may interact with this view.

The next higher abstraction is the *conceptual view,* which describes how the data is organized. Finally, there are possibly several *external views* to a database. These views are seen and used by the user, often through the query language. Taken

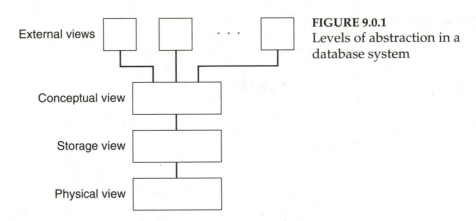

FIGURE 9.0.1
Levels of abstraction in a database system

together, the host language plus the DSL, and the external, conceptual, storage, and physical views, comprise a *database management system* or DBMS.

9.0
IN THIS CHAPTER

The basic models for the conceptual view are:

- Hierarchical model
- Network model
- Relational model

Each will be considered, but since the database paradigm is primarily relational, this model will be presented more fully. In addition, we will look at representing database relationships using semantic models.

9.1
HIERARCHICAL AND NETWORK MODELS

Historically, the first of the conceptual views is the *hierarchical model,* where data is viewed as a tree. One DDL for the hierarchical model is IBM's Information Management System (IMS), with its accompanying DML, DL/I. In the library, the DDL might describe the hierarchy shown in Figure 9.1.1.

A typical database request for a list of all publishers of books that were written by Kurt Vonnegut is:

```
get all PUBLISH.NAME where AUTHOR = 'Kurt Vonnegut'.
```

The difficulty with the hierarchical model is that access to data records is always from the top down. Finding the publisher's name for a particular AUTHOR NAME would involve traveling down the tree through AUTHOR to NAME and then climbing back up

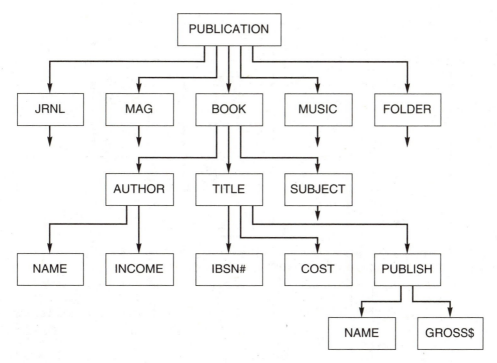

FIGURE 9.1.1
Publications hierarchy

to the BOOK level, and traversing back down through the SUBJECT and PUBLISH levels to NAME. There are ways to hook up a hierarchy across levels, but it is not easy for database users to use these methods.

The obvious solution is to model the database as a graph, where connections can be made between any nodes in any direction. This is called the *network model.* An example is shown in Figure 9.1.2.

The Data Base Task Group (DBTG) of the Conference on Data Systems Languages (CODASYL), which was responsible for the standardization of the business language COBOL, has made a series of proposals for a standard network language. Three languages have been proposed, starting in 1971: a DDL, DML, and a language for defining different views of the DDL. Manipulation of the database is still at the record level, as in the hierarchical model, but making connections is somewhat easier.

EXERCISES 9.1
1. Complete the JRNL branch in the publications hierarchy.
   a. Do you really need to repeat the AUTHOR, TITLE, and SUBJECT fields?
   b. How could you devise a JRNL record to avoid the redundancies mentioned in exercise a above?
   c. Besides wasting space, why is it a bad idea to keep more than one copy of data? Try to think of two reasons.

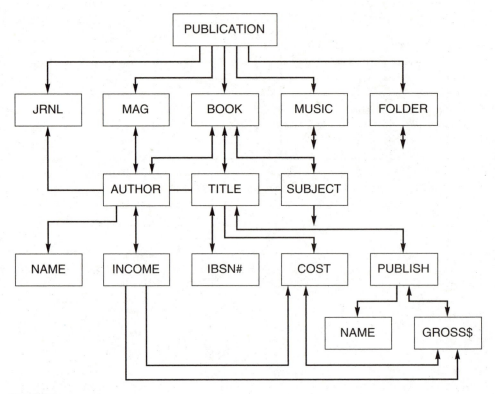

FIGURE 9.1.2
Publications network

9.2
THE RELATIONAL MODEL

Neither hierarchies nor networks provide much structure to the database itself. Form is added in the *relational model.* As we have mentioned, databases are often used by those with little knowledge of computers or mathematics. When most people think of data, it is in the form of a table with rows and columns. A record is then a row in a table. Some possible relations from our PUBLICATION database are shown in Figure 9.2.1.

Notice that we have built-in fields to connect one relation to another. BOOK itself is composed of three *keys* that refer us to the subrelations. The author key AKEY and subject key SKEY are called *foreign keys,* since they are keys to relations other than BOOK. ISBN# is both a *primary key* for BOOK and a foreign key, since it is the primary key for the TITLE relation as well. There are several relational languages, of which the most pervasive is Structured Query Language (SQL).

BOOK

AKEY	ISBN#	SKEY

AUTHOR

AKEY	NAME	PKEY

TITLE

ISBN#	NAME	AKEY

PUBLISH

PKEY	NAME

FIGURE 9.2.1
Publications relations

Manipulating Relational Databases

As with other languages we have seen, mathematical systems of long standing underlie the structure of relational query languages. There really is nothing new under the sun. Here we will view a database as a set of relations, where a relation is a set of tuples (a table). An instance of a relation is a *k-tuple*, where k is the *arity* of the relation. The symbol $t^{(k)}$ is used to indicate an arbitrary k-tuple. For the PUB-LISH relation of Figure 9.2.1, k = 2, and for the other three, k = 3.

So far, we have looked at data descriptions, but not at data itself. Individual records conforming to a particular description are called *instances,* and a collection of instances is a *database.*

We will use the sample library database in Figure 9.2.2 in our examples of the manipulations possible on a database of relations. The AUTHOR-1 relation has three

AUTHOR−1

1001	Smith	MH
1002	Jones	MH
1003	Cohen	BA

AUTHOR−2

1003	Cohen	BA
1004	Brown	MH

PUBLISH

MH	McG-Hill
BA	Bantam

TITLE

0-013	Cats	1002
1-025	Dogs	1002
0-036	Birds	1003
1-324	Cows	1001
2-066	Sheep	1003

FIGURE 9.2.2
Library database

3-tuples, or instances, AUTHOR-2 has two 3-tuples, PUBLISH has two 2-tuples, and TITLE has five 3-tuples.

The Relational Algebra

An algebra is a set with operations defined on it. The relational algebra is defined by the operations allowed on sets of relations. The algebra for the example in Figure 9.2.2 is:

<{AUTHOR-1, AUTHOR-2, PUBLISH, TITLE}, Union, Set-Difference, Cartesian product, Projection, Selection>.

S = {AUTHOR-1, AUTHOR-2, PUBLISH, TITLE} is the set of relations, while *Union, Set-Difference, Cartesian product, Projection,* and *Selection* are the operations on S. We will define these operations below.

Union. Union(A, B) is the set of tuples that occur in A or in B or in both. Union (AUTHOR-1, AUTHOR-2) is:

1001	Smith	MH
1002	Jones	MH
1003	Cohen	BA
1004	Brown	MH

Set difference. The Set-difference of two relations A and B is A – B, the set of relations in A but not in B. Set-difference(AUTHOR-1, AUTHOR-2) is:

1001	Smith	MH
1002	Jones	MH

Cartesian product. The Cartesian product of two relations A and B is the relation A × B, whose first coordinates are those of A, and the last, those of B. Thus if A has k_1-arity and B has k_2-arity, then A × B has $(k_1 * k_2)$-arity. AUTHOR-2 × PUBLISH is:

1003	Cohen	BA	MH	McG-Hill
1004	Brown	MH	MH	McG-Hill
1003	Cohen	BA	BA	Bantam
1004	Brown	MH	BA	Bantam

The Cartesian product is not too useful, because we get duplicate columns and some nonsense relations. For instance, Cohen's publisher is Bantam, not McGraw-Hill. Two variations are implemented for relational databases. The first is the *equijoin,* where only those relations are joined that have equal entries in a specified column. For example, the equijoin$_{PKEY}$ of AUTHOR-2 and PUBLISH is:

		PKEY	PKEY	
1003	Cohen	BA	BA	Bantam
1004	Brown	MH	MH	McG-Hill

The *natural join* eliminates the duplicated column from the equijoin. The natural join of AUTHOR-2 and PUBLISH is:

		PKEY	
1003	Cohen	BA	Bantam
1004	Brown	MH	McG-Hill

Projection. A projection pr oduces a new relation from an existing one, with only a subset of the components or with components rearranged. For example, $_{3,2}$(TITLE) is:

1002	Cats
1002	Dogs
1003	Birds
1001	Cows
1003	Sheep

Only columns 2 and 3 remain, rearranged from 2,3 to 3,2 order.

Selection. Selection σ, as the name implies, selects out those tuples satisfying some condition. For example, $\sigma_{[NAME = 'Cats' \ OR \ NAME = 'Cows']}$(TITLE) is:

0-013	Cats	1002
1-324	Cows	1001

Operations other than the equijoin and the natural join can be defined from these operations as well.

Intersection. $A \cap B$ is shorthand for $A - (A - B)$. So, AUTHOR-1 $\cap$ AUTHOR-2 is:

1003	Cohen	BA

Quotient. $A \div B$ is the relation that factors out tuples from B occurring in A. For example, for relations A and B shown here, $A \div B$ selects those tuples in which all tuples in B match the endings of tuples in A that have the same starting elements. (1,2) appears in the quotient because (1,2,a,b) and (1,2,c,d) appear in A.

A			
1	2	a	b
1	2	c	d
3	4	a	b
3	4	b	c

B	
a	b
c	d

A ÷ B	
1	2

A purely algebraic relational language is Information System Base Language (ISBL), developed by IBM in Britain for use in an experimental system, the Peterlee Relational Test Vehicle. Its better features have since been combined in the SEQUEL language (also known as SQL), which we will look at below, combining both the relational algebra and the relational calculus.

The Relational Calculus

The relational calculus is really two calculi, the tuple calculus and the domain calculus. We already know a good bit about the tuple calculus from Chapter 7 and Appendix A, since it is nothing more than the predicate calculus applied to tuples. Variables will represent tuples. A formula such as (EXISTS $(t^{(k)})$) $A(t^{(k)})$ means, "Is there a k-tuple $t^{(k)}$ such that $A(t^{(k)})$ is true?" The tuples will, of course, need to be part of some relational database.

The tuple calculus. If you recall from Chapter 7, atomic formulas are simply letters such as p and q, or p(x) and q(x). We shall specialize these to relational databases, but otherwise the predicate calculus remains the same. Remember that a formula of the predicate calculus or of the relational calculus can be either TRUE or FALSE. For the relational calculus, atomic formulas are:

1. R(t), where R is a relation and t is a tuple
2. t[i] <comparator> u[j], where <comparator> is a comparison operator such as =, <, or >. t[i] represents the ith component of the tuple t.
3. t[i] <comparator> C, where C is a constant

We will give as examples relational calculus formulas representing the operations of the relational algebra. These are given as sets. The set will be assigned a TRUE value, just in case its members fulfill the condition used in its description. Capital letters such as R or S represent relations, while lowercase letters such as t or u represent tuples. u ∈ R means that the tuple u belongs to the relation R.

Union: R ∪ T = {t | R(t) OR S(t)}

Difference: R − S = {t | R(t) AND NOT(S(t))}

Cartesian product: $R \times S = \{t^{(r+s)} \mid$
$$EXISTS(u \in R)\ EXISTS(v \in S)$$
$$(t[1]=u[1]\ AND \ldots AND\ t[r]=u[r]\ AND$$
$$t[r+1]=v[1]\ AND \ldots AND\ t[r+s]=v[s])\ \}$$

Projection: $_{i_1,\ldots,i_k}(R) = \{t^{(k)} \mid EXISTS(u)\ AND\ R(u)$
$$AND\ t_1 = u[i_1]\ AND \ldots AND\ t_k = u[i_k]$$

Selection: $\sigma_F(R) = \{t \mid R(t)\ AND\ F(t)\}$, where F is a condition on tuples that can be either TRUE or FALSE.

The domain calculus. The tuple calculus as given can yield infinite results. The relation defined by $\{t \mid NOT\ (TITLE(t))\}$ describes an infinite set of tuples, all those not in the 5-tuple relation TITLE. To restrict our definitions to finite relations, we appeal to the domain calculus, which applies to what are called *safe expressions.* We will not give the formal rules for safe expressions here, but refer the interested reader to [Ullman, 1988]. It can be shown that the domain calculus is equivalent to the relational algebra. That is, the set of functions or relations definable using safe expressions is the same set definable through the relational algebra.

There appears to be general agreement that, of the three models mentioned, the relational calculus is by far the easiest to understand and use. The problem with both the hierarchical and network models is that a fairly sophisticated knowledge of links and records is needed to negotiate a database. However, both hierarchies and networks are closer to the physical view of data and provide a basis for very efficient systems.

SQL

SQL stands for Structured Query Language and is pronounced "ess que ell" by some and "sequel" by others. It is sometimes written SEQUEL to enforce the second pronunciation. Its basis is intermediate between the relational algebra and calculus and was originally developed in the early seventies in San Jose, California, by IBM, for the R Database System. It is not fully functional in the sense of being as powerful as a procedural language, but does provide operations sufficient for most database applications. We discuss it here instead of one of the many other possible database languages because there are over 100 commercial products based on it, and because it has been standardized by the American National Standards Institute and the International Standards Organization, the current version being SQL/92 [ANSI/ISO-X3.135, 1992].

Publishing a standard has many advantages in that personnel trained at one location will be able to use their same skills if they change jobs; applications are portable from one machine to another and will be usable for a long time; systems can communicate from one to another; and customers can choose the big or the little version of the same language, depending on their needs. C.J. Date [Date, 1993], however, warns of numerous deficiencies in SQL as it presently exists. The most serious is that it was never really designed in accordance with either the relational algebra or calculus and is filled with numerous hard-to-remember restrictions, ad hoc constructs, and special rules. In other words, SQL is far from orthogonal. Further, [Date, 1995] notes that SQL is moving further from the relational model. He also points out that some features that should be part of the standard have been left as implementation-defined or implementation-dependent. However, "vendors are scrambling to support it, and customers are demanding such support" [Date, 1993].

We will continue to use the library database of Figure 9.2.2, including the PUB-LISH and TITLE tables, but will use the Union of AUTHOR-1 and AUTHOR-2 and call it AU-THOR. We will also leave the third field null in Cohen's record, indicating that his book, *Sheep*, has no publisher as yet. Discussion below follows Date's *Guide to the SQL Standard* [Date, 1993]. In Lab 9.1, you will find some differences, since the implementation is not strictly standard SQL.

AUTHOR

1001	Smith	MH
1002	Jones	MH
1003	Cohen	
1004	Brown	MH

SQL includes both a DDL and a DML. In order to have a database to work with, we must first define it. We will define our library database through a *schema*, as shown in listing (9.2.1).

```
CREATE SCHEMA AUTHORIZATION VANDEKOPPLE                          (9.2.1)

CREATE TABLE PUBLISH ( PNO    CHAR(2)    NOT NULL,
                       PNAME  CHAR(8),
                       PRIMARY KEY ( PNO ) )

CREATE TABLE AUTHOR  ( ANO    CHAR(4)    NOT NULL,
                       ANAME  CHAR(10),
                       PNO    CHAR(2),
                       PRIMARY KEY ( ANO ),
                       FOREIGN KEY ( PNO ) REFERENCES PUBLISH )

CREATE TABLE TITLE   ( ISBN   CHAR(8)    NOT NULL,
                       TNAME  CHAR(8),
                       ANO    CHAR(4),
                       PRIMARY KEY ( ISBN ),
                       FOREIGN KEY ( ANO ) REFERENCES AUTHOR )
```

AUTHORIZATION means that VANDEKOPPLE created this schema. Notice that the data definition includes formatted input. Each table has a field designated as a **PRIMARY KEY**, which cannot be null. This designation must be unique to a row and is the primary way for looking up a record. AUTHOR and TITLE also have **FOREIGN KEY**s that facilitate referencing related tables. The fact that Cohen has no PNO causes no problem, since it does not appear in the PUBLISH table.

The SQL DML has four basic operations: **INSERT**, **UPDATE**, **DELETE**, and **SELECT**. Our next job would be to enter the data into the three tables defined in the schema. For example,

```
INSERT
INTO AUTHOR (ANO, ANAME)
VALUES      (1003, 'Cohen')
```

When Cohen's book is indeed accepted by Bantam, we can:

```
UPDATE AUTHOR
SET    PNO = 'BA'
WHERE  AUTHOR.ANAME = 'Cohen'
```

The **SELECT** statement is generally of the form **SELECT** X **FROM** Y **WHERE** <expression>. One use is to implement the equijoin we saw when describing the relational algebra. We will use our **FOREIGN KEY**s in listing (9.2.2).

```
CREATE TABLE AP                                            (9.2.2)
       AS SELECT AUTHOR.ANAME, PUBLISH.PNAME
          FROM   AUTHOR      , PUBLISH
          WHERE  AUTHOR.PNO = PUBLISH.PNO
```

The following table will result:

AP

Smith	McG-Hill
Jones	McG-Hill
Cohen	Bantam
Brown	McG-Hill

Standard SQL is not particularly suited for selecting a number of rows and performing some operation on them, as it is primarily intended for embedding in procedural languages, particularly COBOL and PL/I, which are not oriented for manipulating tables. One can achieve this sort of iteration by declaring a cursor, which moves around a table like a mouse-controlled cursor moves around a screen.

Suppose Bantam gets sold to some mystery company, to be read from a secret file, and we want to update all rows in PUBLISH where 'Bantam' is the PNAME. While we're at it, we might update the key BA to the first two letters of the new name. This code needs to be embedded in a host language to read in the mystery name and pick off the first two characters. The code in listing (9.2.3) is an outline of a PL/I program to do the job. **EXEC SQL** signals the PL/I compiler to switch to SQL. X and Y are PL/I variables which are written :X and :Y in the embedded SQL code so there is no confusion with SQL variables.

```
EXEC SQL DECLARE C CURSOR FOR                              (9.2.3)
         SELECT  PUBLISH.PNAME, PUBLISH.PNO
         FROM    PUBLISH
         WHERE   PNO = 'BA'
```

```
DECLARE X CHAR(8);        /* PL/I declarations */
DECLARE Y CHAR(2);
EXEC SQL OPEN C;
DO /* for all rows accessible via cursor */ C;
        EXEC SQL FETCH C INTO :X, :Y;
/* read the new name into X & put first 2 letters in Y */
        EXEC SQL UPDATE PUBLISH
                SET PNAME = :X;
                AND PNO   = :Y;
                WHERE CURRENT OF C;
END;
EXEC SQL CLOSE C;
```

In listing (9.2.3), there are five operations with cursors: **OPEN, CURRENT, FETCH, SET**, and **CLOSE. OPEN** sets the cursor at the top of PUBLISH and starts the **SELECT** going over all the rows accessible by the cursor C. **CURRENT** is the row currently pointed to by C. **SET** reads values pointed to by the current value of C, while **FETCH** reads and then moves the cursor to the next row defined for it. **CLOSE** undeclares the cursor.

There are two security measures in SQL, one using a **VIEW** and another called **GRANT**. A **VIEW** can be used to hide some data from users, while operations are **GRANT**ed to them. Most users will probably not be **GRANT**ed **UPDATE** privileges. We can create a **VIEW** of McGraw-Hill ("McG-Hill") authors using:

```
CREATE VIEW MH-AUTHORS AS
        SELECT * FROM AUTHOR WHERE AUTHOR.PNO = 'MH'
```

Many database languages, including the System R version of SQL, include a function for creating an index, e.g.,

```
CREATE INDEX AUTHOR-INDEX
        ON (ANO [order, either ASCending or DESCending]) AUTHOR
```

CREATE INDEX functions directly on the physical database and provides addresses of data rows to speed look-ups. This has been eliminated in Standard SQL, since programs are to be portable from machine to machine. Indexes are created in Standard SQL using the **TABLE** function, i.e.,

```
CREATE TABLE AUTHOR-INDEX
        AS SELECT ANO FROM AUTHOR
```

Two integrity constraints have usually been considered desirable in relational DBMSs. The first is *entity integrity,* which insists that a **KEY**, either primary or foreign, cannot be null. Second is *referential integrity,* which insists that each relation have at least one foreign key to allow relating two or more relations. System R did not enforce either rule, while Standard SQL enforces entity integrity but not referential integrity.

SQL makes provision for concurrency through *transactions,* which are guaranteed to be independent of each other. A transaction terminates normally by executing **COMMIT WORK. ROLLBACK WORK** handles an unsuccessful transaction and returns the database to its state before the transaction began to execute. A **ROLLBACK** must be called by a transaction, and the Standard provides no guidance for transactions running at the time of a system crash or those that terminate without having executed **COMMIT WORK**. Thus these abnormal situations must be handled by the particular implementation.

LAB 9.1: SQL: dBASE IV

Objectives (Labs can be found in the *Instructor's Manual.*)

1. To become familiar with SQL coding for defining and establishing a database for the PUBLISH database.
2. To use the report writing facilities of a popular SQL-based package to produce a short report from the database.

Logic-Based Systems Using PROLOG

Because of the association of relational databases to first-order predicate logic, PROLOG is a natural choice as a query language. As we saw in Chapter 7, facts and rules form PROLOG's internal database. PROLOG can be used as the language to interface with the external relational database, which is to be treated as part of the PROLOG system. By keeping the external database separate, data can still be used by other applications.

In order to see the power of PROLOG's syntax, consider the equijoin example in the query of listing (9.2.2).

```
SELECT AUTHOR.ANAME, PUBLISH.PNAME FROM AUTHOR, PUBLISH
WHERE AUTHOR.PNO = PUBLISH.PNO
```

Here we ask for the author and publisher name for those instances in which the PNO fields match. In PROLOG, this can be written as the query shown in listing (9.2.4).

```
?-author(_,Aname,Pno),publish(Pno,Pname),                    (9.2.4)
    write(Aname,Pname),nl,fail.
```

While early versions of PROLOG were slow and limited, improvements in efficiency have made it sensible to take advantage of its power as a database language.

EXERCISES 9.2

1. Using the library database of Figure 9.2.2, what table results from the equijoin$_{AKEY}$ of AUTHOR-1 and TITLE? From the equijoin$_{AKEY}$ of AUTHOR-2 and TITLE?
2. What is set difference $(A - B)$ if $A =$ TITLE and $B = \sigma_{[NAME = 'Cats' \, OR \, NAME = 'Cows']}$(TITLE)?
3. What is PUBLISH $\times$ TITLE? TITLE $\times$ PUBLISH? Also TITLE $\times$ PUBLISH $\times$ AUTHOR-2?
4. What is the natural join$_{AKEY}$ of TITLE $\times$ AUTHOR-2?
5. If we wish to add ACMPress to the PUBLISH database, would we use SQL **INSERT** or **UPDATE**? Why?
6. Use SQL statements to create the natural join of AUTHOR and PUBLISH.
7. Create an SQL **VIEW** of TITLE giving only those titles by authors Smith or Jones. You first will have to find out from AUTHOR just what those titles are.
8. Use an SQL statement to **DELETE** all authors whose books are published by Bantam.
9. Why is the **fail** predicate used in the PROLOG query of listing (9.2.4)?

9.3
SEMANTIC DATA MODELS

A relational model is certainly easier to use than either a hierarchical or network model, but its tables are still closer to the machine than to many of the natural relationships found in business. Semantic models were first introduced as schema design tools. A schema would be designed and then translated into one of the other three models. Let's look at a semantic model for the library database in Figure 9.3.1.

Semantic models are distinguished by three things. First is the direct representation of object types, called *entities*. Many models distinguish between *abstract* and *printable* or *representable* types. Abstract entities are represented in the diagram by triangles, and subentities by circles with double arrows pointing to the parent type.

The second fundamental mechanism found in semantic models is the notion of *attributes,* or functions between types. For example, lives-at maps AUTHOR into ADDRESS, while is-residence-of maps ADDRESS back to AUTHOR. These attributes are often thought of in the relational sense: AUTHOR lives-at ADDRESS, and ADDRESS is-residence-of AUTHOR.

Third is the ability to represent isA relationships between supertypes and subtypes. Here we have ACADEMIC isA AUTHOR, and EDITOR isA AUTHOR. As subtypes, both ACADEMIC and EDITOR inherit all the attributes of an AUTHOR, including ADDRESS, ANAME, and BOOK. One difference between a semantic model subtype and a subclass in the object-oriented sense is that attributes cannot be redefined. A subentity inherits unchanged all the attributes of the parent entity, while the isA relationships of the library database model subsets of AUTHORs.

There are essentially two sorts of semantic models, entity relationship (ER) and functional data models (FDM). ER tends to emphasize abstract data types, while FDM models are more concerned with attributes related to entities through functions. Figure 9.3.1 represents a combination of both ER and FDM techniques, with ADDRESS and PUBLISHER being structured abstract types, and AUTHOR related to its attributes through functions.

Query languages for semantic databases can be much like SQL, as shown in listing (9.3.1).

```
for each X in AUTHOR                              (9.3.1)
    such that Y = 'Tampa' and
              X lives-at ADDRESS.Y and
              X has-name Z
    print Z
```

Subtypes can be created "on the fly" during program execution, as in listing (9.3.2).

```
create subtype SCIENCE-EDITOR of EDITOR          (9.3.2)
       where EXPERTISE includes SCIENCE
for each X in SCIENCE-EDITOR
       where X has-name Y
       print Y
```

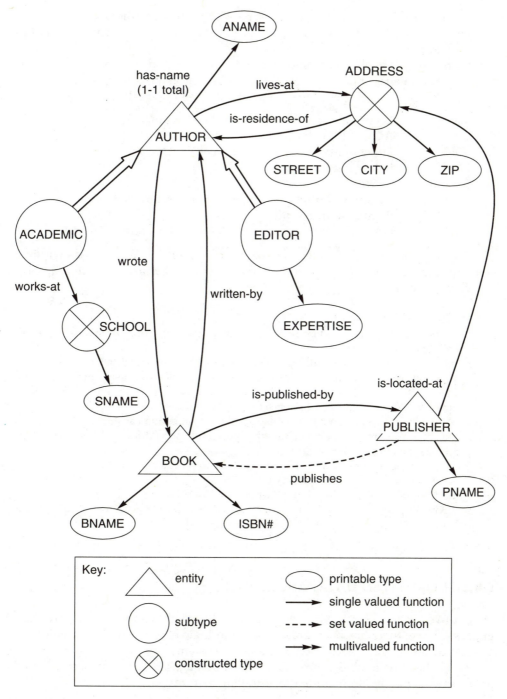

FIGURE 9.3.1
Semantic model for the library database

If we add **record** SCIENCE-EDITOR, the subtype will be added to the database. This is known as a *derived subtype,* since it is derived from properties already existent in the database.

There are a number of implemented semantic data models, especially as front-ends to other database managers. Most run on VAX systems or workstations under either the UNIX or VMS operating systems. Hull and King [Hull, 1987] list these as:

Name	DBMS interface	Implementation language
DAPLEX	ADAPLEX extension	Ada
FQL	Functional data model	Pascal, CODASYL
TAXIS	Relational front-end	Pascal R
Semdal	SEMBASE	C
GEM™	INGRES front-end	Relational Interface Language
ARIEL	Relational front-end	Pascal
Galileo™	GALILEO	VAX machine code

The languages listed above are geared to data-intensive applications within a standard procedural language. Other experimental languages provide graphical interfaces as well.

EXERCISES 9.3
1. In the semantic model of Figure 9.3.1, which function(s) should probably be "1-1 total" besides has-name?
2. a. In Figure 9.3.1, why is there a double-headed arrow from AUTHOR to BOOK?
   b. What would it mean if the arrow from BOOK to AUTHOR was also double-headed?
3. What is the difference between a set-valued (- - -➤) and a multivalued (——➤➤) function? When might you use each?
4. Why is ADDRESS represented as a constructed type, rather than an entity? (Think about this one. Your answer depends on what you think is the difference between an entity and an attribute.)
5. Write queries to the semantic library database to produce:
   a. All authors who works-at CityU
   b. A list of books published by McGraw-Hill (McG-Hill)
6. Redo exercise 5 a different way, i.e., if you didn't already do so, create a subtype for what you want.

9.4
OBJECT-ORIENTED DATABASE MODEL

Descriptive languages offer a better approach to databases than imperative languages. Hence, there has been great interest in logic-based languages, which we discussed earlier, and object-oriented database systems.

As we have seen, objects are fairly close to database entities. Object-oriented database systems should include the following features:

1. Types, classes, and methods
2. Data abstraction and encapsulation

3. Subtypes and inheritance
4. Object identity

The first three have been discussed in Chapters 2 and 4. Type declarations would include record and set types. A subtype might have additional fields and methods defined on that subclass, but would inherit operations defined on the parent type. Because of the possibility of operator overloading, the system should also support dynamic binding.

Object identity indicates that each object has an identity aside from its value. In fact, two objects with the same values could still be distinguished. Suppose that our author database only had fields for ANAME and PNO:

AUTHOR

Smith	MH
Jones	MH
Cohen	BA
Brown	MH

If we had another author whose last name was Jones and publisher was McGraw-Hill, it would not be possible to represent that information in this database. Since a relation is a set, which does not allow duplicate elements, object identity is not supported by the relational model. The additional ANO field would be needed to distinguish the two. It is interesting to note that both the hierarchical and network models do support object identity.

A nice example of an object-oriented database system is the GemStone system, which is marketed by Servio Logic Corp. It has a common DDL/DML called OPAL, which is related to Smalltalk. The system can be interfaced with languages such as C or C++ when writing other applications.

9.5
SUMMARY

The database paradigm is relational, and closely related to logic-based languages. It differs from logic-based languages in that database languages support persistence. By this we mean that the relationships between database entities are preserved off-line. Relational databases and their languages are now the most prevalent, but those based on hierarchies (tree-structured) or networks (graph-structured) still exist.

A database management system (DBMS) usually includes two languages, a data definition language (DDL) and a data manipulation language (DML). The DML is often embedded in another high level language, e.g., an SQL segment within a PL/I program.

SQL is the most-used database language, if not the best. It has provision for concurrency through independent transactions.

9.6
NOTES ON REFERENCES

The three standard theoretical texts on database design and languages are [Wiederhold, 1983], [Ullman, 1988], and [Date, 1995]. The second is most often used as an undergraduate text, perhaps because of its smaller size. Both Ullman and Date emphasize the relational models, with Ullman more theoretical and Date combining applications with theory. Wiederhold's text is divided into three sections, "File Structures and Design," "Database Structures and Design," and "Security and Operations."

The ACM *Computing Surveys* series provides several tutorials on database systems. One of these is an entire volume [Atkinson, 1987] dealing with types and persistence in database languages. Two others, [Hull, 1987] and [Peckham, 1988], are concerned with semantic data models. Hull is a particularly accessible tutorial on semantic notions, including implementations as well as areas of research interest.

[Lucas, 1988] provides a readable treatment of a logic-based system using PROLOG, including examples. Information on object-oriented database systems, including the GemStone system, is available in both [Ullman, 1988] and [Vossen, 1991].

APPENDIX A

Logical Calculi (for Chapter 7)

Logical calculi are systems designed to calculate the truth values of statements according to particular rules. The *propositional calculus* concerns formal reasoning about the truth of statements. The *predicate calculus* includes the propositional calculus and also variables within statements. "Bob is a boy" is a proposition, or statement, and "X is a boy" is a predicate with one variable, X. Propositions are predicates with zero variables. A statement or a predicate is either true or false, never maybe. But at any particular moment in time, we may not be able to determine which!

THE PROPOSITIONAL CALCULUS

The propositional calculus, also called the calculus of statements, is a system for calculating the truth values of new statements assuming the truth of others. For example, suppose we have two propositions, "Fido is a dog" and "Fido is a cat." To save ink, we will assign "Fido is a dog" to the variable p, and "Fido is a cat" to q. A new proposition might be r = p OR q. If either Value(p) is true or Value(q) is true, then Value(r) is automatically true. That is, if we know that Fido is a cat, then certainly Fido is a cat or Fido is a dog. Or we could make the assignment Value(r) = true, without knowing which of p or q is true. This is not as silly as it may seem. Certainly the statement p' OR q' is true if p' = "The Mississippi will breach the levee tomorrow," and q' = "The levee will hold tomorrow." This reflects the natural language meaning of "or".

Variables for simple statements will be p, q, r, s, ... Compound statements can be formed from these using the logical connectives OR, AND, →, and ¬. p → q means if p then q, and ¬p means NOT p.

Each statement will be assigned a truth value of 0 (FALSE) or 1 (TRUE) according to Table A.1.

TABLE A.1
Truth values of the logical connectives

p	q	p OR q	p AND q	p → q	¬p
1	1	1	1	1	0
1	0	1	0	0	0
0	1	1	0	1	1
0	0	0	0	1	1

OR is called the *inclusive-or* since Value(p OR q) = 1 includes the case where Value(p) = 1 and Value(q) = 1, as well as those where only one of p or q is true. Whether Brutus or Cassius or both killed Caesar is called an *instance* of the proposition p OR q, with "Brutus killed Caesar" being substituted for p, and "Cassius killed Caesar" substituted for q. We could just as well substitute "The Sparrow killed Cock Robin" for p. "The Sparrow killed Cock Robin or Cassius killed Caesar" would then be a different instance of the proposition p OR q. An interpretation of p OR q is an assignment of truth values to the propositional variables, p and q. The various possible interpretations of p OR q are displayed in the third column of Table A.1, given the values of p and q shown in the first and second columns. Table A.1 is called a *truth table*.

A comment is needed for the conditional operator p → q. Here p is the premise and q the conclusion of the statement. The notion is that true premises do not lead to false conclusions, thus TRUE → FALSE is assigned the value of FALSE. That both

$$(\text{FALSE} \rightarrow \text{TRUE}) \tag{A.1}$$

and

$$(\text{FALSE} \rightarrow \text{FALSE}) \tag{A.2}$$

are assigned a TRUE value is often confusing. The justification here is that if we start out with false premises, we can't say much about the conclusions. And yet both (A.1) and (A.2) must be assigned truth values. It doesn't make sense to say that "false premises give you false conclusions" is untrue, so we assign (A.2) a value of TRUE. Since we are usually interested in the value of the conclusion rather than that of the premises, we also assign (A.1) a value of 1, since the conclusion is true.

Another way to look at the implication operator, →, is to write p → q in its disjunctive (OR) form, ¬p OR q. The intuitive meaning of ¬p OR q is that q is necessarily true if ¬p is false, i.e., p is true. The truth table for these two forms is:

p	q	¬p	p → q	¬p OR q
1	1	0	1	1
1	0	0	0	0
0	1	1	1	1
0	0	1	1	1

Notice that the last two columns are identical, meaning that the two propositions are equivalent.

When formalizing logic, the first step is to describe what constitutes a valid proposition. This is done recursively with five formation rules as follows:

FR1: A single letter of the alphabet is a proposition. (A.3)
FR2: If p is a proposition, so is ¬p.
FR3: If p and q are propositions, so is p OR q.
FR4: If p and q are propositions, so is p → q.
FR5: If p and q are propositions, so is p AND q.

As we saw above, FR4 is not needed, as → can be replaced by ¬ and OR. You will be asked in exercise A.2 to show that FR5 is not needed either. In fact, only three rules are needed. We can express all statements of the propositional calculus using FR1, FR2, and one of FR3, FR4, or FR5.

A *logical theory* includes all true statements. Some of these are called axioms and are assumed to be true without proof. A thesis is a true statement that is either an axiom, or derivable from the axioms using the rules of inference of the theory. There have been many formulations of the Theory for the Propositional Calculus (PC), which have been shown to be equivalent. A theory is said to be *complete* if all statements that are TRUE are theses. It is *consistent* if no statement that is FALSE can be derived. PC can be shown to be both complete and consistent [see for example, Mendelson, 1979]. One of the best known sets of axioms for PC is that of Whitehead and Russell's *Principia Mathematica* (PM) [Whitehead, 1910].

PM1: (p OR p) → p (A.4)
PM2: q → (p OR q)
PM3: (p OR q) → (q OR p)
PM4: (q → r) → ((p OR q) → (p OR r)).

There are two rules of inference in PM. They are:

- R1 (Uniform Substitution): If p is a thesis, and q is a statement derived from p by substituting every occurrence of a letter, x, by another letter, y, then q is a thesis.
- R2 (Detachment, or modus ponens): If p and p → q are both theses, then q is a thesis also.

Using R1 and PM1, we would have that (s OR s) → s is a thesis of PM, by uniformly substituting the letter s for p. However, (s OR p) → s may not be a thesis since we did not substitute s for *all* occurrences of p. The substitution was not uniform.

We can test the validity of statements using truth tables, or by constructing a proof listing all the true statements as premises, and then deriving the statement we wish to prove through repeated use of the two inference rules.

A truth table for PM2: q → (p OR q), using the values of Table A.1, is shown in Table A.2. Since the last column containing truth values for PM2 contains all 1s, q → (p OR q) is a thesis. A logical thesis is sometimes called a *tautology*, meaning that it is true for any truth-value assignments to the variables.

Let's prove the true statement p OR ¬p, using PM.

Case 1: Assume p   Assumption
         p → (p OR ¬p)   Instance of PM2
         p OR ¬p   R2: modus ponens

TABLE A.2
Derivation of q → (p OR q)

p	q	(p OR q)	q → (p OR q)
1	1	1	1
1	0	1	1
0	1	1	1
0	0	0	1

Case 2:	Assume ¬p	Assumption
	¬p → (¬p OR p)	Instance of PM2
	¬p OR p	R2: modus ponens
	p OR ¬p	Instance of PM3

Proof by Contradiction

There is, however, another proof method that is more applicable to computer solution, known as reductio ad absurdum (reduction to the absurd). Here we assume that the statement to be proved is FALSE and derive a contradiction. We will demonstrate this method to show the validity of PM4 by assuming that it is false, i.e., Value(PM4) = 0.

Step 1: $(q \rightarrow r) \underset{0}{\rightarrow} ((p \text{ OR } q) \rightarrow (p \text{ OR } r))$

We place a value of FALSE (0) under the →, indicating that this implication is assumed to be false. Given the meaning of →, this only occurs when the antecedent is TRUE and the succedent, FALSE. Thus:

Step 2: $(q \rightarrow r) \underset{0}{\rightarrow} ((p \text{ OR } q) \rightarrow (p \text{ OR } r))$
             1   0

We can do no more with the antecedent, (q → r), at this time, so we consider how to make the succedent FALSE. This occurs once again with a true antecedent and false succedent.

Step 3: $(q \rightarrow r) \underset{0}{\rightarrow} ((p \text{ OR } q) \rightarrow (p \text{ OR } r))$
             1   0
                                 1   0

Now (p OR r) has a truth value of 0, only when Value(p) = 0 and Value(r) = 0.

Step 4: $(q \rightarrow r) \underset{0}{\rightarrow} ((p \text{ OR } q) \rightarrow (p \text{ OR } r))$
             1   0
                                 1   0
                                        0   0

We must now make Value(p) = Value(r) = 0 uniformly.

Step 5: (q → r) → ((p OR q) → (p OR r))

$$
\begin{array}{ccccccc}
 & 0 & & & & & \\
1 & & & 0 & & & \\
 & & 1 & & 0 & & \\
 & & & & & 0 & 0 \\
 & 0 & & 0 & & & \\
\end{array}
$$

Next we assign the necessary values to q. Value(q) must be 0, so that Value((q → r)) = 1, as determined in Step 2.

Step 6: (q → r) → ((p OR q) → (p OR r))

$$
\begin{array}{ccccccc}
 & 0 & & & & & \\
1 & & & 0 & & & \\
 & & 1 & & 0 & & \\
 & & & & & 0 & 0 \\
 & 0 & & 0 & & & \\
0 & & & & & & \\
\end{array}
$$

Now Value(p OR q) = 1 (Step 3), and this can only occur with Value(q) = 1, since Value(p) = 0 (Step 5).

Step 7: (q → r) → ((p OR q) → (p OR r))

$$
\begin{array}{ccccccc}
 & 0 & & & & & \\
1 & & & 0 & & & \\
 & & 1 & & 0 & & \\
 & & & & & 0 & 0 \\
 & 0 & & 0 & & & \\
\mathbf{0} & & & & & & \\
 & & \mathbf{1} & & & & \\
\end{array}
$$

We have made bold the two values here because they represent the contradiction of q being both TRUE and FALSE. Thus we "reduced to the absurd" our original claim in Step 1, that Value(PM4) = 0. In logic, a contradiction is a statement that is both TRUE and FALSE. Contradictions do not occur in a consistent theory. However, in a complete theory, every legal statement is either TRUE or FALSE, so PM4 must be TRUE, and Value(PM4) = 1.

We write the entire reduction in a single line by placing the steps above, and the truth values below, the statement.

Steps:	6 2 5	1	5 3 7	2	4 3 4
	(q → r)	→	((p OR q)	→	(p OR r))
Truth Values:	**0** 1 0	0	0 1 **1**	0	0 0 0

THE PREDICATE CALCULUS

The predicate calculus is nothing more than the statement calculus with variables and quantifiers added. Quantifiers are FORALL and EXISTS. For example,

(FORALL X)(IF X is a dog THEN X barks)

and

(EXISTS X)(X is a dog)

are statements of the predicate calculus. "Rex barks" is in the statement calculus, and has no quantifiers. We will look at these differences more closely below.

Relations and Predicates

The propositional calculus lacks expressive power, in that statements are indivisible. We cannot use the same statement in different instances. For example, we might not know who killed Caesar, but do know that he's dead and need a statement stating that "Someone killed Caesar." Then we could substitute either Brutus or Cassius for Someone. Brutus or Cassius is related to Caesar by the relation KILLED. KILLED (Brutus, Caesar) and KILLED (Cassius, Caesar) are two instances of the two-place predicate KILLED. (Notice, we still don't know who did it. That depends on an interpretation, or assignment of truth values to the two instances of the KILLED predicate.)

In mathematics, a two-place (or binary) relation is simply a set of ordered 2-tuples. An example is the relation LESS-THAN, <, which includes (2,3) and (5,7), but does not include (2,2). Other relations may be functions, such as TIMES, *, which is a three-place relation or set of 3-tuples. (3,2,6) belongs to TIMES, but (3,2,5) does not. TIMES is also called a binary function because it has two arguments; in the case of (3,2,6), the arguments are the 3 and the 2. Binary (two-place) relations or functions are often written with their names appropriately between the arguments, e.g., 2 < 3, Brutus KILLED Caesar, or 3 * 2 = 6.

A *predicate* is a relation that can (potentially) be assigned a truth value. It consists of a predicate symbol, such as TIMES, <, or KILLED, and arguments, which may be either variables, constants, or functors. A *functor* is a functional expression that has not been evaluated. TIMES(3,2,X) is a predicate, which is FALSE if 5 is substituted for X, and TRUE if we substitute 6. We may also write

$$\text{TIMES}(3,2,1+Y)) \tag{A.5}$$

if we allow an expression such as 1+Y, to be substituted for variables. What substitution for Y makes this last relation TRUE? If we define a function, PLUS1(Y) = Y + 1, (A.5) can be written TIMES(3,2,PLUS1(Y)). Here PLUS1(Y) is a functor. We need a value for Y that makes the value of the function PLUS1(Y) equal to 6. That (3,2,6) belongs to TIMES constitutes a proof of the statement, "There exists an X and TIMES(3,2,X)." In PROLOG this existential statement would be written

```
WHICH(X : TIMES(3,2,X))
which (_x (times 3 2 _x))
```

or

```
?- TIMES(3,2,X)
```

depending on the dialect being used. It is the job of the PROLOG interpreter or compiler to prove that the variable X may be replaced by 6.

To add predicates to PC statements, we use formation rules FR1–FR3 and add:

FR6: If p is a formula and X is an individual-variable, then (FORALL X) p is a formula.[1]

---

[1]Note that we have changed the designation of a statement from "proposition" to "formula." In many discussions of logic, statements written correctly according to rules FR1–FR3 plus FR6 are called well-formed formulas, or wffs.

Just as we are able to define p AND q as ¬(¬p OR ¬q) (see exercise A.2.a), we can define (EXISTS X) p, as ¬(FORALL X)(¬p). In order to say, "There exists a yellow cat," we could use the convoluted statement, "It is not true that all cats are not yellow." (You were forewarned against the double negative by your high school English teachers for matters of style, not meaning.)

In `IS-A(X, Yellow, Cat)`, X is said to be "free." In `WHICH(X: IS-A(X, Yellow, Cat))`, X is "bound"[2] by the PROLOG quantifier `WHICH` (EXISTS).

Inference rules R1 and R2 still apply to the predicate calculus, and we add two new rules to handle the variables:

- R3 (Uniform Substitution of Variables): If X is an individual-variable, and p is any legal formula, and if q is a formula differing from p only in that all free occurrences of X have been replaced by Y, then (FORALL X)p → q is a thesis, provided the Y did not become bound in q when it replaced X.
- R4 (Universal Generalization): If X is any individual-variable and p and q are formulas, and if p → q is a thesis, then so is p → (FORALL X)q.

In R4, the proposition p may be empty, so an instance of R4 gives us: if q is a formula, then so is (FORALL X)q.[3]

Hughes and Cresswell [Hughes, 1968] demonstrates the trouble you can get into if you ignore the proviso in R3, that the Y did not become bound in q. Suppose p is the statement (EXISTS Y)(X is-a-child-of Y). This, in effect, states that whoever X is, he has a parent (most likely true). Note that X is free in p, while Y is bound by (EXISTS Y). Now if q is (EXISTS Y)(Y is-a-child-of Y), q is FALSE, at least as far as we know. This substitution of Y for X violates the proviso, since it allowed the free occurrence of X to become bound in q by (EXISTS Y). The statement,

(FORALL X)(EXISTS Y)(X is-a-child-of Y) → (EXISTS Y)(Y is-a-child-of Y)

surely cannot be a thesis, since the antecedent is TRUE, but the succedent, FALSE. Fortunately, logic programmers usually need not concern themselves with such problems, but the developers of a language based on logic, such as PROLOG, worried about bindings and scope a great deal.

The First-Order Predicate Calculus

The order of a logical system depends on what value the individual variables, such as X and Y, may have. That is, when we say (FORALL X) p, just which X's did we have in mind? In a first-order theory, we may replace X with a different variable name, as prescribed in R3, or with a constant, called an individual, or with a functor that evaluates to an individual. That is, in the statement IS-A(X, yellow, cat), X may

---

[2]You have already struggled with bindings when you programmed functions and procedures. Variables are either global or local to a procedure, and, if local, are "bound" to the procedure where they are declared.

[3](FORALL X)p can be written as (X)p or (∀X)p, and (∃X)p means (EXISTS X)p. Similarly, ¬(∀X)p means ¬(FORALL X)p, and ¬(∃X)p or ∄Xp means ¬(EXISTS X)p.

only be replaced by another variable, such as Y, by the individual cat Fluffy, Tiger, or MagnifiCat, or by some functional expression $f(X)$ that evaluates to an individual—not by some other relation that would evaluate to TRUE or FALSE.

EXERCISES A

1. Construct a truth table to define the logical connective XOR. p XOR q means that either p or q is true, but not both.
2. a. Using the identity, p AND q ≡ ¬(¬p OR ¬q), use truth tables to show that FR5 of listing (A.3) is not needed.
   b. Using the identity, p → q ≡ ¬p OR q, rewrite the PM axioms (A.4) using only ¬ and OR.
   c. Rewrite the PM axioms using only ¬ and AND.
   d. Rewrite the axioms using only ¬ and →.
3. Use PM to prove the triangle rule:

$$A \rightarrow B, B \rightarrow C \vdash A \rightarrow C$$

   The notation ⊢ means that if both A → B, and B → C are assumed to be true, then A → C can be proved true, i.e., A → C is a thesis. You will find the proof easier if you change each of the implications (→) into the OR form of exercise 2b.
4. Substitute ordinary multiplication (∗) for AND, addition (+) for OR. Show that each of the PM axioms has a value > 0. Here we will define negation as:

p	¬p
1	0
0	1

Here is an example: PM2: q → (p OR q) ≡ ¬q OR (p OR q)

p	q	¬q OR (p OR q)
1	1	¬1 + (1 + 1) 0 + 2 2
1	0	¬0 + (1 + 0) 1 + 1 2
0	1	¬1 + (0 + 1) 0 + 1 1
0	0	¬0 + (0 + 1) 1 + 1 2

5. Use the reductio method in the section on "Proof by Contradiction" to show the validity of:

   a. p OR ¬(p)   (Principle of the excluded middle)
   b. ¬(p AND ¬(p)) (Principle for consistency)
   c. $(p \rightarrow q) \rightarrow ((p \rightarrow r) \rightarrow (p \rightarrow (q \text{ AND } r)))$ (Composition)
   d. $((p \rightarrow q) \rightarrow ((q \rightarrow r) \rightarrow (p \rightarrow r))$
   e. $((q \rightarrow r) \rightarrow ((p \rightarrow q) \rightarrow (p \rightarrow r))$ (d and e are the Laws of Syllogism)
   f. $(¬(¬(p))) \leftrightarrow p$ ($\leftrightarrow$ means "if and only if" (iff). A proof involves two parts: a proof of $(¬(¬(p))) \rightarrow p$, and one for $p \rightarrow (¬(¬(p)))$.

6. Using the PC theses of exercise 5, make appropriate substitutions for the statement letters p, q, and r, to model in PC the following statements:
   a. One either dies of the flu or gets better, there's no two ways about it.
   b. If I pass this course, it means I really studied.
   c. All men are mortal. Socrates is a man, therefore Socrates is mortal.

7. Pick out the free and bound occurrences of variables in:
   a. $(\forall X)p(X,Y)$
   b. $p(X,Y) \rightarrow (\forall X)q(X,Y)$
   c. $((\forall X)(\exists Y)p(Y, X, f(X, Y)) \text{ OR } ¬(\forall Y)q(X, f(Y))$
   d. $((\forall X)((\exists Y)p(Y, X, f(X, Y)) \text{ OR } ¬(\forall Y)q(X, f(Y)))$
   e. $((\forall X)(\exists Y)(p(Y, X, f(X, Y)) \text{ OR } ¬(\forall Y)q(X, f(Y)))$

8. Translate the following statements into quantified statements.
   a. All dogs except pit bulls are gentle with babies.
   b. Some dogs are not gentle with babies.
   c. No one should smoke cigarettes.
   d. Someone should reduce the deficit.
   e. If everyone does his or her share, someone can reduce the deficit.

The lambda Calculus (for Chapter 8)

The lambda calculus(λ-calculus) was developed by Alonzo Church to formalize intuitive notions about functions [Church, 1941]. After the failure of set theory and formal logic to capture all of mathematics, Church attempted to see what mathematical truths could be contained in function theory. His notation, called the lambda calculus, has proven very useful in the theory of functions, and is the basis for the syntax of several functional programming languages, including LISP, SCHEME, and ML.

If we write the expression $(x + 1)$, it can be thought of as either a rule for computation, or as a variable numeric expression. As a number, $(x + 1) = (y + 1)$ will be true just in case $x = y$. However, if we wish to express the notion that the *rule* is the same, no matter what values may be substituted for x or y, we need a new notation, $\lambda x(+ \ x \ 1) = \lambda y(+ \ y \ 1)$. The notation λx indicates that x is *bound* in the expression that follows, $(+ \ x \ 1)$, which is a function of one variable, x. Since $\lambda y(+ \ y \ 1)$ differs only in that the single bound variable has been renamed from x to y, the two expressions represent the same function. In SCHEME, the expression is (`lambda` (x) (+ x 1)). A lambda expression (λxE) is called an *abstraction,* since it generalizes the expression E for any value substituted for x. The other sort of lambda expression is called an *application.* For example, $(\lambda x(+ \ x \ 1) \ 4)$, sometimes written $\lambda x.(+ \ x \ 1) \ 4$, indicates that we are to apply the function $(+ \ x \ 1)$ with 4 substituted for the bound variable x. When $(+ \ 4 \ 1)$ is evaluated, the result will be 5. In the second notation, the "." takes the place of the surrounding parentheses of the first notation.

SYNTAX AND SEMANTICS

The syntax of the lambda calculus is simplicity itself. It has three *improper symbols:* λ, (,); and an infinite list of *variables,* a, b, c, . . ., x, y, z, a_1, b_1, . . ., a_i, b_i, ... A formula is any finite combination of improper symbols and variables. There are four rules for combining the symbols and variables into well-formed formulas (wffs), and three transformation rules. The wff rules are:

1. A variable x is a wff, and the occurrence of x in this wff is free.
2. If F and A are wff's, then so is (F A). An occurrence of a variable in either F or in A or both, is free (or bound) in (F A) if it is free (or bound) in F or in A. An example of this rule is (λx(x) 2), which means that 2 is to be substituted for x.
3. If F is well-formed, and contains at least one free occurrence of a variable x, then (λxF) is well-formed. All occurrences of x in (λxF) are bound. If y is another variable occurring in F, and y is not x, then y is bound or free in (λxF), depending on whether it is bound or free in F. In λx(x+y), x is bound and y is free.
4. A formula is a wff, and variables occurring in it are free or bound, only when this follows from rules 1–3.

Given the formation rules above, lambda expressions involve deeply nested parentheses. x+y is written as $(λx(λy(+((x)y)))))$. This can be abbreviated to $(λx.λy.+ x y)$ when no ambiguity occurs.

Any function of the lambda calculus may be considered as a function of a single variable, using one of two devices. Suppose we have a function, $(λx.λy.+ x y)$, representing ordinary integer arithmetic, the function + applied to the variables x and y. This can be rewritten as $((+ x) y)$, where $(+ x)$ is a function that adds x to its single parameter, y. The other device is to consider $(+ x y)$ as $(+ (x y))$, where the single argument to + consists of the pair of variables $(x y)$. This simplifies proofs about properties of the lambda calculus, since we may assume that all lambda abstractions are single parametered.

Transformation rules depend on whether variables are bound or free, as described above in rules 1–4. The three transformation rules are called alpha (α) conversion, beta (β) conversion, and eta (η) conversion. Alpha conversion allows us to change variable names to avoid name conflicts. We will use the notation [y/x]E to mean, "Substitute y for every free occurrence of x in expression E." An example of alpha conversion is:

$$λx.E \underset{\sigma}{\leftrightarrow} λy.[y/x]E$$

where y is not free in E.

Beta conversion allows us to apply a function (lambda abstraction) to a particular argument. For example, the expression $(λx. + x 1) 4$ reduces to $(+ 4 1)$. The rule for beta conversion is:

$$(λx.E_1) E_2 \underset{\beta}{\leftrightarrow} [E_2/x]E_1$$

The final conversion rule is eta conversion, which can sometimes remove unnecessary lambda abstractions. For example:

$$(λx. + 1 x) \underset{\eta}{\leftrightarrow} (+ 1),$$

since the left and right sides describe the same function. Both beta and eta conversions are called *reductions* when converting from the left to the right side.

A few examples are in order. Suppose we want to reduce $\{λx.[λx. + (- x 1)] x 3\} 9$ using beta reduction. We are using square [], round (), and curly {} for clarity.

$$\{\lambda x.[\lambda x. + (-x\ 1)]\ x\ 3\}\ 9 \tag{B.1}$$
$$\rightarrow \quad [\lambda x. + (-x\ 1)]\ 9\ 3\} \qquad [9/x]\ \text{in}\ [\ldots]$$
$$\rightarrow \qquad + (-9\ 1)\ 3 \qquad\quad [9/x]\ \text{in}\ (\ldots)$$
$$\rightarrow \qquad + 8 \qquad 3$$
$$\rightarrow \qquad 11$$

The next example shows how three LISP functions can be written as lambda abstractions. There are three fundamental LISP functions on lists, **car**, **cdr** and **cons**. (**cons** a b) returns the dotted pair a · b, as described in Chapter 8. If lyst is a list, (**cons** head lyst) returns a new list, with the value of head appended to lyst as the first element. (**car** lyst) returns the first item of lyst, and (**cdr** lyst) returns a list containing everything on lyst but the first element. Thus if lyst = (a b c), and head = 0, the value of (**car** lyst) is a, (**cdr** lyst) is (b c), and (**cons** head lyst) is (0 a b c). Now if you recall our earlier discussion of abstract data types, a data type such as a list can be defined by functions, which are generally related. If we specify that (**car** (**cons** head lyst)) = head, and (**cdr** (**cons** head lyst)) = lyst, any functions will do as long as these relations are maintained. Now suppose we define lambda abstractions:

$$\textbf{cons} \equiv (\lambda a.\lambda b.\lambda f.f\ a\ b) \tag{B.2}$$
$$\textbf{car} \equiv (\lambda c.c\ (\lambda a.\lambda b.a)) \tag{B.3}$$
$$\textbf{cdr} \equiv (\lambda c.c\ (\lambda a.\lambda b.b)) \tag{B.4}$$

Let's check that, in fact, after beta reductions, (**cdr** (**cons** head lyst)) = lyst, as shown in listing (B.5).

$$(\textbf{cdr}\ (\textbf{cons}\ \text{head lyst})) \tag{B.5}$$
$$= (\lambda c.c\ (\lambda a.\lambda b.b))\ (\textbf{cons}\ \text{head lyst})$$
$$\rightarrow \quad (\textbf{cons}\ \text{head lyst})(\lambda a.\lambda b.b))$$
$$= \quad (\lambda a.\lambda b.\lambda f.f\ a\ b)\ \text{head lyst}\ (\lambda a.\lambda b.b)$$
$$\rightarrow \quad (\lambda b.\lambda f.f\ \text{head}\ b)\ \text{lyst}\ (\lambda a.\lambda b.b)$$
$$\rightarrow \quad (\lambda f.f\ \text{head lyst})\ \quad (\lambda a.\lambda b.b)$$
$$\rightarrow \quad (\lambda a.\lambda b.b)\ \text{head lyst}$$
$$\rightarrow \quad (\lambda b.b)\ \text{lyst}$$
$$\rightarrow \quad \text{lyst}$$

So **cdr** is related correctly to **cons**. We leave **car** as an exercise.

This is but one example showing that we really don't need special built-in functions at all, but could get along with lambda abstractions. This in fact is one of the major advantages of the lambda calculus. Church's thesis, which is accepted as true but not proven, states that any effectively computable function can be represented as a lambda abstraction. What has been proven, however, is that the Turing-computable functions (see Chapter 6) and recursive functions are equivalent to the lambda calculus, as are the systems of Markov [Markov, 1954] and of Post [Post, 1943]. It is generally believed that any one of these systems includes all functions that can be computed in finite time.

The lambda calculus has other advantages. One is that evaluation of lambda expressions can be done in any order. What this means is that if a function has several interrelated parameters, say $f(g_1(D)\ g_2(D)\ \ldots\ g_n(D))$, then the g_i can be evaluated in any order without affecting the result of f. In particular, all the g_i could be computed simultaneously, in parallel, returning results to f for the final computation. This is in sharp contrast to the sequential execution of imperative languages. What makes this possible is the lack of side effects in functional languages. The parameter, D, which is shared by all the g_i, will not be affected when any g_i is applied to it, nor when $g_i(D)$ is evaluated.

COMPUTABILITY AND CORRECTNESS

A function is a rule or method for computing a value, given a (single) parameter. A function is computable if the method terminates with a single result. Church's thesis holds that all computable functions are part of the theory of the lambda calculus. The converse of the thesis, however, is not true. Just because a particular function is lambda-definable does not guarantee that it is computable. Attempts to evaluate lambda abstractions that are not computable never terminate.

An example of a nonterminating function is the following lambda application: $(\lambda x.x\ x)(\lambda x.x\ x)$. Substituting $(\lambda x.x\ x)$ for each x in the first expression using alpha reduction, we get the nonterminating result:

$$
\begin{array}{ll}
(\lambda x.x\ x)(\lambda x.x\ x) & \text{(B.6)} \\
\rightarrow\ (\lambda x.x\ x)(\lambda x.x\ x) & \\
\rightarrow\ (\lambda x.x\ x)(\lambda x.x\ x) & \\
\rightarrow\ \ldots &
\end{array}
$$

It has been shown that there is no test function, Halts?(f), that returns YES if a computation of f terminates, and NO otherwise. Even so, the lambda calculus has some nice properties that make it particularly suitable as a basis for functional programming languages. These are:

1. Any recursive function that is expressible in the lambda calculus is equivalent to a nonrecursive lambda abstraction.
2. If two functions are equivalent, they can be reduced through alpha, beta, and eta reductions to the same form, called a *normal form*.
3. For any expression that can be reduced to a normal form, there is a normal order reduction that will produce the form.

The second property is concerned with normal forms, which are just lambda expressions that cannot be reduced further. The third property tells us how to obtain this form if it exists. A *normal order reduction* starts at the left of an expression, reducing from left to right where possible. An *applicative order reduction* reduces the innermost expression first, wherever it may occur. Although normal order may not be the most efficient reduction, it is guaranteed to produce a normal form if one exists. Nonterminating applications, such as $(\lambda x.x\ x)(\lambda x.x\ x)$, have no normal form. The existence of normal forms, and the elimination of recursion, make semantic proofs about the lambda calculus particularly straightforward.

Recall that semantics are involved with what a language means, in contrast to syntax, which is what wffs look like. Two operators are built into the lambda calculus: **APPLY**(E_1 E_2) and **EVAL**(E), which evaluates a user-defined expression. Consider the lambda expression,

$$(\lambda x.+ 1\ x) \tag{B.7}$$

which should increase the value of x by 1.

$$\textbf{APPLY}((\lambda x.+ 1\ x)\ 2) \tag{B.8}$$

is (+ 1 2) = 3.

EVAL(Add1 5) is 6, where Add1 is a function defined by the user to be the lambda expression of listing (B.7). For Add1, the effect of **EVAL** would be:

$$\textbf{EVAL}(\text{Add1 5}) \tag{B.9}$$
$$\Rightarrow \qquad \textbf{APPLY}((\lambda x.+ 1\ x)\ 5)$$
$$\Rightarrow \qquad (+ 1\ 5) = 6.$$

In practice, one of the first extensions to the lambda calculus is a list of constants, containing at least 0 and some of the common functions, such as + and *. Given this enhancement, lambda expressions mean different things in different environments. A lambda variable is assigned at most one value in any environment. However, the same variable *name* may have different values in different environments. You won't be too far off if you think of an environment as a procedure block, with all parameters passed by value. Thus a name x should be thought of as x_{e1}, x_{e2}, etc., where e1 and e2 are different environments. Given the existence of environments, the semantics of lambda expressions can be summed up as:

$$\textbf{EVAL}(k)_e \qquad = \text{constant k in environment e} \tag{B.10}$$
$$\textbf{EVAL}(x)_e \qquad = x_e$$
$$\textbf{EVAL}(E_1\ E_2)_e \ = (\textbf{EVAL}\ (E_1)_e)\ (\textbf{EVAL}(E_2)_e)$$
$$\textbf{EVAL}(\lambda x.E)_e a = \textbf{EVAL}(E) \text{ where a is an arbitrary element of e}$$
$$\textbf{EVAL}(E) \qquad = \perp \text{ where E has no normal form}^1$$

In practice, constants and built-in functions are the same in all environments. For example, **EVAL**(0) = 0, **EVAL**(+) = +, **EVAL**(TRUE) = TRUE, **EVAL**(FALSE) = FALSE, and **EVAL**(IF) = IF. Similarly, **EVAL**(IF TRUE a b) = a, and **EVAL**(IF FALSE a b) = b.

We will also insist that if two expressions E_1 and E_2 reduce to the same form E, then **EVAL**(E_1) = **EVAL**(E_2) = **EVAL**(E). For example, we noticed above that $(\lambda x+ x\ 1) = (\lambda y+ y\ 1)$, and introduced the alpha conversion rule to substitute one variable for another, guaranteeing their evaluation to the same value. However, two functions may return the same values, but not be reducible to each other. For example, $(\lambda x.* x\ x)$ and $(\lambda x.\text{expt } x\ 2)$, where (expt x 2) means x^2, return the same values. Thus **EVAL**($\lambda x.* x\ x$)) = **EVAL**($\lambda x.\text{expt } x\ 2$), but there is no common normal form to which both expressions reduce.

---

[1] The symbol $\perp$ is called "bottom" and is assigned as a value to noncomputable functions.

EXERCISES B

1. Which of the following are legal lambda abstractions?
   a. $\lambda x.x$
   b. $\lambda y(\lambda x.x)$
   c. $\lambda x(\lambda y.x)$
   d. $\lambda x(y\ (\lambda y(+\ x\ y))\ x)$
   e. $(\lambda x.+\ x\ y)$
   f. $(\lambda x.\lambda y.\ +\ x\ y)$

2. Make the following applications, and evaluate the resulting lambda expression where possible:
   a. $(\lambda x.x)\ z$
   b. $(\lambda y.\lambda x.x)\ 6$
   c. $(\lambda y.(\lambda x.x)\ 6)\ 2$
   d. $\lambda x.(y\ (\lambda y.(+\ x\ y))\ x)\ 2$
   e. $(\lambda x.(+\ x\ y))\ 5$
   f. $(\lambda x.\lambda y.\ (+\ x\ y))\ 2\ 5$

3. An abstraction, $\lambda x(\lambda y(E))$ can be written as $\lambda x.\lambda y.E$, as we have seen. It can also be abbreviated as $\lambda x\ y.E$. Rewrite the expressions of exercises 1 and 2 in this abbreviated form.

4. Show that (**car** (**cons** head lyst)) beta reduces to head (see listing (B.5)).

5. Show that given an arbitrary element a, **APPLY**$(\lambda x.(*\ x\ x)a)$ = **EVAL**(expt a 2)).

6. Show that, using eta conversion, $\lambda c.\lambda a.a$ reduces to $\lambda a.a$, and $\lambda c.\lambda a.c$ reduces to $\lambda c.c$.

7. (A challenge) Show that if TRUE = $\lambda x.\lambda y.x$, FALSE = $\lambda x.\lambda y.y$, and the conditional is **COND** = $\lambda p.\lambda a.\lambda b.(p\ a\ b)$ then **EVAL**(**COND** TRUE) = a and **EVAL**(**COND** FALSE) = b. Thus, **COND** can be rewritten as **IF** p **THEN** a **ELSE** b.

APPENDIX C

Software Sources

This appendix contains information about software for PCs running in the DOS environment. Since the Programming Languages course requires a number of different compilers and interpreters, we have chosen inexpensive implementations where possible. Lab assignments and code within the main text have been tested on the software listed below.

No attempt was made to survey all implementations available or make a judgement on the merits of different products.

CHAPTERS 1, 2: VARIABLES, DATA TYPES, AND ABSTRACTION

Pascal

Because of its popularity on college campuses, we used Turbo Pascal Version 7.0 from:

Borland Scholar Program
P.O. #660001
Scotts Valley, CA 95067-0001
(800) 932-9994, ext. 1373

Ada

Code in both the text and the MiniManual has been tested on PCs using the Meridian Ada Compiler, Version 4.1.1 for PC DOS systems, and the Verdix Ada Development System, Version 5.5 for the AT&T 3B family of computers. Both compilers are products of the Verdix Corporation whose address is shown on the next page.

Verdix Corporation
205 Van Buren Street
Herndon, VA 22070
(703) 318-5800 or (800) 653-2522

Free versions of Ada are GWU-Ada/Ed and NYU Ada/Ed. Information about downloading both is available through anonymous FTP in the directory /languages/ ada/compiler/adaed at wuarchive.wustl.edu.

For Win95, UNIX, and OS/2 systems, there is the GNU Ada translator, gnat, from New York University. Use anonymous ftp to obtain information about gnat in the pub/gnat directory at cs.nyu.edu.

CHAPTER 3: BLOCK-STRUCTURED LANGUAGES

C

We used Turbo C from Borland International at the address listed earlier.

CHAPTER 4: OBJECT-BASED LANGUAGES

Object Pascal

Turbo Pascal 7 is an object-oriented extension to Turbo Pascal and the closest you can get to an implementation of Object Pascal. It is available from Borland International.

C++

Turbo C++ is an object-oriented extension to Turbo C. It is available from Borland International.

Java

Java is a simpler C++ with some enhancements as well. It runs on Windows NT/95 and UNIX. The Java Development Kit (JDK) is available free from Sun to schools by anonymous FTP at ftp://java.sun.com/pub/ or from a Mirror site, e.g., ftp://www. blackdown.org/pub/java/pub/ or ftp://sunsite.unc.edu/pub/languages/java. There's a general index for other sources on Java at http://java.sun.com/about.html.

CHAPTER 5: DISTRIBUTED PROGRAMMING

Ada

Addresses for providers of Ada implementations are listed earlier.

C-Linda

C-Linda is available through:

> Scientific Computing Associates, Inc.
> 265 Church Street
> New Haven, CT 06510
> (203) 777-7442

Occam

Occam is available for use with PC add-in boards called transputers. The Transputer Education Kit includes a transputer, an Occam compiler, and documentation for the transputer and the C and Occam languages. It is available from:

> Computer System Architects
> 950 N. University Avenue
> Provo, Utah 84604
> (801) 374-2300

Pascal S

For copies of Pascal S see the *Instructor's Manual*. Source code is listed in an appendix to [Ben-Ari, 1982], or contact:

> Professor Carol Torsone
> Computer Science Department
> St. John Fisher College
> Rochester, NY 14618
> cmt@sjfc.edu

CHAPTER 7: LOGIC PROGRAMMING

PROLOG

micro-Prolog is available from:

> Logic Programming Associates, Ltd.
> 10 Burntwood Close
> London SW18 3JU
> England
> 01-874-0350 (24-hour phone)

In the United States, LPA PROLOG is distributed by Programming Logic Systems, Inc., whose address is shown on the next page.

Programming Logic Systems, Inc.
31 Crescent Drive
Milford, CT 06460
(203) 877-7988

A compiled version of Edinburgh PROLOG is available in an educational version from:

Arity Corporation
30 Domino Drive
Concord, MA 01742
(508) 371-1243 or (800) 722-7489

CHAPTER 8: FUNCTIONAL (APPLICATIVE) PROGRAMMING

SCHEME

There are many versions of LISP available for microcomputers. We chose PC SCHEME Version 3.03 because of its ease of use, closeness to the lambda calculus, and minimal cost. It is available from:

Richard Weyhrauch
Ibuki
P.O. Box 1627
Los Altos, CA 94022
rw@ibuki.com
(415) 961-4996/(415) 961-8016 (FAX)

PC-SCHEME is also available free by anonymous FTP from altdorf.ai.mit.edu in /archive/pc-scheme.

A newer version than PC SCHEME is EdScheme for DOS or 3DScheme and the WinScheme Editor for Windows 3.1 or higher. They are available from:

Schemers Inc.
2136 N.E. 68th Street, Suite 401
Ft. Lauderdale, FL 33308
71020.1774@compuserve.com
(305) 776-7376/(305) 776-6174 (FAX)

CHAPTER 9: LANGUAGES FOR DATABASES

SQL

Lab 9 is written for use with dBASE IV. The implementation is a limited functionality version, available for training and demonstration purposes. dBASE student editions are available from Borland at the address listed earlier.

References

Abelson, 1985   Abelson, H., Sussman, G.J., and Sussman, J. (1985). *Structure and interpretation of computer programs.* Cambridge, MA: MIT Press.

Ada 9X, 1993   *Introducing Ada 9X: Ada 9X project report.* Cambridge, MA: Intermetrics.

Adams, 1992   Adams, J.C., Brainerd, W.S., Martin, J.T., Smith, B.T., and Wagener, J.L. (1992). *Fortran 90 handbook: Complete ANSI/ISO reference.* New York: McGraw-Hill.

Agha, 1987   Agha, G., and Hewitt, C. (1988). Actors: A conceptual foundation for concurrent object-oriented programming. In *Research directions in object oriented programming,* edited by B. Shriver and P. Wegner, pp. 49–74. Cambridge, MA: MIT Press.

Aho, 1979   Aho, A.V. and Ullman, J.D. (1979). *Principles of Compiler Design.* Reading, MA: Addison-Wesley.

Aho, 1986   Aho, A.V., Sethi, R., and Ullman, J.D. (1986). *Compilers: Principles, techniques, and tools.* Reading, MA: Addison-Wesley.

Aït-Kaci, 1983   Aït-Kaci, H., Lincoln, P., and Nasr, R. (1983). Le Fun: Logic, equations, and functions. In *Proceedings of the 1987 Symposium on Logic Programming,* pp. 17–23. Washington, DC: IEEE Computer Society Press.

Andrews, 1983   Andrews, G.R., and Schneider, F.B. (1983). Concepts and notations for concurrent programming. *ACM computing surveys* 15(1): 3–43.

ANSI/IEEE-770X3.97, 1983   *American national standard Pascal computer programming language.* New York: IEEE.

ANSI-1815A, 1983   *Military standard: Ada® programming language.* Washington, DC: American National Standards Institute.

ANSI/ISO-8652, 1995   *American national standard for the Ada programming language.* Washington, DC: American National Standards Institute.

ANSI/ISO-9899, 1990 *The annotated ANSI C standard*, American National Standard for Programming Languages—C, ANSI/ISO 9899-1990 (annotated by H. Schildt). Berkeley, CA: Osborne McGraw-Hill.

ANSI/ISO-9899, 1994 ISO/IEC Amendment 1 to C Standard 9899: 1990 (1994). Geneva: International Standards Org. (ISO).

ANSI/ISO-X3J11, 1986 *Draft proposed American national standard for information systems—Programming language C*. Washington, DC: American National Standards Institute.

ANSI/ISO-X3.135, 1992 *Database language SQL*. Washington, DC: American National Standards Institute, Inc. Also as International Organization for Standardization Document ISO/IEC 9075:1992.

Appleby, 1988 Appleby, K., Carlsson, M., Haridi, S., and Sahlin, D. (1988). Garbage collection for Prolog based on WAM. *CACM* 31(6): 719–741.

Atkinson, 1987 Atkinson, M.P., and Buneman, O.P. (1987). Types and persistence in database programming. *ACM computing surveys* 19(2): 105–190.

Auer, 1989 Auer, K. (1989). Which object-oriented language should we choose? *Hotline on object-oriented technology*. New York: SIGS Publications.

Backus, 1978 Backus, J. (1978). Can programming be liberated from the vonNeumann style? *CACM* 21(8): 613–641.

Bal, 1988 Bal, H.E., and Tanenbaum, A.S. (1988). Distributed programming with shared data. In *Proceedings of the 1988 International Conference on Computer Languages*, 82–91. Washington, DC: IEEE Computer Society Press.

Bal, 1989 Bal, H.E., Steiner, J.G., and Tanenbaum, A.S. (1989). Programming languages for distributed systems. *ACM computing surveys* 21(3): 261–322.

Ball, 1989 Ball, M.S. (1989). Implementing multiple inheritance. *The C++ Report* 1(9): 1–6.

Barnes, 1994 Barnes, J.G.P. (1994). *Programming in Ada*. London: Addison-Wesley.

Barnes, 1996 Barnes, J. (1996). *Programming in Ada 95*. Reading, MA: Addison-Wesley.

Baron, 1986 Baron, N. (1986). *Computer languages*. Garden City, NY: Anchor Press/Doubleday.

Ben-Ari, 1982 Ben-Ari, M. (1982). *Principles of concurrent programming*. Englewood Cliffs, NJ: Prentice-Hall International.

Ben-Ari, 1990 Ben-Ari, M. (1990). *Principles of concurrent and distributed programming*. Englewood Cliffs, NJ: Prentice-Hall International.

Blair, 1989 Blair, G.S., Gallagher, J.J., and Malik, J. (1989). Genericity vs delegation vs conformance vs . . . . *Journal of object-oriented programming* 2(3): 11–17.

Bobrow, 1983 Bobrow, D.G., and Stefik, M.J. (1983). *The LOOPS manual*. Palo Alto, CA: Xerox.

Booch, 1986 Booch, G. (1986). *Software engineering with Ada*. 2nd ed. Menlo Park, CA: Benjamin/Cummings.

Booch, 1994 Booch, G. (1994). *Object oriented design with applications*. 2nd ed. Redwood City, CA: Benjamin/Cummings.

Branquart, 1971 Branquart, P., Lewi, J., Sintzoff, M., and Wodon, P.L. (1971). The composition of semantics in Algol 68. *CACM* 14(11): 697–707.

Brender, 1981 Brender, R.F., and Nassi, I.R. (1981). What is Ada? In *Ada: Programming in the 80's*. Reprinted from *Computer*, 14(6): 17–24.

Brinch Hansen, 1975   Brinch Hansen, P. (1975). The programming language Concurrent Pascal. *IEEE transactions on software engineering* 1(6): 199-207.

Brinch Hansen, 1978   Brinch Hansen, P. (1978). Distributed processes: A concurrent programming concept. *CACM* 21(11): 934-941.

Bryan, 1990   Bryan, D.L., and Mendal, G.O. (1990). *Exploring Ada.* Vol. 1. Englewood Cliffs, NJ: Prentice Hall.

Buzzard, 1985   Buzzard, G.D., and Mudge, T.N. (1985). Object-based computing and the Ada programming language. *Computer* 18(3): 11–19. Also in *Tutorial: Object oriented computing.* Vol. 1, *Concepts,* edited by G.E. Peterson (1987), pp. 115–123. Washington, DC: IEEE Computer Society Press.

Calingaert, 1988   Calingaert, P. (1988). *Program translation fundamentals: Methods and issues.* Rockville, MD: Computer Science Press.

Caromel, 1989   Caromel, D. (1989). Service, asynchrony, and wait-by-necessity. *Journal of object-oriented programming* 2(4): 12–22.

Caromel, 1993   Caromel, D. (1993). Toward a method of object-oriented concurrent programming. *CACM* 36(9): 90–102.

Carriero, 1989   Carriero, N., and Gelernter, D. (1989). Linda in context. *CACM* 32(4): 444–458.

Catell, 1994   Catell, R.G.G. (1994). *Object data management: Object-oriented and extended relational database systems.* Rev. ed. Reading, MA: Addison-Wesley.

Chamberland, 1995   Chamberland, L. (1995). *Fortran 90: A reference guide.* Upper Saddle River, NJ: Prentice Hall.

Chomsky, 1965   Chomsky, N. (1965). *Aspects of the theory of syntax.* Cambridge, MA: MIT Press.

Chomsky, 1966   Chomsky, N. (1966). *Cartesian linguistics.* New York: Harper and Row.

Chomsky, 1988   Chomsky, N. (1988). *The culture of terrorism.* Boston: South End Press.

Church, 1941   Church, A. (1941). *The calculi of lambda conversion.* Princeton, NJ: Princeton Univ. Press.

Clark, 1984   Clark, K.L., and McCabe, F.G. (1984). *micro-Prolog: Programming in logic.* Englewood Cliffs, NJ: Prentice-Hall.

Clark, 1973   Clark, R.L. (1973). A linguistic contribution to goto-less programming. *Datamation* 19(12): 62–63.

C-Linda, 1990   *C-Linda® reference manual.* New Haven, CT: Scientific Computing Associates.

Clocksin, 1984   Clocksin, W.F., and Mellish, C.S. (1984). *Programming in Prolog.* 2nd ed. Berlin: Springer-Verlag.

Cohen, 1991   Cohen, D.I.A. (1991). *Introduction to computer theory.* Rev. ed. New York: Wiley.

Cohen, 1985   Cohen, J. (1985). Describing Prolog by its interpretation and compilation. *CACM* 28(12): 1311–1324.

Cohen, 1988   Cohen, J. (1988). A view of the origins and development of Prolog. *CACM* 31(1): 26–37.

Colmerauer, 1985   Colmerauer, A. (1985). Prolog in 10 figures. *CACM* 28(12): 1296–1310.

Cooper, 1983   Cooper, D. (1983). *Standard Pascal user reference manual.* New York: Norton.

Cooper, 1985 Cooper, D., and Clancy, M. (1985). *OH! PASCAL.* New York: Norton.

Cox, 1984 Cox, B.J. (1984). Message/object programming: An evolutionary change in programming technology. *IEEE software,* January, 1984: 50–61. Also in *Tutorial: Object oriented computing,* Vol. 1, *Concepts* edited by G.E. Peterson (1987), pp. 150–161. Washington, DC: Computer Society Press.

Dahl, 1966 Dahl, O., and Nygaard, J. (1966). SIMULA—An Algol based simulation language. *CACM* 9(9): 671–681.

Date, 1993 Date, C.J. (1993). *A guide to the SQL standard.* 3rd ed. Reading, MA: Addison-Wesley.

Date, 1995 Date, C.J. (1995). *An introduction to database system*s. 6th ed. Reading, MA: Addison-Wesley.

Dauben, 1979 Dauben, W. (1979). *Georg Cantor.* Cambridge, MA: Harvard Univ. Press.

December, 1995 December, J. (1995). *Presenting Java.* Indianapolis, IN: Sams.net.

DeGroot, 1984 DeGroot, D. (1984). *Prolog and knowledge information processing: A tutorial.* Unpublished manuscript, IBM, T.J. Watson Research Center, Yorktown Heights, NY.

Deitel, 1994 Deitel, H.M., and Deitel, P.J. (1994). *C++: How to program.* Englewood Cliffs, NJ: Prentice Hall.

Denning, 1988 Denning, P.J., Comer, D.E., Gries, D. Mulder, M.C., Tucker, A., Turner, A.J., and Young, P.R. (1988). Report of the ACM task force on the core of computer science (Order #201880). Baltimore: ACM Order Dept. Also condensed in *CACM* 32(1): 9–23.

Digitalk, 1986 *Smalltalk/V: Tutorial and Programming Handbook.* Los Angeles: Digitalk, Inc.

Dijkstra, 1968a Dijkstra, E.W. (1968). Cooperating sequential processes. In *Programming languages,* edited by F. Genuys. Reprinted from the Technological University, Eindhoven (1965), pp. 43–112. New York: Academic Press.

Dijkstra, 1968b Dijkstra, E.W. (1968). Go to statement considered harmful. *CACM* 11(3): 147–148.

Duncan, 1990 Duncan, R. (1990). A survey of parallel computer architectures. *Computer* 23(2): 5–16.

Dybvig, 1987 Dybvig, K.R. (1987). *The SCHEME programming language.* Englewood Cliffs, NJ: Prentice-Hall.

Eisenbach, 1987 Eisenbach, S. (ed.) (1987). *Functional programming: languages, tools and architectures.* New York: Wiley.

Ellis, 1990 Ellis, M.A., and Stroustrup, B. (1990). *The annotated C++ reference manual.* Reading, MA: Addison-Wesley.

Emery, 1986 Emery, G. (1986). *BCPL and C.* Oxford, UK: Blackwell Scientific Publications.

Falkoff, 1976 Falkoff, A. (1976). Some implications of shared variables. In *Formal languages and programming,* edited by R. Aguilar. Amsterdam: North Holland.

Feigenbaum, 1983 Feigenbaum, E.A., and McCorduck, P. (1983). *The Fifth Generation: Artificial Intelligence and Japan's Computer Challenge to the World.* Reading, MA: Addison-Wesley.

Feuer, 1982   Feuer, A.R., and Gehani, N.H. (1982). A comparison of the programming languages C and PASCAL. *ACM computing surveys* 14(1): 73–92.

Feuer, 1989   Feuer, A.R. (1989). *The C puzzle book.* 2nd ed. Englewood Cliffs, NJ: Prentice-Hall.

Flanagan, 1996   Flanagan, D. (1996). *Java in a nutshell.* Sebastapol, CA: O'Reilly.

Friedman, 1987   Friedman, D.P. (1987). *The little lisper.* Cambridge, MA: MIT Press.

Gabriel, 1989   Gabriel, R.P. (ed.) (1989). Draft report on requirements for a common prototyping system. *SIGPLAN notices* 24(3): 93–165.

Gallaire, 1984   Gallaire, H., and Minker, J. (1984). Logic and databases: A deductive approach. *ACM computing surveys* 16(2): 153–185.

Gehani, 1986   Gehani, N.H., and Roome, W.D. (1986). Concurrent C. *Software-practice and experience* 16(9): 821–844.

Gehani, 1994   Gehani, N.H. (1994). *ADA: An advanced introduction.* Summit, NJ: Silicon Press.

Genesereth, 1985   Genesereth, M.R., and Ginsberg, M.L. (1985). Logic programming. *CACM* 28(9): 933–941.

Ghezzi, 1987   Ghezzi, C., and Jazayeri, M. (1987). *Programming language concepts.* 2nd ed. New York: Wiley.

Glenn, 1959   Glenn, J., and James, R.C. (eds.) (1959). *Mathematics dictionary.* Princeton: Van Nostrand.

Goguen, 1984   Goguen, J.A., and Meseguer, J. (1984). Equality, types, modules and (why not?) generics for logic programming. *Journal of logic programming* 1(2): 179–210.

Goldstein, 1989   Goldstein, T. (1989). Tutorial: Part I: Derivation. *The C++ report* 1(1): 4–6.

Gordon, 1979   Gordon, R. (1979). *The denotational description of programming languages.* New York: Springer-Verlag.

Gosling, 1996   Gosling, J., and McGilton, H. (1996). The Java™ language environment: A white paper. http://java.sun.com/

Graham, 1980   Graham, S.L., Harrison, M.A., and Ruzzo, W.L. (1980). An improved context-free recognizer. *ACM transactions on programming languages and systems* 2(3): 415–462.

Gries, 1971   Gries, D. (1971). *Compiler construction for digital computers.* New York: Wiley.

Gries, 1981   Gries, D. (1981). *The science of programming.* New York: Springer-Verlag.

Griffiths, 1965   Griffiths, T.V., and Petrick, S.R. (1965). On the relative efficiencies of context-free grammar recognizers. *CACM* 8(5): 289–300.

Grune, 1977   Grune, D. (1977). A view of coroutines. *Sigplan notices* 12(7): 75–81.

Guttag, 1977   Guttag, J.V. (1977). Abstract data types and the development of data structures. *CACM* 20(6): 396–404.

Halmos, 1960   Halmos, P.R. (1960). *Naive set theory.* New York: Van Nostrand.

Harbison, 1995   Harbison, S.P., and Steele, G.L., Jr. (1995). *C, a reference manual.* 4th ed. Englewood Cliffs, NJ: Prentice-Hall.

Harmon, 1985   Harmon, P., and King, D. (1985). *Expert systems: AI in business.* New York: Wiley.

Hayes-Roth, 1985   Hayes-Roth, F. (1985). Rule-based systems. *CACM* 28(9): 921–932.

Helmbold, 1965   Helmbold, D., and Luckham, D. (1985). Debugging Ada tasking programs. *IEEE software* 2(3): 47–57.

Hoare, 1969   Hoare, C.A.R. (1969). An axiomatic basis for computer programming. *CACM* 12(10): 576–583. Also in *Tutorial: Programming language design,* edited by A.I. Wasserman (1980), pp. 500–505. Los Alamitos, CA: IEEE Computer Society Press.

Hoare, 1972   Hoare, C.A.R. (1972). Proof of correctness of data representations. *Acta informatica* 1(1): 271–281.

Hoare, 1973   Hoare, C.A.R. (1973). Hints on programming language design. Technical report no. CS-73-403. Computer Science Department, Stanford University. Stanford, CA. Also in *Programming languages: A grand tour.* 3rd ed., edited by E. Horowitz (1987), pp. 31–40. New York: Freeman.

Hoare, 1985   Hoare, C.A.R., and Shepherdson, J.C. (eds.) (1985). *Mathematical logic and programming languages.* Englewood Cliffs, NJ: Prentice-Hall International.

Hodges, 1983   Hodges, A. (1983). *Alan Turing: The enigma.* New York: Simon and Schuster.

Hofstadter, 1985a   Hofstadter, D.R. (1985). Lisp: Atoms and lists, Lists and recursion, and Recursion and generality. In *Metamagical themas,* pp. 396–424. New York: Basic Books.

Hofstadter, 1985b   Hofstadter, D.R. (1985). Review of *Alan Turing: The enigma.* In *Metamagical themas,* pp. 483–491. New York: Basic Books.

Hopcroft, 1979   Hopcroft, J.E., and Ullman, J.D. (1979). *Introduction to automata theory, languages and computation.* Reading, MA: Addison-Wesley.

HOPL-II, 1993   *The Second ACM SIGPLAN History of Programming Languages Conference* (1993, Cambridge, MA). New York: ACM.

Horowitz, 1984   Horowitz, E. (1984). *Fundamentals of programming languages.* 2nd ed. Rockville, MD: Computer Science Press.

Horowitz, 1987   Horowitz, E. (ed) (1987). *Programming languages: A grand tour.* 3rd ed. New York: Freeman.

Hudak, 1989   Hudak, P. (1989). Conception, evolution, and application of functional programming languages. *ACM computing surveys* 21(3): 359–411.

Hughes, 1968   Hughes, G.E., and Cresswell, M.J. (1968). *An introduction to modal logic.* London: Methuen.

Hull, 1987   Hull, R., and King, R. (1987). Semantic database modeling: Survey, applications, and research issues. *ACM computing surveys* 19(3): 201–260.

Ichikawa, 1991   Ichikawa, T. (1991). Present situation and future prospects on AI utilization in Japan. Japan Information Processing Development Center (JIPDEC).

IEEE-754, 1985   *Binary floating-point arithmetic, IEEE Standard 754.* New York: IEEE Press.

ISO-DP7185, 1980   *Second DP 7185. Specification for the Computer Programming Language Pascal,* May, 1980. Geneva: ISO.

Jackson, 1986   Jackson, P. (1986). *Introduction to expert systems.* Reading, MA: Addison-Wesley.

Jacobson, 1982   Jacobson, P., and Pullum, G.K. (eds.) (1982). *The nature of syntactic representation.* Boston: Reidel.

Jensen, 1974   Jensen, K., and Wirth, N. (1974). *Pascal user manual and report.* 2nd ed. New York: Springer-Verlag.

Johnson, 1988   Johnson, R.E., and Foote, B. (1988). Designing reusable classes. *Journal of object-oriented programming* 1(2): 22–35.

Johnsonbaugh, 1993   Johnsonbaugh, R. (1993). *Discrete mathematics.* 3rd ed. New York: MacMillan.

Jonsson, 1989   Jonsson, D. (1989). Next: The elimination of goto-patches? *SIGPLAN notices* 24(3): 85–92.

Kamin, 1990   Kamin, Samuel N. (1990). *Programming languages: an interpreter-based approach.* Reading, MA: Addison-Wesley.

Karaorman, 1993   Karaorman, M., and Bruno, J. (1993). Introducing concurrency to a sequential language. *CACM* 36(9): 103–116.

Kernighan, 1978   Kernighan, B.W., and Ritchie, D.M. (1978). *The C programming language.* Englewood Cliffs, NJ: Prentice-Hall.

Kerridge, 1987   Kerridge, J. (1987). *Occam programming: A practical approach.* London: Blackwell Scientific.

Knuth, 1967   Knuth, D.E. (1967). The remaining troublespots in ALGOL 60. *CACM* 10(10): 611–617. Also in *Programming languages: A grand tour.* 3rd ed., edited by E. Horowitz (1987), pp. 61–68. New York: Freeman.

Knuth, 1981   Knuth, D.E. (1981). *The art of computer programming.* 2nd ed. Vol. 2, *Seminumerical algorithms.* Reading, MA: Addison-Wesley.

Kowalski, 1985   Kowalski, R.A. (1985). The relation between logic programming and logic specification. In *Mathematical logic and programming languages,* edited by C.A.R. Hoare and J.C. Shepherdson (1985), pp. 11–27. Englewood Cliffs, NJ: Prentice-Hall International.

Kowalski, 1988   Kowalski, R.A. (1988). The early years of logic programming. *CACM* 31(1): 38–43.

Krasner, 1983   Krasner, G. (1983). *SMALLTALK-80: Bits of history, words of advice.* Reading, MA: Addison-Wesley.

Kristensen, 1987   Kristensen, B.B., Madsen, O.L., Moller-Pedersen, B., and Nygaard, K. (1987). The BETA programming language. In *Research directions in object-oriented programming,* edited by B. Shriver and P. Wegner (1987), pp. 8–48. Cambridge, MA: MIT Press.

Kuhn, 1962   Kuhn, T.S. (1962). *The structure of scientific revolutions.* Chicago: Univ. of Chicago Press.

Kuhn, 1970   Kuhn, T.S. (1970). *The structure of scientific revolutions.* 2nd ed., enlarged. Chicago: Univ. of Chicago Press.

Leler, 1990   Leler, W. (1990). Linda meets Unix. *Computer* 23(2): 43–54.

Lesk, 1975   Lesk, M.E. (1975). *LEX-a lexical analyzer generator.* CSTR 39. Murray Hill, NJ: Bell Labs.

Lewis, 1981   Lewis, H.R., and Papadimitriou, C.H. (1981). *Elements of the theory of computation.* Englewood Cliffs, NJ: Prentice-Hall.

Liskov, 1975   Liskov, B.H., and Zilles, S.N. (1975). Specification techniques for data abstractions. *IEEE transactions on software engineering* 1(1): 7–19.

Liskov, 1977   Liskov, B., Snyder, A., Atkinson, R., and Schaffert, C. (1977) Abstraction mechanisms in CLU. *CACM* 20(8): 564–576. Also in *Programming languages: A grand tour.* 3rd ed., edited by E. Horowitz (1987), pp. 254–266. New York: Freeman.

Liskov, 1986   Liskov, B., and Guttag, J. (1986). *Abstraction and specification in program development.* Cambridge, MA: MIT Press.

Louden, 1993   Louden, K.C. (1993). *Programming languages: Principles and practice.* Boston: PWS.

Lucas, 1988   Lucas, R. (1988). *Database applications using Prolog.* New York: Wiley.

McCarthy, 1960   McCarthy, J. (1960). Recursive functions of symbolic expressions. *CACM* 4(3): 184–195. Also in *Programming languages: A grand tour.* 3rd ed., edited by E. Horowitz (1987), pp. 203–214. New York: Freeman.

McCarthy, 1965   McCarthy, J., and Levin, J. (1965). *LISP 1.5 programmers manual.* Cambridge, MA: MIT Press. Also in *Programming languages: A grand tour.* 3rd ed., edited by E. Horowitz (1987), pp. 215–239. New York: Freeman.

MacLennan, 1987   MacLennan, B.J. (1987). *Programming languages: Design, evaluation and implementation.* 2nd ed. New York: Holt, Rinehart, and Winston.

Madsen, 1987   Madsen, O.L. (1987). Block structure and object-oriented languages. In *Research directions in object oriented programming,* edited by B. Shriver and P. Wegner (1987), pp.113–128. Cambridge, MA: MIT Press.

Malpas, 1987   Malpas, J. (1987). *PROLOG: A relational language and its applications.* Englewood Cliffs, NJ: Prentice-Hall.

Mandrioli, 1986   Mandrioli, D., and Ghezzi, C. (1986). *Theoretical computer science.* New York: Wiley.

Mano, 1982   Mano, M.M. (1982). *Computer system architecture.* 2nd ed. Englewood Cliffs, NJ: Prentice-Hall.

March, 1989   March, S.T. (ed.) (1989). *ACM computing surveys* 21(3). Special issue on "Programming Language Paradigms."

Marcotty, 1976   Marcotty, M., Ledgard, H.V., and Bochmann, G.V. (1976). A sampler of formal definitions. *ACM computing surveys* 8(2): 191–276.

Markoff, 1992   Markoff, J. (1992). David Gelernter's Romance with Linda. New York: New York Times, 01/19/92, sec. 3 p.1 c.2.

Markov, 1954   Markov, A.A. (1954). The theory of algorithms. *Trudy matematicheskogo instituta imeni V.A. Steklova.* 42. (in Russian); English translation, Jerusalem: Israel Program for Scientific Translations, 1961.

Mendelson, 1979   Mendelson, E. (1979). *Introduction to mathematical logic.* Princeton, NJ: Van Nostrand.

Meyer, 1988   Meyer, B. (1988). Eiffel: Harnessing multiple inheritance. *Journal of object oriented programming* 1(4): 48–51.

Michaelson, 1989   Michaelson, G. (1989). *An introduction to functional programming through lambda calculus.* Wokingham, UK: Addison-Wesley.

Milner, 1990   Milner, R., Tofte, M., and Harper, R. (1990). *The Definition of Standard ML.* Cambridge, MA: MIT Press.

Milner, 1991   Milner, R., and Tofte, M. (1991). *Commentary on Standard ML.* Cambridge, MA: MIT Press.

Moon, 1986   Moon, D. (1986). Object-oriented programming with Flavors. *ACM SIGPLAN notices* 21(11): 1–16.

Moskowitz, 1989   Moskowitz, R. (1989). Object oriented programming: The future is now. *PC Times,* October 2, 1989, p. 3.

Mueller, 1990   Mueller, R.A., and Page, R.L. (1990). *Symbolic computing with Lisp and Prolog.* New York: Wiley.

Nagel, 1958   Nagel, E., and Newman, J.R. (1958). *Gödel's Proof.* New York: NYU Press.

Naur, 1963   Naur, P. (ed.) (1963). Report on the algorithmic language ALGOL 60. *CACM* 6(1): 1–17. Also in *Programming languages: A grand tour.* 3rd ed., edited by E. Horowitz (1987), pp. 44–60. New York: Freeman.

Nygaard, 1981   Nygaard, K., and Dahl, O-J. (1981). The development of the Simula languages, and Transcript of presentation. In *History of programming languages,* edited by R. Wexelblat (1981), pp. 439–491. New York: Academic Press.

Parnas, 1971   Parnas, D.L. (1971). Information distribution aspects of design methodology. In *Proceedings of the 1971 IFIP Congress,* pp. 26–30. Amsterdam: North Holland.

Parnas, 1972   Parnas, D.L. (1972). On the criteria to be used in decomposing systems into modules. *CACM* 15(12): 1053–1058.

Pascoe, 1986   Pascoe, G.A. (1986). Elements of object-oriented programming. *Byte,* August, 1986. Also in *Tutorial: Object oriented computing.* Vol 1, *Concepts* edited by G.E. Peterson, (1987), pp. 15–20. Washington, DC: Computer Society Press.

Peckham, 1988   Peckham, J., and Maryanski, F. (1988). Semantic data models. *ACM computing surveys* 20(3): 153–189.

Peterson, 1987   Peterson, G.E. (ed.) (1987). Tutorial: Object oriented computing. Vol. 1, *Concepts.* Washington, DC: Computer Society Press.

Peyton Jones, 1987   Peyton Jones, S.L. (1987). *The implementation of functional programming languages.* Hemel Hempstead, Hertfordshire, UK: Prentice Hall International.

Pittman, 1992   Pittman, T., and Peters, J. (1992). *The art of compiler design: Theory and practice.* Englewood Cliffs, NJ: Prentice-Hall.

Plauger, 1996   Plauger, P.J., and Brodie, J. (1996). *Standard C: A reference.* Upper Saddle River, NJ: Prentice-Hall.

Poe, 1984   Poe, M.D., Nasr, R., and Slinn, J.A. (1984). Kwic bibliography on Prolog and logic programming. *Journal of logic programming* 1: 81–142.

Post, 1943   Post, E.L. (1943). Formal reductions of the general combinatorial decision problem. *American journal of mathematics* 65: 197–215.

Pratt, 1975   Pratt, T. (1975). *Programming languages: Design and implementation.* Englewood Cliffs, NJ: Prentice-Hall.

Pratt, 1995   Pratt, T., and Zelkowitz, M.V. (1995). *Programming languages: Design and Implementation.* 3rd ed. Englewood Cliffs, NJ: Prentice-Hall.

ProcSLP, 1986   *Proceedings of the 1986 Symposium on Logic Programming.* Washington, DC: IEEE Computer Society Press.

Randall, 1960   Randall, J.H., Jr. (1960). *Aristotle.* New York: Columbia Univ. Press.

Raymond, 1993   Raymond, E.S. (ed.) (1993). *The new hacker's dictionary.* 2nd ed. Cambridge, MA: MIT Press.

Rees, 1987   Rees, J., and Clinger, W. (eds.) (1987). Revised³ report on the algorithmic language Scheme. Artificial Intelligence Memo 848a. Cambridge, MA: MIT Artificial Intelligence Lab.

Rentsch, 1982   Rentsch, T. (1982). Object-oriented programming. *SIGPLAN notices* 17(9): 51–57. Also in *Tutorial: Object oriented computing*. Vol. 1, *Concepts*, edited by G.E. Peterson (1987), pp. 21–27. Washington, DC: Computer Society Press.

Rich, 1991   Rich, E. (1991). *Artificial intelligence*. 2nd ed. New York: McGraw-Hill.

Richards, 1979   Richards, M., and Whitby-Stevens, C. (1979). *BCPL—the language and its compiler*. Cambridge, UK: Cambridge Univ. Press.

Ringwood, 1988   Ringwood, G.A. (1988). Parlog86 and the dining logicians. *CACM* 31(1): 10–25.

Robinson, 1965   Robinson, J.A. (1965). A machine-oriented logic based on the resolution principle. *JACM* 12(1). Also in *Automation of reasoning*. Vol. 1, *Classical papers on computational logic, 1957-1966,* edited by J. Siekmann and W. Graham (1983), pp. 397–415. Berlin: Springer-Verlag.

Robinson, 1983   Robinson, J.A. (1983). Logic programming—past, present, and future. *New generation computing* 1: 107–124.

Rogers, 1967   Rogers, H., Jr. (1967). *The theory of recursive functions and effective computability*. New York: McGraw-Hill.

Ross, 1923   Ross, D. (1923). *Aristotle*. London: Methuen.

Royce, 1987   Royce, W. (1987). Managing the development of large software systems: Concepts and techniques. In *Proceedings of the Ninth International Conference on Software Engineering,* pp. 328–338. Washington, DC: IEEE Computer Society Press.

Rubin, 1987   Rubin, F. (1987). GOTO considered harmful. *CACM* 30(3): 195–196.

Sammet, 1969   Sammet, J. (1969). *Programming languages: History and fundamentals*. Englewood Cliffs, NJ: Prentice-Hall.

Saunders, 1989   Saunders, J.H. (1989). A survey of object-oriented programming languages. *Journal of object-oriented programming* 1(6): 5–13.

Scholz, 1961   Scholz, H. (1961). *Concise history of logic* (K.F. Leidecker, trans.). New York: Philosophical Library.

Sebesta, 1993   Sebesta, R.W. (1993). *Concepts of programming languages*. 2nd ed. Menlo Park, CA: Benjamin/Cummings.

Sergot, 1986   Sergot, M.J., Sadri, R.A., Kowalski, F., Kriwaczek, P.H., and Cory, H.T. (1986). The British Nationality Act as a logic program. *CACM* 29(5): 370–386.

Sethi, 1989   Sethi, R. (1989). *Programming languages: Concepts and constructs*. Reading, MA: Addison-Wesley.

Shapiro, 1989   Shapiro, E. (1989). The family of concurrent logic programming languages. *ACM computing surveys* 21(3): 412–510.

Shatz, 1989   Shatz, S.M., and Wang, J-P. (1989). *Tutorial: Distributed software engineering*. Washington, DC: IEEE Computer Society Press.

Shopiro, 1989   Shopiro, J.E. (1989). An example of multiple inheritance in C++: A model of the iostream library. *SIGPLAN notices* 24(12): 32–36.

Shriver, 1987   Shriver, B., and Wegner, P. (eds.) (1987). *Research directions in object-oriented programming*. Cambridge, MA: MIT Press.

Shumate, 1988   Shumate, K., and Kjell, N. (1988). A taxonomy of Ada packages. *Ada letters* 8(2): 55–76.

Siklóssy, 1976   Siklóssy, L. (1976). *Let's talk Lisp.* Englewood Cliffs, NJ: Prentice-Hall.

Silvester, 1984   Silvester, P. (1984). *The Unix system guidebook: An introductory guide for serious users.* New York: Springer-Verlag.

Simonian, 1988   Simonian, R., and Crone, M. (1988). InnovAda: True object-oriented programming in Ada. *Journal of object-oriented programming* 1(4): 14–23.

Slater, 1987   Slater, R. (1987). *Portraits in silicon.* Cambridge, MA: MIT Press.

Smedema, 1983   Smedema, C.H., Medema, P., and Boasson, M. (1983). *The programming languages Pascal, Modula, Chill, Ada.* Englewood-Cliffs, NJ: Prentice-Hall.

Sosnowski, 1987   Sosnowski, R.A. (1987). Prolog dialects: A déjà vu of BASICs. *SIGPLAN notices* 22(6): 39–48.

Steele, 1978   Steele, G.L., Jr., and Sussman, G.J. (1978). The revised report on Scheme, a dialect of Lisp. Artificial Intelligence Memo 452. Cambridge, MA: MIT Artificial Intelligence Lab.

Steele, 1984   Steele, G.L., Jr. (1984). *Common LISP: The language.* Burlington, MA: Digital Press.

Steele, 1993   Steele, G.L., Jr., and Gabriel, R.P. (1993). The evolution of LISP. *ACM History of Programming Languages II,* Cambridge, MA: (April, 1993) *SIGPLAN notices* 3(28): 231–270.

Stefik, 1986.   Stefik, M., and Bobrow, D.G. (1986). Object-oriented programming: Themes and variations. *AI magazine,* Winter, 1986: 40–62. Also in *Tutorial: Object oriented computing.* Vol. 1, *Concepts,* edited by G.E. Peterson (1987), pp. 182–204. Washington, DC: IEEE Computer Society Press.

Stroustrup, 1986   Stroustrup, B. (1986). *The C++ programming language.* Reading, MA: Addison-Wesley.

Stroustrup, 1994   Stroustrup, B. (1994). *The design and evolution of C++.* Reading, MA: Addison-Wesley.

Stroustrup, 1995   Stroustrup, B. (1995). *The C++ programming language.* 2nd ed. Reprinted with corrections. Reading, MA: Addison-Wesley.

Sun, 1995   *About Java.* Mountain View, CA: Sun Microsystems.

Suppes, 1960   Suppes, P. (1960). *Axiomatic set theory.* New York: Van Nostrand.

Sussman, 1975   Sussman, G.J., and Steele, G.L., Jr., (1975). Scheme: An interpreter for extended lambda calculus. Artificial Intelligence Memo 349. Cambridge, MA: MIT Artificial Intelligence Lab.

Tanenbaum, 1976   Tanenbaum, A.S. (1976). A tutorial on ALGOL 68. *ACM computing surveys* 8(2): 155–190. Also in *Programming Languages: A grand tour.* 3rd ed., edited by E. Horowitz (1987), pp. 69–104. New York: Freeman.

Tennent, 1976   Tennent, R.D. (1976). The denotational semantics of programming languages. *CACM* 19(8): 437–453.

Tesler, 1985   Tesler, L. (1985). Object Pascal report. *Structured language world* 9(3): 10–14.

TI, 1987   *Revised SCHEME user's guide, tutorial, and reference manual.* Austin, TX: Texas Instruments.

Torsone, 1993   Torsone, C. (1993). Introducing parallel programming to a programming language concepts course. In *Proceedings of the Ninth Annual Eastern Small College Conference,* edited by J.G. Meinke, pp. 66–70.

Tremblay, 1985 Tremblay, J., and Sorenson, P.G. (1985). *The theory and practice of compiler writing.* New York: McGraw-Hill.

Tu, 1986 Tu, H-C, and Perlis, A.J. (1986). FAC: A functional APL language. *IEEE software* 3(1): 36–45.

Tukey, 1977 Tukey, J.W. (1977). *Exploratory data analysis.* Reading, MA: Addison-Wesley.

Turbo C++, 1992 *Turbo C++ version 3.0 user's guide.* Scotts Valley, CA: Borland International.

Turbo 7.0, 1992 *Turbo Pascal 7.0: Programmer's reference.* Scotts Valley, CA: Borland International.

Turbo 7.0, 1993 *Turbo Pascal version 7.0 reference manual.* Scotts Valley, CA: Borland International.

Turner, 1982 Turner, D.A. (1982). Recursion equations as a programming language. In *Functional programming and its applications,* edited by J. Darlington, P. Henderson, and D.A. Turner (1982), pp. 1–28. Cambridge, UK: Cambridge Univ. Press.

Ullman, 1988 Ullman, J.D. (1988). *Principles of database and knowledge-base systems.* Vol. 1. Rockville, MD: Computer Science Press.

Vossen, 1991 Vossen, G. (1991). *Data models, database languages, and database management systems.* Reading, MA: Addison-Wesley.

Warren, 1977 Warren, D.H.D., Pereira, L.M., and Pereira, F. (1977). PROLOG—The language and its implementation compared with LISP. *SIGPLAN notices* 12(8): 109–115.

Warren, 1988 Warren, D.S. (1988). The Warren abstract machine. In *SIGPLAN '88: Advanced implementations tutorial notes,* pp. 1–18. Baltimore: ACM Press.

Watson, 1987 Watson, S.E. (1987). Ada modules. *Ada letters* 7(4): 79–84.

Wegner, 1976 Wegner, P. (1976). Programming languages—the first 25 years. *IEEE transactions on computers,* December, 1976: 1207–1225. Also in *Programming languages: A grand tour.* 3rd ed., edited by E. Horowitz (1987), pp. 4–22. New York: Freeman.

Wegner, 1980 Wegner, P. (1980). *Programming with Ada: An introduction by means of graduated examples.* Englewood-Cliffs, NJ: Prentice-Hall.

Wegner, 1983 Wegner, P., and Smolka, S.A. (1983). Processes, tasks, and monitors: A comparative study of concurrent programming primitives. *IEEE transactions on software engineering* SE-9(4): 446–462. Also in *Programming languages: A grand tour.* 3rd ed., edited by E. Horowitz (1987), pp. 360–376. New York: Freeman

Wegner, 1987 Wegner, P. (1987). The object-oriented classification paradigm. In *Research directions in object-oriented programming,* edited by B. Shriver and P. Wegner, pp. 479–560. Cambridge, MA: MIT Press.

Wegner, 1988 Wegner, P. (1988). Object-oriented concept hierarchies. *Tutorial notes: Object-oriented software engineering.* International Conference on Computer Languages '88. Tutorial presented at the IEEE International Conference on Computer Languages, Miami Beach, FL. October, 1988.

Wegner, 1989 Wegner, P. (guest ed.) (1989). Introduction to programming language paradigms (special issue). *ACM computing surveys* 21(3): 253–258.

Wegner, 1990   Wegner, P. (1990). Concepts and paradigms of object-oriented programming. *OOPS messenger* 1(1): 8–84.

Weiner, 1988   Weiner, J.L., and Ramakrishnan, S. (1988). A piggy-back compiler for Prolog. In *Proceedings of the SIGPLAN '88 conference on programming language design and implementation*, pp. 288–296. Baltimore: ACM Press.

Wexelblat, 1981   Wexelblat, R. (ed.)(1981). *History of programming languages.* New York: Academic Press.

Whitehead, 1910   Whitehead, A.N., and Russell, B.A.W. (1910–1913, 1st ed.; 1923–1927, 2nd ed.). *Principia mathematica.* Vols. 1–3. Cambridge, UK: Cambridge Univ. Press.

Wiederhold, 1983   Wiederhold, G. (1983). *Database design.* 2nd ed. New York: McGraw-Hill.

Wikström, 1987   Wikström, Å. (1987). *Functional programming using standard ML.* London: Prentice-Hall.

Wirth, 1971   Wirth, N. (1971). The programming language Pascal. *Acta informatica* 1(1): 35–63.

Wirth, 1985   Wirth, N. (1985). Turing award lecture: From programming language design to computer construction. *CACM* 28(2): 160–164.

Wolfe, 1981   Wolfe, M.I., Babich, W., Simpson, R., Tholl, R., and Weissman, L. (1981). The Ada language system. *Computer* 14(6): 37–45.

Zilles, 1986   Zilles, B., and Guttag, J. (1986). *Abstraction and specification in program development.* New York: McGraw-Hill.

Index

abstract classes, 167–168
abstract data types (ADTs),
    65–74
  classes of, 91–92
  functional programming
    and, 332
  modularization and, 90–91
  monitors as, 218
  objects and, 150, 170
  private types and, 121
  processes as, 212
  PROLOG and, 316
abstract entities, 390
abstractions, 7, 63–95
  binding and, 39
  lambda calculus and, 405,
    406, 407, 408
  objects and, 92
  OOP and, 150
  variables and, 29, 36
  See also data abstraction
abstract models, 67–69
abstract paradigm, 6
accepted word, 262
access data types. *See* pointers
ACM. *See* Association
    for Computing Machinery
    (ACM)
activation records, 39, 43–45, 61
  exceptions and, 81
  functions and, 85
  parameters and, 90
  recursion and, 80

actor languages, 155
Ada, 117–132
  abstractions and, 71–72
  ALGOL and, 102, 103
  arrays and, 49, 72
  binding and, 39
  blocks and, 42
  box, 124, 126
  circular deadlock in, 240
  Concurrent C and, 231
  context-free grammars and,
    274
  data encapsulation and, 154
  data types and, 30, 47, 48
  Department of Defense
    (DOD) and, 7, 11, 14, 23,
    117–119
  dynamic bounds and, 108
  EBNF and, 276
  as example of block-
    structured paradigm, 6, 8
  as example of object-based
    paradigm, 9
  exceptions in, 82, 128–129
  as extension of third-
    generation language, 13
  generic facility, 116, 120,
    127–128, 163–165
  identifiers and, 37
  integers and, 30
  Java and, 200
  keywords in, 38
  Linda and, 236

Ada (*Cont.*):
  loop control variables in, 42
  modularization and, 91
  Object Pascal vs., 167–168
  OOP and, 152
  operators and, 113
  parameters and, 86
  parsing and, 274
  Pascal and, 115, 119, 124
  pointers and, 35
  pragma, 230
  process units in, 212
  real numbers and, 32
  records and, 52
  rendezvous in, 219, 226–230
  Simula and, 156
  software sources and,
    411–412
  standards and, 24
  strings and, 51
  syntax of, 75
  type checking and, 58, 60
  union types and, 55
Ada 83, 9, 119, 158–162,
    163–164, 179, 194
Ada9X, 119
Ada 95, 9, 37, 119, 158–162,
    1673–164, 179, 194
Ada programming support
    environment (APSE),
    129–131
address binding, 38–39, 88
addresses, 34, 36

ADT. *See* abstract data types (ADTs)
aggregate data types, 30, 47, 48–49
  Ada and, 125
  type checking and, 58
AI. *See* artificial intelligence (AI)
algebra, 4, 382–384, 385
  PROLOG and, 317
  SQL and, 385, 387
algebraic specification, 67, 69–70, 95
ALGOL, 6, 13
  blocks and, 100
  C and, 132
  identifiers and, 37
  syntax of, 75
  type checking and, 58
ALGOL 58, 101, 102
ALGOL 60, 8, 14
  blocks and, 42, 99, 100–111
  context-free grammars and, 274
  Pascal and, 113
  scope and, 41
  Simula and, 156
  trouble spots in, 108–109
ALGOL 68, 8, 19, 111–113
  blocks and, 100, 102–103, 104
  collateral clauses in, 212
  dynamic bounds and, 108
  orthogonality and, 22
  records and, 52
  semaphores in, 215, 221–222
  union types and, 53
ALGOL-W, 113
algorithm
  abstractions and, 70, 75
  ALGOL and, 103
  functional programming and, 330
  OOP vs, 151
aliasing, 87
alpha conversion, 406, 408, 409
alternation
  cooperating processes and, 214
  regular expressions and, 262
  transition diagram and, 264
ambiguous grammars, 272–274
American National Standards Institute (ANSI), 23
American Standard Code for Information Interchange (ASCII), 32

and parallelism, 315
animation, 201
ANSI. *See* American National Standards Institute (ANSI)
APIs. *See* application programming interfaces (APIs)
APL, 12, 26
  arrays and, 50
  binding and, 39
  data types and, 47
  dynamic bounds and, 108
  scope and, 43
applets, 196, 197, 201, 202–203
application programming interfaces (APIs), Java and, 200–201
applicative order reductions, 356, 357
  lambda calculus and, 408
applicative programming, 325–374
  software sources and, 414
APSE. *See* Ada programming support environment (APSE)
arguments, 326, 328, 336
  curried function and, 368
  lazy vs. strict evaluation of, 356–357, 362–363
arithmetic overflow, 19
arity, 304, 381
array descriptors, 50, 51
arrays, 49–51
  abstractions and, 72
  Ada and, 125–127
  aggregate types and, 48, 49
  ALGOL and, 107–108
  APL and, 364
  C and, 142–143
  C-Linda and, 238
  column major order, 50
  conformant, 146
  dynamic bounds, 108
  flexible bounds, 108
  implementation of, 61
  Java and, 197
  LISP and, 332, 335
  process units and, 212
  PROLOG and, 306
  records, 52–53
  row major order, 50
  slice, 125
  type checking and, 57–58
artificial intelligence (AI), 5
  LISP and, 330–331

artificial intelligence (*Cont.*):
  PROLOG and, 301, 302, 317, 318
  SCHEME and, 352
ASCII. *See* American Standard Code for Information Interchange (ASCII)
assembly language, 11, 13, 133
  abstractions and, 74
  Occam as, 220
  translation and, 20
assignments
  parallel processing and, 212
  records and, 53
  subrange data types and, 47
  type checking and, 58
  union types and, 54
Association for Computing Machinery (ACM), 101, 102
associativity
  parse tree and, 272
  PROLOG and, 303
ATN. *See* augmented transition network (ATN)
atoms, 332–334, 336
  in PROLOG, 303–304
  relational databases and, 384
  SCOOP and, 350
attributes, 9, 124
  binding of, 38–39. *See also* binding
  classes and, 162–163
  objects and, 149, 150
  semantic models and, 390
  subclasses and, 162
  variables and, 29, 36
augmented transition network (ATN), 280–281
axiomatic semantics, 17–18, 25, 26
  provability and, 19
axioms, 288, 397

b-tree, 377
backtracking, 295–296, 306, 307, 319
  parallelism and, 315
Backus-Naur Form (BNF), 14–16, 19, 275–276
  ALGOL 60 and, 102, 107, 110
  ALGOL and, 107, 111
  context-free grammars, 275
  parse tree and, 277
  reference language and, 110

Backus Normal Form. *See*
    Backus-Naur Form (BNF)
backward chaining, 297–298
base class, 157, 167–168, 181
BASIC
    context-free grammars and,
        274
    time-share system, 219
    type binding and, 39
    UNIX and, 143
Basic CPL (BCPL), 133–134, 142
BCD. *See* binary coded decimal
    (BCD)
Bell Labs, C and, 133–134
Bernoulli numbers, 119
beta conversion, 406, 408, 408
binary code, 20
binary coded decimal (BCD),
    30, 31
binary point, 31
binding, 29, 38–39
    functional programming
        and, 332
    LISP and, 336, 344, 357–361
    predicate calculus and, 401
    scope and, 40
    time, 38
    type checking and, 58
bits, 6
    Boolean values and, 32
    C and, 139–142
    integer and, 30
    sets and, 56
blocks, 40, 41–42, 61, 99–146
    activation records and, 44
    Ada and, 117–132
    ALGOL 60 and, 99, 100–111
    ALGOL 68 and, 111–113
    C and, 132–145
    exceptions and, 81, 82
    functional programming
        and, 326
    Pascal and, 113–117, 115
    PROLOG and, 319
    records and, 53
    rendezvous and, 219
    strings and, 51
block-structured language
    Ada as, 121
    Pascal as, 42
    software sources and, 412
    virtual machine and, 246
block-structured paradigm, 6,
    8, 99–146
BNF. *See* Backus-Naur Form
    (BNF)

Boolean values, 32–33
    C and, 137
    enumeration types and, 48
    union types and, 55
bound variables, 40
    abstractions and, 87
    arrays and, 50
    lambda calculus and, 405, 406
    predicate calculus and, 401
    type checking and, 58
    See also binding
branching, 74–76
British Standards Institution
    (BSI), 23
broadcasting, 221
buffered message passing, 221
buffers, 220
    Ada and, 227–230
    Concurrent Pascal and,
        225–226
bugs, C language and, 60
buzy waiting, 214
bytes
    Boolean values and, 32
    characters and, 31

C, 6, 8, 13, 132–145
    abstractions and, 85
    ALGOL and, 103, 132
    binding and, 39
    blocks and, 42
    characters and, 32
    data types and, 48, 134–137
    GemStone and, 393
    identifiers and, 37
    integers and, 30
    Java and, 197, 198, 203–205
    Linda and, 236
    objects and, 239
    operators in, 137–143
    Pascal and, 132, 135
    PROLOG and, 302, 318
    reliability and, 19
    semaphores in, 222–223
    Simula and, 156
    strings and, 51
    type checking and, 60
    union types and, 53
    UNIX and, 134, 143
C++, 9, 132
    abstractions and, 72, 85
    classes in, 163, 171–173, 177,
        179
    Concurrent C and, 239
    dynamic binding in, 195

C++ (*Cont.*):
    GemStone and, 393
    inheritance in, 189–193
    Java and, 197, 198, 203–205
    multiple inheritance and,
        182–185, 192–193
    objects and, 239
    OOP and, 152, 153–154,
        160–162, 178
    operators and, 113
    PROLOG and, 302
    Simula and, 156
Cartesian Linguistics, 251
Cartesian product, relational
    databases and, 382–383,
    385
case sensitivity, 37
casts, C and, 136–137
CFGs. *See* context-free
    grammars (CFGs)
character data types, arrays
    and, 49
characters, 32
    abstractions and, 72
    printable (alphanumeric), 32
character strings, aggregate
    types and, 48, 49
Chomsky Normal Form (CNF),
    275, 276–277
circular deadlock, 240
class-based language, 68
classes, 9, 162–175
    abstractions and, 68
    ADTs and, 91–92
    Java and, 198–201
    objects and, 92, 149, 150, 153,
        155
    of processes, 157
    SCOOP and, 349–350
    Simula and, 157
    See also inheritance
clients, 219
C-Linda, 236–239, 413
CLU, 26, 154
CNF. *See* Chomsky Normal
    Form (CNF)
co-routine, 212
COBOL, 11, 13, 65
    databases and, 377, 379, 387
    extensibility and, 23
    identifiers and, 37
    real numbers and, 31
    records and, 52
CODASYL. *See* Conference on
    Data Systems Languages
    (CODASYL)

Code Word Language (CWL), 259

coercion, C and, 144

collateral clauses, 212–213

Combined Programming Language (CPL), 132, 133–134

comma operator, C and, 142–143

Common LISP, 331, 332, 352–354
recursion and, 81, 342
scope and, 43
standards and, 24

communicating sequential processes (CSP)
BSP and, 221
Occam and, 220
rendezvous in, 219

communications channels, 220, 232–235

comparisons, enumeration types and, 48

compile time, 38

compilers, 4, 6, 20, 20
abstractions and, 66
ALGOL and, 103
BCD integers and, 30
C for writing, 144
concurrent execution and, 93
context-free grammars and, 275
extensibility and, 23
functional programming and, 354–362
IDE and, 14
Java and, 197
lazy vs. strict evaluation and, 362–364
lexical analysis of, 252
optimizing, 21, 21
parallel processing and, 315–316
parsing and, 272
PDA and, 252
portability and, 23–24
provability and, 19
recursion and, 79, 81
semantics and, 18
subsets and, 23
very high level languages and, 12, 21
writing/designing, 21, 61

complex numbers
LISP and, 332–334
ML and, 364–365

compound statements, blocks and, 42

computability, lambda calculus and, 408–410

concatenation, 52
transition diagram and, 264

conceptual views (of databases), 377

Concurrent C
Ada and, 231
message passing in, 220
objects and, 239
rendezvous in, 230–232

concurrent execution, 93, 198

Concurrent Pascal, 212, 219, 225–226

concurrent processes
managing partial failure in, 240
Pascal S and, 224
See also parallel processing

concurrent programming, 9, 114, 209
sequential vs., 210
See also parallel processing

Concurrent PROLOG, 9, 315

Concurrent Smalltalk, 239

conditional expression, 337–338

conditionals, 363

Conference on Data Systems Languages (CODASYL), 379

cons, 334–338

consistency, 22, 59
algebraic specification and, 70
theory and, 288

constants, 39
lambda calculus and, 409
PROLOG and, 303

constraints, in PROLOG, 312–313

constructors, 149, 332

content handlers, in Java, 203

context-free grammars (CFGs), 252, 253, 267–279
normal forms and, 275–279
RTNs and, 279–280

context-sensitive grammars (CSGs), 253–254, 279
recognizer, 254
vW-grammar as one, 111

continuation (of exceptions), 81

contour diagram, 41

contradiction, 288, 398–399

control
functions and, 326
in LISP and SCHEME, 337–338, 341–342

control (*Cont.*):
in PROLOG, 308–312

control abstractions, 64, 74–83

control structures, 26, 65

control variables, blocks and, 42

copying, 362

core language, 23

core PROLOG, 302–303, 318

correct resolution, 291
functional programming and, 330
lambda calculus and, 408–410

CPL. *See* Combined Programming Language (CPL)

CPL-BCPL-C, blocks and, 100, 132

CPUs
abstractions and, 66
concurrent programming and, 9
declarative paradigms and, 9
Java and, 198
parallel processing and, 210, 211
state and, 8

crashing, parallel processing and, 240

CSA Transputer Education Kit, 233, 234

CSGs. *See* context-sensitive grammars (CSGs)

CSP. *See* Communicating Sequential Processes (CSP)

curried function, 368

cursor, databases and, 387–388

CWL. *See* Code Word Language (CWL)

dangling else, 75

dangling references, 35

data, store and, 65

data abstractions, 64–74
Ada and, 158
SCHEME and, 336
See also abstractions

Data Base Task Group (DBTG), 379

data container, 152

data definition language (DDL), 10, 377, 378, 379
databases and, 386, 387
OOP and, 393

data domain (D), 65, 67

data encapsulation, 67, 91
    objects and, 92
    See also encapsulation
data independence, 66–67, 91.
    See also orthogonality
data manipulation language
    (DML), 10, 21, 377, 378, 379
    databases and, 386
    OOP and, 393
data processing, 13
data regions, 215
data sharing, 9, 93, 213. *See also*
    parallel processing;
    synchronization
data structures
    abstractions and, 65, 74–83
    C-Linda and, 238
    LISP and, 335–336
    PROLOG and, 304
data system languages (DSLs),
    377, 378
data types, 26, 29–61
    abstract. *See* abstract data
        types (ADTs)
    aggregate, 30, 47, 48–49
    C and, 134–137
    characters and, 32
    data encapsulation and, 154
    LISP and, 329, 332–334
    ML and, 364–368
    primitive, 29, 30–33, 39
    PROLOG and, 316–317
    structured, 47–60
database language paradigm, 10
Database management system
    (DBMS), 10, 26, 378. *See*
    also databases
databases, 377–394
    defined, 377
    instances and, 381–384
    PROLOG and, 389
    querying, 291–301, 377. *See*
        also query languages
    relational model for, 380–389.
        See also relational databases
    searching, 294–301
    semantic models and,
        390–392
    software sources and, 414
dBASE IV, 414
DBMS. *See* database manage-
    ment system (DBMS)
DBTG. *See* Data Base Task
    Group (DBTG)
DDL. *See* data definition
    language (DDL)

deadlock, 215, 218
    ALGOL 68 and, 222
    circular, 240
debugging
    C and, 144
    Java and, 202
    modularization and, 91
    parallel processing and, 240
    PROLOG and, 306
    reliability and, 20
    subrange data types and, 48
    translation and, 21
decidable rule, 249, 257–258
declaration equivalence, 58
declarations
    activation records and, 44
    ALGOL and, 104
    blocks and, 42
    C-Linda and, 238
    iterations and, 78
    name binding and, 38
    type binding and, 39
declarative languages, 7, 9–11,
    283–394
    provability and, 19
definition modules, 91
denotational semantics, 17, 18,
    25
Department of Defense (DOD)
    Ada and, 7, 11, 14, 23, 117–119
    Ada 95 and, 158
    APSE and, 129–132
    Common LISP and, 353
    language, 7, 11, 14, 23
    Pascal and, 115
dereferencing, 34
destructors, 149
detachment, 397
deterministic finite automaton
    (DFA), 264–267
dining philosophers example,
    214–218, 224–225, 231–232
direct naming, 220
discrete data types, 47
discriminants, 54–55, 75–76
discriminated records, 125
discriminated unions, 54, 59
dispatching, 174, 194
display (array), 45
distributed paradigm, 9
distributed programming, soft-
    ware sources and, 412–413
distributed systems, parallel
    processing and, 210, 211
DML. *See* data manipulation
    language (DML)

DOD. *See* Department of
    Defense (DOD)
domain calculus, 384, 385
domain value, functions and,
    325
dotted pair, 334, 337, 354
double-precision real num-
    bers/arithmetic, 32, 61
DSLs. *See* data system
    languages (DSLs)
dynamic arrays, ALGOL and,
    107–108
dynamic binding, 38, 39
    Ada and, 158
    databases and, 393
    OOP and, 150, 158, 193–196
    type binding and, 39
dynamic bounds, 108
dynamic dispatch, 194
dynamic propagation, 81, 82
dynamic scoping, 42–43
    activation records and, 44
    LISP and, 358
dynamic storage, 34–35
dynamic string length, 51
dynamic tags, 174
dynamic type checking, 58

EBCDIC. *See* Extended Binary
    Coded Decimal Inter-
    change Code (EBCDIC)
EBNF. *See* Extended Backus-
    Naur Form (EBNF)
editors, concurrent execution
    and, 93
EdScheme, 414
Eiffel language, 182, 239
elaborated package, 122
elegance, 113, 326, 328
embedded languages, 14
encapsulation
    objects and, 150, 153–155
    process unit and, 212
    See also data encapsulation
Enigma code, 256, 258
entities, 377, 390
entity integrity, 388
entity relationship (ER)
    models, 390–392
enumeration data types, 48
    arrays and, 49
    sets and, 55
environment, 40
    activation records and, 44
    ALGOL and, 103, 106

environment (*Cont.*):
 dynamic scoping and, 42–43
 iteration and, 78
 lambda calculus and, 409
 LISP and, 336
 recursion and, 78–79
 static or lexical scoping and, 41
equijoin, 383, 387, 389
ER models. *See* entity relationship (ER) models
error checking, subrange data
 types and, 47–48
error detection and recovery,
 translation and, 21
error messages, reserved words
 and, 38
ESP. *See* Extended Self-
 Contained PROLOG (ESP)
eta conversion, 406, 408
exception handlers, 19, 20, 26
 Ada and, 128–129
 ML and, 364, 369
exceptions, 19, 20, 81–83,
 128–129, 369
 resumption model, 81, 82
 termination model, 81
excluded middle, principle of,
 291
executable code, error
 detection and recovery
 and, 21
executable module, 20
exemplars, 6, 8. *See also*
 language exemplars
expert systems
 LISP and, 331
 PROLOG and, 302, 317, 318
expressions
 exceptions and, 81
 functions and, 325
 lambda calculus and, 409
 regular, 261–262
Extended Backus-Naur Form
 (EBNF), 16–17, 276–279
 ML and, 369
Extended Binary Coded
 Decimal Interchange Code
 (EBCDIC), 32
Extended Self-Contained
 PROLOG (ESP), 318
extensibility, 23
external views (of databases),
 377–378

FA. *See* finite automata (FA)
FAC. *See* Functional Array
 Calculator (FAC)
facts, 296–297
 PROLOG and, 302, 303–304
 representing negative,
 298–299
FDMs. *See* functional data
 models (FDMs)
fields, 52–55
FIFO assumption. *See* First-In–
 First-Out (FIFO) assumption
fifth generation language, 13
 PROLOG as, 301, 317–318
files
 databases and, 377
 LISP and, 336
File Transfer Protocol (FTP),
 197, 201, 203
final state, 263
finite automata (FA), 252,
 262–267
 context-free grammars and,
 267–268
 PDA and, 268
 RTNs and, 279
finite-state automata (FSA). *See*
 finite automata (FA)
first-class entities, 165–171
first-class functions, funarg
 problems and, 358–361
first-class objects
 functions as, 326, 328–329, 358
 LISP and, 336
first-generation languages, 13
First-In–First-Out (FIFO)
 assumption, 219, 228
first-order function, 328
first-order predicate calculus,
 401–403
fixed point numbers, 31, 32
fixed reals, 123–124
fixed subranges, 47
flexible bounds, 108
floating point numbers, 31, 32,
 123–124
 PROLOG and, 308
 subranges and, 47
folds, 234
foobar, 307
foreign keys, 380, 388
formal languages, 243–282
 Chomsky hierarcy of, 249–256
 defining, 246, 247–248

formal languages (*Cont.*):
 natural vs., 4
 provability and, 19
 semantics and, 17
 types of, 248, 249–250
forms, in LISP, 335–336
formulas, 400, 406
FORTRAN, 8, 13, 14, 37
 activation records and, 44
 ALGOL and, 101, 102, 104, 107
 arrays and, 49
 Backus and, 364
 binding and, 39
 context-free grammars and,
 274
 databases and, 377
 DFA scanner for, 265
 identifiers and, 37
 LISP and, 330
 parameters and, 88
 reserved words and, 38
 type checking and, 58
FORTRAN II, aggregate types
 and, 48
FORTRAN 90, aggregate types
 and, 49
forward chaining, 297–298
fourth-generation languages
 (4GLs), 13, 301
FP, 364
frames, 43. *See also* activation
 records
Franz LISP, 352
free unions, 22, 54–55
free variables, 40
 blocks and, 41, 42
 dynamic scoping and, 42–43
 lambda calculus and, 406
 LISP and, 358, 359
FSA (finite-state automata). *See*
 finite automata (FA)
FTP. *See* File Transfer Protocol
 (FTP)
funarg problems, 358–361
function theory, 5
Functional Array Calculator
 (FAC), 364
functional data models
 (FDMs), 390–392
functional forms, 338–339
functional languages, 13
 features of, 327–330
 garbage collection in, 361–362.
 See also garbage collection

functional languages (*Cont.*):
  implementing, 354–362
functional programming,
  325–374
  APL for, 364
  lambda calculus and,
    405, 408. *See also* lambda
    calculus
  lazy vs. strict evaluation in,
    356–357, 362–363
  ML for, 364–373. *See also*
    Meta Language (ML)
  parallelism and, 362–364
  software sources and, 414
functions, 325–326
  abstractions and, 85–86
  declarative paradigms and,
    9, 10
  defined, 325
  lambda calculus and, 405,
    408. *See also* lambda
    calculus
  Pascal and, 116
  predefined, 38
  semantics and, 18
  types vs., 21–22
  variables and, 29
functors, 304–308
  ML and, 368–369

garbage, 35–36
garbage collector, 35–36
  Ada and, 127
  LISP and, 330, 331, 356,
    361–362
  object-hash table and, 356
  PROLOG and, 316
GemStone system, 393
generality, 22
generative translators, 20
generic data types, 72–73
generic modules, PROLOG
  and, 316–317
generic objects, Object Pascal
  and, 167
generic packages, 164–165
generic procedures and
  functions
  Ada and. *See* Ada's generic
    facility
  Pascal and, 116
generic stacks, in C++. 172–173
geometry, 63–64
global assignments, 10

global variables
  binding and, 39, 40
  functional programming
    and, 329
  Pascal and, 115
goals, 297
Gopher, Java and, 203
goto statement, 19, 74
  Ada and, 122
  ALGOL and, 109
grammars, 245–254
  ambiguous, 272–274
  defined, 246
  for natural languages, 253,
    279–282
  phrase-structured. *See*
    phrase-structured
    grammars
  provability and, 19
  syntax and, 246
  unrestricted, 258–260
grammars over Σ, 247–248
granularity, 363–364
Graph Reduction in Parallel
  (GRIP), 364
Graphical user interfaces
  (GUIs), Java and, 201
graphics, 13–14
ground clause, 294

halting problem, 330
hardware representations, 110
hasA, 179
Haskell (language), 373
heap, 34–35
  Ada and, 127
  dynamic scoping and, 42
  LISP and, 355
heuristics, 331
hierarchical model, 378–379, 385
higher-order function, 328, 368
Higher-Order Language
  Working Group
  (HOLWG), 118
high level languages, 133, 134
Hollerith data type, 49
HOLWG. *See* Higher-Order
  Language Working Group
  (HOLWG)
Hope (language), 356
horn clauses, 10, 290–293
host, 20
host language, 20, 377, 378
HotJava, 196, 201, 202–203

HTML documents, Java and, 201
HTTP. *See* HyperText Transfer
  Protocol (HTTP)
HyperText Transfer Protocol
  (HTTP), 197, 201, 203
hypothesis, 288

IA. *See* Integer Arithmetic (IA)
IAL. *See* International
  Algebraic Language (IAL)
IBM, 21, 32
  ALGOL and, 101
  FORTRAN and, 101, 102
  IMS of, 378
  relational databases and, 384
  SQL and, 385
IBM 370, 30
IBM 704, 326, 330, 334
IBM PROLOG, 316
IDE. *See* Integrated Development Environment (IDE)
identifiers, 16, 37
  Ada and, 226
  ALGOL and, 109
  binding and, 38–39
  enumeration types and, 48
  fields and, 52
  union types and, 54
IEEE. *See* Institute of Electrical
  and Electronics Engineers
  (IEEE)
imperative languages, 97–242
  data types and, 47
  functional programming
    and, 326
  ML and, 364
  variables and, 29
imperative paradigms, 7, 8–9
implementation
  Common LISP and, 353
  databases and, 386
  of inherited classes, 173–175
  monitors and, 219
  PROLOG and, 312–317
implementation modules, 91
improper symbols, 405–406
inclusive-or, 396
indeterminism, 315
indexes
  arrays and, 49, 50
  databases and, 377–378, 388
  type checking and, 58
individuals, as arguments, 328
information hiding, 66–67, 71, 91
  Ada and, 158

information hiding (*Cont.*):
   blocks and, 100
   ML and, 369
   objects and, 92
   OOP and, 150
   Pascal and, 165, 170
   See also data encapsulation;
      encapsulation
Information Processing
   Language (IPL), 330
Information System Base
   Language (ISBL), 384
inheritance
   Ada 95 and, 174
   multiple. *See* multiple
      inheritance
   Object Pascal and, 167–171
   objects and, 92
   OOP and, 150, 155, 177–196
   Simula and, 157–158
initialized variables, value
   binding and, 39
input/output (I/O)
   ALGOL and, 102
   C and, 144
   functional programming
      and, 326
   multiple inheritance and, 184
   PROLOG and, 308
instances, 381–384, 396, 400
Institute of Electrical and
   Electronics Engineers
   (IEEE), 23, 32
   SCHEME and, 331
Integer Arithmetic (IA), 257
integers, 30–31
   abstractions and, 65–66, 72
   characters and, 32
   enumeration types and, 48
   LISP and, 332–334
   PROLOG and, 303, 308
   type checking and, 58
   union types and, 54
Integrated Development
   Environment (IDE), 14
integrity constraints, databases
   and, 388
interleaving, 212, 224
InterLISP, 352–353
International Algebraic
   Language (IAL), 101
International Standards
   Organization (ISO), 16, 385
Internet, 197, 202. *See also*
      World Wide Web (WWW)

interpreters, 4, 20–21, 26
   Java and, 198
   LISP and, 339
   recursion and, 79, 81
intersection, relational
   databases and, 383
I/O. *See* input/output (I/O)
IPL. *See* Information Processing
   Language (IPL)
isA, 179, 390
ISO. *See* International Standards Organization (ISO)
iteration, 75–78, 347–348

Java, 32, 33, 196–205, 207
   animation and, 201
   APIs in, 200–201
   arrays and, 50
   case sensitivity and, 37
   OOP and, 179
   software sources and, 412
   strings and, 52
   type wrappers, 200–201
Java Development Kit (JDK),
   200, 412
jumps, 74

k-tuple, 381
Kernel APSE (KAPSE), 129
keys, databases and, 380
keywords, 36–38
Kleene star, 262, 264
knowledge engineering, LISP
   and, 331

l-value, 137
lambda calculus, 5, 405–410
   Backus and, 364
   functional forms and, 338–339
   functional programming
      and, 326, 327, 329, 330, 347
   SASL, KRC, Haskell, and
      Miranda and, 373
   scope and bindings and,
      357–358
lambda expression, 335–336
LAN. *See* local area network
   (LAN)
language criteria, 14–25
language definitions, 15, 17, 26
   provability and, 19
   semantics and, 18

language descriptions, 14–16
language design, 26
language exemplars, 185–193.
   See also exemplars
language implementation, 6, 26
   abstractions and, 58, 70–71
language paradigms. *See*
   paradigms
language specification, 109–110
language standards, abstractions and, 66
languages. *See* programming
   languages
lazy evaluation, 356–357,
   362–364
lexical analysis, 20, 252, 265
lexical ordering, strings and, 51
lexical scoping, 41, 103
lexical structure (of language),
   246
lifetime, 39, 44
limited private data types, 121
Linda, 9, 236–239
linear-bounded automaton
   (LBA), 254–256
linguistics, 251
linked list, 116
linker, 20
links
   activation records and, 44–45
   databases and, 385
   point-to-point, 9
LISP, 5, 7, 12, 13, 332–352, 374
   abstractions and, 66
   built-in functions of, 336–338,
      407
   data types in, 30, 332–334
   first-order functions and, 328
   funarg problems in, 358–361
   as functional language, 10, 326
   functional programming
      and, 325, 327
   history of, 330–331
   lambda calculus and, 405,
      407
   lists and, 56, 57
   ML vs., 364
   MYCIN and, 317
   operators and, 113
   orthogonality and, 22
   pointers and, 35
   procedure passing and, 112
   PROLOG and, 307, 317, 318
   recursion and, 81
   scope and, 43

LISP (*Cont.*):
    self-modifying functions in, 344–347
    standards and, 24
    translation and, 20, 26
    univ in, 307
LISP dialects, 340, 352–353. *See also* Common LISP; SCHEME
LISt Processing. *See* LISP
lists, 56
    abstractions and, 66
    circular, 191
    exceptions and, 82
    LISP and, 330, 332–336
    ML and, 366
    PROLOG and, 304
literal atoms, 332, 355
literals, 48
loader, 20
load module, 20
load time, 38
local area network (LAN), 9, 210
logic, 4–5
    declarative paradigms and, 9, 10
    PROLOG and, 301
logical calculi, 395–404
logical theory, 397
logic programming, 285–323
    PROLOG and, 297–298, 301–323
    software sources and, 413–414
loops
    abstractions and, 77–78
    blocks and, 42
    transition table and, 264
loosely coupled system, 210, 237
low level languages, 133, 134
LPA PROLOG, 413–414

machine
    target, 30
    theoretical, 18, 247, 312–315
    virtual memory, 38
machine code, 20
    binding and, 38
    Java and, 198
    provability and, 19
    variables and, 29
machine languages, 13, 20
MacLISP, 352–353
macros, 348–352
magnitude, 332–334
mailbox, 220

mainframes, 32
MAPSE. *See* Minimum APSE (MAPSE)
mark-scan, 361–362
mathematics, 4
    abstractions and, 64, 67
    classes and, 162–163
    declarative paradigms and, 9
    functional programming and, 326, 328
    LISP and, 330
    logic and, 285, 301
    notation and, 22
    predicate calculus and, 400
    query languages and, 381
    semantics and, 17–18
member function, 152
memory
    pointers and, 34
    sharing. *See* shared memory
    translation and, 20, 21
    virtual, 38
Meridian Ada Compiler, 411
message passing, 153–155, 213
    managing partial failure in, 240
    Occam and, 232–235
    parallel processing and, 219–221
    tuples and, 236
messages, 152
    Ada and, 174
    objects and, 92
    rendezvous and, 219
    Smalltalk and, 174
Meta Language (ML), 327, 334, 356, 364–373, 374
    call-by-name and, 107
    FP vs., 364
    lambda calculus and, 405
metalanguage, 15, 19, 327
    algebraic specification and, 69
    BNF as, 376
metasymbols, 15, 261, 276
methods, 152, 153–155
    Ada and, 158
    Java and, 199–200
    objects and, 92
    procedures as, 156, 160
    SCOOP and, 350–351
    Simula and, 156
Micro-PROLOG, 302, 303, 413–414
Minimum APSE (MAPSE), 131
MIT Artificial Intelligence Laboratory, 352

mixins, 349–352
ML. *See* Meta Language (ML)
modes, ALGOL and, 112
Modula, 6, 9, 91
    monitors in, 219
Modula-2, 91
    ALGOL and, 102, 103, 113–114
    data encapsulation and, 154
    process units in, 212
    reliability and, 19
    RPCs and, 221
modularization
    ADTs and, 90–91
    Common LISP and, 353
modules, 9
    ADTs and, 90–91
    C and, 135–136
    classes and, 162
    C-Linda and, 238
    concurrent execution of, 93
    data encapsulation and, 154
    executable, 20
    export list, 68, 91
    import list, 91
    interface, 84
    load, 20
    ML and, 368–369
    monitors and, 219
    PROLOG and, 316–317
    stepwise refinement and, 66–67
modus ponens, 288, 397
monitors, 215, 218–219
    Ada and, 230
    Concurrent Pascal and, 225–226
    Java and, 198
    rendezvous and, 219
MULTICS. *See* MULTiplexed Information and Computing Service (MULTICS)
multiple inheritance, 181–185, 192–193
    Java and, 198, 201
multiple processes, 212–213, 220
MULTiplexed Information and Computing Service (MULTICS), 133
multiprocessing, 211, 328
mutual exclusion, 215

name binding, 38–39
name equivalence, 57–58
names, 37
natural join, 383

natural languages
  formal vs., 4
  grammars for, 253, 279–282
  LISP and, 331
  PROLOG and, 302
  provability and, 19
  semantics and, 17
Natural Semantics, 370
negative facts, 298–299
nested block structures, 6, 8, 99
  activation records and, 44
  Ada and, 121
  ALGOL and, 105
  Pascal and, 115
nested statements, ALGOL
    and, 105
network, concurrent execution
    and, 93
Network Implementation
    Language (NIL), 220, 352
network model, 379–380, 385
nondeterministic finite automa-
    ton (NFA), 264–267, 279
nonprocedural programming,
    PROLOG and, 302
Nonselective Top-to-Bottom
    (NTB) Algorithm, 269,
    270–271
nonterminal symbols, 248
normal forms, 275–279, 408, 409
normal order reduction, 408
notation, 22
  functional programming
    and, 326, 328
  functions and, 85, 86
  lambda calculus and, 405
  scientific, 31
NTB Algorithm. See Nonselec-
    tive Top-to-Bottom (NTB)
    Algorithm

object-based languages,
    software sources and, 412
object-based paradigm, 6, 8–9,
    113
object code, 20, 21
object-hash table, 355–356
object identity, 393
object list, LISP and, 332, 355
object-oriented languages, 9
  abstractions and, 5, 92
object-oriented programming
    (OOP), 149–207
  Ada and, 127

classes and polymorphism
    in, 162–175
  databases and, 392–393, 394
  inheritance and, 150, 155,
    177–196
  Java and, 196–205
  LISP and, 331, 348
  newsletters and magazines
    on, 206
  parallel processing and, 239
  Smalltalk and, 175–177
  software sources and, 412
Object Pascal, 151, 156, 186–189,
    160
  abstractions and, 72
  classes in, 165–171
  dynamic binding in, 194–195
  software sources and, 412
Objective-C, 179, 198
objects, 8–9
  abstractions and, 65, 67, 70, 92
  classes and, 163. See also
    classes
  defined, 152
  LISP and, 348–352, 355–356
  ML and, 370
  parallel processing and, 239
  pointers and, 34
  processes as, 156
  programming with, 150–162
  Simula and, 155–158, 156
  state and, 149
  tuples and, 235–239
Occam, 9, 212
  message passing in, 220,
    232–235
  parallel processing and, 362
  software sources and, 413
ON conditions, 81–82
one-to-many message passing,
    221
OOP. See object-oriented
    programming (OOP)
operating system (OS)
  C for writing, 144
  Java and, 198, 200, 202
  parallel processing and, 211
operations
  abstractions and, 65, 67, 70
  lists and, 57
  objects and, 92, 149
  records and, 53
  set, 56
  subrange data types and, 47
  type checking and, 58

operator overloading, 58, 86, 393
operator precedence, 272, 274.
    See also precedence
operators
  abstractions and, 85–86
  ALGOL and, 112–113
  C and, 137–143
  infix notation, 86
  LISP and, 332–334
  prefix notation, 86
  postfix notation, 86
  PROLOG and, 303–308
  shift, 138
optimizing compilers, 21
ordinal data types, 47, 48
Origami folding editor, 234
orthogonality, 21–22, 84
  ALGOL and, 112
  ML and, 369
  SQL and, 386
OS. See operating system (OS)
overloading, 48, 58
  Ada and, 164
  methods and, 92
  operator, 58, 86, 393

P-code, 223
packages, 9, 91
  Ada and, 120–121, 122, 158
  Common LISP and, 353
  data encapsulation and, 154
  Java and, 199, 201
  LISP and, 348–352
  tasks vs., 122
  See also generic packages
paradigms, 1, 6–11
  abstract, 6, 64
  examples of, 7
  OOP and, 149
  for parallel processing, 210–211
Paradox, 162–163, 330
parallel architectures, 315–316,
    326
parallel execution, PROLOG
    and, 319
parallel graph reduction, 364
parallel processing, 209–242
  functional programming
    and, 328, 362–364
  managing partial failure, 240
  OOP and, 239
  PROLOG and, 315–316
  synchronization solutions to,
    221–235

parallel processing (*Cont.*):
  tuples and objects in, 235–239
  two models for, 210
parallelism, 315, 323
  functional programming
    and, 362–364
  granularity of, 363–364
parameters
  abstractions and, 72, 84, 86–90
  actual, 86–87, 88
  ALGOL and, 106, 109, 112
  C and, 135
  call-by-name, 106–107
  call-by-value, 106
  formal, 86–87, 88
  formal vs. actual, 38
  functions and, 325, 326, 329
  lambda calculus and,
    407–408, 409
  name, 89, 106, 108
  objects and, 92
  Pascal and, 116
  PROLOG and, 319
  reference, 87–89
  result, 88
  value, 87, 108
  value-result, 88–89
  var, 22, 38
PARC. *See* Xerox Palo Alto
    Research Center (PARC)
parse tree, 272–279
parsing, 20, 272
  derivation, 248
  PDA and, 252
  PROLOG and, 306
  RTN and, 280
partial failure, 240
partially applicable functions,
    368
Pascal, 6, 7, 13, 26, 113–117
  abstractions and, 65–66,
    71–72, 85
  Ada and, 115, 119, 124
  ALGOL and, 102, 103, 107,
    113, 114
  arrays and, 49, 51, 72, 107
  binding and, 38–39
  blocks and, 42
  BNF and, 15, 16, 19
  C and, 135
  compared with assembly
    language, 12
  context-free grammars, 274
  databases and, 377
  data types and, 47, 48

Pascal (*Cont.*):
  extensibility and, 23
  files in, 377
  functions in, 329
  generality and, 22
  HOLWG and, 118
  identifiers and, 37
  integers and, 30
  interpreters and, 26
  ISO 1980 Revised Standard, 16
  keywords in, 38
  modularization and, 91
  objects in, 160
  orthogonality and, 22
  PDA and, 270–271
  pointers and, 33, 35
  procedure passing and, 112
  pseudocode and, 15
  records and, 53
  semantics of, 19
  sets and, 55, 56
  Simula and, 156
  software sources and, 411
  standards and, 24
  strings and, 51
  syntax of, 19, 75
  type checking and, 58, 59, 60
  union types and, 54, 55
  UNIX and, 143
  See also Concurrent Pascal;
    Object Pascal; Sequential
    Pascal; Turbo Pascal;
    UCSD Pascal
Pascal 74 Standard, 59
Pascal 83 Standard, 59
Pascal-Ada, blocks and, 100
Pascal/R, 377
Pascal S
  Implementation Kit for, 242
  semaphores in, 223–225
  software sources and, 413
pattern matching, 52, 364
PC. *See* predicate calculus (PC)
PC-SCHEME, 414
PDA. *See* push-down automa-
    ton (PDA)
PDP-11, 133
Peano's axioms, 288
persistence, 377
Peterlee Relational Test Vehicle,
    384
philosophy
  logic and, 301
  Turing and, 258
phonology, 251

phrase-structured grammars,
    248, 250–267
  restricted, 253
physical view (of databases),
    377–378, 385
pigeonhole principle, 224
pipes, 220, 223
platform independence, Java
    and, 200, 204
PL/I, 8, 14
  ALGOL and, 107
  context-free grammars and,
    274
  databases and, 387
  dynamic bounds and, 108
  exceptions and, 81–82
  identifiers and, 37
  pointers and, 34
  real numbers and, 31, 32
  strings and, 51
  translation and, 21
  VDL and, 19
PM. *See Principia Mathematica*
    (PM)
pointers, 33–35
  C and, 142, 144
  dynamic scoping and, 42
  Java and, 197
  LISP and, 355
  objects and, 165–171
  OOP and, 178, 181, 186–192
  parameters and, 90
  records and, 53
  strings and, 51
point-to-point link, 9, 220
polymorphism, 162–175
  ML and, 365, 366, 368
  objects and, 92
  OOP and, 150
polytypes, 368
portability, 23, 30
ports, 220
potentially infinite string, 249
power set, 56
precedence, 112
  parsing and, 272
  PROLOG and, 303
predefined character type, 48
predefined functions, 38, 52
predefined packages, 120–121
predicate, 400
predicate calculus (PC), 10, 17,
    288, 395, 399–403
  functional programming
    and, 326

predicate calculus (*Cont.*):
PROLOG and, 302
relational databases and, 384
tuples and, 384
unification and, 293–294
primary keys, 380, 388
primitive data types, 29, 30–33, 39
Principia Mathematica (PM), 288, 397–399
principle of excluded middle, 291
printable entities, 390
private data types, 121
private knowledge, 331
problem solving, LISP and, 331
procedural abstractions, 64, 83–94
procedural languages, 13, 25–26, 156
databases and, 387
functional vs., 326
PROLOG vs., 319
RPCs and, 221
procedure calls, 39
abstractions and, 86–87
activation records and, 44
bound, 193–196
messages as, 152
monitors and, 218–219
remote. *See* remote procedure calls (RPCs)
procedure-oriented language, 8
procedures
abstractions and, 67, 72, 84–90
algebraic specification and, 69
ALGOL and, 104, 112
binding and, 39
blocks and, 99
exceptions and, 81
as methods, 156, 160
objects and, 92
as parameters, 90
Pascal and, 115, 160
PROLOG and, 319
scope and, 40
Simula and, 156
variables and, 29
process units, 212
processes, 209, 212
classes of, 157
Concurrent Pascal and, 225–226
concurrent vs. parallel, 209
multiple, 212–213, 220
as objects, 156

processes (*Cont.*):
Pascal and, 212
processors vs., 211
rendezvous and, 219
synchronization of, 213–221
processors, processes vs., 211
productions
Chomsky Normal Form and, 275
context-free grammar and, 252
context-sensitive grammars and, 253
erasing rules, 253, 260
formal languages and, 247–248
PROLOG and, 302
transition tables and, 264
production system, 248
program specification, 12
program units, 120–121
programming
"in the large," 12–13
modularization and, 91. *See also* modularization; modules
very high level languages and, 12, 353
programming languages, 1, 3, 26
abstractions and, 63, 64
for databases, 377–394
high level, 12, 74
low level, 11–12, 20
mathematics and, 4
for OOP, 149–207
provability and, 18–19
purpose of, 4
reliability and, 19–20
very high level, 12, 353
programs
functions and, 326
in LBA, 254–256
in LISP, 330, 335–336
projection, relational databases and, 382, 383, 385
PROLOG, 9, 10, 12, 13, 301–323
backward chaining and, 297–298
databases and, 394
DEC-10 PROLOG, 302
Edinburgh syntax, 302, 303, 414
functional programming and, 325
lists and, 56
logical calculi and, 401

PROLOG (*Cont.*):
negative facts in, 298
operators and, 113
as query language, 389
relational databases and, 389
SCHEME and, 327
semantics and, 17
software sources and, 413–414
strengths and weaknesses of, 318–319
translation and, 20, 26
proofs, 288–294
functional programming and, 326, 330
lambda calculus and, 406
logical calculi and, 398–399
searching and, 294–301
propositional calculus, 395–399, 400
protocols
Java and, 197, 203
objects and, 92
prototyping, 31
Common LISP and, 353
ML and, 370
provability, 18–19
publication languages, 109
public knowledge, 331
Pure LISP, 85, 352
pure virtual class, 172
push-down automaton (PDA), 252, 268–272
LBA vs., 254
parse tree and, 272
Pythagorean rule, SCHEME and, 349

querying, 291–301
query language, 377, 381–385
mathematics and, 381
PROLOG as, 302, 303–304, 389
for semantic databases, 390–392
queues, 8
abstractions and, 69–70
arrays and, 50
message passing and, 220
monitors and, 218, 219
pointers and, 34
synchronization and, 220
virtual machine and, 246
QUOSET, 317
quotient, relational databases and, 383–384

R Database System, 385
r-value, 137
radix point, 31
railroad charts, 16
raising (of exceptions), 81
random access memory
  (RAM), 8, 11
range value, functions and, 325
RBSs. *See* rule-based systems
  (RBSs)
read-only memory (ROM), 8
real numbers/arithmetic, 31–32
  abstractions and, 72
  characters and, 32
  LISP and, 332–334
  PROLOG and, 308
  type checking and, 58
real time, exceptions and, 81
real-time applications,
  aborting, 19
real-time clock (RTC), 312–315
real-time embeddings, 14
real-time systems, 242
records, 52–55
  activation. *See* activation
    records
  aggregate types and, 49
  components, 52–53
  databases and, 377, 385
  implementation of, 61
  ML and, 367
  OOP and, 160
  pointers and, 34
recursion, 78–81
  activation records and, 44
  ALGOL and, 107
  binding and, 39
  blocks and, 99, 99
  functional programming
    and, 330
  functions and, 326
  lambda calculus and, 407, 408
  left, 311
  LISP and, 331, 338–339,
    341–342, 347
  ML and, 367
  PROLOG and, 304–306,
    308–311
  See also tail recursion
recursively enumerable
  grammars, 258–260
recursive transition networks
  (RTNs), 279–281
rediflow project, 364
reductions, lambda calculus
  and, 406–407

reference counting, 362
reference data types. *See*
  pointers
reference language, 109, 110
referential integrity, 388
refutation complete, 291
regular expressions, 261–262
regular grammars, 251–252,
  260–267
  CDW and, 259
  context-free grammar, 252
  transition tables and, 264
regularity, 22, 116
relational algebra, 382–384, 385
  SQL and, 385, 387
relational calculus, 9, 384–385 .
  SQL and, 385, 386
relational databases
  logic and, 389
  manipulating, 381–385
  PROLOG and, 302, 317
relational model, 380–389
relations
  algebraic specification and,
    69–70
  functional programming
    and, 327–328
  PROLOG and, 317, 327
relationships, databases and,
  377
reliability, 19–20
  Ada and, 119, 158
  monitors and, 219
relocatable code, 20, 38
remote procedure calls (RPCs),
  219, 221, 239
rendezvous, 9, 219
  Ada and, 226–230
  circular deadlock and, 240
  Concurrent C and, 230–232
  message passing and, 220
  pipe and, 220
representable entities, 390
reserved words, 36–38, 226
resolutions, 288–295
  PROLOG and, 304
  searching and, 294–301
responsibility assignment, 83,
  84, 90
restricted phrase-structured
  grammars, 253
resumption model, 81, 82
ring, 66
robotics, LISP and, 331
ROM. *See* read-only memory
  (ROM)

RPCs. *See* remote procedure
  calls (RPCs)
RTC. *See* real-time clock (RTC)
RTNs. *See* recursive transition
  networks (RTNs)
rule-based systems (RBSs), 323
rules
  lambda calculus and, 405, 406
  PROLOG and, 302, 303–304
run time, 38
  analysis (APSE), 131
  binding and, 39
  errors, reliability and, 19
  Java and, 198
run-time system, 4

S-expression (sexpr), 30,
    334–338, 340
  macros as, 348
safe expressions, 385
scalar data types, 122–123, 124
scanners, 252, 265
scanning, 20
schema, 386–387, 390–392
SCHEME, 26, 327, 374
  abstractions and, 66
  bindings and, 358
  call-by-name and, 107
  funarg problems in, 359–361
  functional forms and, 338–339
  Help facility of, 335–336
  IEEE standard for, 331
  lambda calculus and, 405
  lazy evaluation in, 356, 363
  object list in, 355–356
  OOP and, 348–352
  PROLOG and, 327
  recursion and, 81, 341–342
  scope and, 43, 358
  self-modifying function in, 345
  side effects in, 342–347
  software sources and, 414
  type mismatches in, 332, 334
  vectors and strings in, 348
  See also LISP
scientific notation, 31
SCOOPS, 348–352
scope, 39–41, 61
  activation records and, 44
  Ada and, 121–122
  ALGOL and, 104–105
  dynamic scoping, 42
  exceptions and, 81
  lifetime vs., 44
  LISP and, 357–361

searching, 294–301
second-generation languages, 13
selection, relational databases
    and, 382, 383, 385
selectors, 332
self-modifying function,
    344–347
semantic data models, 390–392
semantics, 4, 17–18
    ALGOL 60 and, 102
    analysis, 20
    ATN and, 280
    binding and, 38
    defined, 247
    formal languages, 245, 247
    functional programming
        and, 326, 329–330
    functions and, 326
    lambda calculus and, 405–408
    linguistics and, 251
    ML and, 369–373
    parsing and, 272, 274
    provability and, 19, 19
    syntax vs., 247
semaphores, 215–218, 221–225
    Ada and, 230
    monitors and, 219
SEQUEL, 384, 385. *See also*
    Structured Query
    Language (SQL)
Sequential Pascal (Pascal S),
    223–225
set difference, relational
    databases and, 382, 384
set theory, 5, 6
    abstractions and, 69
    SETL and SETL2 and, 31
set union, type checking and, 58
SETL2, 5, 12
    arrays and, 50
    binding and, 39
    integers and, 31
    sets and, 56
sets, 55–56
    classes as, 162–163
    PROLOG and, 306
sexpr. *See* S-expression
shared memory, 9, 210, 211
    Ada and, 230
    message passing and, 213
    rendezvous and, 219
    synchronization solutions to,
        221–235
side effects
    abstractions and, 85, 87
    ALGOL and, 109

side effects (*Cont.*):
    C and, 144
    functional paradigms and, 10
    functions and, 326, 329
    lambda calculus and, 408
    in LISP and SCHEME,
        342–347
signatures, 368–369
simplicity, 326
Simula, 67, 68, 149, 157
    OOP and, 155–158
    procedure passing and, 112
Simula-Smalltalk-C++/Java,
    blocks and, 100
single solution (PROLOG), 310
single-valued, 325
Smalltalk, 9, 26, 174, 175–177
    abstractions and, 72
    Java and, 198
    objects and, 149
    OPAL and, 393
Smalltalk-72, 176
Smalltalk-80, 177, 179
Smalltalk/V, 179
SNOBOL, 12
SNOBOL4
    binding and, 39
    strings and, 51, 52
software engineering,
    PROLOG and, 302
software sources, 411–414
sound algorithms, 330
source code, 20
    binding and, 38
    branching and, 74–76
    DFA and, 265
    and efficient object code, 21
    memory and, 21
specification, 120–121
Spice LISP, 352
SQL. *See* Structured Query
    Language (SQL)
stack frames, 44
stacks, 8, 99
    arrays and, 50
    ML and, 368
    Object Pascal and, 167,
        170–171
    pointers and, 34
    Turbo Pascal and, 166
    virtual machine and, 246
    See also generic stacks
standard databases, 388
standards, 23–24. *See also*
    portability
standards organizations, 23–24

start state, 263
start symbols, 248
starvation, 214
state, 8–9, 92, 149, 150
    finite automata and, 263
statements
    Ada and, 117
    case, 75
    exceptions and, 81
    for, 77
    if, 75–76
    logical calculi and, 395–404
    Pascal and, 117
    PROLOG and, 303–304
    while loop, 77
static binding, 38, 158
static scoping, 41, 43
    activation records and, 44
    ALGOL and, 103
    dynamic vs., 42
static string length, 51
stepwise refinement, 66–67
storage view (of databases),
    377–378
store, 5
    abstractions and, 65
    imperative paradigms and, 8
strings, 51–52
    aggregate types and, 49
    formal languages and,
        247–248
    LISP and, 348
    potentially infinite, 249
    PROLOG and, 306
strong typing, 58–60
    classes and, 162
    Pascal and, 115–117
structural equivalence, 57–58
structured data types, 47–61
    Ada and, 122–123
Structured Query Language
    (SQL), 385
    databases and, 377, 380,
        385–389
    SEQUEL and, 384, 385
    software sources and, 414
structures
    in ML, 368–369
    in PROLOG, 303
subclasses, 162
subgoals, 297, 310
subprograms, 83–84, 90
    Ada and, 120–121
subrange data types, 47–48
    arrays and, 49, 72
    sets and, 55

subscripts, arrays and, 49
subsets, 23
substrings, 52
subtype principle, 181
superclass, 149, 198–200
swap procedures, 72, 73
symbol tables, 61
symbolic expression, 30
symbols
    finite automaton and, 265
    formal languages and,
        247–248
    lambda calculus and
        improper, 405–406
    in LBA, 254–256
symmetric message passing, 220
synchronization, 213–235
    Ada and, 230
    Java and, 198
    message passing and,
        219–221
    monitors and, 218
    parallelism and, 363–364
    rendezvous and, 219
syntactic analysis, 20
"syntactic sugar," 74
syntax, 4, 15
    abstractions and, 66, 74, 75
    algebraic specification and, 69
    defined, 246
    formal languages, 245, 246
    lambda calculus and, 405–408
    linguistics and, 251
    LISP and, 327, 334
    ML and, 369–373
    parsing and, 274
    PDA and, 252
    PROLOG and, 303–304
    provability and, 19
    reliability and, 19
    semantics vs., 247
syntax diagrams, 16, 277–278
syntax errors, interpreters, 20
syntax tree, 17, 18
Synthese Language Library,
    282

tagged types, 179–180
tags, 54–55, 174
tail recursion, 79, 81
    PROLOG and, 308–311, 315
    See also recursion
target code, 20
target machine, 30

tasks
    Ada and, 120, 121, 212
    circular deadlock and, 240
    packages vs., 122
    process units as, 212
tautology, 397
TCP/IP. See Transmission
    Control Protocol/Internet
    Protocol (TCP/IP)
terminal symbols, 248
terminal/termination state,
    263, 265
termination model, 81
terms, in PROLOG, 303–304
testing, modularization and, 91
text processors, DFAs and, 265
theorem proving
    logic programming and, 301
    ML and, 370
    PROLOG and, 302
theoretical machines
    formal languages and, 247
    PROLOG and, 312–315
    semantics and, 18
theory, 288
    of functions, 405. See also
        lambda calculus
    logical, 397
Theory of Integer Arithmetic
    (IA), 257
Theory for the Propositional
    Calculus, 397
thesis (logical calculi), 397
third-generation languages, 13
3DScheme, 414
thunk, 106
tightly coupled system, 210
time sharing, 211
    concurrent execution and, 93
    monitors and, 219
TM. See Turing Machine (TM)
tokens, 246
    BNF and, 15, 16
    PDA and, 252
    regular expressions and, 261
    regular grammar and, 252,
        265
    scanning and, 20
    translation and, 20
transactions, 219, 388–389
transformation rules, lambda
    calculus and, 406
transition diagram, 263–264
transition tables, 263–264
translation, fast, 20–21

translators, 20–21, 25–26
Transmission Control Proto-
    col/Internet Protocol
    (TCP/IP), 197
transputers, 220, 413
    Education Kit, 413
truth table, 396, 397
tuple calculus, 384–385
tuple space, 235–239
tuples, 36
    arrays and, 50
    functional programming
        and, 328
    ML and, 366, 367
    objects and, 235–239
    relational databases and,
        381–385
Turbo C, software sources, 412
Turbo C++, software sources
    and, 412
Turbo Pascal, 77, 91, 114
    classes in, 165–171
    OOP and, 159–160
    software sources and, 411, 412
Turing-compatible functions,
    407
Turing Machine (TM), 5,
    254–256, 258, 282
    CLW and, 259
    unrestricted grammars and,
        259
type binding, 39, 58. See also
    binding
type checking, 57–61
    ALGOL and, 103
    C and, 135
    LISP and, 334
    PROLOG and, 319
type coercion, 58
type compatibility, 57
type conversions, C and,
    136–137
type equivalence, 57
type extension, 174
types, functions vs., 21–22

UCSD Pascal, 114, 117
unbuffered message passing,
    221
unconstrained arrays, 50, 58, 126
Unicode, 32
unification, 293–294, 304
Uniform Generalization, 401
uniform replacement, 288

Uniform Resource Locators (URLs), 197, 203
Uniform Substitution, 397, 401
uniformity, 22–23
union (in relational databases), 382, 384
union types, 53–55, 59
unit, 91
units of parallelism, 212
univ, 307
universal-fixed type, 123
universal-float type, 123
universal-integer type, 123
universal-real type, 124
UNIX
  C and, 134, 143, 222–223
  Concurrent C and, 230
  Java and, 202
  MULTICS and, 133
  PROLOG and, 318
  semantic databases and, 392
  semaphores and, 222–223
UNIX System Interprocess Communication Primitives, 239
unrestricted grammars, 258–260
URLs. *See* Uniform Resource Locators (URLs)
user-defined data types, 47–48
user-defined exceptions, 82
user-defined expressions, 409
user-defined functions, 332
user-defined operators, 86
utility, concurrent execution and, 93

V operating system, RPCs and, 221
v-table, 173–174
value binding, 39
values
  functions and, 325
  lambda calculus and, 409
  LISP and, 336
  objects and, 149
variable length scheme with fixed maximum, 51
variables, 29, 36–61
  activation records and, 43–45
  ALGOL and, 104
  binding of/bound, 29, 38–39, 40. *See also* binding; bound variables
  case sensitivity and, 37
  control, 42
  lambda calculus and, 405–406, 409
  own, 104
  PROLOG and, 304
  visibility of, 40, 61, 121–122
variant records, 54–55
  Ada and, 124
  Pascal and, 59, 115
VAX, 392
vectors, LISP and, 348
Verdix Ada Development System, 411
very high level languages, 12, 353
virtual facilities (of Object Pascal), 167–168
virtual machine, 38, 246–247

Virtual Method Table (VMT), 167, 174, 186
virtual tables, 193
visible variables, 40, 61
  Ada and, 121–122
VMS, 392
VMT. *See* Virtual Method Table (VMT)
vW-grammar, 19, 111–112

W-grammar. *See* vW-grammar
WAN. *See* wide area network (WAN)
Warren Abstract Machine (WAM), 316
Waterfall model, 129, 130
weak typing, 58–60
wide area network (WAN), 210
Windows 95, Java and, 202
Windows NT, Java and, 202
WinScheme Editor, 414
words, formal languages and, 247–248
word structure, characters and, 31
World Wide Web (WWW), 196, 201

Xerox Corporation, 177
Xerox Palo Alto Research Center (PARC), 176
"yo-yo effect," 186

Zeta LISP, 352–353